2003

CHRONOLOGICAL HISTORY OF U.S. FOREIGN RELATIONS

CHRONOLOGICAL HISTORY OF U.S. FOREIGN RELATIONS

Volume I

1607–1932

by Lester H. Brune

Richard Dean Burns, Consulting Editor

NEW YORK AND LONDON

Editorial Staff:
Laura Kathleen Smid, *Project Editor*
Jeanne Shu, *Senior Production Editor*
Edward Cone, *Copyeditor*
Cynthia Crippen and Melanie Belkin, *Indexers*
Dennis Teston, *Production Director*
Jennifer Crisp, *Cover Designer*
Indiana University Graphic Services, *Cartographer*
Kate Aker, *Director of Development*
Sylvia K. Miller, *Publishing Director, Reference*

Published in 2003 by
Routledge
29 West 35th Street
New York, NY 10001
www.routledge-ny.com

Published in Great Britain by
Routledge
11 New Fetter Lane
London EC4P 4EE
www.routledge.co.uk

10 9 8 7 6 5 4 3 2 1

Library of Congress Cataloging-in-Publication Data

Brune, Lester H.
[Chronological history of United States foreign relations]
Chronological history of U.S. foreign relations / by Lester H. Brune ; Richard Dean Burns, consulting editor.
p. cm.
Rev. ed. of: Chronological history of United States foreign relations. New York : Garland, 1985–1991.
Includes bibliographical references and index.
Contents: v. 1. 1607–1932 – v. 2. 1933–1988 – v. 3. 1989–2000.
ISBN 0-415-93914-3 (set : alk. paper) – ISBN 0-415-93915-1 (vol. 1 : alk. paper) – ISBN 0-415-93916-X (vol. 2 : alk. paper) – ISBN 0-415-93917-8 (vol. 3 : alk. paper)
1. United States—Foreign relations—Chronology. I. Burns, Richard Dean. II. Title.

E183.7 .B745 2002
327.73′002′02—dc21 2002023693

Printed on acid-free, 250-year-life paper
Manufactured in the United States of America

Contents

Volume I
List of Maps vii
Preface ix
Introduction: Brief Overview of U.S. Foreign Relations, 1776–2000 xi

Prologue
I. The American Colonies as Part of the British Empire (1607–1775) 1

The United States Asserts Its Political Independence from Europe
II. Diplomacy During the Revolutionary Era (1776–1788) 7
III. The Federalist Era (1789–1800) 26
IV. The Democratic-Republican Years (1801–1815) 52
V. John Quincy Adams and Foreign Policy (1816–1828) 88

The United States Gains Predominance in the Western Hemisphere
VI. Expanding American Relations (1829–1859) 113
VII. Civil War Era (1860–1868) 190
VIII. The Eve of Empire (1869–1896) 212

America's Initial Moves Toward Global Power
IX. The Imperial Years (1897–1912) 269
X. Wilson and World War (1913–1920) 345
XI. Political Isolation and the Depression Era (1921–1932) 434

Volume II
America's Initial Moves Toward Global Power (continued)
XII. Franklin D. Roosevelt and World War II (1933–1944) 485

Global Relations in the Nuclear Age
XIII. Origins of the Cold War (1945–1952) 599
XIV. Struggles in the Cold War (1953–1968) 664
XV. Détente or Cold War? (1969–1980) 777

From the Cold War to the Post-Cold War Era
XVI. The Reagan Years (1981–1988) 903

Volume III
From the Cold War to the Post-Cold War Era (continued)
XVII. Continuing U.S. Foreign Interventions (1989–2000) 1147

Bibliography 1373
Appendix: Secretaries of State, 1781–2001 1399
Index 1423

Maps

Volume I

North America After 1763 3
The United States After the Treaty of Paris, 1783 18
Louisiana Purchase, 1803 56
Northeast Boundary Settlement, 1842 133
Texas, Mexico, and Oregon Territory, 1836–1848 145
The Mexican War 1846–1848 146
Central America in the 1850s 177
U.S. Interests in the Pacific, 1857–1899 209
Southeast Asia 264
The Philippines, 1899 288
Samoa, 1899 290
Venezuela Boundary Dispute, 1899 293
Alaska Boundary Dispute, 1898–1903 313
Panama Canal Zone, 1903 316
World War I 391
Europe Between Wars, 1919–1937 419
The Far East, 1919–1937 427

Volume II

World War II: Pacific theater 573
World War II: European and North African theater 577
Occupation zones in Germany and Austria 608
Korea, early 1950 649
Cambodia, Laos, and Vietnam, 1954 675
NATO & the Warsaw Pact 680
U.S. Collective Defense Arrangement, 1955 682
The Middle East, 1975 839
Africa, 1978 860
Central America and the Caribbean, 1979 876
Angola and Namibia, 1981 913
Grenada and the Caribbean, 1983 980
Central America, 1984 992
U.S. Air Raid on Libya, 1986 1074

Volume III

Persian Gulf Region 1180
Somalia 1191
Haiti and the Dominican Republic 1204
Post–Cold War Europe and Russia, end of 1991 1209
Bosnia-Herzegovina, 1992 1215
Afghanistan 1286
Indonesia 1312

Preface

The *Chronological History of U.S. Foreign Relations* is designed as a reference for scholars, librarians, students, researchers, journalists, and citizens seeking a straightforward explanation of particular events regarding the United States' relations with other nations. To provide a full contextual understanding of the issues surrounding these events, it also cites events in foreign countries that influenced American decisions.

How to Use These Volumes

Some users of these volumes will be fascinated by the varied and often unusual stream of events in American foreign activity. In that sense the *Chronological History of U.S. Foreign Relations* will be interesting to browse, as well as especially helpful to those who are looking for a quick overview of U.S. foreign relations in a particular time period or who wish to compare time periods. Readers interested in such overviews or comparisons will find the following features especially useful:

Dual Entry Structure: The entry for each event consists of a short heading describing the event and a longer explanation of it. Users can quickly scan headings as a timeline, then slow down at any point to read more in-depth descriptions of events.

Foreign and Domestic Headings: Events in foreign countries that influenced American decisions are identified by italicized headings so that readers can easily distinguish them from domestic events—or even skip over them, if desired.

This reference set is also designed for searchers of information about a specific person, event, or subject in U.S. foreign relations. These users are advised to make use of the following features:

Date Headings: The entire set is organized chronologically, and the entry for each event is preceded by a date heading that indicates the month, day, and year of the event. After finding an event, users can review other events preceding and following it to place the event in its broader historical context.

Cross-References: Many entries are followed by cross-references to related events, referred to by date for easy access.

Index: The analytical index at the back of volume 3 lists countries (except the United States), names, events, and topics. In addition, some key names and terms appear in small capital letters in the text so that a reader scanning the page can find them quickly and easily.

Acknowledgments

The author would like to thank Richard Dean Burns for his expert advice, editing, and picture research, as well as the many presidential libraries and other archives that provided the illustrations, many of which have never been published or widely disseminated previously. Thanks also to Ed Cone, copyeditor, and Laura Smid, project editor, and to Clifford Egan, James I. Matray, and T. Michael Ruddy, who kindly reviewed portions of the manuscript for completeness and accuracy and whose comments were very much appreciated.

Introduction: Brief Overview of U.S. Foreign Relations, 1776–2000

The Continental Congress received aid from various European nations during the American Revolution from 1776 to 1783. France became allied with the Americans in 1778 with the signing of the Franco-American Alliance that provided Americans with financial aid and military equipment. The United States also benefited from British troubles on the European continent; Britain had to maintain sufficient strength on the continent to conduct campaigns against France and Spain while sending contingents to fight American colonists. The British contingents sent to fight in America varied from 1,700 soldiers at the Battle of Lexington in 1776, to 8,000 at the Battle of Saratoga in 1777, to about 1,000 in Virginia and 2,000 in New York during the Battle of Yorktown in 1781. French aid to Americans included the services of French General Marquis Marie Joseph Lafayette and the French navy's blockade of British General Charles Cornwallis' escape by sea while Lafayette's contingents assisted George Washington's army in forcing the British to surrender on October 19, 1781. During the Paris Peace negotiations from April 12, 1782, to January 20, 1783, British negotiators granted the United States territory from the Appalachian Mountains to the Mississippi River in order to prevent Spain from gaining territory along the Mississippi River north of New Orleans.

When the French Revolutionaries imprisoned King Louis XIV and Queen Marie Antoinette of Austria, they provoked war with Austria and Prussia between 1789 and 1792. On February 21, 1793, Great Britain, Holland, and Spain joined in an alliance against the French. During the 1790s, the United States remained neutral but participated in an undeclared war with France (see entries for May 24 and 28, 1798). After Britain joined the war, French conquests continued in Europe, and American neutrality was challenged by the British navy's attempt to blockade American products from reaching France. To maintain its right to trade with any nation and to stop British impressment of U.S. seamen, President James Madison obtained from Congress a declaration of war against Britain on June 18, 1812. During the War of 1812, the U.S. army proved incompetent, allowing British forces to march through Virginia before capturing Washington and burning the White House on August 24–25, 1814. However, with the their failure to capture Fort McHenry, Maryland, the British abandoned their offensive operations, and on October 14, 1814, their ships left for Jamaica while peace negotiations with Americans were underway in Ghent, Belgium. On December 24, 1814, American and British delegates signed the Peace Treaty of Ghent, but before news of the peace treaty reached the contending armies a final battle took place at New Orleans in which General Andrew Jackson's army defeated a British invasion on January 8, 1815.

The Treaty of Ghent's terms maintained the status quo antebellum, but Americans regarded the war as a second revolution to liberate themselves from economic dependence on England. In addition, the British learned to treat their former colonies with more respect in both political and economic terms. The

Monroe Doctrine of December 2, 1923, validated American independence from the British. Drafted by Secretary of State John Quincy Adams, the Monroe Doctrine warned that the independence of any Central and South American nation should not be challenged by Spain or any European power. In addition, no European nation should attempt to colonize territory in the Western Hemisphere.

The War of 1812 and the Monroe Doctrine launched an era of American westward expansion. By 1896, the United States occupied all territory between the Atlantic and Pacific Oceans, north to the 49th parallel and south to the Rio Grande River. Although some Americans attributed this expansion to "God's providence" or "manifest destiny," they actually fought aggressive wars against Mexico and Indian tribes who resisted or refused to be held on reservations. Even four years of Civil War between 1861 and 1865 did not divert American expansion westward.

The U.S. conquest of western lands attracted new agricultural cultivation and the acquisition of mineral resources that promoted the nation's economic growth. By 1896, America's commercial and manufacturing capacities made the United States one of the world's economic leaders; by 1920 the United States had become the world's leader in gross national production.

This industrial growth inspired U.S. manufacturers to seek overseas markets for their goods and to import essential raw materials such as cooper, rubber, and oil. Advocates of overseas ventures drew attention to Spain's repressive measures in Cuba. Aided by reports of Spanish cruelty to Cuban women and the allegation that Spain was involved in the sinking of the USS *Maine* in Cuba's Havana harbor, president William McKinley asked Congress for authority to use armed forces against Spain. Congress responded by passing a Joint Resolution that permitted the president to use armed forces to evict Spain from Cuba (see entry for April 19, 1898). The Spanish American War lasted until December 1898, when Spanish and American delegates signed the Treaty of Paris. Under the treaty's terms, Cuba became a protectorate of the United States and Spain ceded Puerto Rico, Guam, and the Philippine Islands to the Untied States (see entry for December 10, 1898). During 1898, Congress passed a Joint Resolution to annex Hawaii as part of American territory (see July 6, 1898). In 1899, a treaty between the United States, Britain, and Germany awarded the Samoan islands east of 171 degrees longitude to the United States (see entry for December 2, 1899).

President McKinley was assassinated on September 6, 1901, and Vice President Theodore Roosevelt become president. Roosevelt pursued aggressive foreign policies, obtaining the right to build the Panama Canal on November 3, 1903, and continuing the expansion of the United States navy to protect American trade throughout the world (see entry for December 12, 1907).

When World War I broke out in Europe on July 28, 1914, President Woodrow Wilson proclaimed neutrality. From August 1914 until April 1917, Wilson had to deal with controversies about neutral rights, wartime contraband, private loans from American banks to Europeans, and Germany's unrestricted submarine warfare. Because he believed Germany's unrestricted submarine warfare was immoral, President Wilson asked Congress to declare war against Germany. On April 2, 1917, Congress approved a declaration of war against Germany. On April 2, 1917, Congress approved a declaration of war against Germany but delayed a declaration of war against Austria-Hungary until December (see entries for April 2 and December 7, 1917). Because America joined the war against Germany in 1917,

Wilson played a prominent role in the 1919 Paris peace talks by promoting the League of Nations as a collective security mechanism to reduce future worldwide conflict. Senate Republicans opposed U.S. membership in the league, however, because they preferred to enact unilateral U.S. policies to expand American trade without being burdened by the political restrictions of collective security.

Republican presidents pursued isolationist policies from 1920 to 1933. Russia's czarist regime had collapsed in March 1917 and on November 7, 1917, Bolsheviks led by Vladimir Lenin took over the government, vowing to end Russia's participation in the war at whatever cost. After Lenin made peace with Germany on March 3, 1918, leaders of France, Britain, and the United States dispatched troops to Russia in allied interventions that failed to dislodge the Bolsheviks and even helped solidify their power.

Germany established a republic under the Weimar constitution on July 31, 1919, but it experienced problems from the start. Weimar delegates had been required to sign the Treaty of Versailles, which blamed Germany for starting World War I. The "war guilt" clause of the treaty justified the Allies in seeking to collect $33 billion in reparations from a defeated Germany. Together with Germany's economic collapse, this stimulated right-wing opposition to the Weimar government. Faced with massive economic problems, the National Socialist (Nazi) Party, led by Adolf Hitler, gained many middle-class adherents. On January 30, 1933, President Paul von Hindenburg appointed Hitler as German chancellor, and within a year the Reichstag (parliament) had given him dictatorial power.

In East Asia, Japan was also reeling from massive economic dislocations. It became a fascist state when, following the assassination of Premier Yuko Hamaguchi on November 14, 1930, and the assassination of Premier Ki Inukai on May 15, 1932, Japan's military, led by Premier Viscount Makoto Saito, filled all Japanese cabinet ministries with military officers. The military was supported by Emperor Hirohito, who ignored Japan's elected political leaders in parliament (see entry for May 15, 1932). Subsequently, Japanese military generals such as Hideko Tojo led Japan to war against China despite protests from the United States in 1932 and 1937 (See entries for January 7, 1932 and October 5, 1937).

During the 1930s, President Franklin D. Roosevelt contended with an isolationist Congress, which adopted neutrality legislation designed to keep the United States out of war in Europe and Asia. As Japanese and German aggression threatened U.S. interests, President Roosevelt sought to negate the neutrality laws. After winning a third term in 1940, Roosevelt undertook measures to provide lend-lease aid for England and, later, the Soviet Union, which were both at war with the Axis powers of Germany, Japan, and Italy.

Although isolationists opposed U.S. aid to Europe, Japan's attack on Pearl Harbor on December 7, 1941, united the country against fascism in Europe and the Far East. Roosevelt led the nation until his death in April 1945, shortly before the United Nations Organization was chartered. Following Roosevelt's death, President Harry S. Truman and British Prime Minister Winston Churchill, in an agreement with Soviet General Secretary Joseph Stalin, accepted Germany's unconditional surrender (see entry for May 7, 1945). The United States and Britain continued the war against Japan in East Asia until Truman decided to use America's newly invented atomic bomb against Hiroshima and Nagasaki in August 1945 (see entries for August 6 and 9, 1945). Following the bombing of Nagasaki, Japan surrendered on August 15 and signed the official surrender terms in Tokyo Bay on September 2, 1945 (see entry for August 15, 1945). On August 8, the Soviet Union declared war on Japan just before Soviet armies invaded Manchuria. Although the Soviet Union joined the United Nations, this intended collective security arrangement did not end the hostility between capitalist and socialist nations. The socialist-capitalist clash that had begun in 1917 was soon revived following the "strange alliance" of the United States, Great Britain, and the Soviet Union during World War II.

Within five years of Japan's surrender in August 1945, the Cold War had begun between the Western capitalist nations and the communist Soviets and Chinese. As early as March 5, 1946, Winston Churchill delineated the chasm between Western "free states" and the "police states" behind the Soviet iron curtain. A year later, the Truman Doctrine proposed to use American financial and military aid to protect Greece and Turkey from communist threats. The Marshall Plan, which provided economic aid, and the North Atlantic Treaty Organization (NATO), which offered military protection from a possible Soviet military threat, involved the United States in Western Europe. In June 1950, the Korean War began when North Korean armies attacked South Korea and President Truman ordered U.S. forces to support South Korean forces (see entry for June 25, 1950). The Korean War lasted until 1953, when representatives of the United States, North Korea, and South Korea signed an armistice and ceasefire (see entry for June 25, 1953). Although Chinese troops assisted North Korea from November 1950 to 1953, China claimed its troops were "volunteers," a claim meaning China could not participate in signing the 1953 armistice, which created a demilitarized zone at the 38th parallel between North and South Korea. As of 2001, a final peace agreement had not been signed and American troops remained in South Korea. By 1960, the U.S. Asian containment strategy extended from the borders of South Korea through Japan's islands and to the Nationalist Chinese on Taiwan. The Southeast Asian Treaty Organization (SEATO) and the Australian-New Zealand ANZUS alliance completed the U.S. Pacific alliances, while in the Middle East the Central Treaty Organization of Iran, Iraq, and Pakistan linked with NATO members Greece and Turkey.

Between 1950 and 1980, American foreign policy experienced periods of lesser and greater Cold War confrontations with most conflicts occurring in the developing world (Third World) rather than in Europe. Nationalism was a dominate force in Third World countries as they tried to shed their colonial past. By 1960, the U.N. General Assembly had grown to ninety-eight member nations, of which forty-four were from the Asian-African bloc that had recently gained independence.

President Dwight D. Eisenhower tried to relieve tensions with the Soviet Union from 1953 to 1960, yet Eisenhower's "new look" policy emphasized the need for American to maintain sufficient nuclear strike forces to hit the Soviet Union if it became necessary (see entry for October 30, 1953). Moreover, he committed the United States to assisting South Vietnam against North Vietnamese aggression after the French were defeated in Indochina in 1954. Eisenhower's decision escalated the war in Vietnam during the 1960s. In 1961, President John F. Kennedy added American combat support troops to assist South Vietnam and again increased U.S. forces after South Vietnam's leader, Ngo Dinh Diem, was overthrown in 1963 (see entry for November 1, 1963). Following Kennedy's assassination on November 22, 1993, President Lyndon B. Johnson enlarged the number of American forces in South Vietnam and also ordered

United States Air Forces to begin bombing targets in North Vietnam (see entry for March 19, 1965). Neither Kennedy's nor Johnson's policies forced North Vietnam to surrender. In 1969, President Richard Nixon decided to gradually withdraw American forces from South Vietnam while training South Vietnamese troops to defend their nation. Nixon also began secret bombing raids on Cambodia (see entries for March 18 and June 8, 1969). In January 1973, Nixon accepted a compromise agreement with leaders of North Vietnam (see entry for January 27, 1973). The ink was hardly dry on the January agreement before North Vietnamese troops violated the ceasefire in February (see entry for February 9, 1973), but neither Nixon nor his successor, President Gerald Ford, was willing to send more troops to South Vietnam. In April 1975, North Vietnamese forces conquered South Vietnam while American helicopters evacuated the United States Embassy staff from Saigon to a U.S. aircraft carrier off the coast of Vietnam (see entry for April 29, 1975).

During the 1960s, the United States tried but failed to end Fidel Castro's communist regime in Cuba. In 1961, Kennedy's decision to overthrow Castro's forces at the Bay of Pigs incursion by Cuban exiles was unsuccessful. In October 1962, Kennedy thwarted the Soviet Union's deployment of nuclear missiles in Cuba (see entry for October 28, 1962) but did not overthrow Castro.

Nixon succeeded in obtaining détente with the Soviet Union and recognizing the People's Republic of China as the legitimate government of China. Nixon's negotiations with Moscow obtained the Strategic Arms Limitation Treaty (SALT I) and an Anti-Ballistic Missile Treaty (ABM) in 1972, but détente venture floundered with the onset of his Watergate scandal, as well as the public's inability to perceive d tente as a measure to conciliate the Soviet Union. After Nixon resigned as president, President Gerald Ford found that right-wing Republicans, such as California Governor Ronald Reagan, and Democrats, such as Washington Senator Henry Jackson, believed détente was a Soviet design to weaken American resolve to oppose communist governments and to promote Moscow's status in international affairs. Although President Jimmy Carter signed a second Strategic Arms Limitation Treaty (SALT II) with the Soviets in 1979, Carter withdrew the treaty from Senate consideration when Soviet forces intervened in Afghanistan on December 24, 1979, to support the Communist regime against Afghanistan's Islamic mujaheedin rebels seeking to overthrow the communist regime in Kabul, Afghanistan. Carter adopted confrontational policies toward Moscow that essentially ended détente before Ronald Reagan's election in 1980.

Reagan revived a "feel-good" optimism about the nation's future. At the same time that Reagan cut taxes (especially for the wealthy), he launched a $2.2 trillion military buildup and a costly strategic defense initiative (SDI, or "Star Wars") that left the United States with a $5 trillion national debt when President George H. W. Bush took office in 1989. Reagan began his presidency with a strong ideological prejudice against the "evil empire" of the Soviet Union, but became more flexible in dealing with Soviet leader Mikhail Gorbachev after 1985 because the two leaders had a personal rapport. Reagan's personal link plus Gorbachev's desire to end the nuclear arms race led to the 1987 Intermediate Range Nuclear Missile Treaty (INF), which eliminated most INF missiles with strict verification clauses. The repercussions of improved U.S.-Soviet relations relieved Europeans from fear of a superpower war on their continent and enabled the Helsinki Accords of 1975 to promote the growth of democracy in Eastern Europe. The Helsinki Accords and Gorbachev's domestic reform program (perestroika) and openness (glasnost) precipitated protest movements against the Communist regimes in the Eastern European states, leading to democratic reforms during 1989.

In other areas of foreign policy, Reagan initiated no broad, visionary program but often applied U.S. military power in Third World countries. Reagan condoned Israel's invasion of Lebanon (see entry for June 6, 1982) but sent U.S. marines, without a clear mission, to Beirut, where 241 marines were killed when a terrorist bomb blew up the marines' barracks (see entry for October 23, 1983). Reagan immediately ordered military operations against an alleged Communist takeover of Grenada, a small island in the Caribbean. Finally, his alignment with Iraq against Iran during the 1980s backfired when Iraqi President Saddam Hussein invaded Kuwait in August 1990.

Beginning in 1989, Communist nations in Eastern Europe were transformed from Soviet satellites into more democratic governments. The fall of the Berlin Wall on November 9, 1989, was a prelude to the collapse of communist regimes in East Germany, Czechoslovakia, Poland, Hungary, Bulgaria, and Romania, as the Warsaw pact alliance disbanded. Gorbachev resigned on December 24, 1991, after most former Soviet republics had seceded from the Soviet Union. In early 1992, Russia's government, led by Boris Yeltsin, became the successor to the Soviet Union, obtaining the Soviets' permanent seat on the U.N. Security Council.

From 1991 to 2001, Presidents George H. W. Bush and Bill Clinton faced the daunting task of dealing with a series of civil uprisings by nationalists during the post-Cold War era. Through 1991, Bush watched approvingly but passively as bloodless revolutions demolished the Soviet empire and new governments emerged in Eastern Europe. His administration failed to offer sufficient economic aid to assist countries liberated from Communism, especially Russia, in changing their economic institutions from communist, state-owned industries to private, free-market industries.

Bush appeared to make foreign policy decisions on a case-by-case basis rather than according to a larger vision or plan. He backed Chancellor Helmut Kohl's move to reunite Germany and waged war against Panama to remove the corrupt Manuel Noreiga in December 1989. In 1990–1991, he formed a U.N. coalition to prevent Iraq from controlling the oil resources of Kuwait and Saudi Arabia, but he failed to remove Saddam Hussein as president of Iraq, leaving a serious Middle East problem that continued into the next century.

Both Bush and Clinton negotiated formulas for the Strategic Arms Reduction Treaties (START I, II, III), but the fulfillment of these treaties was still pending in 2001. They both pursued Reagan's costly search for a missile defense system, albeit on a less enthusiastic schedule and under new formulas such as the Brilliant Pebbles global positioning system (GPALS) and Theater High Altitude Area Defense System (THAAD). Russian, Chinese, and NATO leaders opposed these missile defense systems as endangering the nuclear arms stability afforded by the 1972 ABM treaty.

Bush's and Clinton's most perplexing problems involved intervention during conflicts in countries where genocide and ethnic cleansing were perpetuated. Bush refused to intervene in the Balkan wars that marked the end of the Federal Republic of Yugoslavia but did everything possible to prevent Haitian refugees from reaching the United States. Nor did Bush help Haiti's democratically elected President Jean-Bertrand Aristide, who was overthrown by a military junta in September 1991 (see entry for September 30, 1991).

Clinton inherited Bush's policies toward the Balkans, Somalia, and Haiti and experienced difficulties himself in solving these problems. U.S. intervention in Somalia became a fiasco in October 1993 after eighteen U.S. soldiers were killed in a hunt for the Somalian warlord Mohammad Farah Aideed. Regarding Haiti, Clinton continued Bush's policy of preventing Haitian refugees from entering the Untied States, but in October 1994 established a coalition of forces under United Nations auspices whose threat to invade Haiti persuaded Haiti's military junta to go into exile while President Aristide returned to Haiti (see entry for October 15, 1994).

During the Clinton presidency, situations in the Congo and the Balkans were most problematic. In the Congo, the United States provided some humanitarian aid, but France agreed to provide most of the United Nation's peacekeeping troops who attempted to end the war in the Congo, a war that involved armed forces from Angola, Uganda, Rwanda, Burundi, and Zambia (see entry for May 18, 1997). In Yugoslavia, Bush and Clinton avoided intervention for five years except for a few American aircraft that joined NATO in 1993 to protect U.N. "safe havens" where Bosnian Muslims or Croats were surrounded by militant Serbs and the Yugoslav National Army (see entry for April 16, 1993). In July 1995, Serb massacres of thousands of Muslims at the safe-haven of Srebrenica finally led Clinton to join NATO in forcing Yugoslav President Slobodan Milošević to negotiate peace arrangements with Croat and Muslim leaders at a meeting in Dayton, Ohio. The Dayton Accords introduced NATO forces in Bosnia to monitor peace, but Milošević's Yugoslav National Army (YNA) and Serb paramilitary units attacked Kosovo's Muslims (Kosovars) who were the dominant ethnic group in the province (see entry for March 5, 1998). Failing to get Milošević to accept peace arrangements for Kosovo, NATO aircraft bombed Serbia and Kosovo for seventy-eight days until Milošević accepted NATO's cease fire and peace terms, including the withdrawal of all YNA and Serb paramilitary units from Kosovo (see entry for June 10, 1999). These NATO attacks precipitated Milošević's loss in the Yugoslav elections of September 2000. The next year Milošević was extradited to The Hague for trial as a war criminal.

Two events vital to U.S. foreign relations occurred in the Middle East and Europe during the 1990s. Peace between Israel and the Palestinians was nearly achieved after the Oslo Accords were signed on September 13, 1993 by Israeli Prime Minister Yitzhak Rabin and Chairman of the Palestine Liberation Organization Yasser Arafat (see entry for September 13, 1993). The Oslo Accords provided for a series of steps leading to a final settlement, with Palestinian Arabs having autonomy in the West Bank and Gaza Strip. Each step in the process caused additional disputes, especially because Israel wanted clearly defined security arrangements before it would relinquish control of all territory it had occupied in the Six-Day War of 1967. Although the Palestine National Authority obtained control of the Gaza Strip and Jericho on May 4, 1994, fulfilling the Oslo Accords became more difficult following the assassination of Israeli Prime Minister Yitzhak Rabin on November 4, 1995. Negotiations on a final settlement failed on July 25, 2000, and a second Palestinian *intifada* began on September 28. Conflict between Israeli forces and the *intifida* continued into the new century.

In Europe, Bush and Clinton succeeded in expanding NATO's membership. In March 1999, former Warsaw Pact members Poland, Hungary, and the Czech Republic were admitted to NATO. Beginning on December 10, 1991, the

European Union agreed to integrate its economy, in part by adopting a unified currency, the Euro, which was put into circulation by all members except Great Britain. EU members also sought ways to unify their military and political decisions, but at the same time were reluctant to give up their national sovereignty. During the 1990s Bush and Clinton negotiated with Canada and Mexico to form the North American Trade Association (NAFTA), a treaty Congress ratified in 1993 (see entry for November 20, 1993) and the United States sponsorship of the General Agreement of Tariffs and Trade (GATT) in 1947 (see October 23, 1947) was modernized into the World Trade Organization after the Uruguay round of GATT negotiations agreed to create the World Trade Organization (see December 14, 1993 and December 1, 1994).

* * *

The third volume of the *Chronological History of U.S. Foreign Relations* was being edited when terrorists struck the World Trade Center towers in New York City and the Pentagon in Washington, D.C., on September 11, 2001. Information about the antecedents of the September 11 tragedy may be found in entries for terrorism and Afghanistan in volumes two and three. The entry for September 6, 1970, explains how terrorists hijacked three commercial airlines: Trans-World Airlines (TWA), British Overseas Airlines (BOC), and Swiss Airlines. Similar hijackings followed during the 1970s, before a climax of four separate hijackings took place in 1985. Another attack important to Americans took place on December 21, 1988, when a terrorist bomb planted on a Pan American airliner exploded over Lockerbie, Scotland, killing 259 passengers and crew and 11 Scottish citizens on the ground.

The terrorism of the 1970s and 1980s grew in terms of suicide bombing attacks. Islamic schools (madressas) in Pakistan and Afghanistan had teachers of the Koran who advocated holy war (jihad) against the ideas of freedom and prosperity in Western Europe and the United States. Beginning in 1979, a military coup led by Nur Muhammad Taraki overthrow the Afghan government of Muhammad Daoud. Aided by advisors from the Soviet Union, Taraki's rebels abducted and killed U.S. Ambassador Adolf Dubs, who became the first victim of violence in Afghanistan. After U.S. President Jimmy Carter claimed Soviet advisors were involved in Dub's assassination, the Carter administration sent small amounts of aid to the mujaheedin rebels who opposed Taraki's regime (see entries for February 14 and December 28, 1979).

During the 1980's, President Ronald Reagan became more aggressive in fighting communism in the developing world (Third World) by increasing U.S. financial and military aid to the mujahideen. The Central Intelligence Agency (CIA) sent billions of dollars' worth of financial and military aid through Pakistan to the Afghan mujahideen. This aid included the U.S. army's most modern defense against low-flying aircraft and helicopters—Stinger anti-aircraft missiles, which enabled the rebels to shoot down aircraft sent to Afghanistan by the Soviet Union. The mujahideen also sold many Stingers for up to $300,000 each, which then ended up in other Middle Eastern and African countries (see entries for June 5, 1986, and May 27, 1988).

After the final Soviet withdrawal from Afghanistan on January 15, 1989, fighting continued between Communists in Kabul and Islamist rebels outside the city. On April 28, 1992, a U.N. mediator supervised the transfer of power from the Communists to a six-member commission of Afghan representatives led by Ahmed Shah Massoud. Expecting the commission to bring peace to Afghanistan, the United States and Saudi Arabia gradually ended their financial aid, beginning in 1992. As this aid ended, the mujahideen financed their actions by forcing local farmers to grow poppies for opium. The opium trade became a prime source of income for rebels, including the Taliban, who were initially just one of several competing groups in Afghanistan.

In 1992, neighboring Pakistan supported the Taliban, hoping to end the rivalry among Afghan warlords and bring stability to Afghanistan. On September 27, 1996, the Taliban captured Kabul, gaining control of Afghanistan except for twelve northern provinces where Massoud's Northern Alliance opposed Taliban rule. As a result of the U.S. bombing campaign after the terrorist attacks of September 11, the Northern Alliance regained Kabul on November 14, 2001.

In 1996, the Clinton administration, uncertain how to deal with the Taliban, refused to recognize their government. There was evidence that Afghanistan harbored terrorists such as Osama bin Laden, who was linked to the bombing of New York's World Trade Center on February 27, 1993. Bin Laden was also linked to the November 14, 1995, bombing at the U.S. Military Training Center in Saudi Arabia that killed five Americans and to the June 25, 1996, bombing that destroyed an apartment building in Dharan and killed nineteen U.S. Air Force officers living there. Two Islamic groups claimed responsibility for these bombings and warned Saudi King Faud to remove all Western influences from Saudi Arabia. The bombings in 1995 and 1996 appeared to be the beginning of terrorist attacks led by Osama bin Laden, who had declared war on Americans because they aided Israel and Saudi Arabia's secular government.

On August 7, 1998, bombs exploded at U.S. embassies in Kenya and Tanzania, killing 213 people, including 12 Americans. On August 15, Pakistan arrested a suspect who confessed that Osama bin Laden led the African operations and intended to bomb American targets around the world. Convinced that evidence indicated bin Laden had masterminded the attacks, President Bill Clinton ordered U.S. navy ships in the Arabian and Red Seas to fire Tomahawk missiles at bin Laden's training camps and other facilities in Afghanistan and the Sudan on August 20, 1998. On October 12, 2000 when two suicide terrorists drove a small boat filled with bombs into the side of the destroyer USS *Cole* while it refueled in Yemen's harbor, killing 17 American sailors. The Clinton administration sent Federal Bureau of Investigation (FBI) agents to Yemen where on November 17, 2000, the FBI cooperated with Yemeni police in arresting two men suspected of planning the *Cole's* bombing.

Lester H. Brune

Prologue

I. THE AMERICAN COLONIES AS PART OF THE BRITISH EMPIRE

Overview, 1607 to 1775

For 169 years before declaring independence, the 13 American colonies were part of the British Empire. Established in accordance with mercantilist policies designed to enhance the motherland's wealth, the colonies would offer benefits not only to their founding companies but also to the English nation. Moreover, the American colonies were part of a global thrust of British commercial interest, a thrust spreading Britain's Empire to every continent and ocean of the world by 1770.

Until 1763, the most significant factor in the development of the North American colonies was London's failure to enforce the strict regulations envisioned by mercantilist theory. First, the internal crisis between the Stuart kings and Parliament stretched over much of the 17th century before Parliament gained control in the Glorious Revolution of 1688–1689. Later, persistent wars with France caused problems for Britain in Europe. Together, domestic and foreign crises diverted British attention from colonial issues to Britain's security needs at home. The colonists profited from England's troubles. Colonial merchants violated the Navigation Acts with impunity, and colonial assemblies gained much local political power without effective complaint from the king.

After the Treaty of Paris in 1763 settled the French Wars for a time, the British government discovered it had lost control over the American colonies, not in theory but in fact. The king's government had never granted the colonists the privileges they assumed for themselves. But, once those privileges were gained, the colonists were unwilling to relinquish what they claimed to be the "rights of all Englishmen." When Parliament passed laws to tax the colonists and used admiralty courts to enforce the mercantilist regulations, the colonists strongly objected.

Although reason called for compromise, the king and Parliament refused to accommodate the colonial arguments. George III desired to reassert his control to strengthen the British Empire. The American colonists resisted. Moderate colonial leaders appealed to reason by petitioning the king to recognize their grievances. Radical colonists eschewed compromise. They formed the Sons of Liberty and organized to gain recognition of their rights by demonstrations and protest if possible or by forceful means if necessary. Because the king continually rejected compromise, the colonial moderates finally had to choose: join the radical's call for independence or loyally accept the king's supreme power. By 1775 most moderates, such as Thomas Jefferson, George Washington, John Adams, and Benjamin Franklin, reluctantly decided to seek independence, joining such radicals as Samuel Adams, Isaac Sears, and Charles Thomson who had foreseen this outcome since 1767.

Beginning at Lexington and Concord on April 18–19, 1775, the king's troops and colonial militia clashed in battle. Before the end of the year, war began in Massachusetts, Virginia, and Canada. All that remained to complete the break was for representatives of the 13 colonies to agree on a declaration separating themselves from the king and government of Great Britain.

May 24, 1607

One hundred and five settlers arrive from England to establish a village at Jamestown, Virginia.

Although all but 32 died from famine and disease during the first seven months, the colony became England's first permanent American settlement. The colonists were sponsored by the London Company under a patent bestowed by King James I (April 20, 1606). During the next 150 years, 13 colonies developed along the Atlantic coast, each founded with grants or charters from the king of England.

August 9, 1619

The First Colonial Legislature convenes at Jamestown.

Called the House of Burgesses, the Virginia assembly represented each of 22 local government units in the colony. This inaugurated a pattern by which each of the 13 colonies developed some type of representative assembly for itself in addition to the various town and county governmental units operating on a local level.

By 1760, each colony had a governor as its chief executive. The governor's precise political power varied from colony to colony but, generally, the colonial assemblies gained a great degree of independent power because they controlled the colony's budget, usually including the governor's salary.

October 3, 1650

Parliament passes the first in a series of Navigation Acts.

Added to, amended, and revised until 1767, the Navigation Acts regulated colonial commerce, industry, and labor. Their purpose was to create and maintain a powerful, self-sufficient British nation and Empire. Colonial economic needs were subordinated to the welfare of England according to these MERCANTILISTIC laws.

February 13, 1689

Parliament declares William and Mary the king and queen of England.

The offer was accompanied by a Declaration of Rights of the people (enacted officially on December 16, 1689). This action, known as the GLORIOUS REVOLUTION, completed Parliament's declaration that James II had broken his contract with the people and its decision to select a king of its choosing to govern Great Britain. This action also ended the eighty-year struggle between Parliament and the Stuart kings in a victory for representative government.

May 12, 1689

The beginning of King William's War (War of the League of Augsburg) inaugurates a series of warfare between England and France.

Although the English and French clashed frequently in the colonies before 1689, this war began a conflict in both Europe and the colonies that finally resulted in the imperial hegemony of Great Britain in North America.

February 10, 1763

British hegemony is confirmed at the Treaty of Paris, which ends the French and Indian War (Seven Years' War).

King William's War ended on September 20, 1697, but was soon followed by QUEEN ANNE'S WAR (War of the Spanish Succession) from May 4, 1702, to April 11, 1713. After 26 years of peace, British conflict began again first with Spain (the War of Jenkins' Ear began on October 19, 1739) and enlarged when France joined Spain in KING GEORGE'S WAR, which ended on October 11, 1748.

The French and Indian War began in the Ohio River valley when British troops fought French forces aided by their Indian allies, beginning on April 17, 1754. The war spread to Europe on May 15, 1756, and later battles were also fought in India and south Asia.

The Treaty of Paris established Great Britain's predominance. France ceded to England all claims to Acadia, Canada, and islands off the Atlantic coast of Canada, except St. Pierre and Miquelon. Great Britain gained all territory east of the Mississippi River except New Orleans. This cession included East and West Florida.

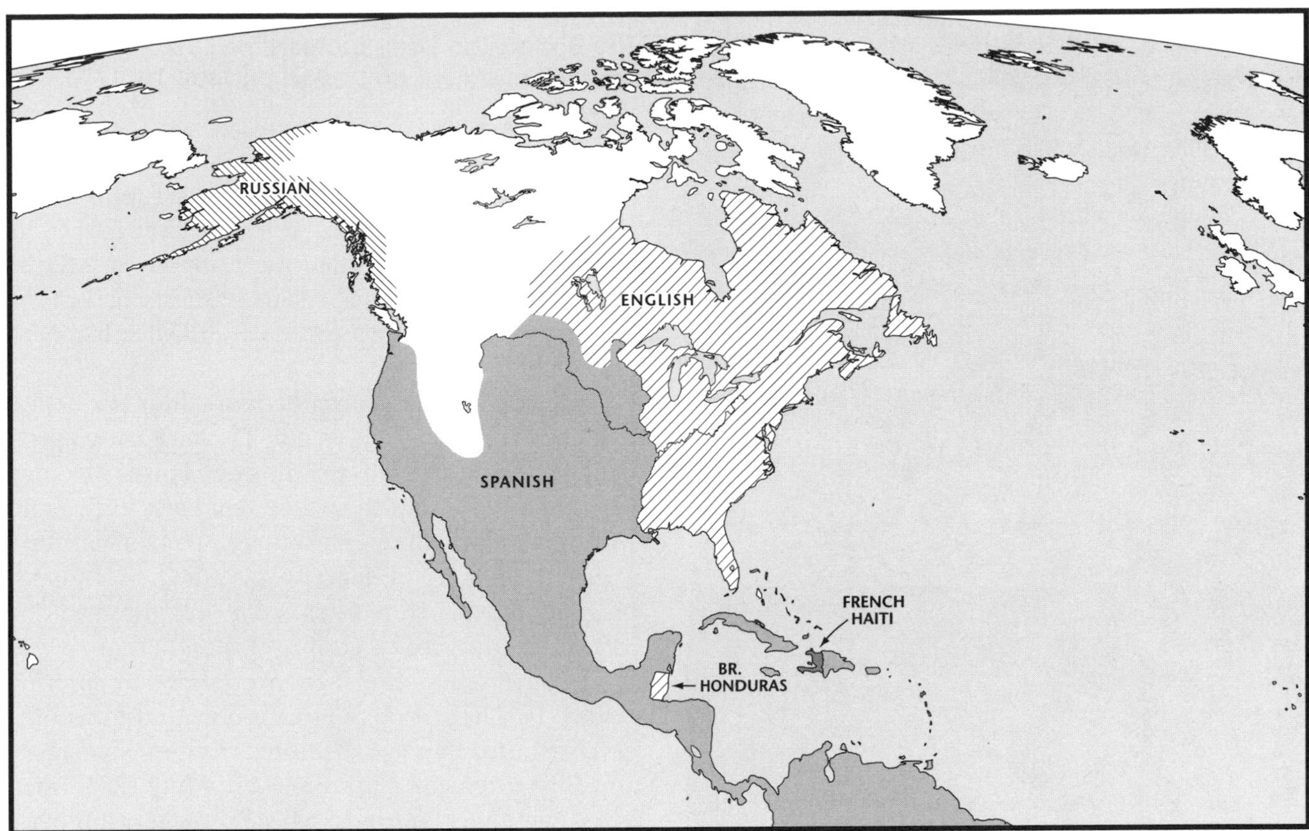

North America after 1763

April 5, 1764

American Revenue Act (Sugar Act) passes Parliament as part of the budget of Chancellor of the Exchequer George Grenville.

This was the first parliamentary law designed specifically to raise money in the colonies by increasing duties on foreign-refined sugar, doubling the duty on foreign goods reshipped from England to the colonies, and adding new items to the colonial import duty list.

More critically, however, Grenville also decided to strictly enforce the Navigation Acts and customs laws, which had not been effectively carried out in the American colonies. He established Vice-Admiralty courts at Halifax where colonial prosecutors could bring suit, placed the burden of proof of innocence on the accused, and generally hoped to end the illicit colonial trade with the French West Indies and between the colonies that violated the navigation laws.

October 7, 1765

Stamp Act Congress convenes in an effort to unite the American colonies in protesting the Stamp Act (passed by Parliament on March 22, 1765).

The colonial leaders claimed the Stamp Act violated their right not to be taxed without representation.

The Stamp Act was the first direct tax levied by Parliament on the American colonies. Its purpose was to require the colonies to bear part of the burden of Great Britain's colonial military expenses. The act affected almost all groups in the colonies: lawyers, innkeepers, land speculators, printers, merchants, and shipowners. Moreover, the king's ministers proposed to enforce the act through the Vice-Admiralty courts, a decision that colonists saw as the violation of their right to trial by jury.

British officials demonstrate their insensitivity to American complaints about the Navigation Acts and then are shocked as violence against them mounts. Library of Congress

August 10, 1767

The Sons of Liberty clash with British troops in New York City.

Led by Isaac Sears, radicals in New York protested General Thomas Gage's attempt to Enforce the Quartering Act (passed by Parliament in 1765). Gage wanted the New York Assembly to provide funds to quarter and supply his soldiers. The Assembly refused, and street demonstrations led to the fight between the Sons of Liberty and British soldiers over the erection of a "liberty pole." Later, on June 6, 1768, the Assembly approved £3,000 for the expenses of Gage's army in New York.

December 16, 1773

The Boston Tea Party protests the Tea Act, which Parliament approved on May 10, 1773.

The Tea Act was not a large tax, but opposition focused on the law as granting a monopoly of tea to the East India Company because the act remitted all British duties on tea sent to America by the East India Company. It also permitted the company to sell the tea directly to its colonial agents. Protests against the Tea Act were made by meetings at Philadelphia, New York, and Charleston.

Boston, however, took the most dramatic action to defy British law. Governor Thomas Hutchinson rejected resolutions of the Boston Town Meeting, which requested that the tea be sent back to England without the local duties having been paid. Thereafter, a group of Sons of Liberty, disguised as Indians, boarded the tea ship *Dartmouth* and dumped the 342 chests of its tea cargo into Boston harbor.

In other cities, similar tea protests led to differing results. In Charleston, South Carolina, customs officers permitted the tea to be stored without payment of any duty; it remained in storage until July 1776, when it was auctioned for funds to benefit the revolutionary cause. In New York City, local Sons of Liberty duplicated the Boston Tea Party by dumping tea into the harbor (April 22, 1774). In Annapolis, Maryland, the tea cargo aboard the ship *Peggy Stewart* was burned in a mysterious fire. A fire also destroyed tea stored in a warehouse in Greenwich, New Jersey.

March 31, 1774

Parliament passes the first of a series of Coercive Acts (called Intolerable Acts by colonial radicals).

The acts sought to force the colonists in Boston to pay for the destroyed tea. The most serious of the Coercive Acts closed the port of Boston and limited sessions of the Massachusetts Assembly and of local town meetings until the cost of the tea was reimbursed.

September 5, 1774

The First Continental Congress convenes in Philadelphia, providing a forum for all of the American colonies to protest jointly British policy and to organize concerted action against Great Britain. All colonies except Georgia were represented.

Moderates in the Congress gained approval for a petition of grievances (Declaration of Rights and Grievances) to seek a compromise with the king. But the radicals led by Samuel Adams obtained approval for a strong protest that claimed Britain sought to "enslave America" and for a resolution advising each colony to raise and train its own local militia. The Congress also approved the formation of local committees to enforce a boycott of British goods if the colonial grievances received no response from the king by December 1, 1774.

April 19, 1775

The first shots of the American Revolution are exchanged between 700 British troops and colonial militia at Lexington and Concord, Massachusetts.

King George had ordered General Gage to take all necessary measures to stop the colonial agitators. Subsequently, on the evening of April 18, British troops left Boston to surprise the colonial leaders and capture their stores of arms and ammunition as well as to arrest the leading rebels, Sam Adams and John Hancock.

Before the day ended, the British destroyed some colonial ammunition stores at Concord but had to retreat from superior colonial militia, numbering nearly 4,000 before the day ended. By sending a 1,000-man reinforcement, General Gage saved the British from surrender, but their losses were heavy. Seventy-three British redcoats were killed and 194 wounded. The colonial minutemen suffered 49 killed and 41 wounded.

May 10, 1775

The Second Continental Congress convenes in Philadelphia to consider action in response to the Lexington and Concord confrontation.

Although the Congress forwarded one last Olive Branch Petition to the king (July 5, 1775) to seek compromise, the moderates' hope for redress of grievance seemed hopeless. Colonial petitions were often sent to the offices of the king's ministers, to Parliament, and to the king since 1765, but except for a small minority in Parliament, the British govern-

First prayer offered in Continental Congress, in Carpenters Hall, Philadelphia, Pennsylvania. Copy of print by H. B. Hall after T. H. Matteson (George Washington Bicentennial Commission). National Archives ment was unwilling to compromise its power over the colonists.

June 15, 1775

George Washington is selected as commander in chief of the Continental Army.

June 17, 1775

The Battle of Bunker Hill is won by the British, but only after they suffer heavy losses, including 242 deaths (compared with 100 colonists being killed).

August 23, 1775

King George III proclaims the American colonists are in rebellion.

An expeditionary force under General Henry Clinton was ordered to be organized against the colonies.

August 23, 1775

Colonial forces under Benedict Arnold and Richard Montgomery begin a campaign to take Canada.

By December, Quebec was besieged, but the campaign failed early in 1776.

The Battle of Bunker Hill, near Boston. Copy of engraving by James Miltan after John Trumbull, published in 1898. National Archives

September 19, 1775

Continental Congress appoints a secret committee to buy war supplies.

Chaired first by Thomas Willing and later by Robert Morris, the committee was authorized to make contracts for the purchase of foreign arms and ammunition. At this time, the Congress also urged local revolutionary committees to export goods to the West Indies, where they could trade for arms and other military needs.

The Secret Committee later became the Committee of Commerce, but it also laid the groundwork for the Committee of Secret Correspondence.

November 29, 1775

Congress creates a Committee of Secret Correspondence to conduct foreign relations.

The leading members of this committee were Benjamin Franklin and Robert Morris. The committee sent agents to Europe to seek loans, alliances, and the purchase of military supplies. By January 1, 1777, 400 merchants had contracted to deliver gunpowder. The committee's agent in London, Arthur Lee, arranged an early French loan through Caron de Beaumarchais and the French foreign minister (see May 2, 1776).

December 11, 1775

Under Colonel William Woodford, 700 Virginia and 200 North Carolina militia defeat British troops under Lord Dunmore at Great Bridge, Virginia.

Dunmore's soldiers retreated to Norfolk.

December 23, 1775

Royal proclamation of George III closes the American colonies to all foreign commerce.

The United States Asserts Its Political Independence from Europe

II. DIPLOMACY DURING THE REVOLUTIONARY ERA

The French Alliance
The Treaty of Paris
Era of Articles of Confederation

1776

January 10, 1776

Thomas Paine's "Common Sense" is published in Philadelphia.

Urging a demand for American independence, "Common Sense" argued that King George had no legitimate right to rule the American colonies. Moreover, Paine asserted, the colonial economy would prosper by severing its political connections with Great Britain.

Paine's pamphlet found a receptive audience in America because independence or complete submission to the British government appeared to be the only alternatives in early 1776. Following the Stamp Act crisis of 1765, political disagreements between the British government and the 13 American colonies grew, finally bursting into intermittent warfare beginning at Lexington and Concord in April 1775. Before 1775 ended, colonial forces undertook an expedition to invade Quebec, and British troops under General Henry Clinton prepared to invade the southern colonies.

Thus, appearing after nearly nine months of hostility, "Common Sense" gave the colonists, now classified as rebels by the king, justification for declaring their independence, a definitive act of revolution against King George's government. Calling the king a "Royal Brute," Paine's essay declared there were neither natural nor religious reasons to justify his right to rule. The English king's hereditary rights derived only from the historic fact that William the Conqueror (1066), a "French bastard landing with an armed banditti," had made himself king against "the consent of the natives."

Paine's essay also described America's relationship to England and Europe in terms that later writers would call "isolationism." He claimed America would flourish economically when it gained independence from Britain. "The agricultural products of the colonies," he wrote, will "always have a market while eating is the custom of Europe.... Our corn will fetch its price in any market in Europe." Moreover, Paine stated, American commerce would prosper best if there were *no political alliances* with any European country. "As Europe is our market for trade, we ought to form no partial connection with any part of it." America's true interest is to "steer clear of European contentions.... Europe is too thickly planted with kingdoms to be long at peace, and whenever a war breaks out between England and any foreign power, the trade of America goes to ruin, because of her connection with Britain." Paine's proposal that America should pursue peaceful commerce with all nations while making political alliances with none became the essence of American political isolationism for over a century after independence was attained.

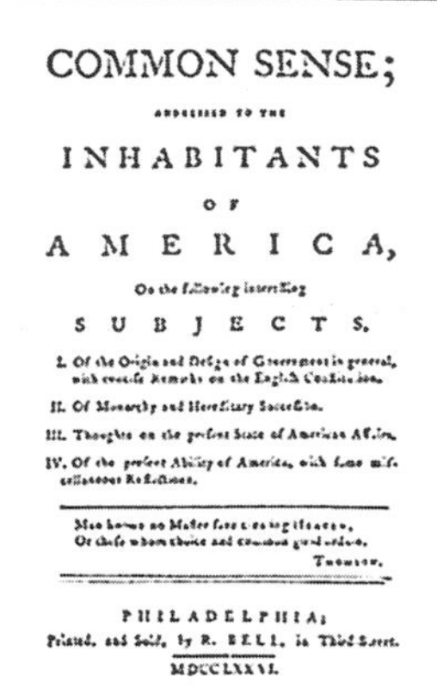

COMMON SENSE;

ADDRESSED TO THE

INHABITANTS

OF

AMERICA,

On the following interesting

SUBJECTS.

I. Of the Origin and Design of Government in general, with concise Remarks on the English Constitution.

II. Of Monarchy and Hereditary Succession.

III. Thoughts on the present State of American Affairs.

IV. Of the present Ability of America, with some miscellaneous Reflections.

PHILADELPHIA;
Printed, and Sold, by R. BELL, in Third-Street.
MDCCLXXVI.

Thomas Paine's *Common Sense*, first published on January 10, 1776, urged colonists to seek independence. Library of Congress

March 3, 1776

The Continental Congress sends Silas Deane to France to seek friendship and aid for the American cause.

A defeated member of congress, Deane had no diplomatic experience. Although he was not fluent in French, he helped create methods for securing military aid and funds from France.

See July 27, 1777.

April 6, 1776

Congress opens American ports to all nations except Britain.

By opening all of its seaports to foreign trade, Congress rejected Britain's Navigation Acts and approved a de facto act of commercial independence. The decree permitted French, Spanish, Dutch, and other nations' ships to trade with the American colonies.

May 2, 1776

King Louis XVI of France orders 1 million livres to be used secretly to supply munitions for the American army.

This assistance resulted from discussions between Arthur Lee and the French foreign minister, the Count de Vergennes. Soon after its founding on November 29, 1775, the Committee on Secret Correspondence instructed Lee to go to Paris because an agent of Vergennes in America, Achard (or Archard) de Bonvouloir, assured the committee of French interest. Lee was also assisted by Caron de Beaumarchais, the author of *The Barber of Seville*, who had some influence at the French court.

Vergennes was eager to aid any enemy of Great Britain because France had fought the British and lost most of its empire as a result of the Treaty of Paris of 1763, and he was desirous of restoring the balance of power in Europe. In offering aid to the American, Vergennes wanted to restore the balance of power in Europe. To fulfill this plan, he persuaded Charles III of Spain to give 1 million livres to the American independence movement in June 1776.

Beaumarchais became the middleman in purchasing the military supplies for America. Under the name of the Rodrique Hortalez Company, Beaumarchais profited from his connections to the French government by providing 40 vessels carrying a substantial amount of French goods to the American insurgents.

June 7, 1776

Independence is proposed.

Richard Henry Lee of Virginia presented a resolution to the Continental Congress, that the United Colonies "are, and of a right ought to be, free and independent states." Lee's resolution included two other important clauses: one stated "it is expedient forthwith to take the most effectual measures for forming foreign alliances"; the second asked that "a plan of confederation be prepared."

Lee's resolution resulted in the appointment of three committees: one, to prepare a declaration of independence; the second, to propose a treaty for use by a diplomatic commission to Europe; and the third, to prepare a constitution for governing the new United States.

See July 2–4, 1776; September 24, 1776; and November 15, 1777.

July 2–4, 1776

On July 2, Congress votes for an independence declaration by 12-0, New York abstaining.

Two days later, Congress approved the committee report prepared by Thomas Jefferson, with the assistance of John Adams and Benjamin Franklin. This

Franklin, Jefferson, Adams, Livingston, and Sherman drafting the Declaration of Independence. National Archives

report provided the text for the Declaration of Independence. The vote on July 4 was, again, 12-0.

July 19, 1776

Congress votes to have the Declaration of Independence engrossed for formal signature by the 55 delegates.

By this time, the Provincial Congress of New York had voted (July 9) to endorse independence, making the declaration unanimous, without abstention.

September 24, 1776

Model treaty for negotiating with European countries is approved by Congress.

This "Plan of 1776" contained basic concepts of maritime law and neutral rights that the new nation pursued throughout its history. Following international ideas frequently used in 18th-century Europe, the Model Treaty's main points were (1) the contention that free ships make free goods; (2) freedom of neutrals to trade in noncontraband items; (3) a restricted contraband list not including foodstuffs and naval stores.

Particularly regarding possible treaties with France and Spain, the committee report hoped to make these only commercial treaties, involving no political or military alliances. It asked France to treat American imports on the same basis as those of French citizens and agreed to give France the most-favored-nation status in American trade.

September 26, 1776

Congress appoints a diplomatic commission to negotiate treaties with European nations.

The three appointees were Benjamin Franklin, Silas Deane, and Thomas Jefferson. After Jefferson declined, Arthur Lee replaced him.

December 26, 1776

American troops defeat the British in a battle at Trenton.

Crossing the icy Delaware River at night and attacking from the north and northeast, Washington's soldiers surprised the British troops camped near Trenton, New Jersey.

Washington's victory came after a series of defeats and retreats by the American armies. In June, the Northern Army retreated from Canada. Later, it lost engagements to the British at Lake Champlain (October 11) and Split Rock (October 13). Washington's army lost New York City (September 12) and retreated across New Jersey to Pennsylvania by December 11. Thus, Washington's attack on Trenton gave the Continental Army one happy note after six months of defeat.

1777

April 17, 1777

Congress reconstitutes the Committee of Secret Correspondence as the Committee for Foreign Affairs.

The committee had no secretary or clerk, however, and its scope of activity was strictly limited.

July 27, 1777

Two famous foreign military officers, the Marquis de Lafayette and Baron Johann de Kalb, arrive in Philadelphia.

These and other European military experts had been recruited by Silas Deane. Together with two other foreign officers, Tadeusz Kościuszko (commissioned October 18, 1776) and Baron von Steuben (commissioned May 5, 1778), these generals aided the colonial war effort. Deane's recruitments, occasionally overzealous, were assisted by the charm, popularity, and renown as a scientist of Benjamin Franklin, who reached Paris on December 21, 1776, and quickly endeared himself to French public opinion.

October 17, 1777

The Northern American Army wins the Battle of Saratoga.

British forces under General John Burgoyne invaded northern New York in an attempt to gain control of the region from the Hudson River to Canada. The American victory prevented this region from falling to British rule. In addition, it caused Lord North to form the Carlisle Commission to attempt to obtain a reconciliation with the colonists in 1778 and to prevent the formation of a French-American alliance. Most writers consider the Battle of Saratoga a turning point in the war. American agents in France noted that Frenchmen reacted as if their troops had defeated the British. Obtaining French assistance and, eventually, the French Alliance of 1778 was made less difficult by the events of October 17, 1777.

The surrender of General Burgoyne at Saratoga. Copy of painting by John Trumbull, 1820–1821. National Archives

November 15, 1777

Articles of Confederation are adopted by Congress.

These articles came from the committee originated in June 1776 as part of Lee's resolution. The committee reported to Congress in July 1776, but the delegates intermittently debated the 13 clauses of the articles for more than a year. After approval by Congress on November 15, they were sent to each state for ratification, a process not completed until March 1, 1781.

December 17, 1777

France recognizes American independence.

Louis XVI's council of state agreed to recognize the independence of the United States.

1778

February 6, 1778

The Franco–American Treaty of Alliance is approved.

The treaty was signed by French Foreign Minister Vergennes and American Commissioners Deane and Franklin. The agreement culminated in nearly two years of French aid to the American cause.

On February 6, two treaties were signed: one, of alliance; the second, of amity and commerce. France recognized American independence, granting it the rights to Bermuda as well as all British colonies on the mainland of North America. The French were free to acquire all British territory in the West Indies. Both parties agreed not to make a truce with Britain without the other's consent.

The commercial treaty gave each ally the most-favored-nation status. The alliance would be "forever," a unique clause; no one knows how it got inserted in the treaty. For the U.S. ratification of the treaty, see May 4, 1778.

impressive enough to lead London's political officials to seek a means to end the war.

The Virginia campaign of Cornwallis in 1781 followed the British success in taking Charleston and securing general control of the Carolinas. Prior to his arrival at Yorktown on August 1, Cornwallis appeared to be in control of the south. He intended to invest Yorktown as a communications base with General Clinton in New York.

The British plans went astray when Admiral de Grasse's fleet arrived on August 30 to blockade the Chesapeake Bay. A British fleet under Admiral Thomas Groves tried but failed to dislodge the French fleet between September 5 and 10, 1781. After Groves withdrew his ships, Cornwallis's loss seemed imminent.

Cornwallis's defeat became certain when Washington's army arrived in Virginia on September 24. De Grasse landed his French troops so that an army of 9,000 American and 7,800 French soldiers besieged Yorktown. Cornwallis held out until October 17 and, following negotiations, surrendered on October 19. Although minor British-American skirmishes occurred during 1782, the surrender at Yorktown proved to be the defeat that aroused the English government to seek peace.

October 20, 1781

Robert R. Livingston is appointed as first Secretary for Foreign Affairs.

Livingston served as secretary until June 4, 1783. The secretary for foreign affairs was the executive in charge of the committee reorganized by Congress in March 1781, after the Articles of Confederation became effective. The committee was appointed by and responsible to Congress, but its daily activity was now conducted by one head. Congress did not clearly define the secretary's duties, and members of Congress frequently interfered with matters of foreign affairs. The difficulties continued throughout the era of the Articles, because the creators of the government feared strong central government and chose to keep most political power under local and state control.

1782

February 27, 1782

The British are ready for peace.

Great Britain's House of Commons voted to cease prosecution of the American war and, on March 5, approved a bill authorizing the king to make peace with the "former colonies." The English had become "sick of the war," leading the House of Commons on March 4 to pass a resolution that considered those who advocated the war as enemies of the king and country.

March 20, 1782

Lord North resigns as Prime Minister.

After barely surviving a vote of "no confidence" on March 15, North resigned. Lord Rockingham, an advocate of peace, replaced North and decided to negotiate with America.

April 12, 1782

Peace negotiations begin.

English-American peace talks began informally in Paris between Franklin and Richard Oswald, an agent for Rockingham's ministry. Oswald bluntly told Franklin that peace is "absolutely necessary," but acceptable details were required.

See June 23 and November 30, 1782.

June 11, 1782

Having recognized American independence, the Dutch loan the new nation $2 million.

On April 19, John Adams, before inquiring about a possible loan, persuaded the Dutch government to recognize American independence. With the government's aid, Adams received a $2 million loan from Dutch bankers that was finalized on June 11, 1782. These two successes did not end Adams's endeavors, and on October 8, he signed a Treaty of Friendship and Commerce with the Netherlands.

See November 30, 1782.

June 23, 1782

John Jay joins Franklin in peace talks.

John Jay arrived in Paris from Madrid and joined Franklin's discussions with Oswald. Unlike Franklin, who preferred working closely with Vergennes, Jay suspected that the French minister placed the French and Spanish interests ahead of the American alliance.

Vergennes wanted to prevent an Anglo-American settlement until France could assist Spain in capturing Gibraltar. In the spring of 1782, French and Spanish forces launched a campaign to conquer Gibraltar, continuing the struggle until failure became apparent by September 30. There was also concern that Vergennes hoped to keep America weak by giving Spain control of the area west of the Appalachian Mountains throughout the Mississippi River valley.

Jay's suspicion of the French plans caused him to bypass Franklin. Jay asked a friend, Benjamin Vaughan, to contact Lord Shelburne, the British prime minister, who gained office after Lord Rockingham died on July 1. Jay's messenger informed Shelburne that if Oswald were commissioned in terms recognizing American independence, the peace negotiation could advance quickly. Jay suggested that by granting independence, Shelburne could benefit England because they would "cut the cords which tied us to France."

Shelburne agreed with Jay's terms, and on September 19, Oswald returned to Paris with an implicit assurance that Great Britain would recognize American independence.

November 30, 1782

Preliminary peace terms are accepted by the British and American peace commissioners in Paris.

On October 26, John Adams traveled from The Hague and arrived in Paris to join John Jay and Benjamin Franklin in finalizing a peace treaty with the British. Henry Laurens arrived in Paris on November 28, just in time to join the other Americans in signing the treaty on November 30.

Prior to the signing of the preliminary agreement, the American delegation agreed not to inform the French, a decision that violated the technical terms of the Alliance of 1778. However, Jay and Adams persuaded Franklin that the French should be told before the final peace treaties were signed. Thus, early in December, Franklin composed a diplomatically astute letter to Vergennes that reported on the American peace terms and expressed hope that the minister would overlook the delegation's lack of "propriety" in not consulting him. Franklin wrote that the American intention was not to break the French Alliance, because this would only benefit England. Then, Franklin cleverly added: "*The English, I just now learn, flatter themselves they have already divided us.* I hope this misunderstanding will therefore be kept secret, and that they will find themselves totally mistaken." The French went along with Franklin's duplicity; Vergennes's agenda was to end the American war and take action to prevent Russia from securing territory from the Ottoman Empire in the Black Sea area.

By secretly agreeing with Britain, the American commissioners demonstrated they were not innocent of the tactics of European diplomatic practice. Partly because Vergennes recognized this, and partly because France was eager to end the war, he accepted

Benjamin Franklin charms French aristocrats at the court of Versailles with his humble manner and homespun dress. Library of Congress

Franklin's explanation. The American delegates secured favorable peace terms from England and successfully maneuvered their diplomacy in the murky waters of European power politics. The peace terms became effective on January 20, 1783.

For the formal signing, see September 3, 1783.

1783

January 20, 1783

Articles of peace become effective.

On this date, Great Britain concluded peace terms with France, Spain, and the United States. Provisions of the agreements also ordered a general armistice on February 4.

See November 30, 1782; April 15, 1783; September 3, 1783.

April 15, 1783

Congress ratifies the preliminary peace terms of November 30, 1782.

After receiving the text of the peace agreement on March 13, some congressmen criticized the commissioners for not consulting with the French. Finally, on April 11, Congress proclaimed the end of hostilities and four days later ratified the treaty.

See November 30, 1782; January 20, 1783; September 3, 1783.

April 28, 1783

Last British loyalists evacuate New York.

During the war, the state governments passed a variety of laws to repress persons loyal to George III. Generally, Loyalists were disenfranchised, exiled, expelled from their offices and professions, and had property expropriated. Over 100,000 Loyalists fled to Canada or Europe, 7,000 alone leaving New York City on April 28.

The British government tried to cover the Loyalist property losses, and the peace treaty earnestly "recommended" that the states reimburse them. Most claims were not paid unless the British government did so, although payment became a diplomatic issue for some time afterward, not being resolved until the 1790s.

July 28, 1783

Francis Dana's mission to Russia ends without success.

Dana arrived at St. Petersburg on August 27, 1781. Because he spoke no Russian or French, he depended on John Quincy Adams, John Adams's 14-year-old son, to translate French for him. Dana and Adams visited most often with the French minister to Russia, the Marquis de Verac, who kept them informed on the Russian court.

As Verac told them, the Russians desired British aid against Turkey and did not wish to antagonize the British by recognizing Dana, the representative of the colonial rebels. As a result, Dana did not present his official papers to the Russian government until February 24, 1783, after the preliminary treaties of peace had been signed in Paris. Even then, Catherine refused to receive Dana, claiming that she must await the final ratification of the treaties. Although Dana argued that the United States had been independent for seven years, Vice Chancellor I. A. Osterman told him that the Russians did not recognize their act of rebellion.

On April 1, 1783, Congress accepted Robert Livingston's recommendation to recall Dana. Livingston did not believe Dana was needed because even if he were recognized, an American representative was unnecessary at St. Petersburg. As soon as Dana received news of his recall, he packed, leaving Russia on August 8.

Notably, Dana did not use his two years to establish contacts that would have established better relations between Russia and America. Although his original commission cited such relations as part of his duty, Dana failed to take the opportunity. He was no bon vivant such as Benjamin Franklin, and his inability to speak or learn Russian handicapped his work.

September 3, 1783

The definitive treaty of Paris is formally signed by Great Britain, France, Spain, and the United States.

Britain's major loss in the war was its 13 former American colonies. Although some Americans criticized the treaty, most historians believe the British were generous, especially since their forces held a strong military position in North America.

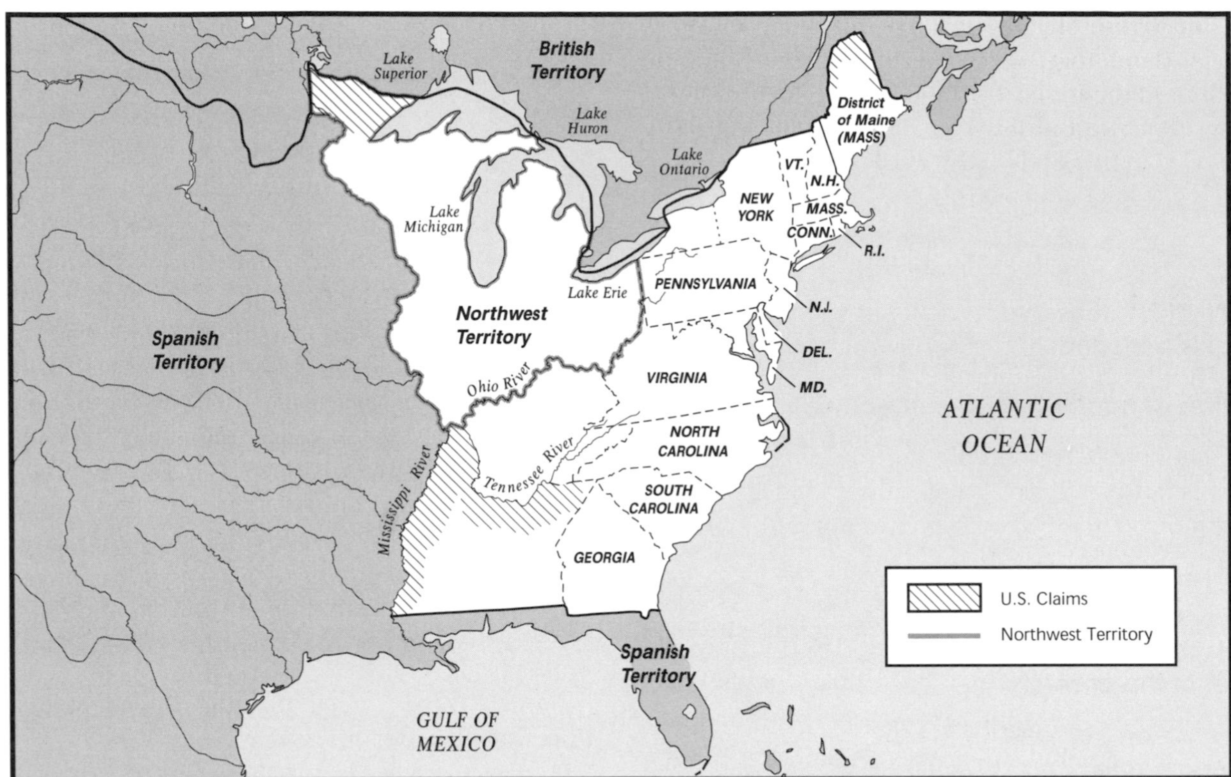

The United States after the Treaty of Paris, 1783

The Americans gained independence and a vast, uncharted area west of the Appalachian Mountains to the Mississippi River. While some boundary disputes remained to be settled, the United States gained the whole Mississippi River region, north to the Great Lakes and east to the St. Lawrence River. A special commission was designated to approve the northeastern boundary between New England and Canada.

In addition, America agreed to "recommend" the reimbursement of Loyalist property damage by the state governments. Great Britain granted American fishermen the "liberty," *not* the right, to fish in Britain's territorial waters, especially the Grand Banks area of Newfoundland. The word *liberty* caused frequent controversy over fishing privileges in future years. For the preliminary peace terms signature, see November 30, 1782.

October 15, 1783

Congress approves an Indian policy for the Northwest Territory.

Recommended by a special committee of Congress, the policy set a boundary between land open to settlement and land temporarily for the Indians. Because the Indians fought for the British against the American colonists, Congress assumed that the Treaty of Paris secured all rights to land in the Northwest to the United States.

The Paris Treaty never specifically mentioned the Indian rights because by a treaty of 1768, the British promised to protect the Indians. Great Britain now claimed that it had not given up Indian rights in the Paris Treaty. The United States obtained *only* the sole right to negotiate for land rights with the Indians. Furthermore, Britain argued that it could not evacuate the Northwest posts until it was assured that Indian rights were protected.

The United States rejected the British view, and Congress drew a boundary whereby it graciously permitted the Indians to remain in certain lands not now needed by the Americans. The boundary cited in 1783 extended up the Miami River in the west, north to the Maumee River, and northeast to Toledo on Lake Erie. Later, in May 1784, Congress shifted the boundary farther west and instructed its peace commissioners to negotiate with each Indian tribe separately in order to divide them and their demands.

The British objected to these unilateral American decisions and, together with demands for payment of debts, used the Indian policy to justify their retention of the Northwest posts.

December 4, 1783

Last British forces evacuate New York City, Long Island, and Staten Island.

General Washington led his troops into the city on November 25, to oversee the final evacuation.

December 12, 1783

Appearing before Congress in Annapolis, George Washington resigns as Commander in Chief of the armies.

This action officially concluded the American Revolutionary War. The revolution succeeded because of wartime diplomacy as well as military action. The French Alliance and French monetary contributions greatly assisted the United States. In the opinion of some historians, the French were the decisive factor in the defeat of Great Britain.

December 26, 1783

American trade with Great Britain is revived.

A British order-in-council permitted the importation of most American manufactured goods under the same terms as before 1776. British merchants profited from this order, for exports to America usually exceeded imports during the next decade. In 1784, British exports to the United States had a value of £3,679,467; imports, £749,345. American diplomats to Britain were not pleased, however, that the British refused to negotiate a commercial treaty with the new nation. The British found they could secure the benefits of trade with the American states without making any treaty concessions. They also closed all British colonies to American trade, although some U.S. merchants smuggled goods into the British West Indies.

See February 24 and April 8, 1785.

1784

February 22, 1784

First U.S. ship sails to China.

Under Captain John Greene's command, the *Empress of China* sailed from New York on February 22,

General Washington resigns his commission to Congress, Annapolis, Maryland, December 12, 1783. Copy of painting by John Trumbull, 1822–1824. National Archives

rounded Cape Horn at the extreme south of South America, and crossed the Pacific, reaching Canton on August 30. It returned in 1785, netting its investors a 25% profit, sufficient to attract future investment in the China trade.

March 1, 1784

Northwest Territory is formed.

Formation of the Northwest Territory began when Virginia ceded its claims to land in the Ohio River valley. Congress appointed a committee, chaired by Thomas Jefferson, to prepare plans for the region between the Ohio and Mississippi Rivers and the Great Lakes.

See April 23, 1784.

April 8, 1784

Secret order of the British Colonial Office instructs the Governor-General of Canada not to evacuate the Northwest Posts.

Although American leaders did not realize it, the British government issued this order to the Canadian officials the night before King George III proclaimed the treaty of peace. The order resulted from the appeals of Canadian fur traders and British military leaders to the British Colonial Office. The fur traders wanted to sustain their profits as long as possible; the military claimed there would be an Indian "butchery" of white men if they were betrayed by their British allies. Although the British ministers claimed the posts were held because U.S. debts were unpaid, this was an ex post facto argument to keep British control in that area.

April 23, 1784

Congress approves the first Northwest Ordinance.

The first instance of U.S. "colonial policy," the ordinance as drawn up by Jefferson's committee, proposed establishing 10 states that would eventually be admitted to the union as equal to the original 13 states. A territorial state would be a self-governing republic and be eligible for full statehood when its population equaled that of the smallest of the original 13 states. The ordinance provided that land would be given free to settlers, a clause that generated intensive debate in Congress over the next three years because land speculators wanted land to be sold in large sections for subdivision by investors.

April 30, 1784

Congress requests power to regulate foreign trade.

Because some states had sent agents to European capitals to obtain commercial treaties, the regulation of foreign trade became a critical issue. Hoping to centralize all foreign-trade regulations in Congress, the Virginia and Maryland legislatures requested that Congress be given power to pass navigation acts.

On April 30, Congress passed and submitted to the states for ratification a request granting it sole authority to regulate foreign-trade for the United States. Without such power, the congressional request asserted, "our foreign commerce must decline, and eventually be annihilated." This request to regulate all foreign commerce was not approved by all the states. The Articles of Confederation required unanimous consent to be amended, and legislators in states such as Massachusetts, Rhode Island, and Pennsylvania refused to ratify the measure because they either feared the increase of central power or preferred to retain their own foreign regulations.

Later, in 1785, a second attempt to amend the Articles by granting commercial powers to Congress was rejected (July 15, 1785). Lack of such power weakened the new government in foreign affairs, especially in gaining a treaty of commerce with Great Britain.

May 7, 1784

Congress approves a basis for commercial treaties with other nations.

Based on the "Plan of 1776" and previous treaties with France, Holland, and Sweden, the new guidelines resulted in a treaty with Prussia (September 10, 1785) and with Morocco (July 17, 1786).

June 26, 1784

Spain closes the Mississippi to American navigation.

The Spanish king instructed the governor of Louisiana to close the Mississippi River under his jurisdiction to all American vessels. Although the significance of this order was not clearly known until 1785, the Spanish orders claimed territory as far north as 32°28′—approximately the mouth of the Yazoo River. The Americans claimed that the Treaty of 1783 placed the boundary at 31° north and granted U.S. citizens the right to navigate the Mississippi and to use the port of New Orleans.

See July 20, 1785.

August 30, 1784

French decree limits American trade with the French West Indies.

The new American government hoped that France would retain open ports for U.S. trade in the West Indies. France had opened these ports during the Revolutionary War, but now, in its first decree following the Treaty of Paris, France chose to limit American trade. By this decree, American ships under 60 tons could import any product except flour, provided the product did not compete with French goods.

Throughout the 1780s, the U.S. minister to France, Thomas Jefferson, tried in vain to persuade the French to drop their trade restrictions. Although the decree of 1784 was revised on October 31, 1784, and in 1787 and 1788, the French continued to place restrictions on exports and imports of U.S. products to the French West Indies.

September 21, 1784

John Jay becomes Secretary for Foreign Affairs.

Following Robert Livingston's resignation on June 4, 1783, Congress delayed the appointment of a new foreign affairs secretary, and the secretary of Congress, Charles Thomson, handled necessary foreign messages. On March 1, 1784, Henry Remsen Jr. was named as undersecretary in charge of foreign dispatches.

On May 7, 1784, after learning that John Jay was returning from Europe, Congress appointed him as secretary for foreign affairs. Because of personal business, Jay did not begin work until September 21, 1784.

1785

February 24, 1785

John Adams is appointed as Minister to Great Britain.

Adams's three years at the court of George III were unsuccessful because English opinion was strongly anti-American. Adams reported that he was treated with "dry decency and cold civility," but the British ministers refused to negotiate a commercial treaty because they knew the Continental Congress was unable to control the trading relations of the 13 American states. Consequently, George III accepted Adams's papers but did not appoint a British minister to the United States.

March 10, 1785

Thomas Jefferson replaces Benjamin Franklin as Minister to France.

For the next four years, Jefferson had no significant problems to settle with France because the Franco-American commercial treaty had been signed earlier. In Paris, Jefferson became a friend of many philosophical radicals who opposed France's absolute monarchy and was an acute observer of the circumstances leading to the French Revolution in 1789.

March 11, 1785

Report on the Barbary powers enables Congress to fix a policy for treaties with these states.

One result of American independence was the loss of British protection for American ships from attacks by the pirates of the North African states of Morocco, Algiers, Tunis, and Tripoli. After the emperor of Morocco inquired about a necessary treaty, Congress appointed a commission on May 7, 1784, to form the proposed treaties. The commissioners were Benjamin Franklin, John Adams, and Thomas Jefferson. On November 11, 1784, this group summarized the Barbary situation in a report to Congress and recommended that in making treaties Congress should set a maximum sum of money for negotiations in the expectation that the American diplomats would pay as little as possible to secure the treaties.

On March 11, 1785, Congress approved the suggestions by defining the powers of the negotiators and authorizing the expenditure of a maximum of $80,000 in concluding the Barbary treaties.

April 8, 1785

Great Britain cuts off most trade between the United States and Canada's maritime provinces.

An order-in-council stated that only livestock, grain, and lumber could be imported into these provinces, and that these commodities must be carried in British ships and be proclaimed by the governor as necessary for the inhabitants. After being renewed several times, these orders became permanent by an Act of 1788.

May 20, 1785

Second Northwest Ordinance is adopted by Congress.

This ordinance provided for surveying the land into townships of 36 square miles, with every 16th section for public education. Land would be sold at public auctions in each area, with prices of no less than $1 per acre.

Soon after passage of the act, Thomas Hutchins, the geographer of the United States, began to survey the Ohio area west of Pittsburgh. Congress also sent agents to the region to make treaties with the Indians, but the largest tribe, the Shawnee, refused to sell their tribal lands. Settlers also began moving into the region, squatting on land that they claimed by right of occupancy. These squatters soon had to fight both Indians and troops sent by Congress to dislodge them from their settlements.

June 23, 1785

Navigation Acts of Massachusetts and New Hampshire discriminate against British ships and products.

According to these state laws, American exports could not leave port in English ships, and all imports arriving in non-American vessels paid double customs duties on their cargoes.

These strict commercial regulations were also passed by other states after it became obvious the Continental Congress did not have the power to regulate foreign trade. The Massachusetts legislature also passed (July 11) a resolution asking Congress to call a convention to revise the Articles of Confederation, the first of several efforts that anticipated the convention of 1787.

July 20, 1785

Jay-Gardoqui negotiations begin in New York.

Congress authorized Jay's discussions with Don Diego de Gardoqui to resolve disputes with Spain regarding the southwest boundary and the navigation of the Mississippi River. This conflict was precipitated when Spain closed the river south of its fort at Natchez. Congress stipulated that Jay must insist on American rights to navigate freely on the Mississippi. Spain's minister instructed Gardoqui that he could not give the United States the right to navigate without cost on the river. For results of the talks, see August 29, 1786.

September 10, 1785

Prussia and the United States sign a commercial treaty.

John Adams began treaty negotiations in Berlin during 1784, but they were completed by William Short, a secretary to Thomas Jefferson, who went to Berlin from Paris. Following the "Plan of 1776" the treaty recognized that privateers were illegal and that "free ships make free goods." In addition, two ideas attributed to Benjamin Franklin were accepted: noncombatants should be given immunity during wartime, and prisoners of war should be treated humanely. A final clause, Article XIII, became an issue before World War I (1914–1918) because it prohibited the confiscation of neutral goods in wartime; goods could be detained but only with compensation for losses.

December 8, 1785

John Adams demands that Britain evacuate the Northwest Posts.

Since his arrival in London during the spring of 1785, Adams had had frequent discussions with British officials on the issues of U.S. debt payment and the frontier posts. No results had been achieved, however. Thus, Adams finally decided to enunciate his demands squarely in a memorial to Lord Carmarthen, England's secretary of state.

The memorial brought no results other than to indicate the friction between the two nations. On February 28, 1786, the British secretary admitted his nation's obligation to withdraw but noted that the United States had not fulfilled any of its agreements on debts under the Treaty of Paris. The British would withdraw only after the debt clauses of the treaty were fulfilled. Under the Articles of Confederation, there was disagreement between the federal Congress and the state governments regarding the debt payment. The debt issue was not resolved until Alexander Hamilton became secretary of the Treasury in 1789.

1786

January 30, 1786

Major Samuel Shaw is appointed as the first U.S. Consul at Canton, China.

Shaw had been an official aboard the *Empress of China,* which completed its first voyage to Canton in 1784–1785. On his return, he sent details about the voyage and Canton to John Jay. As a result, Jay obtained Shaw's appointment as consul from Congress and on January 30 informed Shaw of his new position. Shaw went to China soon after, where, until his death in 1794, he served well in assisting U.S. merchants.

July 17, 1786

Congress ratifies a treaty with Morocco, a Barbary state.

As a consequence of congressional instructions on March 11, 1785, Thomas Barclay negotiated a treaty with the emperor of Morocco. Barclay obtained very liberal concessions from Emperor Sidi Mohamet. Vessels of each nation would be protected from seizure by passes of safe conduct, and commerce would be based on most-favored-nation principles. Consular powers over citizens of each nation were agreed to, and it was also agreed that in case of war, prisoners would not be enslaved.

Most notably, the United States did not have to pay "future presents or tributes" to Morocco. Finally, the emperor agreed to assist the Americans in obtaining favorable treaties with the other North African states.

Barclay did expend £5,000 for expenses, mostly as bribes to various officials. By European standards, however, this sum was small, the treaty obtained being relatively generous.

August 7, 1786

The Continental Congress considers proposals to strengthen the powers of the central government.

States such as Massachusetts instructed their delegates to seek amendments to give Congress control of foreign commerce as well as the right to create federal judges and to force states to pay the funds levied by the central government. Beginning on August 7, Congress debated several such proposals but the delegates could not agree. Because amendments to the Articles of Confederation required a unanimous vote, reforms aimed at improving the government became nearly impossible.

August 29, 1786

John Jay's trade treaty with Spain cannot gain ratification in Congress.

Jay and Gardoqui had been negotiating to obtain a trade agreement since July 20, 1785. Spain was willing to grant trade concessions to America in the Spanish colonies but refused to permit the Americans to navigate the Mississippi River. Spain controlled the river south of Natchez to New Orleans, cutting off southern and western agricultural commerce and trade from the Gulf of Mexico.

The impasse on the Mississippi issue ended on August 29, when a majority of Congress voted to change Jay's instructions to allow him to "forbear" on the demand for the free navigation of the river. The vote in Congress, however, was 7 to 5. Nine votes were necessary to ratify a treaty, and the southern delegates would not yield on the Mississippi issue. As a result, Jay decided that further negotiations were futile. A treaty with Spain was not obtained.

See December 1, 1788.

September 11, 1786

The Annapolis Convention convenes.

Delegates from five states met at Annapolis to consider revising the Articles of Confederation. Nine states had accepted invitations to attend. After the others failed to arrive, the five delegates voted to seek a meeting in Philadelphia on May 25, 1787.

1787

February 4, 1787

"Shays's Rebellion" fails.

The Massachusetts rebellion ended when 4,400 state militia under General Benjamin Lincoln captured 150 insurgents and scattered the rest of 1,200 "rebels," including Daniel Shays, the rebel leader.

Shays's Rebellion began in the summer of 1786 as protests by farmers, many of whom, such as Shays, were veterans of the Revolutionary army. The protests developed after the Massachusetts legislature refused to issue paper money or take other measures to relieve the bank foreclosures that the farmers suffered. To halt foreclosures, the dissidents stopped local courts from sitting in towns such as Northampton and Concord. At Springfield on September 26, Shays's men forced the state Supreme Court to adjourn.

Over the next four months, new state militia were recruited by the governor, but the size of Shays's "army" also increased. Because there was a federal arsenal at Springfield, the Confederation Congress authorized General Henry Knox to raise 1,340 men to protect the arsenal. Though the federal troops were not used, the call for such a force caused panic about "lawlessness of mobs" from many state delegations.

On January 26, Shays led 1,200 men to attack General William Shepherd at Springfield, hoping to defeat him before Lincoln's militia arrived. The "battle" was short. When Shepherd's artillery opened fire, the Shaysites fled. Soon after, Lincoln arrived and his army marched after Shays's rebels, capturing 150 of them at Petersham and crushing the rebellion. Shays fled to Vermont and was later pardoned, on June 13, 1788, by a newly elected governor, John Hancock, whose administration enacted legislation to ameliorate some of the difficulties of the western farmers.

May 25, 1787

Constitutional Convention convenes at Philadelphia.

This meeting had been called by the delegates at Annapolis in September 1786, but its sessions started late because a quorum of seven state delegations was not present between May 14 and 25.

On February 21, 1787, the Confederation Congress had endorsed the Philadelphia meeting by a resolution favoring a convention "for the sole and express purpose of revising the Articles of Confederation."

The convention's work was completed on September 17, 1787.

June 28, 1787

Treaty with Morocco is signed.

This commercial treaty was negotiated with the emperor of Morocco by Thomas Barclay, for the low price of $30,000 in gifts.

The treaty was essential after 1783, because the British navy no longer protected American ships from the privateers off the Barbary Coast of North Africa.

As a result, U.S. ships were raided and their crews held for ransom. Negotiations with agents of Morocco began in 1784, and Congress appropriated $80,000 to be used in solving the problem (May 12, 1785). Barclay's talks were assisted by the king of Spain, who hoped his intervention would induce the United States to change its policy in the Mississippi River valley.

The treaty with Morocco worked well, but the Barbary problem continued; the sultans of Algiers, Tunis, and Tripoli refused to sign the treaty. By 1788, 21 Americans had been enslaved by these pirates. Because the United States had no navy to fight the pirates, Secretary of Foreign Affairs Jay advised Congress to inform each of the 13 states that they should raise money to assist the enslaved Americans, but no state offered any funds. This gave Jay one more reason for advocating changes in the Articles of Confederation that would give Congress power to deal effectively with Algerians and other pirate nations. The Barbary problem continued to damage foreign commerce. By the 1790s, the Barbary pirates had set official ransom rates for prisoners; from $4,000 for cabin passengers down to $1,400 for each cabin boy.

September 17, 1787

Philadelphia Convention approves a new U.S. Constitution.

With George Washington presiding, 55 delegates met in Philadelphia and decided to write a new constitution rather than attempt to amend the Articles of Confederation. Varied proposals were debated by the delegates before arriving at 23 resolutions on July 26 that became the framework for the new constitution. This draft was debated further before the delegates approved the final document on September 17.

The Constitution created a president as chief executive with strengthened powers and established a bicameral Congress. The Congress could levy taxes, pay the national debt, and provide for the common defense and general welfare. Congress could also regulate commerce with foreign nations and between the states. After 9 of the 13 states ratified the document, it would become effective.

October 27, 1787

The first of the Federalist Papers is published to promote the ratification of the Constitution.

Among arguments of the "Federalist" writers, the advantages of the Constitution of 1787 in foreign commerce and the treaty-making process were emphasized. The series of "Federalist" papers was published in New York newspapers between October 27 and April 1788. They were later compiled in a two-volume work titled *The Federalist.* The 85 essays were written by Alexander Hamilton (who wrote 51), James Madison (29), and John Jay (5).

Included in the essays were comments that lauded the Constitution for giving the federal government powers over interstate and foreign commerce, in making treaties, and in providing for national security. As Hamilton wrote in No. 11: "under a vigorous national government, the natural strength and resources of the country, directed to a common interest, would baffle all the combinations of European jealousy to restrain our growth."

1788

September 13, 1788

Eleven states having ratified the Constitution, preparations begin for inaugurating the new government.

Following ratification by the ninth state, New Hampshire, on June 21, 1788, Congress established a committee to prepare for launching the new government. Following the committee's report, Congress on September 13 named New York City as headquarters for the government and instructed each state to appoint presidential electors to convene on February 4, 1789, to choose a president.

The ratification process lasted over a year because some states disputed the Constitution's failure to protect human rights. New Hampshire wanted 12 amendments added regarding individual freedom; Virginia wanted 20 items in a bill of rights; Massachusetts listed 9 desired amendments. American political leaders agreed that the early order of business at the first congressional session in 1789 would be to add civil rights amendments to the Constitution.

By September 13, 11 states had ratified the Constitution. North Carolina and Rhode Island did not approve until after the new government had begun to function, with North Carolina ratifying on September 25, 1789, and Rhode Island on May 29, 1790.

December 1, 1788

Spain grants Americans limited rights to navigate the Mississippi River to New Orleans, provided the users pay the 15% duties charged by Madrid.

Spain granted this concession to encourage western farmers to join James Wilkinson's plans to set up the new state of "Franklin" in the southwest and ally the new nation with Spain. Wilkinson's plots were not successful, but Spain's concessions began a slow increase of Mississippi trade by American farmers.

III. THE FEDERALIST ERA

British Trade
Undeclared French War

1789

March 4, 1789

First Congress under the Constitution is scheduled to meet in New York, but there is no quorum until April 1.

The House of Representatives organized and elected a presiding officer on April 1; the Senate elected a temporary presiding officer on April 6. The first business in the Senate was to count the electoral college ballots. George Washington was the unanimous choice for president; John Adams became vice president. Washington was inaugurated on April 30, 1789.

Washington's First Cabinet: (left to right) Washington, Secretary of War Henry Knox, Secretary of the Treasury Alexander Hamilton, Secretary of State Thomas Jefferson, and Attorney General Edmund Randolph. Library of Congress

May 5, 1789

French Estates General convenes at Versailles.

Although King Louis XVI called the legislative group together to resolve France's economic problems, the three ESTATES soon agreed to meet as one NATIONAL ASSEMBLY on June 17, 1789. The assembly began the French Revolutionary changes in government during the next year.

July 3, 1789

Incident causing the Nootka Sound controversy occurs in the waters off Vancouver Island.

The British government hoped to gain claims to part of the west coast of North America by sending ships and Chinese workers to construct a fort on Vancouver. On July 3, the British ship *Argonaut*, commanded by Captain James Colvert, was seized by a Spanish ship. Spain claimed the entire Pacific coast and said the *Argonaut* and three other British ships were there illegally.

The Spanish action required the British cabinet to consider possible war.

See April 30, 1790.

July 4, 1789

U.S. Congress passes the Tariff of 1789.

This tariff was chiefly a revenue measure, but some features gave moderate protection. One clause gave a 10% reduction in duties to goods arriving in U.S.-built or -owned ships. James Madison failed to obtain discriminatory tariffs between nations having or not having a commercial treaty with America. Hamilton did not wish to discriminate against the British, who had made no treaty with the United States.

From the secretary of the Treasury's perspective, Great Britain would be more inclined to make a favorable commercial treaty with America if the United States repaid its debts and gained Britain's goodwill. Madison's proposal would cause an "economic war" with Britain that the United States could not win.

July 14, 1789

The Bastille is destroyed by mobs in Paris.

As a symbol of the king's absolute power, the Bastille held several political prisoners. The mobs, however, freed all prisoners lodged there.

On the same day, the General Marquis de Lafayette was named commander of the National Guard, and the assembly replaced the Bourbon flag of the gold fleur-de-lis with the tricolor as the flag of France.

July 27, 1789

The State Department becomes the first executive department authorized by Congress.

Originally called the Department of Foreign Affairs, it was renamed the Department of State on September 15, 1789.

John Jay acted as interim secretary of the department until Thomas Jefferson assumed duty on March 22, 1790. Appointed as secretary on September 26, 1789, Jefferson was in Paris as the American minister to France and did not return home until late in 1789 and did not take office until March 22, 1790.

August 24, 1789

The *Columbia*, a trading ship from Boston, sails from the Oregon Territory to Honolulu on its way to Canton, China.

Commanded by Captain Robert Gray, the U.S. merchant ship pioneered a passage across the Pacific that made the stopover at Hawaii popular with U.S. sailors. At first the ships exported sandalwood from the islands, but after the War of 1812, American whaling ships dominated in the central and south Pacific Ocean.

August 27, 1789

The French Assembly issues the Declaration of the Rights of Man.

Like the U.S. Declaration of Independence, this document claimed to be based on the natural rights of men to determine their government.

1790

March 29, 1790

At Washington's request, Gouverneur Morris meets informally in London with Britain's Foreign Minister.

President Washington asked Morris to act informally in London to discover if the British would accept a commercial treaty and friendly relations with America. In meetings during March and April with Prime Minister William Pitt and the foreign minister, the Duke of Leeds, Morris found them friendly but unprepared to negotiate a treaty. Morris did not know at the time, but the British learned through their "spy" in New York, Major George Beckwith, that Washington's cabinet would not approve discriminatory action against England but desired good relations. Beckwith gained this information from Alexander Hamilton, who had befriended the British officer and hoped to gain favors by disclosing information about the pro-British bias of Washington's cabinet.

Because Pitt had inside information on U.S. policy, he did not need to placate Morris by negotiating a favorable commercial treaty or settling the northwest posts issue.

April 30, 1790

British Cabinet risks war over the Nootka Sound incident.

Having received reports of Spanish action against four British ships, their crews, and passengers, the cabinet of William Pitt decided to demand adequate satisfaction for the Spanish outrages. The war never took place because by October 1790, the

Spanish had adopted a conciliatory policy and sought an alliance with England.

The British decision to risk war caused President Washington's cabinet to discuss how the United States should react to an Anglo-Spanish war.

See August 27, 1790.

August 4–12, 1790

Arrangements to pay the French debt are made.

Congressional legislation finalized a schedule of finances for loans from Holland to pay France for funds obtained during the American Revolution. Annual payments of interest and principal were set to conclude all payments on February 1, 1807.

August 27, 1790

President Washington seeks cabinet members' advice on the Nootka Sound controversy.

Assuming a British army might seek to cross U.S. territory to attack the Spanish, the president asked what the U.S. government should do. Secretary of State Jefferson advocated a "watch and wait" policy to allow Americans to bargain with both sides in the event of a crisis. Hamilton desired sympathy toward the British because he believed their trade was indispensable to America.

Because Spain yielded to London in October 1790, the crisis did not require U.S. involvement. The U.S. cabinet papers showed, however, the division between Hamilton and Jefferson, a situation that prevailed until Jefferson's resignation in 1793.

December 15, 1790

Jefferson reports to Congress on the failure of Gouverneur Morris's mission to London.

In Morris's final letters on his mission, he concluded that America should retaliate against British trade and draw closer to France, a policy preferred also by Jefferson.

Congress reacted against Britain as a result of this report and undertook retaliatory commercial acts in 1791.

1791

February 22–23, 1791

Committee of House of Representatives reports a tariff bill to discriminate against Great Britain.

Hamilton and the Federalists opposed this legislation and prevented its passage. American merchants profited from English trade even without a commercial treaty. Nevertheless, many Jeffersonians disliked the way London treated the American requests for trade and better relations, and wanted to place higher charges on British than on other foreign commerce. This would be done by placing a 30 cents per ton duty on ships with commercial treaties and a 50 cents duty on ships without such agreements, including British.

This discriminatory act passed the House but failed in the Senate. Hamilton's Federalist faction in the Senate amended the law to make all foreign duties the same.

March 12, 1791

Jefferson seeks negotiations with Spain on the Mississippi boundary and navigation issues.

To assist the United States in gaining navigation rights on the Mississippi and having the 31st parallel recognized as the southern U.S. border, Jefferson wrote to William Short, the American chargé at Paris, to request French aid as a mediator. France's foreign minister, the Count de Montmorin, agreed and sent a memo to Madrid suggesting such negotiations. By March 1792, the Spanish agreed to negotiate and Jefferson appointed Short and William Carmichael, the chargé in Madrid, to carry out negotiations. For previous problems with Spain in the Mississippi River valley, see June 26, 1784, and July 20, 1785.

June 20–25, 1791

Louis XVI's attempt to flee France is halted at Varennes.

The king was returned to Paris, where he agreed to accept the constitution of 1791, making him the constitutional monarch of France, a position of limited royal power, which neither the king nor his nobles desired.

October 1, 1791

French Legislative Assembly convenes as part of the constitutional monarchy.

Already, however, the new regime was in danger. On August 27, 1791, FREDERICK WILLIAM II of PRUSSIA and LEOPOLD II of AUSTRIA ISSUED the DECLARATION OF PILLNITZ , saying they would intervene on behalf of the French monarchy if they gained the unanimous consent of the European powers, including Great Britain.

November 4, 1791

Ohio Indians defeat forces under General Arthur St. Clair.

This was the second American effort to dislodge the Indians from the territory claimed by Congress on October 15, 1783. During the fall of 1790, U.S. forces under General Josiah Harmar lost to the Indians. In both cases, British arms and ammunition had been used by the Indians, a fact increasing the western settlers' antagonism toward Great Britain.

See May 8, 1792.

November 9, 1791

The first British Minister to the United States, George Hammond, presents his credentials to Secretary Jefferson.

After U.S. attempts since 1783 to have Great Britain assign a diplomatic representative, the British cabinet finally decided to do so in January 1791, largely as a means to counteract "the French party" in America. Hammond was instructed to combat anti-British legislation and to report on the status of the Franco-American Alliance. He had no power to discuss a commercial treaty and could only offer the possibility of future negotiations on the Northwest posts.

Hammond arrived in America in October but waited until Thomas Pinckney was nominated as U.S. minister to England before offering his credentials to Jefferson.

1792

April 20, 1792

France declares war on Austria.

The apparent reason for war was the belief that French royalists-in-exile had persuaded Austria and Prussia to march on Paris, overthrow the revolutionaries, and reaffirm King LOUIS XVI's power. PRUSSIA WAS ALLIED with Austria, joining the Habsburg emperor in the War of the First Coalition against France.

May 8, 1792

The American Congress approves the Militia Act to raise troops to fight the Indians.

In April, 1792, General Anthony WAYNE was made army commander in chief to fight the Ohio Indians. The Militia Act authorized states to enroll all able-bodied free white men between 18 and 45 years of age to operate with Wayne's forces.

June 3, 1792

Gouverneur Morris is formally presented as the Minister of the United States to King Louis XVI.

President Washington appointed Morris minister in 1791, despite evidence that French republicans such as General Lafayette opposed Morris. The appointment was approved by the U.S. Senate on January 12, 1792, and Morris went to Paris from London, where he had many friends among the royalists. Many French republicans thought Morris was an English and Austrian spy.

August 10, 1792

Paris mobs storm the Tuileries Palace, massacre the Swiss guards, and suspend the king's power.

Because the war with Austria was going badly, the leaders of the Paris Commune (city government) believed the king would again try to flee the nation and obtain additional foreign support against the revolution.

After suspending the king's power, the Commune called for the election of a National Convention to form a republic. The Convention sessions began on September 21, 1792.

September 21, 1792

The first French Republic is proclaimed, ending the constitutional monarchy.

September 30, 1792

Great Council of Indian Tribes meets on the Maumee River in Ohio to seek terms of mediation with the U.S. government.

Representatives of the six Nations of Iroquois acted as mediators and secured the demands of the tribes in the Northwest territory. Because of their previous successes against American troops, the Indians insisted on obtaining all land north of the Ohio River, a condition the United States rejected.

By this time, President Washington expressed willingness to negotiate for a transfer of title from the Indians as the British had interpreted the Treaty of Paris (see October 15, 1783). The Indian demand was too extravagant, however, and the United States prepared another military expedition.

December 5, 1792

Washington is reelected President with 132 votes and 3 abstentions.

John Adams is reelected as vice president, although the anti-Federalist opposition gave 50 votes to George Clinton of New York.

1793

January 21, 1793

Execution of Louis XVI, former king of France.

The king's execution by advocates of a republican government aroused the other monarchs of Europe to consult about methods to restore France's legitimate ruler. Great Britain was also discontent with the radical fervor of the French revolutionists whose propaganda decrees called on all people to overthrow their tyrannical kings.

February 1, 1793

France declares war on Great Britain and the Netherlands.

Tension increased between Paris and London during 1792 as a result of the arrest of the French king and the September massacres. In December, the Jacobean radicals in the Assembly promoted the passage of decrees that threatened Britain's Dutch allies. The Jacobins wanted to seize Holland, its fleet, and wealth and persuade the English to eliminate its monarchy.

Following the execution of Louis XVI on January 21, 1793, Great Britain expelled the French ambassador. This provided the Jacobins with a reason to fight, and the French Assembly unanimously voted for war on England and Holland. Soon after, Austria, Prussia, and other European states joined the English against the French.

February 1, 1793

Negotiations with Spain are delayed.

Following Jefferson's attempts to get French aid in negotiating the Mississippi questions with Spain (see March 12, 1791), William Short and William Carmichael arrived in Madrid at a bad moment, just as France declared war on Austria and England, following the execution of Louis XVI. The Spanish royalists had become so upset by the radical events in France that they decided to seek alliance with Great Britain for the first time since 1585. By March 25, Spain allied with England and was at war with France. The mission of Short and Carmichael ended, negotiations on the issues being delayed until 1795, after Spain made peace with France.

April 1, 1793

In Paris, the Committee of Public Safety (CPS) secures control of French political power, suspending the Republican Constitution until the war threat ends.

The committee had nine members but Maximilien Robespierre became, in practice, the dictatorial head of the committee and instituted a Reign of Terror against all opponents of the CPS.

April 19, 1793

Washington's cabinet discusses the nation's neutrality policy in relation to the French Alliance.

Edmund Genet, the new French minister to America, had arrived in Charleston, South Carolina, on April 8, and was expected to submit his diplomatic credentials in the near future.

The cabinet agreed unanimously that neutrality should be maintained. The questions were how to receive the French minister and whether the Treaty of 1778 was still in effect as a consequence of Louis XVI's execution.

As in many matters arising during Washington's first term, Secretary of the Treasury Alexander Hamilton and Secretary of State Thomas Jefferson presented divergent views on the French situation. Hamilton argued the United States was not obligated to the new French government and believed it was in the American interest to sever the alliance and avoid involvement in European quarrels. He advised Washington to issue a statement to Genet that would assert that America did not acknowledge the alliance under the present circumstances. "We have reserved that point for future discussion." In this manner, the alliance could remain inoperative, perhaps forever.

Jefferson disagreed with Hamilton's tactics. He believed America's neutrality should be as benevolent as possible toward France. He claimed the 1778 Treaty was not with the monarch but with the French nation, and the alliance therefore remained in effect. Until France specifically asked the United States to become active militarily, the question of acting under the alliance could be held in abeyance. France might never ask for such help. From his perspective, Jefferson did not believe Washington should make a statement to Genet such as Hamilton suggested.

Following the cabinet session and after considering the written arguments of Hamilton and Jefferson, Washington prepared the Proclamation of Neutrality, which was issued on April 22. Later, on May 8, he received Genet without making any statement regarding the Treaty of 1778.

April 22, 1793

President Washington proclaims a declaration of neutrality.

After studying the arguments presented by Hamilton and Jefferson, Washington selected a moderate policy course. He asserted the United States was at peace with all nations and instructed citizens to avoid hostile acts against any of the belligerents.

See June 29, 1793.

May 22, 1793

Minister Genet requests an advance payment by the United States of debts due France.

On May 18, Citizen Genet was formally received by Washington. Neither party referred to the Treaty of 1778, so the question of American military action was not broached.

The French government needed money, however, and Genet requested the $2,461,513 due to France from loans made since 1778. Previously, France and the United States had agreed on a schedule of payments that would end in 1807. Genet now requested prepayment of the funds so that he could purchase supplies, naval stores, and "other services" in the United States. The "other services" were for the expenses of privateers and an expedition by American mercenaries planned by Genet against Spanish New Orleans.

Washington considered the request for prepayment but agreed with Jefferson not to make the advance except, if Genet desired, an advance of the total payments due for 1793.

June 5, 1793

Secretary of State Jefferson tells the French Minister Genet that his actions have infringed on American sovereignty.

Ever since landing at Charleston on April 8, Genet had undertaken questionable activity for a diplomatic ministry. He commissioned American ships as privateers against British ships and established French prize courts to divide the spoils of captured British ships. Finally, he sought to organize an army under the former American General George Rogers Clark for an expedition against Spanish and British holdings in North America.

Many Americans remembered French aid in the revolution or favored Genet because they opposed the British. Jefferson had first sympathized with Genet but soon realized that his arrogant and extreme actions hurt the French cause in America. Thus, on June 5, he warned Genet to act more circumspectly in his manner and actions, advice that the French minister did not follow.

See August 1, 1793.

June 8, 1793

British order-in-council authorizes the seizure and preemptive purchase of all neutral cargoes of foodstuffs bound for ports under French control.

By an additional order of November 6, 1795, the British announced the detention of all ships carrying French produce or supplies to France or French colonies. These orders violated the neutral right that "free ships make free goods." Very soon, over 300 U.S. ships, mostly in the West Indies, were seized by the British navy and privateers.

June 15, 1793

In the case of *Ware v. Hylton* (3 Dallas, 199), the U.S. Supreme Court rules that state laws are invalid if they infringe on a treaty of the U.S. government.

The case involved a Virginia state law of 1777 that sequestered funds owed to Great Britain. Because the Paris Treaty of 1783 included articles by which the federal government would assist Britain in having its debts paid, the court ruled the Virginia law infringed on this treaty. The court ruled that treaties made in accordance with the Constitution are above state law. This court decision further assisted the Federalist Party policy of funding debts and strengthening the credit of the new nation.

June 29, 1793

The first of a series of newspaper articles is published in which Hamilton and Madison argue the policy of neutrailty and the French Alliance.

The first of Hamilton's seven articles against the French alliance, justifying the Federalist policy on neutrality, appeared on June 29. He wrote under the pseudonym "Pacificus," arguing that the American alliance of 1778 required aid to France only if it were defending itself. Because France declared war on its enemies, Hamilton said it was the aggressor. Moreover, Hamilton claimed that France assisted in the American Revolution because it sought revenge on Great Britain, not because it loved America. Similarly, he said, America must act in its best interest, which was to remain clear of European wars.

Responding to Hamilton in five letters published between August 24 and September 18 by the *Gazette of the United States,* Madison denied that America's desire to be neutral suspended the Alliance of 1778. He attributed such arguments to those who hate our republican government and the French Revolution. Madison also emphasized that the president should consult Congress about treaty obligations because the legislature had jurisdiction over the powers of making war and treaties. Viewing it as an executive function, he said, emanated from British sources favoring "royal prerogative."

In addition to publicly airing the issues of neutrality, these articles and others that debated the policy in various newspapers gave the discussion of proper foreign relations a democratic hearing, raising both passions and ideas between the Federalist and Democratic-Republican Parties being formed.

August 1, 1793

Recall of Citizen Genet is agreed to by Washington's cabinet.

Even after Jefferson's warning to Genet on June 5, the French minister continued to raise volunteers for France and to outfit privateer ships against the British. By August, even Jefferson came to deplore Genet's actions as dampening American sympathy for France.

Jefferson explained the decision to recall Genet in a letter of August 16, sent to Gouverneur Morris, U.S. minister to France. Telling Morris to request Genet's recall, Jefferson wrote that Genet continued to commission privateers, used French consuls to judge prize courts of captured British ships, and used insulting language toward President Washington. In July, Genet had allegedly said he would appeal over Washington's head to the people, although Genet denied this, saying he would appeal to Congress. Most particularly, Jefferson said Genet had conspired to outfit and send off a captured British ship, the *Little Sarah,* renamed the *Petite Democrate,* after explicitly promising Jefferson he would not do so.

Significantly, Jefferson feared Genet might order his privateers to intercept his letter to Morris requesting the recall. Consequently, the secretary of state did not inform the French minister of the cabinet's recall decision until September 15, when he knew the ship carrying his letter to Paris was far out in the Atlantic.

October 8, 1793

The French readily accede to Genet's recall but, in turn, request the recall of Gouverneur Morris.

When Morris presented Jefferson's request for Genet's recall, the Jacobin faction had just replaced the Girondin Party, which had appointed Genet. The Jacobins were just gaining power and added Genet's indiscretions to their attacks on the Girondin Party.

Moreover, the French republicans had desired to renounce Morris's actions for some time, and had the opportunity in October 1793, when Genet's recall was requested. Having been in France before the revolution began in July 1789, Morris had become friendly with members of the king's court. He had been received by Louis XVI in June 1792, just shortly before the king's loss of power in August. Some French republicans thought Morris had conspired to help the king escape to Austria.

While agreeing to Genet's recall, the French government decided to request the recall of Morris as a quid pro quo. They appointed Jean Antoine Joseph Fauchet as the new minister to the United States, instructing him to seek the recall of Morris, who was unpopular with, and unsympathetic to, the French republicans. Fauchet did not arrive in America until January 1794. He waited until April 9, after he was formally received, to request Morris's recall.

The French Jacobins also instructed Fauchet to arrest Genet and return him to France for trial and possible execution. Genet, however, refused to return and secured support to remain in the United States. He married Cornelia Clinton, daughter of New York's governor, George Clinton, and lived the rest of his life in America.

December 31, 1793

Jefferson resigns as Secretary of State.

Although Jefferson had anticipated resigning early in 1793, President Washington prevailed on him to continue in office. Increasingly, however, Jefferson became frustrated with Hamilton's meddling in foreign affairs and openly communicating cabinet "secrets" to British officials. Jefferson wrote Washington on July 31, 1793, that he desired to retire as secretary of state by the end of the year.

1794

January 2, 1794

Edmund Randolph becomes the new Secretary of State.

Randolph had been the attorney general and the only cabinet member who aided Jefferson by not being pro-British. Washington hoped, apparently, that Randolph's appointment would keep some balance of opinion in the cabinet. Randolph was a loyal follower of Washington and usually sought to be nonpartisan among the political factions.

February 17, 1794

The British establish Fort Miami on the Maumee River, 60 miles southwest of Detroit.

The expedition to organize this new fort was sent by Lord Dorchester, governor-general of Canada, a strong advocate of a buffer zone for Indian tribes between the American settlements and British posts in the Northwest and Canada. The effort to create this new fort and Dorchester's efforts to urge an Indian war against Americans increased threats of an English-American conflict in 1794–1795.

March 26, 1794

Congress embargoes all ships in U.S. harbors.

Legislation for a 30-day embargo extended on April 25, for another month, was an attempt to retaliate for British restrictions on neutral trade. The acts were, in fact, restrictive of both French and British trade. One result of this legislation was a British decision to open, temporarily, U.S. trade in the West Indies and to pay Americans for cargo they had confiscated.

April 19, 1794

Senate confirms John Jay's appointment as a special envoy to London to negotiate disputes about trade and the northwest posts.

Jay's appointment caused a lengthy debate in the Senate because the Democratic Republicans claimed Jay had tried to sell out western territorial rights to the Spanish in 1786. Jay's appointment to London was a conciliatory effort, balancing the embargo on trade that Congress passed with a special envoy to negotiate the trade dispute.

See November 19, 1794.

June 5, 1794

Congress approves a neutrality act.

Congress based its act on President Washington's neutrality proclamation of 1793 and the "Rules Governing Belligerents" drawn up in 1793 as instructions to American customs agents. Providing guidelines for neutral action, the law prohibited arming new belligerent vessels in U.S. ports but recognized the legal equipment of foreign vessels. It also prohibited the recruitment of soldiers or sailors within the U.S. territory by a belligerent agent. In many respects, it made activity such as that Genet had taken officially illegal.

June 10, 1794

James Monroe, the new minister to France, receives instructions for his mission.

Despite misgivings by Federalists such as Hamilton, Washington appointed Monroe as minister, and the Senate approved the appointment on May 26. Before leaving for Paris, Monroe received instructions from Washington and Secretary Randolph that gave him little power to negotiate problems with France because they gave him no advantages to offer. He was to seek compensation for French spoliation of U.S. ships and to secure French aid in obtaining a treaty with the dey of Algiers and "free navigation" of the Mississippi from Spain.

Monroe was not, however, given exact information on John Jay's powers in securing a treaty with England. As a result, some commentators thought Monroe was sent to France as a ploy to deceive Paris while Jay made a treaty in London. Regarding the Jay mission, Monroe was told Jay sought redress of spoliation claims and evacuation of the northwest ports.

See January 16, 1795.

July 27, 1794

Thermidorian Reaction Plot overthrows Robespierre and ends the first French Republic.

As virtual dictator of the Committee of Public Safety, Robespierre used the Reign of Terror to attack more and more republicans who disagreed with him. On April 6, he had even executed the notable republican Georges-Jacques Danton, a former CPS member. The men who plotted Robespierre's demise on the 9th of Thermidor (July under the new French calendar proclaimed by the republic) agreed only on removing the dictator. The result, however, brought to power moderates who opposed the Jacobin republicans as well as the Paris Commune. Their new constitution became effective on August 22, 1794, establishing the Directory.

August 14, 1794

James Monroe receives a gala reception from the French National Convention.

Arriving in Paris just after the overthrow of Robespierre, Monroe found the French government in turmoil, with himself the only foreign representative in the city. Not knowing to whom to present his credentials, Monroe appealed directly to the president of the National Convention.

The convention not only greeted Monroe immediately but held a ceremonial expression of fraternity for him as a fellow republican. Following two hours of laudatory speeches, they asked Monroe to send them an American flag to hang beside the French flag in the convention hall.

When Federalists at home heard of the occasion and Monroe's speech in praise of the two republics, they expressed great displeasure with Monroe's "indiscretion." From London, John Jay complained that Monroe's actions would damage the treaty plans he had negotiated with Great Britain.

See January 1, 1796.

April 20, 1794

At the Battle of Fallen Timbers, General Anthony Wayne's forces defeat the Ohio Indians.

The British supplied the Ohio Indians after building a fortress on the Maumee River near present-day Toledo. Because some white renegades accompanied the Indians, a U.S.-British war nearly broke out. General Wayne, however, decided to withdraw after he had defeated the Indians. Thus, the battle brought peace with the Indians in the Ohio territory.

See August 3, 1795.

November 19, 1794

Jay's Treaty between the United States and Great Britain is signed.

While John Jay obtained some trade concessions from Britain, the treaty caused controversy in America because it did not gain U.S. principles of neutral rights or gain more than another promise that Britain would evacuate the northwest posts.

Clauses of the Jay's Treaty included:

1. A mixed arbitration commission to settle the Maine Boundary dispute. The commissioners set the boundary at the St. Croix River, but the decision did not finally settle the dispute.
2. A mixed commission to settle the U.S. Debts to Britain, and U.S. claims for British spoliation of American ships. Following arbitration efforts the monetary issue was settled by a treaty in 1802. The British accepted £600,000 for the debts, and awarded the United States $11,650,000 for damage to ships. The British did not, however, agree to stop their attacks on neutral ships.
3. Open Restricted Trade to West Indies. Though limited to vessels of 70 tons and products other than sugar and cotton, American vessels could trade temporarily in the British West Indies. The British also granted America trade on the basis of most-favored nation.
4. Silence on Neutral Rights. In return for the restricted commercial treaty, Jay did not gain recognition of the British for any of the neutral rights in favor of which the United States had argued since 1778. The list of contraband broadened as Britain desired, and the Rule of 1756 banning any wartime trade that had not been used in peacetime was unchanged. Finally, the British insisted on taking enemy goods from neutral ships, violating the American concept of "free ships make free goods."
5. British to Surrender the Northwest Posts by June 1, 1796. For the problems leading to ratification of the Jay's Treaty, see January 16, 1795, and June 24, 1795.

Angry Republicans denounce Jay's Treaty as inadequate and hang his effigy in Charleston, South Carolina. Library of Congress

1795

January 4, 1795

France reaffirms American trading privileges under the Treaty of 1778.

As a consequence of James Monroe's efforts to harmonize U.S.-French relations, the French DIRECTORY in decrees of November 15, 1794, and January 4, 1795, effectively revoked decrees made in May 1793, which allowed the seizure of goods on neutral ships bound for enemy countries. France also returned to the idea of free ships equal free goods and promised to settle spoliation claims through negotiation.

For a short time in 1795, Monroe appeared to have healed the breach in Franco-American relations.

January 16, 1795

John Jay refuses to let Monroe inform the French about contents of the Jay's Treaty.

During early January, rumors of the English-American treaty spread to Paris, where the French foreign minister believed that as a U.S. ally France should know the treaty terms. At Monroe's request, Jay offered to reveal the terms provided they remained confidential; that is, Monroe should not tell the French. Because the treaty had not been approved by the president or Congress, Jay told Monroe to tell the French simply that the Alliance of 1778 had not been violated, a statement that was not strictly accurate.

Monroe preferred not to know the treaty contents if he could not tell the French foreign minister. Thus, Monroe sought to reassure the French, whose private information on the treaty differed from the statements Jay gave to Monroe. As Monroe wrote to Jefferson, the French blamed Monroe for being untruthful about the treaty.

Secretary of State Randolph did not inform Monroe of the treaty terms until September 1795. By that time, both Monroe and the French had read the treaty in U.S. newspaper accounts that were sent to Paris.

As a consequence of Jay's tactics, Franco-American relations steadily deteriorated in 1795. The suspicious atmosphere surrounding the treaty terms convinced the French that Jay's treaty had indeed violated the Alliance of 1778 and was pro-British.

January 29, 1795

Congress passes a new Naturalization Act.

The new law required five years of residence in the United States before an immigrant could apply for citizenship papers.

June 22, 1795

Spain and France sign peace terms in the Treaty of Basel.

The French agreed to withdraw from Spanish territory they had conquered. In return, Spain ceded Saint Domingue (Santo Domingo) to France.

June 24, 1795

U.S. Senate ratifies the Jay's Treaty.

After news of the treaty reached America in March 1795, intensive debate began both in and out of Congress, with Federalists generally favoring, Democratic-Republicans opposing the treaty. Initially, President Washington was not certain of the value of the agreement but he finally came out in favor of it. The Senate vote of 20 to 10 on June 24 ratified the treaty after suspending the clause covering the restrictions on the West Indies trade.

Although further debate took place on whether the House of Representatives could block the treaty by not approving funds to carry it out, the question became moot when the House voted on April 30, 1796, to approve the necessary treasury appropriations.

August 3, 1795

Treaty of Greenville sets a boundary between Indian lands and land for U.S. settlers in the Northwest Territory.

Twelve Indian tribes in the OHIO-INDIANA region agreed to this treaty, which resulted from the Indians' defeat at Fallen Timbers in 1794.

August 19, 1795

Edmund Randolph resigns as Secretary of State and is replaced by Timothy Pickering.

President Washington suspected Randolph of corruption, believing he had intrigued with the French minister to the United States, Joseph Fauchet, in an effort to block ratification of the Jay Treaty. These charges were never proven and Irving Brant, the biographer of James Madison, contends the charges were not correct.

The appointment of Timothy Pickering placed Federalists in all of Washington's cabinet posts.

August 20, 1795

The first French Republic ends, being replaced by a constitution creating the Directory government.

As a result of the executions during the Reign of Terror and the excessive "wartime" measures used by the Committee of Public Safety, leaders of the THERMIDORIAN REACTION aimed at restoring order to the country. The new government had a two-chamber legislature and an executive office consisting of five directors, whose equality of status would prevent the rise of future monarchs or dictators.

October 27, 1795

Pinckney's Treaty with Spain resolves issues concerning the Mississippi region.

After Spain withdrew from the alliance with England and made peace with France, Spanish Foreign Minister Manuel de Godoy desired to settle the American disputes so that he could concentrate on Europe's problems. Between July and October, Godoy and Thomas Pinckney completed the negotiations resulting in the Treaty of San Lorenzo.

The treaty was a victory for American diplomacy. Spain recognized the 31° north latitude as its boundary and acknowledged that both Spanish and American citizens should have the free navigation of the Mississippi River. American citizens were granted the privilege of transhipping goods at New Orleans free of tax for three years. After three years, the king of Spain might assign another place on the lower Mississippi as an entrepôt. Finally, a mixed commission was set up to arbitrate spoliation claims, and Spain promptly paid the $320,095.07 that the commission awarded to America. The U.S. Senate ratified Pinckney's Treaty unanimously and with little debate.

1796

January 1, 1796

Incident of the French flag causes further Franco-American distrust.

In order to reciprocate Monroe's gift of a flag to France, the French minister to the United States, Pierre Auguste Adet, arranged to present the French tricolors to Washington. The president accepted the flag and proclaimed the day one of "general joy and congratulations."

Adet was disappointed, however, because Washington deposited the flag in the archives rather than display it in the House of Representatives as the French displayed the American flag. Such irritations indicate the deep distrust that had been created between France and Washington's administration.

For background to the flag incident, see August 14, 1794.

March 2, 1796

Senate ratifies a treaty with Algeria to protect U.S. commerce.

The dey of Algiers had, since 1785, attacked U.S. ships and required ransom for captives. American diplomats had tried various means to settle those disputes, but the dey's demands were too costly. In 1792, President Washington commissioned David Humphreys to seek an agreement with Algiers and to ransom Americans held captive by the dey. The treaty was concluded in November 1795 and ratified by the Senate on March 2, 1796.

The Algerian treaty was more expensive than that made with Morocco in 1787. In the first year of the treaty, the United States expended $992,463.25 on ransom, presents, and other tributes to the dey. The Algerian leader promised to assist America in forming treaties with Tunis and Tripoli, but these agreements became costly because of the monetary concessions made to Algeria.

March 10, 1796

James Monroe persuades Charles Delacroix, the French Foreign Minister, not to abrogate the Alliance of 1778.

The French government had asked Delacroix, its foreign minister, to tell Monroe that the treaty ceased to exist when the Jay Treaty was ratified. They claimed the treaty violated neutral rights, accepted Britain's paper blockade of France, and acknowledged Great Britain's contraband list. Each of these, said Delacroix, violated the free-trade ideas of the 1778 Alliance.

Monroe persuaded the French not to act hastily. He told them that 1796 was an election year in America and the November results might lead to more friendly policies toward France. By July 2, 1796, the Directory chose to ignore Monroe's advice.

June 30, 1796

The United States decides to stop the sale of French prizes of war in U.S. ports.

Since Genet's activities in 1793, the French consuls in U.S. ports had accepted and sold the prizes that French privateers took from British ships. After the ratification of the Jay Treaty, the British protested that Article 24 voided the French sale of prizes on U.S. territory.

On May 11, 1796, the House of Representatives approved a resolution ordering the cessation of such sales. Finally, on June 30, Secretary of the Treasury Oliver Wolcott directed customs officers to forbid the entry of such prize property. To the French, this was clear evidence that the Jay Treaty cost France an advantage it previously had under the Alliance of 1778.

July 2, 1796

A French decree announces France will treat American ships precisely as the British.

Complaining that the United States renounced its neutral rights in the Jay Treaty, the French asserted that until America forced Britain to recognize its neutral rights, France would confiscate neutral goods and search neutral ships according to British practice. Although French privateers had frequently violated American neutrality, the July 2 decree was the first authorization of such practices. In effect, the Jay Treaty plus French action nullified the Alliance of 1778. The formality of its existence continued, however, until 1800.

As a consequence of the July decree, French cruisers captured 316 American ships in the Caribbean Sea by the end of 1796. This action continued in 1797 and led to the Franco-American "undeclared war" of 1797–1800.

July 27, 1796

President Washington appoints Charles Cotesworth Pinckney to replace Monroe as Minister to France.

The Federalists had become increasingly critical of Monroe's actions in Paris, and the cabinet advised Washington to remove him. Secretary of State Pickering informed Monroe of this decision by a letter of September 9, 1796, which Monroe received in November, shortly before Pinckney arrived in Paris. The Directory considered the recall of Monroe an affront and refused to accept Pinckney's appointment. In February 1797, Pinckney retired to Amsterdam to await further instructions.

August 11, 1796

British soldiers complete the evacuation of the Northwest posts.

In the Jay's Treaty the British promised to leave these posts, and they arranged to do so by June 1, 1796. The American army requested a delay in order to complete its transport of American troops and supplies to their new stations. The final evacuation was at Fort Niagara on August 11.

August 19, 1796

Spain joins France in war against Great Britain.

The declaration of war followed the signing of the Treaty of San Ildefonso, which allied Spain with France.

September 19, 1796

President Washington issues his farewell address. Making clear his intention not to seek a third term, Washington appeals to the people to rally around the nation, to abjure factional party politics, and to keep the nation free of subservience to any foreign power.

Washington wrote: "The great rule of conduct for us, in regard to foreign nations, is in extending our commercial relations, to have with them as little political connection as possible." In particular, Washington urged American political isolation from Europe, whose interests were remote from the American interest. "Our detached and distant situation invites and enables us to pursue a different course."As one people under an efficient government, he said, the American neutrality will be respected, and "we may choose peace or war, as our interest, guided by justice, shall counsel."

These sentiments were subsequently used as late as 1941 to justify a policy of political isolation from European problems.

October 17, 1796

Peace between France and Austria is made by the Treaty of Campo Formio.

November 15, 1796

The French Minister Adet announces that Paris is suspending diplomatic relations with America.

Shortly before the presidential electors met to cast their ballots, Pierre Adet issued a message of rebuke to President Washington and the Federalist politicians. Adet favored Thomas Jefferson and asserted that if he were elected, French-American relations could be normalized. The Frenchman's attempts to influence the U.S. election were inept and ineffective.

December 7, 1796

Presidential election is won by John Adams; Thomas Jefferson is elected Vice President.

The Electoral College gave Adams 71 votes, Jefferson 68 votes, Thomas Pinckney 59 votes, and Aaron Burr 30 votes.

1797

March 2, 1797

France tightens its restrictions on neutral ships.

The French directors issued a law that allowed its ships to capture all warships carrying goods to Great Britain. This completely annulled the principle in the 1778 Treaty that "free ships make free goods."

Upon learning of this French measure, many Federalists in America, including most of John Adams's cabinet, wanted to declare war against France.

See May 15, 1797.

May 15, 1797

A special session of Congress meets to seek a peaceful settlement with France.

In his message to Congress on May 15, Adams requested preparations for defense as well as a special peace mission to France. He asked Congress for authorization to enlarge the navy for protection of the nation's commerce, to form an army, and to strengthen the militia.

During the special session, Congress acted more moderately than Adams wished. The naval allocations

John Adams, 2nd President of the United States. National Archives

were smaller than requested, the arming of only 80,000 militia was provided, and the construction of forts and artillery along the coast was approved. Congress refused generally to raise taxes as Adams desired. A loan of $800,000 was approved and taxes on salt and stamps set for collection at a later date. For appointment of the peace commission, see May 31, 1797.

May 31, 1797

President Adams appoints a special commission to France to seek a treaty of amity and commerce.

The French government had rejected Charles Pinckney as minister from the United States, and French-American conflict continued on the high seas over questions of neutrality. Adams hoped the special mission would avoid war and establish better relations with Paris. He named two Federalists, Charles C. PINCKNEY and John MARSHALL, and one Democratic-Republican, Elbridge GERRY, as commissioners to negotiate a settlement of pending disputes with France.

See October 18, 1797–February 5, 1798.

Charles Cotesworth Pinckney, ambassador to France. Library of Congress

June 10, 1797

Senate ratifies the treaty with Tripoli.

Patterned after the 1796 treaty with Algeria, this treaty cost the United States $56,486 in 1797, plus annual presents of military stores valued at $12,000.

Elbridge Gerry. Library of Congress

John Marshall. Library of Congress

October 18, 1797–February 5, 1798

W, X, Y, Z Affair in Paris.

Beginning on October 18, 1797, the three American commissioners sent to France on May 31, 1797, conducted unofficial discussions with four agents of French Foreign Minister Charles-Maurice TALLEYRAND-PÉRIGORD. Although Talleyrand met with Pinckney, Marshall, and Gerry on an informal basis on October 8, he refused to grant formal recognition.

Beginning on October 18, the three Americans had private meetings with three of Talleyrand's agents: Jean Conrad HOTTINGUER, Lucien HAUTEVAL, and Monsieur BELLAMY. Early in 1798, a fourth friend of Talleyrand, Pierre Augustin Caron DE BEAUMARCHAIS, also met with the Americans. When President Adams released copies of the American dispatches to Congress, he referred to the four Frenchmen as W, X, Y, Z. In American history, the first three agents' pseudonyms became the basis of referring to the incident as the X Y Z AFFAIR. Beaumarchais as "W" appeared later in the dispatches.

In discussing possible negotiations, Talleyrand's agents suggested that an American loan and bribe of more than $200,000 would permit official talks to begin. The Americans rejected the offer to pay a bribe, as was European custom, before a treaty was signed. They would pay later, although they believed the amount of the requested bribe was too high. In addition, they refused to concede the necessity of a loan to France.

On several occasions, the Americans discussed breaking off all talks. They had not done so by the end of February because Gerry persuaded them to be patient while the French softened their terms.

See January 31, March 19, and April 3, 1798.

November 18, 1797

Spanish royal order opens all Spanish colonies to neutral trade.

After Spain allied with France against England, neutral trade became necessary to Spain's colonies.

The United States was the chief beneficiary of this order. Its trade with Spanish-America increased considerably during the next decade, even though Spain again sought to restrict the trade in 1799, 1801, and 1804. The only measure to hurt this growing trade was Jefferson's Embargo of 1807.

1798

January 31, 1798

The three American commissioners send a memorial to the French Foreign Office.

Because their informal talks achieved no results, Gerry, Marshall, and Pinckney decided to write formally to Talleyrand to signify that they earnestly sought a reconciliation. In the message, they reviewed their grievances and asked permission to present their case to the French, failing which they would have to return to America.

See March 19, 1798.

March 6, 1798

Senate ratifies treaty with Tunis.

This treaty of commerce and protection resembled previous arrangements with Algeria (March 2, 1796) and Tripoli (June 10, 1797). The U.S. payments to Tripoli were $107,000, but no annual tributes were required. Because the Senate made several reservations regarding the agreement, the treaty had to be renegotiated in part. Final Senate ratification of the new treaty occurred on January 10, 1800.

March 19, 1798

Talleyrand answers complaints of the American commissioners in Paris.

This message was a response to a lengthy memorandum sent to the French foreign minister by Marshall, Pinckney, and Gerry on January 31. Talleyrand's response listed all French grievances against America for violating the Alliance of 1778 and signing the Jay Treaty. He also said he could deal only with friendly enemies such as Gerry and not with such pro-British figures as Marshall and Pinckney.

As a result of this memorandum, Marshall and Pinckney left Paris on April 24; only Gerry remained in Paris, trying, he explained, to avoid war.

See July 22, 1798.

March 19, 1798

President Adams gives Congress an unfavorable report on the French mission.

When the president first read the reports from Marshall, Gerry, and Pinckney, which he received on March 4, he was distressed because he believed war or national disgrace faced the nation. By March 19, he had calmed down and did not request a declaration of war.

In his message to Congress, Adams said that a settlement with France appeared impossible. He asked Congress to approve all the defense measures he had requested in 1797. He also revoked President Washington's order that forbade the arming of U.S. merchant ships.

March 23, 1798

Secretary of State Pickering orders the three envoys in Paris to demand their passports and leave France unless they have been officially received and begun negotiations.

March 27, 1798

The Democratic-Republicans in Congress seek to avoid a French war.

Claiming that President Adams's policies seemed to be headed for war, the Democratic-Republicans proposed the so-called SPRIGG RESOLUTIONS. Named for Congressman Richard Sprigg, the resolutions said it was inexpedient to fight France, that Congress should restrict the arming of private American ships, and that seacoast defenses should be built to protect the nation. The Federalists in Congress strongly opposed these resolutions.

April 3, 1798

President Adams sends the W X Y Z dispatches to Congress.

Responding to a request of the House of Representatives on April 2, Adams sent them all the deciphered dispatches received through early February 1798.

Following several secret sessions to discuss the documents, both the House of Representatives and the Senate ordered public distribution of 1,200 of the dispatches. Prior to the public printing, several newspapers published them on April 9 and 10, 1798.

Publication of these messages aroused Federalist demonstrations against France. Many Federalists began to wear a black cockade in their hats in contrast to the red, white, and blue cockade worn by French republicans.

April 7, 1798

Mississippi Territory is organized.

After Pinckney's Treaty was ratified Congress began to plan a territorial government west of Georgia. On April 7, 1798, Congress established a territorial government. Settlement was slow at first because Indians remained in the area and Spain still controlled the seaports of West Florida.

April 27, 1798

Department of the Navy established.

President Adams believed any war with France would be a naval engagement, and he had requested a stronger navy in May 1797. On April 27, 1798, he signed the law creating the Department of the Navy and nominated Benjamin STODDERT as the first secretary of the navy. Congress also authorized the construction of 12 ships of not more than 22 guns each.

May 9, 1798

Presidential proclamation for a day of prayer against French atheism.

Federalists especially had opposed the "excesses" of French republicans who attacked Christian churches and proclaimed worship of the goddess of Reason. To counteract this trend, Adams called for a day of "humiliation, fasting, and prayer for the United States" against the "horror of French atheism."

The Democratic-Republicans ridiculed this Federalist Party ploy. One Boston newspaper editor wrote a "psalm for the Federalist Fast," whose first stanza was:

> Ye Federal States combine
> In Solemn Fast and Prayer
> And urge the powers divine
> To drive us into war.

This 1798 cartoon shows a five-headed Frenchman demanding money from the American negotiators C. C. Pinckney, Elbridge Gerry, and John Marshall to end French seizures of American merchant ships. Huntington Library

May 24, 1798

America's sloop of war, the *Ganges,* sails from Philadelphia.

This ship was a merchant vessel converted to naval service. In 1798, it performed the only extensive naval operations patrolling the coastal waters from Long Island to the Virginia capes.

By the end of 1798, four ships of the U.S. navy had been commissioned for active patrol—the *Ganges*, *United States*, *Constitution*, and the *Constellation*. American ships captured two French vessels in 1798: the schooner *Sans Pareil* on August 23 and the sloop *Jaloux* on September 5. The French captured one U.S. schooner, the *Retaliation*, on November 20, 1798. All this action was in the West Indies.

May 28, 1798

Congressional legislation provides for undeclared war with France.

A series of acts of Congress in the spring of 1798 led to a defensive naval war against France. On May 28, Congress authorized the president to use the navy to "seize, take, and bring into port" French ships near the coastline and intending to attack American ships.

June 13, 1798

Adams signs legislation to tighten the naval laws against France.

The law approved on June 13 embargoed all American commerce with France and its dependencies. It also prohibited French ships from entering U.S. ports unless they were in distress. The law provided that the president could suspend these restrictions if France acknowledged all U.S. grievances.

Adams requested these harsh restrictions, although Secretary of State Pickering wanted the president to request a declaration of war against France.

June 18, 1798

John Marshall returns from France and is greeted as a Federalist hero.

To welcome Marshall, a banquet was held in Philadelphia. During the ceremonies, 16 toasts were raised to his patriotism. One of these became a slogan of Federalist patriots—"Millions for defense but not one cent for tribute."

June 18, 1798

New naturalization law is signed.

President Adams approved a new law changing the period of residence from 5 to 14 years before aliens could apply for citizenship. The act also required all aliens to register with the federal government.

Under Jefferson, Congress repealed this act in 1802, reinstituting the 5-year rule.

June 25, 1798

Alien Friends Act is passed.

This was the first of several Federalist laws passed to repress dissent against the government's policies. Designed to deal with alleged French agents among perhaps 90,000 Frenchmen living in America, the act permitted the president to deport those "dangerous to the peace and safety of the United States." Any alien was liable to arbitrary arrest and deportation whether in time of peace or war. The law would expire in two years unless renewed by Congress.

June 25, 1798

A defensive naval act is signed.

This law permitted U.S. merchant ships to arm and to defend themselves against any French armed vessel trying to stop and search them. Any spoils of war received would be divided between the crew and the ships' owners.

July 1, 1798

Napoléon's army invades Egypt in a campaign aimed eventually against British India.

At first, the French succeeded in their offensive, but they finally were turned back by Turkish forces after a nine-week siege at Acre on May 20, 1799.

July 6, 1798

Alien Enemy Act is passed.

This law authorized the president to restrain, arrest, or deport any alien during the time of declared war. Unlike the Alien Friends Act, this law applied only in time of declared war or invasion.

July 7, 1798

Treaties with French nation are abrogated.

When Adams signed this bill, formal ties with France were practically severed. The issue was whether any nation could arbitrarily and unilaterally end a treaty. Later, when negotiations began with France leading to the convention of 1800, the Adams administration admitted that this bill held no validity.

July 9, 1798

French government embargoes all American ships in French ports.

This decree was the Directory's retaliation for American laws passed during the spring of 1798.

July 9, 1798

Further naval measures against France.

Congress passed legislation to permit the U.S. navy to capture armed French ships and to authorize the president to commission privateers to do likewise.

Notably, in passing this law Congress first defeated a proposal of Peleg SPRAGUE of New Hampshire that would have allowed the U.S. navy to capture both armed and *unarmed* French ships. If approved, Sprague's bill would have been an offensive measure in contrast to the defensive war fought against *armed* French vessels. The House vote against Sprague's bill was 31-52.

July 11, 1798

The Marine Corps is organized.

An act of Congress became effective that authorized a force of men who would be used in the armed ships and galleys of the U.S. navy.

July 14, 1798

Tax is levied to pay costs of undeclared war.

Congress levied this tax on houses and slaves, expecting to raise $2 million. It also authorized the president to borrow $2 million at 6% interest and another $5 million at whatever rate was necessary. Later, Secretary of the Treasury Wolcott found the Federalist bankers desired 8% interest on the $5 million loan, an amount President Adams thought was extravagant.

July 14, 1798

Sedition Act is passed.

This law endeavored to punish criticism of government officials. It provided fines of not more than

A 1798 cartoon in response to the Sedition Act. Matthew Lyon is depicted as attacked by Griswold, a Federalist from Connecticut. Lyon was arrested and imprisoned and fined for publishing a letter criticizing John Adams. Library of Congress

$2,000 and imprisonment of not over two years for conspiracies or for "scandalous statements" against the U.S. government, Congress, or the president. Similar penalties were levied for citizens or aliens who opposed execution of national laws, prevented federal officers from performing their duties, or aided or attempted "any insurrection, riot, unlawful assembly, or combination." The act would be in force until March 3, 1801.

As a result of the Sedition Act, 25 persons were prosecuted and 10 were convicted, all of them Democratic-Republican editors and printers. The Jeffersonian party strongly opposed the Sedition Act and the two Alien Acts of 1798. When Jefferson became president he pardoned all those convicted and Congress restored the fines with interest.

July 22, 1798

In Paris, Elbridge Gerry obtains the first conciliatory words from Talleyrand.

Since April 24 Gerry had stayed in Paris, hoping for some sign of the French government's desire to avoid war. In June, he asked for his passports to leave France but Talleyrand refused to grant safe conduct.

In early July, the French foreign minister finally indicated his willingness to yield. On July 9, he sent a letter to William Vans Murray, the U.S. minister at The Hague, stating that the French desired to reconcile their quarrels with America.

Later, on July 22, Talleyrand told Gerry that France would curb its violence against American ships, and that to effect negotiations no loan would be necessary and President Adams would not need to explain his previous accusations against France. He also agreed to give Gerry his passport so that he could leave France if he desired.

Although C. C. Pinckney, who was in Bordeaux awaiting a ship for America, did not trust Talleyrand, both Murray and Gerry believed that Talleyrand was prepared to accept negotiations with America.

See July 31, 1798.

July 28, 1798

Adams appoints George Washington as Commander in Chief of the army.

This appointment followed congressional legislation on July 16 that increased the army to 12 regiments of 700 men each and 600 light dragoons. This force would become part of the "Provisional Army" of 50,000 men to be formed if full-scale war began or if the president believed national security required it. In addition, 80,000 militia were called to active duty.

July 31, 1798

French Directory takes steps to reconcile the United States.

On Talleyrand's recommendation, the directors issued a decree to abolish some of France's previous naval orders against neutrals. Its July 31 decree revoked the French commissions of privateers in the West Indies, recalled prize court judges who privately profited from the pillage of commercial ships, and ordered respect by the French navy for ships of allied and neutral nations. Finally, the decree ended the embargo on U.S. ships that had been ordered on July 9, 1798.

Talleyrand sent news of the July 31 decree to Gerry, who was at Le Havre waiting to board a ship for his return to America. Thus, when Gerry sailed for home on August 8, 1798, he carried copies of French proposals to bring a rapprochement with America.

See December 8, 1798.

August 1, 1798

British fleet under Admiral Horatio Nelson defeats the French fleet off Aboukir Bay near Alexandria, Egypt.

August 7, 1798–August 29, 1798

George Logan pursues an independent mission to France.

Dr. Logan, a Quaker and a Democratic-Republican from Philadelphia, arrived in Paris on August 7 in an unauthorized attempt to make peace between France and America. Logan's mission was condemned by the Federalists because he undertook the effort with no official sanction. After meeting many French officials, he left France on August 29, carrying letters from Fulwer Skipwith, the U.S. consul general in Paris, to the president and secretary of state, whom Skipwith informed that the French had lifted their embargo and freed some American sailors who had been prisoners of war.

See January 30, 1799, on Logan's Act to forbid such future missions.

October 9, 1798

Adams agrees to Hamilton's appointment as Second in Command of the army.

As early as July, George Washington told the president that he wanted Hamilton to be his inspector general and to have second rank among the army officers. Adams delayed this appointment because he knew Hamilton already had great influence with the president's cabinet members. Finally, Adams yielded and appointed Hamilton because he wished to keep Washington's support.

November 16, 1798

British ship stops and impresses sailors on board a U.S. warship.

HMS *Carnatic*, commanded by Captain John Loring, stopped the U.S. sloop of war *Baltimore*, under Isaac Phillips, as it entered the harbor of Havana, Cuba. Loring ordered a list of the crew and removed 55 men who he claimed were British subjects. He returned 50 of these because Phillips said he needed a sufficient crew to man his ship properly.

This incident indicated that the British as well as the French continued after 1795 to violate America's neutral rights. Secretary of State Pickering protested this violation of an American naval ship but, as was customary, his words to the British were softened because the Federalists desired to retain good commercial relations with Britain, even though such British acts infuriated many Americans as much as French depredations.

The matter of British impressment of sailors especially disturbed Americans. In September 1799, the American agent in Jamaica reported that at least 250 Americans had been pressed into British naval service. Adams's administration protested this incident but avoided any step to embarrass or weaken the British government.

The British claimed the right to impress Americans who were born in British dominions, a claim made by most European nations who did not recognize the right of citizens to change their citizenship. In 1870, the British government agreed to recognize the rights for nations such as the United States to "naturalize"—that is, grant citizenship—to individuals born in another country.

November 16, 1798

Kentucky resolutions against the Alien and Sedition Acts.

Declaring these two acts unconstitutional, the Kentucky legislature stated that if the national government exercised undue powers, each state could "judge for itself" if it would redress or defy such acts of Congress. This resolution assumed that states' rights continued to be supreme because the Constitution of 1787 was a compact. Kentucky did not, however, seek to nullify or obstruct the two disputed laws.

December 2, 1798

Second coalition is formed to fight France.

This new bloc of nations allied against the French armies included Russia, Great Britain, Austria, Naples, Portugal, and the Ottoman Empire.

December 8, 1798

Adams reports to Congress that the French issues remain uncertain.

During the fall months, the president received conflicting reports from Europe regarding the French views. C. C. Pinckney and John Marshall returned with pessimistic and cynical views about Talleyrand and the French government.

In October, Gerry returned from Paris to give optimistic reports of France's changed attitudes and desire to negotiate. And from The Hague, Murray reported that Talleyrand appeared essentially ready to meet Adams's desire to be certain that a new American mission would be received.

Although Adams inclined to appoint a new mission if possible, Secretary of State Pickering continued to advocate a declaration of war. Consequently Adams's message of December 8 referred to possibilities of peace or war. He told Congress the French appeared to desire peace but that the United States could not yet relax its buildup of defensive measures. He preferred to prepare for war while being ready to negotiate if the French gave concrete evidence that they would accept whomever Adams appointed to a French peace mission.

See February 18, 1799.

December 24, 1798

Virginia resolutions oppose Alien-Sedition Acts.

Patterned after the Kentucky resolutions of November 16, but written by James Madison, the Virginia legislation denounced the Alien and Sedition acts, saying the states could "interpose" in order to arrest the "progress of the evil" of such unconstitutional laws. As in Kentucky, Virginia did not seek to nullify the two laws.

1799

January 30, 1799

"Logans Act" is signed by President Adams.

The Federalists proposed this act to embarrass the Democratic-Republicans as a pro-French party. The act provided a fine and imprisonment for any American who corresponded with a foreign government to influence it in a dispute with the United States. The Federalists claimed such contacts sabotaged the administration's foreign policy.

The Logan Act has never been repealed, continuing into the 20th century to restrict private American contacts with foreign governments.

February 9, 1799

First important U.S. naval action against French navy occurs.

The conflict involved two frigates—the USS *Constellation* capturing the French *L'Insurgente.* The French captain tried to avoid the battle because the French governor-general at Guadeloupe, Étienne Borne DESFOURNEAUX, desired U.S. trade and wished to continue treating America as an ally. Nevertheless, the *Constellation* captured its prize, taking it to St. Kitts Island. This infuriated Desfourneaux, who issued his own declaration of war on the United States and ordered all American ships in the Caribbean to be seized.

February 9, 1799

The United States moves to support a revolution against France in Saint Domingue (Santo Domingo).

Toussaint L'OUVERTURE (François Dominique TOUSSAINT), a former Negro slave and former general in the French colonial forces, led his people to declare independence from France in 1797. On November 6, 1798, Toussaint wrote to Adams, telling the president he would open the Saint Domingue ports to U.S. cargo and respect the U.S. navy as a friend and ally.

Although some southern Americans and Federalists feared that the idea of a slave's freedom might spread into the southern United States, Adams and Alexander Hamilton agreed that an independent Saint Domingue would provide valuable

Battle between the U.S. frigate *Constellation* and the French frigate *L'Insurgente*, in the naval war with France. Copy of artwork by Hoff. National Archives

trade for American merchant ships. Adams responded positively to Toussaint's November message. He sent American naval ships to visit Saint Domingue and persuaded Congress to pass a law on February 9, 1799, to open American trade with Saint Domingue. Britain also actively supported independence for Toussaint's government and joined the United States in assisting the revolution.

February 18, 1799

President Adams appoints William Vans Murray as Minister Plenipotentiary to negotiate peace with the French.

Since January 1, 1799, Adams had obtained additional evidence that the French wanted to end the quasi war. His third son, Thomas Bolyston Adams, returned from Europe on January 11, and reported that he, Murray, and John Quincy Adams (minister to Prussia) agreed that the French genuinely sought peace. On February 1, Adams received a dispatch from Murray at The Hague saying that on October 7, 1798, a note from Talleyrand had satisfied Adams's desire to be certain that France would welcome a new U.S. mission. Also on February 1, George Washington, who had been in communication with visitors from Europe, agreed to back Adams's efforts to secure peace. Washington's support may have been the deciding influence, for on February 18, Adams announced Murray's appointment without prior consultation with his cabinet.

Adams accepted one concession to his appointment of Vans Murray on February 18. On the advice of his Federalist Party advisers, he named two other envoys to join Murray on the peace mission: Oliver Ellsworth, chief justice of the Supreme Court, and (after Patrick Henry declined to serve) William Richardson Davie, governor of North Carolina. The Senate approved the appointments on February 25, 1799.

See March 10, 1799, and March 7, 1800.

March 6, 1799

Fries Rebellion begins in western Pennsylvania.

This uprising took place because farmers in that region opposed the new taxes on land and houses. Fries and his followers harassed the tax assessors, and on March 6, 18 of the demonstrators were thrown into jail in Bethlehem, Pennsylvania. Fries led his men to raid the jail and release the prisoners. Adams then decided to send 500 U.S. army troops to put down the "rebellion." Fries was arrested, tried for treason, and sentenced to be hanged in May 1799. On May 21, President Adams pardoned Fries, saying that the demonstrations were not treasonous acts.

March 10, 1799

Adams's cabinet agrees on three conditions that the American commissioners should require France to meet.

These conditions were: (1) France must pay the American spoliation claims; (2) the American ships should not be bound to carry a *role d'équipage* (list of the crew); (3) the United States was no longer bound to guarantee French possessions in the West Indies as required in the Alliance of 1778. The principal new demand was that France must pay the spoliation claims.

June 18, 1799

Coup d'état of the 30th Prairial purges the French directors and puts five new officers in power.

As a result of this coup, Talleyrand resigned on July 20, and was replaced by Count Karl Friedrich Reinhard. The count was a friend of Talleyrand and continued his conciliatory policy toward America.

June 23, 1799

Americans and British continue aid to Toussaint L'Ouverture in Saint Domingue.

On June 23, the United States ended its embargo in the islands and sent ammunition to Toussaint's forces. Both the United States and Britain aided the rebels by keeping French ships out of the island's ports.

October 16, 1799

Adams instructs the three U.S. envoys to proceed to Paris for negotiations.

Since April, Ellsworth and Davie had remained in America awaiting Murray's word that the French would receive them. Because of Talleyrand's resignation, a new uncertainty entered the scene.

On October 15, Adams held a cabinet meeting in which Secretary Pickering and Hamilton (presently an inspector general) wanted to delay or abandon the peace mission. Adams believed, however, that the Directory's representatives had made clear a willingness to negotiate and that the envoys should be sent. On October 16, Adams sent instructions notifying Ellsworth and Davie to leave for France by November 1. Once again, Adams's decisions kept the peace effort alive despite the advice of his Federalist advisers.

See March 7, 1800.

November 9, 1799

Napoléon gains power in France, overthrowing the Directory.

By December 24, Napoléon and his political allies prepared the Constitution of the Year VIII (1799), which was approved in a popular referendum by a vote of 3,011,107 to 1,567.

Napoléon was called the FIRST CONSUL of a three-man executive (government of THE CONSULATE). This gave the appearance of a Roman-style republic with a Senate appointed by the consul, a tribunate that discussed but could not vote on legislation, and a legislature that could vote but not debate. The first consul named a Council of State to administer the government.

The Consulate was Napoléon's first step toward dictatorial power. In 1804, he established an empire, naming himself as emperor of the French. After a popular plebiscite approved the change by a vote of 3,512,329 to 2,569, Pope Pius VII came to Paris to consecrate Napoléon's rule. The emperor himself placed his crown on his head; the pope did not perform that symbolic function.

December 18, 1799

The *Franklin*, the first ship to trade in Japan, returns to Batavia in the East Indies.

The ship *Franklin* was out of Boston, commanded by Captain Deveraux. After reaching Batavia, a Dutch official permitted it to act as the annual Dutch ship that would trade at Nagasaki, Japan.

The *Franklin* left Batavia in April 1799 and acting according to instructions, raised the Dutch flag when it came in sight of Nagasaki. The Dutch had since 1638 been the only Western nation permitted once a year to trade at Nagasaki through the island of Deshima in Nagasaki harbor. Because it needed repairs, the *Franklin* remained in Japan for four months before returning with its cargo to Batavia on December 18, 1799.

Prior to the *Franklin*'s visit under these special circumstances, two U.S. ships that visited Japan to engage in trade had been rejected by the Japanese during the 1790s. These ships were the *Lady Washington* and the *Grace.*

1800

February 1, 1800

Final major naval battle occurs between French and American frigates.

Commanded by Captain Thomas Truxtun, the *Constellation* engaged the French *La Vengeance* in the Caribbean Sea off Guadeloupe. Because *La Vengeance* was en route to France with a cargo of money and carried 80 military passengers and 36 American prisoners, its captain preferred to avoid a battle. Truxtun ordered a chase, catching up to *La Vengeance* and engaging it in a five-hour running defensive action. Night came before either vessel surrendered. The American frigate claimed a victory because it inflicted greater damage on the more heavily armed (38 guns to 54) *Vengeance.*

February 9, 1800

Napoléon orders 10 days of mourning in the French armies to honor George Washington, who died on December 14, 1799.

As first consul, Napoléon wished both to honor Washington and to demonstrate his desire to conciliate the United States. After the period of mourning,

Napoléon ordered a bust of Washington placed in the Tuileries Palace in Paris.

March 7, 1800

Napoléon welcomes the American peace delegation.

Although President Adams had appointed William Vans Murray, Oliver Ellsworth, and William Davie as a peace commission on February 18, 1799, their departure was delayed (and they did not reach Paris until March 2, 1800). The delegates learned that Napoléon had honored George Washington on February 9 and was ready to greet them and to appoint a French peace delegation.

On March 7, the new French ruler received the three Americans in a formal audience. At the same time he announced the appointment of the French negotiators: his brother Joseph Bonaparte, Pierre Louis Roederer, and Charles Pierre Claret Fleurieu. The initial talks of the delegates were set for April 1, 1800.

See October 16, 1799, and October 3, 1800.

May 10, 1800

President Adams dismisses Secretary of State Pickering and appoints John Marshall to succeed him on May 13.

Pickering and other members of Adams's cabinet had always been more loyal to Hamilton than to the president. During the spring of 1800, some Federalists began a plot to replace Adams with another nominee for president in 1800. Adams correctly believed that Pickering was a leading conspirator, and he therefore asked for the secretary's resignation. Four days earlier, Adams had dismissed Secretary of War James McHenry for similar reasons.

May 14, 1800

The French crisis has waned sufficiently for Congress to suspend army enlistments.

On May 14, Adams signed legislation that ended enlistments under the "Provisional Army" bill of June 16, 1798. The law also authorized the discharge of enlisted officers at an early date. Pickering, McHenry, and Inspector General Hamilton opposed this bill and were dismayed that Adams signed it. Under this act the army was officially disbanded on June 15, 1800.

June 14, 1800

Napoléon wins the Battle of Marengo.

This victory over the Austrian forces in northern Italy eventually led to Austria's defeat. With the French army under General Guillaume Brune thrust into Austria from the south and forces under General Jean Victor Moreau attacking via Munich, the Austrians sought peace with Napoléon in December 1800.

October 1, 1800

Napoléon secures the Louisiana territory from Spain in the second Treaty of Ildefonso.

At this time, the first consul planned to make Saint Domingue and Louisiana the center of the French Empire. His unexpected problem was Toussaint L'Ouverture, who refused to give up the independence of his island state.

By the treaty of October 1, Napoléon agreed to add Tuscany in northern Italy to the holdings of the duke of Parma, the brother-in-law of the Spanish king. France would also secure recognition for the duke as king over these domains as the "Kingdom of Etruria." Napoléon had trouble fulfilling these conditions and getting other nations to recognize the new kingdom.

September 30–October 1, 1800

Final signing of the Convention of Morfontaine restores friendly relations between France and the United States.

Known officially as the Convention of Peace, Commerce, and Navigation, the chief clauses of the agreement were:

1. The convention was a peace settlement.
2. The Alliance of 1778 was recognized as not in operation but its exact status and indemnities due as violations were postponed.

3. France would not require U.S. ships to carry a *role d'équipage*.
4. Each side would restore naval vessels they had captured.
5. Arrangements for payment of debts were accepted.
6. America approved maritime rules similar to the neutral rights of the 1778 Alliance. The four main neutral agreements were:
   a. neutral right to trade in noncontraband with any belligerent;
   b. a narrow list of contraband, excluding naval stores;
   c. "free ships, free goods"—except contraband;
   d. neutrals would not trade at blockaded ports (meaning a port "actually blockaded, besieged, or invested").

News of the signing of the Convention of Mortfontaine reached America on November 7, 1800, when the *Baltimore Telegraph and Daily Advertiser* headlined news of the peace agreement. The official copy of the treaty did not arrive until December.

For the U.S. ratification, see February 3, 1801.

Thomas Jefferson becomes President. National Archives

December 3, 1800

In presidential election, the Thomas Jefferson–Aaron Burr electors gain a majority over the Federalists.

Apparently Thomas Jefferson would be elected president, but in February an unusual situation developed because the Democratic-Republican electors gave Burr as many votes as Jefferson (see February 11, 1801).

Adams's loss appears to have been due to Hamilton's attempt to control New York's electoral votes. Hamilton's effort failed on May 1, when Jefferson and Burr secured a majority for the Democratic-Republicans in the New York legislature. Eventually, the eight electoral votes of South Carolina became the deciding votes—votes that went to Jefferson and Burr.

December 16, 1800

League of Armed Neutrality is formed in Europe.

Resembling the league formed during the period of the American Revolutionary War, this league proposed to defend its neutral rights against the British navy. Proposed by Czar Paul I, with the encouragement of Napoléon, the member nations were Russia, Sweden, Denmark, and Norway. Prussia joined on December 18.

Napoléon had used the Convention of 1800 (MORTEFONTAINE) with the United States to urge formation of the league, and Czar Paul hoped America would join. The principal clauses of the league's neutral rights were almost exactly the four neutral principles in the U.S.-French convention of 1800 (see October 3, 1800). Great Britain chose to break the league by retaliation and succeeded in this effort by June 17, 1801.

IV. THE DEMOCRATIC-REPUBLICAN YEARS

Louisiana Purchase
Barbary Pirates War
War of 1812
Treaty of Ghent

1801

February 3, 1801

French Convention of 1800 is ratified with three reservations by the U.S. Senate.

The convention failed to obtain the necessary two-thirds' vote in the Senate because many senators argued that the treaty was unclear regarding the abrogation of the Treaty of 1778 and French indemnity payments. This vote, on January 23, 1801, was 16 to 14.

After discussing the treaty with several senators, President Adams resubmitted it on February 3. The senators now approved the treaty 22 to 9, after adding three reservations. The first reservation definitely required France to pay for damage to U.S. property. The second reworded the treaty to make certain that the Alliance of 1778 and related treaties were abrogated. The third added an article to terminate the convention after eight years.

Final ratification with France awaited further action under Jefferson's administration. For this exchange of ratification, see July 31, 1801. For the treaty terms, see October 3, 1800.

February 9, 1801

Peace Treaty of Luneville between Napoléon and Austria brings the end of the Holy Roman Empire.

February 11, 1801

Jefferson and Burr tie in the presidential balloting of the electoral college.

The Democratic-Republican electors cast two ballots, and their candidate for president, Thomas Jefferson, tied at 73 votes with their candidate for vice president, Aaron Burr.

When the ballots were counted in January 1801, the tie vote required that the Federalists who controlled the lame-duck session of Congress would choose between Jefferson and Burr. Each candidate had supporters in Congress, and 36 ballots were required before Jefferson won on February 17, 1801.

To prevent a recurrence of this problem, Congress proposed the Twelfth Amendment to the Constitution, which was ratified by sufficient states on September 24, 1804.

March 5, 1801

James Madison replaces John Marshall as Secretary of State.

Madison officially began to serve on May 2, 1801, remaining in office throughout Jefferson's eight years as president.

March 21, 1801

Jefferson orders relations with France to be normalized.

Although the final ratifications of the Convention of 1800 had not been exchanged, Jefferson recalled all

U.S. warships, instructed American agents in French colonies to cease all anti-French activity, and resumed commercial relations with France. The laws of 1798 suspending trade with France had ended previously, on March 3, 1801.

May 20, 1801

Jefferson orders the use of naval force against the Barbary states of North Africa.

On May 20, Jefferson placed Richard DALE in command of a squadron of four U.S. navy ships for an expedition to the coast of North Africa.

The settlement of the French "undeclared war" and the construction of an American navy between 1793 and 1800 permitted Jefferson to undertake action he had favored since 1785: USING FORCE, NOT FUNDS, AGAINST THE BARBARY STATES. The Barbary problem arose in 1801 because the pasha of Tripoli claimed America failed to fulfill its treaty terms as interpreted by the pasha. On May 14, 1801, the pasha declared war on the United States, a fact Jefferson did not know when he ordered Dale's expedition.

When Dale left for Africa, he was ordered to pay any necessary annuities to Tripoli if war had not been declared. If war had been declared, Dale should punish Tripoli in order to end the dispute. Dale's instructions involved Algiers, Tunisia, and Tripoli. As previously, Morocco continued to act generously toward Americans.

See August 1, 1801.

June 17, 1801

Britain successfully ends the League of Armed Neutrality of 1800.

Great Britain attacked the league first by an embargo against its members on January 14, 1801; later, on April 2, by fighting and destroying a Danish fleet that claimed neutral rights. The league was further weakened when Czar Paul, its staunchest advocate, was assassinated on March 23, 1801.

July 31, 1801

American and French representatives exchange ratifications of the Convention of 1801.

Jefferson asked William Vans Murray to go to Paris and obtain French agreement to the Senate reservations so that the treaty could be ratified. The only Senate reservation the French objected to was the demand for indemnification. After much discussion, Murray agreed that if France accepted full abrogation of the 1778 Alliance, the United States would yield its indemnity claims. Consequently, the final exchange of ratification took place on this basis.

After Murray's report on the ratification reached Washington, D.C., Jefferson and Madison did not know if the changes on indemnity required Senate approval. Jefferson decided to seek approval and the Senate complied on December 19, 1801, by a vote of 22 to 4.

For the treaty terms, see September 30–October 1, 1800.

USS *Enterprise* captures Tripolitan corsair, 1801. Copy of artwork by Hoff. National Archives

August 1, 1801

United States scores naval victories against Tripoli.

On August 1, the American schooner *Enterprise* captured a small Tripolitan vessel after a three-hour battle. The same day, William Eaton, the U.S. consul to Tripoli, ordered a "paper blockade" against Tripoli. Eaton later reported that the blockade stopped Tripoli's sea commerce for three months even though no American ships were within 300 leagues of the African port.

1802

March 16, 1802

The United States Military Academy is established by Congress.

On July 4, West Point was opened in formal ceremonies.

March 27, 1802

Peace between England and France is concluded by the Treaty of Amiens.

This was the first peace treaty between England and France since 1793.

August 11, 1802

U.S.-Spanish Convention to settle American claims is signed but fails ratification.

After the treaty of 1795 was signed, American and Spanish negotiations continued with regard to claims for the destruction of American ships and property by Spain. On August 11, Charles Cotesworth Pinckney, the U.S. minister to Madrid, signed a treaty that seemed favorable to U.S. claims.

The convention of 1802 was never ratified, because of disputes between the two nations about Florida and the validity of the Louisiana purchase of 1803. The West Florida dispute caused the U.S. Senate to delay its ratification vote for over 18 months after Pinckney signed the treaty. Following Senate approval on January 9, 1804, Spain refused to accept ratification. Because the Spanish government protested America's aggressive action in occupying West Florida, the king refused to settle the American claims.

See October 16, 1802.

October 15, 1802

Spain transfers Louisiana to France.

Although the Treaty of San Ildefonso (October 1, 1800) provided that France would obtain the Louisiana Territory, Charles VI of Spain withheld approval until Napoléon fully transferred Tuscany as part of the Kingdom of Etruria to the king's son-in-law. On October 15, Charles ratified the transfer of Louisiana because the French ambassador to Madrid promised (1) to fulfill the transfer of Tuscany and (2) that France would not transfer Louisiana to a third party.

October 16, 1802

Spain announces suspension of America's right of deposit at New Orleans.

This unilateral action contravened Pinckney's Treaty of 1795, causing Jefferson to protest immediately to Madrid.

The Spanish king ordered this action on July 14, 1802, apparently at the urging of Napoléon. In July, French and Spanish officials had discussed the retrocession of Louisiana to France, and Napoléon did not want the right of deposit open to the United States after France acquired Louisiana.

News of Spain's closing of New Orleans aroused anger among western American farmers. In Washington, Federalist politicians used the issue to attack Jefferson's foreign policy, but most western settlers believed Jefferson would settle the question for them. For the effect of this action on U.S. policy, see April 30, 1803.

November 2, 1802

France fails to subdue the rebellion in Saint Domingue; Napoléon's brother-in-law, Victor Emmanuel le Clerc, dies of yellow fever in the island; Napoléon's dream of an American empire fades.

In 1801, Napoléon believed he could create a French Empire in the Americas. He would easily end the revolution of mulatto and Negro slaves led by Toussaint L'Ouverture and reestablish Saint Domingue—the French part of the island of Santo Domingo—as the center of French America.

In December 1801, a French army of 20,000 veteran soldiers led by Le Clerc sailed for the

Caribbean, landing part of their forces in February 1802. Napoléon had rejected Toussaint's offer to rule Saint Domingue as a slave-free possession of France. Consequently, Le Clerc met stiff resistance from the rebels. By April 1802, Le Clerc had landed 17,000 troops, of which 5,000 were killed and another 5,000 wounded. Then the rainy season began, bringing yellow fever and a malaria epidemic to decimate the French forces.

In May, Le Clerc captured Toussaint by conniving with a disloyal Negro general. Shipping him to France, Toussaint's captors refused to execute him because they did not want a martyr. They let him die slowly in prison by providing little food, clothing, or warmth and no medical attention.

But Toussaint's mistreatment and death did not abate the desire for freedom among the former slaves of Saint Domingue. They continued the fight, causing further havoc for Le Clerc's reinforced army. By November 1802, as Le Clerc lay on his deathbed, only 2,000 French soldiers, out of a reinforced army of 34,000, were healthy enough to function; 24,000 had died and 8,000 had been hospitalized. In his final reports to Paris, Le Clerc said that the attempt to quell the rebellion was doomed.

He was correct. Although a new French general, Donatien-Marie Joseph de Vimeur ROCHAMBEAU, brought another 10,000 troops, the former slaves on the island vowed to remain free. Rochambeau adopted genocidal methods to eliminate the rebels, but the freed slaves retaliated in kind under a new leader, Jean-Jacques DESSALINES. Rochambeau loaded boats with rebels and then sank the vessels to drown the victims. The rebels mutilated the bodies of all white persons they could find.

By April 1803, Napoléon gave Saint Domingue little attention, having decided to end his imperial schemes. Nevertheless, the bloodbath continued on the island until November 18, 1803. Besieged by Dessalines's rebels, ROCHAMBEAU surrendered to an English commander whose navy aided the rebels by blockading French supplies. Dessalines, who had first declared his nation's independence on December 31, 1802, gained control and changed the name of his nation to HAITI. His attempt to stir a rebellion in the Spanish section of the island—Santo Domingo—did not succeed. The island remained divided: Santo Domingo under Spanish rule and Haiti as an independent nation.

1803

April 30, 1803

France cedes the Louisiana Territory to the United States.

In a hastily arranged treaty, Napoléon and France's finance minister, the Marquis BARBE-MARBOIS, concluded a treaty to cede the Louisiana Territory to America. The U.S. agents in Paris were James Monroe and Robert R. Livingston, whom President Jefferson commissioned on January 12, 1803, to offer to purchase Louisiana from France.

Jefferson became concerned about the fate of Louisiana in the spring of 1802 after hearing rumors from Paris that Spain had ceded that territory to France. On April 18, 1802, the president wrote to Livingston, the American minister to France, that if France controlled New Orleans, the United States would have to "marry" itself to the British "fleet and nation."

The fears of western farmers heightened on October 16, after the Spanish intendant at New Orleans suspended America's right of deposit. Seeking some means to resolve the tension, Jefferson decided to send Monroe as minister plenipotentiary to work with Livingston in negotiating the purchase of New Orleans and West Florida. Although Congress appropriated $2 million for the purchase, Monroe was empowered to offer $10 million if necessary.

On April 11, 1803, two days before Monroe arrived in Paris, French Foreign Minister Talleyrand called Robert Livingston to his office. He informed the U.S. minister that France was considering the sale of Louisiana and asked how much America would pay. Startled by the unexpected news, Livingston requested several days for consideration of the offer. Fortunately, Monroe arrived in Paris on April 13, with authority to purchase that territory even though neither he nor Jefferson expected the mission to succeed.

The French decided to sell the territory because Napoléon had abandoned his plans for an empire in the Americas. The bloody effort to defeat the Saint Domingue rebels had been a costly failure in 1802 (see November 2, 1802). In addition, disputes with England over Malta threatened to disrupt the Peace of Amiens and plunge France back into war. Because of his antagonism for the British, Napoléon preferred to have America get control of the Mississippi region.

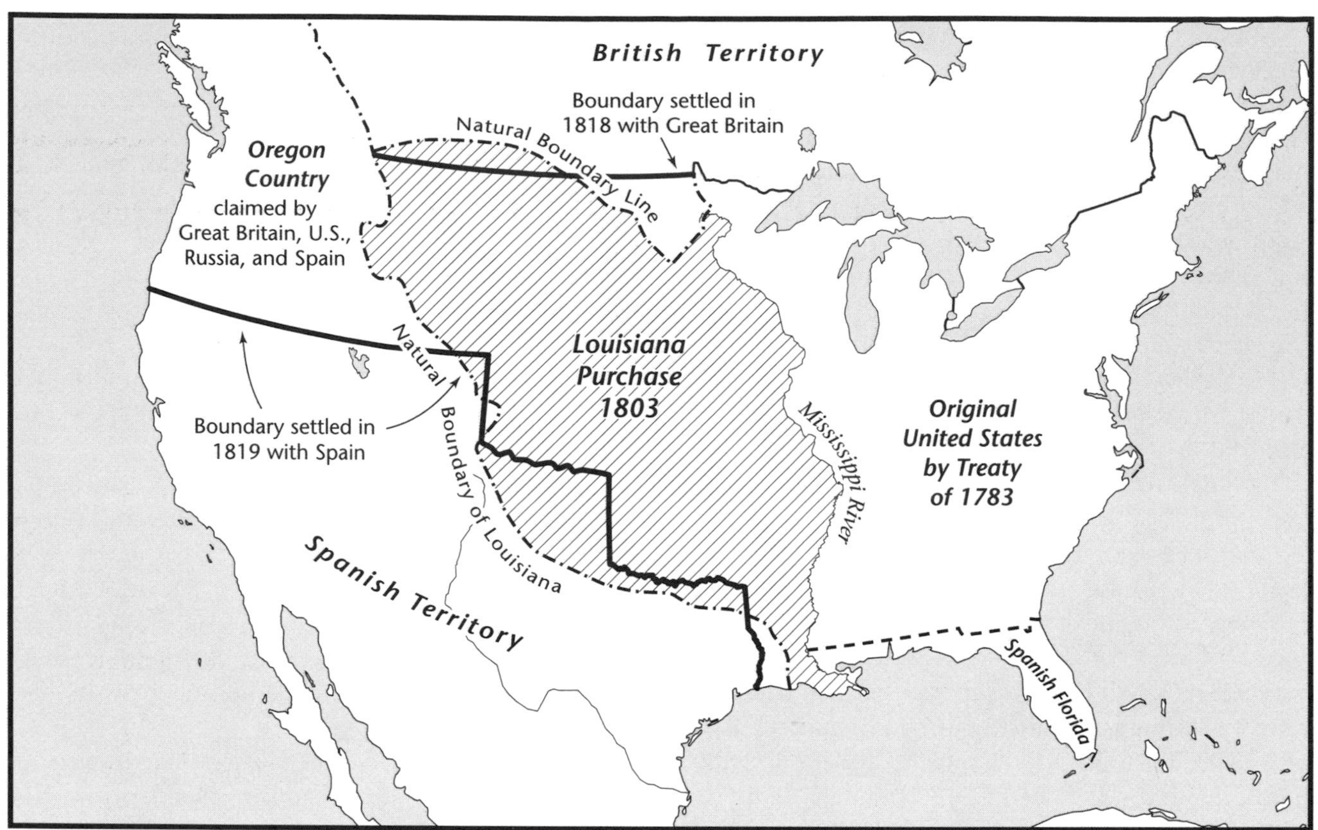

Louisiana Purchase, 1803

Thus, as in 1778, French conflict with the British benefited the United States.

Because Monroe arrived with the power to buy Louisiana, he and Livingston immediately bargained with France's finance minister, the Marquis Barbe-Marbois. They agreed that the United States would pay 60 million francs and assume certain claims of U.S. citizens against France not to exceed 20 million francs. The cost totaled $15 million, which Monroe accepted even though it exceeded the $10 million he was empowered to offer. Monroe reasoned that he had purchased more than New Orleans and West Florida. He received 828,000 square miles of land at about 3 cents per acre. The U.S. Senate agreed, ratifying the treaty on October 20, 1803, by a vote of 24 to 7.

Although the treaty of cession used words identical to the Treaty of San Ildefonso, whereby France received Louisiana from Spain, the western boundaries were not certain and caused future disputes between Spain and America.

For future quarrels with Spain, see September 4, 1803.

For the transfer of the territory to America, see December 20, 1803.

May 12, 1803

British-American Boundary Convention is signed. Coming soon after a favorable commercial decision, better relations are temporarily fostered.

The American minister to Britain, Rufus King, negotiated the agreement that affected three North American boundaries: (1) the St. Croix River border of northern Maine; (2) the U.S. ownership of Campobello and other small islands in Passamaquoddy Bay; and (3) the northwest border between the Mississippi River and the Lake of the Woods. Because of Senate reservations, this convention was not ratified (see February 8, 1804).

In addition to the convention, better relations with Britain were promoted by the *Polly* decision of 1800 by a British court. The *Polly* decision permitted the "broken voyage" concept to apply to the British Rule of 1756 on neutral trade. The *Polly* was an American vessel captured in 1799 by a British privateer, but its prize was ruled against by a British prize court because of the "broken voyage" claim of the owners of the *Polly*. The court ruling, which the Lord Commissions of Appeals Court in London upheld in 1802, was that *Polly*'s cargo was neutral because it went from the French West Indies to a U.S. port where customs duties were paid before the goods were transshipped to Spain. Payment of U.S. duties neutralized the cargo; thus was a "broken voyage" validated even if the cargo's destination was a French allied port.

The *Polly* decision promoted American trade with the European continent because the Rule of 1756 could be evaded by changing belligerent cargo from the French or Spanish West Indies into neutral cargo. This court rule was reversed in the *Essex* decision.

See May 22, 1805.

May 16, 1803

France and Great Britain renew warfare.

The Peace of Amiens of 1802 had not resolved the issues or suspicions between England and France. In particular, the war arose from a dispute over the possession of Malta.

June 7, 1803

Treaty of Vincennes is signed with the Indians.

This treaty, which was made with nine Indian tribes, gave the United States title to land previously disputed along the Wabash River and clearly defined the Vincennes tract, which had been transferred in the Treaty of Greenville of 1795. This treaty was signed at Fort Wayne by William Henry Harrison and the chiefs of nine tribes. The treaty of June 7 was supplemented by treaties of August 18 and 27, 1804, giving the United States land south of the Vincennes tract and north of the Ohio River.

August 31, 1803

Lewis and Clark expedition begins a three-year journey to explore the Louisiana Territory.

Authorized by Congress, Meriwether Lewis and William Clark led a tour whose objective was to cultivate friendly relations with the Indians and extend internal commerce. Their three-year expedition ascended the Missouri River, crossed the Rocky Mountains, and reached the Pacific Ocean by November 7, 1805. It demonstrated the possibility of overland travel to the West Coast and gathered extensive scientific information about the region. Eventually, publicity about their journey stimulated western settlements and commerce west of the Mississippi.

September 4, 1803

Spain protests the sale of Louisiana.

Upon learning of Napoléon's sale, SPANISH minister to the U.S. Marquis de Casa IRUJO (sometimes YRUJO) told President Jefferson that America bought "stolen goods." Irujo's statement represented Spain's first reaction to the sale because the French ambassador to Spain had promised not to resell the territory. By October, however, Napoléon persuaded the Spanish king to comply and Foreign Minister Godoy did so.

Another of Irujo's protests was not easily disposed of: the boundary of West Florida. Jefferson, Secretary of State Madison, James Monroe, and Robert Livingston believed Napoléon's sale included West Florida. Spain argued, however, that West Florida had never been a part of Louisiana. Thus began one dispute over the uncertain boundaries in the west.

See February 24, 1804.

October 10, 1803

Secretary of State Madison orders James Monroe to insist that Great Britain stop the impressment of U.S. citizens.

Out of 46 impressment complaints during the previous year, 43 were against the British. The public outcry against British impressment led Congress to introduce a bill to punish all violators of the American flag. Public opposition to impressment made all future negotiations with Britain difficult. Americans disliked having their citizens kidnapped into the British navy; the British insisted that they could not give up their search for "deserters."

October 31, 1803

Tripoli captures the U.S. frigate *Philadelphia* and its crew of 307 men.

The American naval ship was captured because it ran aground while chasing an enemy ship close to the shore of Tripoli. This capture and the crew's imprisonment made peace negotiations difficult and extended the war with Tripoli.

Since August 1, 1801, the U.S. navy had used a "paper blockade" against Tripoli to limit its raids on American vessels. On June 30, 1803, President Jefferson hoped to pursue the war more vigorously by dispatching six additional U.S. ships to join the fleet off North Africa's coast. He also named Commodore Edward Preble to head the Mediterranean fleet.

The loss of the *Philadelphia* again forced the U.S. navy to use more passive blockade methods until 1805.

See June 10, 1805.

December 20, 1803

France transfers the Louisiana Territory to America.

On November 30, 1803, the Spanish governor of Louisiana gave the keys to the public buildings of New Orleans to a French representative, and France assumed control of the Louisiana territory. Just 20 days later, the French left New Orleans and on December 20 officially ceded the territory to the United States.

1804

February 8, 1804

Boundary Convention with Great Britain is ratified with reservations by the Senate.

Signed on May 12, 1803, the Anglo-American boundary agreement met all the proposals made by the United States. The convention had problems in the Senate because the French cession of Louisiana in 1803 created new difficulties regarding the boundary of the upper Mississippi River. Because Louisiana had not been thoroughly surveyed, many senators hesitated to approve the treaty. Therefore, in spite of Jefferson's favorable recommendation, the Senate's act of ratification reserved its approval of Article V on the northwest boundary.

When the Senate action was presented to Great Britain, its ministry refused to accept the changes. Thus, the 1803 Convention was aborted; the boundary questions remained.

February 24, 1804

Congress passes the "Mobile Act," claiming west Florida is part of the United States.

Jefferson reacted to Spain's claim that West Florida was not part of Louisiana by asking for legislation to make the disputed region American land. Congress complied, and the "Mobile Act" annexed to the Mississippi territorial district *all* "navigable waters, rivers, creeks, bays, and inlets, lying within the United States, which empty into the Gulf of Mexico, east of the river Mississippi." In effect, this annexed West Florida to the United States.

See January 2, 1805.

December 5, 1804

President Jefferson is reelected.

Jefferson received 162 votes to the Federalist Charles Cotesworth Pinckney's 14. For vice president, George Clinton defeated Rufus King by the same vote. The Democratic-Republicans also won control of Congress.

December 12, 1804

Spain declares war on England.

After renewing war with Napoléon, England often attacked Spanish ships because Spain was a French ally. The occasion for war at this time was Britain's seizure of a Spanish treasure ship from South America on October 1, 1804. When word of the capture reached Madrid, the king had little choice but to declare war in retaliation for the British action.

1805

January 2, 1805

James Monroe arrives in Madrid to negotiate the west Florida issue.

President Jefferson hoped that Monroe and Charles Cotesworth Pinckney, the U.S. minister to Spain, would resolve the Florida and U.S. claims issues with the Spanish government. In October 1804, Secretary of State Madison told Monroe to proceed directly to Spain, but the envoy stopped in Paris to seek French aid in the negotiations. He discovered, however, that Talleyrand had persuaded Napoléon to back Spanish claims to West Florida. Spain was a French ally in the war against England and Talleyrand wished to retain Madrid's friendship. When Monroe reached Spain, he realized the negotiations would be difficult.

Without French backing, Monroe had little chance of success. The United States contended that West Florida was already American territory as part of the Louisiana Purchase. Therefore, Monroe could not offer to pay for it. His only available tactic was bluff. On May 12, Monroe met with Foreign Minister Pedro de Cevallo, asking Spain to cede Florida, to recognize the Colorado River as the Texas border, and to ratify the August 1802, claims convention. After Cevallo refused, Monroe asked for and quickly received his passport to leave Spain.

See December 3–6, 1805.

May 22, 1805

The Essex decision affirms a more rigid interpretation of the rule of 1756, thereby causing further British attacks on American merchant vessels.

This decision of Britain's Lords Commissioners of Appeals Court reversed the liberal *Polly* decision of 1802 by restricting the "broken voyage" tactics used by U.S. ships. Going beyond the considerations of the *Polly* case, the *Essex* decision ruled that goods must pay a *bona fide* import duty to be neutralized. If all or part of such duties were rebated to the shipper, the doctrine of *continuous voyage* applied because the cargo's destination was not a neutral nation but a belligerent nation.

The *Essex* carried wine from Barcelona, Spain, to Havana, Cuba, but had stopped first at Salem, Massachusetts. At Salem, American duties were paid but were rebated in part to the ship. A British privateer captured the *Essex* between Salem and Havana, taking the cargo to a British prize court. The lower court's ruling of *continuous voyage* awarded the cargo to the privateer. This ruling was upheld by the appeals court.

Upon learning of the *Essex* ruling, British ships began quickly to raid American ships whose captains thought they were protected by *Polly*'s "broken voyage" doctrine. This caused a rapid increase of U.S. shipping losses and renewed friction between England and America.

For the *Polly* case, see May 12, 1803.

June 10, 1805

Peace with Tripoli follows a successful American expedition across the Libyan desert from Egypt to capture Derna.

An unusual American campaign led to Tripoli's capitulation in the war. As planned by American Consul

U.S. Marines raise flag over Derna ("the shores of Tripoli") and the Pasha of Tripoli sues for peace. National Archives

to Tunis William EATON and Captain Isaac HULL of the U.S. frigate *Argus*, a military force would attack Derna by land after a march across the desert, while the *Argus*, the *Nautilus*, and the *Hornet* bombarded the town with naval guns. In addition, 100 U.S. marines would land to assist Eaton's "army."

In Egypt, Eaton recruited a multinational group of 400 mercenaries for the march on Derna. "General" Eaton's army included 10 Americans, 38 Greeks, 300 Arabs, and a variety of other ethnic groups. He led this often dissident group on a 500-mile journey across the Libyan desert. In spite of shortages of water and food and threats of mutiny, Eaton's men reached Derna and attacked on April 27, 1805. Assisted by the naval bombardment and the marine force, Eaton captured Derna.

While the land-sea operations proceeded, Tobias LEAR, the American general consul for the Barbary States, undertook negotiations with the pasha of Tripoli, which concluded in a peace treaty on June 10. The treaty provided for an exchange of prisoners and the American payment of $60,000 because Tripoli held more hostages. The United States would no longer pay annual tributes, and commerce between the countries would be on a most-favored-nation basis. The U.S. Senate ratified the treaty on April 12, 1806, by a vote of 21 to 8.

August 30, 1805

U.S. naval action leads to a new treaty with the Bey of Tunis.

On April 24, 1805, after a U.S. naval squadron blockaded Tunis, the *Constitution* captured a Tunisian vessel with two prize ships as they attempted to enter their home port. The bey of Tunis protested this action, threatening to declare war. The American naval commodore, John RODGERS, refused to release the ships. He informed the Tunisian ruler that Tunis could no longer infringe on U.S. rights without being punished.

Rodgers's threat had a large naval force to back it because at the end of the Tripoli campaign, seven U.S. warships joined the *Constitution* at Tunis. The bey's challenge to Rodgers ended when the Americans captured another vessel trying to run the blockade. A truce was arranged and a Tunisian ambassador sailed to the United States aboard the USS *Congress* to conclude a treaty with Secretary of State Madison. The peace treaty was finalized on January 7, 1807.

October 21, 1805

The British Navy defeats the Franco-Spanish fleet at Trafalgar.

This battle left the British fleet in general control of the Atlantic Ocean.

December 3–6, 1805

Jefferson's report to congress favors peaceful methods, delays army increase.

In his fifth annual report to Congress on December 3 and a special secret message on December 6, President Jefferson described the need to strengthen U.S. security and his attempts to purchase West Florida from Spain. He told Congress about James Monroe's abortive 1804–1805 mission to Spain and his preference for peaceful methods, although some disputes had to be met "by force."

Specifically, Jefferson explained that "upward of 300,000" able-bodied men between the ages of 18 and 26 could "furnish a competent number" of troops at any time they were wanted. On December 6, he also asked Congress for authority to change the nation's course from peace to war in the degree required but did not request an increase in the size of the army.

Jefferson's special message of December 6 emphasized the possibility of buying West Florida from Spain for $2 million. In response on February 13, 1806, Congress approved the $2 million, but the State Department's attempts to make the purchase did not succeed.

On February 24, 1807, after Monroe negotiated a treaty with Great Britain that Jefferson rejected, Congress authorized the president to enroll 30,000 citizen-soldiers (volunteers) to be on call for two years of duty and serve at least one year. On April 12, 1808, after approving the 1807 Embargo legislation, Congress approved legislation to recruit 6,000 men for the army.

See January 2, 1805; November 27 and December 31, 1806; December 22, 1807; and October 27, 1810.

1806

April 10, 1806

Congress passes a nonimportation act to coerce Great Britain to change its neutrality policies.

American public protest against British attacks on U.S. vessels and its impressment of U.S. sailors increased after England and France renewed warfare in 1803. Congress finally acted on April 10, 1806, because diplomatic talks had failed.

For three years Secretary of State Madison and U.S. Minister to England James Monroe had been unable to reach an agreement with London. Yet the impressment problem grew. The number of American citizens impressed is uncertain but between 3,800 and 6,257 had been forced into the British navy between 1803 and 1812. After the war ended in 1815, Britain released 1,800 Americans from impressment, but these survivors represented only a part of the number impressed.

In order to persuade the British to agree on policy changes, Congress passed three resolutions between February 5 and April 10, 1806. As prepared by Senators Samuel SMITH and John Quincy ADAMS, the first two resolutions protested the Rule of 1756 and the *Essex* decision of 1805 as "unprovoked aggression" and a "direct encroachment upon their [America's] national independence."

The third resolution was the nonimportation act of April 10. As originally proposed, a nearly total nonimporting program was intended. Before congressional passage, however, amendments omitted the most important British imports from the list: cotton and woolen goods, iron and steel. A specific attempt by Adams to include these items was defeated.

Moreover, before approving the act Congress weakened it further by delaying the effective date until November 15, 1806. This date was extended again and the bill did not become effective until December 14, 1807, at the time Jefferson's embargo passed.

As Bradford Perkins's study shows, the English considered the nonimportation act a bluff, and its weak character made it worse than useless. The dilemma facing Congress and Jefferson's administration was that while British maritime policy violated basic neutral rights as interpreted by many Americans, the commercial profits from British trade were too lucrative to be endangered.

May 1, 1806

Jefferson protests a British naval attack that kills an American citizen.

The British ship *Leander*, one of two vessels blockading New York harbor, stopped an American merchant ship to check its cargo. In firing its warning shots, the *Leander* miscalculated and the shot killed John PIERCE, an American sailor.

In addition to his protest, Jefferson ordered all British ships to leave the New York area and demanded that the British court-martial the *Leander*'s commander, Captain Henry WHITBY.

May 16, 1806

The Fox blockade of 1806 is an attempt to conciliate America while coercing France.

Following the death of Prime Minister William Pitt early in 1806, the new ministry of Lord William Grenville sought a more moderating attitude toward the United States. Grenville and his foreign secretary, Charles James Fox, believed Pitt's officials had been too arrogant toward America and had enforced the *Essex* decision too quickly and strictly.

In order to make a few concessions to the United States, Fox recalled the British minister to Washington, Anthony Merry, who had proven quite unfriendly to Jefferson and Madison. To replace Merry, Fox sent David M. Erskine, who had little diplomatic experience but did have an American wife and a reputation as a liberal.

On May 16, Fox and Grenville approved an order-in-council that they designed as both a conciliatory measure toward America and as evidence of stronger measures against Napoléon. The Fox blockade of May 16 placed the entire northern coast of Europe from Brest to the Elbe under blockade. However, the order added that the blockade would be rigorously enforced only from the Seine to Ostend. Elsewhere, neutral ships could visit enemy ports if they carried no contraband or enemy-owned goods and if they visited no other enemy ports. By their relaxed enforcement, Fox and Grenville indicated that the *Essex* decision on continuous voyage would apply only in a limited area of blockade. The European ports on the Atlantic and in Holland and Flanders would be open to American ships.

See May 22, 1805.

The Fox blockade did not satisfy James Monroe and other Americans. Fox had withdrawn a promise to specifically alter the *Essex* decision because of protest from political opponents. With the *Essex* decision intact, the blockade order appeared to enforce the action in the limited place where the British navy could effectively carry out rigorous enforcement. In this context, Fox had added many miles of coastline for future potential blockade. Thus, the Fox blockade did not seem to be a genuine concession to America or other neutral nations.

Subsequently, as Monroe feared, the British in 1807 extended the area proclaimed for rigorous enforcement. On January 1, 1807, an order-in-council ended the Ostend River limitation, and on November 17, 1807, Britain excluded neutral trade from any continental port between Copenhagen and Trieste unless the ship was first searched for contraband by British naval officers.

May 17, 1806

American delegates are appointed to negotiate with Great Britain.

Largely as a consequence of American public concern about neutrality, James Monroe and William Pinkney were named ministers plenipotentiary to obtain a treaty with Great Britain. In Secretary of State Madison's instructions to the two delegates, the three issues identified as critical between the two nations were impressment, definition of blockade, and neutral rights rules on contraband and the continuous or broken voyage.

Madison's instructions also suggested possible compromise positions for the U.S. delegates. These were (1) waiving the concept of "free ships equal free goods"; (2) accepting a flexible definition of contraband; (3) applying the Rule of 1756 to all Direct Trade between a belligerent and its colonies. The delegates could also accept a compromise on impressment as follows: the United States would return all deserters to Britain and the English would not enlist subjects on U.S. vessels. Monroe's and Pinkney's attempts resulted in a treaty on December 31, 1806.

See December 31, 1806.

November 21, 1806

Napoléon's Berlin decree proclaims a (paper) blockade of Great Britain by closing all continental trade with the British.

This decree established Napoléon's Continental System. Later, with the Milan Decree of December 17, 1807, Napoléon theoretically closed all of the European coastline to British Trade. The trade of all neutral nations was damaged by the Continental System and Great Britain's orders for a blockade of Europe. Because the British navy controlled the oceans, its trade restrictions resulted in greater conflict with the United States than did Napoléon's.

November 27, 1806

President Jefferson warns U.S. citizens not to join Aaron Burr's expedition against Spain's territory in Florida and Texas.

Exactly what Burr's purposes were remains a mystery. His opponents claimed he wanted to rule over a new nation created in the western regions. Burr said he raised forces to defend western settlers from the Spanish armies and Indians in the west and southwest.

When Burr's activity first surfaced early in 1806, Jefferson sent a small force under General James Wilkinson to the frontier area of Louisiana and Texas. Wilkinson agreed with the Spanish commander in Texas to respect a neutral zone on the border between the Sabine and Arroyo Hondo Rivers. Apparently, Wilkinson also joined Burr's plot, although their precise agreement is unclear because Wilkinson eventually betrayed Burr.

Nevertheless, in 1806 Burr raised a contingent of volunteer adventurers and marched them from the Ohio river valley to Tennessee. These activities alarmed Jefferson and precipitated his proclamation of November 27, warning Americans that it was not legal to arm in order to attack a foreign nation's territory.

As it happened, Burr's plans had little substance and failed. He reached Natchez with his volunteers but Wilkinson then denounced him and moved his troops to New Orleans to protect the city from Burr. Burr fled but was captured on February 19, 1807. He was tried for treason, but the jury returned a verdict of "not proven." Chief Justice John Marshall, who presided at Burr's trials, ruled that the verdict must stand as "not guilty."

Burr's affair was the most publicized of many western schemes to capture Florida or parts of Texas from Spain. Because of Spain's difficulties in Europe during the Napoléonic era, it was too weak to retain control of its overseas empire.

December 2, 1806

Congress prohibits the importation of slaves after January 1, 1808.

In accordance with the 20-year limit written into the Constitution of 1787, Jefferson recommended this action to Congress. In 1807, Great Britain also outlawed slave trade (and in 1833 abolished slavery in the empire). Subsequently, the British attempted to have America sign an agreement to permit either nation to search suspected slave-carrying ships. The United States refused to do so, largely because of the existing conflicts with Great Britain on neutral rights and impressment.

December 31, 1806

In London, Monroe and Pinkney sign a treaty with Great Britain on neutral rights.

After several months of discussion in London, Monroe and Pinkney obtained a treaty similar to the Jay Treaty of 1794, but one that they hoped would avoid war.

The U.S. delegates failed to achieve the compromise on impressment that Madison had suggested on May 17. Britain's negotiators, Lord Holland and Lord Auckland, argued that the British public insisted on the right to impress deserters. On November 9, the British delegates gave the Americans an official note explaining that British officers would be ordered to be cautious during impressment proceedings to "preserve" American citizens from "molestation or injury." They asked the American delegates to accept this note as final and to attempt to resolve other commercial issues. Monroe and Pinkney agreed and the Treaty of December 31 resulted.

On receiving copies of the treaty, Jefferson and Madison immediately rejected it. Jefferson thought that without an impressment agreement the treaty was worthless. Early in 1807, Secretary Madison instructed Monroe and Pinkney to renew discussion and endeavor to obtain a better treaty. The *Chesapeake* affair changed future discussions, however.

See June 22, 1807.

1807

January 7, 1807

British order-in-council outlaws all neutral trade between ports controlled by Napoléon.

This order was valid if Britain could make an effective blockade of all ports under French control.

May 12, 1807

Secretary of State Madison helps a Christian missionary, Dr. Robert Morrison, receive passage to and consular aid in China.

Having had a trade monopoly in the Far East since receiving its charter in 1600, the British East India Company refused to give Morrison permission to proselytize in China, the English missionary came to America to seek aid. Madison helped him secure passage on an American ship and sent a letter to Edward CARRINGTON, the American consul at Canton, to assist Morrison. When Morrison arrived in Canton, the U.S. missionary effort began in China.

June 22, 1807

The *Chesapeake* Affair nearly causes war with Great Britain.

A British naval ship, HMS *Leopard*, commanded by Captain S. P. HUMPHREYS, intercepted the American navy ship USS *Chesapeake* off Cape Henry near Hampton Roads, Virginia. An officer representing Humphreys boarded the U.S. ship, but the *Chesapeake*'s captain, Commodore James BARRON, stated there were no British subjects on board. Barron refused to be searched, and after Humphreys learned his reply, a conflict ensued. The *Leopard* fired a warning shot across the *Chesapeake*'s bow but Barron refused to yield. Surprisingly and contrary to international practice, the *Leopard* aimed and fired a direct cannonade at the *Chesapeake*. The Americans suffered 21 casualties: 3 dead, 18 wounded. Unprepared to fight, Barron rushed a live coal from the mess hall to fire one wild shot before surrendering. British officers now boarded and searched the ship, and impressed four sailors they claimed were British deserters.

Humphreys's action had been inspired by a recent incident involving British deserters. Early in 1807, several English sailors deserted HMS *Melampus* and allegedly enlisted in the American navy. These sailors deserted when they came ashore to purchase the ship's provisions in March 1807, because the *Melampus* was stationed beyond Virginia's three-mile limit.

Previously, Humphreys asked both the British consul in Norfolk and its minister in Washington for help, but they resisted him. Finally, on June 1, the British naval commander at Halifax, Admiral G. C. Berkeley, issued an unusual order. He told all ships in his command to recover the deserters outside the three-mile limit. Berkeley was later reprimanded for this order.

When Barron's ship sailed on June 22 for the Mediterranean, Humphreys found it a perfect target. The *Chesapeake* was heavily laden with gear and provisions for the transatlantic journey. The *Chesapeake* incident caused cries of protest from Americans. Calls for war against Great Britain required extreme measures by Jefferson to avoid war.

See July 2 and September 5, 1807.

England did not redress its insult until the eve of America's declaration of war in June 1812. The British later admitted that only one of the four impressed seamen was a British deserter. He was tried and hanged by the British in Halifax. The British impressed the other three into their navy even after they were known to be Americans.

July 2, 1807

President Jefferson avoids war by measures intended to compel British changes in policy.

Congress was not in session at the time of the *Chesapeake* incident and the president decided not to call a special session. Jefferson tried to punish Great Britain by expelling all British ships from American waters and prohibiting American intercourse to provision any ship that refused to leave. He also sent a schooner auspiciously named the *Revenge* to London to demand satisfaction from the English government and to bring instructions to U.S. Minister to Britain James Monroe on the settlement of the impressment problem.

Great Britain's reaction to the *Chesapeake* affair was considered insulting. It refused to negotiate impressment and demanded that Jefferson withdraw his order to expel British ships. As a consequence tensions grew between the two nations and multiplied during the next five years.

These years (1807–1812) were the era of Napoléon's peak of power in Europe. Nevertheless, the British refusal to seek a compromise method for dealing with deserters and impressment cannot be excused by Napoléon's status. A settlement along the lines suggested by the Americans would have benefited both nations. The British ministry in 1806–1807 adamantly insisted that the public would not permit a compromise. As the evidence involved in the cases of three of the four sailors taken from the *Chesapeake* showed, the British violated humanitarian principles by their action.

July 7–9, 1807

Napoléon's victories over Prussia and Russia result in the Treaties of Tilsit.

Prussia was virtually controlled by Napoléon; Russia stopped fighting France and agreed to use its good offices to obtain a peace treaty between France and Great Britain. The czar's attempt to mediate peace was not successful.

September 5, 1807

The *Chesapeake* crisis unleashes fear that the British in Canada are encouraging the Indians to attack Americans.

Although General William Henry Harrison, the American commander in the Indiana territory, had no direct evidence of British attempts to seek Indian help if war began, he reported to Washington on September 5 that Indians were attending meetings in Canada and would fight when the British told them to do so. British records show that the governor of Canada desired to use the Indians to help defend Quebec. In January 1808, Shawnee Indians met with Canadian agents at Amherstburg, in Canadian territory near Detroit. They exchanged presents and reestablished good relations with each other, leading subsequently to further British aid for Indians in the Northwest territory of America.

October 17, 1807

The British assert their right to search ships and impress "Deserters."

To emphasize their refusal to negotiate impressment, the British issued an order-in-council to assert the right to recover British subjects from foreign vessels. Significantly, the order did disclaim the right to search warships of another nation, as had happened in the *Chesapeake-Leopard* incident.

November 11, 1807

British order-in-council declares a blockade of all countries under French control, including colonies of those nations.

The only concession Britain made to neutral nations was to permit direct trade with enemy colonies if the ships did not go to any European ports.

December 22, 1807

President Jefferson signs the Embargo Bill of 1807.

In addition to his July 2 decree prohibiting British ships from being in U.S. waters, Jefferson decided to ask Congress to embargo *all* American commerce with the outside world. Although the legislation indicated the bill would preserve American seamen and vessels from perils on the "sea and elsewhere abroad," everyone understood that the law's intention was to coerce Britain and France to repeal their repressive acts against America's neutral trade.

Ograbme (Embargo), or the American Snapping-Turtle. This cartoon was typical of the criticism of Jefferson's embargo policy. Collection of The New York Historical Society

Since 1806, British and French decrees militated against all neutral rights in time of war. In 1807, both nations tightened their prior restrictions. After August, Napoléon ordered enforcement of the Berlin decree and French officials began large-scale seizures of neutral ships in continental ports. Although on December 22 Jefferson did not know the MILAN decree sought to further blockade English trade, Congress and Jefferson knew that since August, many U.S. ships had been seized by France. They also knew about the British blockade order of November 11, 1807, and England's refusal to negotiate with Monroe.

Jefferson and Madison estimated incorrectly that France and Britain needed America's manufactured and agricultural products. They hoped to coerce either England or France to accept America's neutral rights. The embargo was not perceived in Washington as a warlike economic weapon. Thus, Jefferson did not request and Congress did not make any special defense or security preparations in 1807.

One interesting effect of the vote on the embargo was the "recall" of Senator John Quincy Adams by the Massachusetts legislature because he voted for the embargo. On May 8, 1808, the legislature elected James Lloyd Jr. as senator. Adams resigned his Senate seat on June 8 and actively joined the Democratic-Republican party.

1808

March 12, 1808

An amendment to the Embargo of 1807 permits the President to lift the embargo for whichever belligerent repealed its restrictive blockades of neutral commerce.

This was the most significant of several amendments to the Embargo of 1807, passed in an effort to rectify the damage being done to the U.S. economy by the embargo.

Almost immediately after the embargo passed in December 1807, the planter south lost tobacco and cotton exports and the commercial north suffered a business downturn. Protest demonstrations and petitions against the embargo took place all along the coastal states, but especially in New England. The act of 1807 was called the "DAMBARGO"' by its detractors.

Unfortunately neither the embargo nor its amendments brought the anticipated French and English rush to respect neutral rights. The embargo tended to please the French because the British bottled up their navy and merchant ships. The British merchants suffered some loss, but their response was to harden, not soften, their attitude toward U.S. shipping. The one salutary result for the American economy, according to some historians, was that American manufacturing was promoted to fill home product sales to replace British and French imports.

April 17, 1808

Napoléon issues the Bayonne Decree.

Pretending that he was aiding the United States in enforcing its embargo, the French emperor's decree assumed that all American ships in French ports must be British vessels with false papers. Therefore, the French seized the U.S. ships, confiscating $10 million worth of American goods and shipping.

May 21, 1808

Incident between American soldiers and Canadian traders occurs near Niagara.

After 1805, tensions along the U.S.-Canadian borders complemented British-American troubles on the high seas. One incident occurred in May 1808, near the mouth of the Niagara River. Twenty bateaux of Canada's MICHILIMACKINAC COMPANY were carrying goods along the American side of Lake Ontario when a boatload of American soldiers fired at the craft, capturing two of them. The soldiers had been called to act by the local U.S. customs agent, who believed the Embargo of 1807 intended to stop trade across the Canadian border.

The customs officer was mistaken. Therefore, Jefferson ordered the ships to be released and the property to be returned to its owners.

November 22, 1808

Congressional report indicates the Embargo of 1807 has failed.

Throughout 1808, opposition to the cessation of trade grew as the economy of the seaboard states suffered. As a result, a committee of the House of Representatives investigated all aspects of the legislation and its effects on the nation. The report concluded that the embargo had not effectively coerced either European belligerent but had damaged the U.S. economy. The committee reported that America had three choices: (1) to go to war; (2) to submit to the belligerents; or (3) to persevere in a bad policy. But the committee suggested a fourth choice. It believed that America's desire to avoid war but not yield in the principles of neutrality required a "middle course" between the evils of both, which would not "be inconsistent with national honor and independence." The "middle course" recommendation was to end the embargo of all goods and adopt a nonintercourse act to boycott British and French imports. Congress passed such legislation in February 1809.

See March 1, 1809.

December 7, 1808

James Madison wins the Presidential election with 122 electoral votes to 47 for the Federalist Charles Cotesworth Pinckney and 6 for George Clinton of New York.

In 1808, the Democratic-Republicans suffered two splits in their party. "Old" southern Republicans nominated James Monroe, who withdrew his name from nomination; eastern Republicans selected Vice President Clinton. Both of these groups were critical of Jefferson and Madison's foreign policy. They could not, however, gain strong national support, and Madison easily won the election. Federalist power continued to decline as Jefferson's party held the trust of most of the people. For many of them, his domestic program remained sound despite the foreign policy conflict with Great Britain.

1809

January 9, 1809

An enforcement act tightens the implementation of the embargo.

Following publication of the report on the embargo by the House committee, Secretary of the Treasury Albert Gallatin proposed that strict enforcement of the embargo might persuade the European nations of America's serious intentions and, thereby, persuade England or France to yield. In January 1809, Congress tried Gallatin's suggestion by giving U.S. customs agents greater power to stop any illegal trade. Stronger enforcement did not work. It further hurt American business but did not affect British or French policies.

In contrast to Gallatin's idea, some state politicians used the November 1808 report to annul the embargo. Thus, for example, Connecticut Governor Jonathan TRUMBULL contended that because Congress exceeded its powers, state assemblies should "interpose" to protect the people's rights. The Federalists' desire for trade led them to urge the states' rights that Jefferson had invoked in the Kentucky resolutions of 1799. As a result the Non-Intercourse Act was passed by Congress.

See March 1, 1809.

March 1, 1809

Jefferson signs the Nonintercourse Act, which ends the embargo on March 4, 1809.

The nonintercourse law excluded ships and goods of the belligerents from America and forbade U.S. vessels to trade with either warring power. However, the act provided that if either nation ended its commercial restrictions, the president could suspend nonimportation with that nation. The act of March 1 tried the "middle way" proposed by the House report of November 1808. As such, it reflected the continued unwillingness of Congress to yield to either Britain or France.

The Embargo Act of 1807 ended on March 4. American merchants could trade with nations not in the Anglo-French orbit. Madison and Jefferson hoped that the British and French would suffer from the nonintercourse bill because they desired American exports. If so, they might retract their attempts to limit neutral trade.

March 6, 1809

Robert Smith becomes Secretary of State.

He served until April 1, 1811. Smith had been secretary of the navy in Jefferson's cabinet from 1801 to 1809.

April 7, 1809

Erskine Agreement appears to settle the Anglo-American dispute.

As a result of diplomatic exchanges between Washington and London in December 1808, British Foreign Minister George Canning instructed Britain's minister to the United States, David Erskine, to settle pending differences with America by negotiating with Secretary of State Robert Smith. George Canning, the British foreign minister, had on January 23 instructed David Erskine to negotiate with Secretary of State Smith in an attempt to settle pending differences. Following these instructions, Erskine talked with Smith and on April 7 their agreement seemed to have resolved the long-standing maritime problems.

Smith agreed to accept Britain's three conditions for revocation of their orders-in-council. The conditions were (1) withdrawal of Jefferson's "Chesapeake" order of July 2, 1807, as well as all nonintercourse and nonimportation cuts affecting the British; (2) recognition of the Rule of 1756 on continuous voyage; (3) the use of the British navy to enforce American acts prohibiting intercourse with France.

After reaching these three agreements, Erskine decided to go beyond his instructions in order immediately to heal the breach with America. Erskine assured Smith that Britain's orders-in-council would end on June 10, 1809, and that England would send an envoy to conclude formally a treaty of amity and commerce.

The exchange between Erskine and Smith implied that the impressment issue could be readily settled. The United States would prevent English seamen from being employed by American ships and would return deserters to the Royal Navy. The British would have no reason to impress American sailors.

If the Smith-Erskine agreement had been fulfilled, diplomatic relations between the United States and Britain would have been revolutionized. Unfortunately, the optimism of April turned to gloom in August after the British disavowed their minister's agreement.

April 19, 1809

On the basis of the Erskine Agreement, President Madison proclaims the renewal of trade with Great Britain.

The April 7 Erskine-Smith talks indicated that England acceded to certain neutral rights and that the president hoped to end the nation's commercial plight by reopening trade. Because Erskine's statements were disavowed, Madison's proclamation was premature.

See May 30, 1809.

May 30, 1809

Foreign Minister Canning disavows the Erskine Agreement and recalls the Minister from Washington.

Canning's reasons for the disavowal are not certain. Officially, he cited several technical details of Erskine's orders, but largely, Canning seems either not to have expected the American acceptance of his three conditions or to have changed his mind because of political problems in London. Whatever Canning's purpose, he did not accept Erskine's agreement and the breach between the two nations widened again. Canning missed an opportunity to settle long-standing disputes with America.

See August 9 and November 8, 1809, and January 20, 1810.

August 9, 1809

President Madison revives the NonIntercourse act against Great Britain.

News that George Canning disavowed the Erskine agreement reached Washington on August 9. Immediately, the president proclaimed that trade with England was again illegal.

The apparent settlement with Great Britain in April 1809 cheered the Americans. U.S. shippers and merchants quickly acted to renew trade with England. Now their hopes for a peaceful settlement ended and further evidence of London's duplicity seemed apparent. Future negotiations between London and Washington became even more difficult during the next three years.

October 14, 1809

Napoléon's victory over Austrian forces at Wagram (July 5–6) results in the Treaty of Schonbrunn.

Austria now came under French control and agreed to end all alliances with Great Britain. French power on the Continent continued to expand.

November 8, 1809

President Madison rejects Britain's new Minister to the United States, Francis James Jackson.

Jackson, who had treated Denmark harshly prior to Britain's defeat of the Danish fleet in 1807, was appointed to replace David Erskine. Following Canning's advice, Jackson claimed that the Americans tried to trick Erskine into agreeing with them. On meeting with Secretary of State Smith in Washington, Jackson bluntly stated that Smith and Madison knew that Erskine had violated his instructions on April 7. When Smith denied this, Jackson repeated his charge, which, in effect, called them liars.

Jackson was subsequently ignored by the American officials and on November 8, 1809, Madison and Smith sent a curt note to him saying "no further communications will be received from you." Jackson stayed in America until September 1810, meeting with Federalist opponents of Madison and appealing to them to condemn the president.

1810

January 20, 1810

America seeks new negotiations with Great Britain.

After Canning rejected the Erskine agreement of 1809, President Madison seemed uncertain what to do. The U.S. army and navy were in miserable condition. The embargo cut off customs duties and emptied the Treasury, and Congress could agree only to pass resolutions denouncing the British. When Madison asked for funds to outfit the navy and raise a 20,000-man volunteer army, Congress refused because new taxes would be necessary to pay the cost.

By January, the one American hope arose because of a change in the British cabinet. Foreign Minister Canning resigned because he disagreed with Prime Minister Lord Castlereagh and forced the formation of a new cabinet. In London, U.S. Minister William Pinkney had excellent personal relations with the Marquis of Wellesley, who replaced Canning. Pinkney believed Wellesley might agree to satisfactory terms on the problems with America.

Therefore, on January 20, Secretary of State Smith sent Pinkney instructions to renew negotiations to restore amity. He was told first to settle the *Chesapeake* matter, then to arrange for withdrawal of the orders-in-council by Britain.

But Pinkney's discussions with Wellesley were futile. Wellesley did not have cabinet support for an agreement with America, and after Congress passed

Macon's Bill No. 2 on May 1, 1810, the British had even less reason to revise their commercial practices.

March 23, 1810

Napoléon's Rambouillet Decree orders the seizure of all U.S. vessels entering any French port.

This decree was made retroactive to May 20, 1809. John Armstrong, the U.S. minister to France, constantly protested against Napoléon's confiscation of American ships, but as historian A. L. Burt remarked, Armstrong "might as well have prayed to Neptune for the restoration of ships from the bottom of the sea."

May 1, 1810

Macon's Bill No. 2 is designed to coerce England and France into ending their restrictions on neutral trade.

By early 1810, both the Embargo Act of 1807 and the Nonintercourse Act of March 1, 1809, had failed to resolve the American problems regarding neutral rights with the belligerent European powers. The aborted Erskine Agreement of April 19, 1809 (see also May 30, 1809) caused bitter relations between London and Washington. In addition, Napoléon confiscated more U.S. ships, claiming they were disguised British vessels (see March 23, 1810).

Named for the chairman of the Foreign Relations Committee, Nathaniel Macon, Macon's Bill No. 2 attempted to revive American trade while enticing Paris and London to repeal their trade restrictions. Although prohibiting British and French warships from U.S. waters, this bill reopened U.S. trade with all the world. It provided, however, that if either France or Britain ended their trade restrictions, America would give the other nation three months to do likewise. If the second power refused to repeal its edicts, the United States would declare nonintercourse with the recalcitrant nation.

While, in theory, Macon's Bill should have helped solve the trade issues, in practice it caused difficulty. Neither London nor Paris accepted this legislation. Therefore, while New England merchants rejoiced and rushed to renew trade with England, protected by the British navy, the French did not profit from the increased trade. They claimed America had virtually yielded to the British.

See August 5 and November 2, 1810.

May 25, 1810

A military junta in Río de la Plata removes the Spanish viceroy but claims to rule for King Ferdinand VII.

Napoléon's conquest of Spain in 1808 led to many rebellions in Spain's American colonies. Río de la Plata province included Paraguay, Uruguay, and Argentina. This province successfully resisted an English invasion force in 1806–1807, when colonial militia led by Santiago de Liniers chased the British from Buenos Aires. In 1809, a junta in Madrid under Napoléon's direction sent a viceroy to rule, but the local *cabildo* of Buenos Aires removed him from office. A new government was set up under Mariano Moreno. Direct Spanish authority was never restored in this province, from which three separate states later developed.

August 5, 1810

Napoléon claims he will revoke his trade restrictions. At the same time, however, he secretly confiscates U.S. ships.

The events by which the French emperor got the Americans to end trade with Britain began to unfold on August 5, when France's foreign minister, the due de Cadore, talked with John Armstrong, America's minister to France. Cadore told Armstrong that France would end its Berlin and Milan Decrees on November 1, 1810, provided the English revoked their orders-in-council or the United States should "cause their rights to be respected by the English."

Armstrong interpreted this to mean that French trade restrictions would end on November 1. In fact, the revocation of the French regulations depended on the effective end of the British blockade either by English or American action.

Neither Armstrong nor President Madison knew that on August 5, Napoléon also signed the Decree of Trianon. This secret proclamation legitimized (for the French) the confiscation of U.S. ships seized in French ports between May 20, 1809, and May 1, 1810. These ships had reached France after the American Nonintercourse Act of 1809 opened trade with England and France. The Trianon Decree was not disclosed until 1815, becoming one factor in later American claims against France for damage to U.S. property. If this decree had been published in 1810, subsequent U.S. action would undoubtedly have been different.

October 27, 1810

West Florida is annexed.

President Madison issued a proclamation announcing that the area of Florida from the Mississippi to the Perdido River was an American possession. He authorized the military occupation of the region.

This territory had been disputed with Spain because Jefferson believed the Louisiana Purchase included territory east of the Mississippi River to the Perdido River. Negotiations with Madrid had been fruitless, and following Napoléon's conquest of Spain, Madrid's authority in the Americas weakened.

In 1810, a group of southern expansionists led a revolt against Spain, and on September 26 they declared the independent state of the Republic of West Florida. Madison's decree brought this republic into the union.

November 2, 1810

President Madison applies Macon's Bill No. 2 against Great Britain.

Madison's proclamation of November 2 assumed that Napoléon had revoked his Berlin and Milan Decrees as of November 1. The proclamation asserted that the "edicts of France have been revoked because they ceased on the first day of the present month to violate the neutral commerce of the United States." Therefore, he said, unless Britain rescinded its orders-in-council by February 2, 1811, nonintercourse laws would apply against the British.

Whether Madison and Armstrong were not fooled by Napoléon but simply hoped that the acceptance of his August 5 statement would require him to enact it is not certain. Both France and England caused difficulty, and Madison disliked the Federalists' willingness to yield to all British demands on neutral rights. Perhaps he hoped that under pressure of Napoléon's repeal, the British would also placate Washington. He was mistaken, of course. Throughout 1810, as Pinkney's efforts with Wellesley showed, the British were unwilling to compromise with the United States.

1811

January 15, 1811

No-transfer resolution approved by Congress.

Because Spain's conquest by France ended effective Spanish control in Florida, Congress asserted that it would view with "serious inquietude" the effort by a third party to gain control of the southern border of America. Moreover, "certain contingencies" might compel the United States to the "temporary occupation" of the territory with "future negotiations" to determine the outcome. In particular, there was fear in the southern states that England might seek to occupy Florida, which the Americans hoped some day to annex. This "no-transfer" concept anticipated one of the principles later enunciated in the Monroe Doctrine.

See December 2, 1823.

February 28, 1811

William Pinkney, the U.S. Minister to Great Britain, leaves London and is not replaced until the end of the War of 1812.

Pinkney was recalled from his position in reciprocity for President Madison's demand that Britain recall F. J. Jackson on November 8, 1809. Pinkney delayed leaving London for over a year because he hoped to negotiate a settlement of Anglo-American problems with Foreign Minister Wellesley. Because Prime Minister Spencer Perceval opposed any change in England's commercial regulations, the Pinkney-Wellesley talks failed, leaving Pinkney with no recourse but to go home.

In December 1810, Pinkney asked for his passports and a formal audience of leave but did not receive these items of protocol until February. After Pinkney departed, U.S.-British relations reached a difficult position because President Madison offered no replacement for the post of minister to England.

March 2, 1811

Congressional legislation supports Madison's proclamation of nonintercourse with Great Britain.

In accordance with President Madison's proclamation of November 2, 1810, the United States severed trade with England on February 2, 1811. Although Congress had been in session since December, debate on a bill to recognize nonintercourse with England did not begin until February 2.

During the congressional debate, Federalists and Republicans generally argued from a pro-British or pro-French stance similar to that used during the 1790s. The Federalists claimed that Napoléon's message did not precisely repeal the Berlin and Milan Decrees; the Republicans contended they could depend on the "good faith" of France. Unofficial reports from Paris indicated the French had suspended their commercial restrictions, but these reports could be and were interpreted to suit the pro-British or pro-French views of the congressmen.

Finally, as the session of Congress drew to a close, both houses passed an act approving nonintercourse with Great Britain. On March 2, the Senate voted for a previously passed House bill. This act did include one provision overlooked in Macon's Bill No. 2: a provision permitting the president to renew trade with Britain immediately upon learning that it had withdrawn the orders-in-council.

April 6, 1811

James Monroe replaces Robert Smith as Secretary of State.

Monroe would serve as secretary until March 3, 1817. Monroe had extensive experience both in government and in diplomacy. His service included work as a senator (1790–1794) and governor of Virginia (1799–1802), and as the minister to France (1794–1796 and 1803) and the minister to Great Britain (1803–1807).

President Madison asked Secretary Smith to resign in March 1811, because of the intense personal antagonism between Smith and Secretary of the Treasury Albert Gallatin. The dispute caused Gallatin to offer his resignation to Madison because he believed there should be no factional disputes within the president's cabinet. Madison had to choose between Smith and Gallatin and did not hesitate to select the Treasury secretary.

May 16, 1811

An American naval ship attacks a British ship, killing 9 British seamen and wounding 23.

This serious incident illustrated both the problem and the antagonism that prevailed between England and America before the War of 1812.

The attack of the USS *President* on HMS *Little Belt* resulted from a previous British impressment of an American sailor. On May 10, the captain of HMS *Guerriere* stopped and boarded an American ship to impress an alleged deserter. The impressed seaman was considered to be a bona fide American who was unjustly taken by the British. Consequently, other U.S. navy ships began searching for the *Guerriere* to retaliate for its insult to the United States. The search was further complicated because in 1810 the U.S. secretary of the navy informed all naval captains that they were not to permit another insult such as the United States experienced in the 1807 *Chesapeake* affair.

Commodore John RODGERS, commander of the *President,* went out to search for the *Guerriere* on May 16. In the late afternoon, sailing near Cape Henry, his men thought they sighted the British ship. Rodgers ordered a chase and they overtook and fired on the *Little Belt.* Rodgers later claimed the *Little Belt* was mistaken for the *Guerriere* because the ship's structure was that of a corvette and darkness was coming when the ship was sighted. Whatever the exact circumstances, Rodgers and his crew believed they acted to rectify a prior insult by the British against their nation.

Always needing sailors for its ships, Britain insisted that "born an Englishman, always an Englishman," and consequently seized naturalized English-American citizens forced them into the British navy. National Archives

July 3, 1811

The new British Minister informs Secretary Monroe that the English are not ready to withdraw their commercial restrictions.

A. J. Foster, Britain's new minister, began discussions with Monroe on July 3, and it quickly became clear that England had not changed its policy. Foster had been told he should settle the *Chesapeake* affair, but on all other matters he and Monroe disagreed.

The British argued that Napoléon had not definitely repealed the Berlin and Milan Decrees. Moreover, Foster threatened British retaliation if the United States did not end its prohibition on British trade. The *Little Belt* incident, said Foster, would need to be resolved, but he agreed with Monroe to negotiate the *Chesapeake* issue first.

Because Foster offered no new policies, Monroe and Madison became persuaded that the British had no intention of ending their attack on U.S. neutral rights.

July 8, 1811

Revolutionaries in Venezuela proclaim a short-lived independence from Spain.

Creole political leaders in the northern states of South America initially failed in their attempts to obtain independence. One leader in Venezuela, Simón BOLÍVAR, had to retreat to exile among the Caribbean islands after royalist army officers overthrew the rebels on July 25, 1812. Later, in 1816, Bolívar returned to the mainland to lead a more successful revolution for Venezuela as part of a larger state, Grand Colombia.

July 11, 1811

American settlers at Vincennes, Indiana, petition to destroy the Indian capital at Tippecanoe.

Because the Indian leader Tecumseh and his brother, the Prophet, had British aid in organizing tribes of Indians in the western territories, the American inhabitants living near Vincennes met and adopted a resolution to take action against the Indians. Following their meeting, they persuaded General William H. HARRISON to lead an expedition against Tippecanoe. On September 26, Harrison led a force of 1,000 men on a 150-mile march north to the Indian stronghold on the Wabash River (see November 7–8, 1811).

July 31, 1811

In Mexico Hidalgo is captured and executed, ending the first Mexican rebellion against Spanish rule.

On September 16, 1810, Miguel Hidalgo y Costilla, a creole priest, began a revolt in GUANAJUATO. His ill-armed "army" of Indians, mestizos, and creoles was defeated near Guadalajara on January 17. Hidalgo with remnants of his followers was chased until captured on July 31. Hidalgo's disciple Jose Maria MORELOS continued the revolt after Hidalgo's execution by the Spanish.

August 14, 1811

Paraguay proclaims independence from Spain.

Initially in 1811, Paraguay was part of Río de la Plata together with the provinces of Buenos Aires and the Banda Oriental (Uruguay). Unity did not last, however. In 1813, Paraguay renounced all allegiance to Buenos Aires's central government. In 1816, Brazilian troops invaded and took control of the Banda Oriental as Portuguese territory.

September 19, 1811

Joel Barlow arrives in Paris and attempts to have France clarify its actions on neutral rights since 1810.

Although Madison's proclamation of November 2, 1810, assumed that France had repealed the Berlin and Milan Decrees, there was no concrete evidence to back his assumption. Napoléon had not published a definite decree to repeal his Continental System. Moreover, French privateers continued to seize U.S. vessels, and French port officers treated American ships as if the decrees were still in effect. On September 9, Barlow met with the duke of Bassano, the French foreign minister, to demand that France observe the repeal of the decrees and sign a commercial treaty granting reciprocal trading rights to America.

Bassano followed a policy of delay. He reassured Barlow that the decrees had been ended and that France desired to negotiate a commercial treaty. Yet throughout the fall and winter of 1811–1812, Bassano's oral manifestations of good faith were not given evidence in a written treaty or a decree that demonstrated that the Berlin and Milan Decrees had been abrogated. Not until May 1, 1812, after Barlow specifically told Bassano that France must authenticate the repeal of the Continental System, did Bassano act to satisfy those demands.

See May 1, 1812.

November 4, 1811

"War Hawks" dominate the new session of Congress.

When the 12th Congress convened on November 4, there were fewer Federalists and more war-minded Republicans—the War Hawks—present. The Republicans elected Henry Clay of Kentucky as speaker of the House. These Republicans saw the maritime demands of the British as "outrages" to America's national honor and believed that the time for action had arrived.

In addition to Clay, leading Republican nationalists included John C. Calhoun and Langdon Cheves of South Carolina, Felix Grundy of Tennessee, John Adams Harper of New Hampshire, and Peter Porter from western New York.

November 7–8, 1811

Harrison's forces defeat the Indians at Tippecanoe in Indiana.

General Harrison and his 1,000 men had established Fort Harrison on October 28. Soon after, they marched toward the Indian headquarters at Tippecanoe, where the Prophet was in charge of the local tribes. Chief Tecumseh was not present because he was traveling in the south to enlist other tribes to unify against the white Americans.

At Tippecanoe, Harrison's men attacked at dawn on November 7, taking the Indians by surprise. The next day, Harrison ordered his troops to destroy the village. This victory was applauded by western Americans, who consistently claimed the British enticed and aided the Indian attacks on Americans. In Congress, Henry Clay of Kentucky vowed that there would be no peace in the west until the United States drove Britain out of Canada.

November 12, 1811

Britain agrees to settle the *Chesapeake* Affair of 1807.

When the new British minister, A. J. Foster, arrived in Washington during the summer of 1811, his instructions allowed only one area for agreement with the United States: the *Chesapeake* incident. Secretary Monroe and Foster negotiated a settlement signed on November 12. The agreement had the following results:

1. Only two of the four seized sailors were returned to the U.S. navy. Of the other two, one had been hanged in Halifax as a British subject who deserted the navy. The other had been impressed into British naval service, where he died in a hospital. Britain released the remaining two sailors, who reported to duty aboard the *Chesapeake* on July 11, 1812. The British fulfilled this agreement even though the United States declared war in June 1812.

2. The widows and orphans of the men killed when the British fired on the *Chesapeake* were granted "suitable provisions" by the British government.

3. Britain refused to include any statements regarding justification for impressment or future exclusion of such attacks.

November 29, 1811

A request for greater national defense measures is not met by Congress.

At the opening of a new congressional session, the House Committee on Foreign Affairs recommended an increase in defense preparations by Congress. Chaired by "war hawk" Peter Porter, who received advice from President Madison and Secretary of State Monroe, the committee proposed funds to increase the regular army by 10,000 men, to create a volunteer army of 50,000, to construct six new naval frigates, and to allocate $3 million for added defense costs.

Between November and February 1812, Congress did not adequately fulfill these requests. The regular army was authorized an additional 15,000 men but no funds were approved; 50,000 volunteers were also authorized without funds for recruitment; the naval construction program failed to pass; and Secretary of the Treasury Gallatin's request for new taxes to finance the war was rejected. Also, a request for

$3 million to repair naval vessels was decreased to $1 million.

1 8 1 2

March 18, 1812

American "volunteers" led by George Mathews seek to annex East Florida to the United States.

Acting under the congressional legislation of January 15, 1811, Madison had directed Mathews to go to West Florida and arrange to annex East Florida if the Spanish governor agreed or "in case of the actual appearance of any attempt to take possession by a foreign power."

Mathews reported to Secretary Monroe on June 28 and August 3, 1811, that the Spanish governor would not agree to cede East Florida. He added that many inhabitants of the region were ripe for revolt and that with a little assistance, they could overturn the Spanish government. Because Monroe did not answer his letters, Mathews assumed Monroe tacitly approved his activity.

Securing the aid of Captain H. G. Campbell, who commanded a naval fleet in the area, Mathews moved against East Florida on March 18. He took over the town of Fernandino and the island of Amelia, then marched to besiege St. Augustine, the Spanish capital.

Although Madison renounced Mathews's action when he learned of it in April, he did not order Mathews to retreat. As Monroe told the French minister who had protested Mathews's activity, while Mathews had exceeded his instructions, "now that things had reached their present conditions, there would be more danger in retreating than advancing." As a result, on the eve of the War of 1812, Mathews and his "rebels" continued to occupy a portion of East Florida. Southern expansionists hoped that a war with Britain would justify the annexation of East Florida.

April 4, 1812

Congress approves President Madison's request for a full embargo against Great Britain.

After passage of the Nonintercourse Act of March 2, 1811, Madison and Secretary of State Monroe failed to convince Great Britain to repeal its orders-in-council restricting neutral trade. Madison hoped the embargo would bring additional pressure on Britain, which might finally persuade London to end its commercial restrictions.

On April 1, Madison requested a full embargo on British trade for 60 DAYS. The time limit could later be extended but was designed to give the British time to repeal their trade regulations. Before the bill passed Congress on April 4, the Senate changed the time limit to 90 DAYS in order to allow England more time to react.

Madison believed the embargo was justified not only because Napoléon had apparently repealed the French restrictions, but also because English ships had recently seized 18 U.S. vessels worth $1,500,000. The 90-day embargo passed the House by a vote of 70–41, the Senate by 20–13.

April 10, 1812

Congress empowers the President to call a militia of 100,000 soldiers for six months' duty within the states and territory of America.

The clause of this legislation that limited the militia to "duty within" America caused difficulty during the War of 1812 because many recruits refused to fight outside of their home states.

May 1, 1812

The French Foreign Minister shows the U.S. Minister to Paris a copy of the French decree repealing the Berlin and Milan decrees.

Because the British government disputed the claim that France had ended its Continental System on November 2, 1811, the Duke of BASSANO, France's foreign minister, showed Joel BARLOW, America's minister, a copy of an April 28, 1811, decree issued at St. Cloud ending French restrictions on neutral trade.

The April 28 decree showed that Napoléon deceived Madison in 1810. Napoléon had not abolished the commercial restrictions on November 1, 1810, as Madison assumed. The St. Cloud Decree of 1811 stated that in consideration of the act of Congress of March 2, 1811, "the decrees of Berlin and Milan are definitively, and to date from the first of November last, considered as not having existed in regard to American vessels." There had been no decree during the summer of 1810 to repeal the French restrictions. As the St. Cloud document states,

Napoléon acted after the U.S. Congress enactment of March 2, 1811. This did not satisfy the requirements of Macon's Bill No. 2 and did not justify Madison's declarations of November 2, 1810, and February 2, 1811, which said the French had repealed their trade restrictions.

The St. Cloud Decree did not reach Washington until July 13, 1812. By that time, war with Britain had been declared.

Barlow thought and most historians believe the St. Cloud Decree of April 28, 1811, was a spurious document, written in 1812 and predated by the French Foreign Office. Bassano told Barlow that although the decree had not been published, it had been shown to Jonathan Russell, then the U.S. chargé in Paris, and to Louis Serurier, the French minister to the United States. Both men denied this allegation. If Napoléon and his officers had been up to date on Macon's Bill No. 2, they might have better dated the decree for August 1810.

May 8, 1812

Spanish Constitution of 1812 is promulgated.

Written by a national assembly (Cortes) elected in 1810 in those parts of the country liberated by the British army, this constitution became famous as an advanced democratic document. It provided for a one-chamber parliament, universal suffrage, and popular sovereignty. When the British restored Ferdinand VII as king of Spain in March 1814, he agreed to accept the constitution but failed to keep his promise.

The constitution of 1812 became a point of dispute in Spain's American colonies. Some Spanish colonialists preferred the document, but many, such as General Iturbide in Mexico, rejected it as an impractical, revolutionary decree that upset the social order.

May 14, 1812

West Florida is incorporated by Congress as part of the Mississippi Territory.

The United States claimed this territory was part of the Louisiana Purchase despite Spanish objections. In 1810, a group of Americans entered West Florida, captured the Spanish fort of Baton Rouge, and proclaimed the independence of the Republic of West Florida (September 26). A month later (October 27), Madison proclaimed West Florida was an American possession and ordered its military occupation. On May 14, Congress finalized this annexation by making the area from the Mississippi to the Perdido River a part of the Mississippi Territory.

May 27–28, 1812

Conversations of Madison and Monroe with Britain's new Minister to the United States convince them that war is necessary.

The president and secretary of state talked with A. J. Foster over a two-day period and discovered his instructions from London left no hope for British changes with regard to U.S. neutrality. The British categorically insisted on their commercial restrictions and argued that Napoléon had not ended his restrictions. Foster's unyielding orders appeared to make future talks hopeless.

See June 23, 1812.

June 1, 1812

Congress is asked to declare war on Great Britain.

President Madison's request for war emphasized that Great Britain had been consistently hostile to American independence and America's neutral commerce. London had arrogantly rejected American pleas to negotiate on the four basic issues that Madison said justified war. These disputes were (1) impressment of U.S. citizens by Great Britain; (2) violations of American peace and commerce by the British navy; (3) the pretended blockade of almost all European ports that Britain used to plunder American commerce; and (4) Great Britain's "sweeping" and illegal claims against neutral rights in their orders-in-council.

June 18, 1812

Congress declares war on Great Britain.

On June 17, the Senate held two votes regarding a declaration of war. First, the Senate voted 18 to 14 in favor of declaring war on both England and France. After agreeing to reconsider this proposition, the Senate voted a second time to declare war on England by 19 to 13. This version of the declaration was approved by the House of Representatives by a vote of 79 to 49. Madison immediately signed the bill.

In the Senate, the Federalists and the "old Republicans" opposed the war. Generally, an analysis of the congressional vote indicates that all New England states except Vermont opposed the war, as did the maritime states of New York, New Jersey, and Delaware. The vote for war gained strongest support from the west and the south, where the desire to expand American territory into Florida and Canada combined with the issue of neutrality to persuade delegates from these sections to support the war.

According to some historians, the vote on the declaration of war in the House demonstrated that few states solidly opposed the war and that the sectional analysis cited above should be qualified. The House vote by state was:

	For war	Against war
New Hampshire	3	2
Vermont	3	1
Massachusetts	6	8
Rhode Island	0	2
Connecticut	0	7
New York	3	11
New Jersey	2	4
Delaware	0	1
Pennsylvania	16	2
Maryland	6	3
Virginia	14	5
North Carolina	6	3
South Carolina	8	0
Georgia	3	0
Ohio	1	0
Kentucky	5	0
Tennessee	3	0
TOTAL	79	49

James Madison asks for a declaration of war against Britain. National Archives

June 23, 1812

Great Britain conditionally repeals its orders-in-council.

Unaware that the United States had declared war, effective June 18, 1812, Prime Minister Castlereagh announced repeal of the British restrictions on the trade of neutral nations with the provision that the Americans would revoke their prohibitions on British commerce.

Although some historians cite Castlereagh's repeal orders as making the War of 1812 "unnecessary," the British announcement of June 23 did not resolve several basic disputes with the United States. The recognition of the repeal of the orders would have wiped out American spoliation claims against Britain's illegal blockades. Castlereagh's announcement also stipulated his nation's right to reinstitute the orders "if circumstances required."

Finally, and most critical, the British remained unwilling to compromise on the impressment issue. Castlereagh told the U.S. chargé in London, Jonathan Russell, that no ministry could remain in office if it renounced the right of impressment. In sum, Castlereagh's offer at best would have renewed the negotiations that his nation had adamantly refused to qualify for nearly 20 years. British arrogance toward America from the time of Canning's disavowal of Erskine's agreement until June 1812 placed President Madison in constant frustration as he and the U.S. Congress sought the peaceful resolution of the neutrality and impressment issues.

See also August 29, 1812.

June 26, 1812

The Massachusetts House of Representatives claims the war is against the public interest and advises volunteer militia to enroll for defensive purposes only.

Titled an "Address to the Peoples," the Massachusetts resolution revealed the widespread dissent in America against the War of 1812. Later, historian Samuel Eliot Morison would write that the dissent from 1812 to 1815 was the most extensive until the Vietnam antiwar movement of the late 1960s.

Soon after the declaration of war, leading politicians in New England condemned the war. Following the lead of Massachusetts, the Connecticut General Assembly denounced the war on August 25. The governors of these two states also refused to furnish state militia to the federal government. Thus, in contrast to the Vietnamese dissent, protests of the War of 1812 began among the elite power blocks and seeped downward. New Englander commercial interests desired their lucrative British commerce more than they were willing to uphold principles of neutral rights. John Quincy Adams's recall as a senator for approving the embargo of 1807 showed the attitude of the Federalist politicians toward British violations of neutrality.

August 29, 1812

Lord Castlereagh rejects a U.S. peace proposal.

After Congress had declared war in June, Secretary of State Monroe learned that the British were willing to suspend their orders-in-council. Therefore, on June 26, in the same message that informed the U.S. chargé in London, Jonathan Russell, of the war declaration, Monroe instructed Russell to inform the British that an armistice was possible if Great Britain abandoned its paper blockades and impressment and agreed to pay American spoliation claims. Russell informed Castlereagh on August 24, but five days later the prime minister rejected the offer, telling Russell that impressment remained nonnegotiable.

Impressment again prevented negotiations on October 27, 1812. Monroe received an offer to negotiate peace with Admiral Sir John Borlase Warren in Halifax. On October 27, Monroe responded that the United States would negotiate if Britain suspended impressment, a condition Admiral Warren could not accept. Thus, peace feelers achieved no results during the early months of war.

September 14, 1812

The French armies occupy Moscow.

Napoléon's offensive into Russia began in June 1812. Aided by Austrian and Prussian troops, the French were highly successful as the Russians retreated but burned their fields behind them. In September, the czar's armies evacuated Moscow but Alexander would not surrender or accept peace with France. Having secured no peace treaty and with winter approaching, Napoléon had to retreat because his supply lines were too long.

September 21, 1812

Czar Alexander I offers to mediate the Anglo-American disputes.

Having become England's ally when Napoléon declared war on Russia on June 22, 1812, Alexander hoped to end the British-U.S. hostility. On September 21, the czar offered his mediation service to the U.S. minister to St. Petersburg, John Quincy Adams. Both Adams and President Madison accepted the czar's offer, and the president appointed Secretary of the Treasury Albert Gallatin and James A. Bayard to a special mission to St. Petersburg.

The American delegates reached the Russian capital on July 21, 1813, where they waited for England's delegation. Finally, early in 1814, they learned that Castlereagh had rejected the czar's mediation but agreed to begin direct negotiations with the American representatives.

October 19, 1812

Napoléon's armies begin their retreat from Moscow.

Having failed to gain Russia's surrender and not having established suitable supply lines for his army, the French emperor ordered a retreat. What began as a smooth retreat turned into a horrible rout when the Russians counterattacked and the severe Russian winter weather began in November. By the time the French forces reached the Nieman River in mid-December, only 100,000 of Napoléon's original 600,000-man invasion force remained. The "little corporal's" demise had begun.

December 2, 1812

Madison is reelected President.

The election of Madison for a second term was decisive. He received 128 votes to Dewitt Clinton's 89. Elbridge Gerry was elected vice president over Jared Ingersoll by a vote of 131-86.

December 26, 1812

Great Britain declares a blockade of the Chesapeake and Delaware bays.

This was the first of a series of British orders to project commercial war against America. On May 26, Britain extended the blockade from the Mississippi River to Long Island.

Knowing that New England strongly opposed the war, the British permitted commerce with those states to continue. They hoped to exploit New England's dissent against "Mister Madison's War." Not until August 25, 1814, when Britain planned new offensive actions from Canada and at New Orleans, did England extend the blockade to include New England.

December 29, 1812

USS *Constitution* defeats the *Java* in a duel off the coast of Brazil.

From July to December, 1812, U.S. frigates won a series of naval engagements against Great Britain. The USS *Constitution*'s first victory was over the *Guerriere* on August 19. In October, the USS *Wasp* defeated the *Frolic* and the USS *United States* defeated the *Macedonia*.

Capture of the *Guerriere* by the USS *Constitution*. Copy of the engraving by D. Kimberly after T. Birch. National Archives

While the British won some naval engagements, the December loss of the *Java* made His Majesty's Navy realize that a greater effort had to be made against the American navy. In 1813, British ships moved to bottle up U.S. seaports and American ships; England again gained control of the sea in 1814, when it was strong enough to land forces in Virginia and attack America's capital city.

Nevertheless, American ships and privateers won a notable number of individual victories. The British lost about 825 naval and merchant ships during the war.

1813

February 28, 1813

Russia and Prussia form an alliance against Napoléon—The Treaty of Kalish.

This began the formation of a large international alliance that defeated the French emperor's armies in 1814.

March 3, 1813

Great Britain and Sweden form an alliance against Napoléon.

Sweden promised to supply an army of 30,000 men to fight the French.

April 15, 1813

American forces occupy Mobile in West Florida.

U.S. troops commanded by General James Wilkinson moved to the Pearl River, where they displaced the small Spanish garrison without bloodshed. This extended American territory to the Perdido River and was the sole territorial gain not returned after the War of 1812. Wilkinson's move into West Florida finally carried out the military occupation that Madison proclaimed on October 27, 1810.

April 17, 1813

American forces raid and burn York, Canada, in an attempt to get control of Lake Ontario.

In a combined army-navy action under General Henry Dearborn and Captain Isaac Chauncey, the U.S. navy seized British vessels at York while 1,600 troops raided the city by way of Sackett's Harbor. Against Dearborn's orders, his men set fire to various public buildings in York, including the assembly house and the governor's residence. The raid did not get control of Lake Ontario because Dearborn's men returned to Niagara on May 8 after Dearborn became ill. The York raid did, however, become the British pretext for burning Washington in 1814.

June 15, 1813

Great Britain, Russia, and Prussia form an alliance—Treaty of Reichenbach.

Soon after, on August 12, Austria declared war on France and Joined the Alliance. This completed the international coalition to fight Napoléon.

September 10, 1813

U.S. Navy wins Battle of Lake Erie.

Although American naval ships and privateers won many duels against individual British vessels on the high seas, the most critical naval engagement of the War of 1812 was the Battle of Lake Erie.

Captain Oliver Hazard Perry had been ordered to the Great Lakes on February 13, 1813. When Perry reached Presque Isle on the western end of Lake Erie, he discovered no naval preparations had been made. Under his direction, the men constructed five new vessels from local oak trees, barn door hinges, and several yards of canvas. Other parts of the vessels had to be shipped from Pittsburgh. Another five ships were hauled by oxen from the Black River Navy Yard up the rapids of the Niagara River near Buffalo and over to Lake Erie. Perry finally assembled his entire flotilla at Put-in-Bay in August 1813.

Early in September, a British squadron of six vessels sailed toward Perry's forces. Commanded by Captain Robert H. Barclay, the British fleet had a total of 65 guns to Perry's 55. The American ships were, however, superior in tonnage and heavy armaments.

Perry sighted the British at dawn on the morning of September 10, 1813. As the ships sailed into range, fierce barrages of cannon ripped the larger frigates apart. Perry's flagship, the *Lawrence,* was destroyed, forcing the captain to row himself over to raise his flag on the *Niagara.* Eventually Perry's forces prevailed. As Perry reported to his superiors: "We have met the enemy and they are ours."

Oliver Hazard Perry, standing, transfers his command from the *Lawrence* to the *Niagara* during the Battle of Lake Erie. National Archives

Perry's success on Lake Erie permitted General Harrison's forces to cross the lake and invade Canada, securing the western sector of the war for American troops.

October 5, 1813

Battle of the Thames in Canada enables General Harrison to make the northwest frontier secure from Great Britain.

Harrison's successful campaign in the west followed American defeats in 1812, including General William HULL's surrender of Detroit on August 16, 1812, and the massacre of the American garrison at Fort Dearborn (at the site of Chicago) on August 15, 1812.

Prior to Perry's victory on Lake Erie, Harrison had been reluctant to take the offensive because of alleged British strength around Detroit. The defeat of the British fleet permitted Harrison to cross the lake to land in upper Canada on September 27. The British at Detroit were outflanked and had to withdraw. As the British and their Indian allies retreated across southern Ontario, Harrison overtook them at a small town on the north bank of the Thames River. The British and the Indians were decisively beaten, ending British power in the Northwest territory of America. At the battle of the Thames, the Indian leader TECUMSEH was killed. His death and the British loss caused the American Indians to desert their former benefactors and make peace with America.

See July 22, 1814.

October 16–19, 1813

Napoléon loses the Battle of Leipzig.

A combined force of Prussian, Russian, and Austrian armies defeated the French imperial forces near Leipzig in eastern Germany. The conflict is also referred to as the Battle of Nations.

December 7, 1813

Congress embargoes all trade with the enemy.

Madison recommended this measure to Congress because New England ships continued to trade with the British. The merchants of New England supplied beef, flour, and other provisions to the British armies in Canada and to British ships operating off the east coast.

See December 26, 1812.

December 29–30, 1813

The British burn Buffalo and capture Fort Niagara.

Although the British were not able to launch a further offensive in northwestern New York during the war,

Britain (John Bull) dictating trade terms to the Americans. Bull asks for everything except Porter and Perry, two American naval heroes of the War. Library of Congress

the capture of Fort Niagara, which remained in British hands until the war's end, stifled any U.S. plans to attack Canada.

Although the American "war hawks" had urged a "march on Canada," U.S. military efforts in New York were a dismal failure. In the fall of 1812, American plans to invade Canada ended when the New York militia refused to leave the state, first at Fort George on August 23, later at Plattsburg on November 23.

Then a planned march on Montreal failed during the fall of 1813. Forces under General James Wilkinson descended the St. Lawrence to within 90 miles of Montreal but were beaten by the British on November 11. During the same offensive, 4,000 men under General Wade Hampton marched from Plattsburg to the Canadian border. But after attacking a small British force at Chateaugay on October 25, Hampton abandoned the drive and returned to Plattsburg.

The burning of Buffalo on December 30, 1813, was the first sign of a British counteroffensive. Nevertheless, British plans to attack in 1814 by way of Lake Champlain were not successful. In a naval engagement on the lake on September 11, the U.S. fleet under Captain Thomas MacDonough defeated the British, forcing their army to retreat back to Canada.

In brief, throughout the War of 1812 neither belligerent was able to launch significant offensive action in the northern New York–Canadian border area; a stalemate resulted.

December 30, 1813

Castlereagh's offer for direct peace negotiations is received and accepted by President Madison.

The British prime minister's proposal resulted from Czar Alexander's offer of mediation on September 21, 1812. In a memo to the czar on July 5, 1813, Castlereagh rejected mediation but agreed to conduct direct talks with the American delegation. For some reason, Alexander did not inform the Americans, who were in St. Petersburg.

Nevertheless, on November 4, Castlereagh wrote directly to Madison. The president gladly accepted the offer and made plans to send a negotiating team to London. On January 18, 1814, the Senate confirmed the appointments of Bayard and Gallatin, who already waited in St. Petersburg. They also commissioned John Quincy Adams, Henry Clay, and Jonathan Russell to participate in the negotiations.

The peace talks began at Ghent, Belgium, on August 8, 1814. The British delegates were Lord Gambier, Henry Goulburn, and William Adams.

1814

March 13, 1814

Madison asks for the repeal of the embargo of December 17, 1813.

Within a month after Congress embargoed all trade with the enemy, the law's ineffectiveness became obvious. Initially on January 25, 1814, Congress had amended the act when the people of Nantucket claimed they were starving because their personal provisions could not be bought on the mainland of Canada. Worse, however, the law was violated constantly by New Englanders who opposed both the war and the embargo.

Therefore, on March 13, 1814, the president advised Congress to abolish the embargo and all previous nonimportation laws. By April 14, 1814, Congress had followed Madison's request.

March 13, 1814

The victorious allied armies enter Paris; Napoléon is sent to Elba.

Following the Battle of Leipzig in 1813, the allied forces marched across the Rhine and through eastern France with slight opposition. On April 11, the allies accepted Napoléon's abdication and sent him to exile on Elba island in the Mediterranean Sea. The Bourbon heir, Louis XVIII, became monarch of a constitutional regime in France. More than 20 years of war with France appeared to be ended.

May 30, 1814

The European war ends when the first Treaty of Paris is signed.

The Big Four Powers (Austria, Britain, Prussia, and Russia) acted leniently toward France to strengthen the restored Bourbon monarchy. They established French boundaries as they had been in 1789. Allied agreement on the boundaries of other European states disrupted by Napoléon's armies caused greater difficulty. Therefore, the allies agreed to hold a congress at Vienna later in 1814 to settle these boundary issues.

July 22, 1814

Treaty of Greenville restores peace with the Indians in the Northwest Territory.

Following the death of TECUMSEH at the Battle of the Thames in the fall of 1813, the Indians' tribal confederacy disintegrated. Thus, Harrison's success in ending British power in the northwest gradually turned the Indians against their former ally.

The Treaty of Greenville was signed by chiefs of the Delaware, Miami, Seneca, Shawnee, and Wyandot Indians. They agreed to declare war on Great Britain and to act peacefully toward American settlers in the area.

August 9, 1814

Treaty of Fort Jackson ends the Creek Indian wars in Georgia and Alabama.

General Andrew Jackson had soundly defeated the Indians at HORSESHOE BEND on March 27, 1814, killing 800–900 warriors and capturing 500 squaws and children. By the Treaty of Fort Jackson, the Creeks ceded two-thirds of their lands to the Americans and agreed to withdraw from the southern and western parts of Alabama.

Having been inspired by Tecumseh's southern visit of 1811, the Creek Indians began to attack American settlers on July 27, 1813. General Jackson of the Tennessee militia led successful counterattacks on the Creeks, and by the spring of 1814, his forces reached the center of Creek territory at Horseshoe Bend. Jackson's offensive led to the treaty of 1814, which ended the conflict.

August 24–25, 1814

British capture and burn Washington, D.C.

During the summer of 1814, the British decided to enhance their offensive action in upper New York by diverting American forces with raids along the coast of Virginia.

A British raid into the Baltimore-Washington area was planned by Sir Alexander COCHRANE in retaliation for an American raid on York, Canada (April 17, 1813), during which Americans burned the assembly houses and the governor's residence. Cochrane's raid was launched on August 19, when British troops moved up the Chesapeake Bay and landed at Benedict, Maryland. With 4,000 troops, General Robert Ross marched on to Bladensburg, where U.S. forces under General William H. WINDER were routed. Because the U.S. troops fled so fast, one editor referred to the battle as the "Bladensburg races."

Now the British could march unopposed on Washington because the U.S. army and government had fled. The British troops set fire to the Capitol, the White House, all of the department buildings (except the Patent Office), several homes, and the office of the *National Intelligencer* newspaper. On August 25, the British returned to their ships and withdrew from the city.

On August 27, President Madison, his wife, and congressional and departmental officials returned to Washington. The president had followed the army as it left the city. According to some accounts, he spent one night in a henhouse "miserably shattered and woebegone." Dolley Madison escaped from the White House as the British entered, but she rescued the canvas portrait of George Washington painted by Gilbert Stuart. Nevertheless, August 1814, was not a memorable moment of American history.

September 12–14, 1814

The British attack Baltimore, bombarding Fort McHenry.

Following the British attack on Washington, the British fleet sailed from the Potomac to within 16 miles of Baltimore, where British troops under General Robert Ross disembarked on September 12. Although the U.S. militia inflicted severe losses (including the death of General Ross) on the British, redcoats moved on toward Fort McHenry. To support its army, the British fleet bombarded Fort McHenry (September 13–14), but they were not successful in breaking the American defenses. Subsequently, the British abandoned their attempts against the fort and withdrew. On October 14, the British ships left the Chesapeake Bay and sailed for Jamaica.

The bombardment of Fort McHenry on the night of September 14–15 inspired Francis Scott Key's verses of "The Star Spangled Banner." His poem, set to the music of the English song "To Anacreon in Heaven," was designated as the national anthem in 1916 but not confirmed by Congress until 1931.

British bomb Fort McHenry as they attack Baltimore. Library of Congress

December 15, 1814

The Hartford Convention meets in secret sessions to find some means to protest dissent against the War of 1812.

Although not all dissent against the war came from New England, the strongest group of political leaders opposing the war appeared to have been in these states. The Hartford Convention originated with a call for a meeting of dissenting states by the Massachusetts legislature on October 17, inviting delegates from Connecticut, Rhode Island, Massachusetts, Vermont, and New Hampshire. The last two of these states elected delegates at local conventions; the other delegates were elected by their state legislatures. Although some radical dissenters advocated stronger remedies, this was not the intent of the convention. The most notable radical activities during the war were Massachusetts Governor Caleb Strong's inquiry about British aid in case of a dispute with the federal government and John Lowell's call for secession by the 13 original states.

Strong sent a secret mission led by Thomas Adams to visit General John Sherbrooke, Britain's army commandant in Halifax. The delegates asked Sherbrooke how Britain would act if Strong, as governor of Massachusetts, clashed directly with the president of the United States. Sherbrooke had to consult with his superiors in London, from whom he learned on December 13, 1814, that if Madison and the U.S. Senate did not ratify the Treaty of Ghent, which was nearly completed, Sherbrooke could sign a separate peace treaty with any New England state and aid such state in fulfilling its local needs. The approval of the Treaty of Ghent ended these negotiations. Strong's secret mission did not, however, have the knowledge or support of any large New England body.

John Lowell's dissent was more outspoken and public than Strong's. Lowell wrote three pamphlets against the war: "Mr. Madison's War," "Perpetual War, the Policy of Mr. Madison," and "Thoughts in a Series of Letters, in Answer to Questions respecting the Division of the States." The last of these, written in 1813, contained Lowell's argument for the secession of the original 13 states. He proposed to kick the western states out of the union and to draft a new constitution that would protect the maritime and commercial interests of New England and the other Atlantic seaboard states. Lowell's ideas probably led others to attribute his design to the Hartford Convention.

In contrast to the proposals of Strong and Lowell, the Hartford Convention was a body of moderate, not radical, spokesmen against the war. The convention agenda was the drafting of constitutional amendments to protect New England's interests and to permit states to conduct their own military defense. "Crazy Jack" Lowell was not a convention delegate but denounced the members as timid and self-serving men. Thus, in spite of some myths to the contrary, the Hartford Convention's resolutions did not plot secession.

See January 5, 1815.

December 24, 1814

The Peace Treaty of Ghent is signed by American and British negotiators.

The treaty negotiations reached the following key decisions:

1. No Territorial Changes. When talks opened in 1814, the British desired boundary changes, chiefly the establishment of a neutral buffer state for Indians in the northwest between the United States and Canada. Drawing a line west from the south border of Maine to west of Lake Superior, the British proposal would have ceded one-third of the existing U.S. territory to the buffer zone. Not until November 27 did the Americans persuade the British to yield their territorial desires and accept the American position of status quo ante bellum.

The only exception to the status quo was the U.S. acquisition of West Florida, which actually had been Spanish but which the British had been interested in occupying.

2. No Mention of Impressment and Neutral Rights. Because the French had surrendered and ended Europe's lengthy era of war, the delegates agreed that these questions presented problems too difficult to settle.

3. Agreement to Arbitrate Boundary and Fishery Disputes with Future Commissions. These included negotiations on the northeast and Great Lakes boundaries and, in particular, fishing rights along the Atlantic coastal areas of Canada and New England.

4. The Mutual Release of all Prisoners of War and U.S. Subjects Impressed by the British Army. Under the latter clause, the British released 1,800 seamen in 1815.

News of the treaty signing reached New York on February 11, 1815. Four days later, the U.S. Senate unanimously ratified the treaty; Madison proclaimed peace on February 17, 1815.

1815

January 5, 1815

The Hartford Convention adjourns: its report requests states' rights to provide their own military defense in time of war.

The convention's recommendations represented the moderate dissent of men such as George Cabot and Harrison Gray Otis of Massachusetts, who believed that the war was unconstitutional because it affected the "sovereignty of a state." Among the convention's resolutions were the following: (1) citizens should be protected from military service not authorized by the federal Constitution; (2) local federal revenues should be available for local defense costs; (3) an interstate defense system, independent of the federal government, should be used to repel any enemy force; (4) direct taxes and congressional representation should be according to the number of free persons; (5) no embargo should last more than 60 days; (6) a two-thirds' vote should be required to declare war, restrict commerce, and admit new states; (7) naturalized citizens should not hold public office; (8) presidents should be limited to one term of office.

Following the convention, the Massachusetts legislature appointed a committee to go to Washington and ask Madison's administration to provide federal funds for local defenses. En route to Washington, the committee learned of Andrew Jackson's great victory at New Orleans and then the news of the Treaty of Ghent. The war was over and the Hartford Convention discredited.

Because radical dissenters such as John Lowell favored secession as a response to the war, the myth began that the Hartford Convention proposed secret acts to leave the union. The opponents of the Federalist Party suspected and publicized this belief, which appeared in some history books well into the 20th century.

January 8, 1815

Battle of New Orleans: General Andrew Jackson's forces repel a British invasion.

The British attack on New Orleans was part of their 1814 offensive operations. The plan was to gain con-

General Andrew Jackson's victory at the Battle of New Orleans. National Archives

trol of the strategic Mississippi River valley. To effect this, a naval fleet carrying 7,500 army veterans of the fight against Napoléon assembled near Jamaica on December 13, 1814. Commanded by Sir Edward PAKENHAM, the ships took the army to the coastline east of New Orleans at Lake Borgne, where they disembarked.

Hearing about the British naval movements, Jackson's troops had moved to New Orleans from Mobile on December 1. On December 23–24, Jackson ordered his men to construct a line of breastworks between a cypress swamp and the east bank of the Mississippi, where they could defend New Orleans from the British attack. Working long hours, the Americans completed the defense line before Pakenham could attack.

On January 8, 1815, Pakenham sent 5,300 men against Jackson's defense lines. Facing a withering rifle and artillery barrage, the redcoats were driven back with heavy losses. Total deaths in the day's fight were 2,036 British and 8 Americans. The British losses included General Pakenham and two other British generals.

Although the Battle of New Orleans took place after the Treaty of Ghent had been signed, the Americans celebrated their great defensive victory. After a generally disastrous war, which included the burning of Washington, D.C., the nation needed a hero; General Jackson filled the role.

March 1, 1815

Napoléon returns from Elba for 100 days of rule and renewed war.

Landing in southern France, Napoléon marched toward Paris, gaining a growing army en route. After Louis XVIII fled to exile, Napoléon regained control of the French government until he was again defeated by a multinational army at Waterloo.

March 2, 1815

Congress declares war on Algeria; President Madison sends two naval squadrons to the Mediterranean Sea.

Madison requested the declaration of war because the dey of Algiers had broken his previous good relations during the War of 1812. The dey's navy captured an American ship, the *Edwin*, on August 25, 1812, and imprisoned the captain and crew. Attempts to resolve the Algerian problems failed because the dey vowed to capture more American ships and dismissed the U.S. consul from Algeria.

After the Treaty of Ghent brought peace with Great Britain, Madison wanted to redress the Algerian assault on the American vessel. Therefore, after Congress declared war, he sent two naval squadrons commanded by William BAINBRIDGE and Stephen DECATUR to secure an honorable peace for the United States.

March 3, 1815

Reciprocity Act passed by Congress.

This legislation permitted the president to promote and establish duties on foreign ships entering U.S. ports on the same terms that a foreign nation charged American ships entering their ports.

Prior to this act, the United States followed the general European practice of retaliatory discrimination against foreign ships entering U.S. ports. America now began a policy contrary to Europe's mercantilistic practices. Any nation agreeing to *direct trade* with its ports with no discriminatory tonnage duties on American ships would not have tonnage duties levied against its vessels.

Initially, this law provided only for direct trade between nations. In 1817, the Act of 1815 was amended specifically to prohibit trade of foreign ships coming from a third country. But in 1828, reciprocity was extended to include such indirect trade, provided, of course, that the foreign nation permitted indirect trade by American ships on an equal basis.

Reciprocity in shipping duties was successful. By 1830, American ships traded with the major ports of the world without discriminatory shipping regulations.

June 8, 1815

The Congress of Vienna redraws the European boundaries disrupted by the French Wars and restores "legitimate" monarchs who Napoléon had replaced.

The congressional delegates had met in Vienna since September 1814, but Napoléon's "100 Days" interrupted many of their sessions and delayed their agreements.

The congress sought, generally, to restore both the boundary status quo and the legitimate kings wherever possible. Its decisions fostered an era of conservative and reactionary European policies against the political principles of republicanism and the "rights of man" proclaimed during the French Revolution. Its desire to restore monarchs to the territory they held in 1789 led Ferdinand VII, the king of Spain, to seek the aid of Austria and France in regaining the American colonies that had rebelled during the French Wars.

June 18, 1815

The Battle of Waterloo ends Napoléon's 100-day resurgence.

After Napoléon returned to Paris on March 20, the Big Four (Austria, Great Britain, Prussia, and Russia) formed a new alliance to defeat the emperor. At Waterloo, Napoléon's armies were completely defeated. As a result, on June 22, Napoléon again abdicated. This time he was sent to St. Helena in the South Atlantic Ocean as a prisoner of war. On July 7, Louis XVIII returned again to Paris to rule as France's constitutional monarch.

June 29–30, 1815

Algeria accepts American peace terms after successful U.S. naval action.

Commodore Stephen Decatur's naval squadron had sailed from New York on May 20. When he reached Gibraltar, Decatur heard that an Algerian cruiser was nearby, having just returned from an Atlantic voyage.

On June 17, Americans aboard the *Constellation* sighted an Algerian ship and sailed to attack. Chasing down the Algerian vessel, the Americans forced its surrender. It was the *Mashuda,* flagship of Algeria's Admiral Reis Hammida. During the battle, the admiral and 30 of his crew were killed. Decatur's men also captured 400 Algerians.

Two days later, Decatur captured a second ship, the *Estedeo,* and the dey of Algiers agreed to begin peace talks. On June 30, Decatur gave the Algerian delegates the draft of a proposed treaty, which the dey accepted with only a few minor changes.

According to the treaty, the dey released all American prisoners, restored U.S. property seized since 1812, and indemnified the United States with $10,000 for the *Edwin.* In addition, America would pay no future tribute money to Algeria but agreed to make a favorable commercial treaty.

Although the U.S. Senate ratified the treaty on December 21, 1815, the final ratifications were delayed until February 1, 1822. In 1816, the dey asked for changes in the treaty before he would ratify it. The U.S. delegation refused to make any changes, and, facing the guns of Decatur's ships, the dey signed "under compulsion." The six-year delay in final Senate action was caused by an oversight of the State Department, which forgot until 1822 to submit the document for Senate approval.

July 3, 1815

The United States and Great Britain sign a commercial convention.

The American negotiators signed this agreement although the British made no concessions on the West Indies trade, which American merchants desired to open completely. Britain did, however, admit American ships to the East Indies and India. The act also freed direct commerce between the United States and Great Britain from discriminatory duties on goods and tonnage.

August 9, 1815

Commodore Decatur obtains an indemnification from the Pasha of Tripoli.

Sailing to Tripoli after his successful campaign in Algiers, Decatur arrived on August 5 and immediately demanded that the Pasha Yusuf pay America $30,000 for having given Great Britain the prize ships captured by the American privateer ship *Abaellino.* After some negotiations, Decatur reduced his demand to $25,000 plus the release of 10 Christian captives. The pasha accepted the treaty on August 9.

September 1, 1815

America proclaims neutrality in the independence wars between Spain and its colonies in Latin America.

Although neutrality did not offer direct aid to the South American groups seeking independence, it benefited the rebellions in several indirect ways:

1. recognition of belligerency permitted neutral trade with both sides;
2. it encouraged Great Britain's declaration of neutrality;
3. U.S. naval officers operating in the Caribbean and Pacific were instructed to avoid any collision with the Latin American "patriots" and not to favor "the cause of Spain against such a struggle";
4. ships flying insurgent flags could use American ports on the same terms as other foreign ships.

September 26, 1815

The Holy Alliance is formed by Russia, Prussia, and Austria

The emperors of these three powers signed this agreement at the urging of Czar Alexander I. It pledged the rulers to use Christian principles in their relations with each other and with their subjects. Actually, as part of the post-Napoléonic reactions, the alliance opposed the democratic principles of the American and French Revolutions and tried to reaffirm the divine right of kings in Europe. In the public mind, especially in America, the Holy Alliance and the Quadruple Alliance (see November 20, 1815) were the same. The important difference was that the British refused to join the Holy Alliance.

November 20, 1815

Renewal of the Quadruple Alliance.

The four major powers—Austria, Britain, Russia, and Prussia—each agreed to supply 60,000 men if the second Treaty of Paris should be violated. The Second Treaty of Paris, which followed Napoléon's second defeat, was also signed on November 20, 1815.

The Quadruple Alliance also formed a system of congresses of the powers to resolve problems and to discuss common interests of the states. In 1818, the Big Four powers admitted France to their ranks and formed the Quintuple Alliance.

December 22, 1815

A second attempt at Mexican independence fails when Morelos is executed.

As Father Hidalgo's successor in July 1811, Morelos led his rebellious army to victories at Oaxaca (November 25, 1812) and Acapulco (April 12, 1813). On November 6, 1813, Morelos had declared Mexican independence. The second attempt to achieve independence failed, however, because a Spanish army captured and executed Morelos on December 22, 1815.

From 1816 to 1821, Juan Ruiz de Apodaca, the Spanish viceroy at Mexico City, reaffirmed Spanish control by forcing the surrender of other revolutionary leaders.

V. JOHN QUINCY ADAMS AND FOREIGN POLICY

Transcontinental Treaty
The Monroe Doctrine

1816

April 27, 1816

Protective Tariff of 1816.

In contrast to the revenue tariff of 1791, this bill protected certain U.S. products by increases in the tariff rates. Congress placed a 25% duty on most woolen, cotton, and iron manufacturers. Cheap cotton imports were virtually excluded because they received a minimum value of 25 cents a square yard. Duties of 30% were placed on paper, leather, and hats. Although shipping interests opposed the tariff, the War of 1812 had stimulated sufficient American manufacturing to cause most Democratic-Republicans to adopt the protective tariff they had previously rejected when Alexander Hamilton had earlier proposed it. The tariff bill and the chartering of the Second Bank of the United States in 1816 signified the adoption of many old Federalist economic ideas by the Republicans. The tariff of 1816 set a pattern of continuous tariff increases until 1832.

July 27, 1816

U.S. Troops destroy Fort Apalachicola in Spanish Florida territory.

The Americans near the border of Florida decided to retaliate against the Seminole Indians and runaway slaves who would attack U.S. settlements in Georgia and flee into Spanish territory. The British had built Fort Apalachicola during the War of 1812, and it became a center for the Indian raids. Previously, American protests to the Spanish were not successful because Spain was too weak to control the Seminoles.

On July 27, American forces commanded by General Edmund P. GAINES pursued a band of Indians across the Florida border and chased them to their fortress. Gaines's men attacked the fort and destroyed it. Unfortunately, this attack did not stop the Indian raiding parties. It did, however, call national attention to the problems on the Florida border.

July 28, 1816

Combined British-Dutch fleet destroys Algiers.

Following Napoléon's defeat in 1815, European countries adopted the U.S. tactics of joining together militarily to resist the Barbary States. After a year of war against Algiers, an allied force of English and Dutch frigates appeared off the coast of Algeria. They fired a terrific bombardment, virtually destroying the capital city. But the action provided the desired result. The dey agreed to peace terms that ended the depredations of the Algerian privateers, abolished Christian slavery, and released 1,100 European captives held for ransom. During the next 30 years, the fortunes of Algiers led to its conquest by France in 1848.

December 4, 1816

James Monroe is elected President.

Monroe, a Democratic-Republican, defeated Rufus KING, the Federalist nominee, by 184 electoral votes to 34. Daniel D. TOMPKINS of New York was elected vice president. Monroe had a closer contest in gaining his party's nomination during a congressional caucus on March 16, 1816. Younger party members proposed the election of William CRAWFORD. Monroe won the contest by a vote of 65 to 54. Nevertheless, internal political disputes had begun to disrupt the Democratic-Republican Party. The political maneu-

James Monroe is elected President. Library of Congress.

verings multiplied during the eight years of Monroe's presidency.

1817

March 3, 1817

A revised Neutrality Act limits America's indirect aid to the nations rebelling against Spain in Latin America.

The 1817 legislation revised the act of September 1, 1815, to correct loopholes that various European nations complained about to the State Department. In particular, two practices used since 1815 caused difficulty for the United States. One problem arose in December 1815, when a U.S. court prevented U.S. customs agents from seizing an armed ship, the *American Eagle,* which was intended for use by the rebels of Haiti. The neutrality act did not provide any limits on the foreign purchase of armed vessels to be used by rebels. In addition, although a U.S. citizen could not purchase such an armed warship, a foreigner could do so.

To correct these faults, the Act of 1817 made it illegal to sell American-made warships either to the insurgents or to Spain. The new law was neutral but it forbade a practice that had benefited the insurgents for two years.

See April 20, 1818.

March 5, 1817

John Quincy Adams is commissioned as Secretary of State.

Beginning his duties on September 22, 1817, Adams served throughout James Monroe's presidency, until March 3, 1825. Adams was eminently qualified for this post. He had studied in France and the Netherlands, was secretary to the minister to Russia in 1781, and to his father, John Adams, during the Paris negotiations with Britain in 1782–1783. He had further diplomatic service in Prussia (1797–1801), Russia (1809–1814), and Great Britain (1815–1817).

April 28–29, 1817

Rush-Bagot Agreement provides for the demilitarization of the Great Lakes.

Following the Treaty of Ghent, congressional leaders indicated that maintaining a navy on the Great Lakes was folly unless the British intended to do so. Initially, in 1815, John Quincy Adams, the U.S. minister in London, feared that Britain would do so, reporting that London newspapers said the fleet on those lakes would be increased.

Reports of a possible naval race led to discussions in both London and Washington in 1816. Consequently, most of the agreement for the naval disarmament had been worked out by Secretary of State Monroe and British Foreign Minister Robert Stewart, Lord Castlereagh. After Monroe became president on March 4, Richard Rush, as acting secretary of state, conducted the final exchange of notes with Britain's minister to the United States, Charles Bagot.

By the agreement, each nation limited its navy on inland waters to one vessel on Lake Champlain and Lake Ontario and two vessels on the Upper Lakes. None of these ships would exceed 100 tons or have more than one 18-pound gun. A year later, on April 16, 1818, the Senate unanimously approved this agreement.

August 17, 1817

Mission from Buenos Aires finds United States unsympathetic to the cause of Latin American independence.

This "lack of American sympathy" was the conclusion of Manuel H. de AGUIRRE, who came to the United States as a representative of the leader of Buenos Aires, Juan Martin PUEYRREDON; the leader in Chile, Bernardo O'HIGGINS; and the liberator of Chile and Argentina, General José SAN MARTÍN. Aguirre's mission sought recognition for these governments and funds for warships and arms to use in San Martín's Peruvian campaign. Aguirre realized neither objective.

The United States not only refused to recognize the Buenos Aires government, but it also repudiated a loan to Buenos Aires that had been negotiated by a special American agent, Colonel John DEVEREUX. When Aguirre reached Washington, the State Department did not recognize his mission and refused to give him diplomatic immunity.

Aguirre experienced only one small kindness in America. He attempted to purchase two frigates in New York, which the Spanish consul seized in protest. This matter was settled in favor of Aguirre when the U.S. courts forced Spain to return the frigates to him. Not surprisingly, however, Aguirre grew disgruntled with U.S. foreign policy. His final report to his superiors stated that the Americans would not help the rebellions unless it involved the "enriching of their merchants." Although many American citizens sympathized with Latin America's independence, the American government did not.

Aguirre did achieve some results. He successfully encouraged the visit to Buenos Aires of a special American commission, which left in November 1817, to investigate the situation in Latin America. Aguirre's efforts also prompted Henry Clay to seek recognition for the new Latin American governments.

1818

January 1–5, 1818

The Black Ball Lines, a transatlantic packet company, begins regularly scheduled sailing between New York and Liverpool, England.

On January 1, the ship *Courier* left Liverpool for New York; on January 5, the ship *James Monroe* sailed from New York. This began regular monthly sailing from each port on a specified day and at a specified hour. The average crossing time until 1822 was 39 days; by 1848, it dropped to a 33.3-day average. Together with packet lines in American coastal trade and the less regular schedules of other ships, this began the "golden era" of American clipper ships, which lasted until the late 1840s.

January 6, 1818

Andrew Jackson's "Rhea Letter" informs President Monroe he can take Florida from Spain.

General Jackson wrote a letter to the president soon after receiving command of the U.S. forces in the southwest on December 26, 1817.

To clarify his orders from Washington, Jackson asked Monroe to signify to him through such a person as Congressman John Rhea that the possession of Florida would be desirable, "and in sixty days it will be accomplished." When neither Monroe nor Secretary of War John Calhoun responded to Jackson, the general took silence to mean consent.

See April 7, 1818.

February 12, 1818

The independence of Chile is proclaimed.

This declaration had been preceded by revolutionary activity from 1810 to 1818, led by Bernardo O'HIGGINS and José de SAN MARTÍN

March 30, 1818

A resolution of the House of Representatives to recognize the independence of liberated Latin American nations is defeated.

Throughout the United States many citizens supported the South American revolutions against Spain that had grown since 1809. The Spanish king and the Congress of Vienna both claimed that the colonies should be restored to their "legitimate" rulers, a policy that made the U.S. government act cautiously.

For Monroe and Secretary of State John Quincy Adams, recognition caused a dilemma, because while they sympathized with colonial independence, they also wished to negotiate with Spain to settle the boundary questions in Florida and the southwest part of the Louisiana Purchase.

Consequently, Monroe opposed the House resolution favoring recognition. The president argued that the United States must wait until Spain's chances for recovering its colonies were "utterly desperate." Because of Monroe's opposition, the House resolution lost by a vote of 45 to 115.

See April 20, 1818.

April 7, 1818

General Andrew Jackson's attack in Spanish Florida supports America's desire to acquire that territory from Spain.

On April 7, General Jackson's men pursued into Florida a band of Indians who raided American territory. Chasing the culprits to Fort St. Marks, Jackson defeated them and seized the Spanish outpost. Jackson raised the American flag over the fort and court-martialed two English traders whom he accused of aiding the enemy. Following the hasty trial, Alexander Arbuthnot was hanged and Robert Ambrister was shot. Jackson claimed their deaths were an example of the retribution awaiting all such "unprincipled villains" who deluded the Indians into "horrid deeds of savage war."

Jackson did not stop at St. Marks. He marched west to Pensacola and captured that town on May 24. He deposed the Spanish governor, confiscated the royal archives, and put in force "the revenue laws of the United States." Later, Jackson said his one regret was that he did not hang the Spanish governor.

Jackson's aggressive campaign caused consternation in Washington; however, John Quincy Adams used this venture to impress upon Spain that it was too weak to control Florida. Jackson claimed that the "Rhea letter" of January 6, 1818, had sanctioned his action in Florida.

General Andrew (Andy) Jackson. Library of Congress

April 18, 1818

Navigation Act is signed by President Monroe.

This was one of a series of laws limiting British trade to pressure London to open the British West Indies to U.S. commerce. This act closed all U.S. ports to British ships arriving from colonies that were closed to American vessels.

April 20, 1818

A Neutrality Act results from Henry Clay's efforts to recognize the independence movements in Latin America.

The act of 1818 codified existing neutrality laws but also made two changes that favored the patriotic cause in Latin America.

The two changes resulted from Clay's attempt to send a minister to Buenos Aires and the congressional debate that followed his resolution. On March 24, 1818, Clay proposed an appropriation to send a minister to the United Provinces of Río de la Plata. Clay and his opponents in Congress argued the issue in long debates throughout March 1818. Clay claimed that Spanish American independence was the cause of freedom from despotism. In addition, U.S. trade would prosper if it gained free, direct commerce with the new nations. His opposition argued that the new governments were not liberal and democratic and that their products might undersell American products. Eventually, because Monroe's administration opposed Clay's appropriation as long as negotiations proceeded with Spain on boundary questions in

North America, the bill failed in the House by a vote of 115 to 45.

The Neutrality Act of 1818 did, however, enact a law more favorable to the Latin American rebellion. First, it prohibited a foreign state (Spain) from augmenting its warships in ports of the United States. Second, and more important, it omitted previous legislation that prevented arming of American vessels beyond the limits of American waters. Thus, Latin American patriots such as Aguirre could now purchase an unarmed vessel, sail it outside America's territorial waters, and have other ships bring armaments to supply and finish the warship.

While the 1818 neutrality law favored the Latin American governments, the issue of their recognition had not yet been finally resolved. That problem awaited the success of Secretary Adams's negotiation with Spain in 1819.

See November 1, 1818, and March 8, 1822.

October 1, 1818

Great Britain returns Astoria (Fort George) on the Columbia River to the United States.

Because the Treaty of Ghent provided for the return of territory and places occupied by either party during the War of 1812, the United States insisted that Astoria should be returned by the British.

Astoria was established as a trading post in 1811 by John Jacob ASTOR's Pacific Fur Trading Company. It was sold during the war to Britain's North West Company. Renamed Fort George, it was occupied by the British in 1813.

After the war, Astor wished to regain the fort and renew trade in the Oregon territory. At his request, Secretary of State Monroe had informed the British in 1816 that America intended to reoccupy Astoria. Monroe commissioned Captain James Biddle, commander of the USS *Ontario,* to take possession of the fort.

Although Sir Charles Bagot, Great Britain's minister to the United States, protested this action, Lord Castlereagh, the foreign minister who sought good relations with America, ordered the British naval commander in the Pacific to cooperate with Captain Biddle.

On August 19, Biddle's arrival at the COLUMBIA RIVER went smoothly. He went ashore near the fort and nailed up a board painted with an inscription saying he and the *Ontario* had taken possession on behalf of the United States.

October 20, 1818

Convention of 1818 with Great Britain resolves issues on the northeast fisheries, deported slaves, the northwest boundaries and Transatlantic commerce.

Richard RUSH and Albert GALLATIN negotiated this treaty in London with the British delegates, Henry GOULBURN and William David ROBINSON. The treaty provisions included:

1. FISHING RIGHTS—Americans gained permanent fishing rights on the southern shore of Newfoundland, the Labrador Coast, and the shores of Magdalen Island. They could dry and cure fish on Labrador's unsettled coast.
2. DEPORTED SLAVES ISSUE TO ARBITRATION—The British had carried away U.S. slaves during the War of 1812, and the U.S. request for restitution was referred to a friendly sovereign for mediation. The czar of Russia was later agreed on as mediator, and in 1822 he ruled that America should be indemnified. The indemnity was settled in 1826 when Britain paid the United States $1,204,960.
3. NORTHWEST BOUNDARY—A boundary was agreed on at the 49′ north from the Lake of the Woods to the Rocky Mountains. The British refused to extend this line all the way to the Pacific coast. As a result, the Oregon territory west of the mountains was "free and open" to the subjects of both states for trade and commerce during the next 10 years.
4. TRANSATLANTIC TRADE—The two parties agreed to renew the trade convention of 1815 (see July 3, 1815).

The U.S. Senate unanimously approved the Convention of 1818 on January 30, 1819. The convention had not, however, solved two major Anglo-American controversies—impressment and the West Indies trade.

November 1, 1818

Report to President Monroe disagrees on policy for the recognition of the rebellious governments of Latin America.

The three commissioners, Caesar A. RODNEY, John GRAHAM, and Theodorick BLAND, returned from a visit to the Río de la Plata but could not agree on the nature of the new government. In the draft of their report to Monroe on November 1, each of the three offered differing views.

The three-man commission had been appointed by Monroe in November 1817 to obtain firsthand data on the situation in Buenos Aires and Chile. The commissioners returned in July but had difficulty preparing a report because they disagreed. For example, Rodney eulogized the government of Buenos Aires, Graham was lukewarm toward it, and Bland abhorred it.

Monroe had hoped the mission would help to resolve the issue of recognition. Instead, it caused more dismay both in Monroe's cabinet and in Congress, where Henry Clay still advocated immediate recognition of the new "republics."

November 28, 1818

Secretary of State Adams defends General Jackson's Florida venture by blaming Spain.

The Spanish government protested Jackson's attack on Florida in April and May 1818, and almost disrupted Adams's negotiations on boundary issues with the Spanish minister, Don Luis ONIS Y GONZALES.

On November 28, Adams responded to the Spanish protest by blaming Spain for encouraging and sheltering the Indians. Spain, he wrote, must adequately protect its territory from such disorderly raids on America. If such disorders continued, Adams warned Onis, American forces might attack the Indians again to protect Americans. Adams's message concluded that Spain should either reinforce Florida to maintain peace or should cede the area to the United States.

Adams had masterfully turned Jackson's attack into an ultimatum that placed the burden on Spain to strengthen its territorial government or abandon Florida to America. While he agreed to return the Spanish forts to Spanish rule, he let Madrid know what action they could expect if they did not cede Florida to America.

See February 22, 1819.

1819

January 2, 1819

Panic of 1819 begins with reports that cotton prices fell on the Liverpool market.

The drop in the price of raw cotton began in December 1818, but news of it reached Savannah, Georgia, early on January 2, when *Niles Weekly Register* reported that the high price of $32\frac{1}{2}$¢ per pound in October had slumped to 24¢ by mid-December. The 1818 price had averaged 30¢ per pound, but by July 1819 the price had decreased to 14.3¢ per pound at Liverpool.

The rapid decline of cotton prices symbolized the recession more than being the cause of it. Since 1815, inflationary prices on cotton, tobacco, and wool resulted from the return of peace in both Europe and America. Other causes of the panic in the United States were an escalation of land speculation in western land, the poor management of the Second Bank of the United States during the first years after it was rechartered in 1816, and the overissue of paper banknotes by local banks.

The Panic of 1819 affected England and France as well as the United States—a reflection of the growing interdependence of investment, sales, and commerce between the Old and the New World. The Panic of 1819 lingered into the early 1820s and resulted in the passage of bankruptcy laws by several western states.

February 15, 1819

U.S.-British relations become more cordial—a Washington ball honors the departing British Minister, Charles Bagot.

The settlement of the Treaty of Ghent and discussions leading to the Conventions of 1815 and 1818 brought better Anglo-American relations than had existed since 1776.

A ball given on behalf of Charles Bagot illustrated this improved relationship. It was attended by the secretaries of state, war, and the navy; the justices of the Supreme Court; and many senators and representatives. Tables were decorated with flags of the two nations and, as toasts were made to the health of the Bagots, the band struck up "God Save the King," following which the British minister immediately asked for the playing of "Yankee Doodle."

February 22, 1819

The Transcontinental Treaty is signed by Secretary Adams and Spain's Minister Onis.

One of the most critical treaties of the 19th century for the United States, the Adams-Onis agreement resolved boundary disputes that had embroiled Spain and America in quarrels since 1803. The United States was the principal beneficiary of Spain's need to make a peaceful settlement. The treaty ceded Eastern Florida and validated the seizure of West Florida by the United States. It also defined the southwestern boundary of the Louisiana Purchase. The agreed boundary began at the mouth of the Sabine River and zigzagged in a northwesterly direction to the 42° north, which it followed to the Pacific Ocean. Spain also ceded its vague claims to the Oregon territory.

For its part, the United States surrendered its doubtful claims to Texas as part of the Louisiana Purchase and assumed the damage claims of Americans against Spain, which totaled about $5 million. Each government renounced the damage claims of one's citizens against the other's citizens.

The U.S. Senate ratified the treaty unanimously on February 24, 1819. Because of delays by the Spanish government, final ratifications were made on February 22, 1821.

Adams's critics claimed he might have obtained at least part of Texas if he had held out longer. Both Monroe and Adams were most concerned about securing Florida and a definite boundary for Louisiana. Without U.S. yielding on Texas, the treaty of 1819 might have been canceled. Most historians believe that America had again profited from Europe's (Spain's) distress.

February 24, 1819

The House of Representatives defeats four resolutions seeking to condemn Jackson's Florida escapade.

Even though Jackson's decisive acts against the Indians and the "British agents" won the plaudits of crowds in New York and Philadelphia as well as the western states, his political enemies in Congress established a Senate committee to investigate his activity. The Senate committee censured Jackson's "aggression," but its four recommendations condemning Jackson lost in the House after a 27-day debate.

May 26, 1819

The *Savannah* uses some steam power in crossing the Atlantic Ocean.

A sailing ship equipped with collapsible steam-driven paddle wheels, the *Savannah* crossed from Georgia to Liverpool in 25 days. The steam engine was an auxiliary power, however, and operated only 80 hours ($3\frac{1}{3}$ days) of the trip. The collapsible paddle wheels did not prove effective.

The owners of the *Savannah* could not sell the ship in Europe. It was brought home to America, sold at auction, and returned to being a sailing ship in the coastal trade. Not until April 23, 1838, would a British company establish regular steamship service on the Atlantic.

August 10, 1819

New Granada (Colombia) is liberated by Simón Bolívar's army.

After being forced into exile at Jamaica by the Spanish armies in 1815, Bolívar renewed his warfare in 1818, and on August 7 he defeated a royalist army at the Boyaca River. His occupation of Bogotá on August 10 completed the liberation of the country from Spain. On December 17, the three states of New Granada, Quito (Ecuador), and Venezuela formed the confederacy of Great Colombia with Bolívar as president and military dictator. This confederacy broke up in 1829–1830, and New Granada formed its own constitution on February 29, 1832.

1820

January 5, 1820

Cádiz mutiny occurs by Spanish soldiers who had assembled to reconquer the American colonies of the Spanish King, Ferdinand VII.

Since his restoration in 1814, Ferdinand's repressive policies caused much dissatisfaction. Finally, in 1820, the army mutiny demanded the full implementation of the liberal Constitution of 1812. Other rebels joined the Cádiz rebels, marched on Madrid, and captured Ferdinand VII. The king was held as a prisoner until French forces restored his "legitimacy" on August 31, 1823.

March 3, 1820

Missouri Compromise is reached.

After debating the issue for nearly a year, Congress approved the admission of Maine as a free state and Missouri as a slave state and excluded slavery in the Louisiana Purchase north of the line 30°30′.

May 15, 1820

An anti-British trade law is signed by President Monroe.

To compel Britain to liberalize its regulated trade with the West Indies, this act declared nonintercourse for British vessels that traded with any British American colony. In addition, British ships could not take colonial products to England and reexport them to the United States.

May 15, 1820

Congress levies retaliatory duties against French shipping.

Since 1815 the State Department's representatives to France had failed to get Paris to agree to the reciprocal shipping agreement followed by America. The French refused because their government wished to build a large French merchant fleet by levying discriminatory duties on U.S. and other foreign ships.

After failing once again to persuade the French to accept reciprocity, U.S. Minister Albert GALLATIN recommended congressional laws to retaliate in U.S. duties on French ships. On May 15, Congress approved legislation to charge French ships $18 per ton beginning July 1, 1820.

May 15, 1820

Congress acts to strengthen the laws prohibiting the African slave trade.

Persisting violations of the 1807 laws against the slave trade caused Congress to place stiffer penalties on this activity. The 1820 act declared that slave trade was piracy. Violators would not only forfeit their vessels as provided in 1807, but would suffer the death penalty as pirates.

On March 5, 1819, congressional legislation had provided $50 bounties for informers who aided the capture of illegal slave traders in the United States or on the sea.

August 29, 1820

Revolution in Oporto, Portugal, overthrows the Regency.

In 1807, Britain established a regency in Oporto after landing troops to fight Napoléon's army. The Regents replaced King John VI who was in Brazil. After the rebels adopted the Constitution of 1822, inviting King John VI to return as a constitutional monarch. John agreed, leaving his son Dom Pedro to rule Brazil. This action effectively ended Portuguese rule in Brazil.

December 6, 1820

President Monroe is reelected without opposition.

Monroe received 235 electoral votes; there were 3 abstentions and one vote for John Quincy Adams. At the April 1820 caucus of the Democratic-Republicans in Congress, the attendance was insufficient to conduct formal nominations. The Federalist Party had deteriorated to the point that it had no candidate. As a result, Monroe campaigned unopposed.

1821

January 26, 1821

The Congress of Laibach instructs Austria to overthrow the liberal revolution in Naples.

Dominated by the three conservative emperors of Russia, Austria, and Prussia, the Quintuple Alliance of powers formed after the Congress of Vienna devoted itself to eradicating the republican principles of 1789. The French monarch sometimes aided these three emperors; the British delegation rejected the reactionary policies of attempts to preserve absolute monarchs.

A liberal uprising in Naples on July 2 eventually required the attention of the five allies, who consulted to preserve peace in Europe. The king of Naples,

Ferdinand I, was forced by the rebels to accept a liberal constitution that limited the king's power. The Neapolitan rebellion closely resembled the uprising in Spain in January 1820, two events that disturbed the emperors of Russia, Prussia, and Austria.

In order to consider the Spanish and Neapolitan rebellions, delegates of the Quintuple Alliance met at TROPPAU on October 20, 1820. At Troppau, Prince Klemens von METTERNICH, Austria's foreign minister, persuaded all the delegates except the British to accept the Troppau Protocol. This protocol permitted the powers to intervene in any state where revolutions disturbed the peace of Europe. To Metternich, disturbing the peace meant seeking to end "legitimate monarchy." The British rejected such interference, a difference of opinion that gradually weakened and ended the Quintuple Alliance.

As a result of the Troppau Protocol, the five allies agreed to meet at Laibach in January 1821 to consider the rebellion at Naples. At Laibach, again with British dissent, the four European emperors agreed that an Austrian army should restore Ferdinand I to full power. In March 1821, Austria carried out its mission. Marching on Naples, Austria's forces crushed the poorly armed rebels, abolished the constitution, and made Ferdinand an absolute ruler.

The decisions of Troppau and Laibach led British and American diplomats to wonder if the European monarchs would intervene against the Spanish rebellion and, further, against the rebellions in Latin America.

February 24, 1821

Mexican independence is proclaimed.

This bloodless coup d'état was led by conservatives in Mexico who opposed the Spanish Constitution of 1812, which King Ferdinand VII had accepted during the Cádiz revolt. The leader of the coup was Agustín de ITURBIDE, a creole who favored the position of the church and the upper classes, and feared the liberal turn of events in Madrid. Iturbide's forces wished to recognize Ferdinand VII as their sovereign but to reject the Constitution of 1812 in Spain.

A new viceroy from Spain reached Mexico City on August 24, 1821, and agreed in the Convention of Córdoba to accept the new government. However, the Spanish government in Madrid rejected the viceroy's action. As a result, Mexican independence of Spain was maintained. On May 19, 1822, Iturbide was elected emperor of Mexico as Agustín I.

March 6, 1821

Outbreak of the Greek War of Independence from the Ottoman Turkish Empire.

This uprising, led by Alexander HYPSILANTI (YPSILANTI) in Moldavia, was joined by a larger anti-Turkish movement in MOREA. Although both sides committed atrocities and massacres during the next several years, American sympathy was with the Greeks as the "foundation" of Western civilization. In the United States a "Greek fever" brought orations, balls, mass meetings, sermons, poems, and congressional resolutions that supported the Greeks. Nevertheless, Secretary of State John Quincy Adams preferred not to get involved in such European matters and did not openly aid the rebels.

June 24, 1821

Bolívar's victory at Carabobo assures Venezuela's independence.

Since July 5, 1811, VENEZUELA's revolutionaries had constantly struggled against royalists and Spanish forces. In 1815, Spanish troops under PABLO MORILLO appeared to have won, forcing Bolívar to retreat to exile in Jamaica. He returned, however, to fight Spanish forces in Colombia, Ecuador, and Venezuela. His victory at Carabobo in 1821 enabled Venezuela to secure independence from Spain. As conceived by Bolívar, Venezuela was a part of GREAT COLOMBIA. In 1829–1830, Venezuela separated from this confederation and became a fully independent state.

July 28, 1821

The independence of Peru is proclaimed by José San Martín.

Although revolutionary uprisings had taken place in Peru since 1809, the arrival of San Martín with forces from Chile compelled the Spanish viceroy to flee from Lima. This permitted San Martín to gain control of the entire nation, granting it independence in 1821.

November 1, 1821

The U.S. consul at Canton reports the execution of an American seaman by the Chinese: The Terranova Incident.

The American consul in Canton, China, B. C. Wilcocks, reported the events that led to the execution of Francis Terranova, who had been tried and convicted under Chinese law for killing a Chinese woman. Terranova was an Italian seaman on the crew of a U.S. ship, the *Emily,* out of Baltimore.

Following the alleged murder and accusation of Terranova by the Chinese authorities, Consul Wilcocks advised the *Emily*'s captain to settle the matter by a payment to the dead woman's relatives. The ship's officers believed Terranova was not guilty and decided to contest his case in court. Following Chinese legal practice, the trial was held, and Terranova was found guilty and ordered to be punished.

The accused was aboard the *Emily,* whose captain refused to surrender him. In response, the Chinese authorities stopped all U.S. trade at Canton and arrested the *Emily*'s security merchant, the man who conducted financial business for the ship's cargo. This action jeopardized the profits of all American ships at Canton and persuaded the *Emily*'s captain to surrender Terranova. The captain claimed the Chinese agreed not to execute Terranova.

It is not known if the captain's story of a Chinese promise was correct. Wilcocks and other American officials in Canton did not understand the Chinese language and had to rely on local interpreters. The fact was, however, that Terranova was executed according to Chinese custom in murder cases, by strangulation.

At this time, no Western nation had official treaties with China, and Canton was a wide open, wild seaport. The Western traders did not know Chinese law, custom, or language and therefore assumed the Chinese were barbarians. The Chinese, of course, saw the drunken, shoddy seamen as barbarians.

Nevertheless, incidents such as the Terranova case readily persuaded Americans and other Western visitors to China that they could not "trust" the Chinese legal system. As a result, in the Asiatic treaties after 1839, the Western nations required rights of legal extraterritoriality in China, Japan, and most other non-Christian nations.

1822

March 8, 1822

President Monroe recommends recognition of the Latin American republics.

Within two months, Congress appropriated $100,000 to establish appropriate diplomatic missions and to welcome the new republics. The Republic of Greater Colombia was recognized on June 19, and Mexico on December 12, 1822; Chile and Argentina on January 27, 1823; Brazil on May 26, 1824; the United Provinces of Central America on August 4, 1824; and Peru on May 2, 1826.

June 14, 1822

The British Parliament approves the "American Trade Act" to open some West Indies ports to U.S. ships.

This law reflected the desire of many British merchants to effect a "free-trade" program. It opened certain West Indies ports to American ships that imported an enumerated list of U.S. products and carried out a list of colonial products. These U.S. ships and cargoes would be treated on the same terms as British ships.

The law did not really provide free trade. First, its enactment depended on foreign states granting equal and reciprocal advantages to British ships. Second, it reserved Britain's freedom to give preferential tariffs on the listed articles when they were imported from British North America (e.g., Canada). As we shall see, Secretary of State Adams did not believe reciprocity could allow intercolonial preferences and enumerated lists of products. While it was a step toward reciprocity by England, Adams wanted Britain to go further.

See August 22, 1822, and March 1, 1823.

June 24, 1822

U.S. Senate ratifies commercial Treaty with France.

Following the American enactment of retaliatory legislation on May 15, 1820, France agreed to negotiate a compromise settlement to end its discriminatory commercial duties. Secretary of State Adams and French Minister to the U.S. Baron Guillaume-Jean Hyde De Neuville negotiated the treaty. By its terms, each nation would levy a balance of discriminating duties for two years. After that time, an annual lowering of duties would occur until all discrimination ended, or until either party denounced the treaty. In this manner, the American principle of reciprocity was eventually accepted by France.

August 12, 1822

The death of British Foreign Minister Castlereagh enables the liberal wing of the Tory Party to control the cabinet.

The Torys' liberals included Foreign Minister George Canning and Board of Trade President William Huskisson, both of whom wished to end gradually the country's mercantilist system in favor of free trade.

August 22, 1822

President Monroe does not remove all discriminatory duties on British trade.

On August 22, Monroe responded to the British "American Trade Act of 1822" by a proclamation removing the nonintercourse provision of the U.S. act of May 15, 1820. Yet Monroe did not provide for reciprocity to British ships. His proclamation retained a tonnage duty of $1 per ton and a 10% import duty on vessels not privileged by treaty. The British minister to the United States, Stratford Canning, noted this continued discrimination by America and asked Secretary Adams to correct this clause. But Adams, who pursued neomercantilist policy to promote American trade, would not recommend any changes to Monroe. Adams proposed the Act of 1823, which sought greater concessions from Great Britain before the United States accepted reciprocity (see March 1, 1823).

September 7, 1822

Brazilian independence is proclaimed.

Between 1820 and 1821, King John VI of Portugal transferred his government to Brazil to escape the British-controlled regency and the republican ideas being followed at home. But by April 1821, John VI desired to return to Lisbon. Therefore, he named his son Pedro as prince regent of Brazil. To keep Brazil "safe" from Portuguese control, Pedro called a constituent assembly on June 3, 1822, which proclaimed him as the "constitutional emperor of Brazil." This assembly also declared on September 7 that Brazil was independent of Portugal. On December 1, the prince regent was crowned as Pedro I.

October 20, 1822

Congress of Verona approves French intervention in Spain to restore the king.

The delegates of the Quintuple Alliance met at Verona, Italy, to carry out further the Troppau Protocol, which had succeeded against Naples. Because the Spanish rebels of 1820 still controlled Madrid, the allies needed to decide on possible intervention to restore Spain and the Latin American colonies to Ferdinand VII. The Greek Revolution was also on the agenda at Verona.

Although the British delegates continued to oppose intervention in another state's internal affairs, the three European emperors and the French king decided to send a French army to restore Ferdinand VII to power in Spain. They did not, however, indicate any interest at that time in restoring the Spanish colonies to the king.

After the Congress of Verona, Great Britain declined to attend future congresses. On the European continent, the monarchs relied on Prince Metternich's reactionary progress to eliminate liberal ideas. Until 1848, Metternich's system seemed to work.

For the Naples intervention, see January 26, 1821.

1823

February 28, 1823

The House of Representatives resolves that the United States should negotiate to abolish the slave trade.

This House action evolved from a series of investigations of the slave trade problem begun in December 1821. The U.S. legislation of 1807 to prohibit the slave trade had not been enforced, and a congressional act of May 15, 1820, making slave trade an act of piracy did not work. International agreements were needed to stop this trade effectively.

Great Britain had for some time sought the cooperation of other nations in combating the slave trade. In 1818, Lord Castlereagh had proposed such a treaty with the United States. The British offer was rejected because John Quincy Adams refused to allow a foreign ship to stop and search a suspected slave ship.

Adams's objection was the particular point to which the House resolution of 1823 addressed itself. Passed in the House by a vote of 131 to 9, the resolution said the United States should agree to the right of visit and search for the slave trade. It was the only effective way to end slavery under "the law of civilized nations."

The House resolution brought some results. It caused Secretary Adams to reconsider his prior belief that visit and search should not be permitted under any circumstances. Adams agreed to negotiate with Britain a treaty on the slave trade that brought interesting consequences.

See March 13, 1824.

March 1, 1823

Congress passes a trade act that rejects Britain's Conciliatory Act of June 14, 1822.

The trade act of March 1, 1823, offered to treat British vessels on a basis of reciprocity, provided that all American vessels and goods were admitted to British colonial ports on the same terms as British commerce from "every part" of its empire. This provision could not be accepted by Great Britain because it would abolish the preferential tariffs and shipping duties London granted to its colonial trade.

The American law therefore ended an attempt by Great Britain to grant limited concessions to U.S. ships in the West Indies. Parliament responded by assessing new duties and limits on American goods (July 17, 1823) and eventually closed all British West Indies ports to U.S. commerce.

See June 27, 1825.

April 28, 1823

Secretary of State Adams supports Spain's retention of Cuba and Puerto Rico because he fears England may desire to occupy those islands.

Because Cuba and Puerto Rico were all that remained of Spanish control in Latin America, Adams believed that Great Britain might wish to gain control of these islands. The French army invaded Spain to restore Ferdinand VII as king, and the expectation was that England wanted to control Cuba to prevent the Quintuple Alliance from intervening.

Anticipating this possibility, Secretary Adams outlined U.S. policy on the Caribbean situation for Hugh Nelson, the American minister to Spain: (1) the United States was content for Spain to retain Cuba and Puerto Rico; (2) transference of these islands to another power would be viewed with "repugnance" by America; (3) the United States recognized that it might find it necessary to occupy Cuba temporarily to protect it from others.

June 23, 1823

Secretary of State Adams sends instructions to Richard Rush outlining the broad number of important issues requiring British agreement.

Adams recognized, as he told British Minister to the U.S. Stratford Canning during the spring of 1823, that recent great changes in world affairs provided a suitable time for an accommodation between British and American interests.

To seek such an accommodation, Adams sent Richard Rush, the U.S. minister in London, a series of nine lengthy instructions in June and July, covering

John Quincy Adams. Collection of the New York Historical Society

the vital issues with England. Adams hoped each of these could be resolved. They included (1) commercial intercourse; (2) visit and search in the slave trade; (3) the southeast boundary; (4) American consuls in British courts; (5) French interference in the Newfoundland fisheries; (6) the northwest boundary; (7) maritime rights.

In August, when Rush undertook to begin discussing these issues, British Foreign Minister George Canning diverted attention to an immediate issue: possible European intervention in Latin America. Although Rush and other Americans were willing to act in accord with Britain on Latin America, Adams insisted that the Latin American question should not be separated from the totality of Anglo-American issues he outlined for Rush. Unless all or many of these issues were resolved, Adams did not want to act in coordination with London on Latin America. The United States could deal with that matter separately with Latin America, without British aid.

On U.S. Latin American policy, see August 16–20, 1823.

July 1, 1823

The Central American provinces declare independence from Spain.

Revolutionary movements in the captaincy general of Guatemala began against Spain between 1811 and 1814. In 1821, Guatemala accepted Iturbide's offer to become part of Mexico, but the other provinces of Central America refused. For example, San Salvador offered on December 2, 1822, to become a part of the United States.

In 1823, a general assembly of Central America met in Guatemala City. The delegates decided to confederate as the United Provinces of Central America but to permit each state to be sovereign. These states were GUATEMALA, SAN SALVADOR, NICARAGUA, HONDURAS, and COSTA RICA

July 17, 1823

British renew duties on American shipping to the West Indies.

Because Monroe's proclamation of August 22, 1822, did not remove all discriminations on U.S. duties, the British government imposed special duties on U.S. commerce in the West Indies. These fees equaled the 10% duties that America continued to levy on British colonial shipping. The British cabinet under George Canning had endeavored to conciliate American trade laws but failed because of J. Q. Adams's desire for greater English concessions.

See June 27, 1825.

July 17, 1823

America protests Russia's claim to Pacific Coast Territory north of the 51st parallel.

On July 17, Secretary Adams told the Russian minister in Washington, Baron Tuyll, that the United States would contest Russia's right to "any territorial establishment" on this continent, for the Americas are "no longer subjects for any European colonial establishments."

Adams's protest particularly focused on Czar Alexander's ukase of September 4, 1821, which claimed for Russia all Pacific coast territory north of the 51°. This included part of the Oregon territory that Britain and America had agreed in 1818 was open to Anglo-American settlement.

The czar's decree of 1821 sought to extend Russia's early claim of the 55° north down to the 51° north. Under an earlier 18th-century claim to the 55° north, the Russian American Trading Company founded Sitka in 1799. In 1812, the company established Fort Ross just north of San Francisco. The company wanted to move farther south, and although the ukase of 1821 did not include Fort Ross, it included part of the Oregon territory.

Adams's warning to Baron Tuyll led to a series of negotiations that settled on a southern boundary for Alaska in 1824. Nevertheless, this Russian attempt to extend its boundaries was fresh in Adams's and Monroe's minds as they prepared the president's speech to Congress in November 1823.

August 16–20, 1823

Britain's Foreign Minister, George Canning, asks Richard Rush if the United States will join the British in a joint declaration opposing intervention in Spanish America by any European Alliance.

The Congress of Verona (October 1822) sanctioned French intervention in Spain to restore Ferdinand VII, and in the spring of 1823, French armies invaded Spain for that purpose. By August, the French victory was assured.

Canning opposed European intervention in the Americas, and he told Rush, the U.S. minister to Britain, that "the simple fact of our two countries being known to hold the same opinions would, by its moral effect, put down the intention on the part of France."

Four days later, Canning sent Rush a proposed declaration, including these main points: (1) Spain cannot recover the colonies; (2) the question of recognition is but a matter of time; (3) neither Britain nor America aims to possess them, but neither should they be transferred to another power.

Rush had not received instructions in regard to Canning's proposal. He told Canning he would agree, however, provided Great Britain first recognized the independent republics. But Canning was reluctant to grant recognition because Spain had been Britain's ally. As a result, Rush said he had to wait on Canning's request to hear from Washington. Canning did not wish to wait, however.

See October 9, 1823.

August 31, 1823

French armies complete their objective of defeating the Spanish liberals and restoring King Ferdinand VII.

As directed by the Congress of Verona (October 20, 1822), a French army of 100,000 soldiers invaded Spain on April 7, 1823. After capturing Madrid on May 23, they marched southward and finally routed the rebels at Fort Trocadero outside Cádiz on August 31. Ferdinand VII became an absolute monarch unfettered by a constitution. The congress system had once again halted the spread of liberal republican ideals. Those who like to praise Metternich's system should reflect on the reactionary policies it encouraged between 1815 and 1848.

October 9, 1823

The Polignac Memorandum: George Canning warns the French ambassador his nation should not intervene in Latin America.

After Richard Rush refused to make an immediate joint Anglo-American declaration against intervention, Britain's Foreign Minister Canning sought an opportunity to warn the French unilaterally. On October 9, Canning held an audience with the Prince de Polignac, France's ambassador, to tell him that England supported Latin American independence unless the Spanish king negotiated a favorable settlement. He told Polignac that England would recognize the American republics if any attempt were made by an outside power to restrict trade or otherwise intervene in Latin America. To certify that France agreed with Canning, Polignac pledged in a memorandum that France rejected "any design of acting against the colonies by force of arms." The memo was not published until March 1824, after Monroe's speech of December 2, 1823.

December 2, 1823

The Monroe Doctrine is enunciated.

In consultation with John Quincy Adams, President Monroe's State of the Union message embodied a statement on U.S. policy relating to Europe, Russia, and the Americas. Arising from recent consideration of George Canning's proposal to Richard Rush on possible European intervention in the former Spanish Empire, Adams strongly desired a unilateral American statement. Adams wanted the U.S. statement to be based on American national interest as part of an American system in the Western Hemisphere. The Monroe Doctrine's main points are as follows:

1. Noncolonization—The American continents are no longer subjects for future European colonization.
2. Doctrine of Two Spheres—In world politics, the European system differed significantly from the American. One was monarchical; the other, democratic and republican. This sentiment not only expressed antagonism toward European monarchies but stressed the community of interests between the United States and South America.
3. Nonextension—America would consider as dangerous to its peace and safety any attempt of a European power to extend its system into the Western Hemisphere.
4. Noninterference—The United States would not interfere in European affairs or in the existing European colonies in the New World; Europe should not interfere in the Western Hemisphere.

Monroe's speech did not immediately gain the prominence it later attained in American history. After the Panama Congress affair of 1825–1826, it received little attention until 1844, when President James K. Polk revived Monroe's ideas to justify his policies in Oregon and Texas.

December 8, 1823

Secretary of State Adams seeks cordial relations with England.

Although Adams and President Monroe had agreed the United States would make a unilateral statement to oppose European intervention in Latin America, they instructed Richard RUSH in London that this did not negate a desire for good relations with England. Adams wrote that if the Holy Alliance decided, as rumored, to send a 12,500-man army to reconquer Spanish America, the United States and Great Britain could discuss a "further concert of operations to counteract that design."

The Monroe Doctrine had been a unilateral declaration of U.S. policy made to Congress. It was not an appeal to separate foreign governments. Nor did it preclude possible cooperation with other nations (i.e., England) holding common interests in the independence of the Latin American nations.

At the time of these instructions, Adams was unaware of the Polignac memorandum of October 9, 1823. He hoped that George Canning's offer of August 16, 1823, might lead to a general settlement of historic problems between England and America, including neutral rights, impressment, and the West Indies trade. Unfortunately, Canning was not ready in 1823 to negotiate regarding these issues.

The document of December 8, 1823, disproves, as Samuel Flagg Bemis has noted, the myth created by Walter Lippmann on August 22, 1940. Lippmann, a columnist for the *New York Herald Tribune,* asserted that the United States and Britain had made an agreement regarding Latin American intervention on August 23, 1823. He repeated his error in a 1943 book, *U.S. Foreign Policy: Shield of the Republic.* Lippmann supported an Anglo-American alliance against the Axis in 1940. As Bemis asserted, by 1940 an incorrect historic myth was not necessary to promote Anglo-American goodwill in the 20th century.

December 15, 1823

Congressional resolutions on the navy indicate war is not anticipated as a factor in the Monroe Doctrine.

Two resolutions regarding the navy were proposed by Joel POINSETT in the House of Representatives.

The first resolution requested President Monroe to submit plans for a peacetime navy. On January 30, 1824, Monroe offered his plan as prepared by the secretary of the navy. It proposed a navy to protect the neutral rights of America, but did not mention any possible use against Spain, France, or the Holy Alliance in Latin America.

The second resolution asked for an investigation into increasing the size of the navy by adding 10 sloops of war. Poinsett believed more ships were needed because the U.S. navy had only 5 sloops of war but had 30 officers of commandant rank. Poinsett's resolution and the resulting naval bill passed on April 27, 1824, disclose the prevailing thinking about the navy relating to foreign policy.

Poinsett's bill provided for a "police"-type navy to protect merchant ships. The sloops of war Poinsett desired were small warships used basically for protective purposes. In contrast, Richard RUSH in 1822 proposed that the United States establish the strongest navy in the world by constructing 4,000-ton frigates and increasing the caliber of guns accordingly. Rush's idea of a strong, fighting navy was not accepted in 1822 or in 1824–1825.

Nor did the naval bill passed in April 1825 accept Poinsett's proposed increase for police-size sloops of war. The secretary of the navy requested $225,000 for "contingent expenses," but before the bill passed, Congress had cut 25% of this sum.

As Arthur Whitaker has noted, President Monroe's administration depended on the moral force of the warning in his message to Congress. In addition, of course, he and John Quincy Adams knew that the British navy stood between the Holy Alliance and any attempt it might make to regain the Latin American colonies for Spain. Under such circumstances, the United States did not require a large naval force.

December 17, 1823

President Monroe sends a "spy" to Europe to report on possible attempts to intervene in Latin America.

During the fall of 1823, the European powers considered calling another congress of the "concert of Europe" to resolve the Spanish American issue. In November, Britain's foreign minister, George Canning, suggested the United States might wish to send a representative to the congress. Monroe's administration refused to grant such sanction to the "potentates" of Europe. But Monroe did wish to gain detailed information about the proceedings of such a congress.

As a result, he sent a secret agent, Alexander MacRae, to Europe to gather information about the congress and other European intentions. Because the rumored congress was never held, MacRae's mission ended in August 1824, although he made several reports to the State Department, the final report being filed on January 4, 1825.

1824

March 13, 1824

Anglo-American Convention to suppress the slave trade is signed but not ratified.

This treaty was agreed to because Secretary of State Adams changed his mind about using search and seizure of ships suspected of the slave trade. Because of previous disputes with the British on search and seizure, Adams had been wary of permitting this clause in any slave trade treaty.

Adams changed his views in 1823 after debate in the House of Representatives resulted in a House resolution which recognized the need to use search procedures on the high seas in order to end the slave trade. Once Adams altered his opinion and informed Richard Rush in London of his willingness to accept this tactic, Britain's Foreign Minister Canning readily accepted a slave-trade agreement.

In the convention of 1824, the following important clauses were included: (1) persons involved in slave trade are punishable as pirates; (2) the two nations would allow search and visit of each other's merchant ships; (3) a captured ship would go for trial to its country's port; (4) crew members could not be taken from a captured vessel; (5) the officer in command of the capturing vessel is responsible for any abuse of the right of search and seizure.

Final ratification of this convention failed because the treaty became a political football in the U.S. Senate. Adams's political opponent Senator William Crawford accused him of abandoning the nation's traditional opposition to searches and offered an amendment that crippled the convention. The amendment eliminated Article I, which allowed searches both on the African and the American coastlines. Crawford won because two-thirds of the Senate disapproved Article I but passed the remainder of the treaty.

The British would not accept the elimination of Article I and the final ratification failed. As would often be the case, partisanship and not on the merits of a treaty prevailed in the U.S. Senate.

April 17, 1824

Russia accepts 54°40′ as the southern boundary of its territory in North America.

Although John Quincy Adams originally proposed the 55th parallel as the southern boundary, the Russian chancellor, Count Nesselrode, desired 54°51′ to keep the Prince of Wales Island in Russian territory.

The treaty was agreed to in St. Petersburg by Nesselrode and the U.S. minister to Russia, Henry Middleton. In addition to resolving the boundary issue, Russia gave up its claims to Fort Ross in California and accepted the reciprocal right of trade by citizens of both nations along the entire northwest coast for 10 years. The U.S. Senate ratified the treaty by a vote of 41 to 1, and ratifications were exchanged on January 13, 1825.

August 6, 1824

Secretary Adams informs Colombia that if there were a substantial threat to Latin America, the United States could resist only with British cooperation.

Adams's interpretation of Monroe's 1823 message to Congress received an interesting twist after Colombia's foreign minister asked Washington how the United States intended to resist if the Holy Alliance intervened in Latin America. Colombia, he wrote to Adams on July 2, 1824, intended to defend "its independence and liberty against every foreign influence and power." How could the United States help Colombia?

After discussions in the cabinet, Adams composed a cautious answer to Colombia's query. Adams minimized the possibility of any intervention by the Holy Alliance and praised Colombia for its desire to resist all outside influence. The United States could not, however, entertain an alliance with Colombia. Any action of America's would depend on the U.S. Congress and its agreement at the time a threat arose.

Most significantly, however, Adams admitted that the United States could not resort to force of arms without a "previous understanding" with other European powers who would ensure "efficient cooperation in the cause" of Latin American independence. Although Adams did not directly say "with England's cooperation," both he and the Colombian government understood the message. Adams wished to enlarge U.S. prestige in foreign relations, but he also realized that British power was superior at that time.

December 1, 1824

Presidential election results give no candidate a majority.

The demise of the Federalist Party after 1815 combined with widespread opposition to presidential nominations by congressional caucus brought a wide-open political campaign. State legislatures nominated candidates and five nominees sought the presidency. As a result, after the election of December 1, Andrew Jackson had 95 electoral votes; John Quincy Adams, 84; William Crawford, 41; and Henry Clay, 37. John C. Calhoun withdrew as a presidential candidate in September and, consequently, he easily won the vice presidency with 137 votes.

Because no candidate received a majority of votes, the election was submitted to the House of Representatives for a decision early in 1825.

1825

February 9, 1825

John Quincy Adams is elected President by the House of Representatives.

Because the December 11, 1824, electoral college vote gave no candidate a majority, the three leading candidates had to be voted on by the House. Henry Clay, the fourth-ranking candidate, was eliminated, and on January 8, 1825, Clay advised his electors to vote for Adams. In addition, Clay persuaded his Kentucky friends in the House to vote for Adams, while the state legislature instructed them to vote for Jackson. The House vote gave Adams 13 states to 7 for Jackson and 4 for Crawford.

February 16, 1825

Russia and Great Britain sign a treaty recognizing 54°40′ as the southern boundary of Russian holdings on the northwest Pacific coast of North America.

This treaty matched the agreement between Russia and the United States in 1824. It left the United States and Great Britain to dispute claims for land between the 42° and the 54°40′ in the Oregon territory.

March 7, 1825

Henry Clay is commissioned as Secretary of State.

Clay served in this office until the end of John Quincy Adams's presidency on March 3, 1829. In January 1825, Representative George Kremer of Pennsylvania charged that Clay had made a "corrupt bargain" to support Adams's presidential election in return for the office of secretary of state. Clay demanded a congressional investigation of the charge but Kremer refused to appear. There is no evidence of such a bargain (Adams also denied it), but the accusation followed Clay throughout his political career.

March 7, 1825

Joel Poinsett is appointed as the first U.S. Minister to Mexico; his instructions: to buy a boundary for the United States as far west as possible.

Although President Adams had as secretary of state in 1819 negotiated a boundary with Spain at the Sabine River, he and Clay were reluctant to accept this boundary for Mexico. In 1825 and again in 1827, Secretary Clay urged Poinsett to offer a scale of money for any boundary west of the Sabine: the Brazos River, the Colorado River of Texas, the "Snow Mountains" (Sangre do Cristos), or the divide between the Nueces and Rio Grande Rivers.

Mexico refused to alter its boundary unless it were moved farther east. Luis Aléman, Mexico's secretary of state, told Poinsett he was quite ready to change the border: to the Mississippi River.

March 24, 1825

Mexico opens the state of Texco-Coahuila to American immigration.

This law resulted from the previous arrival of American settlers led by Stephen F. Austin, who brought 200 families to Texas in 1821 under a land grant secured by his father, Moses Austin. The Austin plan worked well, and the leaders of the Mexican Republic, established in 1824, hoped the new immigrants would become good citizens of a sparsely populated region of Mexico.

The immigration law combined with promises of free or low-cost land was very successful during the next five years. More than 15,000 Americans flocked into Texas. On April 8, 1830, Mexico passed a law to keep U.S. citizens and slaves out of its territory, but the law could not be effectively enforced along the long Mexican border. By 1836, as Americans in Texas prepared to seek independence, at least 30,000 Americans with over 3,000 slaves lived in northeastern Mexico.

May 7, 1825

President Adams's cabinet discusses the Panama Congress.

Simón Bolívar, in the name of Peru, had issued a circular note on December 7, 1824, inviting independent nations of the former Spanish Empire to a congress at Panama on October 1, 1825. Don Pedro Gual, Colombia's minister of foreign affairs, directed his ambassador to the United States, José Maria Salazar, to inquire if America would be interested in attending the congress. In accord with Gual's instructions, Salazar told U.S. Secretary of State Henry Clay that the Conference would consider principles of the freedom of the seas, but he did not mention a possible military alliance against Europeans. There had even been rumors that Colombia and Mexico planned to attack such distant Spanish possessions as the Canary Islands or the Philippines.

The possibility of a convention on commercial neutrality together with Secretary Clay's influence persuaded President Adams and the cabinet to accept the Colombian request. The United States would go to Panama as a *neutral* nation. Adams and Clay also decided to inform Salazar that the United States could not attend as early as October 1, and would prefer that the congress meet at a later date.

June 27, 1825

Britain enacts legislation that bans all U.S. trade with the West Indies.

By the act of June 27 combined with three subsequent commercial regulations of July 5, 1826, Britain prohibited all U.S. ships from trade with the British West Indies.

Since 1822, Albert Gallatin had been following Adams's instructions to get a commercial treaty opening British colonial ports to America. Britain first passed a law in 1822 that partly opened British West Indies trade, but Adams demanded full reciprocity of trade so that U.S. merchants would be treated equally in all parts of the British colonial empire. England believed that its colonial ports deserved preferential duties while direct U.S.-British trade could be reciprocal.

By a proclamation of August 22, 1822, and a law of March 1, 1823, Adams persuaded President Monroe and Congress to retain discriminatory tonnage duties and import duties on British colonial trade. In retaliation for American discrimination in 1823, Great Britain levied similar tonnage and import fees on July 17, 1823.

Further discussions between Gallatin and Canning failed in 1824. England wanted to be conciliatory and accept some U.S. trade with the West Indies; Adams and Monroe desired reciprocity in both colonial and direct trade. The dispute temporarily ended in 1826 when Great Britain decided to prohibit all U.S. trade with the West Indies. Legal U.S. trade with British colonies in the Caribbean was back to its status of 1793: no trade allowed.

By seeking too much, Adams lost all of the West Indies trade. The United States could retaliate only by closing all U.S. ports to Britain's colonial trade.

See March 27, 1827.

August 6, 1825

Bolivia proclaims independence from Spain.

After revolutionary forces under Simón Bolívar defeated Spanish troops at the Battle of Ayacucho,

Spain agreed to withdraw its last 25,000 soldiers from the region.

October 25, 1825

President Adams and Secretary of State Clay warn France not to attempt to occupy Cuba.

Rumors that the French, whose army controlled Spain, might seek to take over Cuba had become prevalent in 1824–1825. Therefore, Adams decided to warn France and other parties that American policy preferred that Spain should retain Cuba and Puerto Rico. The U.S. minister to France, James Brown, was told to inform the French that the United States would consent to Cuba's occupation by no power other than Spain. He also advised France that in the future, the American government expected to be notified if France planned to reinforce its Caribbean fleet. (In 1824, France had added 28 ships to its American fleet.)

November 2–3, 1825

The United States is invited to attend the Panama Congress.

Although Simón Bolívar, who originated the idea of a congress, intended the meeting to bring unity among the Latin American nations, both Mexico and Colombia sent invitations to the United States on November 2–3, 1825.

In accordance with America's response to a previous Colombian inquiry (May 7, 1825), the opening of the congress had been delayed from October 1, 1825, and would convene in 1826. The invitation from Colombia's Foreign Minister José Maria Gual also clarified the proposed agenda of the congress as follows:

1. agreement on principles of international law;
2. discussion of a continental alliance to enforce the noncolonization principle of Monroe's speech of 1823;
3. abolition of the slave trade;
4. treatment of the Black republic of Haiti;
5. other matters for the good of the hemisphere.

December 5, 1825

The United States and the United Federation of Central America sign a commercial treaty that provides for complete reciprocity.

Since 1815, American negotiators had sought to arrange complete reciprocity of shipping duties with other nations. The treaty with Central America was the first in which each nation accepted the complete reciprocity rule. Secretary Clay was enthusiastic about the treaty. In 1826, he stated: "This is the most perfect freedom of navigation. We can conceive of no privilege beyond it." This reciprocity meant each nation permitted its ships to enter the other's ports on a basis of equality with its own citizens' ships. The U.S. Senate approved this treaty on December 29, 1825, and final ratifications were exchanged on August 2, 1826.

December 26, 1825

President Adams recommends the Senate approve two delegates for the Panama Congress.

After receiving the invitation to the congress on November 2, 1825, Adams and Secretary of State Henry Clay considered the implications of attendance. Clay had been a champion of Latin America's independence, but Adams had been reluctant to be involved there.

By December, Adams realized the potential value of establishing proper contact with the Latin American leaders. He decided to name Richard C. ANDERSON and John SERGEANT as envoys extraordinary and ministers plenipotentiary to the Assembly of American Nations. In his request to the Senate, Adams noted the growing commercial relations of the United States with Latin America. Commerce plus necessary political concerns gave the American nations common interests distinct from Europe's. Therefore, Adams asserted, consultation with Latin American leaders was important.

Adams made it clear, however, that the United States was not interested in forming any alliances or in becoming involved in aggression. Some of Adams's political opponents claimed the president had been converted to Clay's "South American" fever. This charge failed to recognize that both Adams and Clay based their ideas on American national interests. The independence of Latin American nations had been recognized, and their geographic proximity gave America common interests with them. Nevertheless, Adams's apparent change of view and his numerous political opponents in Congress led to intensive debate over the naming of delegates to the congress.

See March 14, 1826.

1826

March 14, 1826

Senate approves delegates to the Panama Congress following six weeks of political invective against Secretary Clay and President Adams.

The Senate debate on Adams's appointment of two delegates to Panama reflected the intense opposition of Martin Van Buren and other political enemies of the administration, not the merits of the request.

The tone of Adams's opponents was set on January 11, when the Senate Foreign Relations Committee opposed sending delegates to Panama. Their report implied that Adams sought to deceive the Senate by emphasizing the neutral rights agenda of the congress (see December 26, 1825). In reality, it said, the Latin American nations intended to commit the United States to a secret and conditional alliance that conflicted with America's traditional neutrality as established under President Washington. With three southern senators on the committee, the report also objected to the agenda items on the recognition of Haiti (the Black republic) and the slave trade.

Despite such opposition arguments, the Senate voted on March 14 to confirm the appointments. Anderson was approved by 27 to 17; Sergeant by 26 to 18. The House of Representatives now had to authorize and appropriate funds to pay the delegation's expenses.

March 30, 1826

Senator John Randolph's bitter accusations regarding the Panama Congress lead to a duel with Secretary of State Henry Clay.

Although the Senate had previously approved the Panamanian delegation, Senator Randolph of Virginia made an emotional and rambling speech against the action of Adams and Clay on Panama. He insinuated that Clay had doctored or forged the invitations of November 2–3, 1825. He and others in the Senate had tried to hold true, Randolph asserted, but they were defeated, "cut up and clean broke down . . . by the combination unheard of 'till then, of the Puritan and the blackleg."

Clay, the alleged "blackleg," immediately challenged Randolph to a duel. Following arrangements made by their seconds, the two met on April 8. After exchanging harmless shots, Clay fired a bullet through the skirts of Randolph's long white flannel overcoat. Randolph fired wildly in the air and rushed to shake Clay's hand. "You owe me a coat, Mr. Clay," he exclaimed. Clay had earned a distinctive status for a Secretary of State: dueling on behalf of a foreign policy.

April 22, 1826

The House of Representatives appropriates $40,000 for delegation expenses to the Panama Congress.

Following the Senate's approval of delegates Anderson and Sergeant on March 14, the House took a month to discuss and authorize the mission's expenses.

In urging quick House consideration for the appropriation bill on March 15, President Adams contended that participation in the congress was "directly deducible" from George Washington's policies. Whenever the United States acted to restrain Europe from intervention in Latin America, said Adams, it did so in America's interests and sense of justice.

May 8, 1826

Secretary Clay's instructions to the Panama delegates permit no alliances but seek to commit Latin America to U.S. policies on international law.

Clay instructed Anderson and Sergeant to seek "good neighborhood" agreements on such fundamental ideas as abstention from wars in Europe, noncolonization, no-transfer of colonies in the Western Hemisphere, freedom of the seas, the right of expatriation and naturalization, commercial reciprocity, and the end of privateers on the high seas. Clay's concepts described much of U.S. policy in the Western Hemisphere but were not presented at the

Panama Congress because the American delegation never arrived.

See July 15, 1826.

July 15, 1826

Panama Congress adjourns with no U.S. delegates present.

The congress convened on June 22, 1826, with delegates from Colombia, Mexico, Peru, and Guatemala. Great Britain sent a commissioner, Edward J. Dawkins, to the meetings as an observer.

During the month's sessions, the delegates approved four treaties of mutual defense and a common army. They also agreed to meet again at Tacubaya, Mexico. These agreements were not ratified, however, except by Colombia.

The British agent Dawkins gained the most from the conference. He kept the delegates informed of Great Britain's interest in both the welfare and commerce of Latin America. London, he said, consistently urged Ferdinand of Spain to be reconciled to colonial freedom.

The U.S. delegates never reached Panama. Richard Anderson, who was the U.S. minister to Colombia, intended to go to Panama. But en route he caught a tropical fever while on a boat in the Magdalena River and died in Cartagena on July 24, 1826. Sergeant refused to attend a summer meeting in Panama, where he knew tropical fever came easily. He resigned his commission but Secretary Clay persuaded him to retain it and go to the congress in the fall. Subsequently, Sergeant went to Mexico City, but the renewal of the sessions scheduled for Tacubaya never took place. In sum, this initial attempt to obtain consultation among nations of the Western Hemisphere did not succeed. Another such attempt did not take place until the 1880s.

August 17, 1826

Argentina is told by the U.S. Minister that the Monroe concept of nontransfer of 1823 does not apply to land transferred as the result of war between two Latin American states. This view is later approved by President Adams and Secretary of State Clay.

The Argentine government asked J. M. Forbes, the U.S. minister at Buenos Aires, if American policy approved land transfers because it was fighting Brazil for the disputed province of BANDA ORIENTAL (Uruguay). Argentina had occupied the Banda Oriental in 1814, but Portuguese troops regained control in 1820. Brazil claimed to have inherited the state from Portugal and took over in 1822. A war began between Argentina and Brazil in December 1825, after rebels in the province agreed to annexation by Buenos Aires.

The Buenos Aires government claimed that England helped Brazil during the war and intended to extend British influence if it defeated Argentina. Forbes rejected this interpretation because he did not believe the circumstances involved a power outside the Western Hemisphere.

Rather than accept Forbes's decision, the Argentine government appealed to Washington for an interpretation. Both Adams and Clay agreed with Forbes but had no opportunity to tell Argentina until July 9, 1828. The delay resulted because Buenos Aires had not sent a minister to Washington for nearly two years.

August 22, 1826

Jedediah Smith leaves Salt Lake on an expedition of the southwest.

His exploration party mapped out a region that, at that time, was northwestern territory of Mexico. Smith's group of 15 men went across the SEVIER valley to the VIRGIN River and on to the Colorado. They trekked across the Mohave Desert into California via the Cajon Pass and reached the San Gabriel mission (Los Angeles) on November 27, 1826. Smith's explorations were probably surpassed only by those of Lewis and Clark in the Northwest territory.

1827

February 17, 1827

The Governor of Georgia successfully prevents President Adams from interference in that state's defrauding of the Indians.

On February 17, Governor George Michael TROUP informed Secretary of War James BARBOUR that the Georgia militia would prevent any federal attempt to interfere with Georgia's right to expel the Creek and Cherokee Indians from land between the Flint and Chattahoochee Rivers. President Adams yielded to the governor, dooming the Indians to loss of their valuable lands.

This incident originated on February 12, 1826, when the U.S. Indian Commissioner Duncan C. Campbell persuaded several Creek chieftains to accept a small sum of money for 4,700,000 acres of their best land. The Treaty of Indian Springs was proclaimed by Adams but was later nullified when the president learned that fraud was involved in Campbell's transaction.

A second agreement, the Treaty of Washington, gave better terms to the Indians and was proclaimed by Adams on January 23, 1826.

In December 1826, Georgia's state assembly opposed the Treaty of Washington and declared the continued effectiveness of the Treaty of Indian Springs. Following the assembly's decision, Governor Troup called out the state militia and wrote to Secretary Barbour that Georgia would execute the Treaty of Indian Springs without federal interference. Preferring not to support the Indian claims by a dispute with Georgia, Adams permitted Georgia's troops to clear the region of the Creek and Cherokee Indians.

Adams's policy had future repercussions. Alabama and Mississippi devised programs to remove the Indians from valuable land that federal Indian treaties had awarded to the Indian tribes.

March 27, 1827

President Adams closes U.S. ports to British vessels coming from colonies in the western hemisphere.

Following the British legislation of June–July 1825, which closed U.S. trade to the West Indies, Adams sent Albert Gallatin to negotiate in London, but Gallatin had no success. Finally, on March 27, Adams acted under the U.S. trade act of March 1, 1823, by setting restrictions against British ships coming from the West Indies. Adams's failure to obtain the partly favorable commerce that Britain offered in the parliamentary act of June 24, 1822, was perhaps one of his major diplomatic mistakes. The West Indies trade became an issue in the presidential campaign of 1828 and contributed to Adams's defeat by Andrew Jackson.

August 3, 1827

The Harrisburg, Pennsylvania, Convention calls for a higher protective tariff.

Because many of the northern and northeastern manufacturers believed the tariff of 1824 did not provide sufficient protection, they decided to lobby for a higher tariff act. A new bill placing high duties on woolen textiles passed the House on February 10, 1827, but the Senate forces led by Vice President John Calhoun defeated the bill.

Because of the Senate action, the protective tariff faction decided to call a convention and petition Congress to pass a higher tariff. About 100 delegates from 13 northern states met at Harrisburg from July 30 to August 3, 1827.

The Harrisburg petition requested a minimum valuation of all imported textiles as well as higher duties on hemp, flax, hammered bar iron and steel, and other goods. Their petition was presented to Congress on December 24, 1827.

August 6, 1827

Anglo-American Convention renews the joint use of the Oregon Territory.

The treaty of 1818 that allowed subjects of both nations to have the "free and open" use of Oregon expired after 10 years. The convention of 1827 extended this principle indefinitely. The convention permitted either nation to abrogate the agreement after one year's notice.

During negotiations on the Oregon treaty between 1824 and 1826, the two parties had agreed on extending the 49° as the boundary from the Rockies to the Columbia River. The region between the Columbia to 49° north was still disputed: Britain desired the north bank of the river; the United States wanted the 49° as the boundary to the Pacific.

September 29, 1827

Anglo-American Convention is signed, agreeing to submit the northeast boundary question to arbitration.

This agreement resulted from negotiations between Albert Gallatin and two British commissioners, H. V. Addington and Charles Grant. These talks were part of a series of discussions on the northeast boundary that had been carried on after the signing of the Treaty of Ghent in December 1814. The Ghent agreement called on commissioners from each country to settle the dispute that originated at the Treaty of Paris in 1783.

By the 1820s the northeast boundary question involved two principal disagreements:

1. A 100-mile gap between Maine and New Brunswick that entailed 7,697,280 acres of land. The British desired as much of the area as possible to build a military road reaching to a warmwater port on the Bay of Fundy. The United States insisted on all of the 100 miles because the state of Maine claimed the area. The Maine authorities argued that Mitchell's Map of 1782, which John Adams used in the 1783 Paris talks, gave the 100-mile territory to the United States.
2. An area of 100,000 acres located at the head of the Connecticut River. The argument centered on which of two streams entering the Connecticut River should be considered as the headwaters.

In the 1827 convention, the two nations agreed to submit both questions to arbitration by some "friendly sovereign or state." According to the convention, each party would present its map with a supporting statement to the arbitrator. Each party could also offer a rebuttal of the other's statement.

Without knowing who would arbitrate, the Senate approved the convention by a vote of 34 to 4. The four objecting senators were from Maine and New Hampshire.

See December 7, 1831.

1828

January 12, 1828

Mexican-American Treaty is signed that recognizes the Sabine River as the boundary.

When Joel Poinsett became minister to Mexico, Secretary of State Clay instructed him to get a boundary "as far west as possible." The Mexicans knew the Americans desired to obtain more of their country and unalterably opposed making any concessions. Thus, Poinsett's offers of $1 million for one-half of Texas or $500,000 for a lesser grant of land made the Mexicans more suspicious of U.S. intentions.

In addition to opposing Poinsett's request for a land cession, the Mexican government refused to approve a commercial treaty until America accepted the Sabine River as the boundary line in accordance with the Spanish-American Treaty of 1819. Poinsett conceded, and on January 12 signed a treaty recognizing the Sabine boundary. The final ratification of the treaty was made in 1832.

May 19, 1828

Congress approves the "Tariff of Abominations."

The tariff of 1828 was an extremely high protective tariff passed because of conflicting political interests. Although this tariff is often considered a political tactic by the Jacksonians to ensure Adams's defeat in the 1828 presidential race, recent scholars contend that Martin Van Buren, Jackson's lieutenant in Congress, desired the high tariff for local New York interest groups, even though the Jacksonians normally opposed high tariffs.

Whatever the political purpose, the tariff hurt foreign imports by protecting American textile manufacturers as well as certain producers of raw materials. Initially, the Jacksonians in Congress designed the tariff to hurt New England textiles, but Senate amendments corrected these deficiencies enough to get New England's congressional votes.

During the 1828 presidential campaign, the tariff was denounced as one of "abominations." The dispute led to a controversy and split Jackson's followers during the 1830s.

December 3, 1828

Andrew Jackson is elected President.

Jackson, who had barely lost the election of 1824 in the U.S. House of Representatives, had organized his followers under Martin Van Buren of New York and John C. Calhoun of South Carolina. With their help, together with that of his western supporters, Jackson won 178 electoral votes; Adams received 83. Calhoun won the vice presidency with 171 votes.

Andrew Jackson. Photo taken by Matthew Brady. National Archives

December 19, 1828

The South Carolina legislature opposes the Tariff of 1828.

A set of eight resolutions that passed the South Carolina state legislature declared the tariff was unconstitutional, oppressive, and unjust.

Over the next two months, three other states followed South Carolina's example by opposing the tariff: Georgia on December 30; Virginia on February 4, 1829; Mississippi on February 5, 1829.

During this same period, John C. Calhoun prepared an essay to defend state sovereignty and minority states' rights. He proposed the right of a state to nullify any act of Congress that was unjust to that state. Titled "The South Carolina Exposition and Protest," Calhoun's essay was appended to South Carolina's resolutions opposing the tariff of 1828. In the essay, Calhoun's views laid the way for the nullification controversy of 1832.

The United States Gains Predominance in the Western Hemisphere

VI. EXPANDING AMERICAN RELATIONS

Oregon Dispute
Texas and the Mexican War
Early Canal Diplomacy
Trade with China and Japan

1829

March 6, 1829

Martin van Buren is commissioned as Secretary of State in Jackson's cabinet

Van Buren assumed his duties on March 28, serving as secretary until May 28, 1831.

August 25, 1829

Renewed effort to purchase Texas from Mexico is prepared by Secretary of State van Buren.

The secretary outlined proposals for the purchase of Mexican land and arguments designed to persuade the Mexicans to sell. Although the instructions were sent to Joel Poinsett, the U.S. minister to Mexico, in August 1829, they were followed by Anthony BUTLER, who replaced Poinsett on October 29, 1829. In fact, Butler, a close friend of President Jackson, seemed to have persuaded the new administration to continue the attempt to buy Texas.

In the August 1829 instructions, Van Buren agreed to raise the sum of $1 million offered by President Adams to "four or even five million dollars." Van Buren believed that the region was of small value to Mexico, especially because of the "notorious lack of confidence between Mexico and the present inhabitants of Texas."

For the next seven years, Butler tried to purchase part of the Mexican territory. Although he often informed Jackson that his mission verged on success, this does not appear to have been true. The more the Americans urged the sale of land, the more the Mexicans refused and became convinced that Washington caused their problems in Texas, where a revolution was brewing. Butler's efforts ceased in 1836, when the Texans declared independence for the Republic of Texas.

November 30, 1829

London Conference grants Greece complete independence from Turkey.

The conferees from France, Russia, and England chose Leopold of Saxe-Coburg to rule Greece. Leopold declined the offer, and in 1832 the powers selected Otto, a Bavarian prince, to be monarch of Greece.

1830

March 28, 1830

Convention of 1830 with Denmark settles American claims.

During the Napoléonic Wars, the French emperor asked Denmark to enforce his Continental System by confiscating American ships. After 1815, Americans claimed that the Danish prize courts unjustly allowed noncontraband goods to be seized. By 1827, the total claims of American merchants were $2,662,280.36.

At first, Denmark argued that decisions of its prize courts could not be reviewed by foreign powers. In 1827, Henry Wheaton, an international lawyer, became America's chargé d'affaires in Copenhagen. He disputed Denmark's arguments, saying that after a prize court made an award, the government of that country was responsible for any unjust award. The Danish government complied and in the Convention of 1830 offered a lump sum of $650,000 to be released from all claims of Americans.

May 7, 1830

America and the Ottoman Turkish government sign a commercial treaty.

In 1829, Secretary of State Van Buren had commissioned three delegates to obtain a trade treaty with Turkey. They were Captain James BIDDLE of the U.S. navy; David OFFLEY, U.S. consul at SMYRNA; and the State Department's Charles RHIND. The treaty gave America the most-favored-nation status and permitted American ships to navigate to and from the Black Sea. One secret article added to the treaty provided that the sultan could consult with Americans about the best means to buy lumber and build ships in America. According to Rhind, this article was necessary so the sultan would know he obtained a concession by granting the commercial treaty. As Rhind expected, the Senate rejected the secret article before approving the treaty on February 1, 1831. The sultan did not dissent, however, and exchanges were finalized on October 5, 1831.

May 28, 1830

An Indian removal policy is passed by Congress.

This program involved making new treaties with Indian tribes located between the Appalachian Mountains and the Mississippi River, to pay the cost of sending the tribes to new land west of the Mississippi. This would permit the eastern region to be settled entirely by the white man. The removal idea had been suggested by John C. Calhoun in 1823 and was used by the state of Georgia in an attempt to get Cherokee land by the Treaty of Indian Springs.

The Georgia action raised questions of federal jurisdiction over Indian treaties. John Quincy Adams had, however, overlooked the fact that Georgia violated the Treaty of Washington and carried out its own treaty with the Indians. In addition, states such as Georgia had difficulty in sending the Indians farther west.

The Indian Removal Act of 1830 resolved the federal-state dispute particularly because President Jackson eagerly carried out the new policy during his two terms of office. By 1837, Jackson's administration concluded 94 treaties to obtain Indian land and remove the tribes to western land. For example, in a treaty of December 29, 1835, the Cherokees surrendered all their land east of the Mississippi, for which they received $5 million plus transportation costs to their new land in the west.

Some Indian tribes refused to be removed. The most notable Indian resistance in the 1830s was the Illinois Black Hawk War of 1832 and the lengthy Florida Seminole War from November 1835 to August 14, 1843. The Indians' only choice was to sign or die.

See Treaty of Indian Springs, February 17, 1827.

July 5, 1830

A French expeditionary army captures Algiers and deposes the dey.

The French attack followed a dispute with Algiers caused when the dey slapped the French consul in the face and refused to accept French demands for satisfaction. The French were not certain about their future plans for Algeria, but throughout the 1830s and 1840s the government of Louis Philippe pursued a constant series of wars against the dey's successor,

Abd el-Kader of Mascara, making the country a de facto protectorate of France.

July 28, 1830

Revolution in Paris overthrows the government of the Bourbon king Charles X.

Following the restoration of the Bourbon dynasty to the French monarchy in 1815, Louis XVIII and his successor, Charles X, had steadily moved toward a more absolute regime, seeking to violate previously established French freedoms. By the summer of 1830, the liberals in the French legislature protested against the king's attempts to abolish these liberties.

On July 28, radical republicans led by the Marquis de Lafayette raised barricades in Paris and took over the Hotel de Ville (City Hall). To withstand the radical action, the French Liberal Party of Adolphe THIERS sponsored a new candidate for the monarchy, LOUIS PHILIPPE, the duke of Orleans.

By July 30, the liberals, acting as a rump legislative body, revised the constitutional document of 1814 to permit the creation of a new constitutional monarchy under Louis Philippe.

October 5, 1830

President Jackson issues a proclamation opening the British West Indies trade on a partially reciprocal basis.

The Jacksonians had protested President Adams's loss of the West Indies trade in 1827, and in 1829 Jackson and Secretary Van Buren moved to settle the trade issue with the British. Louis McLane, the new minister to London, received instructions to inform the British that the recent election showed the American people had rejected Adams's action of 1827. Consequently, the Jackson administration was willing to comply with the British offer of 1822 for a restricted West Indies trade if Great Britain stood ready to return to that basis. McLane presented this offer to England in 1829, but the British were slow to respond to his request.

In May 1830, Jackson asked Congress to approve legislation that would implement his offer to the British, provided they agreed to open the West Indies trade. Because Jackson had not heard from McLane regarding the British response, he wanted Congress to grant him power to open the trade if Britain agreed. Before adjourning in May, Congress gave the president such power.

The congressional act helped McLane in his talks with Great Britain. After learning of the congressional resolution, the British agreed to recede from their order-in-council of July 1825, and to grant a partial opening of the West Indies trade as provided in their 1822 offer. The United States first had to rescind its discriminatory trade laws against Great Britain of 1818, 1820, and 1823. McLane assented and immediately wrote to Jackson that the British would open the West Indies trade as soon as the United States ended its discriminatory duties.

Jackson's proclamation of October 5 followed McLane's agreement by abolishing the American restrictions on Great Britain. On November 5, 1830, the British government revoked the 1825 order that had closed all West Indies trade to Americans. Unlike Adams, Jackson accepted the partial West Indies trade with British preferences for the members of its empire. Otherwise, trade with the West Indies was open on the best terms available since 1783.

For Adams's policy, see March 27, 1827.

November 16, 1830

Era of Whig Party reform begins in England.

Having campaigned on a program to liberalize trade and enlarge the British electorate, the Whigs defeated the Tory government of the Duke of Wellington. A Whig cabinet under Prime Minister Earl Grey took office. During the next two years, Grey's government extended the suffrage and reformed obsolete electoral laws. An era of reform sponsored by the industrial and commercial classes began. Internationally, the British gradually moved to an era of free trade that also sought to enlarge and solidify the British Empire.

1831

April 5, 1831

United States and Mexico sign treaties of commerce and the Texas boundary.

During President Adams's administration, Mexico tied these two treaties together, being ready to accept commercial terms only after the boundary settlement. The boundary treaty signed by Joel Poinsett on January 12, 1828, had to be renewed in 1831 because full ratification had not been made in the allotted time. When the treaty setting the boundary at the Sabine River was agreed to, Mexico also signed a most-favored-nation treaty of commerce. Before the commercial treaty was ratified, two additional technical protocols were added on September 17 and December 17, 1831. The U.S. Senate approved the treaties on March 23, 1832, and final ratifications were exchanged on April 5, 1832.

May 24, 1831

Edward Livingston replaces Van Buren as Secretary of State.

Livingston had been an aide to General Jackson at the Battle of New Orleans and served as senator from Louisiana from 1829 until his appointment as secretary by President Jackson. Livingston served until May 29, 1833, when Jackson sent him to Paris to try to settle the French spoliation claims issue.

Martin Van Buren resigned as secretary to permit Jackson to reorganize his cabinet and drop three of John C. Calhoun's friends from their offices. Vice President Calhoun and Jackson had completely severed their political ties over the tariff issue. As secretary of state, Van Buren gained Jackson's admiration and became the heir apparent to the presidency. Upon his resignation, Van Buren was appointed as minister to Great Britain. When congress returned for its next session in December 1831, John Calhoun led the Senate forces that vetoed Van Buren's new appointment.

July 4, 1831

A treaty between France and the United States settles American spoliation claims.

Claims of each nation for the attacks on their shipping going back to the 1790s had been unsuccessfully negotiated for over 30 years. By the agreement of July 4, France consented to pay 25 million francs in six annual installments for claims due Americans; the United States agreed to pay 1.5 million francs to settle all French claims. In an additional treaty clause, France forfeited its claim to most-favored-nation treatment at New Orleans in return for lower duties on French wine imported to America.

July 20, 1831

Secretary Livingston seeks to discover if a Dutch company has permission from Colombia to build a canal in Nicaragua.

Livingston instructed the U.S. chargé to the Central American States, W. N. Jeffers, to find out if that federated government had granted the Dutch rights to build a canal. If possible, Jeffers was to request rights for U.S. citizens to purchase canal stock. He was also to report to Washington on the feasibility of a canal across Nicaragua and on how long construction would take. Jeffers learned that no Dutch company had been granted canal-building rights. Nevertheless, Livingston's inquiry indicated the early American interest in such a canal connecting the Atlantic and the Pacific Oceans.

September 8, 1831

The Russian army captures Warsaw, ending the Polish revolution of 1830–1831.

By the Treaty of Vienna of 1815, Czar Alexander I granted Poland some autonomy as well as a constitution. However, Poland was placed in a permanent union with Russia and garrisoned by Russian troops. In 1830, Polish rebels successfully expelled the czar's army garrison and declared the Romanov czar was deposed.

Poland's liberation was short-lived. In the summer of 1831, Russian forces invaded and regained control of Warsaw on September 8. Poland lost its constitution and Czar Nicholas I began a policy designed to Russify the Polish people; that is, to eliminate the Polish language and culture in favor of the Russian way of life.

December 7, 1831

President Jackson and the U.S. Senate reject the arbitrator's decision on the northeast boundary.

In accordance with the convention of 1827, William B. Lawrence, America's chargé in London, and Britain's Foreign Secretary Lord Aberdeen agreed to have the king of the Netherlands arbitrate the northeast boundary dispute. Because the Netherlands king was a relative of the British king, the United States preferred arbitration by the Russian czar or the king of Prussia, but both of these rulers refused to serve.

Later historic evidence indicates the United States had the best case; Albert GALLATIN's mistakes are blamed for the United States not proving its case to the king. Gallatin used Mitchell's Map of 1755, which did not define the highlands territory dividing the rivers flowing into the St. Lawrence River and the Atlantic Ocean. Mitchell's Map of 1782, which John Adams used at the negotiations of the Treaty of Paris, clearly delineated the region and demonstrated where the "St. Croix River" began and flowed to the Bay of Fundy. The British had presented "MAP-A" to the arbitrator, but this map did not clarify the issue, a factor that assisted Britain's case.

Because neither "Map A" nor the Map of 1755 settled the dispute, the king of the Netherlands could not make an exact decision. He decided, however, to change his role to that of mediator and proposed the division of the two disputed areas, giving Britain the northern half and America the southern half. This mediation satisfied Great Britain because it received land on which it could build its desired military road. The two states of Maine and New Hampshire were not pleased, and Jackson was not certain what to recommend. The compromise seemed generally acceptable to Jackson, but he did not want to damage his political chances in New England. Therefore, the president offered the arbitration decision to Congress for its "advice" without a recommendation.

After a Senate committee report opposed the arbitrator's decision, the Senate voted to accept that committee report. The committee asserted the United States had no obligation to accept the judgment of the king of the Netherlands because he went beyond his duty in offering a compromise as a mediator. Therefore, the committee advised President Jackson to begin new negotiations with Great Britain. After the Senate concurred with the committee, Jackson followed its advice. The arbitration plan of 1827 had not resolved the northeast boundary dispute.

See September 29, 1827.

1832

January 26, 1832

Falkland Islands crisis between America and Argentina: Jackson sends a minister to resolve the dispute.

On January 26, Jackson and Secretary Livingston decided to send a new chargé d'affaires, Francis Baylies, to Buenos Aires to attempt to resolve a dispute that had arisen in 1831 at the Falkland Islands.

Although possession of the Falklands was contested by Argentina and Great Britain, the Argentine government appointed Louis VERNET as governor of the Falklands in June 1829. Vernet received political and military rights over the islands as well as exclusive fishing rights. In 1831, Vernet used his authority to seize three American sailing ships: the *Breakwater*, the *Superior*, and the *Harriet*. The *Breakwater* escaped from Vernet, who forced the other two ships to accept a fishing license in return for a share of their profits. Vernet also required the ships' captains to allow the *Superior* to continue its work while the *Harriet* was taken as a prize ship to Buenos Aires.

Because the American minister to Argentina had recently died, the protest against Vernet's action was made by George W. Slocum, the U.S. chargé d'affaires. When the Argentine authorities ignored his protest, Slocum enlisted the assistance of Commander Silas Duncan of the U.S. naval warship *Lexington*. Duncan had been sent to the South Atlantic in June 1831, with instructions to "protect the commerce of citizens of the United States by all lawful and honorable means within your power."

Slocum and Duncan issued an ultimatum to Argentina on December 6, 1831. If within three days the *Harriet* was not restored to its captain and compensation agreed to for U.S. property damage, the *Lexington* would go to the Falklands and enforce compliance. The Argentine minister of foreign affairs, Thomas Manuel de Anchorena, rejected Slocum's threat, and on December 10, Duncan's ship sailed for the Falklands.

Duncan's raid on the Falklands succeeded. He disarmed the colonists, looted the settlement, and arrested many of the islanders, including seven of Vernet's lieutenants. Duncan carried his captives to Montevideo, where he told Slocum he would hold them until Buenos Aires met the American demands.

In his annual message of December 6, 1831, Jackson told Congress that three American vessels had been seized. He did not know about the activity of Duncan and Slocum until January. When he found out, he did not object to the vigorous steps they had taken.

On January 26, Livingston instructed Baylies on his negotiations. Baylies was to claim U.S. rights to fish in the South Atlantic and to obtain a treaty recognizing these rights. Argentina would have a choice: it could disavow Vernet, in which case a U.S. naval squadron would break up his colony and take the pirates to Buenos Aires for trial, or it could accept Vernet's illegal acts and make restitution to the United States.

See August 19, 1832.

February 5, 1832

The U.S. Minister to Great Britain, Martin van Buren, requests compensation for slaves taken from a wrecked ship in the Bahamas.

Van Buren's request referred to an American ship, the *Comet,* which was wrecked in the Bahama Islands while sailing from Alexandria, Virginia, to New Orleans. The 164 slaves on board were saved and taken by British officials to Nassau, where they were declared to be free.

Van Buren asked for compensation for the owners of the slaves, contending that this payment was as humane as freeing the slaves. He asked if the British intended to free every slave landed in a British colony by shipwreck or otherwise. If so, he argued, compensation for the property should be paid.

The British government referred the issue to English law officials, and, in 1836, Britain paid claims for property on the *Comet* as well as for another ship, the *Encomium,* which was wrecked in the Caribbean Sea in 1833.

July 14, 1832

Tariff of 1832 does not satisfy the southern nullification proponents.

Although the 1832 tariff freely admitted cheap raw wool and flax and ended some of the features of the 1828 tariff that were disliked by northern manufacturers, the south viewed it as entirely a northern measure. The passage of the act revived Calhoun's doctrine of nullification as published in December 1828. In the south, the idea of nullification had spread, but forces of national unity prevented southerners from using the concept. Passage of the tariff of 1832 caused the forces of nullification to gain strength in southern state governments and led to attempts to reject the tariff bill.

August 19, 1832

Baylies is not able to solve the Falklands dispute with Argentina.

Baylies reached Buenos Aires to confer with its acting foreign minister, Manuel Vicente de Maza, on June 20. During the next five weeks, Baylies's arrogant attitude and the Argentine's outrage at Duncan's activity prevented any settlement of the crisis. De Maza blamed Duncan, not Vernet, for the trouble. Therefore, de Maza demanded U.S. reparations before further negotiations could take place.

By August 14, Baylies realized the talks were fruitless, and he decided to go home. Upon leaving Argentina, he wrote to Livingston that he had "attempted to soothe, and to conciliate and coax these wayward and petulant fools long enough. They must be taught a lesson or the United States will be viewed with contempt through South America."

Baylies's return ended the 1832 American crisis with Argentina over the Falklands. The United States left the rest to Great Britain. The British had long claimed the islands, and after Duncan disarmed the settlers in 1831, London decided it was time to act by occupying the Falklands.

For antecedents of this dispute, see January 26, 1832; for the British action, see December 15 (ca.), 1832.

October 14, 1832

American claims against the Two Sicilies are paid by the convention of 1832.

The U.S. claims against the Kingdom of the Two Sicilies originated when the state confiscated goods under Napoléon's commercial decrees from 1806 to 1814. The United States held that the Neapolitan government was responsible for depredations to American ships; the king's minister contended that the claims occurred when an interloper—Napoléon's brother-in-law Joachim Murat—controlled Naples.

In 1832, John NELSON, the U.S. minister to the Two Sicilies, persuaded the government to settle the claims. Nelson later wrote the State Department that the "friendly visit" of a squadron of American warships aided the negotiations. In the convention, the king of the Two Sicilies agreed to pay America $2,119,230 over a 10-year period at 4% interest.

December 5, 1832

President Jackson is reelected in an overwhelming victory.

Jackson received 219 electoral votes and a popular vote of 687,502; Clay won 49 electoral votes and 530,189 popular votes; William Wirt carried the 7 electoral votes of Vermont; and John Floyd took the 11 votes of South Carolina. Martin Van Buren was elected vice president with 189 votes.

The 1832 campaign was the first to have national nominating conventions: the National Republican Convention nominated Clay on December 12, 1831; the Democratic Party convention endorsed Jackson for a second presidential term and Van Buren for vice president; William Wirt was the candidate of the Anti-Masonic Party.

December 15 (ca.), 1832

British send a sloop of war to reclaim the Falkland Islands.

The British ship arrived at Berkely Sound and ordered the Argentine commander to leave. Because the British had superior firepower, the Argentines evacuated the islands and the British raised their flag at Port Egmont in January 1833.

The British claimed the islands by right of the first sighting by Sir Richard Hawkins in 1594 and by possession in 1765. The Spanish had taken the islands in 1770 but apologized and returned them to England in 1771 after a sharp diplomatic dispute.

The British did not settle the islands, however, and the Falklands had no formal government until 1820, when Argentina claimed them on the basis of former Spanish sovereignty. In 1828, Buenos Aires granted Louis Vernet the control of the islands and the exclusive fishing rights. Woodbine Parish, the British minister, protested Vernet's grant and firmly denied Argentina's right to the islands.

Until December 1832, however, the British did not try to reclaim the Falklands. Even after raising the flag in January 1833, the British did not send colonists to the islands. They did actively renew the dispute with Argentina for the next 10 years. Finally, in 1841, Parliament established a penal colony in the islands and prisoners were sent there.

Subsequently, the Americans agreed that the British claim did not violate the Monroe Doctrine.

See January 14, 1839.

December 18, 1832

Commercial treaty is signed between Russia and the United States.

James Buchanan, U.S. minister to St. Petersburg, and Russia's Foreign Minister Count Nesselrode signed a treaty of navigation and commerce. The treaty followed the earlier American preference for a reciprocal system of navigation duties and port fees. One clause of the treaty extended the commercial provisions to the Kingdom of Poland, which was under Russian jurisdiction during the 19th century. The U.S. Senate consented to the treaty on February 27, 1833, and final ratifications were exchanged on May 11, 1833.

1833

February 12, 1833

Henry Clay introduces a compromise tariff that resolves the nullification controversy.

Controversy over the 1832 tariff caused intense friction between Jackson and Vice President Calhoun during the fall and winter of 1832–1833. South

John C. Calhoun, Andrew Jackson's first vice president, and later secretary of state. Photo by Matthew Brady. National Archives

Carolina adopted an ordinance to nullify the tariffs of 1828 and 1832 (November 24) and a law to enforce the nullification ordinance by raising a military force and funds for armaments. Jackson alerted the federal forts in Charleston (October 29) and issued a Proclamation to the People of South Carolina telling them that nullification was an "impractical absurdity" and that "disunion by armed force is treason" (December 10, 1832). Finally, John C. Calhoun resigned as vice president on December 28 to lead the nullification battle.

Senator Clay saved the day by formulating a compromise tariff that made both sides believe they had won a victory. Clay's bill passed the House on February 26, 1833, and the Senate on March 1. Jackson signed it the next day.

The Compromise Tariff of 1833 expanded the list of free products, including worsted goods and linens, and provided for a gradual reduction of all duties over 20% at two-year intervals from 1834 to 1842.

May 29, 1833

Louis McLane is commissioned to replace Livingston as Secretary of State.

McLane was a senator from Delaware when Jackson appointed him as minister to Great Britain in 1829. He served in London until 1831, returning to America to become secretary of the Treasury, which post he occupied until May 1833. McLane was appointed secretary of state in a political arrangement that sent Livingston to Paris as minister and transferred Attorney General W. J. Duane to the Treasury Department as its secretary.

September 21, 1833

Edmund Roberts completes a successful mission to southeast Asia when he signs commercial treaties on each side of the Indian Ocean. The two treaties are with Siam and Muscat.

President Jackson commissioned Roberts in January 1832 to seek treaties with the kings of Siam and Cochin China. Roberts's visit to Cochin China was not successful, but at his second stop in Bangkok, Siam, he negotiated a treaty that was signed on March 30, 1833.

In Siam, he heard that the ruler Sa'id ibn Sultan of Muscat (Oman) might be willing to make a trade agreement. Roberts crossed the Indian Ocean to the southeast corner of Arabia and obtained a treaty on September 21, 1833.

The Senate consented to the two treaties on June 30, 1834. Final ratifications were exchanged with Muscat on September 30, 1835, and with Siam on May 14, 1836.

1834

February 17, 1834

Convention with Spain resolves a group of claims of American and Spanish citizens.

This is the so-called VAN NESS CONVENTION, which provided that Spain would pay a lump sum of 12 million reales for all outstanding U.S. claims against Spain.

April 22, 1834

In order to maintain constitutional regimes in both Portugal and Spain, France and Great Britain join those nations in a quadruple alliance.

In Spain, the alliance opposed Don Carlos, the pretender to the throne and an advocate of absolute monarchy. The allies defeated the Carlist faction in 1836 and established a moderate, limited monarchy under Isabella II and the constitution of 1837.

In Portugal, the allies combated Dom Miguel, who abolished the Portuguese constitution in 1828 and proclaimed himself as sole ruler. The British and French persuaded Dom Pedro to abdicate as king of Brazil and helped to restore his daughter Maria da Gloria as queen of Portugal. On May 26, 1834, the allies and Dom Pedro defeated Miguel and made Maria a constitutional ruler.

June 27, 1834

John Forsyth replaces McLane as Secretary of State.

McLane resigned his office because President Jackson rejected his advice to take strong measures against France by issuing letters of marque and making reprisals on French property. Roger TANEY, the secretary of the Treasury, opposed McLane's suggestion because he believed it would cause a war for which the United States was unprepared. Jackson agreed with Taney and continued to act in a conciliatory fashion toward France. McLane disliked Taney personally and had felt for some time his influence over Jackson was excessive. As a result, McLane resigned and Forsyth was appointed.

Forsyth had been governor (1827–1829) and senator (1829–1834) from Georgia prior to his appointment. He served as secretary during the remainder of Jackson's administration and during Van Buren's administration, leaving office on March 3, 1841.

For the French issue, see December 1, 1834.

December 1, 1834

In his annual message to Congress, President Jackson asks for power to compel France to pay the spoliation claims required by the treaty of July 4, 1831.

Although the spoliation treaty was 30 months old, the French Chamber of Deputies had not appropriated funds for the 25 million francs owed to Americans. The United States reduced its tariffs as required by the treaty, but the Paris banks would not honor a draft the U.S. Treasury presented for the 1833 payment of the claim. Jackson could understand the political problems involved in getting legislative action. He was more irritated that the ministers of Louis Philippe's government did not urge approval of the funding by the French Chamber.

Initially in 1834, Jackson sent Edward Livingston to Paris with special instructions designed to encourage French payment. This resulted in the ministry getting a vote in the legislature, but the Chamber of Deputies defeated the bill by a vote of 176 to 168.

In the spring of 1834, when news of the chamber's vote reached Washington, Secretary of State McLane wanted Jackson to take immediate reprisals. The president rejected this advice. Not only was the United States unprepared for war, but also Jackson sympathized with America's old friend and the stumbling beginnings of the new Orleanist government. Thus, Livingston was directed to continue for the next several months to urge favorable attention to the U.S. claim.

By December, Jackson still hoped for French compliance but wanted Congress to empower him to take stronger measures if necessary. Consequently, his message expressed the desire for peace and friendship with France but asserted that "these objects were not always secured by surrendering the rights of our citizens or permitting solemn treaties . . . to be abrogated or set aside." If the French chamber did not act properly at its next session, Jackson wanted authority to make reprisals on the French. International law, he claimed, permitted such seizures "without giving just cause for war." Jackson concluded on a less harsh note. "Collision with France," he said, "is to be regretted" because we share her ideals of liberal institutions. Nevertheless, France is wrong and "in maintaining our national rights and honor all governments are alike to us."

1835

April 29, 1835

A rupture in U.S.-French relations results from legislative politics in Paris and Washington: Livingston leaves Paris.

Livingston decided to end his attempt to settle the spoliation problem and leave Paris on April 29 because the French Chamber of Deputies recently passed a bill that affected the dignity and honor of the American president. The chamber agreed to pay the U.S. claims only after President Jackson explained the "offensive phrases" in his congressional message of December 1, 1834.

The rupture in Franco-American diplomacy was actually caused by internal politics in Washington and Paris. The spoliation claim was one pawn used by opponents of Jackson and French Premier Jacques Victor Albert, duc De Broglie. The French chamber sought mischief over the spoliation claim because it heard the news that the U.S. Congress adjourned in March without granting Jackson the powers he requested.

In Washington, Henry Clay and the Whig opposition caused Jackson discomfort. The Whigs controlled the majority of the Senate Foreign Relations Committee and, rather than support the president, wrote a report on January 14, 1835, that condemned his "warlike measures" and refused to grant him authority to make reprisals "at this time." The Senate opposition also prevented passage of a House bill that provided "contingent preparations" for fortifications. Jackson's House majority had rallied to support him, but the Whigs in the Senate adjourned in March 1835 without approving any support for Jackson's French policy.

Until de Broglie's opponents in the French assembly heard about the failure of the American Congress to back Jackson, there seemed to be hope for French settlement of the spoliation claims. The French newspapers did not like Jackson's message of December 1834, but Edward Livingston wrote Jackson that it was just what was needed to prod the French to act. Later, however, the news of congressional inaction inspired de Broglie's political opponents to upset the spoliation problem in April 1835.

In Paris, Louis Philippe's supporters had by 1834 divided into two political factions: a right-of-center party of resistance led by François GUIZOT and a left-of-center party of movement led by Adolph THIERS. The duc de Broglie sought to heal this breach in 1834 by forming a ministry that tried to unite the center deputies against the policies of Thiers and Guizot. In December 1834, de Broglie and his foreign minister, the Count DE RIGNY, did not, however, want to test their popularity by pushing the spoliation issue.

Jackson's message of December 1834 changed de Rigny's views. Although he objected to part of Jackson's harsh terms and recalled the French minister to America as a sign of dismay, he also told Livingston he would ask the chamber for 25 million francs to pay the spoliation claims.

In January, de Rigny submitted his bill to pay the spoliation claims, and Livingston believed most of the French delegates favored it. But in April trouble arose when news arrived that Congress did not support Jackson. One deputy, Antoine Pierre BERRYER, admitted that the chamber's rejection of the claims in 1834 did "not produce a war then, and congress has just adjourned in temper which leaves us nothing to apprehend."

Thus, when debate on the spoliation appropriation began in April, de Broglie's opponents amended the legislation. Eleanor Bernard à VALAZE introduced an amendment that would stop payment of the U.S. claim unless Jackson explained "the offensive phrases" of his 1834 message. The appropriation bill passed the chamber with this amendment.

On April 29, Livingston had no recourse but to obtain his passports and leave Paris. Before leaving, he explained to de Broglie that the 1834 message was an intragovernment communication to Congress, which should not concern the French government. Jackson, he told the premier, sincerely desired good relations with France. But de Broglie's precarious political situation prevented him from acting generously. He could not pay the claims, he said, until Jackson indicated in writing that his words of 1834 were only "bluster." France could not accept the assertion that the president's words were a "privileged communication."

Thus, the spoliation claims reached an impasse. The legislative limits of partisan politics in two governments continued a dispute that the executive officials in both countries desired to end.

See November 6, 1835, and February 5, 1836.

August 6, 1835

U.S. Ambassador to Mexico Anthony Butler is instructed to offer to buy Mexican territory as far west as San Francisco Bay.

Secretary of State Forsyth sent these instructions to Butler soon after Jackson had rejected a fantastic Butler scheme to buy Texas from Mexico.

Butler had returned to Washington in June 1835 to try to convince Jackson and Forsyth of his latest plot to buy Texas. He claimed a priest named Hernandez, who was a close friend of Mexican general Santa Anna's, could arrange the deal. All Butler needed was one-half million dollars "judiciously applied" (through bribery) to obtain negotiations. Jackson immediately rejected this plan. He told Butler to return to Mexico City for one final effort to purchase Texas. The president wanted the sale completed, if possible, by December.

It is not clear why Forsyth wrote the instructions of August 6, 1835. Whether Jackson really believed Mexico would sell more than Texas or whether the president simply wanted to try is not known. All that is certain is the existence of the August 6 message to Butler and Mexico's unwillingness to sell. Indeed, the Mexicans found the U.S. offers insulting. Perhaps the Mexican request in December for Butler's recall is related to the new offer he made.

See December 6, 1835.

November 6, 1835

U.S. Relations with France are completely severed when the U.S. chargé d'affaires decides to leave Paris.

Thomas P. Barton, the U.S. chargé, had continued attempts to settle the spoliation problem after Livingston left Paris in April 1835. Following Secretary of State Forsyth's orders, Barton had asked de Broglie when the United States could expect to receive the money due under the 1831 treaty. After some delay, de Broglie wrote to Barton that the funds were available any time that Jackson satisfactorily explained his previous insults against France.

Finding de Broglie adamant on the matter, Barton asked for his passports and left France on November 6. The French chargé at Washington was also recalled by de Broglie. The premier's recall did not reach Washington for over four weeks, and the chargé left America on January 2, 1836.

December 6, 1835

At Mexico's request, Anthony Butler is replaced as minister to Mexico.

During his six years in Mexico, Butler had wheedled, promised, and boasted that he could eventually persuade some Mexican official to sell all or part of Texas. His activity finally became too obnoxious, and the Mexican government requested that Jackson recall him. He was replaced as minister by Powhatan Ellis, who Secretary Forsyth hoped would improve relations with Mexico.

December 7, 1835

Jackson's annual message to Congress reports on the French issue in firm but conciliatory terms.

While U.S. relations with France had been severed on November 6, Jackson told Congress he would never apologize to France "for the statement of truth and the performance of duty." He desired, however, that France would fulfill its obligations so that "mutual good will" could be restored.

1836

February 5, 1836

France agrees to pay the U.S. spoliation claims.

The duc de Broglie decided to end the dispute with the United States just before he left office in favor of the ministry of Adolph Thiers. Although Jackson's December 7, 1835, address to Congress differed little in tone from that of 1834, de Broglie chose to interpret the message as satisfying the explanation required by the French law of April 1835.

Most likely French political problems influenced de Broglie's decision. Not only had his ministry failed to form a strong center faction but he had involved France in a dispute with Russia. Furthermore, the rise of radical movements in France caused internal problems that Thiers's ministry was to repair if it could.

Because de Broglie accepted Jackson's statement, the French payments under the 1831 treaty began and were completed by 1838. American-French relations improved once again.

March 6, 1836

The Alamo falls to Mexican forces.

The Battle of the Alamo took place because of increased friction between the Anglo-Americans in Texas and Mexico's government. As the Texans began to organize for rebellion, General Santa Anna, Mexico's military dictator, decided to assert his strong rule over Texas.

Mexican forces surrounded the Alamo, an outpost near San Antonio. For 12 days, 187 men led by Colonel William B. Travis held off 5,000 Mexican soldiers. On March 6, the Mexicans stormed the fort and killed all the defenders.

Santa Anna's early successes in Texas continued. On March 27 at Goliad, Texan irregulars under James Fannin surrendered to Santa Anna's superior

An 1885 painting of the storming of the Alamo, probably provides the most accurate view of the event. Library of Congress

force. The Mexicans responded with a massacre of the 300 Texans.

April 21, 1836

Texans win the battle of San Jacinto.

Santa Anna's victories at the Alamo and Goliad first caused panic among the Americans in Texas. Many fled toward the U.S. border with Mexican troops in pursuit.

At San Jacinto, Sam HOUSTON rallied the disorganized Texans and made a surprise attack on Santa Anna's army. Attacking during the Mexicans' siesta time, the Texans caught them unprepared. Santa Anna donned a common soldier's uniform and fled. He was captured in tall grass near the battlefield.

Rather than kill Santa Anna, Houston forced him to sign two treaties on May 14, 1836. One treaty was an armistice under which the Mexican army withdrew from Texas and a peace commission was to be created. The second was an agreement that Texas territory would not extend "beyond the Rio Grande." As soon as Santa Anna reached Mexico City, he denounced the treaties because they were made under duress. The Texans, however, claimed the treaties gave independence to the state of Texas.

December 7, 1836

Martin van Buren is elected President.

The Democratic Party convention nominated Van Buren on May 20, 1835. The Whig Party (a union of the National Republican Party and John C. Calhoun's southern faction) could not agree on a single nominee. The Whigs split and backed three candidates: Daniel WEBSTER, Hugh L. WHITE, and William H. HARRISON.

Van Buren won 170 electoral votes; Harrison received 73; White, 26; and Webster, 14. South Carolina gave its votes to Willie P. MANGUM.

The ballot for vice president produced no majority candidate. The election went to the Senate, where Richard M. Johnson, the Democratic Party nominee, won by 33 to 16.

December 21, 1836

President Jackson sends Congress a message on Texas but takes no stand on the recognition issue.

Although Texas declared independence in March 1836, no nation had yet recognized it. The Texan leaders sent two commissioners, George C. CHILDRESS and Robert HAMILTON, to Washington to gain recognition and possible annexation. Secretary Forsyth talked with the commission in April, but only as individuals, with no official status. Later, on June 25, Forsyth sent Henry M. MORFIT to Texas to gather information on the conditions of the state.

Texas took more steps toward independence before December 1836. David G. Burnet was made provisional president, Stephen F. Austin was named secretary of state, and W. H. Wharton became minister plenipotentiary to the United States.

In preparing his report to Congress, Jackson was most influenced by the strongly divided opinion on the Texas question. Some pro-slavery southern cities, such as Nashville, petitioned for the recognition of Texas. Northern abolitionists adamantly opposed the recognition or annexation of Texas.

Jackson equivocated in his report. He described the current situation in Texas and reminded Congress that at its last session Congress resolved to grant recognition "whenever satisfactory evidence" showed it had a functioning government. Until Mexico or another foreign power granted recognition, Jackson believed the facts did not warrant recognition. However, he implied, Congress could grant recognition if it desired.

1837

March 3, 1837

Congress recognizes the independence of Texas.

Although the slavery issue seriously divided Congress on the question of the annexation of Texas, most American politicians agreed that Texas should become an independent state. In his December 1836 report on Texas, President Jackson left the decision on recognition up to Congress, even though he would have liked another foreign nation to be the first to give recognition. Congress rejected this proposal and, on March 3, approved a resolution that recognized Texas and appropriated funds to send a diplomatic official to represent the United States. Jackson acted quickly. On his last day as president he signed the bill of recognition and appointed Alcie La Branche as the U.S. chargé d'affaires in Texas.

Sam Houston, President of the Republic of Texas (1836–1838, 1841–1844), later elected governor. National Archives

May 10, 1837

Panic of 1837 escalates when the New York banks suspend specie payments.

The panic developed from reckless speculation in land and canal building by state and local companies using loans from British banks. As in 1819, the panic first became evident when the price of cotton fell on the southern market, this time in New Orleans. Unemployment increased in the northeastern states, which led to demonstrations and food riots in New York City in February and March.

The May suspension of specie payments by the New York banks spread to the banks of Baltimore, Philadelphia, and Boston. Many of these banks held federal deposits, and the suspension of bill payments in gold and silver had repercussions that caused many banks to fail.

Most effects of the panic abated by 1840, but some western and southern states continued to suffer from the burden of debts incurred because of the boom in building canals and roads. In addition, after at least seven states and one U.S. territorial government defaulted on loan payments to Britain, a great amount of ill will toward America developed in England.

August 25, 1837

President van Buren rejects a request to annex Texas.

The issue of annexing Texas divided Americans too much in 1837 for Van Buren or any other politician to risk placing such a recommendation before Congress. Although the United States recognized Texas as an independent state, Secretary Forsyth told the Texan representatives that Mexico claimed a state of war existed with Texas.

After this definite decision by Forsyth and Van Buren, which rejected annexation, Texan officials withdrew their offer and pursued Texan development as the Lone-Star State. The annexation question was not raised again in Washington until 1842.

December 29, 1837

The *Caroline* incident causes antagonism between Americans and Canadians living near the northern New York border.

This incident took place because many Americans provided sympathy and assistance for Canadian rebels led by William L. MACKENZIE. The rebels sought independence for Canada from Great Britain but had largely been defeated by the time of the *Caroline* incident.

The *Caroline* was a small American steamer that had carried military supplies across the Niagara River to aid Mackenzie's rebels. In retaliation, a group of British volunteers rowed across the Niagara River on the night of December 29 and set the *Caroline* on fire. At least one American, Amos Durfee, died in the attack.

Although some Americans called for a retaliatory raid on Canada, President Van Buren delayed taking any countermeasures against Canada, and the tension subsided. Nevertheless, the McLeod incident of December 13, 1840, demonstrated that strong anti-British attitudes still existed in northern New York.

See May 29, 1838.

1838

January 5, 1838

President van Buren takes action to calm tensions with Canada.

To restore order in northern New York, Van Buren sent General Winfield Scott on a visit to border areas, where he mediated local problems between the two nations' citizens. Scott also persuaded the governors of Vermont and New York to call out the state militia to help keep order on the border. Although these steps did not entirely eliminate the existing antagonism, the border situation calmed down considerably in New York until the McLeod case of 1840 caused tensions to be renewed.

March 10, 1838

Because of Canadian border problems, Congress revises U.S. neutrality laws.

The *Caroline* incident of December 29, 1837, demonstrated a weakness in American neutrality regulations that permitted the United States to be a supply base for foreign rebellions. This situation had also existed from 1825 to 1836 on the Mexican border, but Congress did not wish to act effectively to stop American aid to Texas. When Mexico protested, President Jackson claimed that it was not possible to enforce U.S. neutrality on the long southern border.

British-Canadian protests brought a more effective attempt by Congress. The law of 1838 allowed the federal government to seize any vessels being used for hostile purposes against a neighboring state. In addition, the government could seize any suspicious vessels, vehicles, arms, or ammunition.

March 24, 1838

Buenos Aires is blockaded by a French naval squadron.

The French had indemnity claims against Argentina that the Argentine ruler José ROSAS refused to pay. These claims, plus French support for Uruguayan rebels seeking freedom from Argentina, led the French chargé in Buenos Aires to request naval assistance.

Because the United States had broken diplomatic relations with Argentina in 1832, there was no American official at Buenos Aires to report on the developments. The United States first took note of the blockade officially when Congressman Caleb Cushing requested the House of Representatives to obtain information on the blockade from the State Department on January 6, 1839.

May 29, 1838

Retaliating for the British sinking of the *Caroline*, an American group loots and burns a Canadian vessel, the *Sir Robert Peel*.

While traveling within U.S. jurisdiction on the St. Lawrence River, the *Sir Robert Peel* was boarded by a party of disguised Americans. The Americans set the boat's passengers ashore, yelling to them, "Remember the Caroline." Then they burned the ship. This was one of many incidents on the U.S. border in 1838 as anti-British emotions swelled. Some groups plotted the destruction of British power in Canada. Because neither London nor Washington had a genuine grievance, none of the incidents resulted in further conflict.

August 18, 1838

Expedition led by Charles Wilkes leaves to explore the South Seas.

The Wilkes expedition surveyed routes of U.S. whaling ships in the Pacific Ocean. In January 1840, Wilkes claimed the discovery of the continent of Antarctica. His ship coasted along the Antarctic barrier from 150° E to 108° E, an area subsequently named Wilkes Land. On his return to America, Wilkes supervised the preparation of a 19-volume report on his expedition.

1839

January 6, 1839

Information about the French blockades of Buenos Aires and Vera Cruz is requested from the State Department by a House of Representative resolution.

The French navy began a blockade of Argentina at the mouth of the Río de la Plata on March 24, 1838. In July 1838, the French navy also blockaded Vera Cruz, Mexico. These actions were interpreted by some Americans as violations of the Monroe Doctrine. Neither received much U.S. attention in 1838–1839.

In both blockades, France justified its action as a means to obtain claims due its citizens by Argentina and Mexico. The House resolution for information had been initiated by Caleb Cushing of Massachusetts. During the House debate on the resolution, Monroe's nonintervention principle was recalled. In 1838, the Monroe Doctrine lacked the sanctity of tradition later given to it; the State Department did not apply it by objecting to French activity.

Also, the United States had its own claims against Mexico as well as the Texan-Mexican problem. Therefore, it sympathized with the French demands for payment. In addition, Senator Henry Clay believed the French blockade at Vera Cruz aided the Texans by diverting the Mexican army. Finally, the French action at Vera Cruz was brief. After landing a few soldiers to demonstrate their serious intent, the French pulled out of the area.

The Argentina blockade dragged on until 1840. On one occasion, the American naval commander in the South Atlantic, Commodore J. B. NICHOLSON, tried but failed to mediate between France and Rosas. Eventually, on October 29, 1840, Great Britain ended the blockade by persuading the two sides to accept the Mackau Convention. This agreement sought to compromise the dispute by arranging periodic payments of French claims. When the Rosas government violated the pact, the French renewed their blockade in 1845.

In Congress, Cushing's resolution was attacked as a Whig Party attempt to embarrass President Van Buren. The resolution failed to pass because the Democrats controlled the House.

January 14, 1839

The Secretary of State interprets the British seizure of the Falklands as outside the intent of the Monroe Doctrine.

Because the Argentine dispute over the Falklands persisted, the Argentine minister to the United States asked Secretary of State Forsyth if the Monroe Doctrine statement against further colonization in the Western Hemisphere did not apply. Forsyth, as apparently President Jackson had done in 1833, argued that the British claim to the island went back to 1771, antedating Monroe's speech to Congress. Therefore he told Carlos M. ALVEAR, the Argentine minister, that the United States had to remain neutral in the dispute.

Alvear also asked for compensation for the destruction inflicted on the Falklands by Commodore Duncan in 1831. Forsyth defended Duncan's action, contending that Vernet had acted irresponsibly toward the U.S. ships. In addition, Forsyth stated that he doubted the validity of Argentina's grant to Vernet, because the British had a valid claim to the islands.

In brief, the Monroe Doctrine was not used against Britain in the Falklands case because the British had held the territorial rights since 1771.

February 27, 1839

"Restook War" on the Maine-Canadian border ends with a Modus Vivendi.

Unlike the *Caroline* crisis of December 29, 1837, the "Restook War" evolved from a dispute on the northeast boundary that had been unsuccessfully argued and negotiated since 1783.

In 1838, Maine's government organized and armed a civil posse to build and maintain fortifications on the boundary line claimed by the state of Maine. Soon settlers from both nations moved into the disputed land and in some cases made counterclaims to the same plots. Clashes between these settlers grew more frequent, especially in the fertile Aroostook River valley, where the Restook War took place.

To resolve the disputes and restore order, President Van Buren sent General Winfield Scott to the area, and Congress empowered the president to call out the militia and enroll 50,000 volunteers if necessary. Scott and a small army occupied the forts built by Maine and negotiated an understanding between the local leaders of Maine and New Brunswick. Each party in the disputed territory agreed to hold only the territory it currently occupied until negotiations between England and the United States could resolve the problem.

April 19, 1839

The American consul at Canton reports the Chinese know the United States does not share Britain's views on the opium trade.

Peter W. SNOW, the consul at Canton, tried to separate American policy from the British as much as possible when the Chinese sought to end the opium trade. Snow had followed the other European consulates on February 26, 1839, when the Chinese executed an opium dealer on the square in front of the foreign consular factories. The foreign officers thought this execution at that place was an insult and took down their nations' flags.

Generally, however, Snow followed advice received in consultation with American merchants in Canton who wished to continue their trade despite British problems. From 1805 to 1839, the U.S. ships had engaged in some opium trade. The Americans brought Turkish opium, which was considered inferior to the Indian opium brought in by the British. While estimates of the opium trade are difficult, Tyler Dennett believes only about 10% of the U.S. trade value to China before 1839 was in opium.

Snow's efforts to separate the United States from British interests had a significant immediate result. During the opium war, other Europeans followed the British consul first to MACAO and later to Hong Kong. Consequently, the U.S. merchants at Canton gained a trade bonanza, carrying much trade of the Europeans between Canton and Macao or Hong Kong without foreign competition in tea and silks. Although the Americans in Canton could not leave their port factories, there was no evidence of ill will between the U.S. merchants and the Chinese.

May 10, 1839

The entire Bible is translated into the Hawaiian language by American missionaries.

The first U.S. missionaries to Hawaii left Boston in 1819, led by Reverend Hiram BINGHAM. In Hawaii, they set up churches and schools and devised a written language for the Hawaiian people so that the Bible could be printed and read. By 1839, the entire Bible was available for the Hawaiians to read.

May 25, 1839

American merchants in Canton petition Congress for an agent to negotiate a commercial treaty with China and a suitable force to protect Americans.

Although the Americans were not directly jeopardized by the Anglo-Chinese war, they believed England would win and gain a treaty with China. The Americans wanted to prepare to retain their equal trade status with the Europeans whenever a settlement was reached. The petitioners did not expect that the U.S. naval force would need to fight but would apply pressure on China as the British often did. The merchants' petition reached Washington in early January 1840, and Abbot Lawrence of Massachusetts presented it to the House of Representatives.

September 6, 1839

Spain demands the release of its ship *Amistad* and the return of Negro mutineers to Cuba.

This Spanish note to Secretary Forsyth resulted from an unusual series of circumstances extending back to June 1839. The *Amistad* left Havana, Cuba, with two Spaniards, José Ruiz and Pedro Montes, and their 50 Black slaves. On the high seas the slaves revolted, killed the ship's captain, and ordered Ruiz and Montes to take them back to their homes in Africa, from which they had recently been captured.

The *Amistad* sailed instead to Long Island Sound, where an American warship captured it and took it to New London, Connecticut. The American captain, T. R. GEDNEY, then sued the owners of the *Amistad* for salvage claims because he rescued the ship from mutiny.

Meanwhile, José Ruiz had been arrested in New York on the charge of enslaving free Africans. Ruiz awaited trial by the courts of New York.

In reply to Spanish protests, Secretary Forsyth explained that the federal government could not interfere with court action in Connecticut and New York. The *Amistad* case was not resolved until March 9, 1841.

November 3, 1839

The Opium War begins between Great Britain and China.

British efforts to persuade China to legalize the opium trade had been rejected by the Chinese between 1836 and 1839. On March 10, 1839, the Chinese commissioner at Canton seized the local opium stores and burned them. This led to hostility between British and Chinese forces that continued intermittently until August 29, 1842.

1840

March 16, 1840

Telling Congress that Americans are "angels of light" in China, Congressman Caleb Cushing begins the myth that America alone respects China's rights and laws.

Cushing spoke in the House of Representatives regarding the British war in China relative to the United States. He told Congress that Americans did not wish to join with England in China. The English conduct in China was outrageous and should not be accepted by Americans. The historian Tyler Dennett concluded that Cushing thus began the myth of U.S. kindness and idealism in China, a myth cherished by many Americans but not based on facts regarding American conduct in the Chinese trade either before or after 1840.

To be sure, there was a difference in U.S. and British attitudes toward the Chinese. Although merchants of both nations sought to profit handsomely from the China trade, the critical difference in the 19th century was the presence of the British navy in sufficient strength to be used when necessary. American activity was primarily through diplomatic or commercial agents. The U.S. naval squadron in the China seas was too small to act effectively and was usually controlled by U.S. diplomats.

For more on Cushing's views, see July 3, 1844.

December 2, 1840

William Henry Harrison wins the Presidential Election.

The Whig Party Convention nominated Harrison on December 4, 1839, and agreed with Thurlow Weed of New York to unite on one candidate. The Democratic Convention nominated Van Buren for reelection but divided on the issue of a vice presidential candidate and selected no one.

Harrison won 234 electoral votes to Van Buren's 60. The Whig vice presidential nominee, John Tyler, also received 234 votes and was elected.

December 13, 1840

Great Britain demands the immediate release of Alexander McLeod: Secretary Forsyth cannot comply.

McLeod, a Canadian deputy sheriff, had been arrested while visiting New York and charged with the murder of Amos Durfee, who died during the British raid on the *Caroline* in 1837. McLeod was in prison awaiting his trial when the British protested to Secretary of State Forsyth and demanded McLeod's release. Great Britain contended that the *Caroline* raid had been an authorized military expedition, and its participants could not be charged with murder.

As in the case of the Spanish ship *Amistad*, Forsyth explained to the British that while he could try to have the case changed to a federal court, New York state had current jurisdiction over McLeod.

While newspaper editors and popular comment in New York and England expressed feelings of possible war, the McLeod incident ended when the prisoner was acquitted. McLeod's trial took place in Utica, New York, during the summer of 1841. Partly because the local prosecutor conducted a weak case, partly because McLeod had an alibi of being five or six miles away from the scene of the *Caroline*, the Utica jury needed only 20 minutes to find him not guilty.

In a belated effort to prevent such incidents in the future, Congress passed legislation in 1842 that gave federal courts jurisdiction over persons accused of a crime committed under orders of a foreign government.

1841

March 5, 1841

Daniel Webster is named Secretary of State by President William H. Harrison.

Following Harrison's death, Webster continued to serve as secretary under President Tyler until May 8, 1843. Webster was one of America's most prominent leaders in the pre–Civil War era. Apart from the northeast boundary treaty he arranged with England when he was secretary, his most significant public service dealt with domestic affairs.

March 9, 1841

The U.S. Supreme Court frees the Africans in the *Amistad* case.

The Spanish owners of the slaves brought to the United States after a mutiny had sued in the courts for return of their property. On March 9, 1841, the highest court of appeal sustained a lower-court action that freed the Blacks to return to Africa. According to the court, Spanish law did not permit slaves; hence, they had not been property of the owners. After the Blacks were freed, anti-slavery groups raised money to permit them to return to their homes in Africa. This case contrasts with the *Creole* case, where U.S. law permitted slavery.

See March 22, 1842.

April 4, 1841

President Harrison dies of pneumonia and is succeeded by John Tyler.

Although Henry Clay and the congressional Whig majority had planned to control Harrison's programs, they could not accomplish this with President Tyler, who constantly quarreled with the Whigs in Congress. As a result, Harrison's early death of pneumonia caused a division in the Whig Party. The dispute in 1841 centered primarily over the Whigs' desire to incorporate the Fiscal Bank of the United States, an institution intended to revive the central bank that the Jacksonians had liquidated.

November 22, 1841

John Quincy Adams denounces China's "tribute trade" as being anti-commercial.

Adams's speech on November 22 demonstrates the ethnocentric Western views of Asian cultures that Americans viewed as "barbarism." He also understood better than did Caleb Cushing (see March 16,

Secretary of State Daniel Webster

1840) the basis of the problem between the Western powers and China.

Adams's speech to the Massachusetts Historical Society explained that the Chinese were a self-sufficient empire that admitted no need for commercial intercourse abroad and held outsiders to be inferior beings. Nations seeking trade with China, he said, were considered to be "tributary nations" who brought gifts and performed a kowtow (ritualistic bow) to the emperor, if he received them. Adams believed that the Chinese practice was an "enormous outrage upon the rights of human nature," and that the Western nations should force the Chinese to stop it. This, he said, was the root cause of England's Chinese war, which was not just over a "few chests of opium."

Adams, of course, saw commerce as a positive good as well as an American right. The Chinese, whose civilization went back to the Ch'in dynasty of 220 B.C. or the Shan era of 2500 B.C., did not find external commerce to be necessary but rather disruptive of China's social order. Throughout its long history, China admitted trade from its neighbors (and even the Italian Marco Polo) on a congenial basis as long as the foreigners followed and respected Chinese customs. The Anglo-Saxons in particular wanted to trade but wished to fix trading terms and refused to kowtow to China's customs in any respect.

Both Adams and Cushing represented American attitudes toward East Asia that have lingered into the present and poorly served U.S. policy in that region of the world.

December 2, 1841

Secretary of the Navy Abel P. Upshur's annual report notes that U.S. Naval officers need higher ranks to take their proper place in diplomatic gatherings.

Upshur observed the valuable role naval officers had in representing the United States, both in conducting explorations at sea and in their duties in many foreign lands. But the government had not provided them titles of rank that gave them equality or better with admirals of other foreign navies. Many American ship commanders were lieutenants or captains, but a few were commodores. Therefore, he desired that Congress add U.S. naval ranks for officers to attain, such as admiral.

Upshur also advocated the creation of naval bases in the Pacific Ocean. The United States, he contended, needed a naval establishment in Hawaii, where many U.S. ships stopped, and somewhere on the Pacific coast between the Columbia River and the Guayaquil. Such a Pacific coast base would of course be at the expense of Mexican territory, which contained valuable ports in that region.

1842

January 29, 1842

Secretary Webster objects to British action in the *Creole* case, arguing that Britain's colonial authorities should aid the shipowner in cases where mutineers (even if slaves) come to British ports.

The *Creole* was a U.S. ship carrying a cargo of slaves from Virginia to New Orleans. At sea, the slaves mutinied and forced the ship's mate to go to Nassau in the Bahama Islands. The British freed all the slaves except the 19 who led the mutiny. These 19 were kept at Nassau on criminal charges.

In his note to Edward Everett, the U.S. minister in London, Webster argued that the law of nations obliged local authorities to aid the ship's owners and crew of a mutinied vessel, and to protect the ship's property, including slaves, until the ship's lawful voyage continued. Webster demanded an indemnity for the conduct of the Nassau officials and assurances of correct conduct in the future.

Although Webster argued against British action on the legal basis that the hospitality of port officers should require them to oppose mutiny and protect property, some anti-slavery spokesmen such as Joshua Giddings contended that Webster's protest was in favor of slavery.

See March 22, 1842.

March 22, 1842

Joshua R. Giddings fails to obtain congressional legislation to prohibit the coastal trade in slaves.

Because of the *Creole* case, against which Webster protested to the British, Giddings, a Whig congressman from Ohio, presented legislation restricting the American coastal trade in slaves, a proposal that stimulated intense opposition from southern representatives. Giddings assailed Webster and argued slaves had a right to recover their freedom by any means and should not again be enslaved.

Giddings's propositions failed to pass, but the debate in Congress required Webster to explain to the British Minister Lord Ashburton that his argument, not Giddings's, reflected the American reasons for desiring to make certain that British port officials respected U.S. property that entered their ports because of distress on the high seas, whether mutiny or bad weather.

March 30, 1842

The Whigs under Tyler reinstitute a protective tariff at the level of 1832.

This measure passed Congress following the lapse of the gradual tariff reductions provided under the Compromise Tariff of 1833. The Whigs retained tariff levels of duties of between 23% and 35% until their defeat in the election of 1844.

June 28, 1842

Texas and Great Britain ratify treaties concerning commerce, opposition to the slave trade, and the public debt.

These three treaties between Britain and the Republic of Texas had been pending since 1840 because the Texas legislature was reluctant to approve the slave-trade agreement. Great Britain insisted that the slave trade must end before it would approve a commercial agreement. By June 28, the Texas legislature agreed and the treaties were fully ratified. The "public debt" convention had two important parts: (1) Britain would mediate with Mexico to recognize Texans independence; (2) after gaining such recognition, Texas would assume £l million of Mexico's debt to Great Britain.

The increased contact between Texas and such foreign nations as Great Britain and France caused some Americans to urge the annexation of Texas. Both President Tyler and former President Jackson believed the United States had to act quickly to make Texas a state.

August 9, 1842

The Webster-Ashburton Treaty is signed to settle the northeast boundary dispute.

To persuade the representatives of Maine and Massachusetts to relinquish their claim to over 3 million acres of land on their borders, Secretary of State Webster accepted a map that others knew to be false. Either because he was eager to settle the long-standing quarrel or because of neglect, Webster's negotiations gave Britain land to which the United States held a valid title.

There were two curious circumstances of the Webster-Ashburton negotiations:

1. The British Foreign Office and two Americans misled Webster regarding the maps used in the lengthy border dispute. John Adams used a copy of Mitchell's Map of 1782 at the Paris Peace Conference of 1782–1783. This map validated the U.S. claims in the area of the "St. Croix" and Connecticut Rivers. Although Webster did not have a copy of the 1782 map, the British Foreign Office did and it had been seen by Jared Sparks, a Harvard scholar, and by Edward Everett, the U.S. minister to London. Neither Sparks nor Everett told Webster about the existence of the 1782 map. Later, they explained they had pledged as gentlemen not to reveal the privileged information about the British files.

Sparks, who was an Anglophile, misled Webster even more by telling him of another map that validated the English claim. This map was, said Sparks, by a French cartographer, "d'Anville," and had been found in the papers of the Count de Vergennes, the French foreign minister in 1782. Although he did not have a copy of the d'Anville map, Sparks gave Webster a map on which he drew from "memory" a red line marking the 1782 agreement. He gave this map to Webster, who used it to convince the representatives of Maine and Massachusetts that their land claims were wrong.

The British, of course, willingly accepted the d'Anville map line as drawn by Sparks. It gave them the land they needed for a military road to the Bay of Fundy, their principal objective during the negotiations. The action or inaction of Sparks and Everett is questionable at the least. Why Everett gave a gentleman's word precedence over the interest of the nation he represented is a difficult question to answer. Sparks's action seems even more duplicitous. He not

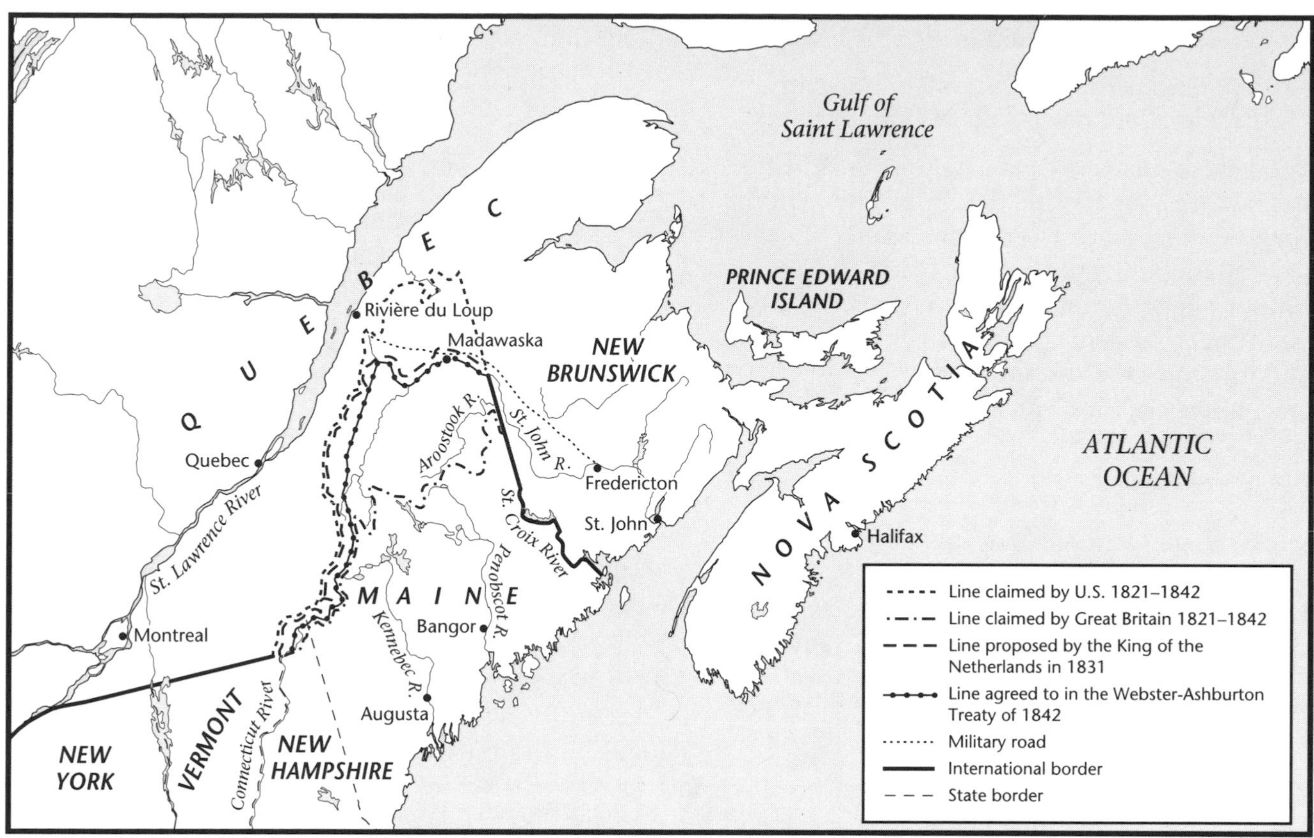

Northeast Boundary Settlement, 1842

only provided Webster with data on a nonexistent French map, but he also accepted $14,500 from Lord Ashburton for "expenses" to travel to New England to convince the Maine-Massachusetts leaders that they should accept British claims by showing them his d'Anville map. One historian estimates that expenses for such a visit in 1842 would have been about $450.

2. In the Webster-Ashburton Treaty, the United States received less land than the king of the Netherlands arbitration had awarded America in 1831. Maine got 4,489,600 acres of land; New Brunswick got 3,207,680 acres. In the Connecticut River valley, the United States retained its fortress at Rouse's Point near Lake Champlain and received most of the 100,000 acres under dispute. The United States paid Maine and Massachusetts each $150,000 plus the expenses they incurred in defending the area since 1783.

Whatever the dubious character of Webster's Treaty, the northeast boundary was finally settled. The U.S. Senate ratified the treaty on August 20, 1842, and final ratifications were exchanged on October 13, 1842. One year later, Americans learned the truth about the existence of Mitchell's Map of 1782 in the Foreign Office files. It was disclosed during a debate in the British House of Commons.

August 29, 1842

Federal courts are given jurisdiction over illegal acts committed under orders of a foreign government.

Because the case of Alexander McLeod on December 13, 1840, raised the issue of state court jurisdiction when an accused person claimed to have acted on behalf of a foreign nation, Congress passed legislation to give federal justices power to issue writs of habeas corpus and to discharge from custody persons claiming a foreign government connection. Appeals from federal justices would go through the U.S. circuit courts to the U.S. Supreme Court. Any proceeding against the accused by a state would be null and void.

August 29, 1842

Great Britain wins the Opium War, forcing China to accept the Treaty of Nanking.

The British victory occurred after the British seized several Chinese ports and the city of Chinkiang on the Grand Canal leading to Peking. Sir Henry POTTINGER dictated the Treaty of Nanking, by which China ceded Hong Kong to Britain, opened five ports to European trade under Western consular supervision, established uniform import tariffs, and paid Britain a £21,000,000 indemnity. The five ports opened to Western trade were Canton, Shanghai, Amoy, Foochow, and Ningpo.

October 20, 1842

U.S. Navy Commodore Thomas A. C. Jones captures Monterey, California, because he believes Mexico and the United States are at war.

By the fall of 1842, reports were prevalent of war in Texas or Vera Cruz, or of action by the French or British in California. Thus, rumors could be mistaken for fact. Such tension led the U.S. naval commander of a squadron in the Pacific Ocean to make a preemptive raid on Monterey in 1842. Commodore Jones misconstrued a report he received about relations between Washington and Mexico City and became persuaded that war had broken out. Fearing that British ships in the area would try to capture California, Jones decided to move immediately.

Jones sailed to Monterey harbor and demanded the town's surrender. The defenseless officials complied and, fortunately, Jones's "victory" took place without bloodshed. He hoisted the U.S. flag and declared California to be annexed to the union. The next day he learned that there was no war. Only slightly embarrassed, he lowered the flag, apologized to the local authorities, and sailed away. The State Department had to express its regrets to the Mexican government and Jones was reprimanded by his superiors.

December 7, 1842

Secretary of the Navy Upshur again urges Congress to support a naval force adequate to protect American commerce.

As in December 1841, Upshur's annual report provided a lengthy explanation for having American naval squadrons in many parts of the world and urged Congress to provide the ships and funds to improve those fleets. He wrote: in the Pacific Ocean, America can scarcely expect five or six small vessels to protect our commerce and coastline. In the East Indies, "it is owing more to our good fortune than to our strength" that our merchants do not suffer because we have only two ships in that region. And in Africa we have no ships but need "at least eighty guns" to work with England in patrolling the slave trade. Off the African coast, "several of our vessels have been captured and their crews barbarously murdered." Vessels are needed to protect these U.S. ships. In brief, said Upshur, Congress should determine that our navy be enlarged. "A commerce, such as ours, *demands* the protection of an adequate naval force."

On December 20, 1842, President Tyler further emphasized Upshur's remarks by giving Congress a special report on the increased U.S. trade with Hawaii and China.

Upshur succeeded somewhat in improving the U.S. navy's well-being from 1841 to 1843. He reorganized the navy's administration, shifted its building program to steam-powered ships, and received the largest funding ever given to the navy: $6,588,894 in fiscal 1842. He encouraged the development of the warship *Princeton* as the first six-bladed, screw-driven warship, and the *Michigan* as the first iron warship with a side wheel in 1843. He encouraged Robert Livingston's experiments in building a "shot and shell proof" warship, but the project was not successful and was abandoned in 1854.

December 30, 1842

A "Monroe Doctrine" for Hawaii is implied in a report to Congress by President Tyler.

In his message, Tyler asserted that the United States had a special interest in Hawaii (the Sandwich Islands), and although America did not desire to possess the islands, the United States would look with dissatisfaction on their occupation by any other nation. Finally, he recommended the appointment of a U.S. consul for Hawaii.

The president's report resulted from efforts by Hawaiian agents to gain recognition of the independence of a new government in the islands, as well as British and French interests in controlling islands in the Pacific Ocean. In August 1842, the French had taken over the Marquessas Islands and Tahiti, and later sent a naval ship to visit Hawaii.

The Hawaiian government of King KAMEHAMEHA III had also been seeking U.S. recognition in 1842. Peter BRINSMADE, an agent of the king, visited Washington and talked with Secretary of State Webster on April 8, 1842. While Webster did not agree to grant recognition, he expressed interest in knowing more about the government and also gave Brinsmade a letter of introduction to the U.S. minister in London. Brinsmade's mission included visits to London and Paris to gain recognition by these nations of King Kamehameha's government.

Tyler's recommendation that a consul be sent to Hawaii implied the United States would grant recognition. On March 3, 1843, with congressional approval, Tyler appointed George BROWN as the U.S. consul in Honolulu.

1843

March 3, 1843

Congress approves sending a resident commissioner to China.

President Tyler requested the authority to appoint a commercial and diplomatic representative to China and to have $40,000 appropriated for the mission's expenses. Congress approved this with amendments that no person in the mission would have a salary of more than $9,000, and that the appointment should be with the Senate's advice and consent.

After Edward Everett, the U.S. minister to England, declined the appointment, Tyler named Caleb Cushing, a loyal Whig who was also familiar with China.

June 24, 1843

Abel Parker Upshur becomes Secretary of State after Webster resigns.

After Webster resigned because he disapproved of Tyler's energetic attempts to expand into Mexican territory, the president appointed Upshur, who was closer to Tyler's anti-Whig, anti-Jacksonian political ideas. He favored U.S. expansion, as his messages to Congress demonstrated when he served as secretary of the navy in 1841 and 1842.

Upshur's service as secretary of state proved to be brief. On February 28, 1844, he was killed by a gun that exploded aboard the naval warship *Princeton* on the Potomac River.

See February 28, 1844.

August 23, 1843

Mexican Minister of Foreign Affairs J. M. Bocanegra complains about American efforts to annex Texas.

Having learned about debates in the U.S. Congress in favor of annexation and Secretary of State Upshur's attempts to obtain a treaty with Texas, Mexico's foreign minister sent a note to Waddy THOMPSON, the U.S. minister to Mexico, protesting against U.S. efforts to annex a "province of Mexico." He notified Thompson that Mexico had so far refrained from declaring war on America but that such a war could come if the United States persisted in its schemes.

The next day, Thompson responded that he was astonished that the foreign minister used newspaper rumors to accuse America. Nevertheless, because of Mexico's threat of war, Thompson said he could offer no explanations under such veiled threats. If Mexico wanted to intimidate, threats would not work; if it wished to warn Washington, this act was not supported by fact. The U.S. minister's response attempted to conciliate Bocanegra without answering his complaints. Under Secretary Upshur's orders, Thompson hoped to persuade Mexico to settle claims it owed to U.S. citizens.

For 1843 U.S. discussions about annexation of Texas, see February 15, 1844.

September 23, 1843

President Santa Anna announces that after six months foreigners will be forbidden to have any retail business in Mexico.

While the United States protested against these limits on U.S. business activity as violating the commercial treaty with Mexico, Bocanegra defended the actions because he said all nations should have such limitations. This decree was another of many small antagonisms building up between Mexico and America between 1843 and 1846.

September 26, 1843

President Tyler renews diplomatic relations with Argentina by appointing Harvey M. Watterson as chargé d'affaires at Buenos Aires.

Tyler had two reasons for wishing to renew intercourse with Argentina: he desired a commercial treaty with that nation and he feared that Great Britain's interference in South American politics gave England too many trade concessions. Generally, Tyler disliked England and was suspicious of its activity everywhere, but especially in Texas.

Argentina also had reasons for accepting Tyler's offer to renew relations. In its Río de la Plata troubles, Buenos Aires faced an informal coalition of France, England, Brazil, Uruguay, Paraguay, and Chile. Rosas's regime needed a friendly nation. Consequently, Rosas accepted Watterson's credentials, and Argentine-American relations were healed.

Watterson's stay in Argentina was short. The U.S. Senate rejected his nomination in June 1844, and Secretary John Calhoun appointed William Brent Jr. to replace him.

September 28, 1843

Secretary of State Upshur instructs the U.S. Minister to Britain to help the English government understand both the "philosophy of slavery" and that the United States will not abolish slavery.

Having become dismayed by British attempts to abolish the slave trade, Upshur believed he should "educate" Englishmen about the value of slavery to the social order as well as the American economy. In a private note to Edward Everett, the U.S. Minister to England, Upshur expressed his belief that England wanted to revive its West Indies trade and would use that area and Texas to dump its surplus manufactured goods. He also told Everett that a free state on America's southern border would greatly disturb the South and ruin both Southern agriculture and Northern industries.

Generally, Upshur was an intense Anglophobe as well as being strongly pro-slavery. His discontent with British policy in Texas prevented an early solution of the Oregon question with Great Britain. Everett had written Upshur in August 1843 that Lord Aberdeen was willing to make a treaty at the 49° north. Upshur delayed a response until October, and Aberdeen decided to send a new minister to Washington, Richard Pakenham, to settle the Oregon boundary with the United States.

September 30, 1843

The U.S. Consul informs the State Department that China will grant America most-favored-nation status.

Before Caleb Cushing arrived to negotiate a treaty with China, Commodore Lawrence Kearney had contact with Chinese officials in Macao who told him that the emperor would grant all foreign nations the same commercial rights as the English received in 1842 and that the five Chinese ports would be open on an equal basis for all. This foundation of the "open-door" policy was a deliberate Chinese choice explained to the British when the Treaty of Nanking was made. Kearney's role in this process was to discover the Chinese desire to grant any trading nation equal privileges. These were not mentioned in the 1842 treaty but were part of the British supplemental treaty of 1843 negotiated after September 1843. On his arrival in 1844, Cushing had little more to do than formalize the Chinese agreement.

December 16, 1843

U.S. Navy punishes an African region where several Americans were allegedly murdered.

After learning that an entire crew aboard an American schooner had been murdered by a tribe, Great Beribee (in present-day Ivory Coast), President Tyler sent a naval squadron under Commodore Matthew C. Perry to punish the Africans. Perry attacked and destroyed four villages at Great Beribee and killed its "gigantic chief," King Crock 0.

Commodore Perry, with U.S. Marines, admonishes Nigerian villagers for their raids on neighbors. National Archives

1844

February 15, 1844

Texas says it is willing to negotiate a treaty of annexation.

Throughout most of 1843, W. S. Murphy, the U.S. chargé in Texas, and Secretary of State Upshur urged Texas officials to help prepare an annexation agreement. They told Anson Jones, Texas secretary of state, and Isaac Van Zandt, Texas minister to the United States, that President Tyler favored annexation and that the Congress, which would meet in December 1844, would favor a treaty. Upshur desired to speed up the process of annexation because he believed England was on the verge of winning the favor of Texas to remain independent, as implied by the Treaty of 1842.

See June 28, 1842.

In order to bring Texas to the negotiating table, Upshur had to arrange to protect Texan security in the interim between the start of negotiations and the treaty ratification. On January 17, 1844, Upshur assured Van Zandt that America would protect Texas during the interim months of treaty preparation. Upshur practically guaranteed that annexation would be approved and promised to aid Texas if Britain or Mexico caused any difficulties.

Thus, when Anson Jones informed Murphy that Texas was satisfied and would negotiate annexation, Upshur and Tyler seemed to have prepared the way to completion of a treaty. Jones told Murphy on February 15 that J. P. Henderson would go to Washington to assist Van Zandt in the final negotiations.

Two unanticipated factors delayed the treaty process. First, Secretary Upshur died in an accident in February 1844, and second, Tyler's connections with Congress were too tenuous for him to guarantee quick ratification of a treaty. Nevertheless, in February the process began for the final annexation of Texas.

February 28, 1844

Secretary of State Upshur is killed when a naval gun explodes accidentally.

During his term as secretary of the navy, Upshur took pride in helping to develop new naval equipment. Among these was a new battleship, Princeton, which carried a wrought-iron cannon, the Peacemaker, capable of firing a 225-pound projectile.

On February 28, President Tyler entertained groups of dignitaries with a cruise on the Potomac River aboard the *Princeton.* Throughout the morning, the Peacemaker was often fired to demonstrate its ability and amuse the guests. After lunch, several guests including Upshur went back on deck to watch the gun fired once more. This time the cannon burst, as often happened. Upshur and Congressman Thomas Gilmer of Virginia died instantly, and several other observers were stunned by concussions. Later, a naval court of inquiry exonerated everyone involved, reporting that the gun burst was an unfortunate accident.

March 6, 1844

John Caldwell Calhoun becomes secretary of state following Upshur's death in a naval accident.

Calhoun had been a prominent American politician since being elected to the House of Representatives from South Carolina in 1808. A former vice president (1829–1832), he served as senator from South Carolina from 1832 to 1843. He served as secretary of state until March 10, 1845, when he returned to his Senate seat.

April 12, 1844

Secretary of State Calhoun signs a treaty to annex Texas to the union.

The treaty of annexation had been sought by the Tyler administration for more than a year prior to the beginning of negotiations after February 15, 1844. Secretary Upshur's death postponed the process several weeks, a factor that became important because the Senate vote on the treaty had to be delayed until after the party nominating conventions were held in May 1844. The treaty, signed on April 12, did not reach the Senate until June 8, 1844.

April 18, 1844

Secretary of State Calhoun informs the British Minister that America signed the Texas annexation treaty to forestall the dangers of British influence to abolish slavery in Texas.

This memorandum from Calhoun to Pakenham, the British minister to the United States, was a reply to the December 26 note of Lord Aberdeen, which reply had been delayed because of Upshur's death in February.

Aberdeen's December instructions to Pakenham were an attempt to explain that England had no designs on Texas or on slavery in that state. He admitted the British would prefer slavery to be ended everywhere, but they wanted Mexico and Texas to make their peace arrangements without any outside interference.

Calhoun's response asserted America's concern that Britain constantly tried to procure the end of slavery everywhere. Nations to whom slavery was a positive good, such as the United States, had to protect themselves from such encroachments. In the case of Texas, Calhoun said, the United States was particularly concerned that British pressure would compel Mexico and Texas to make the end of slavery a condition of recognition. The Texas treaty, he said, had been concluded as the most effectual means to avoid the British threat.

While Calhoun's letter to Pakenham made a case for U.S. slavery and the Texan annexation as a reaction to British designs on that area, the disclosure of the Pakenham note from Calhoun caused anti-slavery forces to claim they had proof that the Southern states wanted Texas in order to enlarge the slaveholders' influence. As a result, annexation became a strong political issue between the Whigs and the Democrats during this presidential election year and at the May nominating conventions.

May 1, 1844

The Whig National Convention nominates Henry Clay for president without reference to the Texas issue.

The Whigs' lack of an annexation platform resulted from uncertainty about the best political policy on this issue. Clay first opposed the annexation of Texas but by July made a statement that straddled the issue, saying he favored Texas annexation "with common consent of the Union, and upon just and fair terms." Nevertheless, the Whig senators defeated the Texas annexation treaty on June 8, 1844.

May 24, 1844

First telegraphic message is sent from Baltimore to Washington, D.C.

Although Samuel F. B. MORSE devised a practical telegraph in 1832, many experiments had to be conducted to make it operational, including invention of the Morse code in 1838. Morse and Alfred Vail worked on constructing the telegraph system, which became operational between Baltimore and Washington on May 24, 1844. During the 19th century, the increased speed of communications altered diplomatic intercourse by permitting foreign offices to readily contact both their own and foreign diplomats. The telegraph soon made such communications possible within the American and European continents.

May 29, 1844

The Democratic Convention nominates James K. Polk for President on a platform to annex both Texas and Oregon.

During the convention, Van Buren led on the first presidential ballot but lacked the necessary two-thirds' majority. Finally, Polk, a dark horse candidate from Tennessee, was nominated. Seeking to appeal to both Northern and Southern voters, the Democratic policy on expansion called for the "reoccupation of Oregon and the reannexation of Texas."

President Tyler initially sought to run as a third-party candidate, but on August 20 he withdrew as a nominee and supported the Polk ticket.

June 8, 1844

The Texas annexation treaty is rejected by the Senate.

The defeat of the treaty by the Senate is usually attributed to the delay in voting until after the May nominating conventions and, perhaps more pertinent, to Calhoun's note to Pakenham of April 18, 1844. Calhoun's note seemed to tie the slaveholders directly to the Texas question and caused the Whigs to believe they had a campaign issue to defeat the Democrats. Thus, the Whig senators had little difficulty in defeating the Texas treaty. The Senate vote was 35 against the treaty, 16 for the treaty. Nevertheless, there is no doubt the vote reflected a political bias, not the merits of the treaty.

July 3, 1844

The Treaty of Wanghia is signed with China.

After five months of negotiation, Caleb Cushing and the governor-general of Kwangtung and Kwangsi, Kiying, signed a commercial treaty. The treaty with China gave the United States trading rights equal to those granted to England in the Treaty of Nanking (1842). Together with the promise Kiying made to Commodore Kearney in 1843 (see September 30, 1843), this treaty enunciated the "open-door" principle that China would trade with all nations on an equal basis, that is, equal to rights previously granted to England.

In the treaty that Cushing signed at Wanghia, a small village near Macao, the United States gained some provisions that England had not secured. These included the American right to employ Chinese teachers and to purchase Chinese books; a specific extraterritoriality clause placing U.S. citizens who committed a crime in China under the legal jurisdiction of the U.S. consul and U.S. law, and Chinese who committed a crime against an American under Chinese law and jurisdiction; and the recognition of opium as contraband, in which products Americans would not trade.

The issue of extraterritoriality was of particular interest in the Chinese treaty of 1844 and thereafter—Cushing's prejudice against the laws of "Mohammedan and Pagan Governments" led him to believe it was not safe to commit the lives and liberties of U.S. citizens to their courts. Thus, extraterritoriality protected Americans from the "sanguinary barbarism" or "phrenzied bigotry" of Asians and Africans. Cushing's ethnocentrism contrasts with the comments of other "realistic" appraisers of extraterritoriality who saw this legal device as an alternative to the occupation of foreign territory.

July 18, 1844

Britain decides to delay a joint Anglo-French attempt to keep Texas independent.

On July 18, British Foreign Minister Lord Aberdeen accepted the advice of Richard Pakenham, Britain's minister to the United States, to delay a proposed Anglo-French effort until after the 1844 election in America.

Although British diplomats frequently told U.S. representatives that they did not wish to interfere in Texas, the records show this was not true. In May and June 1844, Lord Aberdeen, in conjunction with advice from Paris, discussed the question of Texas's recognition by Mexico with both Ashbel Smith, the Texas minister to London, and Don Tomas Murphy, Mexico's representative.

On June 22, Pakenham advised Aberdeen that recent political events in America made it impractical for France and England to proceed with their plans at present. Both Pakenham and the French minister in Washington agreed that the presidential contest between Clay and Polk made the Texas situation the key to the election. Consequently, Pakenham wrote, England and France "have everything to gain by the success of Mr. Clay," who opposed immediate annexation. If the British plans became known without U.S. consent, Clay's campaign would be damaged.

Lord Aberdeen and the French planned in 1844 to guarantee the independence of Texas and to oppose annexation "to the last extremity." France and Britain would require Mexico to recognize Texan independence and a suitable boundary line. In this process, the British and French would seek U.S. approval but did not expect to receive it. Most significantly, Britain dropped its previous insistence that Texas abolish slavery.

The Anglo-French plan was aborted by events. The French agreed with Aberdeen's July 18 request to delay the plan until after the election. Clay's defeat in 1844 made their plot more difficult to pursue. The recognition proposals did not die, however, and the Anglo-French diplomats made a last-minute effort to keep Texas a separate nation in the spring of 1845.

See July 4, 1845.

September 29, 1844

The Vorhees naval incident disrupts U.S. relations with Argentina.

Just one year after the United States reestablished relations with Argentina, an incident in the Río de la Plata again caused trouble. Because Buenos Aires continued its attempt to defeat the rebels in Uruguay, their navy blockaded the sea approaches to the port of Montevideo. On September 29, a U.S. naval vessel, the *Congress,* commanded by Captain P. F. Vorhees, was damaged by gunfire from an Argentine ship chasing a blockade runner.

Believing the attack unjustified, Captain Vorhees ordered the seizure of the Argentine ship, the *Sancola,* and its crew. Vorhees held the crew and ship as prisoners, claiming the vessel should be tried for flying a false flag.

Vorhees had clearly overreacted. Watterson, the U.S. chargé at Buenos Aires, reported to Calhoun that the captain's act should not be upheld. Even before Calhoun could respond, Commodore David Turner, commander of America's South Atlantic squadron, came to the region and refused to back Vorhees's action. Turner told the Rosas government that the United States respected its blockade and that Vorhees would be punished. Later, on December 28, Calhoun wrote the new U.S. chargé, William Brent, to express America's regrets for Vorhees's mistaken actions. Vorhees was court-martialed and suspended from the navy for three years.

October 31, 1844

General Santa Anna is overthrown as ruler of Mexico.

The career of Santa Anna resembled a roller coaster from 1833 to 1855, as he was in and out of office again and again. On this occasion the new regime of José J. Herrera impeached him in December 1844 and exiled him to Cuba on June 3, 1845.

December 3, 1844

President Tyler's annual message recommends that Congress pass a joint resolution to bring about Texas's annexation.

The message reported that Mexico had renewed war against Texas and was preparing an invasion. It also emphasized that Polk's election as president demonstrated that the American people desired to annex Texas.

December 4, 1844

James K. Polk is elected president in a campaign highlighted by the Texas annexation issue.

Polk received 170 electoral votes to Henry Clay's 105. The popular vote in the election has led historians to form a variety of conclusions about the intent of the electorate. Polk's popular vote was 1,337,243; Clay's, 1,299,062. A third candidate, James C. Birney of the Liberty Party, received 62,300, votes which technically gave Polk a minority of the popular vote with 23,819 votes less than a majority.

The analysis of the pro-annexation vote is more complex, however, because during the campaign Clay issued a statement that could be interpreted as favoring annexation. Clay wrote that he personally did not object to annexation and would "be glad to see it without dishonor—without war, with the common consent of the Union, and upon just and fair terms." As often is the case, the analysis of the U.S. election returns in 1844 is an imprecise business. Those favoring expansion in 1844, such as President

President James K. Polk. Copy of engraving by H. W. Smith. National Archives

Tyler, claimed the people's vote favored the annexation of Texas.

1845

February 20, 1845

Britain's alleged hypocrisy regarding slavery is disclosed by President Tyler in a report to Congress.

Tyler claimed that while Great Britain urged other nations to abolish slavery and the slave trade, British citizens profited from captured slave ships by refusing to return captured Africans from slave ships to their homes in Africa.

Tyler reported details of British business activity in Brazil and the Caribbean islands to verify his beliefs. The Brazilian slave trade was part of a complex series of financial-trade deals. First, English investors bought a cargo in America for transportation to England in U.S. ships. From England the cargo of goods intended for exchange in Africa would be transshipped to Brazil. In Rio, a new crew boarded the ship to cross to Africa and exchange the cargo for slaves that were brought to Brazil.

Americans were participants in this trade, said Tyler, and Congress should legislate to stop the U.S. activity. But British investors were behind the whole scheme in the U.S.-English-Brazil-African trade.

Perhaps worse, said Tyler, British ships that took slaves off other nations' ships did not free the slaves to return them to their homes. Black Africans were taken to the West Indies to become "trade apprentices" under "virtual slave-like" conditions. Moreover, the captain and crew of ships that stopped slave ships received a bonus according to how many pounds per capita the slaves weighed.

Perhaps intentionally, Tyler sent this bitter report to Congress just before he left office in March 1845. Polk's administration had to deal with the resulting objections from London.

March 1, 1845

Texas is annexed by a joint resolution of Congress.

Following Tyler's recommendation of December 3, 1844, a resolution of annexation passed the House on January 25, by a vote of 120-98. In the Senate, an amendment empowered the president to negotiate a new treaty that could be ratified by the Senate or adopted by joint resolution. In this form, the Senate approved the bill 27-25 on February 27, and the House concurred on February 28, 132-76. President Tyler signed the resolution on March 1, 1845.

March 3, 1845

Congress grants subsidies to promote oceanic steamship lines of the United States.

Government subsidies went to American companies to develop steamships to compete with British hegemony in the use of such oceanic trade and passenger ships. During the 12 years this act was in effect, about $14,500,000 was granted to establish steamship lines to Le Havre, Bremen, Liverpool, and Panama. Except for the Panamanian route, the attempt was unsuccessful.

The attempt to compete directly with well-established British transatlantic steamships was an error.

Routes such as that to Panama needed to be developed but were neglected. The two subsidized American lines needed more financial aid each year and were poorly managed. In addition, the emphasis on speed for the ships made them costly and in constant need of repair. Two other American lines, the Vanderbilt Line and the Inman Line, had excellent management and operated profitably without subsidies by 1860.

March 6, 1845

President Polk commissions James Buchanan as Secretary of State.

Buchanan had been a representative and senator from Pennsylvania since 1821, a service interrupted once when he was U.S. minister to Russia in 1832–1833. He served as secretary throughout Polk's four years as president.

July 2, 1845

The British Minister rejects Polk's offer to divide Oregon at the 49th parallel.

Since 1818, American diplomats had offered to settle the Oregon boundary issue at the 49° north. The British had insisted on the Columbia River as the dividing line.

Although some of Polk's political followers now wanted to extend the boundary north to 54°40′, the president and Secretary of State James Buchanan decided to reiterate America's traditional offer to England. On July 2, Buchanan called in Richard PAKENHAM, the British minister to the United States, and proposed settlement of the Oregon boundary at the 49° north.

Rather than refer the offer to London, Pakenham stood on his country's previous decisions and rejected the offer. This was, of course, a diplomatic mistake, and London disavowed Pakenham's rejection. The British minister attempted to adjust his error by an offer to arbitrate the Oregon dispute, but Polk refused, claiming Britain must make some concession on the issue before it would be reconsidered.

July 4, 1845

A special convention in Texas accepts annexation under the terms of the U.S. Congress's joint resolution.

As soon as the joint resolution passed Congress on March 1, Secretary of State Calhoun sent instructions to Andrew Jackson DONELSON, the chargé d'affaires in Austin, to invite Texas to accept union under the joint resolution. President Anson Jones of Texas decided to

The Patriots Getting Their Beans. This 1845 cartoon illustrates that the Texas and Oregon questions aroused strong feelings among Americans. Library of Congress

call a special convention to make the final decision on this proposal.

Only one shadow came across these developments, a British attempt to get Texas to accept recognition from Mexico provided it would never allow itself to be annexed by a third power. The British successfully persuaded the Mexican government to accept this proposal, and in June the Congress of Texas considered it together with the joint resolution of the U.S. Congress.

Texas sentiment in favor of joining the United States was overwhelming. By a unanimous vote, the Texas Congress rejected Mexico's offer and approved the joint resolution. On July 4, a special Texas convention confirmed Texas's approval of annexation by the United States. On October 13, a popular referendum in Texas also approved annexation. To finalize the entire process, the U.S. Congress passed a resolution admitting Texas as a state on December 29, 1845.

October 10, 1845

A "naval school" opens at Fort Severn, Annapolis, Maryland.

This school to train naval officers became known as the U.S. Naval Academy in 1850. It was founded by Secretary of the Navy George Bancroft.

October 17, 1845

American influence in California is urged by Secretary of State Calhoun's instructions to the U.S. consul at Monterey.

The United States formally opened a consulate in California on April 2, 1844, appointing Thomas O. Larkin as consul. Larkin had built a prosperous trading business in California after immigrating there, but he favored the eventual U.S. takeover of the region. He had written glowing reports on California for newspapers in Boston and New York and, in 1844, wrote to the State Department regarding the new French consulate and activity by Britain's Hudson's Bay Company. He also observed that by 1844 almost 500 Americans lived in the province, and they talked about playing the "Texas game" soon, i.e., rebelling from Mexico.

Buchanan's instruction to Larkin on October 17 encouraged the consul's interest in the "Texas game." He told Larkin to counteract all foreign influence in California and to forward details about the "leading" citizens, trade, and "character" of immigration. Furthermore, Calhoun asked Larkin to gain friends for the United States and to assure them that if California declared its independence, "we shall render her all the kind offices in our power as a sister republic." Buchanan indicated the president had no desire to "induce" the Californians to become free; yet if they wished to unite with us, "they would be received as brethren, whenever this can be done without affording Mexico just cause of complaint."

November 10, 1845

The Slidell Mission—John Slidell is sent to Mexico to buy territory from Texas to the Pacific Ocean.

Following Santa Anna's overthrow by Herrera on November 10, 1845, Mexico's new Foreign Minister Peña a Peña informed the United States that the government would receive a commissioner who could settle Mexican-American disputes "in a peaceable, reasonable and honorable manner." Polk appointed John Slidell to go to Mexico City as envoy extraordinary and minister plenipotentiary.

In instructing Slidell, Secretary of State Buchanan first stated that the Rio Grande should be insisted on as the southern boundary. Slidell should offer to purchase territory in any of four alternative agreements outlined as follows:

1. the Rio Grande and all of California and New Mexico for $25 million plus acceptance of all claims of U.S. citizens;
2. the Rio Grande and all of New Mexico and California excepting Monterey for $20 million plus U.S. claims;
3. the Rio Grande and New Mexico for $5 million plus U.S. claims;
4. the Rio Grande boundary for the assumption of U.S. claims.

For the outcome of Slidell's mission, see March 1, 1846.

December 2, 1845

President Polk's annual message to Congress calls for annexing "the whole Oregon Territory" and for keeping England out of California.

The president told Congress that his attempt to compromise with Britain on the Oregon territory had been rejected. This offer was now withdrawn "and our title to the whole Oregon territory asserted and, as is believed, maintained by irrefragable facts and arguments." He asked Congress to authorize sending Britain the one year's notice needed to end the "joint occupancy" and to permit him to extend U.S. laws to the "American citizens in Oregon." Polk appeared to have closed the door to compromise with the British and to have asserted the U.S. claim to the northern border at 54°40′, the southern boundary of Russian-America.

Regarding California, Polk's speech reacted to rumors of British designs on that province. Mexico, he said, could not effectively control California. Polk assumed the British would try to occupy it to thwart U.S. expansion. To avoid this, Polk warned the European powers that North America was not open for colonization. Saying he reaffirmed Mr. Monroe's "wisdom and sound policy," he announced to the world that the United States would consent to no future European colonies in North America.

In addition, Polk's speech asserted that if part of California desired to join the United States, "this will be a question for them and us to determine without any foreign interposition." Thus, in California and in Oregon, Polk asserted his desire to act to enlarge the American nation by whatever means were necessary.

Some writers refer to this speech as having enunciated "Polk's Doctrine" because he emphasized no future European interference on the North American continent, whereas Monroe implied that his doctrine included all of the Western Hemisphere.

December 20, 1845

Robert Peel's ministry returns to control of the British government.

The British government temporarily ended a crisis resulting from shifts of the old Whig-Tory alignments to a Liberal-Conservative alignment during the 19th century. Peel's liberal conservatism favored a lowering of tariffs to offset Whig policies. Nevertheless, the Whig leader Lord John Russell forced Peel's resignation on December 5. Russell could not, however, get votes to form a ministry, and Peel returned to office on December 20.

Because Peel now experienced opposition from a more conservative Tory group led by Benjamin Disraeli, Russell agreed to give Peel some assistance in his effort to repeal the Corn Laws. In particular, Russell agreed to silence, temporarily, Lord Palmerston, whose nationalistic, saber-rattling foreign policy demands not only hindered Peel but alarmed many British businessmen who saw Palmerston as irresponsible. Among other policies, Palmerston had criticized Peel's weakness in North America. He claimed Peel capitulated to the United States in the Webster-Ashburton Treaty and should make no concessions on the Oregon territory. Thus, the "silencing" of Palmerston early in 1846 permitted Peel to modify his Oregon policy and to accept a compromise.

December 27, 1845

"Manifest Destiny"—a term coined by John L. O'Sullivan—comes into vogue to define America's right to "possess the whole of the continent which providence has given us."

The term "manifest destiny" became popular after its use in a New York *Morning News* editorial on December 27, in connection with the Oregon territory. Earlier, O'Sullivan used the phrase in an unsigned editorial for the July-August edition of *The United States Magazine and Democratic Review.* It was first used in Congress on January 3, 1846, in a speech by Robert C. Winthrop of Massachusetts. Generally, the term became the popular expression by which Americans could moralize their expansion across North America as a type of "divine" predestination or "evolutionary" design. After 1898, some expansionists explained the taking of Pacific islands by a slightly altered term, "inevitable destiny," taking the American civilization beyond the continent.

1846

January 2, 1846

In Mexico City, President Herrera is overthrown by General Mariano Paredes, who is anti-American.

This coup d'état continued the series of such upheavals that had kept Mexico in political turmoil since 1836. Paredes's return to power had been largely due to his claim that Herrera was too friendly to America. Thus, Paredes would not recognize Slidell and informed him of this decision on March 1, 1846.

January 13, 1846

Polk orders General Zachary Taylor to take up positions on the Rio Grande River.

Polk took this action on the basis of Slidell's notification that Herrera refused to negotiate with him. News of Paredes's coup had not yet reached Washington.

Taylor's order to move to the Rio Grande symbolized Polk's rejection of Mexico's claim that the Neuces River was the correct border. Texas had claimed the Rio Grande border ever since Santa Anna's armies retired below that river in 1836. Otherwise, Mexico had a better claim to the Neuces boundary according to its organization under former Spanish and Mexican rulers. Neither side had a large settlement in the area, although south of the Neuces Corpus Christi was an American settlement and Mexico had a few scattered ranches in the region.

Nevertheless, Polk insisted that the Texan claim was correct, and Buchanan's instructions to Slidell reflected this demand. When General Taylor and his 3,900 U.S. soldiers entered Texas in July 1845, Taylor was told to take positions south of the Neuces but to avoid disturbing any Mexican ports or settlements. Taylor had positioned his forces at Corpus Christi until March 1846, when he received Polk's orders of January 13.

February 26, 1846

President Polk is willing to consider a compromise on Oregon at the 49° north latitude.

Secretary of State Buchanan wrote Louis McLane, U.S. minister to England, that President Polk would give the "utmost respect" if Great Britain offered to compromise on Oregon at the 49° north. This message indicated Polk's readiness to change his demand for all of the Oregon territory, which he insisted on after Pakenham rejected his compromise offer of July 2, 1845.

By February 1846, Polk and Buchanan changed their hard line because of the Mexican problems and because McLane informed them, in January, that Britain's Foreign Minister Aberdeen was preparing measures for defending Canada and taking "offensive

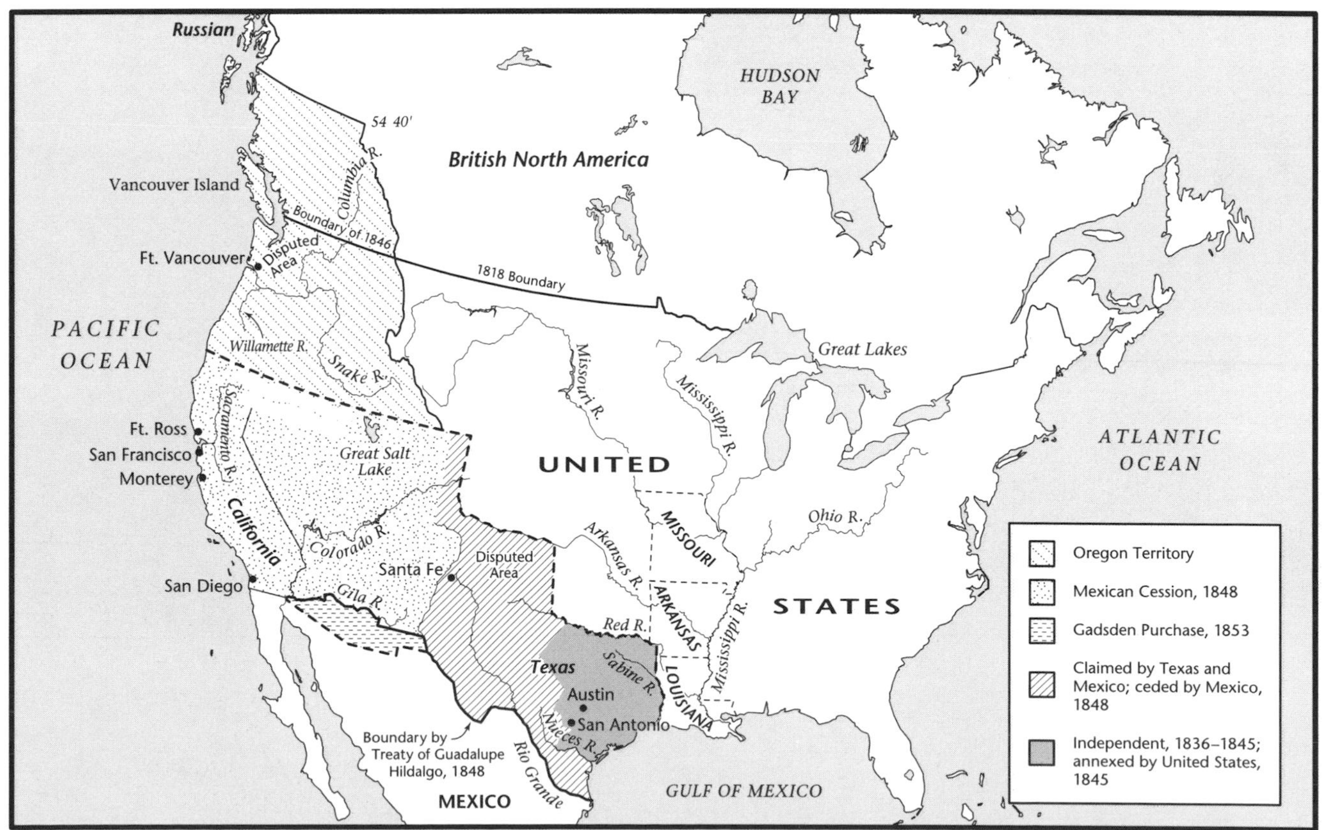

Texas, Mexico and the Oregon Territory, 1836–1848.

measures" against the United States. While Buchanan did not indicate to McLane that Polk would negotiate with Britain, he said the president would submit a British compromise offer to the Senate for its advice. In a separate personal note to McLane, the secretary said he believed the Senate would approve such a compromise. In this fashion, Polk attempted to straighten out the British lion's tail that he had twisted in his December 1845 speech to Congress.

See June 6, 1846.

March 1, 1846

Slidell's offer to negotiate is rejected by the Mexican government.

This was the second time that Slidell's attempt to be recognized had failed. When Slidell arrived in Mexico City in December 1845, President Herrera's opponents criticized him for appeasing the Americans, and he could not risk accepting Slidell's credentials. Rumors in Mexico disclosed that Slidell wished to purchase Mexican territory, and Mexico's foreign minister told him they could settle only the Texas issue. Officially on December 20, Mexico's Council of State rejected Slidell because they said his credentials should be as "minister" only, not as a special envoy.

Because Slidell knew that a coup d'état was being plotted against Herrera, he retired to Jalapa, near Vera Cruz, and did not leave Mexico. The coup took place in mid-December, and General Mariano Paredes assumed office. After a brief wait to permit the government to be organized, Slidell offered his credentials to the new minister of foreign relations, J. M. Castillo. But Paredes was less inclined than Herrera to accept Slidell. The coup leaders had accused Herrera of "seeking to avoid a necessary and glorious war." Indeed, Mexico's military leaders constantly contended they could defeat the Americans. Mexico had a vastly larger army, and its European advisers usually supported the belief that they had a military force superior to America's.

Following consultations by the Mexican Council of State, Castillo informed Slidell on March 1 that he could not be recognized. Slidell was not surprised. On January 12 he had written the State Department that

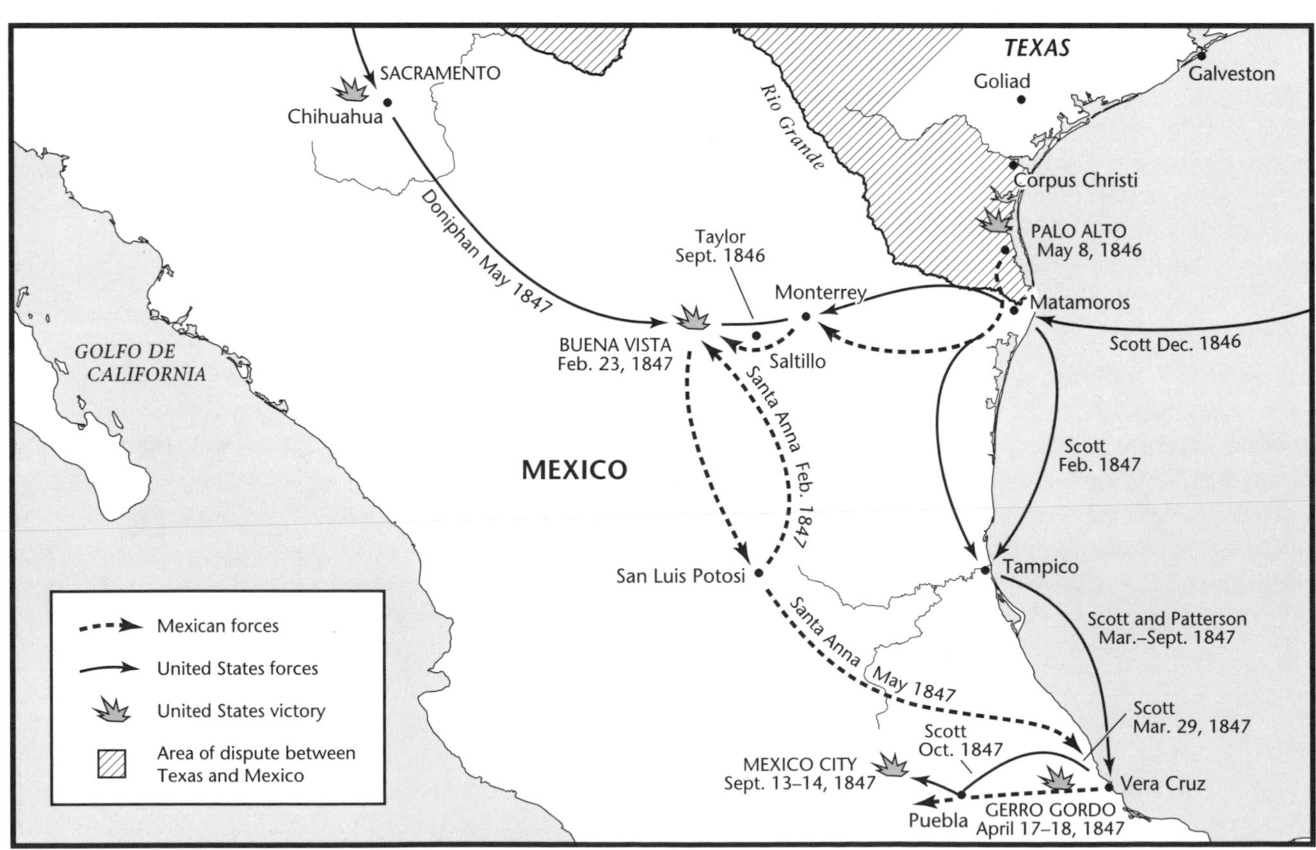

The Mexican War, 1846–1848.

he did not expect the Paredes regime to negotiate with him. Slidell left for home, reaching Washington on May 8, 1846.

March 30, 1846

"Polk's Doctrine" does not extend Monroe's principles to affairs in Argentina.

President Polk's indication to congress in his speech of December 2, 1845, that he was concerned with foreign intervention only in North America was further reiterated by Secretary Buchanan in an incident at the Río de la Plata. The French and British renewed their blockade of Buenos Aires because the Argentine government failed to fulfill its agreement with France of October 29, 1840. The United States protested the blockade, which began in September 1845, but Buchanan told the U.S. chargé in Buenos Aires, William Harris, that America could not be the "guardian" of all South America. The United States had more vital interests elsewhere.

The March 30, 1846, instructions to Harris elaborated on the views of Polk and Buchanan. The significant part of the memorandum stated: "Whilst existing circumstances render it impossible for the United States to take part in the present war; yet the President desires the whole moral influence of this Republic should be cast into the scale of the injured party. We cordially wish the Argentine Republic success in its struggle against foreign interference."

April 25, 1846

The first fighting of the Mexican War: Mexican cavalry attacks 63 U.S. soldiers in the disputed territory, killing 11 and wounding 5 Americans.

This clash occurred after troops from both armies entered the disputed territory between the Rio Grande and Neuces Rivers. General Taylor followed Polk's orders of January 13 and moved his forces to the north bank of the Rio Grande on March 28. They erected Fort Texas across the river from the Mexican town of Matamoros. On April 12, Mexican troops established Fort Paredes near Matamoros and warned Taylor to withdraw his army to the Neuces River. In addition, Taylor blockaded the Rio Grande at its mouth to assure his supply lines, which the Mexicans refused to guarantee.

On April 23, Mexico's President Paredes learned of Taylor's blockade and, calling it an act of war, proclaimed the existence of a "defensive war" against America. The next day, General Mariano ARISTA, commander of Fort Paredes, notified Taylor that hostilities had begun and sent Mexican patrols across the Rio Grande.

On April 25, a Mexican force of 1,600 crossed the river above Taylor's fortifications and came upon a company of 63 Americans, led by Captain Seth THORNTON. The Mexican cavalry attacked, killing and wounding 16 Americans and capturing 9 others. News of this skirmish reached Washington, D.C., on May 9, 1846.

April 27, 1846

With congressional approval, Polk notifies Great Britain that Oregon's present status will end in one year, expressing hope there may be an "amicable adjustment" of claims.

The resolution of Congress to terminate the "joint occupation" of Oregon had been softened between the time of its introduction to Congress on January 5 and its passage on April 23. By the spring, most Democrats and Whigs favored a compromise with Britain. Calhoun and the southern bloc had Texas and would accept a small Oregon; Clay and the eastern business groups represented by the Whigs feared a costly war with England. Only a few midwest congressmen such as Senator Edward A. HANNEGAN of Indiana and William ALLEN of Ohio held out for the 54°40′ boundary.

To open the door to compromise with Britain, the resolution ending "joint occupation" included loopholes to allow Polk to negotiate. Polk was not "directed" but "authorized" to give England the year's notice. Wording on the U.S. "rights to all Oregon" was deleted. The hope for an "amicable adjustment" was added. British Minister Pakenham, whose haste in 1844 led to the current situation, took note of the conciliatory efforts. After the resolution passed the Senate by 42 to 10 and the House by 142 to 46, a compromise appeared to be certain.

April 28, 1846

Notification of the termination of the Oregon Treaty is sent to London.

The day after Polk's signature of the congressional resolution, Secretary of State Buchanan dispatched the notice and instructions to Louis McLane, U.S.

minister to England. He told McLane to inform the British that Polk was willing to consider a suitable British proposal in order that friendly relations could continue. Together, the resolution and instructions gave British Foreign Minister Aberdeen sufficient cause to prepare a compromise. The dispatch of April 28 was presented to Aberdeen on May 21, 1846.

May 8, 1846

John Slidell returns from Mexico City and urges "chastisement" of Mexico.

Although Polk was ready to act vigorously against Mexico in February when he first learned that Paredes and Herrera had refused to accept Slidell's papers and negotiate, he delayed taking drastic steps until he knew the British dispute over Oregon might be resolved (see April 27, 1846). Polk also waited for Slidell's return to Washington to obtain direct data about the situation in Mexico. On his return, Slidell was, of course, upset by the poor treatment he had received in Mexico City. He believed that Mexico needed a show of American force to persuade it to capitulate on the boundary issues.

The next day, Saturday, May 9, Polk's cabinet met. The president told them he intended on Tuesday to send Congress a recommendation of war against Mexico. Only Secretary of the Navy George Bancroft opposed Polk's announcement. Bancroft wanted to wait until Mexican forces "committed a hostile act to justify war." Soon after the cabinet adjourned, Polk received news of the Mexican attack of April 25.

May 11, 1846

Polk asks Congress to declare war on Mexico because, he says, the Mexican army has "shed American blood upon American soil."

Polk's message to Congress was prepared over the weekend after John Slidell returned from Mexico and as news of the skirmish in the disputed territory reached Washington. Slidell's return led to a cabinet meeting in which the decision for war was agreed to be given to Congress on Tuesday, May 12. On the evening of May 9, after the cabinet decision, the news of Mexico's April 25 attack reached Polk, and he decided to send his message to Congress on Monday, adding news of the killing of five Americans.

The May 11 message summarized the long series of Mexico's offenses against America, emphasizing Mexico's refusal to recognize or negotiate with Slidell. His speech climaxed with the startling news of the April 25 Mexican attack, news to stir the souls of all patriots. Despite American patience, Polk said, "Mexico has passed the boundary of the United States, has invaded our territory, and shed American blood upon American soil. She has proclaimed that hostilities have commenced, and that the two nations are now at war."

May 13, 1846

War is declared after Congress approves legislation with a minimum of debate.

The House of Representatives approved the war bill on May 11, by a vote of 174-14. One notable amendment that the House defeated stated that the measure did not signify approval of Polk's decision to order U.S. troops into the disputed territory between the Neuces and Rio Grande Rivers.

In the Senate, the only discussion focused on John C. Calhoun's opposition to the bill's preamble, which said "a state of war exists." Calhoun abstained from voting for the bill because he contended "a state of war" did not exist until Congress recognized it. In the Senate, the vote was 40 to 2 with 3 abstentions including Calhoun's.

On May 13, Congress also authorized the president to enlist 50,000 volunteers and appropriated $10 million for army and navy expenses.

Although President Polk's Whig opponents in Congress supported the war effort, they later complained bitterly that Polk deceived them in his May 11 speech by stating that American blood was shed on American soil. One notable example of the Whig complaint was made by a freshman congressman from Illinois, Abraham Lincoln, who at the opening of the congressional sessions in December 1847 introduced a series of resolutions asking the president to identify the exact "spot" on American soil where the first blood was shed. Clarifying his charges in a speech on January 12, 1848, Lincoln challenged Polk to respond to his inquiries, claiming that the war was "unnecessarily and unconstitutionally commenced" in 1846. A major result of Lincoln's opposition to the war was that the Whigs did not renominate him for Congress in 1848.

May 18, 1846

General Taylor crosses the Rio Grande to occupy Matamoros.

Taylor's battles against Mexico were successful after the initial loss to the Mexican cavalry attack on April 25. On May 8, he defeated a 6,000-man Mexican army at Palo Alto with 2,300 U.S. troops. As the Mexicans retreated, Taylor pursued them. At a ravine called the Resaca de la Palma, his troops caught and defeated the Mexicans, chasing them across the Rio Grande. On May 17, General Arista evacuated the Mexican fort at Matamoros, and the following day Taylor occupied the city.

June 6, 1846

The British Parliament repeals the Corn Laws, an act that generally provides a free-trade policy for Great Britain.

The repeal of the Corn Laws marked the successful advocacy of free trade by the Manchester School of economists, who believed free trade would aid both workers and factory managers by making available cheaper food and cheaper raw materials. Generally, Britain followed free-trade policies until the end of the century.

June 6, 1846

Britain offers to accept the 49° north as the Oregon boundary.

By February 1846, Lord Aberdeen was ready to resolve the Oregon issue. Lord Palmerston had agreed not to complain (see December 20, 1845), and with news of the abrogation by the United States of the Convention of 1827, Aberdeen also learned that Polk was willing to compromise. On June 6, the British minister to America, Richard Pakenham, presented the British offer, agreeing to draw the Oregon boundary at the 49° north. Only a few details remained to be worked out to settle the dispute.

June 12, 1846

The U.S. Senate advises the President to accept Britain's compromise proposal on Oregon.

By the time McLane notified Lord Aberdeen of the congressional resolution of April 27, 1846, the British foreign minister had taken action essential to obtaining English acceptance of, in general, the 49° north latitude as a suitable compromise. Several factors influenced Aberdeen's decision: (1) the fur trade of Hudson's Bay Company on the Columbia River declined and caused the company to move its headquarters to Vancouver Island, away from contentious American settlers; (2) the repeal of the Corn Laws and the low U.S. Tariff of 1846 by the Polk administration heralded an increase in Anglo-American trade; (3) peace societies in England and America actively petitioned their representatives to avoid war; (4) Lord Palmerston, the energetic opposition spokesman in Parliament, was persuaded by his liberal colleagues not to attack a compromise on the Oregon issue.

In Washington, Polk's first inclination was to force Britain to give up its right to navigate the Columbia River, but a majority of his cabinet members suggested that the president refer the offer to the Senate for advice, making it responsible for accepting or rejecting the British proposal.

Surprisingly, the Senate moved quickly. On June 12, after only two days of debate, it approved the offer by a vote of 38 to 12. Although some Whigs claimed the Democrats betrayed the western interests, the United States received the boundary it had sought since 1818.

"What? You Young Yankee Noodle, Strike Your Own Father?" A British view of the Yankee at the time of the Oregon boundary dispute. *Punch*, 1846

June 15, 1846

Great Britain and the United States sign a treaty to settle the Oregon boundary.

After the U.S. Senate on June 12 indicated its agreement with Lord Aberdeen's compromise proposal, Richard Pakenham, the British minister to the United States, and Secretary Buchanan easily agreed on a treaty. Three days later the Senate ratified the treaty by a vote of 41 to 14, and the treaty was proclaimed on August 5, 1846.

The Oregon Treaty provided for (1) extending the 49° north as the boundary except that the entire Vancouver Island would be British; (2) free navigation of the channel and straits of Juan de Fuca for both parties; (3) free navigation of the Columbia River by the British. Part of this water boundary had to be redefined in 1873.

July 30, 1846

The Democratic administration of Polk returns to a revenue tariff: the Walker Tariff.

This measure was the first revenue bill since the Tariff of 1816 began a protectionist trend. The Compromise Tariff of 1833 had been designed to reduce tariffs gradually over a 10-year period, but when this era ended, the Whigs reinstituted protective rates in 1842. The Walker Tariff of 1846 reduced the minimum valuation for products and substituted specific for ad valorem duties. A few commodities had no duty.

For previous tariff bills, see February 12, 1833, and March 30, 1842.

August 10, 1846

The Senate defeats the "Wilmot Proviso," an amendment designed to exclude slavery from any territory acquired from Mexico.

David Wilmot, a Democratic Party representative from Pennsylvania, introduced his amendment to a bill that appropriated $2 million to facilitate negotiations that might end the Mexican War. Wilmot and other "free-soil" advocates desired to prevent slavery from being authorized in any new American territory. Wilmot's amendment passed the House of Representatives, but both the amendment and the bill were lost in the Senate by the adjournment of Congress on August 10.

The Wilmot Proviso was again added to an appropriations bill in February 1847, but the Senate defeated it on March 1, 1847. Although Congress never approved Wilmot's amendment, it became a part of the political platform of the Free Soil Party and, later, the Republican Party.

August 15, 1846

General Stephen Watts Kearny proclaims New Mexico is part of the United States.

This proclamation followed General Kearny's occupation of Las Vegas. His "Army of the West" left Fort Leavenworth on May 15, two days after the declaration of war, and marched down the Santa Fe Trail to Las Vegas. On August 1, he warned Governor Manuel Armijo and residents of the area not to resist, offering protection to those who cooperated with him.

Mexico had an estimated 4,000 troops in the area, but they dispersed and offered no resistance to American troops until early 1847, when they were suppressed at TAOS by Colonel Sterling Price and his men. By September 25, 1846, Kearny was ready to move on to California.

August 16, 1846

An American effort to end the Mexican War quickly fails when Santa Anna breaks his promise to arrange peace terms.

From his exile in Cuba where he fled after being expelled by the Mexican government on June 3, 1845, General Santa Anna informed President Polk that for $30 million he could return to power in Mexico and arrange peace terms on the basis of a boundary to include the Rio Grande and San Francisco Bay.

In order to get Santa Anna's help, the U.S. navy permitted him to pass through their blockade and go to Vera Cruz on August 16. Once in Mexico, Santa Anna refused to carry out his proposal. Rather, he denounced all efforts to appease the United States and raised troops to march on Mexico City. On December 6, Santa Anna was elected president of Mexico, and soon after, he led an army against General Zachary Taylor in northern Mexico.

September 25, 1846

After capturing Monterey, General Taylor proclaims an eight-week armistice.

Taylor's northern army moved from the Rio Grande to the San Juan River on July 14. He then advanced to Monterey, which fell on September 25 after a four-day siege.

Taylor's armistice was declared without Polk's consent, and when Washington's officials found out, the War Department told him to end it. The armistice ended on November 13, after which Taylor captured SALTILLO, the capital of Coahuila, on November 16, 1846.

December 12, 1846

The United States and New Granada (Colombia) sign a treaty giving America the right-of-way across Panama.

This TREATY OF NEW GRANADA was signed by Benjamin A. BIDLACK, U.S. minister to New Granada. The government of New Granada requested a treaty with the United States to protect it from British designs in the Caribbean and the Isthmus of Panama. This was a commercial treaty that included a clause giving the United States the right-of-way across Panama. The U.S. Senate ratified the treaty on June 3, 1848, and full ratifications were exchanged on July 12, 1848.

1847

January 13, 1847

The Treaty of Cahuenga ends fighting in California.

Both U.S. army and navy forces plus local citizens had been active in California since June 1846. Parties of U.S. settlers attacked Mexican forces and captured Sonoma on June 14 in the "Bear Flag Revolt." About the same time Commodore John D. SLOAT sailed his Pacific Coast naval force to California. On July 7, Sloat seized Monterey while other naval forces under Commander John B. MONTGOMERY took San Francisco and a third group under Lieutenant James W. REVERE occupied SONOMA (July 9).

Commodore Robert F. STOCKTON, who replaced Sloat in July, issued on August 17, 1846, a premature declaration that California was annexed to the United States. It was premature because Mexican forces had rallied under Captain José Maria FLORES and regained control of southern California by October 29.

On November 25, after Kearny reached California with 100 men, U.S. forces led by Stockton regained their lost territory by taking San Pascual (December 6), San Diego (December 29), and Los Angeles (January 10, 1847).

The last Mexican forces, led by Andres PICO, surrendered on January 13, 1847, and signed the Treaty of Cahuenga. By May 31, 1847, a government had been set up for California with Colonel Richard B. MASON as governor.

February 22–23, 1847

General Taylor defeats Santa Anna's forces at the Battle of Buena Vista, ending the northern campaign.

Although Taylor lost 9,000 of his experienced troops by transfer to General Scott's Vera Cruz expedition, he disobeyed instructions to hold a defensive line at Monterey and advanced in an offensive toward Agua Neuva. Santa Anna marched 15,000 men toward Taylor's army, and they met in a valley three miles north of the hacienda of Buena Vista. Taylor, with 4,800 men, refused a demand to surrender, and in a hard-fought battle he forced Santa Anna to retreat.

Following this engagement, Taylor held his defensive lines in the north until he requested relief from his command on November 26, 1847.

March 27, 1847

Vera Cruz surrenders to Major General Winfield Scott.

The surrender of this city on the Gulf of Mexico ended a siege by U.S. naval batteries and U.S. army forces that began on March 22. After the Mexicans refused to surrender, Scott's army landed south of Vera Cruz on March 9 in the first large-scale amphibious action of U.S. military history. The troops came ashore in special landing boats assembled first at Sacrificios Island. Two weeks of fighting secured the beaches and gave the army a secure position before the siege of the city began.

Once Vera Cruz fell, Scott prepared his force of 9,000 men for the march on Mexico City.

Major General Winfield Scott at Vera Cruz. Copy of lithograph by Nathaniel Currier, 1847. National Archives

July 27, 1847

The Independent Republic of Liberia is established.

Liberia was founded on the west coast of Africa as a colony for American slaves in 1822. These former slaves had been freed with compensation to their American owners by the American Colonization Society. This group's policy was to purchase slaves' freedom and return them to Africa. After 1830, U.S. abolitionists and most former slaves objected to the colonization principle. Great Britain in 1847 was the first nation to recognize the new government.

August 24, 1847

The Armistice of Tacubaya is timed to permit Santa Anna to consider peace proposals following General Scott's victories, which brought American forces within five miles of Mexico City.

After capturing Vera Cruz on March 27, Scott's armies won a series of encounters at Cerro Gordo (April 17–18), Jalapa (April 19), Perota (April 22), and Puebla (May 15). After resting at Puebla to reinforce his army, many of whom became ill with smallpox, Scott continued his advance on August 7 and set up new headquarters at Ayotla on August 11. Although the American forces were, as usual, outnumbered by Mexican troops by 2 to 1, they defeated Santa Anna's positions at Contreras (August 19–20) and Churubusco (August 20), which caused the Mexican withdrawal to Mexico City. These victories over Mexico's larger armies were attributed to the military skills of General Scott and other officers such as Robert E. Lee.

Before attacking Mexico City, the armistice was arranged to discuss peace proposals with Mexico's president, Santa Anna.

September 7, 1847

The Armistice of Tacubaya ends after Mexico rejects the peace offers of Nicholas P. Trist.

President Polk appointed Trist on April 15, 1847, for a secret mission to arrange peace with Mexico. The secrecy of his mission became known quickly in Washington (April 20), even though Trist traveled to Vera Cruz under an assumed identity. Objecting to Trist's mission, General Scott believed the diplomat should not have precedence over military authority. Subsequently, British diplomatic aid was needed to reconcile the dispute between Trist and Scott and to arrange the armistice.

Trist began talks with former Mexican President Herrera on August 27, under the armistice of Tacubaya. Polk had instructed Trist to obtain both the Rio Grande boundary and territory including San Francisco. He was also to negotiate for lower

California and transit rights across the Isthmus of Tehuantepec.

After 10 days of discussion with Herrera and the other Mexican delegates, it became apparent to Trist that Santa Anna was stalling for time and was not willing to grant any of the American demands. Therefore the talks were ended on September 7. Scott renewed war against the capital city of Mexico the next day.

The Land of Liberty. A British satire of American the boastful American: a leering, cigar-smoking, unprincipled Yankee, guarding his almighty dollar and title to Oregon and Texas. Note references to slavery, debt repudiation, dueling, fighting with knives in Congress, and pillaging churches in Mexico. *Punch*, 1847.

September 14, 1847

Mexico City is captured; the American flag is raised over Mexico's national palace.

General Scott's final military victories in Mexico City came quickly after the armistice ended on September 7. General William J. Worth made a successful raid on the Mexican gun foundry at Molino del Rey (September 8), and on September 13, American storming parties scaled the rocky slopes of the fortification at Chapultepec and captured the strategic hill leading to the western city gates of San Cosme and Belen.

The next morning, American infantry and marines broke through the city walls and gained control of Mexico City. The U.S. Marines reached the "Halls of Montezuma", where they raised the American flag.

November 22, 1847

A new Mexican government asks Trist to negotiate peace under the terms he presented previously.

After the capital city fell, a group of moderate Mexican political leaders formed a new government under interim President Pedro Maria Anaya on November 11. Santa Anna had tried to besiege the American garrison at Puebla but failed on October 12. He then fled the country, leaving Mexico with no government until Anaya took over on November 11.

Although President Polk had recalled Trist from his peace mission on October 6 (the news reached Mexico on November 16), General Scott and Edward Thornton of the British legation persuaded Trist to remain and negotiate a treaty. Realizing that Polk could not fully understand the situation, Trist agreed and informed the Mexican leaders that he would negotiate with them.

December 23, 1847

France gains control of Algeria with the surrender of Abd El-Kader.

In 1848, Algeria was organized into three departments and given representation in the French parliament (revoked in 1852, after Napoléon III became Emperor).

1848

January 1, 1848

British Naval forces aid the Mosquito Indians in seizing the city of San Juan (Greytown) at the south of the San Juan River in Nicaragua.

This was one of several British ventures in Central America designed to assist British interests in getting rights to move their trade across the isthmus.

February 2, 1848

The Treaty of Guadalupe Hidalgo is signed by Trist and the Mexican commissioners.

Formal negotiation of the peace treaty did not begin until January 2 at a village outside Mexico City. Although Trist's discussions were not officially authorized, President Polk decided to submit the resulting treaty to the Senate, which ratified it on March 10, 1848. Ratifications were exchanged on May 30, and Polk proclaimed the treaty in effect on July 4, 1848.

The principal terms of the treaty were:

1. The U.S.-Mexican boundary was to go up the Rio Grande to New Mexico, across the Gila River to the Colorado River, and then to the Pacific Ocean. The treaty added 1,193,061 square miles, including Texas, to the U.S. domain.
2. The United States paid Mexico $15 million and assumed claims of American citizens totaling $3,250,000.

February 8, 1848

A Congress of the Pacific States of South America forms a confederation for protection from a threatened European intervention.

This congress met at Lima, Peru, from December 11, 1847, to March 1, 1848, and created an antimonarchist agreement against a new Spanish threat. The Spanish danger arose because a former president of Ecuador, General Juan José FLORES, organized a military expedition in Spain to regain the American colonies for Spain's monarch.

The Flores expedition aborted late in 1848, because Great Britain intervened and refused to allow the general's ships to leave Spanish waters. The five South American states that formed the confederation were New Granada, Ecuador, Peru, Bolivia, and Chile. They agreed to meet again in case of future threats to their independence.

For the U.S. reaction to this confederation, see May 13, 1848.

February 22, 1848

A revolution in France leads to Louis Philippe's abdication and the establishment of the Second Republic.

This Paris uprising inaugurated a series of republican rebellions throughout Europe; some were successful, others were not. Generally, the revolutions of 1848 ended the conservative era of Prince Metternich, which typified European politics between 1815 and 1848. After 1848, many European states moved to abolish or restrict their kings' power.

In France, Louis Philippe abdicated on February 24, permitting radical republicans at the Paris city hall to proclaim a republic. Disorders and riots continued throughout the summer of 1848 in various French cities. Finally, a constitution was approved and the Second Republic began. It had a one-chamber legislature and a strong president. On December 10, Louis Napoléon, the nephew of Napoléon I, won election as president of the republic.

February 28, 1848

Richard Rush, the U.S. Minister to France, quickly recognizes the new Republican government of France.

Rush, who assumed his position in Paris only in July 1847, indicated America's displeasure with the policies followed by Louis Philippe's government and its preference for a republican regime that would end the monarchy. Contrary to the advice of other nations' diplomatic delegations in Paris, Rush did not wait for instructions from Washington but rushed to be the first foreign representative to congratulate the French on restoration of republican government.

Although Rush's action was unprecedented, Polk and Buchanan supported his enthusiasm. On March 31, Secretary of State Buchanan wrote Rush that Polk would have regretted it if any other nation had preceded America in promoting the French republic.

March 4, 1848

The promulgation of a liberal constitution by Charles Albert, King of Piedmont, inspires Italy's unification plans.

Following the advice of Count Camillo Benso di CAVOUR, Charles Albert issued a constitution that established a parliamentary-cabinet government patterned after that of Great Britain. This act eventually brought other Italian liberals, followers of MAZZINI and GARIBALDI, into the Piedmontese effort to unite all Italian states into one nation.

March 7, 1848

The Yucatán province of Mexico seeks the protection of the United States, but President Polk refuses.

The Yucatán's agent in Washington, Don Justo SIERRA, appealed for American aid because of an Indian uprising that Sierra said threatened to exterminate the whites. If the United States would assist them, Sierra said, the Yucatán would surrender its sovereignty to the United States.

Polk would have refused the offer immediately, but he understood that the Yucatán's agents made similar invitations to France and England, a suggestion that alarmed the president. Therefore, Polk sent the Yucatán's request to Congress for advice. Some Southern expansionists favored the annexation of the Yucatán. Polk's supporters followed the president in opposing this request and in restricting U.S. expansion to the southwest and Oregon. Nevertheless, the decade of the 1850s saw several various proposals to expand U.S. territory into the Caribbean or Central America.

March 13, 1848

Republican uprisings in Vienna, Prague, and Budapest cause the resignation of Count Metternich, whose pro-monarchist methods symbolized European politics from 1815 to 1848.

The demonstrations in the three largest Habsburg cities began in Budapest, where liberals led by Lajos (Louis) KOSSUTH demanded a responsible government. The riots expanded to Vienna after Austrian troops fired on a student protest rally that broke out in Prague on March 15.

The early successes of the republicans did not last. Metternich's replacement was Prince Felix SCHWARZENBERG, an iron-willed royalist. He persuaded the Emperor Ferdinand to resign in favor of his 18-year-old son, Francis Joseph I. The royalists rallied in Prague and Vienna. An army under Prince Alfred Windischgratz bombarded Prague and crushed the Czech rebellion on June 17. Next, Windischgratz and Baron Joseph Jellachich forced the liberals in Vienna to submit. Hungary gave the Habsburgs more problems and held out for another year.

See August 9, 1849.

May 13, 1848

Secretary Buchanan supports South American efforts against European intervention.

In 1848 an American Congress met in Lima, Peru. As proposed by the U.S. delegation, the Congress approved resolutions to unite against General Flores's intended expedition being organized in Spain. On May 11, Buchanan informed the U.S. consul at Lima that Spain's government disclaimed any connection with Flores's plans. On May 13, 1848, the secretary informed Van Brugh LIVINGSTON at Quito, Ecuador, that the United States was concerned with any projects similar to Flores's that challenged Latin American independence. While the United States could not guarantee or ally with any group, it did use "all moral means" to discourage European interference in Latin America. Therefore, while the United States sympathized with the objectives of the Lima confederation of February 1848, the United States did not directly associate itself with such an alliance.

May 18, 1848

Opening session of the Frankfurt National Assembly of Germany.

Following a series of liberal uprisings in many German states in March 1848, a committee of 53 liberals arranged elections to be conducted for a constituent body for all Germany. This group of 830 delegates began meeting on May 18. The parliament eventually proposed a constitutional emperor in 1849, but its status deteriorated after April 21, 1849, when

Frederick William of Prussia rejected its offer to serve as emperor.

June 17, 1848

The Polk administration offers $100 million to purchase Cuba from Spain.

The idea of buying Cuba had been suggested to Secretary Buchanan by John L. "Manifest Destiny" O'Sullivan of the New York *Morning News* in a letter of March 19, 1848. The question was discussed by Polk's cabinet in May and June 1848, after the U.S. consul in Havana, R. B. Campbell, indicated that the creole leaders in Cuba desired to be annexed to America.

Secretary Buchanan opposed the scheme because he thought it would hurt the Democrats in the 1848 election. But Polk and other cabinet members wished to pursue the idea of buying Cuba, and on June 17 Buchanan sent instructions to the U.S. minister to Spain, Romulus M. Saunders, to offer to purchase the island. The secretary wrote Saunders that the United States feared another foreign power might seek to get Cuba and the United States could not permit such a contingency. Saunders could offer Spain $100 million in 10 annual installments for the cession of Cuba to America.

Spain refused to sell. The Spanish foreign minister told Saunders he would prefer to see Cuba sunk in the ocean before he would transfer it to any other power. This, of course, indicated that England would not easily be able to get control of the island.

August 5, 1848

President Polk appoints A. J. Donelson as Minister to the federal government of Germany.

Andrew Jackson Donelson, the U.S. minister to Berlin, received this appointment in the expectation that the Frankfurt Parliament of 1848 would succeed in uniting Germany under a liberal republican regime. Donelson had reported the details of the 1848 uprisings in the German states but foresaw the reluctance of the rulers of the German states to give their prerogatives to a federation.

Prussia's king, Frederick William, sent Baron Roenne as its envoy to America to replace the Prussian minister, Baron Gerolt. One interesting sidelight was Roenne's request for U.S. naval aid in planning a German navy. Initially the Polk administration agreed to assist, but when war developed between the German states and Denmark, this aid was withdrawn (see April 10, 1849).

August 21, 1848

Congressional legislation empowers U.S. ministers and consuls in China and Turkey to judge and punish U.S. citizens who commit crimes in those nations.

This law was necessary because American commercial treaties with China (July 3, 1844) and Turkey (May 7, 1830) contained EXTRATERRITORIALITY provisions. These treaty clauses exempted American citizens from trial and punishment by the governments of China and Turkey, placing such authority in the hands of U.S. consuls assigned to cities in each empire.

November 7, 1848

Zachary Taylor wins the Presidential election.

General Taylor received the Whig Party nomination on June 7 and campaigned on his military character and reputation to avoid the slavery issue. The Democratic Party could not agree on one nominee. At its Baltimore convention on May 22, the Democrats nominated General Lewis CASS for president. Cass ran on a platform that denied that Congress could interfere with slavery in the states.

The Democratic split occurred at the Baltimore convention over the seating of delegates from New York. Neither New York group took part in the convention, and on June 22 one New York group, the "Barnburners," who favored the Wilmot Proviso, met at Utica, New York, and nominated Martin Van Buren for president. Van Buren also got the support of the Free-Soil and Liberty Parties at a convention in Buffalo, New York, on August 9.

Van Buren did not carry a single state in the election, but his supporters divided the Democratic Party vote in New York, permitting Taylor to win New York's 36 electoral votes. New York's votes were the number needed by Taylor, who won 163 votes to Cass's 127 votes.

Congress was also badly divided in the 1848 election. In the Senate the Democrats held a majority of 10. In the House, however, no party held a majority, and a division between Northern and Southern Whigs

During General Zachary Taylor's campaign for president, opponents criticized his Mexican War record. Library of Congress

caused additional difficulties. The Whigs had 105 representatives and the Democrats 112, but 13 Free Soilers held the balance of power in House party votes.

1849

January 31, 1849

Commodore James Glynn is ordered to go to Nagasaki to require Japan to release eight American seamen; he succeeds.

The U.S. seamen had been rescued by the Japanese from a shipwrecked American whaling ship, the *Lagoda,* which had struck a shoal in the Sea of Japan. The seamen had not been well treated by the Japanese, who kept them imprisoned at Nagasaki. Upon hearing of the seamen's plight, U.S. Commissioner at Canton John W. Davis and the head of the U.S. navy squadron in China, David Geissinger, agreed that the men should be freed.

Thus, on January 31, Geissinger ordered Glynn to go to Nagasaki and effect the prisoners' release in a "conciliatory but firm" fashion. Using the aid of Dutch officers at Deshima in the bay of Nagasaki, Glynn obtained the release of the men. Apparently the seamen were ill treated because the Japanese believed they were American spies who had been sent to overthrow the government. During the 1840s, French, British, and Russian ships had arrived in various parts of Japan, and the Japanese had grown exceedingly suspicious if not fearful of these foreigners.

Commodore Glynn returned to America in 1851 and received a hero's welcome for having freed the Americans. At President Taylor's request, Glynn prepared a report on his experiences. The report included the recommendation that the United States should obtain a commercial treaty with Japan as soon as possible.

March 7, 1849

John Middleton Clayton is commissioned as Secretary of State.

Clayton had been a senator (1829–1836) and chief justice (1837–1839) for Delaware. He was best known as a scientific farmer. He was serving a second term as senator from Delaware when President Taylor selected him as secretary, a position he held until July 22, 1850.

April 10, 1849

Secretary Clayton questions the Prussian use of a ship being outfitted in the United States.

A vessel named the *United States* had been purchased by Prussia with the assistance of the U.S. navy under an arrangement provided in 1848 by President Polk. Since that time, war had broken out between Denmark and Prussia over Schleswig-Holstein; this brought the warship issue under U.S. neutrality provisions, especially after Denmark protested against the American assistance.

Clayton told Baron Roenne, the Prussian minister, that the ship could not sail from New York unless he declared it would not be used against any government at peace with the United States. Eventually, Roenne gave bond that the *United States* would not be used in the present war and the ship was released from New York.

June 12, 1849

The American-owned Panama Railroad Company secures a concession from Colombia to build and operate a railroad across the Isthmus of Panama.

The New York–chartered Panama Company was headed by William H. Aspinwall, John L. Stephens, and Henry Chauncey. Aspinwall was the president of the Pacific Mail Steamship Company, which had grown to be a leading American shipping concern during the 1840s. This company's ships carried passengers from New York and San Francisco to porterage across Panama and now planned to build the first transcontinental railroad in the isthmus.

Although Aspinwall failed in 1850 to persuade Congress to subsidize his venture, the Panama Company went ahead with its plans, completing the project in 1855.

See January 28, 1855.

June 21, 1849

Elisha Hise signs a treaty with Nicaragua to obtain exclusive U.S. rights to a canal through Nicaragua.

President Polk had sent Hise as a special envoy to Central America to obtain data about recent British activity in response to a complaint from Nicaragua. Hise learned the details of the British occupation of San Juan (Greytown) in 1847 and had become convinced that England planned to control any canal route across Nicaragua.

Without authorization, Hise decided to make a treaty with Nicaragua because it sought protection from British encroachments. The treaty gave U.S. citizens the exclusive right to build and fortify a Nicaraguan canal. The United States agreed to protect Nicaraguan territory.

Hise's treaty was never offered to the U.S. Senate for ratification. Secretary of State Clayton did not want to guarantee Nicaraguan territory and said Hise had exceeded his authority. Clayton sent E. George Squier to replace Hise.

See October 16, 1849.

August 9, 1849

The Hungarian Republic is crushed by Austrian and Russian armies.

Following the 1848 rebellions in the Habsburg Empire, the revolutions in Prague and Vienna were ended in six months by Austrian armies. In Budapest, however, the rebels defeated General Jellachich's forces, driving them out of Hungary in October 1848.

Early in 1849, the Hungarians continued to resist the imperial army. In January-February, General Windischgratz reconquered Budapest and most of Hungary. In March, however, the Hungarian General Arthur GORGEI rallied his followers and in early April liberated the nation from Austria once again.

On April 13, a Hungarian diet met and proclaimed a republic, electing Lajos (Louis) KOSSUTH as president the next day. The republic was short-lived, however. Austria secured assistance from Czar Nicholas I of Russia. As Russian armies under General Ivan PASKIEVICH invaded from the north, Austrian forces under General Julius HAYNAU attacked from the west. Gorgei's forces resisted fiercely but were outnumbered. On August 9, the Hungarians lost decisively at the battle of Temesvar and Gorgei surrendered on August 13. Kossuth resigned as president on August 11 and fled to Turkey.

The Austrians inflicted bloody vengeance on the Hungarians. Despite promises of clemency to Gorgei when he surrendered, the assize of ARAD convicted the rebel leaders of treason. Nine Hungarian generals were hanged; four were executed by a firing squad.

October 16, 1849

The British Navy seizes Tigre Island near Honduras.

The British seizure of this island in the Gulf of Fonseca on the Pacific coast of Honduras was another incident in the U.S.-British contest for canal rights in Central America.

E. George Squier, who replaced Hise as American consul in Central America, agreed with Hise's assessment of British design to control that region. The British Minister Frederick CHATFIELD was applying pressure on Honduras to grant Britain canal rights by demanding that Honduras settle debts owed to Great Britain. To forestall the British, Squier persuaded Honduras to cede Tigre Island to America for 18 months, during which time Squier hoped to make a canal treaty.

To counteract Squier's deal with Honduras, Chatfield ordered a British ship under Captain J. A. PAYNTER to seize Tigre Island and raise the British flag. Paynter seized the island on October 16, 1849. The British held the island until Foreign Minister Palmerston disavowed the act in February 1850 as part of the negotiations preceding the Clayton-Bulwer Treaty of 1850.

November 7, 1849

French President Louis Napoléon ends a Franco-American dispute of "honor."

An incident known as the Poussin Affair between America and France illustrates how an affair of national respect develops from words into near war. The incident arose because of a diplomatic exchange of notes between Secretary of State Clayton, French Minister to the United States William Fell POUSSIN, and later French Foreign Minister Alexis de TOCQUEVILLE and President Taylor.

The affair began as a simple claim by a French citizen for 500 bales of tobacco that the U.S. army had seized during the invasion of Mexico. Although a U.S. military court had paid a claim with interest, the Frenchman wanted greater compensation and appealed to Poussin for help. Clayton first responded that he believed the military court claim was sufficient. But Poussin persisted and, seeking to argue the merits of the court case, he wrote harshly to Clayton. The United States should honorably pay its debt, he wrote, and not brand the "character of an honest man," as Poussin claimed the court had done.

Somewhat exasperated, Clayton preferred to talk about the matter with Poussin. Clayton's request for an audience seemed to be offensive to Poussin. Clayton had written: "I lose not a moment in requesting you to repair to this city without unnecessary delay."

In subsequent messages, such slights multiplied between Poussin and Clayton and soon involved President Taylor and Foreign Minister de Tocqueville. Another incident occurred 30 days later, when the French insisted that a U.S. navy officer should be severely reprimanded and complained of the indignity inflicted on a French ship by the U.S. national marine. President Taylor, an old military man who disliked Poussin's implications affecting U.S. honor and dignity, told Clayton to protest to Paris. Clayton asked Tocqueville to review his minister's conduct and act appropriately. But the French foreign minister continued to back Poussin. He admitted that perhaps Poussin had "too much spirit," but Clayton had not been courteous in his observations about the minister.

By September, a major diplomatic crisis had grown from nothing. The United States asked Paris to recall Poussin; France refused to recognize W. C. Rives, the U.S. minister, who did not reach Paris until September 27 (Rives had been appointed by Taylor in March 1849). On this note, the affair continued into November, when Clayton instructed Rives to leave France and sever diplomatic relations if he had not yet been received by Tocqueville.

Before Clayton's final note reached Rives, President Louis Napoléon decided to stop the diplomatic sniveling. He received Rives on November 1, and, as the U.S. minister reported to Clayton, told the American that republicans should not act like monarchists over such affairs. With a republic such as America, Napoléon said, "he was ashamed to make the first advance." Further, he hoped his step in receiving Rives would be viewed in America "as a special mark of his consideration."

Clayton and Taylor agreed with the French president. Napoléon's action reached Washington in time for Taylor to mention France with "unusual praise in his speech to Congress of December 1849." While Rives thought Napoléon might have had ulterior motives for his change of policy, the French president certainly acted wisely in laying to rest an inconsequential affair. Under the "old diplomacy" of the 19th century such conflicts of words were often exaggerated beyond their necessity and often caused a war or a near-war crisis.

December 4, 1849

President Taylor recommends the admission of California as a state.

Because he believed Congress did not need to legislate for the U.S. territories on such issues as slavery, Taylor sent agents to tell California and New Mexico to organize their own governments.

California organized a government during the fall of 1849. Because its population grew rapidly to over 100,000 after the discovery of gold (January 24, 1848),

California needed to establish law and order quickly. A Monterey Convention adopted a constitution on October 13, and the people ratified it on November 13. Their new government was ready to function by the time Taylor recommended California's admission as a state.

Taylor's proposal caused political problems. California's constitution placed it in the "free" state category. Its admission would upset the political balance in the Senate, where, in 1849, there were 15 slave and 15 free states represented. As a result, California's application for admission led to intense political wrangling in 1850 because of Southern opposition.

1850

April 19, 1850

The Clayton-Bulwer Treaty provides an Anglo-American agreement on a Central American canal.

By this treaty, the United States and Great Britain tried to settle a series of disputes regarding each nation's interest in a canal or trade route in the isthmus region of Central America. The two nations agreed that (1) neither would seek exclusive control of such a canal; (2) a canal would be open to all nations on equal terms; (3) the canal would be neutralized; and (4) neither nation would exercise dominion over Nicaragua, Costa Rica, the Mosquito Coast, or any part of Central America.

The treaty climaxed disputes between the two nations in Central America that began in 1847 and increased after the discovery of gold in California made such a canal more essential. In January 1848, Britain forced Nicaragua to renounce the city of San Juan (Britain called it Greytown) at the mouth of the San Juan River. The British also extended their protection over the Mosquito Indians down the coast, south of Belize.

Although the Mexican War diverted American attention from the isthmus in 1848, President Polk had sent Elisha Hise to Nicaragua to obtain data about British intentions. Hise exceeded his authority, however, because he signed a treaty with Nicaragua to protect it from other powers and to receive an exclusive American right-of-way for a canal.

Secretary Clayton refused to send Hise's treaty to the Senate and sent E. George Squier to replace him. Squier obtained a similar treaty but one that protected the rights of Cornelius Vanderbilt, whose Atlantic and Pacific Shipping Company wanted a right-of-way in Nicaragua. Squier's treaty also omitted an American guarantee of Nicaraguan independence.

Although Clayton did not approve either the Squier or the Hise treaties, he used them to pressure Sir Henry Lytton Bulwer, British minister to the United States, and Foreign Minister Palmerston to make a joint agreement regarding the isthmus. The one problem of negotiation that faced Clayton and Bulwer was the British claim about protection of the Mosquito Indians, which the United States rejected. This matter was resolved by an oral U.S. statement disclaiming the British Mosquito rights and by inserting into the treaty a clause that said neither party would make "use of any protection" to indirectly seek control over areas of Central America.

With the above understanding, the treaty was signed on April 19, 1850. The U.S. Senate approved it on May 22 by a vote of 42 to 11. But the British delayed ratification until an agreement was made to exclude British Honduras from the term "Central America." The final treaty ratifications were exchanged on July 5, 1850.

This treaty soon became unpopular and open to dispute, as subsequent Anglo-American diplomacy would demonstrate.

For Hise treaty, see June 21, 1849; see also April 30, 1852.

July 7, 1850

U.S. demand for a claims settlement causes a break in relations with Portugal.

An illustration of President Taylor's firm nationalistic policy, Secretary of State Clayton's vigorous attempt to settle a series of U.S. claims extending back to the War of 1812 caused difficulty with Lisbon. The oldest U.S. claim, that of the owners of the privateer *General Armstrong,* had been abandoned with Britain by the Treaty of Ghent of 1815 but continued to be demanded of Portugal for a violation of neutrality. Five other cases claimed by shipowners were less difficult to settle in the negotiations.

As soon as he took office in 1849, Secretary Clayton asked the U.S. minister to Portugal, George W. Hopkins, to obtain an immediate settlement. Hopkins's efforts were fruitless, and in March 1850, Clayton instructed the newly appointed minister to

Portugal, James Clay, to try to liquidate all claims for some "round sum." In July 1850, Clayton asked the secretary of the navy to send further orders to Clay aboard an American warship. This ship would await Clay, and if settlement was not reached within 20 days, Clay should break relations by leaving Lisbon on the naval ship.

On July 7, Portugal offered to settle all claims excepting the *General Armstrong* case, for which it requested arbitration. Because Clayton had instructed him not to accept arbitration, Clay refused the July 7 offer. He immediately demanded his passports and left Lisbon on the U.S. warship a few days later.

Relations with Portugal remained strained for another year. In 1851, President Millard Fillmore and Secretary Webster turned aside Taylor's uncompromising stance and agreed to submit the *General Armstrong* case to arbitration. The arbitrator ruled against the American shipowners, a ruling that was accepted and ended all U.S. claims cases against Portugal as of 1851.

The American Rover-General who Tried to Steal a Cuba. The British chide Americans as they are expelled. *Punch,* 1950

July 8, 1850

Spain releases all but three Americans arrested in an attempt to invade Cuba—the first López venture.

Because there had been rumors of revolutionists in Cuba, some Southern U.S. expansionists hoped to promote an independence rebellion in Cuba. In August 1848, Secretary of State Clayton learned about a group being organized by Narciso López for action in Cuba. Clayton and President Taylor opposed these illegal acts and successfully halted the expeditionary vessels, the *Sea Gull* and the *New Orleans.*

As a result, López shifted his activity from New York to New Orleans, where he organized another plot against Cuba. López used expert legal advice to evade the authorities, and his three ships left New Orleans on May 1, 1850, and eluded U.S. naval ships sent to stop him. One ship, the *Creole,* landed a group of men at Cardena, Cuba, where they burned several buildings before the Spanish chased them back to their ship. They fled to Key West.

The other two vessels stopped at Contoy, a small key off the Yucatán coast. Although this was Mexican territory, Spanish officials seized 40–50 men who were aboard these ships and took them to Havana for trial.

At this point, Secretary Clayton protested to Spain, arguing that these crews could not be arrested by Spain on Mexican territory. Clayton also persuaded Taylor to warn Spain that he would ask Congress to declare war if the U.S. prisoners were executed.

To emphasize the U.S. threat, Taylor ordered a U.S. naval ship under Commodore Charles Morris to go to Havana and warn the captain general of Cuba not to harm the American prisoners. The United States also protested through the U.S. minister in Madrid and the Spanish minister to Washington, Calderon de la Barca.

While Clayton protested, the trial of the prisoners took place before a Spanish naval court in Cuba. In July, the court released all but three of the prisoners. The captain and mate of the *Georgiana* and the mate of the *Susan Loud* were given prison terms. In October 1850, however, the queen of Spain pardoned the three

Americans as a "proof of friendship to the United States."

July 9, 1850

President Taylor dies in Washington of cholera morbus. Millard Fillmore takes the oath of office on July 10.

July 22, 1850

Daniel Webster is given a second appointment as Secretary of State by President Fillmore.

Webster served in the office until his death on October 24, 1852.

Webster's appointment in 1850 symbolized President Fillmore's desire to emphasize and try to resolve domestic American issues rather than be concerned with foreign expansion. Webster and Fillmore desired a compromise with the South on the slavery question rather than to defy the slaveholders as the William Seward faction advocated. Thus, Webster looked at diplomatic questions in relation to the domestic crisis developing in America and the need to preserve the union.

Clayton had resigned as secretary following Taylor's death on July 9. He was apparently glad to have a good excuse to resign because he had wearied of the burdens of the office and because a kidney disease was endangering his health.

September 9, 1850

The Compromise of 1850 admits California as a free state and organizes the territorial governments of New Mexico and Utah under "popular sovereignty."

On September 9, a lengthy political dispute in Congress ended with the first of a series of five laws passed as part of the so-called Compromise of 1850. In addition to admitting California and organizing the territories of Utah and New Mexico, the compromise included the Fugitive Slave Act of September 18 and the Act to Abolish the Slave Trade in the District of Columbia of September 20. The compromise intended to solve the basic divisions between the slave and free states. It did so only temporarily because disagreement about the compromise grew during the next decade.

December 21, 1850

Secretary of State Webster informs Austria that Americans were proud to have supported the Hungarian attempt to win independence from the Habsburg Empire.

Webster's note in behalf of the Hungarian republic of 1849 responded to a protest of U.S. activity made by the Chevalier HULSEMANN, Austria's chargé d'affaires in Washington. Hulsemann contended that an American agent had interfered in Austrian affairs. The agent he referred to was A. Dudley MANN, whom President Taylor sent on a special mission to Hungary on July 18, 1849. Taylor instructed Mann to obtain information about the Hungarian uprising of March 1848, and about the republican efforts of the rebellious army.

Hulsemann on September 30, 1850, objected in particular to the portion of Mann's instructions that allowed him to recognize the Hungarian republic if conditions made it feasible to do so. Hulsemann wrote that he had not planned to protest until President Taylor's message of December 1849 expressed sympathy for the Hungarians and Taylor released the correspondence of Mann to the Senate on March 28, 1850.

Webster's response to Hulsemann reflected the growing pride of Americans that the "Young America" movement exemplified in an exaggerated style. As Webster explained, he wanted to "tell the people of Europe who and what we are" and "to touch national pride" so that he might "make a man feel *sheepish* and look silly who should speak of disunion."

Although part of Webster's reply to Hulsemann argued the confidentiality of U.S. instructions to its diplomatic agents, his telling remarks described America as a lighthouse for republican ideas in all the world. The United States, he wrote, was a "successful example of free government" such as the monarchs of Europe dreaded when the Austrian rulers previously denied the "lawfulness of the origin" of the American government. The United States, exclaimed Webster, was not disturbed by monarchical denunciation. The U.S. republic was a rich, fertile land "in comparison with which the possessions of the Habsburgs are but as a patch on the earth's surface." The United States was ready to take its chances on retaliation by Austria and would continue to express its opinions "freely and at all times on world events because the only principles of government which meet the demands of the present enlightened age are the civil liberties of Americans."

The purpose of Webster's letter is seen in the widespread publicity he gave to the dispatch to Hulsemann. Americans without regard to party praised Webster's response. Nevertheless, Webster's note to Hulsemann did not signal a change in America's nonintervention policy toward Europe: opinions, yes; actions, no.

1851

July 14, 1851

A New York to San Francisco transportation route opens service by way of Nicaragua.

The Accessory Transit Company (ATC) of Cornelius VANDERBILT and associates organized this travel service. In 1849, Vanderbilt, Joseph L. WHITE, and Nathaniel J. WOLFE received a charter from Nicaragua giving them an exclusive right-of-way for a canal through that country.

After extensive surveys showed that a canal through Nicaragua was impractical, Vanderbilt changed his older Atlantic and Pacific Ship Canal Company to the ATC and obtained transit rights for a route through the lakes and rivers of Nicaragua. This route opened on July 14, 1851, with one steamship, the *Prometheus*, operating between New York and San Juan del Norte and another ship, the *Pacific*, on runs between San Francisco and San Juan del Sur. The route operated as follows: (1) a 9-to-10-day steamship trip from New York to Nicaragua; (2) a river steamer up the San Juan River to Lake Nicaragua with one porterage at the Saltillo Rapids; (3) a steamer for 119 miles across the length of Lake Nicaragua; (4) a mule cart ride for 12 miles to the Pacific coast; (5) steamship from Nicaragua to San Francisco. By 1854, the mule ride was replaced by luxury carriages drawn by four mules down a macadamized road.

Vanderbilt's Nicaraguan route was shorter than Aspinwall's Panamanian route (4,531 to 4,992 miles) and faster by about four days. Consequently, the ATC profited greatly and ended the monopoly of the isthmian travel held by Aspinwall's Pacific Mail Steamship Company. In 1855, however, the completion of a railway across Panama revived that route because the time was cut to a difference of only two days and the train was much more comfortable than the transit across Nicaragua.

For Aspinwall's railroad route, see June 12, 1849, and January 28, 1855.

August 16, 1851

Colonel William Crittenden and 50 other Americans are executed in Cuba for attempting to overthrow the Spanish government.

Crittenden and other American volunteers had been recruited for their venture against Cuba by General Narciso LÓPEZ, head of Cuban refugees in the United States. LÓPEZ had been trying for two years to march on Havana. He told his U.S. recruits that Cuba was ripe for revolution and that as soon as a force landed on the beaches near Havana, his comrades in Cuba would rise up in masses to join the rebels and overthrow Spanish rule.

López's expedition of August 1851 was his third and largest attempt. His first try ended on August 11, 1849, because President Taylor ordered federal authorities to intervene. The second failed on May 19, 1850, although many of his men landed at Cardenas, Cuba.

President Fillmore tried to stop López's activity by a proclamation on April 25, 1851. Fillmore warned American citizens that it was illegal to prepare and launch such expeditions against another country. The Southern expansionists who were eager to annex Cuba to America did not heed the president.

López's third and last expedition sailed for New Orleans on August 3, 1851. The ships reached a beach 60 miles from Havana and nearly 200 men went ashore. Their cause was hopeless. The uprising of Cubans that LÓPEZ promised never materialized. On August 13, Crittenden and 50 of his patrol were caught. The next day a military court tried them and on August 16 the Spanish authorities executed them. LÓPEZ fled but was captured on August 28, together with 162 Americans. The Spanish publicly garroted LÓPEZ; the 162 prisoners were sent to Spain.

In New Orleans, Americans rioted to protest Crittenden's execution. The demonstrators marched on the Spanish consulate and wrecked the building. For this reason, Spain refused the U.S. State Department's request for the prisoners' release until the Americans paid for the damage to the consulate. Congress voted an appropriation of $25,000 to pay the damages, and the prisoners taken to Spain were freed.

December 2, 1851

Louis Napoléon's coup d'état ends the Second French Republic and leads to the establishment of the Second Empire one year later.

Declared to be Emperor Napoléon III on December 2, 1852, the new French ruler began an activist foreign policy in an attempt to duplicate the international successes of his famous uncle.

December 5, 1851

Americans give a great public reception to Lajos Kossuth, the Hungarian patriot and exiled republican leader.

Kossuth had fled Hungary on August 11, 1849, after the Austro-Russian armies defeated the Hungarian rebellion. He went to Turkey, where the United States interceded to secure his release and visit to America in 1851.

"*Fast Friends.*" (Left to right) England, Kossuth, and America. *Punch*, 1950

During Kossuth's visit, Webster's note to Hulsemann of December 21, 1850, was recalled again as Americans denounced European monarchs and praised the cause of republican government. No foreigner since Lafayette received such favors as Kossuth did. President Fillmore entertained Kossuth at the White House on December 5, and on January 7, 1852, Congress organized a banquet supported by members of all political parties. At the banquet, Webster praised Kossuth and offered good wishes for "Hungarian independence, Hungarian self-government, Hungarian control of Hungarian destinies."

The public favor did not translate into government support for Kossuth. The Hungarian leader wanted America to join with Great Britain to forcibly prevent Russian interference in Hungary and to help him fund his rebellious forces in a new effort against Austria. As Webster wrote a friend, "I shall treat him with all personal and individual respect, but if he should speak to me of the policy of 'intervention,' I shall 'have ears more deaf than adders.'" In a few weeks the celebration ended; the serious part of Kossuth's mission to America failed. U.S.-Austrian relations were strained for a time, but after Webster's death on October 24, 1852, diplomacy between the two nations became normalized again.

Kossuth experienced difficulties with other Hungarian exiles in America. They claimed he was arrogant. Consequently, Kossuth moved to England, where he continued to speak on behalf of Hungarian independence.

1852

January 10, 1852

The leader of the young America movement endorses Stephen A. Douglas for the Democratic Presidential nomination.

According to the January 10 issue of the *New York Herald,* George N. SANDERS, who had begun in 1851 to call for a Young America movement to match the Young Italy and Young German movements in Europe, decided to propose Senator Douglas as the appropriate Democratic candidate for president in opposition to such "old fogy" Democrats as Lewis Cass and William Marcy.

Sanders had become editor of the *Democratic Review,* the main backer of Young America. The group was an informal alignment of youthful

Democrats who wanted a vigorous, nationalistic policy for the United States that would fulfill the American mission to support the spread of republics throughout the world.

The term "Young America" had first been used by Edwin de Leon in a commencement address at South Carolina College in 1845. After the Mexican War ended and the 1848 republican revolutions took place in Europe, the concept of Young America received more support in the United States.

The movement appears, however, to have had more bark than bite. Sanders and others were outspokenly in favor of republican revolutions and U.S. expansion but made little headway in politics. Sanders sought in vain to get financial aid for Lajos Kossuth. After President Pierce appointed him as the U.S. consul in London in 1853, the U.S. Senate rejected his nomination. The movement did not get Douglas nominated in 1852 and gradually lost its luster and following by 1854.

March 16, 1852

U.S. policy in China succeeds in having the Shanghai settlements internationalized.

Ever since Shanghai had been opened as a Western port in 1844, U.S. and British consuls disputed Britain's claim to be the sole authority regulating land purchases and other details of daily life in the ports of China. Britain had dominated the port of Canton before 1839, and by the Treaty of Nanking of 1842 England had sole control of Hong Kong. Therefore, the United States advocated the internationalization of foreign settlements in the new ports, that is, the Western nations working together with no one nation in control.

To achieve internationalization, the U.S. consul first obtained Chinese recognition that the U.S. treaty of 1844 gave America rights equal to British rights to occupy land. On March 16, 1852, the Chinese officials accepted this concept when they completed the sale of land to an American by going through the office of U.S. Vice Consul Edward Cunningham, rather than through the British consul as in the past. Soon after, Cunningham issued a circular letter to other U.S. consuls in China asking them to maintain this agreement at the other four treaty ports.

Although the British consul protested this action on March 23, 1852, the British government in London accepted the international concept in May 1853. As a result, a municipal law code was prepared for the international settlement at Shanghai, a code for Westerners to follow in their conduct of business as well as in buying and selling land in China. One vital clause of the code recognized Chinese sovereignty over the land in the International Settlements. China received a small annual tax, and all land deeds had to have the Chinese seal of authority. Furthermore, the municipal government received its authority to rule from the Chinese government.

April 30, 1852

The Webster-Crampton Convention clarifies parts of the Clayton-Bulwer Treaty.

While the Clayton-Bulwer Treaty resolved the issue of isthmian canal rights, other Anglo-American relations with the Central American states became confused after 1850 with regard to boundary questions. Following Bulwer's retirement as minister to the United States because of ill health, Secretary of State Webster and the new British minister, F. T. Crampton, continued to discuss these affairs in a conciliatory fashion. Eventually, the two agreed to sign the convention of 1852 to resolve problems of Central America.

By this convention, the British ceded Greytown (San Juan) to Nicaragua. Great Britain also agreed to continue assistance to the Mosquito Indians for three years before turning their protection over to Nicaragua. The treaty required the concurrent approval of Nicaragua's government. It objected to the parts of the treaty concerning possible canals through its territory. Subsequently, because of Nicaraguan opposition, the Treaty of 1852 was not ratified. Plans for a possible canal in Nicaragua had to be postponed.

In 1852, Nicaragua seemed to be satisfied with the potential income it would receive from Vanderbilt's isthmian transportation facilities, which had begun operation on July 14, 1851 (see that date). In addition, Vanderbilt's surveys for a canal revealed that substantial problems were involved in building a canal through Nicaragua. Vanderbilt conducted his activity quite independently of the State Department.

See March 12, 1857.

June 30, 1852

Webster fails in a final effort to obtain Mexican approval for an American railroad across the Isthmus of Tehuantepec.

In August 1850, Webster and Mexican officials began a series of negotiations to obtain concessions that would assist a group of Americans who had purchased a grant to build a railroad in the Tehuantepec isthmus. In 1850, Secretary of State Clayton's attempt to secure these privileges had failed, as would Webster's, because of Mexican fears that another part of its territory would fall to the United States. On May 22, 1851, the Mexican Congress repealed the land grant that the Americans had been assigned in 1846.

Nevertheless, on June 30, 1852, Webster tried once again to clear the air by proposing guarantees to Mexico that the United States would not take over the territory and the railroad could be used by all nations on an equal basis. Once again, the Mexican government rejected Webster's entreaties.

Because of Webster's failure, American railroad interests began more seriously to seek a method to obtain a railroad running entirely in U.S. territory from New York to California. In the long run the expense of such railroads seemed increasingly better than the isthmian connections heretofore attempted. Such projects gained support from the Republican Party in 1860 when its campaign platform agreed to sponsor government aid for a transcontinental railroad.

November 2, 1852

Franklin Pierce is elected President in a major victory for the Union Democrats and a defeat indicating the demise of the Whig Party.

The Democratic Party nominated Pierce at its Baltimore convention on June 1, 1852. Its platform gained the support of the Southern Union Rights Party because it affirmed the Compromise of 1850, opposed any congressional action regarding slavery, and endorsed the states' rights ideas of the 1799 Kentucky Virginia Resolutions. In addition, Pierce favored the expansion of U.S. territory.

At Baltimore on June 16, the Whigs named General Winfield Scott as their candidate. Although the Whigs' platform generally imitated that of the Democrats, the party had already divided seriously on a sectional basis. Former Southern Whigs had joined the Union Rights Party; many Northern Whigs joined the Free Soil Party.

A third presidential candidate was named by the Free-Soil Party—John P. HALE. Its platform condemned both slavery and the Compromise of 1850, and favored free homesteads and unimpeded immigration.

Although the Free-Soil Party received no electoral votes and few popular votes (156,149), its Northern votes cost the Whigs several states gained by the Democrats. Pierce received the electoral votes of 27 states (254 votes); Scott won only 4 states (42 votes).

November 5, 1852

Commodore Matthew Perry receives instructions for obtaining a commercial treaty from Japan.

Previously, Japan allowed only one Dutch trading ship each year to make contact with Japan, a policy going back to 1638, when the TOKUGAWA dynasty of SHOGUNS deported all Europeans and isolated itself from "barbaric" Western influence. During the 1840s, several proposals had been considered by U.S. merchants and consuls in China regarding a new treaty with Japan. The *Lagoda* incident of January 31, 1849, further inspired such American action.

By 1852, President Fillmore agreed to a Japanese mission and appointed Commodore Perry of the U.S. navy to command a naval expedition. Because Secretary of State Webster was ill, Perry took the unusual step of preparing his own instructions, which, of course, the State Department approved. Because Daniel Webster had previously prepared instructions for Commodore J. B. AULICK to conduct the mission, the differences between a diplomatic and a military structure for such a mission may be compared. Aulick's mission had been planned in 1851 but was cancelled when he became ill.

A vital area of difference between Webster and Perry related to the approach to make in meeting Japanese officials. Webster had taken the advice of U.S. consuls in China by avoiding all references to the previous treatment of American sailors as in the *Lagoda* incident. In contrast, Perry wrote that Japan's conduct toward shipwrecked sailors was an act of a "weak and semi-barbarous people," who may be considered "as the common enemy of mankind." Japan must be held to act more properly in the future because its disregard for persons in distress was not tolerable.

Nevertheless, Perry's objectives were the same as those of Webster in 1851: (1) to gain protection of distressed seamen; (2) to open one or more Japanese ports for trade; and (3) to obtain rights to purchase coal for ships.

To accomplish his task, Perry desired a fleet of five steamers and six or more sailing ships. Japan would be assured of American friendship but must be informed that the United States required "positive assurance" there would be no more incidents such as those experienced by the *Lagoda, Morrison,* and *Lawrence,* all U.S. ships whose crews were mistreated. If conciliatory words did not seem to be sufficient, Perry would warn the Japanese that if any further American seamen were mistreated, Japan "will be severely chastised."

Perry had given himself wide powers to treat with Japan. His instructions were approved by Acting Secretary of State C. M. Conrad on November 5, 1852. He sailed from Norfolk, Virginia, for Japan on November 24, 1852.

See February 15 and July 8–13, 1853.

November 6, 1852

Following Webster's death on October 24, Edward Everett is commissioned as Secretary of State.

Everett had been a Unitarian minister and professor of Greek literature at Harvard before serving as a congressman from Massachusetts from 1825 to 1835. He was a minister to Great Britain from 1841 to 1845 and president of Harvard University from 1846 to 1849. He served as secretary of state until March 3, 1853.

November 16, 1852

The United States reverses its previous claims and recognizes Peru's rights to the Lobos Islands.

These islands, which were off the coast of Peru and held valuable guano deposits, had been used by Americans and protected by a U.S. naval force. Webster supported the American claims when he first learned of them in 1852, but later, on the basis of Peruvian objections, he realized he had been hasty in his original opinion and before his death began a formal paper that his friend and successor Edward Everett used to acknowledge Peru's claim.

On November 16, Everett spoke to the minister of Peru in Washington and explained that the United States withdrew its earlier claims and now recognized without a doubt Peru's claim to the Lobos Islands.

December 1, 1852

The United States refuses to join England and France in a Treaty to protect Spain's retention of Cuba.

The talk of Southern American annexationists and the action of the LÓPEZ expeditions inspired France and Great Britain to prepare an agreement to disclaim "now and for hereafter" any intention of possession of or assuming dominion over Cuba. The French and British ministers at Washington presented this agreement to Secretary Webster on April 23, 1852, and requested that the United States join in a tripartite pact to keep the status quo in Cuba.

Some consideration had been given to this request before Webster's death, but a final response had to be made by Secretary Everett. Everett's note rejected the request that the United States join in such an agreement. Not only was the U.S. tradition to avoid political alliances, but the United States had a greater interest in Cuba's status than either of the European powers.

Everett noted that the United States had previously stated its desire that no power but Spain should hold Cuba. Furthermore, the United States had no present intention of possessing Cuba. Nevertheless, the American government could not fix the fortune of Cuba "now and for hereafter." Future circumstances might easily change the views of all three powers regarding Cuba. Thus, while the United States did not want France, England, or Spain to assume incorrect inferences from this rejection, the president believed that at present there should be no change in Cuba. Thus, Everett decisively closed the door to any trilateral action on Cuba with France and England.

1853

January 20, 1853

British forces capture and occupy Rangoon and Pegu in Burma, ending a British war against the Burmese.

February 8, 1853

Anglo-American claims convention settles all outstanding claims of the two nations.

Because the Treaty of Ghent in 1815 had settled prior spoliation claims, the Convention of 1853 involved only a variety of small claims between citizens of each nation. American claimants received $329,734.16, British claimants, $277,102.88.

February 10, 1853

The Secretary of the Navy recommends that Congress subsidize or encourage the operation of a steamship line to China by the great circle route.

This interesting proposal of Secretary of the Navy John P. Kennedy was derived from a report written by Lieutenant M. F. Maury of the U.S. Naval Observatory.

Kennedy advocated a steamship route across the Pacific from California to China by a northern route bypassing Hawaii because it was shorter. Maury's calculations showed that a great circle route from Panama to China was 1,200 miles shorter than a route by way of the Sandwich Islands (Hawaii). He also noted that such a route from Monterey, California, to Japan was closer than a line from Panama to Honolulu.

To establish this route, Kennedy urged Congress either to set up a direct government agency to subsidize the company or to encourage individual enterprise to undertake the project.

February 15, 1853

Commodore Perry receives permission to occupy the Liu-Ch'iu (Ryukyu) Islands if Japan does not willingly open them to the United States.

These islands lay off the coast of China between the Japanese Islands and Formosa. Americans in the 19th century usually referred to them as the "Lew Chew" Islands, which was an Americanized version of the Chinese Liu-ch'iu. In the 20th century they are usually referred to as either the Loochoo or Ryukyu Islands.

During his voyage to Japan, Perry had written to the secretary of the navy to describe U.S. naval needs in the Pacific Ocean. He particularly recommended the U.S. occupation of the Ryukyu Islands "for the accommodation of our ships of war and for the safe resort of merchant vessels of whatever nation."

As a naval strategist, Perry believed that in the Pacific Ocean, the United States needed ports as a refuge, trade base, and place for forts in case of war with a European nation. The United States, he said, had to protect our "vast and rapidly growing commerce" to fulfill the destiny of our "ambitious longings of increased power, which are the natural concomitant of material success."

On February 15, 1853, Secretary of State Everett responded that the president approved occupying the Ryukyu Islands but cautioned Perry not to take supplies without paying for them and "to make no use of force, except in the last resort or in defense, if attacked, and for self-preservation."

On July 11, 1854, Perry signed a treaty with the "King of the Lew Chew Islands." This document recognized the king's government as independent of both China and Japan, opened the port of Napa to American trade, and provided for the safety of distressed sailors. This treaty was approved by Congress on March 3, 1855, and the treaty proclaimed on March 9, 1855. The Japanese assumed the obligations of this treaty on November 5, 1872.

March 7, 1853

President Pierce commissions William Learned Marcy as secretary of state.

Marcy held a variety of political positions before becoming secretary of state. He had been a senator (1831–1833) and governor (1833–1838) of New York; served on the Mexican Claims Commission (1840–1842); and was secretary of war (1845–1849). He served Pierce throughout his four-year term of office.

June 1, 1853

An American diplomatic dress circular is issued by Secretary of State Marcy.

Prompted apparently by Senator Charles Sumner, Secretary Marcy sent a circular letter to all U.S. representatives abroad encouraging them to wear a "simplicity of dress" when they attended official functions. In line with ideals of "True Democracy," U.S. officials should follow the example of Benjamin Franklin, "our first and foremost representative at a royal court," in wearing "the simple dress of an American citizen."

Actually, Marcy's guidelines for dress permitted U.S. diplomats some degree of judgment about what they wore. The official could conform to the customs of the country he was accredited to if he deemed that most suitable. But Marcy hoped to convince the U.S. representatives that simple dress was most appropriate for our citizens.

July 8–13, 1853

Perry's naval expedition is anchored near the city of Uraga in the Bay of Edo (Tokyo).

Perry's fleet of two steamships belching black smoke from their stacks, and two sailing ships, arrived in Japanese waters to seek a treaty with Japan's emperor. Not knowing what to expect, Perry's ships arrived with their decks cleared and ready for war, if necessary.

On arrival, the commodore isolated himself like an Oriental potentate and demanded to be received by high-ranking agents of the imperial government. When low-ranked Japanese officials told him through intermediaries to go to Nagasaki, he refused. He informed these minor officers that if a direct messenger of the emperor would not come to receive the president's letter, he would land with a force sufficient to deliver it himself. If the emperor refused to accept the president's letter, Perry would consider it an insult requiring redress for which he would not be accountable.

Perry's threat brought the emperor's first counselor, the Prince of Idzu, to the site, and Perry went ashore to deliver the president's letter.

Back aboard his ship, Perry took his fleet farther into the bay to within seven miles of the city of Tokyo. He then notified the Japanese that he would return in the spring with more ships to receive the emperor's response. Over the fall and winter, Perry's fleet went to Napa in the Ryukyu Islands. He also ordered Commander John Kelly to go to the Bonin Islands

Commodore Matthew Perry lands near Tokyo. National Archives

and took possession of Baily Island in the name of the United States. Although Great Britain claimed this island, Perry maintained that a U.S. navy captain named Coffin had reached Baily first in 1823, four years before the British.

July 23, 1853

The Pierce Administration reaffirms Fillmore's policy of Status Quo on Cuba.

The Cuban situation had become so unsettled since 1848 that its annexation by the United States seemed to be foreordained. President Polk had tried to purchase the island, the López expeditions tried to "liberate" it, and the weak Spanish local rulers in Cuba not only failed to quell disturbances, but made matters worse.

Nevertheless, in a July 23 message to Pierre Soulé, U.S. minister to Spain, Secretary Marcy instructed him not to offer to buy Cuba but as much as possible to maintain the neutrality followed by President Fillmore. Marcy's memorandum did note that American policy on Cuba hinged on U.S. security. He believed, however, that at present U.S. policy was (1) to oppose Cuba's transference to another power; (2) to be neutral regarding Cuba; (3) to be disinterested in obtaining Cuba; (4) to hope for an independent Cuba; (5) to settle with Spain the claims for U.S. property damage in Cuba.

See April 3, 1854, for changes in this policy.

September 7, 1853

The Taiping rebels in China capture Shanghai and directly affect the western settlements.

Led by a Chinese mystic, the T'ai (Great) P'ing (Peace) soldiers fought to overthrow the Chinese emperor and establish a new dynasty. The rebels captured Nanking in March 1853 and marched on Shanghai, which fell to the rebels on September 7.

The collapse of the imperial authority in Shanghai left the Western powers uncertain as to whom to pay the customs duties owed to China under their treaties. Initially, the British and Americans collected the fees, intending to forward them to the proper government when order was restored. Other nations stopped collecting the fees, each allowing its nation's ships to unload and sell goods without paying the treaty fees. On January 4, 1854, U.S. Commissioner in China Humphrey Marshall decided to stop collecting the customs fees so the American shippers would not be discriminated against by nations that had already stopped their collections.

Westerners in China were uncertain whether they should oppose or promote the Taiping. Some missionaries sympathized with the rebels because their leader inspired his followers with biblical verses and some Christian ideas. Other Western agents believed their treaty rights with the emperor would be jeopardized if the Taiping took over, because they were not certain whether the rebels would honor the treaties. After 1858, when Peking extended the Western treaty privileges, most of the China "experts" decided to support the imperial authority against the Taiping.

September 12, 1853

U.S. Minister to London James Buchanan is given full power to negotiate a settlement of Central American problems with Great Britain.

Anglo-American issues in the area just south of Mexico had been developing since 1848. The Clayton-Bulwer Treaty of 1850 solved only part of the difficulty because questions about British rights persisted.

On July 2, 1853, Marcy's initial instructions to Buchanan on his mission to London outlined what Marcy deemed to be British violations of the Monroe Doctrine. In particular, Marcy's concerns included the British extension of its Belize's territory, British claims to protectorship over the Mosquito Indians, and British jurisdiction over Ruatan and other islands in the Bay of Honduras. If possible, Marcy preferred to exclude Britain from all these areas and even contested its claims to Belize.

After reaching London, Buchanan sought further authority to negotiate an agreement on Central America with Lord Clarendon, Britain's foreign minister. On September 12, Marcy granted Buchanan such power. The negotiations with Clarendon continued for two years but were not successful in formulating a treaty to resolve these issues.

September 26, 1853

U.S. protection for persons seeking U.S. citizenship is claimed by Secretary of State Marcy: the Martin Koszta Case.

On September 26, Secretary Marcy answered Austrian demands for the deliverance of Martin Koszta by refusing to deliver him and upholding American officials who defended Koszta from forcible repatriation by Austria.

Koszta was born in Hungary but fled to Turkey after the failure of the Hungarian rebellion in 1849. When Turkey refused to extradite Koszta to Austria, Austrian and Turkish officials agreed to permit him to come to America. On July 31, 1852, Koszta renounced his allegiance to any other state and took an oath declaring he intended to become a U.S. citizen. After living 23 months in America, Koszta took a business trip to Smyrna (present-day Izmir), Turkey, where the U.S. consul gave him a letter of safe-conduct. Before he left Turkey, however, a group of paid men seized him and threw him into the harbor, where an Austrian ship, the *Huszar,* waited to pick him out of the water.

While the U.S. consul protested, Koszta was rescued by an American warship that happened to arrive at Smyrna. Captain David N. Ingraham, who commanded the U.S. navy vessel *St. Louis,* had learned about the incident and informed the commander of the *Huszar* that the guns of the *St. Louis* would be used if Koszta was not released. This threat resulted in Koszta's release to the custody of the French consul at Smyrna and eventually to America.

On August 29, 1853, the Austrian chargé in Washington, Chevalier Hulsemann, wrote to Secretary Marcy to demand Koszta's return and satisfaction for the "outrages" of the U.S. officials in Turkey. Marcy's reply refused Hulsemann's demands. He argued that Koszta's declaration of intent to be a U.S. citizen, not only in America but also on receiving his safe-conduct pass in Smyrna, placed him under American protection.

Interest in Marcy's decision was widespread both in America and in Europe. His reply to Hulsemann was translated into German and 1,000 copies were distributed in Europe. In 1854, Captain Ingraham was honored by a resolution of Congress and by a commemorative medal struck in his behalf on August 4.

December 30, 1853

The Gadsden Treaty between Mexico and the United States is signed.

Negotiated by General James Gadsden, who became U.S. minister to Mexico in July 1853, this treaty contained important agreements as follows:

1. Adjustment of the southern boundary gave the United States 26,670 square miles of land south of the Gila River. Joint commissions would be established to mark the exact boundary.
2. The United States received free transit across the Isthmus of Tehuantepec for mail, merchandise, and troops.
3. For the above considerations, the United States paid Mexico $10 million.
4. Article XI of the Treaty of 1848, which required the United States to prevent Indian incursions into Mexico and to restore Mexicans captured by the Indians, was abrogated.

After minor amendments, the U.S. Senate ratified the agreement and President Pierce proclaimed it on June 30, 1854.

1854

January 18, 1854

William Walker's filibustering expedition against Mexico fails.

Walker, who became a celebrated hero in the United States for his various efforts to "liberate" and "republicanize" parts of Mexico and Central America, had landed "emigrants" from California in Lower California on November 3, 1853. Arriving because he claimed some Mexican citizens of the region invited him to protect them from the raids of Apache Indians, Walker proclaimed the independence of Lower California at La Paz. On January 8, Walker and his men moved some forces to Sonora, Mexico, and proclaimed on paper the annexation of the province to his "nation."

By this time Mexican officials had protested to Washington and California, claiming the United States helped outfit, supply, and protect Walker's rebellion. These protests led U.S. officials to shut off Walker's food and supply line from California and to prevent further mercenaries from reinforcing Walker's "emigrant" group.

Because his supplies dried up, Walker decided on January 18 to move his men as quickly as possible back to the United States to avoid the anger of Mexican troops on their way to Sonora. Walker crossed the border and surrendered to U.S. officials in San Diego. In California, Walker was a hero, and a local jury found him innocent of any criminal wrongdoing. He was freed to launch another expedition a year later in Nicaragua.

See October 15, 1855.

February 28, 1854

The *Black Warrior* incident at Havana creates a crisis in U.S.-Spanish relations.

The *Black Warrior* was a side-wheel steamer that had operated in coastwise trade between New York City and Mobile, Alabama, since August 25, 1852. Because its sea route required a regular stop at Havana, Cuba, an agreement had been made with Cuban authorities to grant a concession exempting the vessel from the need to make a cargo manifest for the Havana authorities.

For some unexplained reason, after 17 uneventful voyages by way of Cuba, the Cuban port authorities on February 28 contended that the *Black Warrior* had violated port regulations, which required a manifest. The ship's captain, James D. Bulloch, appealed to the captain general, who ruled Cuba for Spain, but the appeal was rejected. The *Black Warrior*'s captain and crew had to abandon the ship to the Cubans.

Although the ship was returned to its captain by the end of March 1854, the news of this insult spread to America during the next month, causing both official and unofficial American protests and demands for satisfaction from Spain. On March 15, President Pierce told Congress that the case had been presented to Madrid. The United States demanded both an indemnity and a vindication of U.S. honor.

The incident was an illustration of frequent minor wrongs done to Americans and other foreigners by corrupt Spanish-Cuban authorities. As such, it was one factor that caused President Pierce to change his policy toward Spanish maintenance of dominion over Cuba.

See April 3, 1854.

March 28, 1854

Crimean War begins. A British-French alliance fights to prevent the Czar from forcing his demands on Turkey and occupying the Danubian provinces along the Black Sea.

The war lasted until Czar Alexander II agreed to preliminary peace terms on February 1, 1856.

March 31, 1854

Commodore Perry and Japanese officials sign the Treaty of Kanagawa.

Perry returned to Tokyo Bay with a fleet of seven ships on February 13, 1854, earlier than he had proposed to Japan in 1853. The Japanese were willing to negotiate a treaty, but Perry first demanded that his fleet be allowed to come to the city of Tokyo. The Japanese objected for they wished to keep the ships at Uraga, as

Commodore Perry arrives to sign the treaty allowing U.S. ships to enter Japanese ports. National Archives

far as possible from Tokyo. Finally, a compromise was accepted. Perry could bring his fleet as far as Yokohama, and discussions took place at the small port town of Kanagawa.

The treaty was brief: the two countries declared they followed a spirit of amity; Japan opened for limited trade the ports of Hakodate in Hokkaido and Shimoda, on the coast south of Tokyo Bay; a U.S. consul could have residence at Shimoda; and a most-favored-nation trade clause was approved. Principally, however, the treaty provided for Japan's good treatment of shipwrecked or distressed sailors.

There were two notable omissions in the treaty. No extraterritoriality clause was included because Perry did not like the way this clause permitted many crimes by Westerners in China to go unpunished. Second, the Americans did not receive rights to obtain coal in Japan, although this had been one of the basic objectives of Perry's mission.

Perry succeeded in obtaining a treaty at least partly because Japan was ready to open its doors. Japan's internal politics had reached the point where its merchants desired contact with the West. After Perry's first visit in 1853, shogunal advisers used Perry's threat to persuade the council to negotiate with Perry. Japan's council also ended restrictions on shipbuilding by Japanese in order to permit the construction of naval vessels and steamships. These internal developments in Japan moved rapidly toward the historic Meiji Restoration of 1868.

April 3, 1854

American policy on Cuba is changed when Secretary of State Marcy proposes to buy Cuba from Spain.

On April 3, Marcy instructed the U.S. minister at Madrid, Souel, to seek to buy Cuba for up to $130 million. Marcy said President Pierce had changed U.S. policy and desired to obtain Cuba either by purchase or by using some other means to "detach" it from Spain. The meaning of "detach" was not clarified by Marcy.

Two factors influenced Marcy and Pierce to change their policy: (1) the *Black Warrior* incident of February 28, 1854, for that Souel had previously been told to seek an indemnity and to gain satisfaction for the insult; and (2) a crisis in the Spanish government that Souel, on February 23, had reported would probably bring a more liberal regime to power, one willing to sell Cuba.

April 28, 1854

Secretary of State Marcy informs the British Minister to the United States that America will be neutral in the Crimean War.

Marcy's note to F. T. Crampton, Britain's minister, recited the basis and contents of the neutrality act of April 20, 1818, which governed U.S. neutrality. Because it became a later issue with Britain, it is important to note that Marcy informed Crampton that foreign nations could not recruit Americans to fight in a war in which the United States was neutral.

See June 9, 1855.

May 30, 1854

Kansas-Nebraska Bill is passed by Congress, allowing for the possible extension of slavery in the west through popular sovereignty.

When Senator Stephen A. Douglas of Illinois introduced this bill on January 23, 1854, the question of the extension of slavery was revived in Congress. Douglas argued that the people living in a territory should decide the issue of slavery in their future state. The 1854 bill applied specifically to the territories of Kansas and Nebraska, both of which were north of the line dividing slave and free states as approved in the Missouri Compromise of 1820. The law made it possible for slavery to be extended and stimulated intense antagonism between slaveholders and abolitionists. Some historians believe this bill was a vital factor in bringing the Republican Party into being in July 1854, to oppose the extension of slavery.

June 5, 1854

The Anglo-American Reciprocity and Fisheries Treaty—the Marcy-Elgin Treaty—is signed.

Work on a treaty regarding the Northeast fisheries and U.S.-British trade began during Fillmore's administration in 1852. Its conclusion was not certain until Lord Clarendon of Great Britain sent the earl of Elgin to Washington as a special envoy in May 1854.

The treaty granted American fishermen more "liberty" than the prior treaty of October 20, 1818. They were restricted only from fishing in the rivers and mouths of rivers on the Northeast Canadian coast. Canadians received reciprocal rights on the east coast of America as far south as Norfolk, Virginia. Generally, the treaty favored Americans in the business of fishing, lumber, and manufacturing because it also included rights of reciprocal free trade between the two nations. The treaty also provided that either party could abrogate the document on a year's notice. Later, the United States did so.

See March 17, 1866.

July 6, 1854

Meeting at Jackson, Michigan, adopts the name Republican for a new party dedicated to an anti-slavery program.

This meeting, which founded the modern Republican Party, consisted of representatives of groups of former Whigs and Free-Soilers, as well as anti-slavery Democrats. The Jackson meeting evolved from an earlier meeting of representatives of these three political factions at RIPON, Wisconsin, on February 28 to oppose the Kansas-Nebraska bill. The RIPON meeting suggested the forming of a party with the name "Republican."

Following the Jackson convention, other state meetings were held throughout the Northern states. Party membership spread widely by the end of 1854. In 1856, the Republican Party was large enough to nominate a candidate for president.

October 18, 1854

The Ostend Manifesto favors the U.S. purchase of Cuba or "Wresting it from Spain."

The report known as the Ostend Manifesto resulted from a weeklong meeting of the American ministers to Spain, France, and Great Britain. They had convened their discussions at Ostend, Belgium, on October 9, but because publicity about their conference generated much newspaper attention, they adjourned and moved their sessions to Aachen in Prussia.

The three ministers—Pierre Soulé, minister to Spain; James Buchanan, minister to England; John Y. Mason, minister to France—met because of an August 16, 1854, request from Secretary of State Marcy that they discuss the European situation relative to Cuba. Marcy's opinion had been that Britain would not obstruct an American takeover of Cuba, but France, under Napoléon III, was an unknown factor. Moreover, he thought the Crimean War so occupied those nations that they could not object strongly.

Souel, who had charge of the ministers' meeting, also knew that Secretary Marcy was greatly upset because Spain had rejected the U.S. demands for an indemnity and satisfaction in the case of the ship *Black Warrior*, which had had trouble at Havana (see Marcy to Souel on June 22, 1854).

Against the background of the *Black Warrior* case, previous British-French interests in Cuba, and the Crimean War, the three U.S. ministers met from October 12 to 18 at Aachen to discuss Cuba in American relations. In their report, which reached Washington on November 4, 1854, the three diplomats made two primary recommendations:

1. The United States should make an "immediate and earnest effort" to purchase Cuba at a price not exceeding $120 million.
2. If Spain would not sell, the United States must consider whether Spain's possession of Cuba endangered American peace and "the existence of our cherished union." If it did, "we shall be justified in wresting it from Spain" just as a person would tear down the burning house of his neighbor if there "were no other means of preventing the flames from destroying his own home."

October 24, 1854

Calais incident—France refuses to admit Pierre Soulé to its territory.

After attending the meeting that resulted in the Ostend Manifesto, Soulé went to London before returning to Madrid. He decided to make his journey to Spain by taking a boat to Calais, France, and to proceed on to Paris and Madrid. At Calais, however, French officials refused to admit him. After sending a message to Mason, the American minister to France, Soulé returned in anger to London.

In Paris, Mason learned of the French action before receiving Soulé's note. The French minister of foreign relations, Drouyn de LHUYS, had informed Mason that Napoléon III did not find it agreeable to have Soulé on French soil. De Lhuys stated that France believed Soulé communicated with its enemies and on December 14, 1853, had injured the French ambassador to Spain, the marquis de Turgot, in a duel. Turgot was permanently crippled by Soulé's bullet in his thigh.

Mason protested the French action at Calais and on November 1, de Lhuys told Mason that Soulé would be allowed to travel through France to Spain provided he did not "tarry" in Paris.

This incident not only indicates the tension that occurred in France over the news of the Ostend Manifesto, but also tells something about Soulé's reputation, which apparently was bad both in Spain and in France. In fact, on September 9, 1854, Horatio S. PERRY, secretary of the U.S. legation in Madrid, wrote to Secretary of State Marcy to warn him that someone other than Soulé might be able to buy Cuba from Spain. While Soulé had many talents, Perry wrote, he was not a good diplomat and had isolated himself from the diplomatic circles in Madrid.

Because Soulé is usually considered to have been the instigator of the Ostend Manifesto, his personal inclinations seem to have played a significant role in American diplomacy regarding Cuba and Spain in 1854.

November 13, 1854

The Pierce administration responds to the Ostend Manifesto by approving the possible purchase of Cuba but rejecting the alternatives of "Cession or seizure" of the islands unless there were imminent danger to U.S. security.

In general, Marcy's note of November 13 repealed the policies he had first cited to Souel on July 23, 1853: the United States considered the purchase of Cuba the best solution, a tripartite policy with Great Britain and France was not accepted, and Spain needed to give some assurance of ending the misconduct of its Cuban officers.

In a concluding paragraph, Marcy seemed almost but not quite to rule out the use of American force to gain Cuba. A war to take Cuba would require that the present situation be a menace to America so that the president could request such a contingency. Apparently, the desire to expand U.S. territory to include Cuba was still present; but how to accomplish the task honorably and without war was the problem.

This cartoon highlights domestic opposition to the Ostend Manifesto. Library of Congress

December 18, 1854

Spain's Cortes rejects America's offer to purchase Cuba.

On his return from Ostend to Madrid in November, Soulé talked with the new Spanish foreign minister, Don Claudio Anton DE LUZURIAGA. The minister agreed to have the U.S. offer to buy Cuba considered by the Spanish Council of State, the Cortes. Yet even before the date set for the Cortes discussion, Soulé heard that Spain would not approve his request. On December 17, he wrote to Secretary Marcy in Washington asking to be relieved of his mission.

Soulé's expectations were evident in the Cortes session of December 18. The members accepted de Luzuriaga's advice that "to part with Cuba would be to part with the national honor." As in the case of the attempt to purchase Mexico, the U.S. State Department found that an offer to buy even undesirable territory from its owner is not a simple affair.

1855

January 28, 1855

An American-owned railway opens operations across the Isthmus of Panama.

This railway resulted from the concession granted by Colombia on June 12, 1849, to the Panama Railroad Company of New York, headed by William Aspinwall.

The new railroad route rivaled the ATC route that Vanderbilt had constructed across Nicaragua (see July 14, 1851). Construction of the road cost $8 million, but during its first six years of operation the railway company made a profit of $7 million. The line was 47.5 miles long from Aspinwall (Colón) on the Atlantic Coast to Panama City. Estimates were that as many as 6,000 workers and engineers died of cholera and other diseases during the four years of construction. Although Vanderbilt's route was shorter by both distance and time, the Panama route became popular because the ship and short train ride was more comfortable than the Nicaraguan journey.

March 1, 1855

An act of Congress seeks more formally to organize the diplomatic service of the United States.

For the first time, congressional legislation provided for the various diplomatic ranks and fixed the salaries of these persons. It established regulations for issuing passports and prescribed the duties of American consular offices.

President Pierce's administration objected to some of the provisions of this law, and on August 18, 1856, Congress approved new legislation to satisfy technical shortcomings of the 1855 act. In particular, the president wanted the law to specify his right to appoint, evaluate, and remove diplomatic officers.

Under the 1855 act, Secretary of State Marcy issued the first book of consular instructions for U.S. diplomats, entitled *General Instructions to the Consuls and Commercial Agents of the United States.*

March 3, 1855

The official documents surrounding the Ostend Manifesto are published by the House Committee on Foreign Affairs.

The Pierce administration had tried to maintain secrecy regarding many of the affairs about Cuba in 1854, but news reports and comments from Europe caused distrust as well as anxiety in America. The papers published in March 1855 were selected and edited by Marcy and Soulé. The original manuscripts were not fully examined until historians reviewed the State Department files during the 1920s—70 years later. The full account indicates that both Marcy and Soulé sought almost any means to get U.S. control over Cuba. How much Pierce is to be implicated in the composition of Marcy's instructions to Soulé, Buchanan, and Mason is not certain.

June 9, 1855

Secretary of State Marcy believes Britain is violating American neutrality by recruiting soldiers for the Crimean War.

According to Marcy, numerous reports indicated that the British minister to the United States, F. T. Crampton, helped British consulates in various U.S. cities to recruit Americans. The consuls would provide money for the Americans to travel to Canada, where they would officially enlist in the British army.

In particular, Marcy wrote to U.S. minister Buchanan in London to discover from Lord Clarendon, Britain's foreign minister, how he could approve his support of Crampton's attempt to recruit in violation of the American neutrality law of 1818. Marcy had learned from J. Savile Lumley, the British chargé in Washington, that Clarendon approved recruitment because the British Parliament passed a Foreign Enlistment Act on December 23, 1854.

Buchanan presented Marcy's complaint to Clarendon in July 1854, but the British minister's explanation was not satisfactory. Clarendon said that the recruitment attempts had ceased, but Marcy knew they had not. The dispute over British recruitment continued until 1856, for which see May 27, 1856. Historians who have researched British files know that Clarendon did not give Buchanan an honest answer in July 1855, when he told him recruitment had ceased.

October 15, 1855

William Walker conquers Grenada and takes control of Nicaragua's government.

Walker, an American adventurer, began his attack on May 4, 1855, when he landed with 56 mercenaries on the Pacific coast of Nicaragua. His project was aided by the Accessory Transit Company (ATC), which provided passage on its steamships from San Francisco and supplies for Walker's "army." The ATC operated the transportation route across Nicaragua but was dissatisfied with the political and legal disorders of Central America and encouraged Walker's belief that he could unite that region under one strong government.

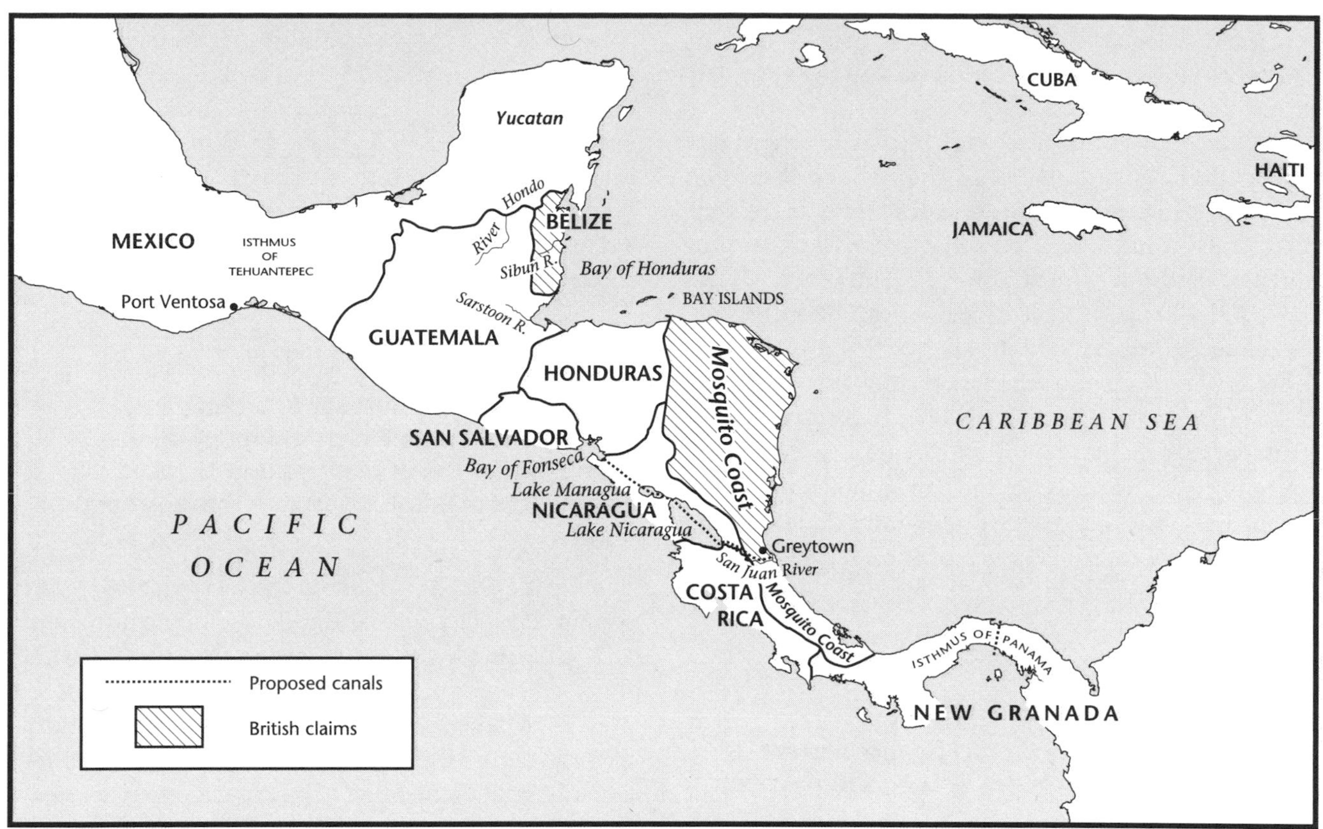

Central America in the 1850s.

After establishing a base on the coast and receiving 500 more "emigrants" from California, Walker marched on the capital city, Grenada. Even though Walker's attack began in September, more than three months before reaching the city, the Nicaraguan government was unprepared to fight. Walker besieged the city, which fell to his forces on October 15. Walker declared the state had been "liberated" and made Patricio Rivas the provisional president of Nicaragua.

Although some accounts of this conquest allege that Cornelius Vanderbilt assisted Walker because Vanderbilt owned the ATC, this is not accurate. Vanderbilt retired from the ATC presidency in 1853 and left the company in the hands of two subordinates, Charles Morgan and Cornelius K. Garrison. These two men had manipulated the company's stock to get a controlling interest for themselves. By enlisting Walker's aid, Morgan and Garrison apparently believed they could complete their elimination of Vanderbilt's interest in Central America. But Vanderbilt returned from Europe in 1855, heard of his associates' plot, and decided to destroy their financial plans.

See May 15, 1856, and May 1, 1857.

1856

February 13, 1856

U.S. court ruling is accepted that gives a consular treaty precedence over the U.S. Constitution—the Dillon Case.

On February 13, 1856, Secretary of State Marcy accepted a court ruling and expressed regret to France for a case that had been under dispute since June 26, 1854.

The conflict arose in April 1854 when Patrice Dillon, the French consul in San Francisco, refused to accept a court order to appear as a witness in a trial before a California court. Even when subpoenaed by a U.S. District Court, Dillon protested by claiming immunity under the French-American consular convention of February 23, 1853, one clause of which exempted French diplomats from orders of U.S. courts. Dillon's protest included closing the consulate at San Francisco.

When first confronted with the problem, Marcy argued that Amendment 6 to the U.S. Constitution allowed defendants to call witnesses and that the consular convention could not disqualify the constitutional provision. In California, however, Judge Ogden HOFFMAN Jr. ruled in favor of Dillon because the Constitution gave a treaty ratified by the U.S. Senate special status as the law of the land.

Consequently, Secretary Marcy had to retract his previous arguments and offer his regrets to the French government. The case provided an important caution for future State Department negotiators, who had to consider more carefully how a proposed treaty related to the U.S. Constitution.

April 16, 1856

The Declaration of Paris regulating international law is adopted by the powers as part of the peace process ending the Crimean War.

The four rules regarding naval action on the high seas that the Paris congress adopted were as follows:

1. privateers must be abolished;
2. neutral flags cover enemy goods, excepting contraband;
3. neutral goods under an enemy's flag cannot be captured, excepting contraband;
4. blockades must be effective to be binding; that is, there must be sufficient force to prevent access to an enemy's coast.

Following the conference, the French government solicited the adoption of these rules by other nations. The United States was one of the few nations not to agree. The powers who originated the Declaration of Paris were France, Great Britain, Austria, Russia, Turkey, and Piedmont Sardinia.

For U.S. decision, see July 28, 1856.

May 15, 1856

The United States recognizes the Nicaraguan regime of William Walker and Patricio Rivas.

Walker's "filibustering" expedition that captured Grenada in October 1855 appeared to have gained him control of the Nicaraguan government. Nevertheless, U.S. recognition of Walker's regime caused British resentment. London aided Costa Rica, Honduras, and Guatemala—Central American nations that disliked Walker's government. This early American recognition led the local populace to believe that Walker's acts abetted by the Accessory Transit Company were, in reality, American-sponsored efforts to gain control of Central America.

May 27, 1856

Because Britain continues to violate U.S. neutrality laws, the Pierce administration dismisses the British Minister and revokes the exequaturs of British consuls in three American cities.

Since June 9, 1855, when Secretary of State Marcy sought British explanation of their recruitment of U.S. citizens for the British army, the English diplomats continued to violate the law by recruiting. On May 27, Marcy informed the British government that its minister to the United States, Crampton, and its consuls at Philadelphia, Cincinnati, and New York City had been dismissed from the country because they violated the sovereign rights and municipal laws of America. He dismissed these four men after Lord Clarendon, Britain's foreign minister, refused to recall them as Marcy had requested on December 28, 1855. Marcy said U.S. law enforcement officers in New York, Ohio, and Pennsylvania had sufficient evidence of the consuls' illegal actions.

In England, the American action stimulated much debate in the House of Commons. The British ministry was, however, sustained in a vote of confidence on July 2, 1856. Significantly, however, the British did not take the usual action of requesting the recall of the U.S. minister to England, G. M. Dallas. This apparently indicated that Clarendon realized there was some justice in the American dismissal of the British officials.

May 29, 1856

United States enters into treaty with Siam.

This treaty of amity and commerce gave the United States the most-favored-nation arrangements concluded by Great Britain on April 18, 1855. The treaty provided for consuls and the right to trade throughout the kingdom. The United States, like other Western powers, received extraterritoriality provisions whereby U.S. citizens were legally responsible only to U.S. law as administered by U.S. consuls.

July 28, 1856

Secretary Marcy informs the French Minister that America cannot accept the four rules of international law adopted at Paris on April 16, 1856.

In a memorandum to the French minister to the United States, the Count de SARTIGES, Marcy gave two basic reasons for objecting to the four rules: (1) the United States contended that all private property at sea, excepting contraband, should be exempt from capture; and (2) ending all use of privateers left small-navy nations at the mercy of large-navy nations.

Although Marcy objected to the complete abolition of privateers in wartime, the United States never used them in war subsequent to April 1856. During the Civil War, however, the Confederate government made effective use of privateers against Union commerce.

November 4, 1856

James Buchanan is elected President.

As the Democratic Party candidate, Buchanan received 174 electoral votes. The Republican Party candidate, John C. Fremont, received 114 votes with a popular vote of 1,335,264 to Buchanan's 1,838,169. The Whig Party nominee, Millard Fillmore, received only 8 electoral votes.

November 16, 1856

American gunboats are ordered to destroy the Chinese barrier forts near Canton.

In December 1855, Peter Parker had arrived in China, appointed by President Pierce to negotiate a new commercial treaty. At Canton, Parker learned that the Chinese refused to negotiate with the United States, Great Britain, and France.

After conflict broke out between British, French, and Chinese forces in Canton, Parker called for a U.S. naval ship to evacuate American citizens. As a U.S. ship approached Canton, Chinese guns of the Barrier Forts fired at the Americans.

The next day, November 16, Commodore Lucius H. Foote, commander of the American Asiatic squadron, ordered his gunboat commanders to demolish the Barrier Forts. The gunboats did so on November 17 and 18, much to the delight of the British and French. The gunboat diplomacy forced the Chinese to undertake negotiations in 1857.

See June 18, 1858.

December 13, 1856

America and Persia (Iran) sign a commercial treaty.

Following Senate ratification of this Persian treaty on March 10, 1857, President Buchanan requested funds to open a legation in Tehran. Because Congress refused to pay these expenses, there was no U.S. legation in Persia until 1883.

1857

February 5, 1857

A liberal revolution in Mexico ends when a federal constitution is adopted.

The revolutionaries overthrew Santa Anna as military dictator on August 9, 1855, and began a series of political and religious reforms designed to establish a democratic republic. The reforms attempted to break the power of the church by ending its great land holdings and to abolish the corruption of the political-military groups that had vied for power since 1821. The liberal constitution established Mexico as a federation that decentralized some of the political power to the provincial governments.

The republic under President BENITO JUÁREZ was barely created in 1857 before the conservative forces rallied against it. A civil war began that lasted until December 22, 1860. During the civil war, Juárez moved his capital city to Vera Cruz while the conservatives occupied Mexico City. The United States recognized the liberal regime on April 7, 1859, hoping Juárez would retain his position.

March 3, 1857

Tariff of 1857 returns the United States to a revenue tariff.

The Walker Tariff Act of 1846 had established the Democratic Party proposals for a revenue tariff. Since that time no general tariff revisions had occurred, but under President Taylor the Whigs had by 1850 raised some duties to a protective level. The

1857 tariff reversed this trend of piecemeal protection by a general overhaul of the tariff to reinstitute its nonprotective features.

The 1857 act enlarged the list of free items and generally reduced tariffs to an average of 20%. This Democratic Party policy provided the Northern manufacturing interests with another reason to support the Republican Party's platform for a protective tariff in 1860.

March 6, 1857

Lewis Cass is named Secretary of State.

Among Cass's previous political duties were secretary of war (1831–1836); minister to France (1836–1842); and senator from Michigan (1845–1857). Cass served as secretary until December 14, 1860. Generally, however, historians believe he was largely a figurehead as secretary because President Buchanan preferred to direct foreign affairs. Cass served over 40 years in public life and grew lethargic in his old age. Cass was ably assisted in some of his duties after 1857 by Assistant Secretary of State John Appleton and Attorney General J. S. Black.

March 10, 1857

Dr. Peter Parker recommends American possession of Formosa.

Parker, the U.S. commissioner in China since December 1855 and a former medical missionary, wrote to the State Department on March 10 to justify an American seizure of the island of Formosa, a Chinese possession off the coast of China near Amoy.

Parker's request originated from a suggestion of Gideon Nye Jr., an old friend of the commissioner. Nye had established a trading company in Formosa that had a monopoly of the camphor trade, but his company had been having problems with the natives, who were dissatisfied with their pay and working conditions. Nye even suggested to Parker that the company would set up an independent "government" in Formosa if it could be assured of American backing.

Parker's memos to the State Department in February and March did not explain the details of Nye's interests in Formosa but hoped to convince Washington of that island's strategic value. He did not believe that China could long retain control of the island and wanted the United States to own it, "particularly as respects the great principle of the balance of power." England had already established outposts of empire, Parker said, at Gibraltar, Singapore, Hong Kong, and elsewhere. Thus, it could not object to American control of Formosa.

In addition to Nye's interests in Formosa, Parker's own inclinations were to affirm his nation's strong interest in obtaining a controlling influence in East Asia and China. Since his appointment as commissioner in 1855, Parker had urged an aggressive policy toward Chinese authorities. On his way to China in 1855, he visited London and Paris, whose officials reported to the State Department that they were shocked by the aggressive tactics Parker advocated to control China. Parker had been a medical missionary in China since 1834 but developed no sympathy for Chinese political leaders and merchants, who considered him to be a "foreign devil." His suspicions of the Chinese were enhanced in 1855 and 1856 when his attempts to negotiate a new treaty and to visit the emperor in Peking had been rejected.

At the time Parker wrote his proposal to the State Department, his attempt to persuade the U.S. naval commander in China, Commodore James Armstrong, to agree on the occupation of Formosa had not been successful. Armstrong saw value in having a coaling base in Formosa but said the size of the U.S. navy in Chinese waters made the project impractical. Moreover, he could not act without approval of his Washington superiors.

As Armstrong's response implied, Washington did not share Parker's concern for an active policy in China. Although Secretary of State Cass never specifically answered Parker's request of March 10, Cass informed the commissioner that the United States could not take warlike steps without the approval of Congress. Furthermore, he told Parker, the U.S. naval forces in China were not intended for aggressive purposes.

Thus, while not approved, Parker's proposal is significant as a request of an official and former Chinese missionary's view of China. In addition, it indicated President Buchanan's unwillingness to accept "aggressive action in the Pacific" in 1857.

March 12, 1857

U.S. Senate amendments to an Anglo-American Convention prevent clarification of U.S.-British interests in Central America.

In 1856, British Foreign Minister Lord Clarendon and the U.S. minister to Great Britain, George M. Dallas, signed a treaty to resolve previous political disputes regarding the isthmian transportation routes. The convention provided equal rights for both parties for either of two proposed routes and settled British boundary claims in the area of Belize and Nicaragua. These disputes had not been solved satisfactorily in the Clayton-Bulwer Treaty of 1850.

Although the U.S. Senate finally approved the convention, it tacked on an amendment that Britain rejected. This amendment sought to meet objections of some senators regarding islands in the Bay of Honduras. Britain claimed these islands as a separate colony, but in 1856–1857 Clarendon was negotiating a new treaty with Honduras to gradually relinquish British control. The Senate amendment asserted that the islands had always been under Honduran sovereignty. In addition, the amendment rejected Britain's right to abolish slavery in those islands.

The Senate approved the Dallas-Clarendon agreement with the amendment by a vote of 32 to 15, barely two-thirds. Great Britain refused to accept the amendment, however, and the treaty was never ratified. The British contended that they were in the process of resolving the status of the islands with Honduras and that a convention with a third party, the United States, should not interfere with British-Honduran arrangements.

See June 24, 1881.

April 10, 1857

The United States refuses to join England and France in obtaining new treaties with China.

Because of their experiences in China since 1842 and the threat of the Taiping Rebellion, England, France, and the United States informally agreed that their original treaties with China should be revised. Therefore, between March 1 and March 30, 1857, the British minister to the United States, Lord Napier, discussed with Secretary of State Cass the possibility of joint action by the three powers in China. Napier pointed out that America profited greatly from the Chinese trade opened by England in 1842 and that a joint agreement in China would benefit all three nations. France, he said, was willing to cooperate, and Napier asked the United States to join them in an allied declaration of objectives in China, to appoint a minister to negotiate with them, and to increase the size of U.S. naval forces in the South China Sea.

On April 10, Cass told Napier that the president would not work with other nations in a joint treaty or in a threat of force but would appoint a minister to obtain a new treaty. Cass said America could not declare war without congressional approval and preferred to deal with China on a bilateral basis. The U.S. secretary also cautioned the French and English to act with moderation toward China and permit "those changes which time gradually brings about."

In May, President Buchanan acted in accordance with Cass's remarks to Napier. He appointed William B. Reed as minister plenipotentiary to China to negotiate a treaty, informing Reed not to ally with England and France but to find an opportune moment to press American claims for Chinese reparations to property damage and a treaty revision. Needless to say, the United States hoped to profit from British and French pressure on China. Cass instructed Reed that "the United States seeks only the enlargement of opportunities for trade, it does not desire territory or to interfere in Chinese affairs."

April 11, 1857

The United States signs a treaty with Denmark ending the sound dues that Denmark had collected for over 400 years.

The "Sound Dues" were fees levied by Denmark on all shipping passing from the North Sea to the Baltic by way of two straits known as the Great Belt (Skagerrak) and the Little Belt (Kattegat). Various diplomats in Europe often discussed ending the dues, but until 1855 no one acted to pressure Denmark to change its practice.

The Pierce administration decided to act. First, it persuaded Congress to approve giving one year's notice to end the U.S. commercial treaty with Denmark of April 26, 1826. Next, Secretary Marcy delivered this notice to be effective in 1855 and informed the Danish government that the "Sound Dues" should be changed.

Denmark called a conference of delegates from European nations that met in Copenhagen to settle the issue. Although the United States refused to attend the conference, it accepted its results. In suspending future dues, the delegates agreed that each nation would pay a fixed sum to capitalize a fund that would maintain the channel services with buoys, lighthouses, and other safeguards. In the treaty with Denmark of April 11, 1857, the United States accepted these conditions and its share for payment of the fund, which was $393,011. After Senate ratification and House appropriations of money, this fee was paid and the "Sound Dues" ceased.

May 1, 1857

William Walker's regime in Nicaragua is overthrown.

After 18 months of power, Walker's downfall came at the hands of a coalition Central American army assisted by Great Britain and Cornelius Vanderbilt.

Although the Central American army defeated Walker, his trouble began because Charles Morgan and Cornelius Garrison, his Accessory Transit Company (ATC) allies, tried to outwit Cornelius Vanderbilt. When Vanderbilt returned from retirement in 1855, he determined to defeat his former associates' attempt to get control of the ATC (see October 15, 1855). First Vanderbilt rallied his financial friends in New York to support him in regaining the controlling interest of the ATC. Then he decided to eliminate Walker and his allies in Nicaragua.

Walker, Garrison, and Morgan had further angered Vanderbilt by playing their trump card. Early in 1856, the Walker-Rivas government of Nicaragua annulled the ATC charter to operate in Nicaragua and confiscated the ATC property.

Vanderbilt had not been "pure" in his dealings with Nicaragua, so Walker could justify the charter's annullment. In particular, Vanderbilt had in 1851 arranged the ATC account books so that, technically, the ocean steamships profited but the transport lines across Nicaragua did not. This manipulation exempted the ATC from paying Nicaragua any income due under the 10% of the company's profits on the transit route. In annulling the ATC charter, Walker cited this financial shortcoming. Once the ATC charter had ended, Walker chartered a new company set up by Morgan and Garrison that would take over Vanderbilt's route and property.

Walker had miscalculated. Vanderbilt's financial powers and ties with London were too great for Morgan and Garrison. Vanderbilt stopped his ATC steamships from operating between Nicaragua and the New York–San Francisco ports. Without passengers at San Juan del Norte and San Juan del Sur, the Nicaraguan transit route could not operate successfully.

Vanderbilt also gave financial backing to British efforts to unite the Central American states against Walker. With Britain's political sanction, the governments of Honduras, El Salvador, Guatemala, and Costa Rica gathered a united armed force to attack Nicaragua under the leadership of Rafael Carrera of Guatemala. After being duly trained, this army attacked Nicaragua and besieged the capital city of Grenada early in 1857. Rather than surrender to his enemies, Walker, on May 1, 1857, traveled to the Pacific coast and surrendered to Commander Charles Henry Davis of the U.S. navy.

The navy brought Walker safely to America, where he received a hero's welcome. The U.S. public did not know of the various financial dealings behind Walker's rise to and fall from power. To them, he was a gallant adventurer who tried to establish a more civilized republican government in a disreputable Central American state. Thus, Walker the hero was freed to conduct two more attempts to control Nicaragua before being shot by an execution squad in 1860.

See September 12, 1860.

June 17, 1857

The United States and Japan sign a new commercial agreement.

This convention resulted from negotiations between the U.S. minister to Japan, Townsend Harris, and the Japanese representatives of the shogun. Harris arrived in Japan on August 21, 1856, but was not welcomed by the Japanese, who tried to persuade him to leave. Nevertheless, he took residence at a temple in Shimoda and with the aid of a Dutch interpreter, C. J. Heusken, obtained a treaty that improved on the one Commodore Perry signed in 1854.

In particular, the treaty of 1857 granted America the rights that other European countries had gained in their treaties made after Perry "opened" Japan's door. Great Britain signed a treaty in October 1854; Russia, in January 1855; and the Netherlands, in January 1856. By the most-favored-nation clause of Perry's treaty, the gains made by these three nations were incorporated into the treaty of 1857.

The important parts of the 1857 treaty were as follows:

1. Nagasaki became an open port;
2. extraterritorial rights were given by Japan. Like Perry, Harris disdained these rights but Secretary of State Marcy told him in 1855 that the U.S. Senate would not ratify an Asian treaty lacking extraterritoriality;
3. Americans could reside at Shimoda and Hakodate;
4. the value of the Japanese ichibu was fixed at $34\frac{1}{2}$ cents, whereas Perry had valued it at one dollar.

Harris considered the treaty of 1857 a stopgap measure as he continued to negotiate a more elaborate agreement that added to the 1857 treaty. This was completed on July 29, 1858.

•

July 17, 1857

America again wants to purchase Mexican territory.

Claiming that money from the sale of land might help Mexico's new republican government to survive, Secretary of State Cass instructed U.S. Minister to Mexico John Forsyth to offer to purchase Lower California, Sonora, and the area of Chihuahua north of the 30° latitude. Forsyth was authorized to pay up to $15 million for all these areas.

In addition, Cass sent Forsyth the draft of a treaty for a canal route across the Isthmus of Tehuantepec. This treaty would strengthen the ambiguous working of the Gadsden Treaty regarding U.S. rights to a canal route. In addition, a Louisiana company called the Tehuantepec Company planned to send representatives to Mexico to verify its right to construct a canal. Forsyth was asked to aid this venture.

Knowing the precarious status of Juárez's government, Forsyth hesitated to follow his instruction of July 17, 1857. After Secretary Cass reprimanded him for not acting, Forsyth finally presented the offer in November 1857. As expected by Forsyth, the Mexican foreign minister told him the offer was insulting and strongly rejected any proposal to sell Mexican land.

1858

May 28, 1858

Russia and China sign the Treaty of Aigun.

By this agreement, the Russian and Chinese governments accepted a border on the Amur River as far east as the Ussuri River. Each nation was given navigation rights on both of these rivers. The exact border on the Ussuri River and from that river to the coast was retained for future negotiations.

This treaty resulted from Russia's rapid expansion into eastern Asia, which began during the 1840s. In 1847, Czar Nicholas I sent General Nikolai N. Muravev to consolidate Russian territory in Siberia. Muravev founded the city of Petropavlovsk in the Kamchatka peninsula in 1849 and Nikolaievsk at the mouth of the Amur River in 1850.

Russia's interest in East Asia also brought its officials to Canton and Shanghai in 1857–1858, where Count Putiatin joined the French, British, and American delegates at Tientsin.

The Treaty of Aigun was negotiated by General Muravev and the Chinese official I. Chang. Although the Chinese emperor refused to ratify this treaty, it was validated by a Sino-Russian treaty of November 1860.

June 11, 1858

The British agree to stop their naval ships from forcibly visiting American ships in search of slaves or for any reason in time of peace.

Following the Crimean War, the British sent many of their small vessels that had been employed in that war to the coast of Africa and the Gulf of Mexico to search American and other nations' merchant ships suspected of the slave trade. More than six incidents of forcible search of U.S. ships occurred in 1856 and 1857, leading the Buchanan administration to a series of protests to the British government.

On April 10, 1858, Secretary Cass sent a lengthy note to Lord Napier, the British minister to America, that objected strongly to English practices. Cass wrote that the independence and honor of the United States was threatened when a foreign naval officer boarded its vessels, assumed command, examined its papers, and sent it to port at his pleasure for trial. The United States had ordered its naval ships to protect all U.S. merchant ships from the British practice. Therefore, a serious collision could occur if the British did not change their policies quickly.

In his note of April 10, Cass said that if an officer had just suspicion that a ship was a slave ship flying false flags, the officer must be held responsible at his risk for his actions. If that officer deported himself properly, did no injury, and returned peacefully if he was in error, there could be no just complaint. Generally, however, this had not been the practice of British officers, who arrogantly boarded ships, threatened the people on board, and treated the captain and crew as if they were guilty.

On June 9, the British Foreign Minister Lord Malmesbury accepted the principles described by the U.S. note of April 10, 1858. They could not justify their officers' actions, for the navy had been told to stop its practice of forcibly visiting U.S. ships.

This ended the controversy. Great Britain receded from a policy of active pursuit and visit of American ships suspected of the slave trade. The United States returned to its agreement in the Webster-Ashburton Treaty for joint Anglo-American patrols off the African coast, but this tactic was not effective.

June 18, 1858

Treaty of Tientsin—profiting from the Anglo-French war against China, the United States signs a new treaty with China.

Following in the wake of Anglo-French naval action against China, the U.S. Minister William B. Reed signed a treaty at Tientsin, a small city on the Pei-ho River between Peking and the coast of the Yellow Sea.

As British and French naval ships fought China in 1857–1858, the diplomats of those two nations were joined by American and Russian officials who sought to gain new treaty provisions from China. French and British ships had bombarded Canton for a second time on December 28, 1857, and forcibly occupied that city in early January 1858. (For the first Anglo-French bombardment and an incidental U.S. action, see November 16, 1856.)

The envoys of the four powers and the French-British fleet then proceeded first to Shanghai and later to the mouth of the Pei-ho River, which led toward Peking. The Chinese sent minor commissioners to Taku, and although the British and French refused to deal with these men, Reed and Russia's envoy, Count Putiatin, began conferences with them.

Because China refused to send more prominent imperial negotiators, the French and British ships attacked and overthrew the Chinese forts at Taku on May 20. The Anglo-French ships then proceeded up the river on May 29. Reed and Putiatin followed behind in a Russian steamer named *Amerika,* which flew the flags of both America and Russia.

The Chinese were now subdued. Two high-level officials representing the emperor came to Tientsin to arrange treaties with all four powers. Russia obtained its first commercial treaty with China on June 13. The United States signed a treaty on June 18, Britain on June 26, and France on June 27. Because the Russian and the American treaties contained most-favored-nation clauses, the two nations received the same commercial benefits as Britain and France.

The important terms of the Treaty of Tientsin were as follows:

1. Foreign representatives had rights to reside in and visit Peking. While the other three powers agreed to continue using letters to the emperor, the British insisted on residence, and all powers eventually received such rights.
2. When the Taiping Rebellion ended, the Yangtze River would be open to navigation by foreign ships.
3. China's interior was open to foreigners. The British treaty said foreigners may go anywhere "for pleasure, or for purposes of trade." Furthermore, foreign citizens were under extra-territoriality provisions that made them immune from Chinese law. In reporting this clause, Reed told Buchanan that "no greater wrong could be done to a weak nation" than to exempt citizens who commit crimes from local law.
4. Seven new Chinese ports were opened for trade.
5. Foreign tonnage duties were reduced, and the rights of exportation allowed foreign ships to carry coastal trade. This clause damaged coastal trade by Chinese ships.
6. Christian missionaries were freely permitted to teach, worship, and convert Chinese without interference from the government.

Although Minister Reed recognized the grave inequalities these treaties forced on China, later Americans ignored these blatant disregards for Chinese rights under the "open door." Americans often believed the open door treaties benefited China; the Chinese saw them as "Unequal" treaties signed under duress. They condemned Americans as well as the other Western powers because the United States desired all the prerogatives given to England. As S. Wells Williams, the U.S. chargé in China, wrote to Secretary of State Cass: "It is quite a mistake to suppose that the rulers of China have any regard for one nation more than another; that they are more friendly, for instance, towards the Americans than towards the English; they may, perhaps, fear the English and Russians more than they do the Americans, but they would be glad if none of them ever came near them."

July 29, 1858

Commercial treaty signed between the United States and Japan; it serves as a model treaty for regulating Japanese relations with the Western powers for over 40 years.

In contrast to the treaty of 1857, which principally repeated the essence of Japan's treaties of 1854–1856 with the West, the Treaty of 1858 provided more extensively for Japan's relations with the United States and became the structure used by Japan for treaties with European nations.

During a year of discussions in Tokyo, U.S. Minister Harris gained the trust of the Japanese, convincing them that the United States, unlike England, France, and Russia, did not desire territory but wished to help preserve the independence and territorial integrity of Japan. He advised them about the use of tariffs and customs duties and of the need to strengthen their defenses to protect themselves. Thus, he said, Japan, unlike China, would be able to develop its commercial relations with the West in a more positive way to benefit Japan.

Within Japan, the treaty being discussed by Harris and representatives of the shogun caused conflict between the Japanese daimyos who surrounded the emperor's court at Kyoto and those nobles who supported the shogunate. From February, when a draft of the treaty was accepted by the shogun's negotiators, until June 1858, the shogun's representatives hesitated to sign the treaty because the emperor refused its terms. Only after news reached Tokyo of the treaties of Tientsin that the Anglo-French forces required the Chinese to sign in June 1858 did the Japanese officials agree to sign the U.S. treaty. At that time, Harris agreed to include terms for Americans to act as mediators for Japan in dealing with France and England.

The principal parts of the 1858 treaty were as follows:

1. an exchange of diplomatic representatives and consuls between Tokyo and Washington;
2. the opening of six Japanese ports with U.S. consuls at each;
3. permission for Americans at these six ports to reside, lease land, erect homes and warehouses, and freely practice their religion;
4. a fixed tariff that ranged from a low 5% on the staple goods needed by U.S. whaling ships stopping in Japan to a high of 35% on alcoholic spirits;
5. an invitation to the Japanese to study U.S. naval construction and to buy warships in America;
6. U.S. assistance as mediator with foreign powers and by the "friendly aid" of U.S. navy vessels and U.S. consuls;
7. opening of Yokohama, Nagasaki, and Hakodate as supply depots for U.S. naval ships;
8. prohibition of the opium trade.

August 2, 1858

Government of India Act by the British Parliament places political control of India under the crown of Britain.

The British East India Company, which originally controlled relations in India, was transferred to a governor general of India who was appointed by and directly responsible to the British cabinet.

November 8, 1858

The United States and China sign a convention to regulate tariffs and trade relations.

The Anglo-Chinese treaty secured by Lord Elgin in June 1858 granted Great Britain certain trade concessions that under the most-favored-nation agreement now accrued to America. Chinese tariffs were reduced to 5% ad valorem, and the foreign customs controls of Shanghai were extended to all ports open to Chinese trade. The treaty legalized the opium trade but set import duties on the drug. As U.S. Minister to China Reed explained, he included this "evil" in the U.S. treaty because he hoped it would end the smuggling in which U.S. ships had become involved.

November 8, 1858

Sino-American claims convention is signed.

The U.S. Minister William Reed presented to the Chinese envoys a group of claims for the loss of property of U.S. citizens since the treaty of 1844. China agreed to pay up to 500,000 taels from deductions on duties paid by U.S. ships at the ports of Canton, Foochow, and Shanghai. The American consul would deduct 20% of the paid duties and report these charges to China until the claims were paid in full. The payment process was fulfilled by February 27, 1860, with U.S. citizens receiving a total of $489,694.78.

1859

April 7, 1859

The United States recognizes the liberal, constitutional Mexican government of Benito Juárez.

When the conservatives in Mexico attacked the republican forces and drove them from Mexico City in early 1858, the U.S. minister to Mexico was uncertain what course of action to take. Finally, in June 1858, Minister John Forsyth suspended relations with the government of President General Miguel Miramon. Forsyth asked the State Department for advice, explaining to Secretary Cass that the regime was intensely disrespectful to Americans. President Buchanan told Forsyth to leave Mexico but withheld recognition from the Juárez government, which had moved to Vera Cruz.

Buchanan sent a special agent, William M. Churchwell, to Mexico on December 27, 1858, to inquire fully about the political conditions. Churchwell reported favorably on the Juárez government and on March 7, 1859, Cass commissioned Robert McLane to go to Mexico and grant recognition if the Juárez government "seemed likely to maintain itself."

On April 7, McLane presented his credentials to President Juárez, conferring recognition on the republic at Vera Cruz.

April 29, 1859

The War of 1859 begins when Austria invades Piedmont in northern Italy.

By May 12, France declared war on Austria to comply with its alliance with Piedmont. The conflict ended on July 12 by an agreement between Napoléon III of France and Austrian Emperor Franz Joseph. Nevertheless, this short war led to the unification of Italy under the Piedmontese ruler King Victor Emmanuel because the Austrian invasion led many Italian city-states to join with Piedmont.

See March 17, 1861.

May 19, 1859

A southern commercial convention at Vicksburg, Mississippi, resolves that laws prohibiting the slave trade should be repealed.

This Southern decree conflicted with U.S. legislation against the slave trade. In foreign relations, the United States had expressed opinions opposing the slave trade but had never signed a treaty such as Great Britain advocated to visit and search ships as the effective method to end the slave trade. The British claimed that many foreign slave ships used the American flag fraudulently to protect themselves from visit and search at sea.

The Vicksburg Convention wanted the federal government to end all enactments against the slave trade in favor of protecting the South's "peculiar institution."

June 25, 1859

Americans are indirectly involved in the second Anglo-French war against China—the incident at Taku.

As in the signing of the Treaty of Tientsin of June 18, 1858, the U.S. minister to China and the U.S. navy had difficulty in remaining aloof from the use of violence in China in 1859.

President Buchanan commissioned John E. Ward to replace William Reed as minister to China in 1859. Ward's first duty was to exchange final ratifications of the 1858 treaty with China. In May 1859, when Ward arrived in Hong Kong, he discovered that Britain and France were claiming that China had not fulfilled the 1858 treaties and they expected to apply military pressure once again.

Ward went to Shanghai, where he met the three Chinese commissioners who had negotiated the 1858 treaties—TAN, KWEILIANG, and HWASHANA. Ward told them he had a personal letter from President Buchanan that he wished to deliver to the emperor. Although the U.S. treaty did not specify that the exchange of ratification would be in Peking, the Chinese envoys agreed to take Ward to Peking as soon as the French and British delegations were ready to go.

When the British Commissioner Sir W. F. A. Bruce arrived at Shanghai, questions of proper protocol arose. The Chinese wanted the British and French forces to evacuate Canton *before* ratification took place. In addition, they wished the delegations to travel to Peking by a land route through Pentang without their military forces. The French and British objected to both these requests. They would evacuate Canton *after* ratification and would go to Peking by way of the Pei-ho River with their gunboats accompanying them as far as possible.

After the British and French left Shanghai with their fleet for the Pei-ho River, Minister Ward boarded the U.S. frigate *Powhatan,* commanded by Commodore Josiah TATTNALL, and proceeded to the Pei-ho River, where he arrived on June 21.

Ward soon faced the same problem Reed had faced in 1858: how to obtain Chinese concessions without becoming involved with the Anglo-French use of force. The Chinese had strongly barricaded the mouth of the Pei-ho River and reinforced their gun batteries at TAKU. While the French and British prepared to destroy the barricades, Ward decided on an independent course of action and with Commodore Tattnall boarded a small chartered steamer, the *Toeyman,* to try to pass the barrier and make contact with Chinese officials for a peaceful talk.

On June 24, Ward's plans went awry. As they proceeded toward the Pei-ho, the *Toeyman* ran aground in a falling tide, leaving their ship in danger of being fired on by the Chinese shore batteries. A British vessel came alongside to pull the *Toeyman* free but the attempt failed. Not until evening did the *Toeyman* float free and return below the mouth of the Pei-ho. Fortunately, the Chinese withheld their fire.

The next day, a battle ensued between the Anglo-French fleet and the Chinese. Both the barricades and Chinese guns were stronger than expected, and before the day ended, Commodore Tattnall and the *Toeyman* aided the British. When the British requested aid, Tattnall was reported to have told Ward, "blood is thicker than water," and he would "be damned if he'd stand by and see white men butchered before his eyes" by Chinese.

With Ward's approval, the *Toeyman* began towing some British junks into the positions desired by British naval officers. Other American sailors helped load British guns and rescued wounded sailors. The next day, the British and French ministers returned to Shanghai. Ward, however, made contact with Chinese envoys and gained permission to visit Peking.

See August 22, 1859.

June 27, 1859

The United States reaffirms its traditional views of neutrality as a result of the war of 1859 in northern Italy.

Although the European war lasted only from April 29 to July 12, Secretary of State Cass decided to assert American principles on the law of nations and against unjust practices interfering with American commerce. Therefore, Cass sent a circular note to American ministers in Europe informing them of these U.S. principles.

These principles as defined by Cass emphasized the right of a neutral to have its ships and property protected from the ravages of war between other nations. Stopping, examining, and seizing neutral cargo should not be condoned. Regarding blockade, Cass believed this was valid if held to a particular port where it could be effective. But, he wrote, a war against trade by blockade of a coastline was not rational or compatible with international law. Finally, Cass wanted the contraband list narrowly limited to arms and munitions. Belligerents had no right to add to the list. Therefore, the United States would decide for itself what was proper contraband.

This memo is of special interest because of subsequent American practice during the U.S. Civil War. Cass, of course, did not know that in less than two years the United States would be at war.

July 25, 1859

Anti-American manifestos appear in Central America.

The U.S. minister to Nicaragua, Mirabeau B. LAMAR, reported that a manifesto of the presidents of Nicaragua and Costa Rica had requested that England and France should protect them from American intervention wherever necessary.

This manifesto, which was one of many being circulated among the Central American states against the United States, represented a reverse "Monroe Doctrine" seeking European, not American, protection in Latin America. William Walker's Nicaraguan ventures and the American involvement on Walker's behalf left a long-term residue of ill will in Central America. While the U.S. State Department contended that it had acted properly, the early recognition of Walker's government, the American financial schemes, and the "emigrant" mercenaries from California suggested a plot. Moreover, Walker's reception as a "hero" in America and the failure of U.S. courts to punish him or extradite him caused Central America justifiably to see a U.S. plot in Walker's activity. Not only had the Democratic Party platform of 1856 praised Walker, but President Buchanan had also pardoned him after his return to America in 1857. For many years after Walker's defeat, Costa Ricans celebrated May 1, the day of his defeat, as a great event in their nation's history. In contrast, U.S. diplomatic messages to the State Department during the 1850s show a lack of sense that something was wrong with American policy toward Central America.

July 30, 1859

U.S. attempt to purchase Mexican territory fails.

Since April 7, 1859, U.S. Minister McLane had discussed with Juárez the possible sale of Lower California, Sonora, and part of Chihuahua as well as the transit rights across the Isthmus of Tehuantepec. Juárez seemed willing to negotiate. Whether this was to maintain good U.S. relations while all European governments recognized the conservative regime in Mexico City or because Juárez might have ceded Lower California (at least) is not known. Ultimately, Juárez would not sell any territory.

Regarding the transit rights, McLane now followed Secretary Cass's instructions to seek the right for America to use troops to protect the right-of-way on any canal that was constructed. Juárez would not consider this idea but suggested a military alliance with the United States to protect his government and, therefore, the canal rights. This suggestion was impossible for Buchanan to accept. The United States would protect the canal and U.S. property but could not make an alliance in favor of any particular Mexican government, not even a republican one such as Juárez led.

Thus, McLane's proposals were unacceptable. Washington's relations with Juárez remained friendly, however.

See December 19, 1859.

August 22, 1859

U.S. Minister Ward returns to Shanghai, having visited Peking and exchanged treaty ratifications at Pehtang.

Soon after Anglo-French naval forces failed to break the Chinese barricade at Taku on June 25, 1859, U.S. Minister Ward was contacted by Chinese emissaries who said they would escort him to Peking by way of PEHTANG. Ward agreed and, not realizing that overland travel by sedan chairs was proper for high officials, he and his aides traveled in carts such as lesser tribute-bearing envoys traditionally used when visiting Peking to do homage to the emperor.

Regarding another symbolic technicality, Ward stood firm and was therefore refused an audience with the emperor. Before taking Ward to meet the emperor, his Chinese hosts told him that he must be ready to kowtow to the emperor. The usual tribute kowtow was three kneelings and nine prostrations before his imperial highness. The envoys told Ward he could modify his number of kneelings before the emperor. Ward had heard of the kowtow and objected. He refused to bow or kneel in any fashion. An impasse resulted. Since he could not see the emperor, Ward asked for transportation back to Shanghai.

On the way back, however, the Chinese officials persuaded Ward to exchange ratifications at Pehtang even though he had not given Buchanan's letter to the emperor. Ward did so, stopping at Pehtang long enough to officially complete the Treaty of Tientsin.

December 14, 1859

Juárez and McLane sign two treaties regarding U.S. transit rights in Mexico and the enforcement of treaties—Congress does not ratify them.

The "Treaty of Transits and Conventions" guaranteed U.S. possession and enjoyment of the Tehuantepec canal route for which the United States paid $4 million: $2 million to Mexico and $2 million for claims of U.S. citizens against Mexico. The "Convention to Enforce Treaty Stipulations" permitted the United States to defend its territorial and commercial rights in Mexico against outside interference, that is, against any European attempt to control Mexico.

Buchanan presented these treaties to the U.S. Senate on January 4, 1860. They were sent to the Senate Committee on Foreign Relations but were never acted on by the Senate.

December 19, 1859

Buchanan seeks congressional authority to intervene in Mexico to aid Juárez and secure the Mexican indemnities due American citizens.

As part of his annual message to Congress, President Buchanan reviewed the Mexican situation. The civil war, he said, had created anarchy in Mexico. Great Britain threatened to occupy Vera Cruz to secure its claims against the government, and American commercial interests suffered severely from the chaos. By helping Juárez regain Mexico City, the United States would be certain to have the claims of Americans satisfied. Moreover, the president wrote, if we did not try to save Mexico from disorder, some other nation might attempt to do so, forcing America to interfere under more difficult circumstances.

Buchanan's request for authority to intervene in Mexico fell on deaf ears in Congress. The slavery question and the many domestic difficulties within America prevented U.S. politicians from seriously concerning themselves with Mexico. John Brown had raided Harper's Ferry on October 16–18, 1859, and the Kansas issue still required attention in Washington. Mexico's problems seemed far distant compared with these developments at home.

VII. CIVIL WAR ERA

Relations with Neutrals
France in Mexico
Alaska Purchase

1860

January 23, 1860

French-British commercial treaty initiates a free-trade policy on the European continent.

England had adopted a free-trade policy in 1846 and hoped to persuade other nations to follow. This treaty with France, which was part of Napoléon III's move to liberalize the empire, was one significant success of British efforts to promote free-trade policies by other governments.

March 24, 1860

Antiforeign samurai assassinate Ii Naosuke, leader of the pro-Western shogunate in Tokyo.

Ii's death resulted from the growing conflict in Japan between the Tokugawa shogun in Tokyo and the pro-emperor daimyo at the imperial palace in Kyoto. To stop the threat at Kyoto and reassert the shogun's power, Ii had assumed leadership of the Tokugawa on May 30, 1858, acting in the "great elder" tradition of the Ii clan.

The assassination of Ii by anti-Western samurai was a serious setback for the shogunate and enabled the antiforeign Choshu and Satsuma daimyo at Kyoto to enhance their influence and pave the way for the ultimate fall of the shogunate in 1867–1868. In the early 1860s, the Kyoto-Tokyo dispute erupted into a pro- and anti-Western argument, causing Kyoto extremists to devise a program to "cherish the emperor" and "expel the barbarians." This led directly to assassinations and attacks on Western personnel living in Japan.

See January 22, 1861 and July 16, 1863.

May 17, 1860

Japan's first mission arrives in America to exchange treaty ratifications and display Japanese culture.

A gala Japanese party of 77 officials including two ambassadors arrived at San Francisco on May 17, 1860. Following a week of social sessions with California officials, the Japanese took a steamer to Washington by way of the Panamanian railway route. During the remainder of the year they visited New York, Philadelphia, and Baltimore, where they displayed Japanese products and cultural items to Americans, including lacquerware, tea, and silk goods.

August 31, 1860

Secretary of State Cass warns the French Minister his country should not interfere in Mexico.

As evidence showed the growth of French influence in the conservative government of President MIRAMON in Mexico City, President Buchanan and Cass believed Paris would intervene against the Juárez government at Vera Cruz (see April 7, 1859). The French held claims against Mexican debts for which Cass admitted they deserved justice, but Cass told the French that an attempt to occupy parts of Mexico or to interfere in the Juárez-Miramon struggle "would give great dissatisfaction to the United States."

On two other occasions in 1860, Cass warned England and Spain against intervening in Mexico's internal affairs. In July, the English minister to the United States asked Cass if America would join

Britain and France in trying to settle the Mexican problem. Cass replied that the United States never interfered in the domestic affairs of an independent state and particularly opposed any intervention in Mexico.

In September 1860, Cass cautioned Spain about interference in Mexico. Madrid had sent Juárez a strong demand for the immediate payment of its claims and implied that an attack on Vera Cruz might be required. Cass informed the Spanish minister to the United States that his country could pursue its just indemnities but must not disturb the delicate political dispute in Mexico

September 12, 1860

William Walker is executed in Honduras; his Central American ventures end.

Following his overthrow in Nicaragua on May 1, 1857, Walker made two final attempts to gain power in Central America. In November 1857, he led an expedition that sailed from Mobile, Alabama, to the coast of Costa Rica, where U.S. navy Commodore Hiram PAULDING stopped his ship and arrested Walker. Paulding returned Walker to New Orleans, where he was indicted for violating U.S. neutrality laws. President Buchanan pardoned him of any crime, an action resulting from Walker's continued heroic status in the eyes of the U.S. public.

In Walker's final adventure, his ship again escaped from naval observers at Mobile in August 1860. Loaded with mercenaries, it reached the coast of Honduras, where, unfortunately for him, a British warship captured Walker and turned him over to Honduran authorities for violating the waters of that state. In Honduras as in other Central American countries, Walker symbolized the diabolical schemes of Americans against their governments. Walker was tried by a Honduran court on charges of planning violent rebellion. He was found guilty and was executed by a firing squad on September 12, 1860.

October 12, 1860

Peking, China, is occupied by 17,000 Anglo-French troops.

China's imperial government could not withstand the dual military threats of the Taiping Rebellion and foreign forces. In addition, after 1855, secret society bandits known as the NIEN attacked the Ch'ing imperial armies in the region west of the Great Canal, and Muslims in Yunnan Province revolted to gain religious independence.

Against the English and French, the Ch'ing rulers desired to keep the foreigners out of the capital city as a symbol of China's and the emperor's power. Consequently, when the British and French envoys arrived to take up residence in Peking in 1859, imperial forces stopped them (see June 25, 1859). The Anglo-French force had retreated temporarily to Shanghai but returned in 1860 with a larger force. The combined Anglo-French forces of 101 warships, 130 troop transports, and 16,800 soldiers plus a coolie corps of 2,500 Cantonese forced their way up the Pei-ho River and defeated an imperial army commanded by Mongol General Prince Senggerinchin. The emperor fled beyond the Great Wall to JEHOL, and allied forces occupied Peking on October 12.

Lord Elgin, the British envoy in charge of the Peking expedition, intended to remain in the city long enough to obtain a definitive agreement for foreign residence at the "heavenly" city, as allowed by the 1858 treaties. His plans changed, however, after a gang of Chinese extremists attacked and killed 20 Anglo-French delegates on their way to negotiate with Prince KUNG, the emperor's brother. Elgin decided he had to make a violent reprisal against China. Therefore, he ordered his troops to destroy 200 buildings of the Imperial Summer Palace, which was situated northwest of Peking.

Soon after this reprisal, Prince Kung signed a new convention with England and France that added a few concessions to the 1858 treaties. The British secured the Kowloon peninsula opposite Hong Kong; the French gained rights for Catholic missions to hold property in the interior of China.

November 6, 1860

Abraham Lincoln is elected president, the division in the Democratic Party almost making the results certain.

The Democratic Party split occurred on May 3 when the Charleston Convention adjourned because eight Southern state delegations withdrew. The convention reassembled at Baltimore on June 18 and nominated Stephen A. DOUGLAS for president. Those delegates who withdrew at Charleston met again on June 28 and nominated John BRECKINRIDGE for president. In addition to these two Democratic candidates, John BELL was nominated by the Constitutional Union Party, while at Chicago on May 16, Abraham Lincoln was selected by the Republican convention. Lincoln's platform appealed to the eastern and western sections of the nation. It favored internal improvements, a homestead law, and a protective tariff. It denounced the slave trade and the extension of slavery in any territory.

In the election, Lincoln received 180 electoral votes; Breckinridge, 12; Bell, 39; and Douglas, 12.

President Abraham Lincoln, 1964. Mathew Brady Collection. National Archives

December 12, 1860

In protest against President Buchanan's unwillingness to reinforce Fort Sumter, Secretary of State Cass resigns.

Ever since he had been secretary of war during the nullification controversy of 1832, Cass had believed the union must be preserved. Thus, in November Cass urged the president to send troops and warships to defend the federal forts at Charleston, South Carolina. Buchanan refused and Cass resigned, saying the president's cabinet should be in unanimity at this "perilous juncture of the nation's history."

Jeremiah Sullivan BLACK replaced Cass on December 17, 1860, serving for the brief period until Lincoln's inauguration on March 4, 1861. The former attorney general, Black was one of Buchanan's few close friends, yet he too could not persuade the president to maintain the Southern forts. Buchanan believed that the south would more easily compromise if the forts were not reinforced. Black did, however, convince the president to support Major Robert ANDERSON after he moved out of Fort Moultrie on the mainland and shut the federal troops in the less pregnable Fort Sumter on December 27, 1860.

See April 13, 1861.

December 22, 1860

Benito Juárez's liberal forces defeat the conservatives and regain Mexico City.

In spite of this victory, Juárez continued to suffer from the foreign pressure of the French government, which demanded payment of the debts due to France. The civil strife had disorganized the Mexican economy and finances, making these payments impossible.

See December 17, 1861.

1861

January 22, 1861

C. J. Heusken, interpreter for the U.S. Minister to Japan, is assassinated on the streets of Tokyo.

Heusken's murder was the seventh killing in 18 months by antiforeign Japanese associated with the anti-shogun groups at Kyoto. Although U.S. Minister Townsend Harris chose to remain in Tokyo and obtain a reparation from the shogun of $10,000 for Heusken's mother, the British, French, Dutch, and Prussian representatives left the city until the Japanese government could guarantee their safety.

See March 24, 1860.

March 1, 1861

Abraham Lincoln is inaugurated as President.

In his inaugural speech, Lincoln said he did not intend to interfere in states where slavery existed. He would not, however, countenance secession because "no state, upon its own action, can lawfully get out of the Union."

March 2, 1861

The Morrill Tariff brings the triumph of protection policy.

As advocated by the Republican Party in the campaign of 1860, the Morrill act levied high tariffs to protect American manufacturing, a policy followed generally for the next 50 years. Duties were increased from 25% to 30% in the 1861 act, but subsequent additions raised the average duties to 47% by February 24, 1869.

March 5, 1861

William Henry Seward is commissioned by President Lincoln as Secretary of State.

Seward had been a leading figure in the Republican Party. He lost the party's nomination for president in 1860 to Lincoln largely because some Republicans believed his intemperate speeches against slavery would hurt the party in doubtful states.

On December 8, 1860, Lincoln asked Seward to become secretary of state. Seward readily accepted because he thought the "incompetent" Lincoln would need a "prime minister" to rule. It took only one month after the inauguration for Lincoln to let Seward know that the president was the nation's leader. Nevertheless, Seward served Lincoln well and continued to be secretary under President Andrew Johnson following Lincoln's assassination in 1865. Seward remained in office until March 4, 1869.

Seward held some notable foreign policy ideas. He wanted a vigorous expansion program for the nation, especially in the Pacific Ocean, which he believed would replace the Atlantic as the "chief theater of events in the world's great hereafter." Seward's interests were shown during his administration of the State Department by the purchase of Alaska and an attempt to open Korea to trade.

March 17, 1861

Italy is united under King Victor Emmanuel of Piedmont.

Following the Austrian attack against Piedmont on August 29, 1859, Parma, Modena, Romagna, and Tuscany joined Piedmont to combat Austria. When the war ended, only the southern part of Italy remained to be united.

In 1860, Giuseppe Garibaldi led an invasion of Sicily and Naples and overthrew the king. Consequently, Piedmont's Premier Count, Camillo di Cavour, sent Piedmont's armies south where they defeated the papal forces and joined Garibaldi's men to prepare for a triumphal entry into Rome. Their final plan failed, however. Napoléon III sent French troops to protect the pope and Rome from Italian control.

With only Rome separated from complete Italian unity, an Italian parliament met and, on March 17, proclaimed the Kingdom of Italy under Victor Emmanuel with a government based on the Piedmontese constitution of 1848. Rome was taken by Italian forces in 1870 after France withdrew its troops to fight in the Franco-Prussian War.

April 1, 1861

Secretary Seward proposes a "foreign war panacea" to stimulate national unity.

Combining the recent French and Spanish threats in Mexico and the Caribbean with America's domestic crisis, Seward suggested to Lincoln that an energetic pursuit against these European powers might raise the specter of war, or bring actual war, which would gen-

William Henry Seward, Secretary of State. National Archives

erate a national spirit capable of reuniting the South to the Union.

On March 31, Seward received a dispatch from C. J. Helms, U.S. consul in Havana, which indicated that Spain had sent several companies of soldiers on transports headed for Santo Domingo. According to the secretary, this indicated a possible French-Spanish plan to gain power in the Caribbean and use it to overthrow the liberal Mexican leader, Benito Juárez. To counter this threat, Seward proposed to demand an immediate explanation from Madrid and Paris, and to inquire where Britain and Russia stood on the question of Mexico. If Spain and France did not respond, Lincoln could ask Congress to declare war.

Seward's foreign proposals contrasted with his advice to Lincoln to refuse to reinforce Fort Sumter. If any Southern fort were maintained, he wanted it to be Fort Pickens in Florida, whose status would indicate to France and Spain the American concern in the Gulf of Mexico.

Lincoln did not accept Seward's proposal. He said all America's previous policies had included no suggestion of war to Spain or France, and such a change should not be hastily advised. He also said he would decide on Sumter's fate as soon as he had examined all factors and opinions. Seward's "panacea" is usually considered to be his one rash act as secretary of state; he matured in office and acted with competence in most other cases.

April 13, 1861

Fort Sumter falls to Confederate forces—the Civil War begins.

After deciding to resupply Sumter, Lincoln notified South Carolina on April 6 that the ship being sent to the fort carried nothing but provisions. The Charleston leaders feared, however, that if a ruse were not involved in the maneuver, the provisioning of Sumter would mean a prolonged federal occupation of the fort.

Therefore, after Major Anderson said he would surrender only when his supplies ran out, General Pierre G. T. Beauregard decided to take the fort. South Carolina's shore batteries began firing on April 12 at 4:30 A.M. and after 34 hours of bombardment Anderson surrendered on April 13. On April 15, Lincoln declared that the Confederate attack on Sumter indicated that an "insurrection" existed and he called for 75,000 volunteers to join the Union army.

April 19, 1861

Proclaiming a blockade of the South, Lincoln forbids all trade with the seceded states.

Although President Lincoln claimed the Southern states could not secede and that there was only an insurrection of individuals in the South, he and Seward realized the value of a blockade although a declaration of blockade recognized a state of war.

While the attempt to blockade 3,550 miles of Southern coastline could only be a "paper" blockade, the U.S. navy tried to make it effective. Although it was not prepared for war in April 1861, the navy gathered a collection of ships to patrol the coast in July 1861. In August, a large ship construction program began, including seven ironclad gunboats. The blockade appeared to become more effective during the next several years. It is believed that in 1861 a blockade runner had about 1 chance in 10 of being captured; by 1863 the odds of capture were 1 in 3.

May 19, 1861

Spain declares the annexation of the Dominican Republic and occupies the island.

The Spanish had been waiting to take over this area since 1844 when the eastern half of Santo Domingo rebelled against Haiti. In early 1861, Madrid officials persuaded the Dominican president to ask for annexation. In May Spain accepted this request to prevent Haiti from controlling the entire island.

Seward knew of this offer on April 1, when he made his "panacea of war" suggestions to Lincoln. He had informed the Spanish minister to the United States that the United States would consider the occupation of Santo Domingo as an unfriendly act.

May 21, 1861

The United States insists that Great Britain's neutrality requires it to stop all intercourse with "domestic enemies" of the United States.

Secretary of State Seward sent Charles Francis Adams as U.S. minister to England, instructing him on May 21 that he should not communicate with British officials if they had any intercourse with Southern agents.

Although British Foreign Secretary Lord John Russell had met early in May with William L. Yancey and Pierre A. Rost, two Confederate agents, he informed Adams that he had no intention of seeing these agents again.

On May 13, Great Britain declared neutrality, and on June 1, 1861, it forbade armed ships of either belligerent from bringing prize ships to British ports. This order was a particularly hard blow at Confederate privateers who preferred British prize courts.

Despite Britain's declaration of neutrality, British shipyards continued to construct warships for the South.

See April 4, 1863.

July 18, 1861

The United States withdraws its proposal to adhere to the Declaration of Paris of 1856 on neutrality.

As soon as the Civil War began, both Seward and Confederate President Jefferson Davis tried to use international law to serve their interests. On April 17, Davis offered to issue letters of marque for privateers to raid Northern shipping. Seward on April 24 sent word to Paris and London that the United States would accept the Declaration of Paris, which President Buchanan had rejected in 1857. The declaration of 1856 outlawed privateers. Before 1861, the abolition of privateers did not benefit the United States because of its small naval force. After April 18, the privateers' legality aided the South more than the North.

When the U.S. ministers to London and Paris, Charles Francis ADAMS and William L. DAYTON, presented Seward's offer to their respective host governments, neither the British nor the French would accept the U.S. request unless the present circumstances of war were excluded. Lord Russell contended that Britain did not recognize the Confederate government but did accept a status of belligerency in America. Therefore, Britain had to be neutral and could not permit a change in the status of prewar conditions.

On July 18, in final discussions, the British and French required the U.S. ministers to agree to exempt the South from the Paris Declaration. Adams and Dayton rejected these terms and did not sign the treaty. Secretary Seward concurred with the action of these U.S. representatives.

October 24, 1861

First transcontinental telegraph message is transmitted from San Francisco to Washington, D.C.

This successful communication line resulted from the Pacific Telegraph Act of June 16, 1860, which authorized construction of a telegraph line from Missouri to San Francisco.

October 31, 1861

Napoléon III's attempt to establish an empire in Mexico begins with the Convention of London.

This convention was agreed to by France, Great Britain, and Spain in a coordinated attempt to force the Mexican government of Benito JUÁREZ to pay the debts due the three European nations. The three powers sent a combined force to Vera Cruz in December 1861, but soon thereafter the English and Spanish troops withdrew, permitting Napoléon to fulfill his ambition of controlling Mexico as part of a

French empire. In signing the Convention of London, the powers had agreed not to interfere in Mexico's right "to choose and constitute freely the form of its government." This was not, however, Napoléon's real intention because early in October 1861, he had secretly decided to make the Austrian Archduke MAXIMILLIAN the ruler of Mexico.

December 17, 1861

Vera Cruz, Mexico, is occupied by French, British, and Spanish forces.

Acting under the Treaty of London of October 31, 1861, the three European nations took Vera Cruz to demand Mexican payment of its foreign debts. Because the French pursued attempts to get political power in all Mexico, the Spanish and British withdrew their forces by April 8, 1862; the French continued to plan an attack on Mexico City.

See June 7, 1863.

December 26, 1861

Secretary of State Seward resolves the *Trent* Affair by releasing the four confederates taken from the *Trent* and praising England for finally recognizing the U.S. interpretations of neutral rights.

Seward's note to the British releasing James M. MASON, John SLIDELL, and their two secretaries, George EUSTICE and James MACFARLAND, was a political masterpiece in which Seward yielded the substance but gained the U.S. principles of neutrality.

The four Confederates had been aboard the British mail steamer *Trent* bound from Havana for St. Thomas in the Danish West Indies. They had reached Havana aboard a Confederate blockade runner and intended to continue from St. Thomas to England as diplomatic officials of the Confederate government. Returning from duty off the coast of Africa, Captain Charles WILKES, commander of the U.S. navy warship *San Jacinto,* learned that Slidell and Mason were on board the *Trent* and decided, with no orders from Washington, to seize them. Just after the *Trent* left Cuban waters, Wilkes's ship overtook it and, after firing two shots across its bow, forced it to stop. Boarding the *Trent,* Lieutenant D. M. FAIRFAX ordered the Confederate envoys to be seized and taken to the *San Jacinto.* Wilkes then sailed off, returning home to Fortress Monroe in the United States.

On Wilkes's arrival home, he and his crew were greeted as heroes. The secretary of the navy congratulated Wilkes and the *New York Times* suggested that America should "consecrate another Fourth of July to him." The Northern wave of approval for Wilkes in November 1861 came because the North needed "heroes" since the Union armies had not fared well against the Confederacy since April 1861. Therefore, any good news was exaggerated.

In England, Foreign Minister Lord Russell sent orders to Lord Lyon, the British minister to the United States, to protest the seizure even though many people in Britain realized that America had simply applied the belligerent rights usually upheld by Great Britain. The *London Times* editor wrote that the United States acted on its strict rights as a belligerent and that "unwelcome as the truth may be, it is nevertheless a truth, that we ourselves established a system of International Law which now tells against us."

Look Out for Squalls. Britain's strong stand on the *Trent* affair is portrayed here with the swaggering, sharp-nosed, cigar-smoking Yankee. *Punch,* 1861

Not until December 26 did Seward respond to the British protest. To help insure that the British had no cause to grant recognition to the Confederate government, Seward agreed to release the prisoners to Great Britain. He explained that Captain Wilkes had made only one minor error: he failed to take the Confederate agents as "contraband" of war to a prize court for a decision on their fate. Because Wilkes overlooked this technicality, the United States would graciously release the prisoners.

Seward continued by saying that he was pleased that in Lord Russell's note, the British had adopted the American principles on neutrality by asking the United States to do what Britain had so often failed to do in the past. At last, he stated, Britain recognized the correctness of American claims in an issue that "for more than half a century alienated the two countries . . . and perplexed with fears and apprehensions all other nations." Thus, Seward implied, Russell recognized that since the era of Napoléon's wars the United States had been right and England wrong on neutral rights and belligerent rights.

The Confederate warship *Alabama* sinks after a battle with the USS *Kearsage* in June 1864. National Archives

1862

June 5, 1862

In the Treaty of Saigon, the Annamese Emperor agrees to French control over the three provinces of Cochin China.

French missionaries had been active in Annam since 1615 and had been favored by the Emperor Gia Long, whom they helped secure power in 1802. Subsequently, however, the Emperor Minh-Mang and his successors tried to eliminate Christian missionaries by persecution. Under Napoléon III, France again sought power in Annam by occupying Saigon in 1858. This occupation plus the control of Cochin China was recognized by the emperor of Annam in the Treaty of 1862.

July 31, 1862

The warship *Alabama* leaves England despite American attempts to detain it.

A British shipbuilder constructed the *Alabama,* which was launched on May 15, 1862. Although Great Britain claimed neutrality, this was the second vessel that nation built for the Confederacy. Early in 1862, the *Florida* left England after English authorities informed U.S. Minister Adams it was an Italian ship. Under the name *Oreto,* it cleared Liverpool for Palermo but steamed to Nassau, where it was armed with cannon and rechristened as the *Florida* for the Confederate navy.

In the case of the *Alabama,* Adams obtained extensive evidence proving the ship was bound for the Confederacy, but the Liverpool authorities rejected his evidence. Adams referred the case to the foreign secretary, Lord Russell, who did not act for five days. When Russell finally sent orders to Liverpool to hold the *Alabama,* his message arrived too late. Having foreseen Russell's probable action, the crew boarded the *Alabama* under the pretense of a trial voyage with party guests on board. The *Alabama* then steamed to the high sea, sending the guests back to port in a tugboat.

When the Civil War ended, the U.S. damage claims against Britain for constructing ships to sell to the Confederacy were referred to as the "Alabama claims." This term was largely in respect to the *Alabama*'s success against American merchant ships. Before being destroyed by the USS *Kearsage* in June 1864, the *Alabama* burned, sank, captured, or released under bond over 60 merchant ships.

September 21, 1862

A U.S. adventurer, Frederick T. Ward, organizer of China's "ever victorious army," is killed in the Battle of Tzeki.

Ward, who had been commissioned a general in the Chinese imperial army in 1861, played a leading role in the restoration of the power of the Ch'ing dynasty during the 1860s.

Following the Anglo-French occupation of Peking in October 1860, two factors permitted the reassertion of Ch'ing power. Reformers led by Prince Kung and the Empress Dowager Tz'u-hsi, who ruled for her young son after the death in 1861 of the Emperor Hsieng-feng, agreed to appease the Western powers who in turn assisted the Ch'ing. Second, a new commander of the Chinese army, Tseng Kuo-fan, profited from the assistance of Western military men in strengthening the Chinese army and defeating the Taiping and other rebel groups.

Frederick Ward was the Western military leader selected to aid Kuo-fan. Ward previously fought in Nicaragua with William Walker and had come to China in 1859 to work on a Yangtze steamship. At the request of Chinese in Shanghai, Ward raised a force of mercenaries in 1861 to fight the Taiping. After his army of Filipinos captured Sunkiang from Taiping, Kuo-fan commissioned Ward as a general to recruit and train Chinese to fight Western-style warfare.

Although the British authorities first tried to stop Ward by arresting him in May 1861, he escaped. The British Admiral Sir James Hope realized that Ward's methods could be the means for preserving the Ch'ing rulers with whom Great Britain made its treaty arrangements. Thereafter, with the aid of French and British authorities and Shanghai merchants, Ward trained an army of 4,000 Chinese. He named his force the Ever Victorious Army and used amphibious tactics on the Yangtze River to recapture Anking and Tsingpu in 1861 and 1862. By the time Ward died in the battle of Tzeki on September 21, an effective force of Western-trained Chinese had been established to work with Tseng Kuo-fan in defeating the Taiping.

Following Ward's death in September 1862, his chief subordinate, Henry A. BURGEVINE, was appointed general of the Ever Victorious Army, but he proved to be incompetent. In March 1863, a British adventurer, Charles G. "Chinese" GORDON, took control of Ward's army, using it to destroy the Taiping forces by 1864. Although Gordon attained more attention from British publicists, Frederick Ward had the honor of showing that the Chinese could be trained in Western methods and of inaugurating the initial victories of the Ever Victorious Army. Gordon simply completed Ward's plans.

September 23, 1862

President Lincoln issues the preliminary Emancipation Proclamation as a means of preventing foreign recognition of the Confederate government.

After the Confederate armies won a succession of victories over the Union forces during the first year of war, many in Great Britain and France began to believe that the Confederates deserved political recognition. The Union losses had also prevented Lincoln from acting to "free the slaves" because he and Secretary Seward wanted such an act to follow a victory.

On September 17 at Antietam, General George B. MCCLELLAN forced General Robert E. LEE to pull back from Maryland into Virginia after one of the war's bloodiest battles: the Union casualties were 2,108 killed and 9,549 wounded; the Confederate losses were 2,700 killed and 9,029 wounded.

McClellan's "victory" provided the opportunity for Lincoln to announce that as of January 1, 1863, the slaves would be freed in all areas still in rebellion. Lincoln did not free slaves in the border states, which remained in the Union. He also rejected proposals for full emancipation or compensated emancipation. The most significant result of the emancipation announcement was its effect on public opinion in England, where it appeared to liberals as though Lincoln's armies fought to liberate the slaves as well as to preserve the Union. In the Northern states, the "radical" Republicans expressed dismay at Lincoln's limited measure, which had not effectively liberated one slave. The president contended that he was being consistent because since 1861 he had acted to keep as many states as possible from joining the "insurrection." The British public mistook Lincoln's lesser purpose as being his major purpose for fighting the Confederacy.

See October 5, 1862, and November 1, 1862.

October 5, 1862

In England, William Gladstone speaks in favor of recognizing the Confederate States of America.

By the summer of 1862, the dearth of cotton began to be felt in England and many British political leaders considered recognizing Jefferson Davis's government. Before news of Lincoln's announcement of emancipation reached London (see September 23, 1862), Prime Minister Lord Palmerston and Foreign Secretary Lord Russell informed a young, rising Liberal spokesman, William Gladstone, that they were prepared to recognize the Confederacy and offer to mediate in the American war.

On October 5, Gladstone tested British public opinion on recognition in a speech at Newcastle. He spoke favorably of the Confederate military success and asserted that Davis had created not only an army and navy but "greater still a nation."

Shortly after, news of Lincoln's decree reached England and caused Russell and Palmerston to reconsider their plans.

See November 1, 1862.

November 1, 1862

Napoléon III proposes that Britain, Russia, and France offer mediation in the U.S. Civil War—Britain and Russia refuse.

Napoléon had a general sympathy with the Southern cause but hesitated to recognize the Confederate government unless England did. As a step toward recognition, Napoléon proposed that the three European powers offer mediation, assuming that if it failed, the Confederacy would be ready for recognition.

Earlier in 1862, British Foreign Minister Russell seemed congenial to such a cooperative effort. By November 1, however, Russell and Prime Minister Palmerston decided they could not join Napoléon's effort. Owing partly, if not largely, to the British public's favorable reaction to Lincoln's notice of emancipation in September 1862, the British leaders felt that the increase in English support for the North made any pro-Southern action inadvisable. In addition, Lee's loss at Antietam and the increased importations of cotton from Egypt and India began to lessen English dependence on the Southern product. Because Russia opposed Napoléon's idea, Russell used that excuse to back away from his earlier acceptance of the French plan. The British never again came close to granting recognition to the Confederate government.

1863

January 1, 1863

President Lincoln issues the Emancipation Proclamation.

This decree formally liberated all slaves in areas still in rebellion but freed no slaves under federal military jurisdiction. Nevertheless, as when the "preliminary" decree was issued on September 23, 1862, this act won wide public support in England and France.

Writers during the civil rights movement of the 1960s and 70s criticized the proclamation for not immediately terminating the slavery system. While this criticism has some merit, it fails to recognize that there could be no retreat from the process set in motion by the proclamation which did shortly end slavery in the United States.

Emancipation Proclamation announces that slaves in rebel areas are free.

January 22, 1863

A Polish uprising begins; Russian troops suppress it.

With great severity, the Russians put down an uprising that began on January 22, 1863. Led by Napoléon III, the governments of France, Great Britain, and Austria threatened to intervene on behalf of the Poles. Bismarck, however, promised the czar that Prussia would cooperate in suppressing the revolt and sent four Prussian army corps to the Polish frontier. With Bismarck's support, Czar Alexander II ignored the other diplomatic protests and proceeded to act vigorously against the insurrection. After suppressing the opposition in Poland by May 1864, the czar abolished Polish autonomy and took action against Roman Catholic clergy, which caused a rupture in Russia's relations with the Vatican. This uprising also played a role in the preparations for the formation of the First International Communist Party of Karl Marx and Friedrich Engels.

February 6, 1863

Secretary of State Seward rejects a French offer of mediation.

Napoléon III's offer had been made on February 3, through the French minister to the United States. Seward refused the request and on March 3, 1863, a congressional resolution asserted that such mediation offers were "foreign intervention" in American affairs.

Napoléon's offer was surprising because France had considered but never actually recognized the Confederate States of the South. Both Seward and Lincoln denied the need for foreign recognition or intervention because they argued that the Civil War was an act of rebellion by the Southern states.

April 4, 1863

The United States protests that the British government continues to allow Confederate ships to be built.

The U.S. minister to England, Charles F. Adams, heard that a British shipyard had completed construction of a raiding ship, the *Alexandra,* that was scheduled to be put to sea. He protested that this was the third vessel built by English shipyards for the Confederate states, two others having been completed in 1862—the *Alabama* and the *Florida.* Together with other Southern raiders, these Confederate ships by 1865 had destroyed 257 ships and caused 700 American vessels to transfer their registry to foreign flags. These casualties ruined the U.S. merchant marine, which had been highly effective between 1815 and 1860. For the next half-century, U.S. merchant shipping lagged behind that of other commercial nations.

In the case of the *Alexandra,* the British government seized the ship but its owners took the issue to British courts, which released the ship from custody. The British proceeded to change their laws toward ship construction. By September 1863, the government developed more effective means to stop future ships from joining the Confederate navy.

See September 5, 1863.

June 7, 1863

French troops occupy Mexico City.

After seizing Vera Cruz in December 1861, Napoléon III believed the Mexicans would rise up to assist him against Juárez, but this never happened. In addition, the British and Spanish forces left Vera Cruz in 1862. Nevertheless, the French pushed on. With an army of 28,000 and a foreign legion of 78,000 Belgians and Austrians, the French marched on Mexico City, taking it on June 7, 1863.

During the next year, France established a monarchical government and selected the Archduke Maximilian of Austria as emperor. Maximilian assumed authority on April 10, 1864, after signing a convention by which Mexico would pay the expenses of the French army of intervention from December 17, 1861, to July 1, 1864, a cost of 270,000,000 francs at 3% interest. The new Mexican empire began with serious financial burdens added to the existing foreign claims against the government.

July 4, 1863

The Union armies win significant victories at Gettysburg and Vicksburg.

On the same day, General Lee's army lost at Gettysburg, Pennsylvania, and General Grant's army won at Vicksburg, Mississippi. Lee's loss ended his attempts to invade the North; Grant's victory permitted his forces to capture Port Hudson, Louisiana, on July 8, and split the Confederacy into two parts.

Lee wanted his Northern invasion to succeed in order to demonstrate to British and French leaders that they should recognize the Southern government. His defeat coupled with Grant's victory ended any remaining possibility of foreign recognition.

July 16, 1863

A U.S. warship sinks two Japanese gunboats in retaliation for the killing of five Americans aboard the U.S. vessel *Pembroke*.

This U.S. merchant ship was traveling near the Straits of Shimonoseki in May 1863, when gunboats of the Choshu daimyo fired on it, killing five and wounding six sailors. The Choshu attack resulted from an internal political struggle in Japan between the shogun at Tokyo and the imperial court at Kyoto.

During the spring of 1863, the Prince of Choshu persuaded the emperor to issue an edict expelling all barbarians by June 25, 1863, and ordering the shogun to carry out the edict. Knowing they could not fulfill this order even if they chose to, the shogun's representatives warned the U.S. Minister Robert H. Pruyn and other Western representatives of the impending problem.

In May 1863, the Prince of Choshu decided to demonstrate how to defeat the barbarians. His gunboats and shore batteries on the Inland Seas near Shimonoseki began to attack any passing foreign ships. Choshu's first victim was the *Pembroke*.

By coincidence, the U.S. navy's warship *Wyoming* stopped at Yokohama early in July while it was hunting for the Confederate warship *Alabama* in the Pacific Ocean. Learning about the attack on the *Pembroke*, the *Wyoming*'s Commodore McDougal decided to go to Shimonoseki, capture the Choshu gunboats, and turn them over to the shogun's forces. The shogun approved of the action, for his representatives had moved quickly to indemnify the United States for the *Pembroke* incident with a payment of $10,000.

Near the straits, however, the Choshu shore batteries began firing at the *Wyoming* and McDougal chose to attack. His guns fired on and sank a Japanese brig and a steamship. A few days later, a French naval vessel steamed to Shimonoseki, where it landed a small force of men who burned a village of the Choshu and destroyed one gun battery and much ammunition.

A major effect of these Western retaliatory attacks was the lessening of Choshu influence in Kyoto. On September 30, 1863, troops of the Satsuma and Aizu daimyo chased the Choshu out of Kyoto and gained a dominant influence over the emperor.

For internal Japanese divisions, see March 24, 1860; for further gunboat diplomacy against Japan, see September 23, 1864, and June 25, 1866.

August 11, 1863

Cambodia accepts France as its protector.

After gaining control of Cochin China in the Treaty of June 5, 1862, French forces moved westward into Cambodia, a kingdom that had constantly been threatened by Annam to the east and Siam to the west. King Norodom of Cambodia agreed on August 11 to accept French protection and to allow French traders to control the use of the Mekong River.

September 5, 1863

The U.S. Minister to England is more successful in firmly opposing British ship construction for the Confederacy.

Following instructions from Secretary of State Seward, C. F. Adams warned Lord Russell, Britain's foreign minister, that if the ironclad ships under construction for the Southern rebels were delivered to them, the United States would consider it an act of war.

Acting perhaps in light of the recent Union army victories at Vicksburg and Gettysburg, Russell ordered the ships (the "Laird rams") to be held in Liverpool until the British government took control of them in October. In May 1864, the British government purchased them for the British navy.

About this time, the French government also enforced its neutrality by selling six ships built for the Confederacy to other European governments.

Yet while the British government was more diligent after 1863 in trying to prevent its ships from reaching the Confederate navy, it was not always successful. During the next 18 months, at least three other cruisers joined the Confederate navy: the *Georgiana*, *Georgia*, and *Shenandoah*. The *Shenandoah* was second only to the *Alabama* in effectively raiding Union merchant ships.

Never captured, the *Shenandoah*'s captain surrendered his ship to the British at Liverpool after the Civil War ended.

September 24, 1863

Two Russian warships arrive at New York, the first of its fleet coming to New York and San Francisco during the fall of 1863. Americans incorrectly believe the Czar sent the ships to support the United States against British and French interference in the Civil War

Between September 24 and October 12, 1863, Russia's two major naval fleets sought safety in American ports. At the time, Britain and France had threatened to interfere in Russia on behalf of the Polish rebellion. Fearing possible war, eight Russian warships came to New York, six to San Francisco. The Russian naval leaders sent the vessels to the neutral American ports until the crisis with London and Paris ended in 1864. They did not want the ships to be captured if war began.

Russia's reason for sending its ships to American ports was kept secret from the United States. As a result, many Northern politicians and news editors believed the Russian ships arrived to help the Union cause in the Civil War. The year 1863 had been bad for the Union army. In addition, the British and French were rumored to be ready to aid the Confederate states. Thus, the Northern journalists greeted the Russian naval officers as heroes who favored the United States. Secretary of the Navy Gideon Welles was quoted as saying, "God bless the Russians." When the Russian spokesman simply stated that his nation's ships were in American ports for "no unfriendly purpose," news editors interpreted his cautious words as being designed not to offend London and Paris. Consequently, until the Russian fleets were recalled to their home ports during the spring of 1864, Americans wined, dined, and praised the Russian crews and officers. The Russians could not appear ungracious and did not explain their real reasons for coming to the U.S. ports.

In 1915, historian Frank A. Golder's research in the Russian archives disclosed the actual reason for the Russian naval visits to New York and San Francisco in 1863. As Golder noted, however, American belief in Russia's support provided a big boost for Northern morale during the pessimistic war situation of 1863, even if it was mistaken.

1864

April 4, 1864

The U.S. House of Representatives passes a resolution protesting the French action in Mexico.

This resolution indicated the growing U.S. opinion against French policies. Throughout 1862 and 1863, the American press noted what was happening in Mexico, but the exigencies of the Civil War prevented any strong responses. In 1864, as the Southern military threat diminished, advocates of strong action against Napoléon III increased.

The House resolution that passed on April 4, just before Maximilian took over as emperor on April 10, indicated the developing American resentment against France. Passed by a vote of 109 to 0, the House resolution said Americans were not "indifferent spectators of the deplorable events" in Mexico. The United States, it said, would never acknowledge a monarchical government erected in this hemisphere by any European power.

Although the U.S. minister to Paris, William Dayton, informed the French that a resolution of Congress did not speak for the president, the French should have received the message about future U.S. policy once the Civil War ended. Napoléon III was, however, neither the competent nor the sensible ruler his uncle had been.

April 14, 1864

Peru and Spain go to war after a Spanish fleet seizes the Chincha Islands near Peru.

These two countries had engaged in lengthy controversies because Spain refused to recognize Peru's independence. In 1865, Peru signed alliances for aid with Chile, Bolivia, and Ecuador, finally forcing Spain to abandon hostilities on May 9, 1866. The war continued on a diplomatic level until 1871, when Spain signed separate treaties with each of the four nations while the United States acted as mediator.

May 21, 1864

American policy regarding French activity in Mexico is to protest sufficiently to maintain U.S. interests against France until the Civil War ends.

When John BIGELOW replaced William DAYTON as U.S. minister to France, Secretary of State Seward outlined the policy he and Lincoln had followed after the French occupied Mexico City in June 1863. America had to avoid the two extremes of doing nothing and protesting so harshly that France would recognize and form an alliance with the Southern Confederate government.

Consequently, Seward wrote to Bigelow that the United States must persist in sufficiently protesting French actions in Mexico and must avoid compromising any U.S. interests. Nevertheless, America could not "gasconade about Mexico when we are in a struggle for our own life." Until the war ends, the secretary said, the United States must withhold vigorous threats against the French.

July 4, 1864

An immigration act permits contracts to be let for foreign labor to increase the flow of cheap labor into America from Europe.

Under this act, companies or shipowners could advertise in Europe to pay for an immigrant's passage to America under a contract for the person to work a maximum of 12 months to pay for passage. This act was often abused by illegal contract stipulations. Generally, however, it stimulated an upsurge of immigrants from southern, eastern, and central Europe during the next 50 years.

September 23, 1864

Following naval action by the Western powers against the Choshu Daimyo at Shimonoseki, the shogun agrees to keep Yokohama Port and the Inland Sea open to trade.

For nearly five years, samurai led by the Choshu and Satsuma daimyo sought to gain control over Japanese policy by securing influence at the imperial court in Kyoto. These daimyo fostered an anti-Western program, seeking once again to isolate Japan from Western contact.

These internal struggles had already caused an incident with the American ship *Pembroke* (see July 16, 1863). Following that event, U.S. Minister to Japan Pruyn obtained a $32,000 indemnity from the shogun at Tokyo. Nevertheless, despite Western protests against many attacks on their persons and property by agents of the daimyo, the court at Kyoto decreed the closing of Yokohama to Western trade.

To assist the shogunate in counteracting daimyo influence, the Western powers launched a naval expedition against the powerful Choshu Prince of Nagati at Shimonoseki in the Inland Sea. Led by the British Minister Sir Rutherford Alcock, a flotilla of nine British, four Dutch, three French, and one American vessels attacked the fortress of Shimonoseki from September 5 to 8, 1864. Both President Lincoln and Secretary Seward approved American participation in the expedition, although this did not have precedent in either China or Japan. U.S. Minister Pruyn rented a merchant steamer, the *Ta-Kiang*, equipping it with naval guns from the USS *Jamestown*. Sailors from the *Jamestown* manned the *Ta-Kiang*. The *Jamestown* did not participate because it was a sailing ship, which was of no value to the expedition.

Western gunboat diplomacy succeeded after four days of naval bombardment, and the daimyo's guns were silenced. A landing party destroyed the gun batteries and the Choshu seemed to be crushed. Because British ships had, in a separate action, bombarded the Satsuma fortress at Kagoshima and persuaded the Prince of Satsuma to end his antiforeign policy, the daimyo attempt to close Japan's doors to the West ended.

On September 23, 1864, the shogun agreed to abrogate the decree closing Yokohama port. He also ordered that the Inland Sea remain open to Western ships and assumed an indemnity of $3 million to pay the expense of the naval action against Shimonoseki. The Western nations promised to remit the indemnity if the Inland Sea remained open and secure for Western trading vessels. Because the shogun delayed action in enforcing his agreements, a second naval expedition had to be launched by the Western powers.

See June 25, 1866.

October 19, 1864

Confederate agents violate the neutrality of the U.S. Canadian border by an attack on St. Albans, Vermont.

Since 1862, Confederate agents used Canada as a sanctuary to stage raids into the New England states. The pillaging of St. Albans on October 19 was such a serious attack that Secretary Seward and President Lincoln decided to try to end this activity.

On October 19, Confederate army Lieutenant Bennett H. Young led 25 Confederate agents from Canada to raid St. Albans. The Confederates burned homes, robbed a bank of $200,000, and shot two U.S. citizens, one fatally. Citizens of St. Albans formed a posse and chased the culprits into Canada, where Canadian authorities arrested the raiders. The next day, however, a Canadian judge released the captives because Lieutenant Young produced papers showing he acted on orders of the Confederate War Department.

The raid and the Canadian court decision greatly concerned Secretary Seward. In consultation with the president, Seward informed Great Britain that the United States was giving the necessary one-year notice to withdraw from the Rush-Bagot disarmament convention of 1817. President Lincoln sent a division of the Union army to guard the border against further incursions.

As a result of these actions, British officials in Canada undertook more effective means to prevent future raids. The most significant of these was passage of Canada's Alien Act, by which they expelled foreigners who aimed to engage in military operation against a nation friendly to Canada. Because no other serious incident occurred, Secretary Seward notified the British in 1865 that he was withdrawing the notice to end the Rush-Bagot agreement.

November 8, 1864

Abraham Lincoln is reelected President.

A Republican Convention (also called the National Union Convention) at Baltimore had nominated Lincoln for president and a War Democrat, Andrew Johnson, for vice president. The Democratic Party chose General George McClellan and George H. Pendleton as its candidates. Although the Democratic platform called for the immediate end of the war and the creation of a Federal Union of States, McClellan repudiated this plank. Nevertheless, Lincoln easily won the election by a total of 212 to 21 electoral votes.

November 28, 1864

The Chivington Massacre of Indians enables Colorado Troops to win the Cheyenne-Arapaho War.

Colorado and Dakota had been organized as territories in 1861. The resulting influx of settlers caused an Indian war that climaxed on November 28, when 450 Indians were slaughtered by the Colorado militia under Colonel J. M. Chivington, for whom the massacre is named. The Indians surrendered in 1865 and were moved to reservations in the Dakota territory of the Black Hills.

1865

April 9, 1865

The Confederate army of General Lee surrenders at Appomattox Court House.

After General Grant's forces surrounded General Lee's armies of Virginia, the two generals met on April 9 and Lee accepted Grant's surrender terms.

Lee's surrender virtually ended the Civil War, although other Southern armies had to surrender. The last official resistance ended on May 26, when General Kirby Smith surrendered to General Edward R. Canby at New Orleans. Confederate President Jefferson Davis was captured in Georgia on May 10, 1865.

April 14, 1865

President Lincoln is assassinated; an attempt to kill Secretary of State Seward fails.

Lincoln's death was tragic not only for personal reasons, but also because his effective presidential leadership ended. His desire to conciliate the Southern states could not be managed by Andrew Johnson, who took the oath of office after Lincoln died early in the morning of April 15. Consequently, the radical abolitionist Republicans in Congress gained political control and punished the South during the "reconstruction era" from 1866 to 1877.

About the same time that John Wilkes Booth shot Lincoln, Booth's coconspirator Lewis Powell

General Robert E. Lee (right) surrenders to General Ulysses S. Grant at the Appomattox Court House. Library of Congress

(alias Payne) fought his way into Seward's bedroom and slashed several times with a knife at Seward's throat. Although the secretary was severely cut, an iron brace placed on Seward's shoulders to set his broken jaw saved his life. (Seward had broken his jaw in two places in an accident on April 5, an accident that now saved his life.) At Seward's home, his two sons, a nurse, and a State Department messenger were all wounded by Powell. On July 7, Powell was one of the four persons hanged for the assassination plot against Lincoln and Seward. Booth died in a barn near Bowling Green, Virginia, on April 26.

May 1, 1865

A nationalist uprising in Santo Domingo succeeds in defeating the Spanish.

From 1862 to 1865, Spain committed 28,000 troops to maintain control of Santo Domingo. Nationalist forces in the island fiercely opposed these Spanish forces, and on May 1, 1865, the Madrid government gave up its attempt to control that state.

December 5, 1865

Secretary of State Seward applies more pressure on France to remove its army from Mexico.

After the Civil War ended in April 1865, Seward endeavored to resist advocates of strong or rash action against France and to gradually pressure France to leave without American military action. General Grant was an ardent advocate of war if necessary against France, and he ordered General Philip Sheridan to take 50,000 troops to the Texas-Mexican border. Grant also persuaded General James M. Schofield to organize a mercenary force to go to Mexico and fight the French. Only action by Seward kept Schofield from going ahead with his plan. Appealing to Schofield's vanity, Seward asked him to act as a special envoy to Paris. Schofield's best service, Seward told him, would be to "get your legs under Napoléon's mahogany and tell him to get out of Mexico."

During the fall and winter of 1865–1866, Seward applied increasing pressure on the French to leave Mexico. On December 5, he instructed John Bigelow that while America wished to continue "sincere friendship" with France, the Mexican situation jeopardized this policy until Napoléon III would "desist from the prosecution of armed intervention in Mexico." Soon after, in a note of February 12, 1866, Seward told Bigelow to request France to set a limit for French withdrawal from Mexico.

Historians are unsure exactly how much Seward's policy affected Napoléon's decision to withdraw relative to other factors. Two weeks after Napoléon learned of Seward's December 5 note, he sent orders to Marshal Bazaine to prepare for a withdrawal of French forces. By late 1865, other developments also played a role in Napoléon's decision, including French public opinion against the war, the cost of the occupation, and, perhaps not least of all, the constant attacks by Benito Juárez's forces on the French in Mexico.

See April 5, 1866, and March 12, 1867.

1866

March 17, 1866

America terminates the Marcy-Elgin Treaty of 1854.

The reciprocity treaty of 1854 had provided some degree of free trade and regulated fishing rights between America and Canada. The treaty provided that either party could abrogate it after 12 years, and this the United States chose to do in 1866.

The apparent cause for the treaty abrogation was the intense feeling in the Northern states that the British had tried various means to aid the South during the Civil War, thereby to break up the union of states. Britain's most notable acts were the construction of Confederate ships and the St. Albans raid from Canada in 1864. A simple way for America to retaliate after the war was to end the 1854 treaty.

Letting Him Slide. Napoléon (holding Emperor Maximilian of Mexico): "I am really very sorry, but I must let go, or you might pull me over!" *London Fun*, 1866

April 5, 1866

Paris newspapers announce that Napoléon III has decided to withdraw French troops from Mexico.

This was the first official notice to the French and the Americans of a decision the emperor made in January. According to the dispatch, the troops would be gradually brought home over a period of 19 months. It actually required only 11 months after the official publication.

See March 12, 1867.

May 31, 1866

An Irish Fenian brotherhood unsuccessfully attacks Canada from New York.

The Fenian Society had organized to fight for Irish independence from Great Britain. On May 31, several hundred members of this group crossed the Niagara River and engaged Canadian militia. They were repulsed and fled back to New York. A second Fenian attack was planned for May 25, 1870, at which time the U.S. marshal for Vermont arrested the leaders of the brotherhood.

One of the unforeseen results of the Fenian activity in North America and Canada was the Treaty of 1870, by which England recognized the right of the United States to naturalize as American citizens persons born elsewhere.

See May 13, 1870.

June 25, 1866

Following a second naval expedition against Japan, the United States signs a joint tariff convention with Japan.

This second episode of gunboat diplomacy in Japan was, like the first in 1864, initiated by the British minister to Japan. After Townsend Harris left Japan in 1862, U.S. diplomatic leadership in Japan passed to the British, who, as in China, took aggressive charge of Western interests. Harry Parkes replaced Alcock as the British minister in 1865 but continued Alcock's vigorous policy in Asia, even though Britain's Foreign Minister Lord John Russell preferred a moderate policy.

Parkes instituted plans for a second military expedition after the Japanese defaulted on their $3 million Shimonoseki indemnity payments. Upon securing the approval of the French, Dutch, and American representatives in Japan, Parkes organized a fleet to go to Osaka, where they would be closer to Kyoto. America had no naval vessel available, and the U.S. chargé, A. L. C. PORTMAN, who headed America's delegation after Robert Pruyn resigned in April 1865, went to Osaka on a British warship.

After the joint naval fleet reached Osaka early in November 1865, Parkes informed the imperial court that Japan had a choice. It could fully pay the indemnity or meet three conditions: (1) the emperor's approval of the Western treaties; (2) a new tariff set at 5%, replacing the 20% import duties; and (3) opening the ports of Hiogo and Osaka. If the emperor selected the three conditions, the treaty powers would remit $2 million of the Shimonoseki indemnity. When the emperor appeared to be delaying his response, Parkes sent a message to him demanding an immediate reply or threatening to "act as we may judge convenient."

The emperor capitulated. He agreed to ratify the previous treaties and to revise the tariff. He requested, however, that the ports not be opened until a later time.

The various agreements of the emperor were written into a convention signed by the four powers as a joint treaty on June 25, 1866.

For previous activity, see September 23, 1864.

June 27, 1866

The Seven Weeks' War begins between Austria and Prussia.

The war ended quickly after Prussia won a decisive battle at Königgrätz (Sadowa; after 1918, known by the Czech name Hradec Kralove) on July 3. The war determined that Austria would be excluded from Germany. The North German Confederation organized Hanover, Hesse, Nassau, and Frankfurt under Prussian leadership. The southern German states remained independent until 1871.

July 27, 1866

Transatlantic cable goes into effective operation.

This undersea cable system between England and the United States was first opened on August 16, 1858, but became inoperative after three weeks. Cyrus FIELD, the American businessman who planned the cable, had to subscribe additional funds to correct his first mistakes and lay a second cable. This was completed on July 27, 1866, when a cable line began transmitting permanently.

The cable line affected foreign relations because as its use became common, the State Department could make faster contact with its European representatives. One of its first uses was to obtain rapid communication between Washington and St. Petersburg in negotiating the sale of Alaska by Russia in March 1867.

November 16, 1866

Joint action with France against Korea is proposed by Secretary of State Seward.

Seward suggested French-American action to J. F. BERTHEMY, the French minister to America, on November 16, after receiving such a proposal four days earlier from Anson BURLINGAME, the U.S. minister in China. Burlingame reported that the French seemed prepared to take action to redress their complaints against a Korean massacre of French Catholic missionaries and several of their converts. In addition, the American merchant ship *General Sherman* had recently been burned and its crew murdered by Koreans. When Seward offered his idea to Berthemy, the French minister had not heard of the East Asian events and asked for time to refer the proposal to Paris.

The U.S.-French venture never took place. By the time Seward's offer reached France, Admiral Roze had led a naval expedition to Korea, burning a village but obtaining no satisfaction. The Asians saw this as a French defeat, but in France, Napoléon III's newspapers called it a victory and the government promoted the admiral to a better naval post. Thus, France was unwilling to act again in Korea.

Seward and Burlingame decided to limit their efforts to a protest against the attack on the *General Sherman*. Until March 29, 1885, the United States had not learned exactly what took place to cause the *Sherman*'s destruction. In 1885, the U.S. consul reported the results of his investigation of the event. Evidently, the Sherman ran aground in the Ta-dong River. When a band of Koreans arrived with the intention of helping, the crew mistook the Korean advances as an attack and began to fight the Koreans. In retaliation the Koreans sent a burning raft down the river and set the ship afire. Some crew members died in the fire, and others were probably killed by the Koreans.

1867

March 12, 1867

The last French troops withdraw from Mexico.

As planned a year earlier and announced on April 5, 1866, Marshal Bazaine gradually ended the French army's support for the monarchy of the Emperor Maximilian in Mexico. After the French departure, Maximilian refused to abdicate and Juárez's forces captured him. He was executed before a firing squad at Queretaro on June 19, 1867.

The French departure appeared to be a diplomatic triumph for Secretary Seward. It also enabled the Monroe Doctrine to gain popularity in America, although Seward had never referred to Monroe's policies during his discussions with France.

This cartoon pokes fun at Seward's purchase of Alaska—a transaction some called "Seward's Icebox" or "Seward's Folly." *Leslie's Illustrated*, 1867

March 30, 1867

Russia sells Alaska to the United States.

The Treaty of March 30, which ceded Alaska to the United States, was readily arrived at because both Russia and America were willing to agree. Although U.S. State Department personnel frequently discussed the possible purchase of Alaska during the 1850s, no one seriously considered doing so until 1865, when the Confederate cruiser *Shenandoah* destroyed two whaling ships in the Bering and Okhotsk Seas off Alaska. Secretary Seward had long been interested in America's future commerce in the Pacific and saw the value of having possible naval bases in the north Pacific.

Fortunately, Russian leaders decided to sell Alaska in 1867. The Russian-American Company was in poor financial condition, and the government found it difficult to defend the territory from any possible enemy. The czar's advisers preferred a sale to the United States rather than England because America would serve as a buffer zone between British Canada and Russian Siberia. From previous discussions between Baron Edouard de Stoeckel, Russia's minister to the United States, Assistant Secretary of State William H. Appleton, and Senator William Givin of California, Russia knew the United States would be interested in Alaska.

In March 1867, Baron Stoeckel had friends inform Seward that Russia was interested in selling Alaska. Eagerly accepting the idea, Seward called on Stoeckel and offered to purchase the area. Following some haggling about price, Stoeckel and Seward agreed on $7,200,000. To speed up the process, Seward persuaded the Baron to use the new Atlantic cable to contact St. Petersburg. Stoeckel did, and on March 29 he stopped by to tell Seward that Russia would sell.

Preferring not to delay, Seward sent for office clerks and Senator Charles Sumner, chairman of the Senate Foreign Relations Committee. The treaty was drawn up and signed at four A.M. on March 30. With Sumner's support, the U.S. Senate easily approved the treaty on April 9, 1867, by a vote of 37 to 5.

Obtaining the approval of the House of Representatives for the appropriation to pay the purchase price required more time and effort. Some congressmen believed the selling price was too high; others complained that Alaska was worthless. The purchase was called "Seward's Icebox," and the precedent of acquiring land that was not contiguous to other U.S. territory was denounced. From the perspective of later years, the House debates on the purchase seem inane or "pure politics" against Seward and President Johnson. Surprisingly, Baron Stoeckel lobbied vigorously for the bill and used Russian gold to buy "friendly votes." Seward employed newspaper stories to educate the public about Alaska's strategic situation.

Eventually, on July 14, 1868, the House approved funds for the purchase by a vote of 113 to 43. Some writers believe a critical factor was Russia's transfer of the territory to the United States on October 18, 1867. This act permitted the U.S. flag to be raised over Alaska and enabled some opponents of the bill to be persuaded that "once it was ours, we cannot lower the flag."

June 13, 1867

Two U.S. Naval ships conduct a retaliatory raid on Formosa.

This attack on Formosa resulted from the murder of the entire crew of the U.S. ship *Rover*, which was wrecked on the south coast of Formosa in 1867. After learning about the *Rover*'s loss, Secretary Seward ordered the U.S. Minister to China S. Wells WILLIAMS, to investigate the incident and inform the Chinese government that while the United States did not wish to seize any part of Formosa, China should more effectively control the area.

At the same time, however, the secretary of the navy (probably with Seward's agreement) ordered Rear Admiral Bell to make a punitive raid on the area of Formosa where the attack had taken place. Using the U.S. warships *Wyoming* and *Hartford*, Bell bombarded the coast and sent a landing party of 181 men to punish the "savages" of the area. They chased the natives into the hills but could not catch them. The American casualties numbered 1 killed and 14 cases of sunstroke. In 1874, the Japanese used the

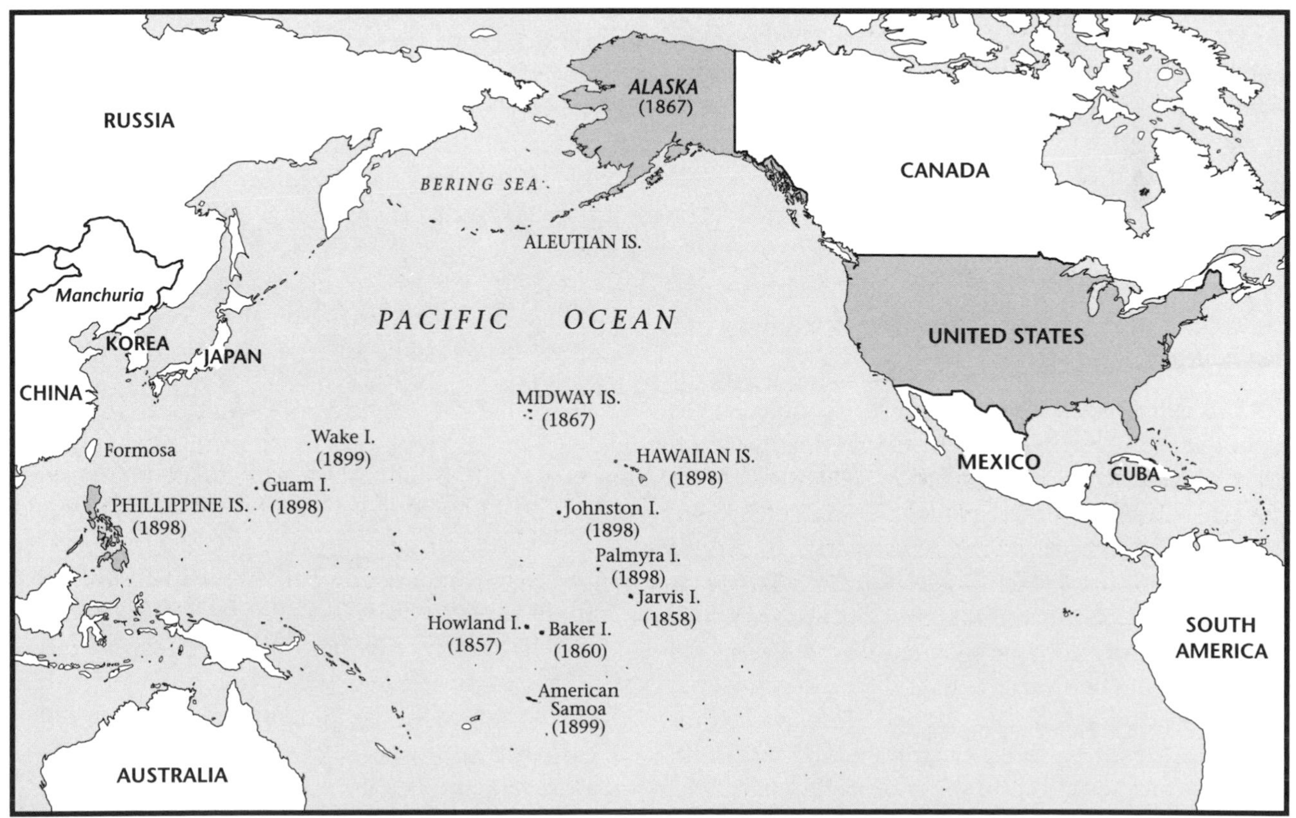

U.S. Interests in the Pacific, 1860s.

U.S. example of 1867 to rationalize their attack on Formosa, which made it part of Japanese territory.

June 21, 1867

U.S. treaty with Nicaragua provides for free transit across that state between the two oceans.

Sometimes referred to as the DICKINSON-AYON TREATY, this was a commercial treaty that included a clause affirming U.S. transit rights across Nicaragua. Secretary of State Seward had hoped to gain exclusive canal rights, but Nicaragua would not grant this privilege. The Senate ratified this treaty on January 20, 1868.

July 1, 1867

The Dominion of Canada is created by the British North America Act.

This act provided for the unity and partial independence of all Canadian provinces under the English crown. To some extent, this legislation resulted because some political spokesmen in both Canada and the United States argued that Canada should be annexed to the United States. In July 1866, a bill introduced in the House of Representatives provided for the admission of Canada to the union; it was not approved, however.

August 28, 1867

The United States takes possession of Midway Island, West of Hawaii.

The U.S. navy ordered Midway to be occupied at the request of the China Mail Steamship Company, which saw it as a valuable coaling station 1,000 miles from Hawaii. Fulfilling these orders, Captain William REYNOLDS landed and took possession of the island in the name of the United States. Formerly known as Brooks Island for its discoverer, it was renamed Midway because it was about halfway between San Francisco and Yokohama.

Because the attempt to dredge Midway's harbor became too costly, it never became a useful seaport. In 1903 it became a station on the transpacific cable line. Midway proved more valuable as an air base when air routes crossed the Pacific Ocean after 1930.

September 30, 1867

The U.S. Senate rejects a reciprocity treaty with Hawaii.

Secretary of State Seward sought this agreement to promote American commerce in the Pacific. Political opponents of President Johnson led the Senate action that vetoed the treaty.

October 24, 1867

The United States signs a treaty to purchase two West Indies islands from Denmark that the Senate rejects.

Secretary of State Seward signed this treaty after he had cruised "for his health" in the Caribbean, visiting various islands. Seward and Secretary of the Navy Gideon WELLES saw the islands as a strategic naval base on the sea lanes between Europe and a future isthmian canal. Denmark was willing to sell these indefensible outposts, and the United States agreed to buy St. Thomas and St. John islands for $7.5 million, subject to a plebiscite by the inhabitants.

Although the plebiscite approved the treaty and the Danish Riggsdag (parliament) and king ratified it, the U.S. Senate never acted on the treaty. Although the House of Representatives had no direct authority over treaties, a House resolution in November 1867 stated that the country's financial condition made the purchase of territory "inexpedient" unless "there is a greater present necessity for the same than now exists." A hurricane and an earthquake at St. Thomas in 1869 made the purchase more unpopular. Finally, in 1870, the Senate Foreign Relations Committee unanimously opposed the treaty of 1867. The Virgin Islands remained as Danish possessions.

1868

January 3, 1868

The Japanese Emperor assumes direct control of the nation, ending the Tokugawa shogun's power.

Although some opposition to this decree caused fighting in 1868, the emperor, backed by the new leaders of the Choshu and Satsuma domains, successfully inaugurated the MEIJI ("Enlightened Rule") of the emperor.

May 16, 1868

By one vote, the U.S. Senate fails to find President Andrew Johnson guilty of high misdemeanors as charged.

The Senate tried Johnson after the House of Representatives voted on February 24, 1868, to impeach Johnson on 11 charges, including alleged violations of the Tenure of Office Act and Command of the Army Act.

July 28, 1868

Burlingame Treaty is signed between China and America.

Secretary of State Seward negotiated this treaty with Anson Burlingame, the former U.S. minister to China, who now acted as an envoy of the Chinese to visit Washington, London, and Paris. Burlingame led a party of 30 Chinese that arrived at San Francisco in February 1868. In their journey to Washington, the mission was wined, dined, and cheered by crowds of Americans as Burlingame used his best showmanship to acquaint Americans with China's civilized manners.

The Treaty of 1868 was a supplement to the Treaty of Tientsin of 1858. It provided for Chinese consuls in America and tolerance for Chinese religious practice in the United States, and permitted China to employ U.S. engineers. The treaty recognized the right of unrestricted immigration of Chinese to America, an article that California desired in 1868 because there was a demand for cheap Chinese "coolie" labor for railroad construction.

Generally, in his mission to America and Europe, Burlingame hoped China would be recognized as a nation equal to Western nations. The problem with this belief in the late 19th century was that China did not have the strong central government necessary to enable it to deal with the West on an equal basis.

After signing this treaty with America, Burlingame continued his mission to several European capitals to "educate" Europeans about China. Tragically, however, Burlingame never made it back to Peking. He died of pneumonia in Russia on February 23, 1870.

October 10, 1868

Outbreak of the Ten Years' Civil War in Cuba.

A rebel group led by Carlos Manuel de CESPEDES proclaimed a revolution at Yara and demanded such reforms as the end of slavery, guarantees of personal liberties, and rights for Creoles as well as peninsulares. The war was often savage and terrorist-style and influenced various U.S. activities in the next decade.

November 3, 1868

Ulysses S. Grant is elected president.

The Republican Party Convention nominated Grant for president on May 20, 1868. Its platform endorsed radical reconstruction policies, condemned President Johnson, and favored Negro suffrage. The Democratic Convention selected Horatio SEYMOUR for president on a platform that attacked radical Republican policies in the Southern states.

Grant won 214 electoral votes to Seymour's 80. Three Southern states did not participate in the election, and six other states were under domination of the radical leaders. The absence of these Southern votes resulted from the radical reconstruction program that regulated the return of Southern states to full status in the union.

VIII. THE EVE OF EMPIRE

The Caribbean and South America, Hawaii, Samoa, and the Pacific

1869

January 3, 1869

The Japanese Emperor holds an audience with U.S. Minister R. R. van Valkenburgh in Tokyo.

This reception, which the emperor granted in 1869 to each of the foreign representatives in Japan, indicated that the MEIJI RESTORATION had achieved some stability. Following the first imperial decree of the emperor, which assumed the shogun's authority in January 1868, political fighting had continued in Japan and sometimes threatened the lives of foreign representatives. But the young samurai leaders of the Satsuma and Choshu domains strongly backed the emperor and strengthened the central government. Although the Tokugawa navy did not surrender until May 1869, the emperor and his political supporters had, by early 1869, achieved sufficient stability to promote effectively their efforts to adapt Western ideas to Japanese traditions.

January 14, 1869

America and Colombia sign a treaty granting Panamanian Canal rights to the United States; the treaty is later rejected by the Senates of both nations.

Gaining exclusive canal rights was a major goal of Secretary of State Seward. On March 2, 1868, he instructed U.S. Minister to Colombia Peter J. SULLIVAN to negotiate a treaty for U.S. canal rights. As the talks progressed, Caleb Cushing went to Colombia to assist Sullivan, and on January 14, 1869, a treaty was signed at Bogotá with Foreign Minister Miguel Samper. The treaty provided the United States rights to a strip of land 20 miles wide to build a canal in Panama. America would have control but not sovereignty over the canal.

Neither the Senate of Colombia nor of the United States ratified the treaty of 1869. The Colombian senators opposed the treaty because they feared the canal could be closed by the United States in time of war, even if Colombia were neutral or, as some observers noted, because they were outraged because they did not immediately receive bribes for granting the canal privileges. The American senators opposed ratification either because they claimed the treaty violated the Clayton-Bulwer Treaty of 1850 or because they opposed anything connected with President Johnson's administration.

Only the province of Panama seemed eager to obtain a U.S. canal. Its provincial legislature disagreed with the Colombian Senate's action and threatened to secede from the nation. This Panamanian reaction persuaded President Grant to sign another treaty on January 20, 1870.

March 5, 1869

President Grant commissions Elihu B. Washburne as secretary of state for a five-day term.

Washburne's brief term in the State Department ended when Grant, as planned, appointed him as minister to France. The appointment was typical of Grant's desire to appoint good if incompetent friends to worthy positions. The president held special affection for Washburne, who, as the congressman from Grant's home district in Illinois, helped promote the president's military career. Washburne needed more impressive credentials to become minister to France, and the appointment as secretary of state provided that requirement.

March 11, 1869

Hamilton Fish is appointed to replace Washburne as Grant's secretary of state.

Fish was unexpectedly asked to be secretary of state after James F. Wilson, whom Grant planned to name, became angry with the terms of the Washburne appointment and refused the office. Fish was a well-to-do businessman in charge of his family fortunes in New York, and he carried his conservative habits of caution and patience into his eight years of service under President Grant.

April 13, 1869

The U.S. Senate rejects the Clarendon-Johnson Treaty to settle indemnity claims between Britain and America.

This agreement proposed to settle all claims between citizens of the two nations made since the Convention of 1853, including the "*Alabama* claims" of the Civil War years. Lord Clarendon, England's foreign minister, and Reverdy Johnson, the U.S. minister to Great Britain, negotiated this agreement, which was signed on January 14, 1869. President Andrew Johnson sent it to the Senate just before his term of office ended in March 1869.

Although the treaty covered all claims from 1853 to 1869, the British refused to express regret for constructing ships for the Confederate states. Moreover, the question of naming arbitrators for the claims was left to chance. These shortcomings plus the opposition in Congress to everything connected with President Johnson made ratification of the treaty almost impossible.

In a celebrated anti-British speech, Charles Sumner, chairman of the Senate Foreign Relations Committee, devastated the treaty. The treaty, he argued, accounted for only a small fraction of British debts. England should pay not only $15 million for the value of American ships and cargo destroyed by English-built ships, it should also pay at least $110 million for the collateral costs to U.S. shipping, such as the insurance rate increase and American ships that changed to foreign registry or were driven from the seas. Sumner noted that American commercial shipping decreased from carrying 65.5% of U.S. foreign trade in 1860 to 27.7% in 1865. Finally, the senator contended that if the Confederacy had not been encouraged by the British, the war would have ended in July 1863, following the Battle of Gettysburg. Consequently, the British should pay an additional $2 billion to cover one-half the cost of the war to the Union treasury. Sumner's bill for Great Britain's indemnity totaled $2,125,000,000. Perhaps, Sumner implied, England should cede Canada to America to compensate for these indemnities.

Sumner's speech and political antagonism to President Johnson made the merits of the treaty of little consequence. The Senate rejected the treaty by a vote of 54 to 1.

May 10, 1869

First transcontinental railroad is completed at Promontory, Utah. The rail lines are joined between the Union Pacific Railway, which was built westward from Nebraska, and the Central Pacific Railroad, coming eastward from San Francisco.

The construction of this railway was heavily subsidized by loans and grants from Congress under the Pacific Railroad Act of July 1, 1862. This was the first of five transcontinental lines established between 1860 and 1900.

July 12, 1869

The Rose-Fish talks end in an understanding that moves toward better U.S. relations with Britain and Canada.

Anglo-American relations cooled considerably after Charles Sumner's attack on Great Britain helped to defeat the Clarendon-Johnson Treaty on April 13, 1869. Nevertheless, political leaders on each side of the Atlantic preferred to improve relations. Both Prime Minister William Gladstone and President Grant advocated friendly intercourse. This view was shared by Secretary of State Fish and Canada's finance minister, John Rose, when they met in Washington on July 8–12, 1869, to consider a reciprocity treaty. Any U.S.-Canadian agreement hinged on better Anglo-American relations, so their discussions turned to the "*Alabama* claims."

Fish told Rose that, while Sumner's extravagant claims in his recent speech did not reflect U.S. policy,

Americans did hold a sense of grievance that required an expression of regret by England as well as an indemnity for its failure to remain neutral in certain Civil War activity. Rose understood and suggested that a special mission to the United States might be the best means to display British concerns and to settle the various disputes.

On the basis of these talks, Rose during the next year returned to England, where he was knighted by Queen Victoria. There he also talked with friends about the American viewpoints. Rose's interests, together with the outbreak of the Franco-Prussian War in 1870 and tensions with Russia about Turkey, caused Gladstone in November 1870 to seek an end to Britain's difficulties with America.

See February 7 and May 8, 1871.

November 17, 1869

The Suez Canal officially opens.

This canal again made the Middle East the center of an important trade route between Western Europe and East Asia.

November 29, 1869

President Grant's military aide signs a treaty to lease Samana Bay and to annex the entire Dominican Republic.

Since 1865, Dominican presidents had sought the protection of the United States against possible invasion by Haiti, their neighbor on the island of Hispaniola. During a Caribbean cruise in the fall of 1867, Seward discussed the purchase or annexation of the city of Santo Domingo with Dominican authorities. The secretary made no treaty, however, because of the bad reaction he received from the purchase of Alaska and because President Johnson's enemies in Congress opposed treaties of annexation. Twice in early 1869 (January 13 and February 1), the House of Representatives defeated resolutions to authorize the United States to protect or annex Santo Domingo.

The hopes of those who favored the American takeover of Santo Domingo did not die, however. In July 1869, Brigadier General Orville E. BABCOCK signed an agreement looking toward annexing the city. Secretary of State Fish personally opposed the annexation of Santo Domingo, but to gain a free hand in the *Alabama* claims negotiations with Great Britain, he agreed to allow Babcock to proceed with his venture.

The two treaties that Babcock signed with the Dominican Republic gave the U.S. Senate a choice of two alternatives: one, to lease Samana Bay as a naval base; or two, to annex Santo Domingo to the United States.

Grant wholeheartedly supported Babcock's treaty, but the senators did not. Because of a misunderstanding, Charles Sumner, chairman of the Senate Foreign Relations Committee, failed to support Grant, and the annexation treaty was disapproved by a vote of 28 to 28. The treaty to lease Samana Bay was not voted on by the Senate.

December 6, 1869

Notice that the United States does not recognize a state of belligerency in Cuba is part of President Grant's annual message.

The Cuban insurrection, which began in 1868, received great attention in America during 1869. Americans generally supported Cuba's independence movement. Cuban exiles in the United States disseminated anti-Spanish propaganda, held mass meetings, and organized filibustering attempts to invade Cuba. In addition, Americans lost property in Cuba, while naturalized American citizens of Cuban birth were imprisoned and sometimes tried by a military court and executed. Yet there was little U.S. interest in the annexation of Cuba as there had been in the 1850s.

Grant's message concluded a year of cabinet discussions and informal negotiations that led to two different nonevents on the Cuban issue. First, on June 29, 1869, Secretary of State Fish instructed the U.S. minister in Madrid, General D. E. Sickles, to use American services to negotiate a settlement of Cuban problems on the basis of independence and the abolition of slavery. The Spanish informed Sickles that they intended to enact reforms in Cuba, and that if the rebels surrendered their arms, a referendum on independence could be held. They rejected Fish's offer to negotiate a settlement with the rebels.

On August 19, an impulsive act of President Grant's could have caused an international crisis. During a vacation trip, several of Grant's more bellicose and pro-Cuban friends persuaded him to draw up and sign a proclamation recognizing Cuban belligerency. Grant sent this declaration to Secretary Fish to countersign and promulgate. Fish, however, knew that the Cuban rebel government was nothing except fugitive leaders collecting under palm trees and, therefore, he filed the decree rather than issue it. The president almost forgot about the decree, but Fish later convinced him that it should not be proclaimed because other European powers refused to recognize the rebels.

Therefore on December 6, Grant and Fish agreed to inform Congress that the United States could not at present intervene in Cuba despite American sympathy for Cuban independence. Nor, he added, could the United States recognize a belligerent situation in Cuba until the insurgents established a satisfactory political organization. Generally, he said, the United States would retain its freedom of action regarding future events between Cuba and Spain.

1870

January 20, 1870

Colombia and America sign a treaty for U.S. canal rights in Panama; the U.S. Senate rejects it as amended.

Following the failure of the U.S.-Colombian treaty of January 14, 1869, President Grant asked Stephen A. Hurlburt, the U.S. Minister to Colombia, to attempt to form a new treaty to obtain the Panamanian site for a U.S. canal. The treaty agreed to in Bogotá on January 20, 1870, resembled the Treaty of 1869 in most particulars. This time, however, Colombia's Senate approved the treaty with the significant amendment that in time of war, the canal had to remain open to the ships of all nations. The U.S. Senate would not accept the amended treaty because the United States wanted to be free to use the canal as a military lever in time of war. Therefore, the United States still had no rights for a canal through Panama.

May 13, 1870

Anglo-American treaty recognizes the right of naturalization of citizens.

The American claim to naturalize as U.S. citizens persons born in another country had been long disputed between England and the United States. During the late 1860s the attacks by Irish-Americans in the Fenian Society against Canada and British rule in Ireland renewed the naturalization question. By the treaty of May 13, 1870, Great Britain recognized America's naturalization system and established principles on which to validate these procedures when naturalized persons went abroad.

June 16, 1870

A House resolution to recognize Cuban belligerency is passed after amendments to subvert its intent.

As the Cuban rebellion entered its second year, pro-Cuban groups in America lobbied Congress to recognize the insurgents. Despite President Grant's report against recognition in his message of December 6, 1869, a group of congressmen introduced a resolution to recognize a state of war between Cuba and Spain that by implication recognized the Cuban government.

Secretary of State Fish and President Grant opposed this resolution and fought to defeat the proposal. Grant sent a special appeal to Congress against interference in Cuba, but after the House Committee on Foreign Affairs recommended its approval, its passage seemed certain. Grant's Republican Party leaders then proposed a series of amendments to the resolution that indicated U.S. sympathy for the Cubans and protested against Spanish policies. The clause to recognize the rebels was dropped. In this amended form, the resolution passed on June 16 by a vote of 101-88.

July 14, 1870

Tariff of 1870 lowers some duties but retains protective features for industrial products.

By 1870, not only the minority Democrats in Congress but also some Republican Party reformers advocated a lower tariff than the 47% rates reached in 1869. The 1870 tariff law placed some items, mostly imported raw materials, on the free list but made only small reductions in duties. By 1872, the reformers reduced tariffs by 10%, but these reductions were abolished in 1875. A tariff to protect U.S. manufacturing became a cardinal principle of U.S. politics by the 1870s.

July 14, 1870

Secretary of State Fish reaffirms the "no-transfer" corollary of the Monroe Doctrine.

Following the Senate's defeat of the treaty to annex Santo Domingo, the secretary believed he should issue a memorandum to indicate to Spain and other nations that no territory in the Western Hemisphere could be transferred to a European power and that the status of an independent Santo Domingo should be maintained. He asked U.S. ministers to make this policy clear to the European governments where they resided.

July 19, 1870

French declaration of war on Prussia becomes a war against all German states.

The French hoped to regain their prestige in Europe by humiliating Prussia. Not only did Emperor Napoléon III fail to do so; the war was a disaster for France. After the French declared war, Prussian armies allied with the southern German states to launch an invasion of France. After Napoléon III capitulated at the battle of Sedan on September 2, the French legislative assembly pronounced the end of the empire and proclaimed a republic with a provisional government led by General Louis Trochu. Following their victory at Sedan, the German armies easily defeated General Trochu's ineffective army and began the siege of Paris on September 19.

With the siege of Paris in place on January 18, 1871, all German states, excepting Austria, agreed to unite and proclaimed William I of Prussia as the German emperor during a ceremony at the Palace of Versailles outside Paris. Ten days later, the French provisional government signed an armistice that permitted the German army to have a victory parade down the Champs-Elysées in Paris.

In the aftermath of the war, the French were unable to agree on a suitable government, continuing a provisional regime with Adolph Thiers as the chief executive. For the next four years, radical republicans from the Paris Commune and monarchists in Bordeaux could not agree on a new French constitution. See February 28, 1875.

August 19, 1870

Italian unity is completed when French forces withdraw from Rome, permitting Italian troops to enter the city and annex Rome to Italy on October 2, 1870.

1871

February 7, 1871

Opening session of the Joint High Commission to settle questions of British-American-Canadian relations.

A commission to resolve claims, the fisheries question, and boundary disputes between the three major English-speaking nations had been suggested by Sir John Rose in a conversation with Secretary of State Fish between July 8–12, 1869. Rose returned to America in January 1871 as Britain's minister to the United States. He and Fish immediately set out to resolve pending disputes along the lines of the 1869 discussions.

Although Senator Charles Sumner threatened trouble, Fish and President Grant decided to proceed with talks to solve the problems and agreed to appoint a special commission to meet in Washington. This commission, which prepared the Treaty of Washington by May 8, 1871, consisted of these delegates: (1) for the United States, E. Rockwood Haar, former attorney general; Supreme Court Justice Samuel Nelson; and Senator George H. Williams of Oregon; (2) for Great Britain, Earl de Grey, marquess of Ripon; Sir Stafford Northcote; Sir John A. Macdonald; Sir Edward Thornton; and Oxford Professor Montague Bernard.

April 5, 1871

The movement to annex Santo Domingo ends even though an investigating committee reports favorably on the proposal.

Following the Senate's defeat on June 16, 1870, of the treaty to annex Santo Domingo, President Grant continued seeking some method to accomplish this project. On December 5, 1870, his annual message to Congress included estimates of the island's great value to American commerce and defense strategy, as well as the possibility of a European power leasing Samana Bay. He also requested Congress to establish a commission to negotiate a new treaty looking toward Santo Domingo's annexation by a joint congressional resolution.

Although the investigative commission was set up, Grant's feud with Charles Sumner on this matter resulted in the demise of the annexation plan. The congressional resolution to establish a commission to visit Santo Domingo and report on annexation passed in January 1870, even though many of Grant's supporters questioned the use of the "Texas" tactic. This commission visited the island, returning in late February to prepare the report that the president sent to Congress on April 5, 1871. This report favored annexation, but by the time it was printed, Sumner's attack on the proceedings caused Grant finally to forsake the project.

Sumner, chairman of the Senate Foreign Relations Committee, had become thoroughly opposed to the scheme to annex Santo Domingo. Sumner and Grant engaged in a personal dispute on Santo Domingo because of a misunderstanding about the December 3, 1869, treaties. Grant had expected Sumner to support the treaty but the senator did not do so. Once Grant's will was challenged he reacted stubbornly, a trait shared by Sumner. Consequently, when the new Congress assembled in early March 1871, Grant prevailed on Senate Republicans to deny Sumner his seat on the Foreign Relations Committee.

Therefore, Sumner prepared to do battle and succeeded in ending Grant's Dominican plans. On March 27, the senator submitted resolutions against the use of military power by the chief executive. His resolutions did not pass but their debate gave Sumner the occasion to deliver a blistering denunciation of Grant's methods in the Santo Domingo situation. He claimed U.S. naval forces had coerced the Dominicans into favoring annexation and declared that Grant wished to ship freed Southern slaves to that Caribbean island.

Sumner's speech, together with the Senate's previous opposition to the annexation of Santo Domingo, won the day. By April 5, Grant knew the treaties could not pass Congress, even though the investigation committee favored the project. Therefore, the president sent the report to Congress, recommending only that it be published to inform the public on the merits of his case. Grant regretted his failure to annex the islands but never again proposed an annexation treaty.

April 30, 1871

The U.S. Army struggle to defeat the Apache Indians begins in Arizona.

This Indian war in New Mexico and Arizona began when an army unit massacred over 100 Apaches at Camp Grant, Arizona. The conflict caused frequent border problems with Mexico because the Apaches often fled into northern Mexico, from where they staged raids. The Apache war did not end until the capture of GERONIMO, the Apache chief, in 1886.

Geronimo (ca. 1829–1909) was the most famous of Apache war chiefs. National Archives

May 8, 1871

The Treaty of Washington creates an arbitration tribunal to settle the "*Alabama* claims" dispute between Great Britain and America.

The Senate's rejection of the Clarendon-Johnson Treaty on April 13, 1869, left the Anglo-American claims argument for further discussions by the Grant administration. Because the president tended to agree with Sumner's policy of linking a large indemnity bill to the Canadian transfer concept, he and Fish adhered to this policy until November 1870. Finally, the growing dispute between Sumner and Grant over Santo Domingo enabled Secretary Fish to convince Grant that Sumner's indirect indemnities policy was too extravagant. About the same time, December 1870, Fish learned that the British were again willing to negotiate Anglo-American disputes regarding claims, the fisheries question, and the San Juan de Fuca border in the Northwest.

After Britain's new minister to the United States, Sir John Rose, arrived in Washington on January 9, 1871, he and Secretary Fish exchanged views and, by February 3, decided to form a joint high commission to agree on a method for resolving the Anglo-American disputes (see February 7, 1871).

On May 8, 1871, Fish and Rose signed the Treaty of Washington as prepared by the commission of five representatives of each nation. The important parts of the treaty were as follows:

1. the expression of regret by Her Majesty's Government "for the escape . . . of the *Alabama* and other vessels from British ports and for the depredations committed by those vessels";
2. creation of a tribunal of five persons to arbitrate the "*Alabama* claims." This section of the treaty established three rules to be followed by the tribunal, the most critical of which stated it was the duty of a neutral government to prevent the departure of any vessel of war intended for use against a friendly nation. This rule virtually conceded the American claims for damages done by Confederate ships built in Great Britain (see July 31, 1862).
3. the readmission of U.S. citizens to inshore fishing privileges in Canada and the opening of U.S. waters north of the 39° to Canadian fishing;
4. submission of the San Juan Island dispute to the German emperor for arbitration.

The U.S. Senate ratified the Treaty of Washington on May 24, 1871, by a vote of 50 to 12. The arbitration tribunal met in Geneva, Switzerland, and issued its findings on September 14, 1872. The German emperor issued his ruling on the boundary question on October 21, 1872.

May 16, 1871

An American naval officer fails to open Korea to foreign trade.

Acting under the direction of Frederick Low, U.S. minister to China, U.S. navy Captain Robert Shufeldt commanded a U.S. squadron of ships that went to Korea. Shufeldt planned to steam up the Han River to Seoul and force the Koreans to accept a treaty. As the U.S. ships entered the mouth of the Han, a Korean force awaited them and blocked their entry. Shufeldt decided to abandon the project in 1871 but made a second and successful attempt on May 22, 1882.

September 3, 1871

Sino-Japanese commercial treaty is signed at Tientsin.

This was the first treaty made between these two East Asian countries. Generally, China refused to grant Japan the terms forced on the Chinese by Western nations. Japan did not obtain a most-favored-nation status and the customs collection privileges given to Europeans and America. Clauses on extraterritoriality provided for bilateral obligations, so that while Japanese in China were under Japanese law and consuls, Chinese in Japan were under Chinese law and consuls. The Western nations disliked one treaty clause that provided for a defensive alliance between the two nations, but in practice the alliance was of no value except as a form of oriental courtesy.

1872

May 22, 1872

President Grant asks the Senate to approve a treaty with Samoa; the Senate takes no action.

The president sent a special message to Congress to recommend the ratification of a treaty with Samoa made by Commander Richard W. Meade of the U.S. navy. Although Meade made this treaty with the Tutuila chiefs without being instructed to do so, Grant believed it had advantages because on September 20, 1871, he received a report from a New York steamship company that described the Samoan harbor at Pago Pago as one of the best in the entire Pacific Ocean. The steamship company of William H. Webb, who sent the report to Grant, had a sea route between San Francisco and Australia and needed coaling facilities in the South Pacific.

Apparently by coincidence, Meade's treaty with Samoa was exactly what Webb desired. It gave the United States exclusive rights to a coaling station in Pago Pago and placed the natives under American protection. The Senate failed to act on the Samoan Treaty of 1872. The prevailing mood in Congress opposed the expansion of U.S. responsibilities.

The Samoan project did not die, however, because both Webb and the U.S. Navy Department desired a naval station in that area. Samoa was approximately halfway between Hawaii and Sydney, Australia, making it a perfect stepping stone between California and England's possessions in the southwestern Pacific Ocean.

A Still Bigger Claimant. Politically-minded Yankee cleverly inflates Alabama claims with air-producing bellows. *Punch,* 1872

September 14, 1872

The arbitration tribunal in the "*Alabama* claims" issues its report.

The tribunal members were Charles Francis Adams (United States), Sir Alexander Cockburn (Great Britain), Justice Jacques Staempfli (by the president of Switzerland), the Viscount d'Itajuba (by the emperor of Brazil), and the tribunal president, Count Frederic Sclopis of Italy. After the group opened its sessions on December 15, 1871, it experienced only one major problem: the indirect indemnities question claimed by the United States.

Somewhat to Great Britain's surprise, the Americans presented the large category of indirect claims proposed by Charles Sumner on April 13, 1869. Secretary of State Fish did not expect to obtain these doubtful claims but introduced them in order that the tribunal would dismiss them as invalid. Of course, this proposal also had the political purpose of silencing Sumner. Fish's expectations were fulfilled. The arbitrators ruled that indirect claims were not admissible. In all other respects, the American claims were awarded by the tribunal. The United States received $15.5 million in gold for damages. Although British representative Cockburn dissented from the agreement, the British government did not protest. It paid the indemnity within one year.

October 21, 1872

As arbitrator, the German Emperor rules in favor of the U.S. claim in the northwest border dispute at San Juan Island.

When Great Britain and America settled the Oregon boundary question in 1846, the precise boundary for the islands in the straits between Vancouver Island and the mainland was not certain. Eventually, the United States claimed that the Canal de Haro was the border and placed San Juan Island in the United States. England claimed that the strait of Rosario was correct and that Canada possessed all islands northwest of that strait. While the British offered to compromise the settlement, the United States objected. In the Washington Treaty of 1871, the arbitrator was instructed to decide which channel was meant by the 1846 treaty and not to propose a compromise of the two claims.

The German emperor ruled in favor of the Canal de Haro Straits, placing all of the San Juan archipelago inside American territory.

November 5, 1872

Japan obtains control over the Ryukyu (Liu-Ch'iu) Islands.

Although the Japanese emperor claimed these islands had always been in his domain, until September 1872 the Japanese government had not in recent times taken effective jurisdiction. On November 5, 1872, the Japanese agreed with the United States to accept obligations for the Ryukyu Islands that were contained in a U.S. treaty of February 15, 1853, signed between Commodore Perry and the "King" of the Liu-Ch'iu (Lew Chew) Islands.

November 5, 1872

Ulysses Grant is reelected President.

Grant campaigned against two prominent opponents: (1) Horace GREELEY, the nominee of a splinter group of Liberal Republicans who advocated civil service reform and reserving public lands for actual settlers in contrast to the pork barrel tactic of granting lumber and mineral rights to corporations that contributed most (through bribery) to a congressman's welfare. Greeley also received the backing of a splinter Democratic Convention and the Liberal Colored Republicans; (2) Charles O'CONNOR, the nominee of the "Straight" Democratic Convention.

Grant won easily, obtaining 286 electoral votes to Greeley's 66. Greeley died on November 26, and in December his electors divided their ballots among four other men.

1873

February 12, 1873

The first Spanish republic is proclaimed and King Amadeo I abdicates.

The Spanish republicans had been elected to the Cortes in August 1872, because the pro-monarchy Carlists did not vote. The republic survived only two years, being overthrown on December 29, 1875, by generals who proclaimed Alfonso XII as king.

August 6, 1873

Japan receives full equality in negotiations of a postal convention with America.

In this treaty, signed in Washington, the United States agreed to help organize a Japanese postal system. In spite of the dissatisfaction of European diplomats, the United States took additional steps toward limiting its extraterritoriality provisions in Japan. In subsequent years, the U.S. government ordered Americans in Japan to conform to that nation's hunting regulations of 1874, press laws of 1876, and quarantine regulations in 1878 and 1879. Each of these acts by the U.S. State Department helped Japan move toward gaining equal diplomatic status among the world powers.

See July 25, 1878.

August 27, 1873

Secretary of State Fish urges Spain to reform its policies in Cuba.

Fish had become increasingly concerned about the corrupt government of the Spanish captain general in Cuba and, together with many Americans, sympathized with the rebellious groups fighting against Spain since 1868.

On October 29, 1872, Fish told the U.S. minister to Spain, D. E. SICKLES, that Spain should end the extortion practiced in Cuba and carry out its laws to end slavery. Hardly had Sickles reported that King Amadeo's government agreed to clean up the Cuban problems than a republican revolution forced the king to abdicate on February 12, 1873.

Spain's republican leaders talked about instituting reforms both at home and in the colonies of Cuba, Puerto Rico, and the Philippine Islands. Early in June, however, Secretary Fish learned that the Spanish had decided to defer enacting reforms in the colonies until they had improved their domestic situation. Fish did not accept this idea, and on June 27 he warned the Spanish that they must accept responsibility for the poor conditions in Cuba and the inefficient captain general in charge there.

By August 27, Fish issued his sternest warning to the Spanish. Citing that certain groups in America wanted to invade Cuba to restore order, he said he hoped that President Grant would not have to encourage these groups by announcing the hopelessness of expecting Spain to bring reforms in Cuba. Thus, on the eve of the *Virginius* affair of October 31, 1873, relations between Spain and the United States had deteriorated greatly.

September 18, 1873

Panic of 1873 begins when Jay Cooke's banking firm fails.

Although this bank's failure keyed the business decline from 1873 to 1876, the economic downswing resulted from long-term railroad speculation and a lower European demand for U.S. farm products. The movement of much U.S. industry to concentrate its power in pools, trusts, and holding companies began during this panic. For example, John D. Rockefeller's Standard Oil Company of Ohio made agreements to concentrate control over 90–95% of refined oil in the Standard Oil Trust between 1873 and 1879.

November 29, 1873

The "*Virginius* incident" in Cuba is calmed when Spain agrees to indemnify the United States.

At a time when U.S.-Spanish relations had become tense, a Spanish cruiser near Cuba captured an alleged American ship, the *Virginius,* and carried its crew and passengers to Santiago, Cuba. The Spanish captors asserted that the ship transported a large cargo of armaments and that the passengers were soldiers recruited by the Cuban revolutionary committee in New York City to invade Cuba.

Although the Spanish government hastened to tell the Cuban officials not to impose a death sentence on the crew or passengers without authorization from Madrid, the notice arrived too late. On November 7 and 8, 1873, 53 of the men captured aboard the *Virginius* were executed, including the ship's captain and 36 crew members. The arrival of a British warship, the *Niobe,* on November 8 prevented more executions. Captain Lorraine of the *Niobe* trained his guns on the city and warned the authorities he would destroy it if any further executions occurred. Lorraine acted because 19 British as well as Americans made up the crew and "passengers" of the *Virginius.*

If the United States had desired to take Cuba to end the difficulties of that island, this incident would have offered an excellent opportunity. In America, indignation rallies against Spain took place all along the eastern seaboard. The *New York Sun* urged war and condemned Spain. There was, however, no desire for war in the United States. Although Secretary of State Fish sent Madrid a virtual ultimatum to demand an apology and redress in 12 days, the State Department learned about the dubious ship registry of the *Virginius* and Fish then moderated his initial outburst.

Between November 27 and 29, Fish and the Spanish minister to the United States, Admiral José Polo de Bernabe, reached an agreement. Polo said Spain would surrender the *Virginius* and all prisoners who had not been executed. Spain would also pay an indemnity, the exact amount of which would be negotiated.

President Grant accepted the Fish-Polo arrangement, and on December 8 the remaining captives returned from Santiago. Spain eventually paid an indemnity of $80,000 to families of the executed Americans. On December 22, Secretary Fish informed Polo that the *Virginius* should not have flown the American flag. The ship had obtained U.S. registry through fraud because Cuban exiles owned and controlled the ship and falsely claimed U.S. citizenship.

For nature of relations between Spain and Cuba, see August 27, 1873.

1875

January 30, 1875

America and Hawaii sign a reciprocity treaty that gives the United States a virtual protectionship over the islands.

The commercial terms of this treaty provided for almost free trade of products between the United States and the islands. In particular, there were no duties levied on Hawaii's unrefined sugar imports to America. The political parts of the treaty asserted that the trade relations of the two signatories would not be extended to any other nation. Further, Hawaii agreed not to lease or dispose of any of its territory to a third power. The Senate approved the treaty on March 18, 1875.

When the 1875 treaty was extended in 1884, the United States received the use of Pearl Harbor as a coaling and naval station.

See December 6, 1884.

February 25–July 16, 1875

The Third French Republic is created by the passage of three separate laws in the National Assembly.

These enactments of the assembly finally settled the political arguments among monarchists, republicans, and socialists that had beset the French during the four years after their defeat by German armies in 1870–1871. The republic, said Adolphe Thiers, France's chief executive, was "the government which divides us least." Thus, the Third Republic was established, lasting until the Nazi German invasion of 1940.

March 18, 1875

The difficulty of policing Indian raids along the U.S. Mexican border is explained in Secretary of State Fish's note to Mexico's Foreign Minister.

As the U.S. army in the west applied increased military pressure against the Indians after the Civil War, the problem of Indian raids began on both sides of the southwest border of America. At first the State Department simply sent information on particular cases to Mexico City. In response the Mexican government sent notices of Apache raids into northern Mexico from U.S. territory. In January 1875, the military forces of each nation in the region arranged to cooperate in fighting the hostile Indians, but little was accomplished to end the problem.

Fish's note of March 18 indicated the difficult parameters of the problem, using the excuses that Mexico frequently made to Washington. Fish noted the difficulty of patrolling a vast, sparsely populated area with the border population "comprising, but too often lawless persons of the nationalities of each of the coterminous states, and refugees from the laws of all nations." People living in the area would, he said, simply have to be aware of the risks. Thus, the problem could be described but it could not be resolved.

April 12, 1875

Secretary of State Fish recognizes the new monarchy of Spain, saying de facto recognition of governments is "the only true and wise principle and policy."

In Spain a group of generals overthrew the first Spanish republic and installed Alfonso XII as king on December 31, 1874. While many Americans, including Fish, expected reforms to be made by the republican government, they often were dismayed by the failure of its reforms both in Spain and in Cuba.

On April 12, 1875, Fish instructed Caleb Cushing, U.S. minister to Spain, to present his papers to the new king because the U.S. practice was to recognize a de facto regime. The de facto principle had been established by Secretary of State Thomas Jefferson in 1793, and was generally followed until Woodrow Wilson's administration from 1913 to 1920.

Fish recognized the new regime largely because he wanted to urge it to end the Cuban insurrection by making needed reforms.

See August 27, 1873, and March 1, 1876.

May 10, 1875

A crisis causing a possible French-German war ends when Russia and Great Britain warn Bismarck not to attempt a preventive war.

This "war scare" began in April 1875, as a result of German dissatisfaction with a new French army law that seemed to be preparing French forces for an attack on Germany to avenge their 1871 defeat. The immediate cause of the crisis was the publication of an article entitled "Is War in Sight?" in the *Berlin Post.* The French claimed the *Post* article was inspired by Bismarck to create circumstances that would justify war.

While Britain's ambassador to Berlin, Lord Odo Russell, warned Bismarck against war, the visit to Berlin of Russian Czar Alexander II and Prince Alexander Gorchakov was most effective in ending the crisis. Bismarck desired Russian loyalty to the Three Emperors' League, a military convention between Germany, Russia, and Austria, formed 1872–1873. The German chancellor realized Russia would not permit Germany to fight a "preventive war" against France. The crisis ended following the Russian visit on May 10, 1875.

July 5, 1875

Insurrection against the Ottoman Turkish Empire breaks out in Bosnia and Herzegovina.

This conflict began three years of acute difficulty in the Balkans and the eastern Mediterranean, a crisis involving all the major European powers. British and French policy endeavored to uphold the

Turkish Empire, "the sick man of Europe," while Russia encouraged the Pan-Slavic movement in the Balkans and sought to profit from the Ottoman Empire's breakup.

November 25, 1875

Great Britain gains control of the Suez Canal, purchasing all company shares of Khedive Ismail of Egypt.

The Suez Canal Company built the canal under the direction of a Frenchman, Ferdinand de Lessups. In 1875, British Prime Minister Benjamin Disraeli arranged to purchase all company shares held by Egypt's Khedive Ismail, giving Britain majority control of the company despite French objections. Desiring to control this strategic place on the route to India and East Asia, the British Parliament approved Disraeli's purchase even though Disraeli had not consulted them before making the purchase.

1876

February 7, 1876

A special U.S. interoceanic canal commission recommends a canal route through Nicaragua.

Between 1868 and 1872, the State Department tried various means to obtain canal rights on the Darien route through Panama, the lake route through Nicaragua, and the Tehuantepec route through Mexico. Because these diverse negotiations had not brought satisfactory results, President Grant appointed a special Interoceanic Canal Commission on March 10, 1872, which was asked to study the three canal plans and to recommend the "best" route. Between 1870 and 1872, Secretary of the Navy George M. Robeson also commissioned several naval officers to explore each of the three isthmian routes. While the navy investigations aided the commission's work, the president's commission had the most significant responsibility of recommending one route.

Both the U.S. navy's and the commission's investigations agreed that the only real options were the Nicaragua or Panama routes. The Mexican route was found to be wholly unsuitable, owing especially to the reports of Captain Robert W. Shufeldt of the U.S. navy. His report indicated that to transverse the Tehuantepec region for 144 miles, 140 locks raising ships to a height of 754 feet would be required. Obviously, the construction of such a canal was prohibitive because of cost and technical problems.

Of the Darien and Lake Nicaragua routes, the commission preferred the latter. Both routes seemed feasible according to the navy reports of Commander Thomas Selfridge (Darien) and Commodore Edward P. Lull (Nicaragua). Owing largely to the influence of Admiral Daniel Ammen, the commission opted for Nicaragua. According to the commission report, the use of canals and the lakes in Nicaragua required less extensive excavations, and the climate of the area was better than Panama's.

The commission's report diverted most U.S. attention to the Nicaraguan route for the next 20 years. Nevertheless, advocates of Panama continued to argue for their route and eventually won.

February 26, 1876

Japan and Korea sign a treaty that recognizes Korea as independent of China.

This treaty also gave Japan both commercial and extraterritorial privileges in Korea. Three Korean ports were opened to Japan and a Japanese representative would have residence in Seoul. Japan's actions effectively opened Korea to trade with Western nations.

March 1, 1876

America fails to obtain foreign support to end the Cuban insurrection.

The failure of Secretary Fish to coordinate pressure on Spain with other European nations' support was noted in a memorandum by Fish to Caleb Cushing, U.S. minister to Spain.

As the Cuban uprising entered its seventh year in 1875, Fish wanted Spain to grant independence to Cuba to stop the difficulties Americans experienced because of the insurrection. American estates in Cuba had been destroyed, the Spanish captain general's administration used bribery and extortion, and Americans of Cuban birth visiting in the island had been abused and sometimes executed. On November 5, 1875, Fish had outlined these and other complaints against Spain in instructions to Cushing. He also told Cushing to urge Madrid to grant Cuba independence and to abolish slavery in the Spanish colonies. Finally,

Fish threatened that if Spain did not bring order in Cuba, it might be "the duty of other governments to intervene."

To obtain support for his threat, Fish sent copies of the November 5 message to the U.S. ministers in England, France, Russia, Germany, and Italy, telling them to relay its contents to their host governments and request statements of support for the U.S. complaints against Spain.

European backing did not materialize. Most crucial to Fish's cause was English cooperation, but it was not available. Britain's foreign minister, the earl of Derby (Lord Stanley), recognized the validity of Fish's complaints but was not willing to make proposals that he believed Spain could not accept. The French refused to join American protests because they thought the Spanish king had too many internal problems to give attention to Cuba. Russia, Germany, and Italy, nations with slight interest in the Caribbean, offered somewhat favorable support to Fish, but their responses were not strong enough to assist the United States.

Fish's project suffered equally because of the conciliatory but dilatory methods of the Spanish government. Spain, as in the past, promised much but never acted effectively to change conditions in Cuba. Spain agreed to pay the $80,000 indemnity for the U.S. citizens killed in the *Virginius* incident of 1873 but instituted no reforms of the conditions in Cuba.

Thus, Fish's attempt to rally European opinion to coerce Spain did not succeed. In a March 1, 1876, message to Madrid, Fish again recited the U.S. charges against Spanish policy in Cuba. Spain responded on April 16 by informing Cushing that it would try to resolve the disorders in Cuba. Spain's attempt was not, however, to reform conditions in Cuba but to suppress the rebellion.

See February 10, 1878.

June 30, 1876

Serbia declares war on Turkey.

This episode of the Near Eastern problem resulted from the slaughter of thousands of Bulgarians by Turkish irregular troops. Bulgaria had launched an uprising for independence from Turkey. In declaring war on June 30, Serbia expected to receive Russian assistance. Russia did not immediately respond, however, and until the Serbs appeared on the verge of complete defeat in September, the czar did not act effectively.

See January 20, 1877.

October 31, 1876

Sioux Wars end when U.S. forces capture chiefs Sitting Bull and Crazy Horse.

The battle on October 31 ended the second war against the Sioux. The first war occurred from 1866 to 1868, when the U.S. army attempted to build a road from Fort Laramie, Wyoming, to Bozeman, Montana. On April 29, 1868, the Sioux and the United States signed a treaty to provide a permanent reservation for the Indians in the Dakota territory.

In August 1875, the discovery of gold in the Black Hills of Dakota brought more white men into the territory provided for the Sioux in 1869. In addition, surveyors for the Northern Pacific Railroad recommended a railway route through Sioux territory. During the Second Sioux War, the Indians achieved their famous victory over General George A. CUSTER at the Little Big Horn (June 25, 1876), but U.S. forces were too strong for the Sioux chiefs, who were finally defeated on October 31, 1876.

November 7, 1876

Presidential election results in disputed electoral votes between Hayes and Tilden.

This election marked the return of sufficient Democratic Party strength throughout the nation almost to enable Samuel J. TILDEN to win. Tilden was nominated by the Democratic Convention at St. Louis on June 29, 1876. The Republican Convention nominated Rutherford B. Hayes on June 16. Two third-party candidates whose votes were not sufficient to affect the election were General Green Clay SMITH of the Prohibition Party and Peter COOPER of the National Greenback Party.

Although Tilden won the popular vote for president by 250,000 votes, the Republicans challenged the electoral vote because of disputed elections in four states: Florida, Louisiana, South Carolina, and Oregon. Each of these states reported two sets of electoral returns on December 6. The dispute required an unusual settlement in early 1877.

See March 2, 1877.

November 20, 1876

In Mexico, Porfirio Díaz overthrows President Lerdo de Tejada and soon assumes absolute power.

The coup d'état by Díaz ended the Mexican republic, which had high hopes but troubled times under Benito Juárez. Following the death of Juárez in 1872, Tejada became president and endeavored to safeguard Mexico's liberal reforms. Social and economic problems continued, however, and the ascension of Díaz on November 20 brought a return to a reactionary military dictatorship, although Díaz often acted in an enlightened manner. Except for the years 1880–1884, Díaz ruled Mexico until 1911.

December 23, 1876

Turkey proclaims a constitutional monarchy; the liberal effort is short-lived.

After overthrowing the Sultan Abdul Aziz on May 30, 1876, a group of reformers led by MIDHAT PASHA prepared a constitution based on a sultan who was limited by parliamentary-style representatives with an independent ministry. In August, Sultan Abdul HAMID II accepted the constitutional concept with Pasha as the prime minister, and the document was proclaimed on December 23. The constitution declared the indivisibility of the Ottoman Empire and granted freedom of press, conscience, and education as well as a representative parliament.

Although the constitution of 1876 indicated one possible direction for reform in Turkey, it did not last long. On March 19, 1877, the sultan suspended the parliament and reasserted his absolute power. Midhat Pasha had been dismissed on February 5, and he was later found guilty of murdering the Sultan Abdul Aziz in 1876. Only British intervention prevented Midhat's execution in 1881.

1877

February 1, 1877

Fish and Grant accept the British nominee for the commission to settle the U.S.-Canadian fisheries issue.

According to the terms of the Treaty of Washington of May 8, 1871, a commission of three persons was to be appointed to meet at Halifax to resolve the Northeast coast fisheries problem. In addition to the U.S. and British delegates, the third commissioner would be a neutral person acceptable to both countries. If a neutral person could not be agreed on by October 1873, the Austro-Hungarian ambassador at London would choose the third commissioner.

The October deadline passed without a decision because the United States feared that the Austro-Hungarian ambassador would select a pro-British nominee. In July 1875, Britain named Sir Alexander I. GALT as its commissioner, but not until August 1875, did Fish name Ensign H. KELLOGG of Massachusetts as America's delegate.

Until February 1, 1877, Fish would not agree on a third person. Thus on that date the British minister to the United States, Sir Edward THORNTON, expressed surprise when Fish informed him that America would accept Maurice Delfosse, the Belgian minister to the United States and a person whom the British had suggested in 1873.

The American agreement on the Halifax commissioner came just before Grant's presidential term concluded. Apparently, Grant and Fish wanted the Treaty of Washington to be entirely fulfilled before they left office in 1877.

March 2, 1877

Hayes is declared to be elected president.

Because two sets of electoral ballots had been reported by four states on December 6, 1876, Congress had to determine some method to decide the election victory. Because the Republican Party controlled the Senate and the Democratic Party controlled the House, an Electoral Commission of 15 members was set up to decide the dispute. As it happened, the Republicans held an 8-to-7 majority on the commission and their votes favored the election of Hayes, who received the disputed votes, thereby winning the election by 185 to 184 electoral votes.

To avoid a continued congressional contest of the commission's decision, the Republican leadership persuaded Southern Democrats to support the commission by promising to (1) withdraw all federal troops from the South and end radical reconstruction policies; (2) appoint one Southerner to the cabinet; and (3) appropriate funds for internal improvements in the South, specifically, funds to construct the Texas and Pacific Railroad to the Pacific coast. This pact with the Southern Democrats enabled Congress to ratify the Electoral Commission's decision and permit Hayes to be inaugurated as president on March 5, 1877. By April 1877, Hayes withdrew the last federal troops from the Southern states.

March 12, 1877

William Maxwell Evarts is commissioned as secretary of state by President Hayes.

Evarts had little experience abroad but was highly qualified by character and the profession of law for the position of secretary of state. Hayes appointed Evarts despite the opposition of the machine-Republican politicians such as Roscoe Conkling of New York and Simon Cameron of Pennsylvania, whose corrupt practices had, from Evarts's viewpoint, seriously damaged the reputation of the party of Abraham Lincoln. In foreign relations, Evarts's principal distinction before 1877 was service as legal counsel to the "*Alabama* claims" commission, which met at Geneva in accordance with the Treaty of Washington of 1871. Evarts served as secretary of state throughout Hayes's term of office.

April 24, 1877

Russia declares war on Turkey.

This war resulted from the crisis that arose in July 1875, when Bosnia and Herzegovina began a rebellion against Turkey. After the Conference of Istanbul failed on January 20, 1877, Russia secured an Austrian agreement to remain neutral in a Russo-Turkish conflict. Great Britain made a final, unsuccessful attempt to persuade Russia and Turkey to disarm, and Russia went to war. This war greatly disturbed the British, who wanted to prevent Russia from spreading its influence from the Black Sea region southward into the Mediterranean Sea.

June 1, 1877

President Hayes orders American army forces to patrol the Mexican border and to pursue and punish by crossing into Mexico if necessary.

The Mexican-Texas border incursions continued to present difficulties during the early years of the government of Díaz, which had gained power in Mexico on November 20, 1876.

Although Secretary of State Fish had clarified the enormous difficulties of preventing cross-border attacks on March 18, 1875, Secretary of State Evarts either did not comprehend or know about Fish's understanding of the problem. Soon after taking office on May 16, 1877, Evarts demanded that the Díaz government suppress Mexican bandits before the United States would grant recognition to the regime. Mexico, in turn, refused to act until diplomatic recognition was granted.

Evarts, President Hayes, and Secretary of War Alexander Ramsey decided the United States should undertake its own border defense at the risk of violating Mexican territory. Consequently, in the order of June 1, 1877, the secretary of war directed Brigadier General Edward O. C. Ord, the commander in Texas, that he was free, when pursuing marauders or on their "fresh trail," to take U.S. forces "across the Rio Grande, and to overtake and punish them."

Díaz reacted in rage to this American order. He dispatched Mexican forces to the border to ward off the Americans, telling the Mexican commander: "You will repel force by force should the invasion take place."

During the summer and early fall of 1877, raids by Mexican bandits into Texas and by Apache Indians and outlaws into Mexico continued. In many instances these were followed by incursions of Mexican troops violating the U.S. border or American troops chasing bandits into Mexico.

Gradually, however, commercial and business interests in Mexico City and the United States feared war could result from these diverse incidents, and both governments took steps to end the problems.

See March 23, 1878.

June 15, 1877

The Halifax Commission convenes on the fisheries dispute, later deciding in Britain's favor.

This commission was established under terms of the Treaty of Washington of May 8, 1871. The three members were appointed on February 1, 1877, and met at Halifax, Nova Scotia. Their charge was to decide what, if any, monetary value the Americans received above the value the British received for the fishery privileges granted by the Treaty of Washington of 1871.

After five months' study, the commissioners voted 2 to 1 that for a 12-year period the United States had received $5.5 million excess value over the British; therefore, America should reimburse Britain by that amount. Although U.S. commissioner Ensign Kellogg dissented from the award, the United States decided it was honor-bound to pay and did so on November 21, 1878, although in making the payment it admonished Britain that it did not consider this a "just measure" of the privileges granted to American fishermen. As an anticlimax, a Canadian professor, Henry Youle HIND, reported in 1878 that the British case presented to the Halifax commissioners used false statistics. Although several congressmen noted this argument, Hind's information did not attract much attention in America and had no effect on the fisheries question.

1878

January 17, 1878

A U.S.-Samoan treaty is signed in Washington; the Senate ratifies it on January 30.

Following the failure of the Meade Treaty with Samoa of May 22, 1872, President Grant sent Colonel Albert B. STEINBERGER as a special agent to gather more data about a naval base in the Samoan Islands.

Steinberger did more than is usually expected of a diplomat to prepare Samoa for a second treaty with America. He first reported to President Grant in 1874 in favor of the great commercial future of Samoa. More important, he worked closely with the feuding native tribes of the islands to end their strife and organize a government. His work and friendship with the natives proved to be so successful that by 1876 he became a sort of "prime minister" among the tribes.

Steinberger's success caused jealousy among the British and German envoys who sought to control Samoa for their countries. German commercial interests had been active in the islands since 1847, and although Steinberger tried to cooperate with Godeffroy and Sons, the German trading house, the German consul in the islands, Thomas Weber, disliked Steinberger. To a lesser degree, the British had become interested in Samoa because of missionaries and trading interests coming from New Zealand.

In 1876, the British and German consuls decided they must supersede the success of Steinberger's influences. Especially at Weber's urging, the British arrested Steinberger and deported him on a British warship. Steinberger's influence continued in the islands, however. Following his arrest a group of chieftains sent LE MAMEA to Washington to solicit U.S. protection against Germany. In 1877, Le Mamea negotiated with Assistant Secretary of State Frederick W. Seward and they agreed to a treaty on January 17, 1878.

The treaty that the U.S. Senate ratified on January 30 provided rights for the United States to establish a naval and coaling station at Pago Pago. The United States also agreed to employ its good offices on behalf of Samoa if any third country interfered with the chiefs on the island.

February 8, 1878

The British send their fleet to protect Istanbul from Russian conquest.

After the outbreak of the Russo-Turkish War on April 24, 1877, British officials feared the czar's army might capture Istanbul. The Russians were assisted by armed forces from Romania, Bulgaria, Serbia, and Montenegro, national groups seeking independence from the Ottoman Empire. From July to December 1877, Turkish forces successfully defended southern Bulgaria before the Russians overran the Turk fortress and moved toward Istanbul. The Russians' success persuaded Britain to send a fleet to the Aegean Sea while warning Moscow to stop its offensive outside Istanbul. Britain's fleet reached the coast near Istanbul on February 8. The Russian army never entered Istanbul, and March 3, 1878, Turkey's Sultan Abdul Hamid and Russian officials signed the Treaty of San Stefano. The treaty's harsh terms were opposed not only by the czar's Balkan allies but also by Britain and France. To avoid another war, delegates from all parties met in Berlin. The Treaty of Berlin was signed on July 13, 1878. Its principal clauses were as follows:

1. The "Big Bulgaria" authorized by the San Stefano Treaty became a small autonomous principality whose prince had to be approved by the Ottoman sultan.
2. Serbia gained independence but had to withdraw from Kosovo and most of Albania.
3. Romania and Montenegro became independent.
4. Austria would administer Bosnia and Herzegovina.

The Treaty of Berlin resolved the Balkan problems for the next 30 years.

See October 6, 1908.

February 10, 1878

Spain ends the Cuban rebellion by the convention of el Zanjon.

Following 10 years of intermittent conflict in Cuba and protests from the U.S. government, the Spanish military quelled the rebellion by persuading some of the Cuban leaders to sign the Convention of El Zanjon. The Spanish victory materialized after King Alfonso XII defeated the supporters of Don Carlos as claimant to the Spanish throne. The Carlist opposition ended in February 1876, about the time that U.S. Secretary of State Fish sought European cooperation to persuade Spain to grant independence to Cuba.

After strengthening his government at home, Alfonso XII commissioned General Arsino Martinez de Campos to be captain general of Cuba and bring order to the colony. Campos succeeded in Cuba by the judicious use of military force, bribes to certain Cuban leaders, and promises of amnesty and reforms. He also negotiated the Convention of El Zanjon with the rebels. The convention contained Spanish promises to abolish slavery in Cuba and to institute administrative reforms that would benefit the Cuban people.

Slavery in Cuba was gradually abolished by 1886, but the other reforms were never carried out. The former corrupt practices of the military officials and the captain general's agents returned to plague Cuba during the next decade. Nevertheless, Campos's activity gave Cuba relative calm for the next 15 years.

See March 1, 1876.

March 23, 1878

America recognizes the Díaz regime in Mexico.

Although in 1877 Secretary of State Evarts pursued a strong legalistic battle against recognition of the Mexican government until the border disputes were resolved, he changed his policy after U.S. commercial groups urged Congress to end the border tension by recognizing Díaz. Early in 1878, the Senate appointed a commission to promote U.S.-Mexican trade, and the House considered resolutions to grant recognition on both January 11 and March 11, 1878.

As a result, Evarts on March 23 adopted the views of the commercial spokesmen. He instructed U.S. Minister to Mexico John W. Foster to recognize the government and to request reciprocal border-crossing privileges as a method to end the incursion along the Rio Grande border. Díaz would not accept such an agreement unless America first withdrew its military order of June 1, 1877, which permitted U.S. troops to enter Mexican territory. An impasse resulted. Border incidents continued and anti-American agitation grew so intolerable in Mexico City that on Mexico's national holiday, September 15, Foster considered fleeing from the American legation.

Fortunately, while pulling Uncle Sam's beard, Díaz also gave order to Mexican society and ended many, if not all, border attacks. By the end of 1878 relative peace prevailed on the border, and in October 1879, General Ord recommended the withdrawal of the June 1, 1877, order.

See June 1, 1877, and February 24, 1880.

May 18, 1878

Colombia grants a French company under Ferdinand de Lesseps exclusive rights to construct a Panama Canal.

The man whose organizational abilities had constructed the Suez Canal gained the right from Colombia to establish a company to build and operate the Panama Canal.

July 25, 1878

An American-Japanese commercial treaty gives Japan greater control over its foreign relations.

This treaty was one of Japan's steps toward obtaining equality of treaty terms with the Western powers; that is, treaties negotiated on a basis of mutual respect, not military force, as had occurred when China, Japan, and Korea were "opened" to Western commerce by Western gunboats.

In 1871, Japan sent a special mission to the United States headed by Prince Tonomi Iwakura. The mission visited various Western nations to gain a respect that might free their nation from the unequal treaties. The prince made an excellent impression in the United States, and beginning with the Postal Convention of August 6, 1873, America treated

Japanese diplomats with an equal status not yet accepted by European nations.

More specifically, the Treaty of 1878 resulted from the efforts of John A. Bingham, U.S. minister to Japan, who encouraged the Japanese to end the unequal treaties. On Bingham's advice the exact treaty decisions were negotiated in Washington between the Japanese minister to the United States, Yoshida, and Secretaries of State Fish and Evarts.

The important parts of the treaty of 1878 were as follows:

1. the treaty abrogated U.S. participation in the multinational tariff convention of June 25, 1866, replacing it with the bilateral tariff treaty of 1878;
2. Japan regained the right to regulate its coastal trade;
3. Japan received tariff autonomy to control its own import duties;
4. the principle of reciprocity of trade was used regarding certain products;
5. article 10 provided that the convention of 1878 would be in effect only when Japan gained similar treaties with other nations who had signed the Convention of 1866. This article preserved U.S. most-favored-nation status until all nations revised their commercial treaties with Japan.

Although European nations, especially Great Britain, protested America's independent action ending the 1866 convention, by 1880 the European powers undertook to formulate equal treaties with Japan. The process did not end, however, until the treaties of 1894.

See November 22, 1894.

1879

July 12, 1879

The German Empire adopts a protective tariff law for both industry and agriculture.

Heretofore, the Germans had followed free-trade principles. During the 1870s, when there was a fall in the prices of agricultural produce, those persons who suffered an economic loss blamed foreign competition. Because the new industrial leaders of Germany had a large representation in the German Reichstag (parliament), they influenced the move away from free trade as a means of better competing with other nations after 1879.

October 7, 1879

Germany and Austria sign a dual alliance.

This is the first of the alliances formed by German Chancellor Otto von Bismarck. As part of his realpolitik, Bismarck hoped to secure Russian and Austrian support against France. The Dual Alliance was one part of that policy. Reconciling Austrian and Russian interests in southeast Europe became more difficult, however.

1880

February 24, 1880

The Texas-Mexican border disorder ends and the United States withdraws its military order to pursue bandits into Mexico.

Although the Díaz administration gradually brought social order to Mexico including the Rio Grande border, Secretary of State Evarts reluctantly moved to stop the U.S. military violations of Mexican territory.

In February 1879, a group of American businessmen visited Mexico, where they were graciously received and favorably impressed by Díaz. The Mexican ruler had adopted a program to develop his nation's resources by seeking U.S. loans and investments, and American commercial groups became eager to cooperate. Evarts remained skeptical, however, and argued in March 1879 that the new government remained indifferent to U.S. demands for the end of border incidents.

But stability did return to the border, and in an October 1879 report to the War Department, General Ord stated his belief that the June 1, 1877, military order was unnecessary at present. Evarts and President Hayes used Ord's report to justify the withdrawal of the June 1 military order on February 24, 1880. In his announcement, Evarts wrote that the president was satisfied that Mexico was determined to maintain the border's security and to "observe its international obligations in preventing invasions of our territory." U.S.-Mexican relations now improved, and American investments thrived in Mexico until the Revolution of 1911 against Díaz.

March 8, 1880

America's concern about de Lesseps's Panama Canal project is expressed in a report of the Select Committee on an Interoceanic Canal of the House of Representatives.

Since May 18, 1878, when the Frenchman Ferdinand de Lesseps secured permission from Colombia for a canal, U.S. opinion expressed opposition to the control of a Panama canal by France or any other European power. In early 1880, de Lesseps visited Washington to attempt to reassure Americans of his intentions. He held a conference with President Hayes and testified before the House Select Committee.

Apparently, however, American politicians still suspected the Frenchman's motives. On March 8, after de Lesseps's visit, both President Hayes and the Oceanic Committee issued statements that reasserted the Monroe Doctrine as opposing foreign control of any isthmian canal. Arguing that such a canal would be "virtually a part of the coastline of the United States," Hayes declared that American policy required that a canal must be under American control.

The House committee used more details to express the same desire for U.S. control of any isthmian canal. Its report specifically asserted that the European control of a canal or a state through which the canal crossed was contrary to the Monroe Doctrine. It also proposed a resolution requiring the president to abrogate any treaty that conflicted with America's right to control such a canal.

In addition to de Lesseps's Panama Company, which began excavations during the 1880s, two American projects tried to promote canals in Nicaragua and Mexico. The Mexican Tehuantepec project had been revived by James B. Eads, an imaginative American engineer. Eads planned to build a railway to carry ships across the isthmus, but after obtaining a concession from Mexico, he could not raise sufficient funds to finance his scheme.

More possible of completion was the project of the Maritime Canal Company of Nicaragua. This venture had the support of Ulysses Grant, Admiral Daniel Ammen, and other notable Americans. It obtained a 99-year concession from Nicaragua stipulating that construction must begin in 3 years and the canal be finished in 10 years. To help raise funds, the Maritime Company tried to obtain a federal charter, but opposition from Eads, de Lesseps, and the U.S. transcontinental railway lines kept Congress from approving a charter. The company also sought funds in Europe but failed. Consequently, by 1884, the Nicaraguan canal project went out of business. De Lesseps's construction activities made Panama the only area where plans had been translated into earth-moving during the 1880s.

October 27, 1880

America makes an unsuccessful attempt to mediate the war of the Pacific.

War broke out in February 1879 when Chile seized the Bolivian port of Antofagasta and Peru came to aid Bolivia. The dispute between these three nations centered on an area along the Pacific Ocean where rich mineral deposits had been found in the mid–19th century. The old Spanish borders for the rocky and desert area were indefinite. Therefore, Chile sought to establish its rights by conquest, and its superior armed forces enabled Chile to capture Tarapaca province during the summer of 1880, cutting Bolivia off from the ocean, as well as the Peruvian provinces of Tacna and Arica.

Because France and Great Britain had interests in all three nations, they approached the United States to suggest a joint mediation. Secretary of State Evarts refused their offer but agreed that the United States alone would mediate the quarrel. The three Latin American nations also agreed, and their delegates met with the U.S. ministers to Chile, Peru, and Bolivia. The talks took place on board the U.S. warship *Lackawanna* off the coast of Arica.

The failure of mediation was reported to the State Department on October 27. The U.S. minister to Peru, Isaac P. Christiancy, wrote Secretary Evarts that Chile demanded the entire province of Tarapaca, where the richest nitrate deposits lay. Bolivia and Peru could not accept this demand and a compromise was impossible. Each side made further accusations against the other, and fighting resumed in southern Peru.

For further American efforts in this war, see January 26, 1882.

November 2, 1880

James A. Garfield is elected President.

Because Rutherford Hayes had pledged in 1876 not to seek a second term, the Republican Party's field was wide open for presidential nominees. Therefore by June 2, when the Republican Convention began in Chicago, two main factions had been formed. One, led by James G. BLAINE and known as the "Half-breeds," opposed the nomination of Ulysses Grant, whom Roscoe CONKLING and the "Stalwart" Republicans backed. The struggle for the nomination grew heated, and on the 36th ballot a dark horse was selected, James A. GARFIELD of Ohio. Garfield won the nomination because Blaine threw his support to him. To appease the Stalwarts and retain party unity, Chester A. ARTHUR was selected to run for vice president. The Republican platform included planks seeking civil service reform, a protective tariff, and the restriction of Chinese immigration.

The Democratic Convention of June 22 nominated Winfield Scott HANCOCK for president, approving a platform that differed from the Republican because it advocated a revenue tariff. Two other candidates who gained a small fraction of votes were James B. Weaver of the Greenback Labor Party and Neal Dow of the Prohibition Party.

The election of November 2 was close. Garfield's plurality of votes was 10,000 out of 9 million votes cast; however, his electoral college margin was more comfortable, 214 to 155.

November 17, 1880

A treaty with China permits America to restrict Chinese immigration.

This treaty repealed the section of the 1868 Burlingame Treaty that permitted unrestricted Chinese immigration into America. Since that date, strong anti-Oriental prejudices had developed in the states along America's Pacific Coast. Some states had tried to pass discriminatory legislation against the Chinese, and California experienced anti-Chinese demonstrations.

In 1879, Congress passed the "Fifteen Passenger Bill" to limit to 15 the number of Chinese arriving in one ship. President Hayes vetoed the bill but set up a commission to go to China and negotiate a new treaty. The commissioners were John T. SWIFT, later a minister to Japan; W. H. TRESCOT; and James B. ANGELL, president of the University of Michigan.

Because the Chinese had internal problems with the European powers and local reformers that absorbed most of their attention, they did not object to a new treaty. The only proposal rejected by China was the prohibition of Chinese immigration. Therefore, the November 17, 1880, treaty allowed the United States to "regulate, limit or suspend" but

In Denver, strong anti-Chinese feelings erupt in a brutal riot. Library of Congress

not prohibit Chinese immigration. Another clause in the treaty accepted by the United States prohibited the opium trade. Great Britain was pressuring China to permit more opium imports, and the Chinese hoped the U.S. prohibition would enable them to compel the British to halt the opium traffic. The Pacific Coast states of America were not satisfied with the Treaty of 1880 because they wanted Chinese immigration to be prohibited.

See May 6, 1882.

1881

March 5, 1881

James G. Blaine is appointed Secretary of State by President Garfield.

Because Blaine led the "Half-breed" Republicans who opposed Grant's nomination in 1880, his appointment renewed the factional strife within the Republican Party. Garfield stimulated even greater controversy by naming William H. Robertson as the New York customs collector, contrary to the wishes of the "Stalwart" leader and New York boss, Roscoe Conkling. This party friction made it impossible for Blaine to survive as secretary following Garfield's death in September 1881.

Blaine had little foreign experience to qualify him as secretary. His appointment was due to his status in the Republican Party and his service as speaker of the House from 1869 to 1876. Blaine's international attitudes, which influenced him in 1881 and again from 1889 to 1892 during his second term as secretary, were his distrust of Europe, especially England, and his desire to improve relations and commerce with Latin America.

May 12, 1881

France occupies and establishes a protectorate over Tunisia.

This French colony was one of the first colonies established by a European power in North Africa. Before World War I began in 1914, North Africa became an area of intense friction among France, Germany, Italy, and Spain.

June 2, 1881

Great Britain pays America an indemnity for damages to U.S. fishermen in 1878.

Not long after the Halifax Commission of June 15, 1877, awarded Britain $5.5 million to settle the northeast fisheries dispute, a group of U.S. fishermen suffered heavy losses when their fishing equipment was destroyed by Canadians in Newfoundland.

On a Sunday in January 1878, several American fishing boats seined for herring in Fortune Bay, Newfoundland. Suddenly local inhabitants attacked them, tearing away their nets and forcing them to go home. The Canadians claimed it was illegal to fish on Sunday in Newfoundland, a law violated by the Americans.

Secretary of State Evarts protested to England, arguing that the Treaty of Washington took precedence over local fishing laws. Evarts gave the British minister to the United States a bill of $105,305.02 for damages to American fishing equipment. In 1878, however, Evarts's complaints were ignored by Great Britain. Foreign Minister Lord Salisbury refused to admit any British fault.

Great Britain's attitude toward America changed when William Gladstone returned to office as prime minister on April 28, 1880. Lord Granville, the Liberal foreign minister, agreed that the Newfoundland citizens should not have taken the law into their own hands and paid £15,000 reparations to the United States on June 2, 1881.

June 18, 1881

The Three Emperors' League is formed by Germany, Austria, and Russia.

The league was a defensive alliance because if any of the three powers were attacked, the other two would remain neutral. One important agreement was to consult with each other before changing the status of Turkey. These clauses of the treaty remained secret in 1881.

June 24, 1881

Secretary of State Blaine seeks a revision of the Clayton-Bulwer Treaty.

The activity of Ferdinand de Lesseps and others seeking a canal across Central America concerned U.S. political leaders during the 1880s. Both President

Hayes and the House Select Committee on Interoceanic Canals indicated their awareness of these interests, and their statements implied that the canal should be under American, not joint, control. Not surprisingly, therefore, Secretary Blaine, who was sometimes referred to as "Jingo Jim," urged Britain to modify the Clayton-Bulwer Treaty of 1850.

To obtain a treaty revision and inform the European nations of U.S. policy, Blaine sent instructions to James Russell LOWELL, U.S. minister to Britain, and circulated copies of the June 24 memo to all U.S. ministers in Europe. Blaine argued that in light of the changed circumstances since 1850, America alone should supervise the canal. America, he said, would guarantee freedom of transit to all nations. Although Blaine's note ignored the Clayton-Bulwer Treaty, he told Lowell in a special note that the treaty of 1850 needed to be changed and the British should be asked to negotiate.

Blaine's retirement following Garfield's death ended his attempt to revise the treaty. His successor, Frederick Frelinghuysen, failed to budge the British and tried to circumvent their agreement.

See March 8, 1880, and December 10, 1884.

July 2, 1881

President Garfield is assassinated by a disappointed Republican office seeker.

Charles J. GUITEAU, a mentally unstable Republican "Stalwart," shot Garfield while the president was at the Washington, D.C., railroad station. The shot did not immediately kill Garfield, who lingered until September 19, 1881. Guiteau was convicted of murder on November 14, 1881, and executed on June 30, 1882.

September 19, 1881

President Chester A. Arthur takes office after Garfield's death.

Arthur, a staunch political opponent of both Garfield and Blaine, eventually appointed an entirely new cabinet. He asked Blaine to remain for a while as secretary of state, even though Blaine had resigned. Blaine agreed and remained in office until December 18, 1881.

November 8, 1881

Mexico refuses Secretary Blaine's offer to arbitrate its border dispute with Guatemala.

The Mexican-Guatemalan disagreement went back to 1823, when the province of CHIAPAS elected to join Mexico. Guatemala claimed the Mexican government had coerced the native population because they really had been part of Guatemala under Spanish rule.

When the government of Guatemala asked Blaine to intervene in 1881, the secretary agreed because he sympathized with that smaller state and feared the Guatemalans might otherwise seek European aid. Therefore on June 7, 1881, Blaine informed Mexico that he would offer his good offices in order that the concept of the "right of conquest should not be used in the Western Hemisphere." He suggested a diplomatic solution or arbitration to settle the quarrel.

Mexico refused Blaine's entreaties. Mexico disliked the Guatemalan proposal for a type of U.S. protectorship for that state and believed Blaine favored Guatemala. On November 8, when Blaine withdrew his offer of aid, he told Mexico he regretted that they could not join America in the use of friendly methods to settle their problems. Eventually, therefore, Guatemala entered direct negotiations with Mexico and had to yield the province of Chiapas to Mexico.

November 29, 1881

Secretary of State Blaine proposes a Pan-American conference for 1882—his successor as Secretary aborts the proposal.

One project that Blaine had suggested to President Garfield before his assassination was a conference to promote good relations with Latin America. Garfield's death delayed the invitation, but with President Arthur's approval Blaine invited 18 American nations to meet in Washington on November 24, 1882.

The proposal was not carried out by Blaine's successor, Frederick Frelinghuysen. In January 1882, Frelinghuysen wrote to William Trescot in Chile that he did not believe a conference was needed and that the president "prefers time for deliberation" on the subject. The official withdrawal of Blaine's invitation was made in August 1882. Fortunately for Blaine, his idea was revived in 1888, and he became the secretary of state who hosted the meeting in 1889.

December 12, 1881

President Arthur names Frederick T. Frelinghuysen as secretary of state.

Like James G. Blaine, Frelinghuysen had little experience in foreign affairs and had refused President Grant's offer to nominate him as minister to Great Britain in 1870. He had been a New Jersey senator from 1866 to 1869 and 1871 to 1877, and a lawyer for the New Jersey Central Railroad and the Morris Canal and Banking Company. Quite unlike Blaine's, Frelinghuysen's personality was passive, reserved, and cautious. He served as secretary from December 19, 1881, to the end of Arthur's term of office on March 6, 1885.

1882

January 26, 1882

Secretary Frelinghuysen releases documents on the Chile-Bolivian conflict at the moment Blaine's appointed negotiator is attempting to settle the dispute—U.S. politics damages U.S. diplomacy.

Shortly before Blaine left office in November 1881, he and President Arthur agreed to send William H. Trescot to mediate the War of the Pacific between Chile, Bolivia, and Peru. The war began in 1879 as a border dispute between Chile and Bolivia during which Peru supported its ally, Bolivia. The Trescot mission was the second U.S. mediation attempt, the first having failed on October 27, 1880.

For two years, U.S. policy in the War of the Pacific was poorly conducted. Following his election, Garfield replaced two veteran diplomats in Chile and Peru, Thomas A. Osborn and Isaac P. Christiancy, with two political "spoils" appointees: Stephen A. Hurlburt and Hugh Judson Kilpatrick. Neither Hurlburt nor Kilpatrick was familiar with the complex details of the Chile-Bolivia-Peru dispute.

Hurlburt, especially, acted in a manner that eventually, but too late, brought a rebuke from Secretary Blaine. Upon reaching Peru, Hurlburt issued a warning to Chile not to annex any Peruvian territory because the United States would not permit it. This declaration won acclaim for Hurlburt from Peruvians but did not represent U.S. policy or interests in that area. Nevertheless, Hurlburt continued to make personal policy. First, he invited Chile's arch rival, Argentina, to send a minister to Peru. Second, he formulated a convention with Peru to create a U.S. naval base at Chimbote, Peru. Both of these acts irritated Chile and made U.S. mediation of the war difficult, if not impossible.

But the worst was yet to come. To salvage the U.S. respect lost by Hurlburt, Secretary Blaine and President Arthur agreed to send an outstanding U.S. diplomat, William H. Trescot, to head a mission to the three warring countries. Trescot's instructions were to pressure Chile to lessen its demands on Bolivia but also to conciliate Chile by disavowing any American intention to affront it and by rebuking Hurlburt for statements against Chile's position. Generally, Trescot hoped to allow Chile to obtain the territory it deserved but to do so through peaceful means, not war.

The Trescot mission barely reached Santiago, Chile, before Frelinghuysen replaced Blaine and decided to reverse Blaine's Latin American policies. Apparently Frelinghuysen, an ardent "Stalwart" Republican with visions of being the party's presidential nominee in 1884, wanted to discredit Blaine's policies. He did it in a most disgraceful fashion, by publishing all diplomatic correspondence regarding the 1879 to 1882 discussions on the War of the Pacific, including a message recalling the Trescot mission before Trescot received notice of that fact.

Frelinghuysen released the diplomatic correspondence on January 26 but never cabled Trescot, who was in Chile. On January 31, Trescot met with Chile's foreign minister, José M. Balmaceda, to continue negotiations, during which the Chilean diplomat had previously yielded several concessions. This day, however, Trescot barely began outlining a proposal when Balmaceda stopped him and interjected: "It is useless.... Your instructions from Mr. Blaine have been published, and others are on their way to you modifying your original instructions in very important particulars." One of which Trescot now learned was his mission's cancellation. Trescot was shocked and surprised. The Chilean legation in Washington had cabled news of the January 26 events to Balmaceda, who, in turn, informed Trescot.

Knowing that Frelinghuysen would not use American influence to pressure Chile to compromise, the Chilean military officers now proceeded to obtain as much territory as possible from Peru and Bolivia.

Trescot returned home, being replaced by Cornelius Logan on June 26, 1882.

As a consequence of American ineptness, British influence grew in South America. Chile resented America's attempt to override its interests; Peru felt its interests had been sacrificed when Hurlburt's policy announcements were disavowed. Bolivia had no chance to regain any of its previous territory on the Pacific coast. For the Treaty of Ancon, which ended the War of the Pacific, see October 20, 1883, and for the truce of Valparaiso, see April 4, 1884.

May 6, 1882

A Congressional act suspends Chinese laborers from immigration for 10 years.

This law resulted from the continued agitation in Pacific coast states to exclude Asiatic immigration. Although the Sino-American Treaty of November 17, 1880, permitted the suspension of immigration, the U.S. commissioners who drew up this treaty considered a five-year suspension as within the spirit of the treaty. President Arthur vetoed a 20-year suspension bill prior to passage of this 10-year bill in 1882.

This legislation also prohibited any state from granting citizenship to the Chinese. Nevertheless, many prejudiced citizens of the Pacific Coast were not satisfied with the Act of May 6, 1882, and continued to urge greater restrictions on the Chinese (see July 5, 1884).

May 20, 1882

A triple alliance is formed by Germany, Austria, and Italy.

This alliance was defensive in purpose, providing that if any of the allies were attacked, the other nations would join in the war to support their ally. Italy desired this alliance to prevent a French invasion as a means of "liberating" Rome from the Italian union.

May 22, 1882

Korea and the United States sign a commercial treaty.

The Korean treaty was negotiated by U.S. navy Captain Robert Shufeldt and the Chinese viceroy in charge of Chinese-Korean relations, Li Hung-chang. The United States received trading rights and extraterritorial privileges similar to those granted by Korea to Great Britain in 1883 and Russia in 1884. The U.S. treaty became possible after Japan forced Korea to sign a treaty on February 26, 1876.

September 15, 1882

The British occupy Cairo, Egypt.

To protect the Suez Canal, the British and French had assumed dual protection of Egypt on November 18, 1876. The Europeans hoped to rule through the political office of the khedive of Egypt, but on February 1, 1881, a nationalistic uprising of Egyptian officers attempted to overthrow the khedive. To promote the continued authority of the Khedive Tewfik, the British sent naval ships that bombarded Alexandria on July 11, 1882. The British then moved on to Cairo and captured the city on September 16, defeating the nationalistic military group.

British problems were just beginning, however, as they struggled to bring order to Egypt and the Sudan while retaining control over the region in opposition to the desire of Egyptian nationalists.

1883

February 14, 1883

The first U.S. Minister to Persia is appointed.

Funds for a legation in Tehran that Congress had refused in 1857 were finally provided in 1882. Therefore on February 14, Secretary of State Frelinghuysen appointed Samuel G. Benjamin as minister resident to Persia. Congressional proponents hoped Benjamin would protect U.S. missionaries in Persia, but as minister, Benjamin endeavored to encourage further commercial activity. However, President Arthur and Frelinghuysen appear to have ignored his efforts. Persia is renamed Iran on March 21, 1935.

February 22, 1883

Congressional legislation is passed to repay Japan the indemnity awarded America for the Shimonoseki incident of 1864.

Because a Japanese noble had fired on a joint Western naval force and an American ship at Shimonoseki in 1860, the Western nations received an indemnity from Japan. The U.S. share was $785,000.87, an amount that Congress on February 22 voted to return to Tokyo because Japan had been forced to pay this damage claim under duress.

See September 23, 1864, and June 25, 1866.

March 3, 1883

The Tariff of 1883 retains protectionist principles.

In 1882, as often happened after 1866, politicians talked about lowering the tariffs to help reduce American consumer costs of both European imports and American manufactured goods. For example, a McCormick Company reaper produced in Galena, Illinois, cost the Illinois farmer $210 as a result of the American protective duties. McCormick sold the same reaper in England for $100 to meet the competitive free-market prices of Great Britain. This was one type of complaint by U.S. farmers' organizations between 1870 and 1900, as they advocated lower tariffs.

Because of tariff reform agitation, President Arthur appointed a nine-man Tariff Commission on May 14, 1882, to obtain recommendations for lowering the nation's tariff duties. On December 4, 1882, the commission recommended a variety of substantial tariff reductions that its report appeared fully to justify.

Nevertheless, the commission proposal was not adhered to by Congress in drawing up the Tariff Act of 1883. Neither congressmen nor the business interests they represented showed any willingness to accept significant reductions in tariffs that affected them. Consequently, tariff protectionism continued. While the general duty average dropped 5% in the 1883 bill, tariff rates continued to be between 35% and 40% on most items.

U.S. Salutes Foreign Ships with Peashooters. The obsolete ships of the U.S. Navy drew ridicule and satire from those who desired a modern fleet. *Harper's Weekly*, 1881.

March 3, 1883

Congress authorizes the building of a modern "steel" navy.

In 1881, a naval board reported to Congress that the U.S. navy ranked 12th among the world's naval powers. It recommended the gradual elimination of obsolete wooden ships held over from the Civil War and the construction of steel cruisers.

On March 3, 1883, Congress authorized the building of three steel cruisers. The building of a "new" navy was further enhanced in 1886.

See August 3, 1886.

June 30, 1883

The United States notifies Great Britain that the fisheries section of the 1871 Treaty of Washington will be terminated in two years, as of July 1, 1885.

The Treaty of 1871 permitted abrogation of the fishery clauses upon two years' prior notice. The U.S. government had been dissatisfied with the large award given to Canada by the Halifax Commission in November 1877 and with British reluctance to pay reparations in the Newfoundland incident of January 1878. Therefore, Congress recommended and President Arthur agreed to end the fishery treaty in 1885.

For the consequences of this revocation, see March 3, 1887. Also see June 15, 1877, and June 2, 1881.

October 20, 1883

The Treaty of Ancon ends the War of the Pacific between Chile and Peru.

The U.S. role in this war grew less after the Trescot mission ended on January 26, 1882. The new U.S. minister to Chile, Cornelius A. Logan, played a small role in persuading Chile to moderate its demands and to bring Peru to new peace discussions. Nevertheless, the internal conditions within the two warring nations motivated their peace treaty.

By the Treaty of Ancon, Chile obtained Tarapaca and possessed Tacna and Arica for 10 years. In 1893, a plebiscite in these provinces would be conducted to determine their future status. The plebiscite never took place, however, and this dispute continued into the 20th century. Bolivia did not sign a truce with Chile until April 4, 1884.

1884

April 4, 1884

Chile and Bolivia sign the Truce of Valparaiso.

This agreement provided for the cessation of hostilities for an indefinite period. Bolivia lost TARAPACA and its only access to a seaport as well as the province of Atacama. Later, in 1892, Chile afforded Bolivia the use of a railway from Antofagasta to Oruro, which gave Bolivia access to the Pacific coast. A peace treaty to end the War of the Pacific was signed on October 20, 1904.

June 6, 1884

France gains control over all of northern Vietnam by the Treaty of Hue.

This treaty completed France's gradual expansion over Vietnam. After gaining protectorship over Cambodia on August 11, 1863, the French explored and conquered the region of the Mekong River. They captured Hanoi on the Red River in 1874 but temporarily evacuated the city. An insurrection in Hanoi in 1882 brought back French forces, which reconquered Hanoi as well as the entire provinces of Tonkin and Annam. In the Treaty of Hue, native rulers recognized French control over their territory.

Although the Chinese contested French authority in Tonkin, the French defeated China in a brief Sino-French war in 1885. China conceded French authority over Indochina by the Treaty of Tientsin on June 9, 1885. The French later occupied Laos in 1893.

July 5, 1884

Congress tightens American restrictions on Chinese immigration.

Many Americans in the Far Western states were dissatisfied with previous laws on Chinese immigration and promoted attempts fully to exclude Orientals. During the presidential campaign of 1884, Chinese exclusion became a critical issue, and Congress decided to amend the act of May 6, 1882. The new law strengthened exclusion by defining "laborer" to include "hucksters, peddlers, drying or preserving shells or fish for any type of consumption." The law also required that Chinese who lived in America before 1882 but returned to visit China must obtain a visa from a U.S. consul *before* leaving China to return to America. This law of Congress kept the letter but not the spirit of the U.S. treaties with China of 1868 and 1880.

November 4, 1884

Grover Cleveland is elected President, the first Democrat since James Buchanan won office in 1856.

The Republican Convention at Chicago had nominated James G. BLAINE for president on June 6. The reform "Mugwump" Republicans rejected Blaine's candidacy, and many of them supported the Democratic candidate, Grover Cleveland. The campaign of 1884 became known as perhaps the filthiest in U.S. history. The Democrats catalogued Blaine's corrupt political bossism in detail; the Republicans charged that Cleveland had fathered an illegitimate child, a charge Cleveland admitted.

Because of the close election margin, Blaine believed his failure to disavow a follower who criticized the Catholic Church cost him the vote of Irish Catholics in New York, where he lost the state by only 1,149 votes. The electoral vote was Cleveland 219 and Blaine 182. New York's electoral vote would have given Blaine the victory.

December 6, 1884

In renewing the American-Hawaiian Reciprocity Treaty, the United States secures a base at Pearl Harbor.

The treaty of 1884 renewed the agreement of January 30, 1875, but added one significant clause. The new article gave America the exclusive right to enter the harbor of Pearl River and establish a naval coaling and repair station. Hawaii accepted this article as a means for gaining the two-thirds Senate majority necessary to renew the commercial reciprocity treaty. Secretary of State Bayard assured Hawaii that the base would be required only during the seven-year term of the treaty. With the addition of the naval base agreement, the Senate ratified the treaty on January 20, 1887.

December 10, 1884

A Nicaraguan treaty granting America exclusive canal rights is presented to the Senate; it is not ratified.

Secretary of State Frelinghuysen decided to send a canal treaty with Nicaragua to the Senate because he failed to obtain British concessions to revise the Clayton-Bulwer Treaty. Like Blaine in 1881, Frelinghuysen had tried in 1882 to convince Great Britain to agree to change the 1850 treaty. Frelinghuysen introduced the new argument that the 1850 treaty's intent was to obtain British capital to pay for the canal, a consideration that, he said, did not apply in 1882. The British would not accept this unique argument and refused to negotiate.

Consequently, in 1884 Frelinghuysen undertook negotiations for canal rights with Nicaragua's minister to the United States, Joaquin ZAVALA. They concluded a treaty on December 1 that gave America the exclusive rights over a Nicaraguan canal. The United States was granted a 2.5-mile-wide strip of land for the canal. In addition, the two countries would form a "perpetual alliance" by which America would protect Nicaraguan territory.

President Arthur quickly sent the Frelinghuysen-Zavala treaty to the U.S. Senate, which rejected it on January 29, 1885, by a vote of 32 to 23. The senators argued that the treaty violated the Clayton-Bulwer Treaty and that the "perpetual alliance" could not be accepted.

On February 23, the Senate voted to reconsider the treaty, but following his presidential inauguration, President Grover Cleveland withdrew the treaty. Cleveland strongly objected to the alliance clause of the treaty.

December 22, 1884

Reciprocal trade treaties with Spain and Santo Domingo are sent to Congress—Frelinghuysen's substitution of treaties for tariff reductions fails.

Secretary of State Frelinghuysen argued that bilateral trade agreements to reduce tariffs were preferable to legislation to reduce tariffs. Thus, in 1883 and 1884, he signed tariff reciprocity treaties with Mexico, Santo Domingo, and Spain. Although Congress rejected the Mexican treaty in March 1884, the secretary pursued his concept by negotiating treaties with Spain and Santo Domingo.

The Spanish treaty related to imports of sugar and tobacco from Cuba and Puerto Rico; the Dominican treaty related to sugar. As proposed in the treaty, these products would enter the United States free of duty. In return, American agricultural and industrial products would be duty-free in the two Spanish colonies and Santo Domingo.

Frelinghuysen had not, however, persuaded other politicians to accept his policy. The Spanish treaty was withdrawn from the Senate by President Cleveland on March 13, 1885. The Dominican treaty was never acted on. Thus, the attempt to replace tariff reform with reciprocal treaties did not succeed during the 1880s.

1885

February 26, 1885

America participates in the Berlin Conference on the Congo.

Germany and France arranged the multinational conference at Berlin to discuss commercial privileges in the Congo River region of central Africa. The United States became involved largely through the efforts of Colonel Henry S. SANFORD, a former Florida real estate speculator who had become an agent for King Leopold II of Belgium in his schemes to exploit the Congo. In November 1883, Sanford visited Washington, where he talked about the Congo with the Republican leadership. Subsequently, on April 22, 1884, the United States became one of the first governments to recognize the International Association of the Congo as a territorial power. This association consisted of a group of European companies that had organized to develop the commercial potential of central Africa. It was financed especially by Leopold II of Belgium.

Because the United States recognized the association, it was one of 14 states invited to the Berlin meeting. For the American delegation, Frelinghuysen appointed John A. KASSON, the U.S. minister to Germany, as head of the delegation. The other members were Colonel Sanford and Henry M. STANLEY, the newsman who "discovered" David Livingston after a famous search through the jungles of Africa in 1869. The secretary of state instructed Kasson to work for "unrestricted freedom of trade" in the Congo but to avoid interference in European politics, two orders difficult to reconcile.

Nevertheless, when the Berlin Conference adjourned on February 26, Kasson believed he had achieved these goals. The General Act issued by the conference provided free trade and neutrality for both the Congo and Niger River basins, abolished slavery and the slave trade, and set standards for the colonial occupation of territory. Shortly after the conference, the International Association of the Congo was recognized as the Congo Free State by the European powers.

See May 2, 1885.

March 6, 1885

Thomas F. Bayard is appointed secretary of state by President Cleveland.

Bayard was a Delaware lawyer who had been a senator from 1869 to 1886 and a potential Democratic Party presidential nominee since 1876. His appointment as secretary principally reflected his high standing in the Democratic Party. Bayard, like Cleveland, often spoke in moralistic terms that cloaked his real concern for the national interest and successful party politics.

March 27, 1885

At the conclusion of a Paris conference of Egypt, Great Britain has gained an understanding with Germany on North Africa and Samoa in the South Pacific.

Following its military intervention against Egyptian nationalists on September 15, 1882, Great Britain had military difficulties in the Nile valley as well as diplomatic issues with France and Germany between 1882 and 1888.

Problems arose in the Sudan when a new uprising occurred against Britain and Egypt's khedive. Led by an alleged Arab prophet, the Mahdi Mohammed AHMED, the Muslims in the Sudan fought several successful battles prior to the Mahdi Ahmed's death on June 21, 1885.

Diplomatically, the British sought international aid to refinance the khedive's loans and the war against the Mahdi. In 1884, Great Britain held an international conference during which the European powers were asked to reduce their interest on Egypt's loans. Opposition from the Franco-German entente prevented the success of the conference. Chancellor Bismarck of Germany and French Premier Jules Ferry frustrated England's plans because France hoped to regain control in Egypt and agreed to support Bismarck in East Africa against the British.

Hardly had the London Conference ended on August 2, 1884, than the British moved toward calling a second conference to solve their Egyptian problems. The conference became a necessity after January 26, 1885, when the Mahdi Ahmed captured Khartoum, a city located on the lower Nile River, where both French and British interests were concerned. The French conducted the 1885 sessions at Paris since Premier Ferry sought to advance his role as a European leader.

The Paris Conference brought limited success to England, but not France. The conferees agreed on March 27 to reduce the khedive's interest rates, but at French insistence a new loan was floated under international control. More significantly in the long term, the British completed an agreement with Germany that served to erode the Franco-German entente of 1884 and reconciled London and Berlin.

The Anglo-German entente settled friction between the two states in East Africa and Samoa as well as Egypt. The Germans supported England in Egypt in exchange for British aid in East Africa and the South Pacific, especially Samoa. The results of this understanding influenced U.S.-German relations in Samoa. In Egypt, England gained sufficient support to challenge France and reach more substantial control over the Suez Canal on October 29, 1888.

See June 25, 1887.

March 30, 1885

A Russian attack on Afghanistan forces in Penjdeh nearly causes war with Great Britain.

Located at a strategic juncture between Persia, India, and Tibet, Afghanistan was of great concern to the British, who considered it as a buffer zone between South Asia and Russia. The war was avoided in 1885 by a Russo-British agreement in which the czar's government formally accepted Afghanistan as a neutral region separating the two great European powers.

April 18, 1885

China and Japan agree that both nations will withdraw their troops from Korea.

The Convention of Tientsin was signed by Prince Hirobumi Ito of Japan and Li Hung-chang, China's viceroy in Seoul. This was a victory for Japan because China heretofore had claimed sole protectorship over Korea and excluded foreign powers' internal intervention.

May 2, 1885

Leopold II, King of Belgium, becomes ruler of the Congo Free State in Central Africa.

This African colony had been built as a personal enterprise of Leopold II. During the next 20 years, Leopold became notorious for his merciless treatment of the native population in the Congo.

November 13, 1885

Serbia declares war on Bulgaria.

Another round in the perennial problems of the Balkans from 1870 to 1914 began when Serbia attacked Bulgaria because it feared the loss of territory in Macedonia. On September 18, 1885, Bulgaria had assumed control over Eastern Roumelia, and Serbia believed Bulgaria planned to expand further. A temporary peace between Serbia and Bulgaria was signed in the Treaty of Bucharest on March 3, 1886. Nevertheless, the incident demonstrated to Great Britain a need to try to resolve problems in the Balkans before such quarrels escalated into Russian intervention on behalf of Bulgaria.

See February 12, 1887.

The World's Plunderers. The rapacious act of European imperialism draws the scorn of an American cartoonist. *Harper's Weekly*, 1885

1886

January 1, 1886

The British annex all of Upper Burma.

By this action, Great Britain gained control of all Burma, a status that the Chinese recognized in a convention with Great Britain on July 24, 1886. By the agreement, Burma preserved its trade with China by continuing decennial tribute missions to Peking. In all other respects, Great Britain controlled Burma as a colony of its empire.

April 29, 1886

President Cleveland recommends to the Senate an extradition treaty with Japan.

His treaty was sent to the Senate shortly before the European powers began a treaty revision conference with Japan. Because of the U.S. treaty of 1878 and other independent American policies toward Japan, the United States had only an indirect influence on the conferences led by Great Britain to discuss tariff agreements and give Japan an equal status among the world powers. The revision process was hampered during the 1880s and 1890s because Japan slowly increased its demands against the European nations and America.

The April 29 treaty with America provided for the end of provisions of extraterritoriality as well as for the mutual exchange of criminals who had fled to either of the two treaty nations. The U.S. Senate approved the treaty with amendments on June 21, 1886. Japan accepted the amendments, which were minor changes in phrasing, and the treaty was proclaimed on November 3, 1886.

August 3, 1886

Congress provides for additional steel naval vessels, enabling Secretary of the Navy William C. Whitney to initiate a beneficial naval reorganization.

Secretary Whitney used his four-year term of office to realign the navy's bureaucracy for a modern naval force and to obtain the construction or authorization for 22 new steel ships. Whitney aligned the navy program with American steelmakers, which encouraged the industry to obtain contracts for the heavy ship plates and huge naval guns used by the modern navy. Whitney set a program in motion that continued for the next 20 years and gave the United States the third-largest navy in the world by 1900.

1887

January 9, 1887

The British protest American seizure of Canadian pelagic sealing ships: beginning of fur seal controversy.

On January 9, Lord Sackville-West, the British minister to America, told Secretary Bayard that the British government could not condone the seizure of three British Columbian sealing schooners by revenue cutters of the U.S. Treasury Department.

Upon investigating the incident, Bayard learned that the Treasury Department claimed the ships were killing fur seals in Alaskan territorial waters and that the Treasury Department ships had begun in 1886 seriously to enforce restrictions against pelagic sealing, that is, against killing seals as they swam in the ocean rather than when ashore. This Canadian practice developed after 1880 because the value of seals for fur increased and the United States restricted the killing of seals on the Pribilof Islands to the Alaska Commercial Company.

The sealing business began to develop after the United States acquired Alaska in 1867. The seals congregated on the four small Pribilof Islands to breed between May and November of each year. To save the fur seal herd, Congress had in 1870 granted the Alaska Commercial Company a 20-year lease of the islands in return for rental payments and royalties on the sealskins used. In addition, the company agreed to slaughter no more than 100,000 male seals each year and only on land. This company monopoly prospered as the price per skin quadrupled by 1880. The restricted killings also enabled the herd to flourish.

The Alaskan company's prosperity also generated competition. By 1880, not only Canadians but sealers from Germany, Norway, Sweden, Japan, Great Britain, France, and Russia began killing seals in the North Pacific. Since the Pribilof Islands were off-limits to foreign sealers, these nations had to harpoon or shoot the seals at sea. This was a wasteful tactic because almost half of the seals shot in the water could not be recovered and female as well as male seals were indiscriminately killed.

To protect the seals and the Alaskan company monopoly and its payments to the U.S. Treasury, U.S. customs ships began seizing all ships in the vicinity of the Pribilofs. The Treasury Department acted on the basis that the Bering Sea was mare clausum, a sea closed to foreign ships, just as Chesapeake Bay would be.

Neither the Canadians nor their mentors, the British, recognized the American right to close the Bering Sea or to seize ships beyond a three-mile limit of Alaskan waters. Sackville-West's protest of January 9, 1877, exemplified the international problem not only about who owned the sealing areas around the Pribilofs but also about how to restrict the seal hunt to preserve the seals' existence. Secretary of State Bayard decided in August 1887 to call for an international meeting to resolve the seal question. After Canada refused to cooperate in this conference, the U.S. Congress authorized the president to seize any vessels in the Bering Sea.

See March 2, 1889.

February 8, 1887

Indian tribes are no longer recognized as legal entities as a result of the Dawes Severalty Act.

Prior to this act of Congress, Americans had since the earliest colonial days dealt with Indian tribes as if they were foreign nations with whom treaties were negotiated or war was necessary to force acceptance of a treaty. The Dawes Act ended this practice, and the United States preferred to deal with the Indians as individuals thereafter. Thus, the act divided the tribal lands among individual Indian members, 160 acres per family and 80 acres per single adult. The Indians could not dispose of their land until after 25 years, when their ownership would become unrestricted.

February 12, 1887

The British sign the first of a series of agreements on the Mediterranean with Italy, Austria, and Spain.

These agreements supported British control of the Mediterranean against French and Russian interests by securing the cooperation of other Mediterranean nations. The agreements consisted of an exchange of notes among the four nations during the spring of 1887.

The notes provided for the status quo in the Adriatic, Aegean, Black, and Mediterranean Seas. Austria and England declared their mutual interests in the Near East; Spain and Italy accepted British protection of Egypt and the Suez; England supported Italy and Spain in separate parts of North Africa. In sum, the British established a Mediterranean policy to reinforce their naval authority in the face of threats from Russia in the Aegean and Black Seas and France in the eastern Mediterranean and Egypt.

On December 12, a second series of notes between Britain, Austria, and Italy again provided for the status quo in the Near East, by agreeing that Turkey should not cede any privileges to Russia in Bulgaria or the straits between the Black and Aegean Seas.

February 20, 1887

Germany, Italy, and Austria renew the Triple Alliance.

Some changes in the original alliance of 1882 were necessary in 1887 to recognize Italy's concern for help against France in North Africa. Germany agreed on the status quo in the Near East, except that Austria could annex Bosnia and Herzegovina if it desired.

The Triple Alliance was further solidified by a German-Italian military agreement of January 28, 1888, in which Italy would aid Germany in case of a Franco-German war.

March 3, 1887

The northeast fisheries dispute with Canada causes Congress to empower the President to bar Canadian ships, fish, or other products from American ports.

The act of Congress that President Cleveland signed on March 3 resulted from Canadian interference with American fishermen throughout 1886.

Following the U.S. termination on July 1, 1885, of the 1871 fishery agreement, Secretary of State Bayard and the British agreed to continue the agreement on a modus vivendi until the start of the next fishing season in March 1886. After that time, however, the Canadians lost their duty-free importation of fish into the United States and, in retaliation, Canadian police boats vigorously enforced laws prohibiting U.S. fishing in Canadian waters by seizing U.S. ships that violated the laws. The U.S. fishermen in New England protested, but attempts to settle the question did not prove satisfactory.

Therefore, Congress decided to act to more strictly prohibit Canadian commercial activity on the eastern coast of America. This dispute became further complicated by an Anglo-American-Canadian dispute over the fur seals in the Pribilof Islands of the Bering Sea, a dispute that paralleled the fishery problem. Because of these dual problems, Cleveland did not immediately enforce the act of March 3, 1887, seeking instead to resolve the problem in negotiations that began with Britain on November 22, 1887.

For the results of these talks, see February 15, 1888.

June 18, 1887

Germany and Russia sign the Reinsurance Treaty.

This treaty was Chancellor Bismarck's attempt to retain close relations between Berlin and St. Petersburg. The Three Emperors' League had provided these relations until 1886, when Austria refused to renew the agreement because of disputes with the czar in southeast Europe. Therefore, to preserve Germany's tie to Russia, Bismarck obtained the secret treaty of June 18. This agreement promised the neutrality of either nation in the event that the other went to war with a third nation.

June 25, 1887

A Washington conference convenes to attempt to end a crisis in Samoa, but the delegates fail to agree.

The conference delegates were Secretary of State Thomas Bayard and the German and British ministers to the United States: Frederick von Alvensleben and Sir Lionel Sackville-West. Bayard requested the meeting as a means for solving problems among the three governments in Samoa.

Since January 17, 1878, when the United States obtained Pago Pago as a naval station, disputes among Germany, England, and the United States had grown in Samoa, owing largely to German demands. In 1879, the consuls of the three nations with interest in Samoa agreed to form a council to regulate the town of Apia, the center of foreign activity. Although unauthorized to do so, the American consul cooperated with the British and Germans.

By 1885, however, the German consul disliked the anti-German attitude of local native chiefs and decided to assert German control over Apia. German forces seized Apia and the Mulinuu peninsula, and forced King Malietoa to sign a treaty accepting a German-Samoan administration.

The British government backed the Germans' Samoan action in return for German support against France in Egypt. This fact, combined with assurances that the Germans would not disturb American rights in the islands, led Bayard and Cleveland to avoid a conflict in 1885.

The status quo did not last in Samoa, however. The Germans encouraged a rebellion against Malietoa by chief Tamasese. They also raised the German flag in Apia and did not permit Malietoa's flag to fly. As a result, in May 1886, Malietoa invoked the U.S. treaty of 1878 and asked the U.S. consul in Samoa, Berthold Greenebaum, for assistance. Greenebaum reacted quickly and without authorization from Washington. He raised the U.S. flag over Samoa's public buildings and proclaimed Samoa was under American protection.

On June 1, 1887, Secretary Bayard learned of Greenebaum's action in Samoa and quickly disavowed it to the German minister. Bayard proposed that the present consuls of all three countries in Samoa should be recalled and that Germany, Great Britain, and the United States should send delegates to Washington to end the crisis. Thus, on June 25, 1887, the Washington Conference began.

A month of meetings by the three delegates in Washington brought no solution to the Samoan problem. The United States desired to retain genuine Samoan autonomy by recognition of King Malietoa and his local assembly as the sole authority in the island and by adding three foreign advisers to serve on the king's council. Von Alvensleben proposed recognition of Tamasese as king to serve with an adviser appointed by the power with the largest material interest in Samoa: Germany.

The U.S. and German positions were so far apart that an impasse resulted. Secretary Bayard suggested that the conference adjourn for several months, and the Germans and British agreed. Soon after, however, the Germans took aggressive action in Samoa to enforce their solution on the local population of the island.

See August 19, 1887, and October 11, 1887.

August 19, 1887

The Germans use force to gain control of Samoa.

The unwillingness of Secretary Bayard to accept German authority over Malietoa's government led the Germans to use direct action against the Samoan king. On August 19, four German warships arrived at Apia; after King Malietoa rejected their demands for political rights, they declared war on Samoa and landed 100 marines. Malietoa fled to the bush but later surrendered and was deported by the Germans. The rebel chieftain King Tamasese took power, but real control of the island passed to the king's adviser, a German appointee named Brandeis.

According to the report of Harold M. Sewall, U.S. consul at Apia, Malietoa was much loved by the Samoan population. Tamasese, the local renegade who received German support, was as unpopular as the Germans. As Sewall described Malietoa's deportation on October 10, 1887, it was a day of mourning in Samoa. The local chiefs were "all in tears" as they held their last talks with the king. Then, "as Malietoa walked to the wharf large crowds of people followed, crying and clinging to him as if they could not give him up."

For the official U.S. reaction to the German aggression, see October 11, 1887.

October 11, 1887

Secretary Bayard orders strict U.S. neutrality in the German aggression against Samoa.

Apparently Samoa was so far away, and the plight of the Samoan people who detested the Germans was so little felt in Washington in 1887, that Secretary Bayard and Cleveland agreed for more than a year to do little to oppose Germany's disregard for the U.S. policies expressed at the Washington Conference.

On October 11, Bayard informed Harold Sewall in Apia to preserve U.S. neutrality and sent the same message to G. H. Pendleton, the U.S. minister to Berlin. Bayard proposed the election of a new king in Samoa, but Chancellor Bismarck informed Pendleton that Tamasese was a newly elected king. Pendleton had been instructed to protest Germany's "unaccountable proceedings." The United States also sent a warship, the USS *Adams,* to Apia on October 20, 1887, but took no further action until news of a native rebellion against Germany that began on September 4, 1888, caused a crisis in German-American relations leading to a new conference.

See February 5, 1889.

1888

February 15, 1888

The Bayard-Chamberlain Treaty on fishing rights is signed.

This treaty developed from discussions of a British-American commission whose work began on November 22, 1887. The U.S. delegates were Secretary of State Bayard, William PUTNAM of Maine, and James B. ANGELL, former U.S. minister to China. The British representatives were Colonial Secretary Joseph CHAMBERLAIN, Canadian Finance Minister Charles TUPPER, and the British minister to America, Sir Lionel S. SACKVILLE-WEST.

The treaty of February 15 provided that Americans could fish in Canadian bays and waters and granted fishermen's rights and duties in the inland waters. Article XV stated that if the U.S. Congress granted Canadians duty-free fish sales, the Americans would be allowed to buy supplies, trans-ship catches, and board new crews in Canada's inshore waters: rights greatly desired by U.S. fishermen.

The stroke of genius in the 1888 negotiations came from Joseph Chamberlain. Fearing that the U.S. Senate, which Cleveland's Republican opposition controlled, would not ratify the treaty, Chamberlain requested and Bayard approved a modus vivendi to accompany the treaty. This agreement said that for two years pending ratification of the treaty, Americans who purchased annual licenses could enter Canadian waters and use the three privileges spelled out in Article XV. If necessary, this modus could be renewed after two years.

Chamberlain's foresight proved to be invaluable in settling the fishery issue. As he expected, the Republican Senate defeated the treaty on August 21, 1888, by a vote of 27 to 30. Nevertheless, the proffered licenses of the modus vivendi worked. U.S. fishermen willingly bought them, and after the first two years the agreement was extended every two years until 1912, when a permanent settlement of the dispute was achieved.

March 12, 1888

U.S. Treaty with China excludes Chinese laborers from immigration for 20 years; the U.S. pays China an indemnity for the deaths of Chinese in America.

Throughout the 1880s and 1890s Chinese immigration and labor continued to be an issue in the Western states of America. In 1885, anti-Chinese riots in Rock Springs, Wyoming, and Tacoma and Seattle, Washington, resulted in deaths and injuries to several Chinese. The Chinese government promptly demanded that the U.S. government indemnify China for these incidents. Congress, however, was reluctant to grant President Cleveland funds to pay any Chinese claim.

In 1887, when the United States asked China to accept a new immigration treaty, the Chinese refused to do so unless Washington paid the Chinese damage claims. The Americans agreed, and the treaty of 1888 contained two major portions: one provided that the United States would indemnify China $276,619.75 for the property and lives harmed in the anti-Chinese riots; the second provided that China would accept a 20-year prohibition on the immigration of Chinese laborers to America.

The 1888 treaty was never ratified. The U.S. Senate insisted on an amendment to prohibit the return to America of 20,000 Chinese residents who had gone to visit China. The treaty of 1880 was not renewed until March 17, 1894, when China accepted another 10-year suspension on the immigration of Chinese laborers.

May 10, 1888

A pan-American conference is authorized by an act of Congress.

This congressional resolution was a belated reaction to James G. Blaine's invitation of November 29, 1881, to conduct an inter-American conference in Washington. After Secretary Frelinghuysen withdrew the invitation in August 1882, President Arthur agreed to have a special commission investigate the potential for a future conference. On December 31, 1884, the special commission reported in favor of a conference, advising that all countries except Chile favored such a meeting.

Although President Cleveland was not enthusiastic about such a conference, enough Democrats joined Republicans to approve the act of May 10, 1888. Secretary of State Bayard followed this law by sending invitations in July 1889, asking 18 Latin American states to attend the conference in 1889. Eventually, only Santo Domingo refused to attend.

See October 2, 1889.

October 21, 1888

The "Murchison" letter of British Minister Sackville-West damages Grover Cleveland's presidential campaign.

Lord Sackville-West wrote a private letter to "Charles F. Murchison," a pseudonym for George Osgoodby, who claimed to be a former Englishman naturalized as an American citizen. "Murchison" wrote to Sackville-West for advice on how to vote in the Cleveland-Harrison election of 1888. The British minister replied in favor of a vote for Cleveland.

Sackville-West had blundered into Osgoodby's trap. Osgoodby was a Republican who had written to both Sackville-West and Sir Charles Tupper to solicit their attitude on Cleveland. When Sackville-West responded, Osgoodby sent the letter to Republican

The Real British Lion. A cartoonist plays on the American's widespread anti-British feelings in the 1880s and 1890s. *New York Evening World*, 1895

leaders, who published it in many U.S. newspapers on October 21.

The British minister's letter hurt Cleveland's campaign because Anglophobia had been heightened in 1887–1888 by the fishery and Bering Sea controversies with Canada and Great Britain, in addition to the usual Irish sentiment against England. Although President Cleveland immediately declared Sackville-West persona non grata and gave him his passports on October 24, the damage had been done to Cleveland's reelection hopes. The earlier Republican charges that Cleveland had bowed to the British flag in the disputes with Canada seemed to have been verified. Cleveland lost in particular the Irish-American vote in New York, the state whose electoral vote largely enabled Benjamin Harrison to win on November 6, 1888.

October 29, 1888

The Suez Canal convention is signed.

At a conference at Istanbul, the major European powers agreed on operations of the Suez Canal. The canal would be open to merchant and war vessels in time of war and peace and would not be blockaded. The British remained free, however, to use their forces to maintain order in Egypt and the Sudan. Although the French continued to try to exert influence in Egypt, the British gradually asserted sufficient strength to end the role of France in most Egyptian affairs and to recapture the Sudan.

November 6, 1888

Benjamin Harrison is elected President, defeating Grover Cleveland in a close race.

The Democratic Convention nominated Cleveland for reelection on June 5, having proposed lower tariffs as the key issue in the campaign. The Republican Convention on June 19 selected Benjamin Harrison, whose platform was the retention of a protective tariff and Civil War veterans' pensions as contained in a bill that Cleveland had vetoed. Other nominees were Alson Streeter for the Union Labor Party, Robert H. Cowdrey for the United Labor Party, and Clinton B. Fisk of the Prohibition Party. During the campaign, the "Murchison" letter of British Minister Sackville-West created an Irish reaction against Cleveland and influenced many votes in the key state of New York (see October 21, 1888). In the election results, Cleveland received 5,540,050 popular votes to Harrison's 5,444,337. By carrying New York and Indiana, Harrison earned the most electoral votes, winning by 233 to 168. The other three presidential nominees received a total of 399,830 popular votes.

1889

February 5, 1889

President Cleveland accepts Bismarck's offer to settle the Samoan crisis at a conference in Berlin.

A German-American crisis occurred in January 1889, because Germans in Samoa seized an American boat during a native uprising.

Germany's assertion of control under Governor Brandeis and King Tamasese in August 1887 had never been popular with Samoan natives. Subsequently, on September 4, 1888, a Samoan chief named Mataafa led a rebellion against the government.

To suppress the rebels in December 1888, a German force landed at Fangolili near Apia but was ambushed by the rebels. Twenty Germans died and 30 were wounded in a disastrous attack. The Germans struck back quickly. German warships shelled the Samoan coast, burning and destroying property with no regard for ownership. Eventually an American boat became involved. The U.S. vice consul in Apia wired Washington: "Americans in boat flying American flag seized in Apia Harbor by armed German boat, but released. Admiral with squadron necessary immediately."

U.S. Marines guard the American consul's quarters during the Samoan crisis. National Archives

The consul's cable about the incident reached America on January 5, and on January 12 the Navy Department dispatched Rear Admiral Lewis A. Kimberley to Samoa aboard the flagship *Trenton* to join up with the *Nipsic* and *Vandalia* in Samoa. On January 15, Cleveland submitted news of the affair to Congress, asserting that German activity in Samoa was "inconsistent with every prior agreement or understanding" made with the United States.

On February 27, Congress appropriated $500,000 to protect U.S. interests in Samoa and $100,000 to build an effective naval base at Pago Pago. By the end of February, however, the crisis had calmed. Germany did not want war with America, especially not in the Pacific. On January 21, Bismarck invited Britain and the United States to meet in Berlin to settle the Samoan problem. On February 5, President Cleveland agreed.

For earlier events, see October 11, 1887; for the conference results, see June 14, 1889.

March 2, 1889

President Cleveland signs legislation claiming U.S. jurisdiction over the Bering Sea and the right to arrest pelagic sealers who violated the area.

Asserting a claim that was not recognized by international law and practice, this legislation resulted from a sealing dispute with Canada that began on January 9, 1877. Subsequently, the attempt to hold an international conference on sealing had failed because Canada refused to cooperate. Throughout 1888, the United States did not arrest any sealers, but the intensified American feelings against Britain and Canada during the presidential campaign of 1888 caused Congress to consider some method for combatting the Canadian "slaughter of fur seals."

On March 22, 1889, President Benjamin Harrison, as required by the law of March 2, warned all sealers that any pelagic sealers entering U.S. dominions "in the waters of the Bering Sea" would be liable to arrest. This American declaration led to a serious crisis with Great Britain that peaked during March 1890, before a modus vivendi was agreed to in 1891.

See June 15, 1891.

March 5, 1889

James G. Blaine is commissioned as secretary of state by President Harrison.

In his note requesting Blaine to accept this office, Harrison stated his desire to emphasize a policy to improve relations with Central and South America during his term of office. This suited Blaine personally because it would fulfill an objective he had begun as secretary to President Garfield in 1881. Blaine served as Harrison's secretary of state until June 4, 1892.

May 31, 1889

A naval defense act is passed by the British Parliament.

Fearing the growing sea power of France and Russia, Lord Salisbury's ministry recommended and Parliament approved a two-power naval standard; that is, the British fleet would be as strong as the fleets of the two next-strongest naval powers. During the 1890s, however, Germany, not France or Russia, became the power with which Great Britain had to compete in naval expansion.

June 14, 1889

The United States, Germany, and Great Britain resolve the Samoan crisis: The General Act of Berlin is signed.

Following the February 5 decision to meet at Berlin, all developments led to a relatively simple resolution of the Samoan problem. Even a natural disaster, a devastating hurricane that hit Apia in March 1889, forged an emotional bond that helped the competing powers settle their difficulties. During the hurricane, three German and three American warships at Samoa were destroyed, and only one British ship in Apia survived. Among the 150 persons killed in the disaster were 49 Americans.

The delegates at the Berlin conference were, for America, John A. Kasson, George H. Bates, and William W. Phelps; for Germany, Count Herbert Bismarck (the chancellor's son), Baron Frederick von Holstein, and Dr. Richard Kravel; for Britain, Sir Edward Malet, Charles S. Scott, and Joseph Crowe.

The conference convened on April 29, 1889, and by June 14 had agreed on treaty terms as follows:

1. King Malietoa was restored.
2. The Apia council used from 1879 to 1887 would be restored to include the king, a Samoan chairman, and one representative from each of the three foreign powers.
3. The three powers would also appoint a chief justice of Samoa to settle disputes about the status of the king of Samoa or between the king and one of the three powers.

In effect, the United States joined a three-nation protectorate over Samoa. This was the first time in its history that the United States helped govern an overseas people.

While the Berlin agreement provided commercial equality for the three powers in Samoa, it did not give autonomy to the Samoan government. The chief justice appointed for Samoa had wide legal authority over the island. Thus foreigners controlled all land titles, taxes, and the municipal government of Apia. Finally, Chief Mataafa, who led the rebellion against German control, was not eligible to become king of Samoa even if the natives preferred his leadership.

October 2, 1889

The first international American conference (Pan-American Conference) convenes in Washington.

Thirty-seven delegates representing 18 American states met together to discuss commercial treaties and arbitration procedures for settling future disputes. Ten delegates represented the United States including the delegation head, John B. HENDERSON, and two captains of American industry, Clement STUDEBAKER and Andrew CARNEGIE.

Secretary Blaine welcomed the delegates in a rousing speech. He indicated his hope that the meeting would establish a basis for confidence, respect, and friendship among the American nations and foster peace and understanding in future relations so that "friendship and not force, the spirit of just law and not the violence of the mob, should be the recognized rule of administration between the American nations and in American nations."

Blaine then invited the delegates to travel on a special train for a tour of 41 U.S. cities. The tour demonstrated the vastness of U.S. factories and their mechanical marvels. The delegates attended parades and saw the firing of a natural gas well during the 6,000-mile journey.

The delegates returned to Washington for more serious business on November 18, 1889. During the sessions, the delegates agreed on only one significant agenda item. Blaine's proposal for a customs union to end tariff barriers was replaced by a clause to promote reciprocity treaties. His advocacy of a system to arbitrate disputes failed because some delegates feared the United States would dominate the process. Finally, however, the delegates agreed to create the Pan-American Union to encourage cooperation among the American nations. In 1907, Carnegie donated funds to house the Pan-American Union in Washington, D.C.

1890

March 18, 1890

Bismarck is dismissed as Chancellor by Emperor William II of Germany.

Bismarck's dismissal influenced German policy because while he desired to retain good relations with Russia, William II wanted closer relations with Austria and Britain, both of whom sought to restrict Russian activity in southeastern Europe. The effects of Bismarck's dismissal were first seen June 18, when Germany refused to renew its Reinsurance Treaty of June 18, 1887, with the czar. Subsequently Russia, having lost all of its agreements with Germany, turned to France and developed an entente.

October 1, 1890

The McKinley Tariff ends previous reductions and stimulates gains for protectionists.

Throughout the 1880s, reformers demanded a lower tariff even though Congress reduced rates by only 5% between 1883 and 1889. When the tariff of 1890 was presented to Congress, Senator McKinley said it would lower tariff rates. During the next six months, however, the special-interest groups amended the bill, and by October 1, the approved tariffs were higher than before. In contrast to the average duties of 47% in 1869, the McKinley Tariff duties averaged 49.5%.

One section of the McKinley Tariff permitted the president to negotiate reciprocity agreements for certain commodities of other nations. For example, sugar and tropical products would be duty-free, provided that the countries exporting those products did not levy duties or other import fees on American agricultural and other export products.

1891

January 1, 1891

Civil war begins in Chile after President José Manuel Balmaceda announces he will extend the budget without congressional approval.

President Balmaceda undertook a series of reforms in Chile following his election in 1886. Gradually, however, his early supporters deserted his program and, after they gained control in Congress, refused to appropriate funds for the government's program. When the president tried to circumvent Congress by ruling by decree, a group known as the Congressionalists instituted a struggle to overthrow Balmaceda, whom they called a dictator.

See August 28, 1891.

March 3, 1891

Congress enacts legislation for copyrights to protect authors.

The copyright bill passed by Congress would protect authors from having their works issued by so-called pirates. Great Britain ignored a petition by 56 British authors for copyright protection. The law of 1891 did not fully protect American works from being pirated because many nations did not recognize the international copyright agreements.

March 31, 1891

The New Orleans "mafia" murders: Italy's Minister leaves Washington because his demands for redress are delayed.

A dispute between the United States and Italy occurred in 1891 because 11 Italians had been lynched by a New Orleans mob. The incident began when New Orleans police arrested 11 Italians for the murder of New Orleans Chief of Police David C. Hennessy. The chief had undertaken a concerted effort in 1890 to investigate, arrest, and punish members of the Sicilian Mafia who had arrived recently in New Orleans, where they practiced their habits of crime, vendettas, and murders, chiefly of fellow Sicilians. Hennessy's activity met with some success, an achievement that led to his murder in the fall of 1890.

Nineteen Italians had been indicted for Hennessy's murder, but in January 1891, six who had jury trials were acquitted or freed on technicalities. Because rumors circulated that the Mafia had intimidated jury members, a citizens' Committee of Fifty conducted its own inquiry. According to the subsequent committee report, evidence presented at the trial overwhelmingly indicated that the acquitted as well as those still awaiting trial were guilty.

The Committee of Fifty publicized its findings and called for a demonstration for justice on March 14, 1891. A mass meeting of 6,000 to 8,000 citizens formed, and after several speeches against the Mafia, they marched on the jailhouse. Because local police agreed with the mob, the jail was easily captured. The mob dragged out the prisoners and publicly lynched eleven of them.

In Italy the news of the lynching caused widespread expressions of outrage. The government instructed its U.S. minister, Baron Francesco Fava, to ask the United States to punish those guilty of the lynching immediately, to pay an indemnity, and to promise to protect all Italians in New Orleans. Secretary of State Blaine explained the U.S. federal legal system to Fava, telling him the State Department would instruct Louisiana Governor F. T. Nicholls to provide protection for the Italians.

Ten days later, Fava again saw Secretary of State Blaine, but few details of the events in New Orleans had reached Washington. Fava was upset at the delay and demanded "immediate" satisfaction from Blaine. When, on March 31, Blaine could report only that an investigation was underway but that no solution had resulted, Fava said he had been recalled as minister by Rome and was leaving the United States.

For the next 12 months, Italy had no diplomatic representative in Washington and relations cooled between the two nations. In Louisiana, a grand jury received information on the lynching, but no indictments were made and no one was ever brought to trial. In the late 19th century, lynchings were commonplace in the South, although usually they were against Black Americans, not Italians. Thus, the failure to prosecute lynchings was not unusual.

On April 12, 1892, Blaine sent Italy a note of regret and offered $24,330.90 for an indemnity to the families of the three Italian citizens who died in the New Orleans lynching. The investigation disclosed that the other eight men who had been lynched were naturalized Americans whose families could not receive an indemnity.

June 15, 1891

Britain and the United States sign a modus vivendi on the Bering fur sealing dispute.

The fur seals dispute between Canada and America increased in intensity after Congress authorized the arrest of pelagic sealers in the Bering Sea on March 2, 1889. Although the Americans allowed all five of the arrested Canadian sealers to escape in 1889, the potential arrest of Canadians allowed ill will and discord to continue. Moreover, diplomatic exchanges between Secretary Blaine and Lord Salisbury in 1889 and 1890 failed to resolve the problem. Blaine argued that the law of March 2 was based on the principle of the public good (*contra bonos mores*), not on a closed sea (*mare clausum*), and that the pelagic killing of seals must stop. Salisbury, who was both prime minister and foreign minister of England, contended that American jurisdiction ended at the three-mile line and said the United States violated all precepts of the law of the sea by arresting Canadians on the high seas.

Attempts to reach a compromise had also failed. Blaine suggested an agreement to ban pelagic sealing at certain periods each year, but Canada responded that America should also limit its land killings on the Pribilof Islands. Salisbury's request that both land and sea killings be restricted caused a dilemma for Blaine. In 1890, the North American Commercial Company secured a lease on the Pribilof sealing when the Alaska Company's lease expired. Blaine had close friends and political allies as stockholders of the new company and did not want to limit their rights to kill seals. Subsequently, the sealing season of 1891 passed in a stalemate and the slaughter of seals continued on land and at sea.

In June 1891, both Blaine and Salisbury were prepared to arbitrate and agreed on a modus vivendi for one year. By the agreement, the North American Commercial Company would kill only 7,500 seals in the Pribilofs in 1891, and there would be no pelagic sealing. On February 27, 1892, this compromise was extended for a second year during which an arbitration convention was accepted.

See August 15, 1893.

A seal pleads for peace and a closed season on sealing. *Punch*, 1891.

July 4, 1891

The United States disputes with Chile over the ship *Itata*.

A series of American difficulties with Chile began when the United States captured the *Itata*, a naval vessel of a rebel group in Chile, and brought it to San Diego, California.

A rebellion had begun in Chile on January 1, 1891, between President Balmaceda and the Congressionalists. The rebels had captured the *Itata*, and in May 1891 they arrived at San Diego to obtain supplies and weapons. Balmaceda's government protested to the United States, and on May 5 the State Department asked a U.S. federal marshal to board the *Itata* and inspect it for violations of U.S. neutrality. The *Itata* steamed off with the marshal on board, later dropping him ashore. After reaching international waters, the *Itata* rendezvoused with another ship to load a cargo of arms and ammunition.

Asserting that the *Itata* crew had violated U.S. neutrality, President Harrison ordered the U.S. Navy to pursue the *Itata* and return it to the United States.

The U.S. navy vessel *Charleston* did not find the *Itata* until it reached Irquique, Chile, where the Americans forced the *Itata* to surrender. The rebels claimed its cargo had been transshipped, but the American commander followed orders and returned the captive ship to San Diego.

In October, after the rebels successfully overthrew Balmaceda, the United States released the *Itata* to the provisional regime. Later, a U.S. court ruled that the navy had erred in detaining the *Itata.*

August 28, 1891

To the dissatisfaction of Chile, the U.S. Minister protects exiles of the former regime.

Between January 1 and August 1891, Chile's Congressionalists faction fought the supporters of President Balmaceda. Gaining control of the Chilean navy, the rebels captured the rich nitrate region of the north. Their forces moved south in July, and after a fierce struggle they captured Valparaiso on August 28. Several days later, the revolutionists set up a new government in SANTIAGO under Admiral Jorge MONTT.

The fall of Valparaiso caused the Balmacadists to scamper for cover. Several of the former politicians fled to the U.S. legation, where Patrick EGAN, the U.S. minister, gave them a haven and political asylum. Because the new government desired to prosecute the former leaders, they asked Egan to release the Chilean exiles. Egan refused, causing new disputes to develop between the United States and the Congressionalists' regime in Chile.

See October 16, 1891.

October 16, 1891

In Chile, a mob attacks 117 U.S. Navy seamen, killing 2 and wounding 17.

Relations between Chile and the United States, which had become cool on July 4, 1891, worsened after an incident at Valparaiso resulted in the death of two Americans on shore leave from the U.S.S. *Baltimore.*

At a time when U.S. relations with Chile were already tense, Captain Winfield S. SCHLEY's ship, the *Baltimore,* arrived at Valparaiso, where 117 seamen were granted shore leave. At the True Blue Saloon, a riot began when a Chilean allegedly spat in the face of a drunken U.S. sailor. The brawl quickly spread throughout the waterfront, and local mobs attacked Americans wherever they appeared. Later, the American sailors claimed the attacks had been planned by Chile, but if so and by whom is not known. Aided by local police, the Chileans used knives and bayonets as well as fists against the Americans. One of the two dead Americans received 18 wounds. Yet no Chileans were seriously wounded in the fray.

Captain Schley quickly wired news of the attack to Washington, explaining that the U.S. sailors were unarmed and did not provoke the attack. Not unexpectedly, the U.S. public reacted in anger and a war scare occurred in early January 1892, before Chile agreed to pay reparations.

See January 25, 1892.

1892

January 25, 1892

Chile agrees to make reparations for the U.S. sailors attacked in Valparaiso: talk of war ends in America.

Between October 16, 1891, when Chilean mobs attacked 117 American seamen, and January 25, 1892, the dispute over this incident became a matter of words and honor with some Americans who called for war against Chile.

Although the State Department protested in October to Chile, requesting an indemnity and apology, the Chilean government requested time to investigate the incident. However, President Harrison and Secretary of the Navy Benjamin TRACY wanted quick action because Chile had insulted the uniform and flag of America. Secretary of State Blaine counseled the president to be patient, and the matter quieted down.

On December 11 the dispute flared anew. On December 9, Harrison's annual message to Congress had announced that Chilean police were involved in the assault on the American flag and prompt Chilean reparations would be required. Two days later, Chile's fiery foreign minister, Manual A. Matta, responded to Harrison's speech with a protest to Washington that Matta published in local newspapers. Matta asserted that the president's charges about the police were insincere and "deliberately incorrect." Further, Matta stated, Chile would prevail despite "the threats that come from so high." Thus, Matta's insults against President Harrison were added to the dispute, raising tempers higher in both Chile and America.

In the United States, Theodore Roosevelt called for war and U.S. navy yards worked overtime to complete new warships. The body of one of the two slain seamen was laid in state in Independence Hall, Philadelphia, an honor previously given only to Abraham Lincoln and Henry Clay.

Nevertheless, the crisis gradually ebbed after January 1, 1892, when Luis PEREIRA replaced Matta as Chile's foreign minister. Pereira knew Chile could not risk war with the United States and sought to conciliate America without sacrificing his own political life in Chile. After talks with Patrick EGAN, the U.S. minister to Chile, Pereira agreed to pay an indemnity for the October incident and to permit Egan to conduct the Chilean refugees who were harbored in the U.S. embassy to a safe exile. Regarding the details of the October riot, however, he said that the Chilean courts had found blame on both sides. The court therefore had indicted one U.S. seaman as well as two Chileans. It also absolved the police from having participated in the riots.

Neither President Harrison nor Secretary Blaine accepted Chile's response to the riot. No Chileans had been hurt, they argued, and this indicated that the Americans were victims. Moreover, Secretary Blaine insisted that Chile must fully withdraw the allegations against President Harrison made by Foreign Minister Matta in December. To reinforce these views, President Harrison laid the dispute before Congress on January 25, 1892. The president informed Congress that Chile had attacked the "uniform—the nationality" of America. Congress, he said, should take "action as may be deemed appropriate."

Fortunately, on the day that Harrison spoke to Congress, Pereira and Egan met again and Chile fully capitulated. Pereira reported that Chile would not only pay reparations but "absolutely withdraws" the accusations by Matta, "which are offensive in the judgement of your government." On learning of Pereira's new response, Harrison felt satisfied. On January 26, the president withdrew his previous message to Congress, informing it that relations with Chile had been healed.

Chile followed through on its agreement during the next year. Three Chilean citizens received prison sentences for the October riots. In July 1891, Chile offered and Washington accepted a reparations payment of $75,000.

July 29, 1892

John Watson Foster becomes secretary of state.

Secretary of State Blaine resigned from office on June 4, 1892. Although Blaine gave no reason for his unexpected resignation, the apparent cause was a lingering illness that had begun in 1887 and become severe during six months of 1891. Blaine died on January 27, 1893, less than eight months after resigning from office.

Foster was eminently qualified to be secretary of state. He had served as minister to Mexico for seven years, to Russia for two years, and to Spain for two years. In 1890, he became a minister plenipotentiary to negotiate reciprocity treaties, and in 1892 he acted as an agent in the Alaskan fur-seal arbitration. He served as secretary until the end of Harrison's term in March 1893, and later filled various other duties for the State Department.

November 8, 1892

Grover Cleveland defeats President Harrison in his bid for reelection.

A major foreign policy issue of the campaign was the tariff. Nominating Cleveland on June 21, the Democratic Convention's platform favored a revenue tariff. Nevertheless, Cleveland had straddled the issue of protectionism in the campaign by advocating "tariff reform" but not specifically "revenue only." In renominating Benjamin Harrison on June 10, the Republican Party came out solidly for a protective tariff. During the election, two additional candidates were James B. Weaver of the growing Populist Party and John Bidwell of the single-issue Prohibition Party. Cleveland's victory in the electoral vote was 277 to Harrison's 145.

November 19, 1892

The Panama scandal erupts in Paris when French authorities take legal action against Ferdinand de Lesseps and his associates.

De Lesseps had formed the Panama Company to underwrite the construction of a canal in the isthmus of Central America. Corruption and mismanagement had caused the company to collapse in February 1889, and its investors lost 1.5 billion francs.

An extensive investigation took place before legal action began against de Lesseps and his partners on November 19, 1892. The trial, which ended February 9, 1893, made public the findings of the investigation, which revealed that the company gave lavish sums to newspapers and members of parliament to secure their cooperation. Furthermore, the government had tried to cover up the affair.

On February 9, the court of appeals levied large fines and a prison term on de Lesseps and his friends. They were never punished, however, because on June 15 France's highest appeals court ruled that the three-year statute of limitations on such crimes had expired before the trial.

1893

January 17, 1893

A coup d'état in Hawaii overthrows the queen, and the new government requests annexation to America.

The Honolulu "revolution of 1893" culminated a dispute between the pro–American-dominated legislature and Queen Liliuokalani. The queen had since 1887 endeavored to regain the full royal authority that her brother, King Kalakua, had sacrificed to wealthy white residents. To combat the queen, the legislators desired American annexation, a process favored by Secretary of State Blaine and John L. Stevens, the U.S. minister to Hawaii.

Throughout 1892, Stevens informed the State Department about the annexation proposals. He also requested instructions about how far the U.S. navy and the minister could go in intervening to protect American interests. Neither Blaine, Harrison, nor, later, Secretary Foster responded to Stevens's questions, and by their silence, Stevens inferred their consent for him in whatever fashion was necessary.

The queen and the legislature had deadlocked in their struggle for power until November 1892, when the legislature appeared to win by forcing the queen to accept a cabinet favorable to the pro-Americans. The queen was not easily defeated, however. On January 14, Queen "Lil" had prorogued the legislature and dismissed its cabinet appointees. The legislative faction retaliated by proclaiming a constitution and immediately petitioning U.S. Minister Stevens for protection. Stevens acted swiftly. He asked U.S. navy Captain Gilbert C. Wiltse of the USS *Boston* to land troops in order to save U.S. property.

On January 16, a battalion of marines landed and deployed at the U.S. legation and the consulate. But the main group of marines took two pieces of artillery to the Hawaiian government's office building and the royal palace, Arion Hall. With this U.S. support, the next day the revolutionists occupied the government buildings, proclaimed a new regime, and received recognition from Stevens. The queen surrendered, claiming she had yielded to American force and expected Washington to renounce Stevens's interference in Honolulu.

On January 19, the provisional government dispatched a commission to Washington that would request annexation terms. On February 1, Stevens announced that the United States would protect Hawaii, but two weeks later Secretary of State Foster disavowed Stevens's protectorate. Foster's act was the first notice that Hawaii might not yet be "ripe" enough for America to pluck.

See May 31, 1894.

March 6, 1893

Walter Quintin Gresham is appointed as secretary of state by President Cleveland.

Although Gresham was a Republican who had been considered a possible presidential nominee in 1888, Cleveland selected him as secretary because they agreed on a compromise tariff. Gresham had almost no foreign experience, having been an Indiana lawyer and judge. His previous federal service was as postmaster general and secretary of the Treasury under President Arthur.

March 30, 1893

Thomas F. Bayard becomes the first American to hold the rank of ambassador when the Senate confirms his appointment as ambassador to Great Britain.

Congress had provided for the appointment of ambassadors in one clause of a regular appropriation bill approved on March 1, 1893. The bill permitted the president to designate such rank provided that the foreign government involved had a representative of the same rank in Washington. Because this applied to England, Cleveland commissioned Bayard as an ambassador. During his term of office, Cleveland also commissioned ambassadors to Paris, Berlin, and Rome.

April 21, 1893

The panic of 1893 results from the decline of U.S. gold reserves and fears of U.S. industrial surpluses that require foreign markets.

As with many economic recessions, the Panic of 1893 resulted from long-term causes precipitated by an immediate difficulty. In the case of the Panic of 1893, the announcement that U.S. gold reserves had fallen below the $100 million mark on April 21 led to a downturn in the overall economy. By June 27, stocks on the New York exchange fell seriously, and before the year ended 491 banks and 15,000 commercial institutions failed.

Factors other than the gold decline contributed to the severity of the 1893 panic. After the British banking house of Baring Brothers failed in 1890, British investors unloaded U.S. securities for gold. The McKinley Tariff of 1890 cut imports and decreased U.S. customs revenue, as had the veterans' pension grants of the Harrison administration.

The Cleveland administration blamed the depression on both the silver purchase act, which it repealed, and the McKinley Tariff, which it revised, but many observers cited the surplus of U.S. industrial products that needed foreign export markets. Of course, both the revised tariff and the undergirding of the solid gold dollar by the repeal of the silver act aided American exports, which soon increased.

Generally, the panic of 1893 aided the U.S. imperial thrust of the 1890s by stimulating the belief that foreign markets for American surplus products were necessary to maintain U.S. prosperity. Populists and other anti-imperialists preferred free silver coinage in order to reduce consumer costs at home. They argued that foreign markets would not be essential if Americans could afford to buy American industry's manufactured products. Nevertheless, both Cleveland Democrats and the Republicans attributed the Panic of 1893 to surplus production and urged foreign policies that would create foreign markets. The markets that seemed to offer the greatest potential for U.S. products were in South America and China.

See October 30, 1893, and August 28, 1894.

August 15, 1893

The arbitration commission in the sealing dispute rules against the United States on all counts.

The arbitration commission had been approved by an Anglo-American treaty of February 29, 1892. It was charged with determining damages claimed by Canada for seizures of sealing vessels and for imposing future sealing regulations. The commissioners were, for America, Supreme Court Justice John M. Harlan and Senator John T. Morgan of Alabama; for Britain, Lord Hannen and Canada's attorney general, Sir John S. D. Thompson; and from other nations, French Senator Baron Alphonse de Courcel, Italian Foreign Minister Marquis Emilio Visconti Venosta, and Minister of Sweden and Norway Gregers Gram.

After meeting and hearing arguments from April 4 to August 1893, the commission issued its rulings on August 15. It decided the following:

1. The United States lost all damage cases and had to pay Canada $542,169.26.
2. Pelagic sealing was banned in a 60-mile area surrounding the Pribilofs.
3. Pelagic sealing was banned from May 1 to July 31 in the seas north of the 35° latitude and east of the 180° longitude.

This arbitration decision ended most American-Canadian disputes regarding seal killings. The agreement did not, however, provide sufficient protection for the seals, only slowing the process of their extermination.

An incidental consequence of this arbitration illustrates the "cost" of U.S. party politics. On August 21, Secretary of State Gresham offered and the British ambassador accepted the lump sum of $425,000 to settle the award (item No. 1 above). Congress, however, refused to pay this sum, owing largely to the partisan enmity of Republicans toward President Cleveland. Consequently, a mixed commission was established to set the proper damage claim, and in December 1897 it awarded Great Britain $473,151.26, which Congress had to appropriate. Thus, in addition to the expense of a new commission, Congress appropriated $48,151.26 more than if it had accepted Gresham's August 21, 1893, proposal.

Also see June 15, 1891.

October 30, 1893

Congress repeals the Sherman Silver Purchase Act of 1890.

President Cleveland called a special session of Congress on June 30 to repeal the silver act, which he believed to be a major cause of the drain on U.S. gold reserves announced on April 21, 1893. The Sherman Act had required the U.S. Treasury to purchase 4,500,000 ounces of silver each month and to issue legal tender notes redeemable in either gold or silver. This act increased the supply of paper money but weakened the federal gold reserve.

Acting on Cleveland's request, the House passed the repeal law on August 28, but the bill became delayed in the Senate. Many Democrats favored the silver purchase act and split with Cleveland on the issue. Eventually, Republicans and Cleveland Democrats in the Senate approved the silver repeal on October 30, 1893. The resulting Democratic Party split caused problems for Cleveland during his remaining term of office and made the silver issue a major factor in the election of 1896.

1894

January 4, 1894

A Franco-Russian alliance is formed.

This alliance resulted because Germany's diplomatic efforts deteriorated after William II took charge and dismissed Bismarck on April 28, 1890. William II spurned Russian attempts to renew their Russo-German agreement in 1891. Consequently, Russia moved into France's waiting arms to form an alliance. France began to court the czar by offering favorable loans, and their friendship was further encouraged by naval visits. On August 1, 1892, French military leaders visited St. Petersburg to draft a military convention that, after lengthy discussions, was finally agreed to in an exchange of notes between December 27, 1893, and January 4, 1894.

The Franco-Russian agreements had two principal parts: (1) if Germany attacked either nation, the other would use all available forces in assistance of the victim; and (2) if any member nation of the Triple Alliance (Germany, Austria, Italy) mobilized, France and Russia would mobilize without delay. The other clauses of the agreements concerned plans for combined general staffs, troop numbers, and means for secret communication.

At this time, Russia did not wish to sever all ties with Germany. Therefore, it negotiated a tariff treaty with Berlin on March 16, 1894, which settled several long-standing commercial disputes between Russia and Germany.

January 29, 1894

A U.S. admiral prevents a rebel blockade and assists the Republic of Brazil to defeat monarchists.

When Brazil established its republic in 1889, the United States applauded and quickly recognized the new government. On February 15, 1891, the United States signed a commercial reciprocity treaty with the new government. Thus, when a group of monarchists led by Brazilian naval officers undertook a rebellion in September 1893, the United States sympathized with the republicans.

Having gained control of the navy, the rebels tried to blockade the Brazilian coast, an action that the United States as well as most European nations opposed. Nevertheless, owing apparently to England's sympathy for the rebels, no other nation sought to break the blockade until the United States acted. On October 11, U.S. Minister to Brazil Thomas S. Thompson asked Rear Admiral Oscar Stanton, whose ship was near Rio de Janeiro, to break the blockade. When Stanton refused, the Navy Department recalled him, sending a new naval officer who took command over a reinforced American naval squadron at Rio.

The new U.S. commander, Rear Admiral A. E. K. BENHAM, first broke the blockade by loading U.S. goods from ships onto barges that transported the cargo to Rio's harbor. This scheme worked so effectively that the Brazilian rebels took steps to stop it. A clash eventually occurred in January 1894. After the U.S. merchant ship *Amy* was fired on, Benham warned the rebel leader, Admiral Saldanha da Gama, that he intended to escort U.S. merchant ships to the harbor and would fire on any ships trying to interfere. Two days later, January 29, the USS *Detroit* escorted a U.S. merchant ship into the harbor, where a rebel Brazilian vessel fired an unloaded warning shot across the bow of the merchant vessel. The American captain of the *Detroit* quickly fired a cannon directly at the rebel ship, informing its captain that if he did not surrender, his ship would be sunk.

The Brazilian surrendered and the blockade was broken. The British naval captain at Rio followed Benham's lead and agreed to help break the blockade. This destroyed the Brazilian rebels' most effective weapon against the republic and saved the government of President Moraes Barros. The U.S. navy maintained five of its six Atlantic squadron warships in the vicinity of Rio for several months to assure the safety of U.S. merchant ships and the security of the Republic of Brazil.

Queen Liliuokalani. Library of Congress

May 31, 1894

The United States refuses to annex Hawaii but accepts the revolutionary regime of 1893 as Hawaii's rightful government.

Although President Harrison and Secretary of State Foster had quickly approved a treaty of annexation with Hawaii during February 1893, the Democrats in the Senate prevented ratification of the treaty. The treaty approved by Foster and the Hawaiian commissioners would have annexed the islands, prohibited Chinese immigration, and given Queen Liliuokalani an annuity. The Democrats, however, followed President-elect Cleveland's request to permit him to handle the Hawaiian question after his inauguration.

On March 4, 1893, Cleveland withdrew the treaty from the Senate and appointed James H. Blount as a special commissioner to investigate the Hawaiian situation. Blount went to Honolulu, replaced Stevens as minister, and proceeded to undo most of Stevens's action of January 17, 1893. He withdrew the marines and lowered the U.S. flag in Honolulu. Then Blount undertook a four-month series of interviews with royalists, revolutionaries, businessmen, and many Hawaiian natives. On July 17, 1893, Blount reported privately to Cleveland against annexation. But the report was not released until November 1893, just before Congress convened.

Blount's report argued that the rebellion lacked popular support. He censured Minister Stevens's activity and stated that the native Hawaiians deplored the new regime. Because the "undoubted sentiment of the people is for the queen," he predicted the new government could survive only a year or two. Blount believed and persuaded both Cleveland and Secretary of State Gresham to agree that the 1893 uprising was immoral and did not represent the island's people.

Unfortunately for the queen, her attitude during the fall of 1893 cost her sympathy among the American public. To repair the damage done by Stevens in 1893, Cleveland had sent Albert S. Willis as minister to Hawaii to placate Queen Liliuokalani. On October 16, Willis expressed Cleveland's apology to the queen, telling her America disavowed the conduct of Stevens and the U.S. Marines in 1893. He told the queen that the president hoped she would grant amnesty to revolutionists and regain her rightful status. To Willis's conciliation, however, the queen reacted in rage. She refused any amnesty, telling Willis the rebels "should be beheaded and their property confiscated."

In America, reports of the queen's harsh words aided the pro-imperial, pro-annexation viewpoints and damaged Cleveland's sympathetic efforts. Although the queen in December sought to retract her statements, she could not diminish the antagonism she caused on the American mainland. On December 18, Cleveland sent Blount's report to Congress and informed the legislators that he had abandoned the February 1893 annexation treaty. He told Congress he could support neither the queen nor the revolutionists and said he would accept any "moral plan" Congress could devise for Hawaii's future.

Congress could not agree on a positive course of action. By early 1894, public opinion in America expressed antagonism toward both Stevens and Queen "Lil." For some, Stevens acted immorally; for others, the queen was "the Tiger protégé of Mr. Cleveland," who "proposed to celebrate her restoration with a holocaust." Consequently, both houses of Congress passed resolutions against annexation. The House censured Stevens; the Senate exonerated him. Both houses agreed that America should not interfere in the domestic affairs of another nation. Nevertheless, much American sentiment favored the Hawaiian Republic.

See July 4, 1894.

July 4, 1894

The Republic of Hawaii is proclaimed in Honolulu.

The pro-American leaders who overthrew Queen Liliuokalani refused to accept President Cleveland's suggestion that they restore the queen's power. Rather, they adopted a constitution and established a republic under President Sanford B. Dole. One clause of the constitution authorized the president to conclude a treaty of commercial or political union with the United States whenever possible. The United States formally recognized the republic on August 7, 1894. A royalist uprising failed in January 1895, assuring the republic's success until 1898, when the United States annexed the islands.

August 1, 1894

Sino-Japanese War begins.

This war resulted from a long rivalry for control of Korea. It was a complete triumph for the Japanese, who won easy victories over the Chinese army and navy at Port Arthur (November 21) and Weihaiwei (February 12, 1895). During the war the British invited Germany, France, Russia, and the United States to make a joint intervention on behalf of China. Both Germany and the United States were unwilling to participate.

See April 17, 1895.

August 28, 1894

The Wilson-Gorman Tariff is approved by Congress.

President Cleveland intended that this tariff would provide duty-free raw materials to supply U.S. industry and to expand foreign markets with less expensive products. Congressman William L. Wilson, chairman of the House Ways and Means Committee, believed duties on raw materials raised the price of manufactured goods and hurt the export trade.

The House passed the bill with duty-free materials as proposed, but the Senate emasculated the tariff act. On February 1, 1894, the House bill had provided a long list of duty-free items of industrial raw materials. But in the Senate, special-interest groups led by Senator Arthur Gorman deleted everything from the list except copper, lumber, and wool.

Although dissatisfied with the duty-free list, Cleveland allowed the bill to become law without his signature because it generally reduced tariffs from the high average of 49.5% in the McKinley tariff to an average of 39.9%. The bill remained protective in nature. The resulting dispute over the tariff further split the Democratic Party on the same lines as had the repeal of the silver act in 1893.

November 4, 1894

In midterm elections, the Democrats lose control of both houses of Congress.

These elections were a disaster for the divided Democratic Party. They lost 113 seats in the House to give the Republicans control by 244 seats to 105. In the Senate, the Democrats lost only 5 seats, but this was sufficient to give the Republicans a 43-39 majority.

November 22, 1894

A commercial treaty with Japan concludes the U.S. policy begun in the Treaty of July 25, 1878, of granting Japan diplomatic equality.

Because of Article 10 of the 1878 treaty, which withheld the convention's effect until other powers revised their treaties with Japan, the Tokyo government had to work throughout the 1880s to obtain European recognition of Japan's equality. In particular, Britain's agreement to grant equal treaties and end extraterritoriality was the prime requisite of Japan's search. It fulfilled this mission when Great Britain signed a revised tariff and commercial treaty on July 16, 1894. Other European nations and the United States could now finalize their revised treaties with Japan. America did so on November 22.

As in the case of the British treaty, extraterritorial rights would end gradually over a five-year period, foreign land leases were confirmed, and a more conventional Japanese tariff was permitted. As a result, Japan's relations with Great Britain became very close after 1894, while the role of the United States in initiating the action to establish the equal treaty status for Japan was either ignored or forgotten in Japan during the next decade.

Because of previous concerns in America about the immigration of Japanese laborers, the United States also insisted that the 1894 treaty should include a clause recognizing the right to regulate immigration. Although Japan opposed such limitations, it accepted a supplementary clause stipulating that the United States had the right to enact laws regulating immigration of laborers between the two countries.

November 30, 1894

The Turkish sultan invites America to join a commission to investigate the Armenian massacres: U.S. participation does not materialize.

International protests had complained against the sultan's inhumane assaults on Armenian insurrectionists in the Sassoun District of the Turkish Empire during September 1894. To placate these protests, the sultan offered U.S. Minister Alexander W. Terrell an invitation for America to participate in an international commission of inquiry.

Upon learning of the invitation, President Cleveland dismissed the idea out of hand. Terrell wired Washington that American participation could provide information that might better protect American interests, and Cleveland finally agreed to appoint a commissioner. The Turkish government had, however, disliked Cleveland's original rejection and informed Terrell that the inquiry commission membership was filled. Thus, no American representative participated in the inquiry about the Armenian incidents.

The Armenian massacres had brought many refugees to America, where they and their sympathizers formed lobbies for U.S. intervention on behalf of the Armenians after 1894. The chief of these groups became the United Friends of Armenia, which was founded at Boston in 1894. In November 1894, the Armenians had no constituency to pressure President Cleveland, but this changed during the next 10 years.

1895

February 20, 1895

Arbitration of the British-Venezuelan boundary dispute is recommended by a joint resolution of the U.S. Congress.

This unusual congressional resolution, which interfered in a dispute between two other nations, resulted from effective lobbying efforts by William L. SCRUGGS. A former U.S. minister to Venezuela whom President Benjamin Harrison had dismissed on bribery charges, Scruggs became a special agent for Venezuela to plead its case against Great Britain's boundary claims.

In 1894, Scruggs printed a pamphlet for distribution in Washington titled "British Aggression in Venezuela, or the Monroe Doctrine on Trial." His pamphlet described the long-standing boundary question in terms favoring his client, Venezuela. The precise boundary between British Guiana and Venezuela had not been clearly defined either when the region was part of the Spanish Empire or following the South American liberation era in the early 19th century. The area was largely uninhabited jungle, although a few English settlers had moved into the border region during the 1840s following a boundary survey by Robert Schomburgk, the SCHOMBURGK LINE. The discovery of gold during the 1870s inspired increased settlement and made the area more valuable to both sides in the dispute.

During a British-Venezuelan quarrel over the boundary in 1887, the United States had offered to mediate, but negotiations began between London and Caracas; these lasted for several years. In 1894, these talks reached an impasse because Britain refused to discuss any land east of the Schomburgk Line. Venezuela insisted on negotiating the entire area as far east as the Essequibo River. Scruggs argued that the British survey had extended the territory of a European power and therefore threatened the Monroe Doctrine's injunction against colonization after 1823.

Having brought the issue to the attention of several influential politicians in Washington, Scruggs persuaded Congressman Leonidas F. Livingston of Georgia to introduce the joint resolution for arbitration of the dispute on January 10, 1895. With few revisions, the resolution passed both houses of Congress unanimously on February 20, 1895. The resolution described the boundary problem and "earnestly recommended" arbitration by "both parties in interest." Together with Scruggs's lobbying efforts, the resolution brought the Venezuelan problem to public attention in America, becoming one critical factor impelling President Cleveland to take an active role in urging Britain to settle the dispute.

See July 20, 1895.

February 23, 1895

The Cuban rebellion resumes after Spain suspends the island's constitutional guarantees of 1878.

Following a decade of civil war during the 1870s, Spain promised in the Treaty of Zanjon of February 10, 1878, to give the Cubans greater autonomy in local affairs. These promises were only partly carried out, however, and tension increased between the Spanish colonial officials and the Cuban Creole population.

Early in 1895, Spain's military leader in Cuba, General Calleja, announced the suspension of civil rights in order, he said, to preserve necessary order. By February 23, several Cuban rebel factions undertook a new civil war against Spain. The principal leaders of these disunited groups were Maximo Gomez, Antonia Maceo, and José Marti.

April 17, 1895

The Treaty of Shimonoseki ends the Sino-Japanese War in Japan's favor.

The two nations had declared war on August 1, 1894, after Japan intervened during an uprising of the Tonghak Society in south Korea and seized the Korean queen. Japan appointed a regent to rule in Seoul who also declared war against China on July 27, 1894.

Japan easily defeated China in battles near Pingyang (September 16), Port Arthur (November 21), and Weihaiwei (February 12). The Chinese army and navy could not continue the war and accepted a peace treaty on April 17, 1895.

By the treaty, China recognized Korea's independence and ceded Formosa, the Pescadores Islands, and the Liaodong Peninsula to Japan. China paid an indemnity of 200 million taels and opened four ports to foreign commerce.

The Sino-Japanese war affected the future of both countries. For Japan, an important consequence was its discovery of a new friend: Great Britain. Because Russia feared increasing Japanese power on continental Asia, the czar opposed the terms of the Treaty of Shimonoseki. Obtaining the backing of the French and Germans, Russia advised Tokyo that it should retrocede the Liaodong peninsula to China. Japan reluctantly agreed to do so but decided to seek a European ally to assist in future incidents. Great Britain seemed to be the best potential ally not only because of its power status but because London had refused to join the Russian protest regarding Japan's acquisition of the Liaodong peninsula. Tokyo began to nurture the British relationship, sowing the seeds for the Anglo-Japanese Alliance of 1902.

China's internal reform movement grew as a result of the Japanese defeat. Japan had previously been a tribute state to Peking, making the 1894 war a humiliation for the imperial government. Subsequently, nationalistic Chinese groups reinvigorated their earlier attempts to reform or eliminate the Ch'ing Dynasty. The way leading to the Revolution of 1911 became open for the reformers.

April 27, 1895

A Nicaraguan dispute leads Great Britain to occupy the town of Corinto: President Cleveland is criticized for being ineffective in protecting the Monroe Doctrine.

The British seizure of Corinto climaxed several years of argument between Nicaragua and England regarding the status of the Mosquito Indian Reserve. Although the United States had hoped the Clayton-Bulwer Treaty of 1850 would settle the question of British rights on the Nicaraguan coast, London continued to act as protector of the Mosquito Indians from Nicaragua's discriminatory policies. A crisis in 1878 resulted in an arbitration by the emperor of Austria, who in 1881 awarded economic and political autonomy to the Mosquito Reserve. During the next decade this autonomy, assisted by British guidance, provided greater security to the region, making its port city of Bluefields a desirable location for both British and American merchants.

Nevertheless, Nicaragua was dissatisfied with the 1881 settlement and sought greater control over both the Indians and the municipality of Bluefields. Consequently, in 1893 Nicaraguans sent General C. A. LACAYO to regain control of the area and establish martial law in Bluefields.

Lacayo's rule dismayed the American and English merchants in Bluefields. They applied to their respective governments for a redress of their complaints. London responded by sending Captain A. G. Howe of the warship *Cleopatra* to Bluefields on March 5, 1894. Howe sent British marines ashore and forced Lacayo to accept a provisional government that included Howe, the British consul, and General Lacayo. Washington acted less quickly but eventually sent the U.S. warship *San Francisco* to Bluefields. Secretary Gresham also instructed Ambassador Bayard in London to find out what the British intended to do in Nicaragua.

British Foreign Minister Lord Kimberley informed the United States that England did not plan to remain in control at Bluefields. He offered to act cooperatively with the United States to settle the crisis. Gresham refused because he wanted to secure control for Nicaragua over the entire area and disliked Howe's rule in Bluefields.

While London and Washington exchanged views during the fall of 1894, Nicaraguan natives staged a rebellion against the provisional government established by Captain Howe. The British protested against these uprisings and on February 26, 1895, demanded reparations and an apology from the Managua government. Nicaragua appealed to Washington for assistance, but Gresham informed Nicaragua that he could not act because the British were not in conflict with the Monroe Doctrine.

While the United States abdicated its responsibility, Britain decided to take charge. Therefore on April 27, British marines again landed, this time at Corinto. Once British forces were in place, they negotiated an agreement that again provided for a mixed British-Nicaraguan authority over the Mosquito Reserve. The British marines withdrew on May 2, and order was restored in Bluefields.

In the United States, news editors and the Republican opposition denounced Cleveland's pro-British policy as weakness and appeasement. As in the Hawaiian revolution of 1893–1894, U.S. imperialists complained that Cleveland did not protect American commercial interests abroad.

June 8, 1895

Richard Olney is selected as secretary of state to replace Gresham, who died of pneumonia on May 28.

Gresham died unexpectedly after becoming ill during April 1895.

Olney, who had been Cleveland's attorney general prior to his appointment as secretary of state, was a corporation lawyer who specialized in railroads and had many intimate friends among wealthy businessmen. He had no prior experience in foreign affairs and was not accustomed to the delicate aspects of diplomatic conciliation. In this respect, he was the extreme opposite of Gresham. Olney served as secretary until the expiration of President Cleveland's term on March 4, 1897.

June 12, 1895

American neutrality laws are applied in the Cuban rebellion against Spain.

Since the rebellion began on February 23, 1895, U.S. citizens had sympathized with the revolution, and exiled rebels in U.S. cities had organized filibuster expeditions to Cuba. As a result, President Cleveland on June 12 proclaimed American neutrality and admonished Americans not to enlist in or help organize any military expeditions against Spain.

Enforcing the proclamation was impossible. Rebel groups organized in America and arms were continually smuggled to the rebels. A study completed in 1909 indicated that 71 filibusters were organized between 1895 and 1898, one-third of which reached Cuba. In addition, 50% of the boats smuggling ammunition to Cuba were successful.

June 25, 1895

Joseph Chamberlain becomes Great Britain's colonial secretary, inaugurating an energetic program to enhance the nation's imperial power and to foster Anglo-Saxon unity with America.

As a member of Lord Salisbury's cabinet, Chamberlain served as colonial secretary until July 11, 1902. His concept of foreign relations included a belief in Anglo-Saxon racial power that was widely held during the era of social Darwinism from 1880 to 1910. He desired greater cooperation with the United States. Having married an American woman, he was an ardent champion of rapprochement with America, hoping that some day, in his words, the "Stars and Stripes and the Union Jack should wave together over an Anglo-Saxon alliance."

July 20, 1895

The United States intervenes in the British-Venezuelan boundary dispute as an American "duty" under the Monroe Doctrine.

The joint congressional resolution of February 20, 1895, which urged Britain and Venezuela to arbitrate, launched an escalation of American involvement after Richard Olney replaced Gresham as secretary of state.

Shortly before his illness, Gresham decided to comply with the congressional resolution by sending notes to London and Caracas to encourage arbitration. He wrote instructions to Ambassador Bayard in London, telling him to use tactful pressure to persuade Britain to negotiate. On May 26, Acting Secretary of State Edwin F. VAL gave Venezuela's minister, José Andrade, a similar note requesting that his government pursue negotiations with Great Britain. Each of these notes was perfunctory in tone, however.

After Secretary Olney took office, the boundary dispute became a means for Olney to exert a stronger stance against England. Olney received President Cleveland's approval to demand that Great Britain negotiate a settlement under U.S. auspices. Thus, on July 20, Olney instructed Ambassador Bayard to demand that Britain submit the entire boundary issue to arbitration. Olney asserted that America had to intervene in the dispute under terms of

> a doctrine of American public law, well founded in principle and abundantly sanctioned by precedent, which entitles and requires the United States to treat as an injury to itself the forcible assumption by any European power of political control over an American state.

Using arguments that were remarkably similar to those of William Scruggs, Olney said Britain wanted to force Venezuela to surrender land designated by the British survey of 1840—the Schomburgk Line. This unilateral British extension of land violated Olney's interpretation of Monroe's policy. Olney never specifically mentioned the Monroe Doctrine, but that policy was the only set of U.S. "rights" to which Olney could be referring.

As designed by Olney, the American intervention would enable Britain and the United States to determine the proper boundary. Although Olney accepted Venezuela's belief that the entire border area had to be discussed, he did not act as an ally of that nation. Olney believed that Venezuela would have to accept whatever agreement the United States made. Thus, the secretary wrote Bayard on July 20, "Today the United States is practically sovereign on this continent, and its fiat is law upon the subjects to which it confines its interpretations." Olney acted in America's interests, not Venezuela's, a viewpoint that did not endear him to the Latin American nations but that anticipated future U.S. unilateral interventions.

There were political, economic, and strategic reasons for the new Cleveland-Olney policy in Latin America. Politically, President Cleveland and the Democrats needed to regain public support for their perceived weakness in Hawaii and Nicaragua. Economically, American businessmen and investors sought commercial positions in Latin America that a strong U.S. policy could foster. Strategically, American plans for a future canal in the isthmus of Central America made the Caribbean Sea vital to U.S. security. In Venezuela, the U.S. navy considered the mouth of the Orinoco River as a strategic area that Great Britain should not acquire.

After Bayard presented Olney's message to the British government, the English requested a delay during which they could fully consider the U.S. position. For the results of Olney's July instructions see December 17, 1895.

See February 20, 1895.

August 5, 1895

Lord Salisbury's attempt to improve British-German relations fails because Emperor William II misunderstands Salisbury's proposals.

Salisbury explored the possibility of establishing better relations with Berlin to counteract the Franco-Russian alliance. Meeting with William II informally at the Cowes Yacht Races, Salisbury suggested to William that the Near Eastern problems might be solved if the Ottoman Empire were partitioned and Russia gained Istanbul. The kaiser reacted too naively, however, not perceiving that Salisbury's hint implied a revolution in British policy; the kaiser thought Salisbury wished to involve Berlin in the difficult problems of southeastern Europe and the Mediterranean Sea.

Therefore, William rejected Salisbury's opening gambit without consideration. Soon after, German diplomats helped William understand the British attempt and the kaiser unsuccessfully tried to arrange another meeting with Salisbury. Thus, the moment for a diplomatic shift in Europe passed. In Berlin, Baron von Holstein, an imperial adviser who detested the British, gained more influence and constantly prevented future attempts at a German-British détente. Thereafter, Anglo-German relations deteriorated in the years before 1914.

October 1, 1895

The Ottoman Turkish government massacres Armenians who demonstrate in Istanbul.

The secret revolutionary society of the Armenians had initiated terrorist attacks against the Turks in 1894. In reaction, the Kurdish cavalry of the sultan ferociously killed many Armenians, inspiring foreign protests and an investigation. The commission recommended reforms for Turkey, but these could not be enforced.

In 1895, Armenian leaders carried out a massive and provocative antigovernment demonstration in Istanbul. Again, Turkish forces attacked the demonstrators and caused many deaths. Once again, the Western powers, headed by the British, tried to pressure the sultan to reform his government and end the persecutions. The Russians made plans in November to send forces to the Bosporus to seize Istanbul before the British arrived. But the French refused to aid the czar, and the Russian army was inadequately prepared for war. Therefore the czar canceled the plans against Turkey.

After a British squadron assembled near Istanbul, diplomatic pressure by the European powers forced the sultan to agree to reform his Armenian policy. These measures were only partly carried out, leading to more demonstrations and killings on August 26, 1896.

See November 30, 1894.

November 15, 1895

U.S. missionary property is plundered in Turkey.

Turkish nationalists began anti-Western attacks on foreign missionaries during the 1890s because they believed that Christians from the West influenced converts, students, and Turkish minority groups to rebel against the government. The national uprisings by Bulgars, Armenians, Arabs, and Greeks seemed to be inspired by missionaries who opposed the Turkish sultan.

During the many disorders and assaults on Western property and missions, two American missions were attacked in November 1895. On November 15, a mob attack at Marash burned down one mission building while looting three others. Soon after, a mob at Harput plundered two schools and the home of a missionary. The total damage during the two attacks was estimated at $100,000, and the U.S. minister to Istanbul, Alexander Terrell, demanded an indemnity from the sultan's government.

Christian missionary influence had become quite extensive in Turkey. By 1900, the U.S. Mission Board had 29 missionary stations and 162 missionaries in Turkey. American churches had set up 36 boarding schools with 2,700 students; 398 primary schools with 15,000 students; and 6 junior colleges and at least 3 four-year colleges—Robert College, the Istanbul Woman's College, and the Syrian Protestant College. Together with other European missionaries, these groups transmitted Western values in politics as well as religion, nationalism being one of these political values.

For Turkish action on the indemnity, see December 24, 1900.

December 17, 1895

President Cleveland informs Congress that Great Britain refuses to arbitrate the Venezuelan boundary and asks Congress to establish a commission to examine and settle the dispute.

President Cleveland and Secretary Olney waited for over five months for Britain's response to their July 20 note demanding arbitration. Finally, Olney

The British ultimately preferred arbitration to "humble pie." *Punch*, 1896

received the response on December 6 from Britain's ambassador, Sir Julian PAUNCEFOTE.

The British response was in two parts. First, the prime minister denied that the Monroe Doctrine permitted American intervention in the Venezuelan dispute and that the doctrine was international law. America's only right, he said, was the right of any state to intervene if a dispute touched its national interest. Second, Lord Salisbury observed that throughout the 19th century Britain had been willing to arbitrate. Its one qualification was an unwillingness to arbitrate about land inhabited by 40,000 British subjects, that is, about the area east of the Schomburgk Line, where settlers had built homes after 1840.

Because Olney detected a defiant tone in Britain's reply as well as its rejection of arbitration for the "entire area," he wrote a special message that the president delivered to Congress on December 17. Cleveland's speech asserted the U.S. right to intervene under the Monroe Doctrine, which, Olney claimed, was applicable to the Venezuelan dispute. And because Britain refused to arbitrate, Cleveland asked Congress to appropriate funds for a U.S. commission to investigate and report on the proper boundary. On the basis of this report, the president concluded that it would be America's duty to resist "as a willful aggression" any land or territory Britain holds that "we have determined of right belongs to Venezuela." Although his speech was harsh toward England, it also contained sufficient latitude to enable him to untwist the British lion's tail if it seemed necessary. For example, the president had only expressed his "opinion" of America's duty and the United States would resist only "after investigation."

Nevertheless, the president's warlike terms aroused many Americans to attack Great Britain. By December 20, Congress unanimously approved $100,000 for the boundary commission's expenses. The Irish National Alliance offered to give Cleveland 100,000 men to conquer Canada. Theodore Roosevelt said he hoped the "fight will come soon." The *New York Sun* headline read: "War if Necessary."

Other calming influences soon prevailed, however. On Wall Street, American securities fell by one-half billion dollars in December. The New York Chamber of Commerce passed a resolution against the "war craze," and a convocation of Baptist ministers declared that war to save the Armenians from the Turks was more viable than against Britain for Venezuelan land. Even Joseph Pulitzer of the *New York World*, who complained about Cuba, thought that the boundary line did not menace America and if persisted in, "it will be a colossal crime."

For the outcome of the investigation commission's work, see November 12, 1896.

1896

January 1, 1896

A Venezuelan boundary commission is appointed by President Cleveland.

Acting under congressional authority he had requested on December 17, Cleveland appointed five persons plus a staff of historians to investigate the Venezuela–British Guiana boundary. The commission began work immediately and researched the British files for data on the question. But the commission never completed its study. In October 1896, Great Britain and the United States agreed to form an arbitration commission to judge the dispute. The boundary commission abandoned its work.

See November 12, 1896.

January 3, 1896

Germany's Emperor William II congratulates the Dutch Boer leader for repelling a British attack: the Kruger Telegram.

The British had experienced difficulty with the independence demands of the government of President

Paul Kruger of the South African republic. As a result, the British financier Cecil Rhodes and the Scottish adventurer Leander S. Jameson planned to stage a revolution against Kruger on December 29, 1895. Although Rhodes decided to postpone the uprising, Jameson and 660 men invaded the Transvaal (Dutch republic) but were defeated by Kruger's forces on January 2.

The next day the German kaiser sent Kruger a telegram, congratulating him on suppressing the revolt. The British people and government were enraged at William II's act, which they considered to be intervention in an internal problem. British-German antagonism in colonial affairs increased as a result of this incident.

January 15, 1896

An Anglo-French agreement guarantees the independence of Siam.

Since 1885, the French had attempted to extend their control westward from Saigon along the Mekong River. But the British desired to have a buffer state separating Burma and French Indochina. Their differences were settled on January 15, 1896, when Britain recognized French claims to all territory east of the Mekong River, and both nations recognized the independence of a somewhat smaller nation of Siam than had existed before 1893.

March 1, 1896

Italy suffers a disastrous defeat from the Ethiopian army: the Battle of Adua (Adowa).

The loss ended nearly a decade of Italian effort to expand its foothold along the Red Sea. Italy's Prime Minister Francesco CRISPI began an imperialist campaign in northeast Africa in 1886. After losing to an Ethiopian force at Dogali on January 25, 1887, Crispi backed King MENELEK as heir to the Ethiopian throne and assisted his rise to power in November 1889. Menelek refused, however, to accept Italy's protectorship and raised an army to challenge Italian claims. War began in 1895, and once again, the Italian army lost on December 1 at Amba Alagi.

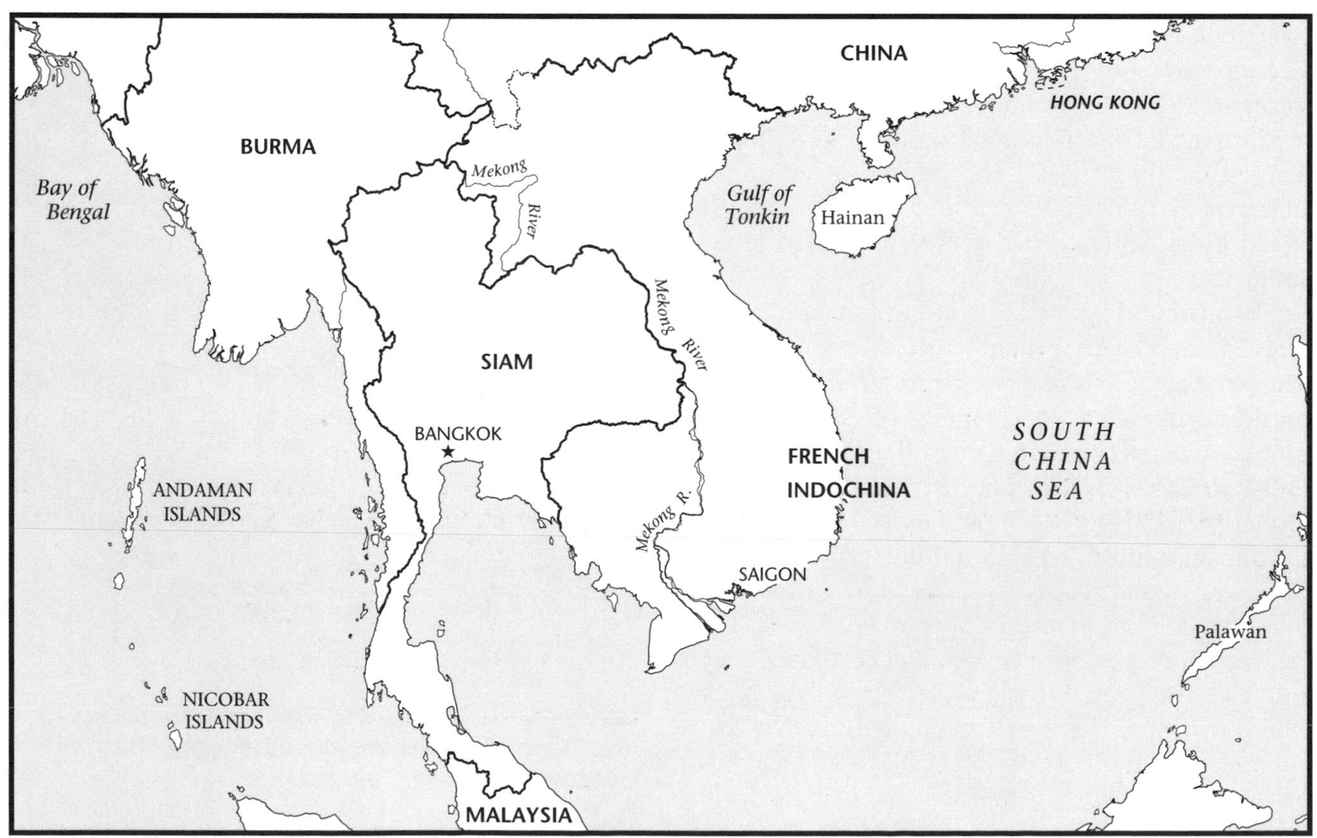

Southeast Asia, 1896

Crispi decided that Italian honor required a victory and organized a new army under General Oreste Baratieri late in 1895. Baratieri's forces attacked Ethiopia early in February, and on March 1, the two nations' armies met at Adua. The Ethiopian troops decimated Italy's 25,000 men. Those who were not killed were taken for ransom in one of the worst colonial disasters for a European army during the imperial era.

In the Treaty of Addis Ababa, Italy recognized the independence of Ethiopia but retained the colony of Eritrea on the Red Sea. During the 1930s Italian leader Benito Mussolini sought again to avenge Italy's honor against this small African nation.

See October 3, 1936.

April 4, 1896

Secretary of State Olney offers American assistance to Spain to mediate with the Cuban rebels.

Heretofore, Olney and President Cleveland had stayed aloof from the Cuban-Spanish conflict. They acted on April 4 to avoid a more precipitate intervention that congressional proponents of the Cuban cause had prepared. A strong stand against Spain was passed as a congressional resolution on April 6, and Cleveland preferred to act earlier.

In September 1895, Olney reported to Cleveland that the Cuban rebellion was causing the same difficulties it had between 1868 and 1878. The current rebellion began on February 23, 1895, and Spain's authorities in Cuba could not maintain order. Cubans who were naturalized Americans were arrested and some had been executed by the Spanish. Cuban rebels burned American property or extorted money from U.S. landowners for protection from destruction. Gunrunners left regularly from U.S. soil, but the navy could not capture most of them. Moreover, Olney reported, nine-tenths of the Cubans supported the rebels. "The property class," he wrote, "to a man is disgusted with Spanish misrule." Spain's local rulers collected enormous taxes but burdened the islands with a $300 million debt and did not protect the lives and property of the people.

Thus on April 4, 1896, Olney urged Spain's minister in Washington, Enrique Dupuy de Lome, to accept the offices of the United States to obtain reform in Cuba and end the war. America, he told de Lome, could not permit another 10 years of Cuban insurrection and all the "distressing incidents" resulting therefrom. Cuba should be given autonomy so that a just end of the war would result.

Not surprisingly, as in the 1870s, Spain rejected America's offer. Madrid was determined to exterminate the Cuban rebels, a tactic that failed before and would fail again.

April 6, 1896

A congressional resolution calls for recognition of belligerent rights for Cuba's rebels and asks the President to offer aid to Spain in granting Cuban independence.

Although several individual congressmen had previously called for Cuban independence or U.S. aid to the Cuban rebellion, this was the first sign that Congress generally wanted to act on behalf of Cuba. These resolutions were not acted on by President Cleveland, who did not consider recognition to be justified and feared that following the congressional recommendation would be a step toward war with Spain. To forestall the interference of Congress, Cleveland and Secretary Olney had offered to mediate the Cuban dispute on April 4, 1896. Spain refused, but the president believed he had taken sufficient action in regard to the resolution of Congress.

May 23, 1896

Western interests in China increase as England and Germany secure loans comparable to loans obtained by France and Russia in 1895.

In Europe as in America following the depression that began in 1893, the China market was visualized as a great potential area for Western investments and commerce. A Franco-Russian financial group collaborated in providing a 400 million franc loan to the Chinese imperial government on July 6, 1895. Shortly afterward, an Anglo-German financial group began negotiations in Peking that led to a £16 million loan on May 23. The Anglo-German loan was made for 36 years at 5% interest.

June 3, 1896

China and Russia sign a treaty granting the czar special rights in Manchuria.

By this treaty, Russia made a 15-year defensive alliance with China in return for the right to build and operate the Chinese Eastern Railway across northern Manchuria. This grant enabled Russia to link its trans-Siberian railway with Vladivostok by crossing Manchuria. The treaty antagonized Japan, however, because Tokyo believed control of the Manchurian railway would enable Russia to dominate the exploitation of Manchuria's iron and coal mines.

August 16, 1896

Gold is discovered in the Klondike area of Alaska.

There had been gold discoveries in British Columbia and the Yukon at various times since 1861. For example, there was some excitement when gold was found in 1887 on Forty Mile Creek in U.S. territory. Comparatively, however, these early discoveries did not stimulate the feverish rush of prospectors who moved into Canada and Alaska after August 1896, when gold was found near Dawson, Canada, 50 miles east of the Alaska border.

August 26, 1896

The Turkish massacres of Armenians are renewed following another nationalist attack.

The reforms that the Ottoman sultan agreed to after October 1, 1895, satisfied neither the Turkish officials nor the Armenians. At the same time, Turkey experienced trouble with Greece, whose government wanted to take over Crete.

On August 26, Armenian rebels attacked an Ottoman bank in Istanbul, which they seized and threatened to blow up. Although the rebels left the bank intact, the Turkish military began a three-day slaughter of thousands of peaceful Armenians. The Western powers again intervened to stop the killings but could not agree on a united plan to end Turkey's internal problem. The disorders continued in Turkey, and intermittent massacres were reported throughout the next 12 months.

For Turkey's troubles with Greece, see April 17, 1897.

October 21, 1896

A Cuban "concentration camp" policy is established by General Valeriano Weyler.

Having received orders from Madrid to suppress the rebels, General Weyler adopted the tactic of moving all Cubans living in combat areas to fortified towns. He hoped to separate peasant support from the rebels. In addition, anyone found outside the forts could be arrested and tried for treason.

These camps became enclaves of active revolutionaries, sympathizers, and neutrals. People of both sexes and many ages were confined in barracks where they had inadequate food and sanitation facilities. Many of those who were tried by military courts were executed or died of disease, starvation, or ruthless treatment by Spanish soldiers. Nearly 400,000 people—25% of Cuba's population—are believed to have died in the concentration camps between 1896 and 1898.

U.S. newspapers reported a variety of horrible incidents that took place in the concentration areas. Women were strip-searched and tortured; children were mistreated; the innocent and guilty received equally bad punishment. The conditions were bad, but the "yellow press" of the 1890s exaggerated many accounts of incidents in "Butcher" Weyler's camps.

November 3, 1896

William McKinley is elected president, receiving 271 electoral votes to William Jennings Bryan's 176.

The campaign of 1896 has become well known for having the gold standard as its main issue. Other issues were present, however, because Bryan's nomination received support from the Populist Party, which advocated antitrust laws and the end of injunctions against labor unions as well as the free coinage of silver. McKinley, the Republican nominee, advocated a high protective tariff and a vigorous foreign policy including the control of Hawaii. McKinley won a majority of the votes even though four minor parties ran candidates for president.

William McKinley, 25th President, campaigned from his front porch. Library of Congress

November 12, 1896

An Anglo-American agreement provides terms for an arbitration treaty between Venezuela and England.

Secretary of State Olney and British Minister to the United States Sir Julian Pauncefote began talks in February 1896 and met intermittently until July, when Olney agreed to change the one point necessary to obtain a British compromise. Rather than require the arbitration of all disputed areas, Olney agreed to exclude any land occupied by either party for a minimum of 60 years. While the British preferred a five-year occupational exclusion, Pauncefote obtained Lord Salisbury's approval on the basis of 50 years occupation, a term the English believed would protect their 40,000 settlers. Olney concurred with the 50-year term.

According to the agreement signed on November 12, the five arbitrators would include two appointees of the U.S. Supreme Court, two appointees of the British supreme court, and a fifth member agreed to by these four or selected by the king of Sweden and Norway.

Secretary Olney had to persuade Venezuela to sign the treaty prepared for it by the United States and England. Venezuela was at first dismayed that Olney had not continuously consulted it. This dissatisfaction ended when Olney and Salisbury agreed to add a sixth arbitrator to be named by Venezuela. The Caracas government signed the treaty on February 2, 1897. For results of the arbitration, see October 1, 1899.

December 30, 1896

Dr. José Rizal, the Philippines nationalist leader, is executed by the Spanish.

José Rizal y Mercado became the Filipinos' outstanding national spokesman during the years prior to his execution. The first Filipino uprising against Spanish rule occurred in 1872. Native soldiers at the Cavite arsenal revolted, killing their Spanish officers and demanding independence. The Spanish used force to suppress the rebellion, making large-scale arrests and imprisoning or executing all suspects in the plot.

During the 1880s, Rizal together with Marcelo de Pilar, Lopez Joena, and Apolinaro Mabini formed the "young Filipino Party" to protest against the powers of the Catholic friars and Spain's economic and political controls. In 1891, Rizal founded the Liga Filipino in Hong Kong, opening a league branch in Manila the next year.

On August 26, 1896, the league and a group called the Supreme Worshipful Association of the Sons of the People (the Katipunan) began an insurrection. The Katipunan was a native Tagalog organization that had its headquarters in Cavite Province under Emilio Aguinaldo.

Spain immediately sent a 28,000-man army to destroy the revolutionaries. In an intensive 52-day campaign the Spanish quelled the uprising and captured Rizal. The Filipino leader had gone to Spain in search of support for his nation. Spanish police arrested him in Barcelona and sent him to Manila for trial. Rizal was judged guilty of treason and executed on December 30, 1896. Rather than subduing the nationalists, Rizal's execution created a martyr. Within a year the insurrection revived.

See December 27, 1897.

America's Initial Moves Toward Global Power

IX. THE IMPERIAL YEARS

Spanish War
Panama and Caribbean Interventions
Interests in the Far East

1897

January 11, 1897

An Anglo-American arbitration treaty is signed; the U.S. Senate rejects it.

Throughout the Venezuelan crisis with Great Britain, Secretary of State Richard Olney and British Ambassador Sir Julian Pauncefote had discussed details for an arbitration treaty to settle future difficulties. Among both British and American leaders, the concept of arbitration had been considered for some time. During the 1880s, 200 members of Britain's House of Commons petitioned the U.S. government to form a general arbitration committee. In 1890, a concurrent U.S. congressional resolution favored such a treaty because many pro-arbitration groups urged Congress to promote arbitration.

Not surprisingly, therefore, the Venezuelan controversy seemed to demonstrate the need for an arbitration process, leading Olney and Pauncefote to begin negotiating a treaty. This treaty was agreed to and signed on January 11. It provided for arbitration of all disputes between the two nations. In cases of territorial claims, there would be a referral to an arbitration court of six members, but if any one member dissented, the awards would not be binding. Even then, before hostilities began the nations would seek the mediation of a third power.

The U.S. Senate would not ratify the treaty. Both President Cleveland and President-elect McKinley recommended acceptance of the treaty, but the Senate vote fell three short of a two-thirds majority—43 to 23. Seven Western and five Southern states opposed the treaty, 22 of the 23 opposing votes coming from these states. Nevertheless, the general support for an arbitration treaty gave evidence of greater cooperation between the two major English-speaking nations.

March 5, 1897

John Sherman is appointed as secretary of state by President McKinley.

Sherman had no significant qualifications to serve as secretary of state. He had been secretary of the Treasury under President Hayes (1877–1881) and a congressman (1855–1861) and senator (1861–1877 and 1881–1897) from Ohio. According to historians, Sherman, who was 74 years old in 1897, was nearly senile at the time of his appointment. McKinley apparently honored him with the secretaryship in order that Marcus HANNA, the president's campaign organizer and indispensable promoter, could replace Sherman as an Ohio senator.

Sherman became ill during the spring of 1898 and resigned from office on April 27, 1898.

April 17, 1897

Greece and Turkey go to war; European powers intervene to stop the conflict.

The Greco-Turkish conflict arose from Greek claims to the island of Crete and territory in Macedonia that Turkey occupied. Following an uprising in Crete on February 2, 1897, the European powers landed troops on Crete on February 15 and held the island in "escrow for future settlement."

Objecting to the European arrangement, the Greeks protested and on April 17 attacked Turkey in Macedonia. The war resulted in a Turkish victory, and by armistice terms of May 19 the sultan retained Macedonia. Subsequently, the European powers decided to turn Crete over to Greece and named Prince George of Greece as governor of the island in November 1898. The powers involved in these decisions were Great Britain, France, and Russia, the latter two generally agreeing with London's terms.

May 5, 1897

A Japanese warship arrives at Honolulu to support Japan's demand for the end of immigration restrictions.

The Japanese minister to Hawaii, H. SHIMAMURA, had been instructed to demand that Hawaii change its discriminatory immigration practices, and the warship *Naniwa* was sent to emphasize the serious intent of Japan's demand.

The Republic of Hawaii's government feared the large influx of Japanese because 24,407 Japanese laborers came to Hawaii between 1886 and 1896. To counter this influx, Hawaiian officials rejected 1,174 Japanese immigrants during March 1897. It was this practice that Tokyo protested.

Tensions grew in Honolulu because shortly after the *Naniwa* arrived, Minister Shimamura told a newsman that he hoped Hawaii would accept his reasonable requests. If not, he would leave and "you know what follows. I hope it will not reach that point." Because Japan had gained confidence in its Pacific affairs after defeating China in 1895, Tokyo believed it could obtain concessions from Hawaii.

For the outcome of this incident, see June 16, 1897, and December 22, 1897.

June 16, 1897

The United States and Hawaii sign a treaty of annexation.

Because the Republican Party platform of 1896 favored the annexation of Hawaii, two Hawaiian agents, Francis M. Hatch, Hawaii's minister to the United States, and W. O. Smith, called on William McKinley early in 1897 and found the president-elect ready to promote annexation. At McKinley's request, Secretary of State John W. Foster began to negotiate a treaty even before McKinley took office. By June 16, the negotiations had been completed and a treaty signed. However, the U.S. Senate did not act immediately on the treaty. Although the Senate Foreign Relations Committee reported in favor of the treaty on July 14, the Senate adjourned before voting on the measure.

In the meantime, Japan protested the American treaty with Hawaii. Believing that Secretary of State Sherman had promised the Japanese minister to the United States, Toru Hoshi, that U.S. annexation was not contemplated, Tokyo said the treaty changed the status quo in the Pacific and endangered its existing treaty rights with Hawaii. Consequently, Sherman sought to compromise with Japan before Congress convened again in December.

See December 22, 1897.

July 7, 1897

The Dingley Tariff raises rates to a new high in U.S. history.

The Republican Party leaders disdained the lower Wilson-Gorman Tariff of 1894 and had campaigned in 1896 on a platform advocating a protective tariff. The Dingley Tariff achieved their goal, raising rates to reach an average of 57%, compared with the McKinley Tariff of 1890, which averaged 49.5% and the Wilson-Gorman average of 39.9%. This bill also surpassed the average of 50% reached by the 1828 "Tariff of Abominations."

September 18, 1897

The U.S. Minister to Spain tells the Spanish Foreign Minister that America insists on action to bring order in Cuba, giving Madrid until November 1, 1897, to provide such assurances.

The U.S. minister to Spain, General Stewart L. Woodford, had been appointed by President McKinley. On July 16, Secretary Sherman instructed him to emphasize to the Spanish government that it must stop the destructive war in Cuba. The war, Sherman wrote, caused "disturbances in the social and political condition of our people," and Spain must make immediate progress toward solving Cuba's problems.

When Woodford reported these U.S. views to Spain's foreign minister on September 18, he issued a virtual ultimatum to Spain to offer America assurances by November 1, 1897, that it would act to resolve the Cuban rebellion. Otherwise, America would feel free to do whatever it "deems necessary to procure peace and order in Cuba."

Woodford issued this request to Spain at a difficult moment in Spanish history, because the ministry was in transition from the Conservative to the Liberal Party.

See October 4, 1897.

October 4, 1897

A liberal ministry replaces the conservatives in the Spanish government.

On October 4, Spanish Liberals under Prime Minister Paaxedes Mateo Sagasta took office. They replaced the Conservative ministry, which had ended when Prime Minister Canovas del Castillo was assassinated on August 8, 1897.

Sagasta's party had been critical of "Butcher" Weyler's methods in Cuba and immediately replaced him with a more conciliatory officer, General Ramon Blanco.

October 6, 1897

The "Cuban girl martyr" is rescued by a reporter for the *New York Journal*.

The story of Evangelina Cisneros was one of the sensational stories used by William Randolph Hearst's newspaper, the *New York Journal*, in competition for circulation with Joseph Pulitzer's *New York World*. In a series of articles during 1897, the *Journal* graphically described the imprisonment of Evangelina, niece of Cuba's rebel president, as she defended her honor and virtue from her lascivious Spanish captors; these articles exemplified yellow journalism at its worst. As the *Journal* championed the "Cuban girl martyr," the paper's subscriptions from women readers grew by the hundreds. In addition, American antagonism toward Spain grew.

On October 6, Evangelina's story achieved a tremendous climax. A Hearst reporter rescued her from a Cuban jail and whisked her to safety in America. Hearst's readers exulted at her escape from the cruel Spanish, and sympathy for the Cuban rebels multiplied.

Evangelina's story was but one of the sensational yellow-journalistic reports used by Hearst, Pulitzer, and other American newspapers to inflame American opinion and bring on the "splendid little" Spanish war in 1898.

November 14, 1897

The Germans occupy Kiaochow peninsula and Tsingtao, China.

The Germans had sought some means to obtain concessions in China since 1895. In early November, the murder of two German missionaries in Shantung provided a rationale for the German navy to land forces in Kiaochow. As a result, on March 6, 1898, a Sino-German convention gave Germany a 99-year lease in the bay area and the right to develop mines and build the Tsingtao-Tsinan Railway in Shantung. The German action led other European powers to obtain special concessions from China between March and June 1898.

See July 1, 1898.

November 28, 1897

The new Spanish government approves a series of reforms designed to solve problems in Cuba.

Prime Minister Sagasta, the Liberal leader in Madrid, replaced General Weyler with Ramon Blanco as captain general of Cuba and in early November issued decrees to reform other conditions in Cuba.

On November 13, Spain began to alleviate the reconcentration policy; on the 25th, plans for

Cuba's political autonomy were adopted; and on November 28, Madrid ordered the release of all Americans who had been arrested in Cuba. The U.S. minister to Spain, General Woodford, believed that the Spanish-Cuban situation looked better than ever. His optimism was short-lived, however.

See January 12, 1898.

December 22, 1897

Japan withdraws its protest against the U.S. annexation treaty with Hawaii.

Following the signing of the U.S.-Hawaiian Treaty on June 16, 1897, Secretary Sherman and the State Department endeavored to placate Japan's protest opposing Hawaii's annexation. A series of talks were held among Tokyo, Washington, and Honolulu to solve the problem. On December 22, Japan withdrew its protest and the United States agreed not to discriminate against Japanese commerce and subjects in Hawaii. In addition, Hawaii agreed to pay Japan $75,000 as an indemnity for its actions against Japanese immigrants during March 1897.

Emilio Aguinaldo (ca. 1864–1964). National Archives

December 27, 1897

A Filipino uprising against Spain ends when Emilio Aguinaldo leaves for exile in Hong Kong.

Following the execution of José Rizal on December 30, 1896, Aguinaldo became the foremost leader of the rebellion in the Philippines. Aguinaldo had especially led the KATIPUNAN organization, which claimed between 100,000 and 400,000 Filipino natives as members.

After Rizal's execution, native rebellions spread from Cavite to the provinces of Pangasinan, Zambales, and Ilocos. Throughout 1897, intermittent fights had been costly to both sides. Eventually Spain's representative, Fernando Primo de RIVERA, agreed to negotiate with Aguinaldo, and they concluded the pact of Biai-na-Bato. By this truce, fighting ended and Aguinaldo left for exile in Hong Kong. The Spanish agreed to deposit 400,000 pesetas in a Hong Kong bank as a guarantee of bringing reforms to the Philippine Islands. When the reforms had been devised, Aguinaldo and his lieutenants could return to Manila and use the Hong Kong funds for educational and social purposes. If Spain did not enact the necessary reforms, Aguinaldo could use the money to purchase arms for his men to renew the independence struggle.

Following Aguinaldo's exile, the Spanish reneged on their promises. The money seemed to be a bribe to the exiles because no reforms were enacted. Aguinaldo and his followers decided to prepare for a renewal of their insurrection.

See May 19, 1898, and September 9, 1898.

1898

January 12, 1898

Spanish conservatives in Cuba denounce the liberal reforms of November 1897 by rioting in Havana; the USS *Maine* is sent to Havana.

Spanish-born colonists and army officers in Cuba opposed the November 28 reforms instituted by Liberal Prime Minister Sagasta to bring peace to Cuba. In particular, they disliked the decree that removed General Weyler and made Ramon Blanco captain general of Cuba. The conservatives preferred the hardline repression of the rebellion conducted by Weyler.

On January 12, these Spanish "loyalists" rioted in Havana to protest against Blanco and "appeasement" of the rebels. The army joined the protests, defying the government and joining the conservatives in shouting "Death to autonomy! Death to Blanco!"

These riots convinced Fitzhugh Lee, the U.S. consul in Havana, that Sagasta's reforms could not be effectively carried out. Lee believed greater disorder was imminent in Cuba and advised Secretary of State Sherman that a U.S. warship might be needed in Havana to protect Americans.

On January 24, the Navy Department dispatched the battleship *Maine* to Havana. Although Lee had suggested sending a battleship, he now informed Sherman that its arrival was premature. Consulting with Spanish officials, Lee decided, too late, that an American warship in Havana might raise the hopes of the rebels that American aid was coming. But once the *Maine* reached Havana, U.S. authorities thought it should remain until the situation in Cuba became more certain.

Pictorial version of a mysterious explosion aboard the USS *Maine*. Library of Congress

February 9, 1898

The Spanish Minister to Washington criticizes President McKinley in a letter published by the *New York Journal*.

The *Journal* had a sensational news scoop on February 9 by publishing a letter written by Dupuy De Lome, the Spanish minister, in which the president was described as "weak and a bidder for the admiration of the crowd." McKinley, de Lome asserted, catered to all groups. He was "on good terms with the jingoes of his party" but always left the door open to retreat to a more popular position if necessary.

The *Journal* obtained the letter from a Cuban revolutionist who had stolen it from the mail going through Havana on its way to the Madrid government. The comments were in a letter not intended for the public. Nevertheless, de Lome resigned his position immediately because he knew the letter's publication damaged the Spanish government in the existing crisis about Cuba.

February 15, 1898

The American battleship *Maine* is destroyed in the harbor at Havana, Cuba.

The *Maine* went to Havana following riots in Cuba on January 12, 1898. On February 15, a mysterious explosion aboard the ship damaged the vessel and it sank quickly; 260 officers and crew were killed. Although the Navy Department urged Americans to reserve judgment on the incident until a naval court of inquiry could report, jingoists such as Assistant Secretary of the Navy Theodore Roosevelt told reporters that the president should order the fleet to Havana because "The *Maine* was sunk by an act of dirty treachery on the part of the Spaniards." American newspapers preferred Roosevelt's view, with Hearst's *New York Journal*'s headlines saying "The *Maine* was destroyed by Treachery" and its editor calling for American intervention.

For the naval court report, see March 28, 1898.

February 25, 1898

Commodore George Dewey of the U.S. Navy's Asiatic squadron is ordered to make offensive operations against the Philippines if war begins with Spain.

Assistant Secretary of the Navy Theodore Roosevelt sent the order to Commodore Dewey because contingent U.S. war plans were to seize Manila in the event of war with Spain. Roosevelt believed such war was imminent in February. Since 1876, American naval officers had investigated Manila's defenses, and in 1896 a naval intelligence officer, Lieutenant William M. Kimball, prepared plans to capture Manila. Thus, for U.S. navy officials Roosevelt's order was no surprise, nor was Dewey's early victory at Manila on May 1, 1898.

March 8, 1898

The British seek U.S. cooperation in protecting China's open door; America refuses.

During the winter of 1897–1898, Great Britain became concerned that Russia, Germany, and other powers had begun to undermine the open door policy of equal trading rights in China by seeking territorial concessions. German action in Kiaochow Bay (November 14, 1897), Russia's desire for Port Arthur, and the Japanese attempt to gain special rights in Korea and Manchuria after the Sino-Japanese war—all these activities indicated that spheres of influence were replacing the Chinese open door policy.

As a result, on February 4, Colonial Secretary Joseph Chamberlain had proposed to Prime Minister Lord Balfour that England should approach the United States for cooperation in maintaining the open door in China. Balfour agreed, and on March 8 Minister to the United States Sir Julian Pauncefote discussed the matter with Assistant Secretary of State William Day.

Either because he was unwilling to alter the U.S. tradition of acting alone in foreign affairs or because the Cuban crisis made the particular moment too difficult for consideration of a firm position on China policy, President McKinley and Day gave Pauncefote a bland reply. The United States, Day told Pauncefote, did not approve of special concessions for one power in China. Yet they could not join Britain in supporting a reassertion of these principles because they saw no immediate threat to the open door in China. The British were dismayed with this response and decided to seek their own concessions at Weihaiwei.

See July 1, 1898; for the subsequent change in U.S. concerns for the open door in China, see September 6, 1899.

March 9, 1898

Congress appropriates an additional $50 million for national defense that could be spent at the President's discretion.

This act had bipartisan support in Congress, and the Democratic Party leader, William J. Bryan, thought $100 million should be appropriated. This bill reflected the growing belief in America that war with Spain was near.

March 16, 1898

A joint congressional resolution to annex Hawaii is presented to the Senate by the Foreign Relations Committee.

The senators who favored the annexation of Hawaii had decided on the "Texas-tactic" of a joint resolution because the Hawaii Annexation Treaty of June 16, 1897, was unable to get two-thirds approval in the Senate. During January and February, while the discussion of the Spanish crisis continued, anti-imperialists and American sugar interests were able to muster more than one-third of the Senate votes. Thus, although President Dole of Hawaii arrived to lobby for the annexation treaty that Hawaii had ratified on September 6, 1897, neither Dole nor the Republican Senate leadership could persuade enough senators to gain ratification.

To replace the treaty, Senator Cushman K. Davis offered the joint resolution of annexation as part of a committee report that tried to justify the need for annexation. The report struck hard against Japanese interests in Hawaii, asserting, "The policy of Japan toward Hawaii will become aggressive and determined so soon as the United States refuses to annex." America, the report said, cannot allow another foreign people to take Hawaii, and the question is "what foreign people shall control Hawaii."

In the spring of 1898, the Spanish crisis prevented a Senate vote on Davis's joint resolution. Soon after Commodore Dewey captured Manila, however, a new joint resolution resulted in Hawaii's annexation.

See July 6, 1898.

March 17, 1898

Senator Redfield Proctor, a former peace advocate, tells Congress his visit to Cuba confirmed the need to indict Spain for its Cuban policy.

Senator Proctor's speech, which appeared to be based on reason, not sensationalism, was considered by many to mean that war was certain. Before visiting Cuba, Proctor did not believe what the newspapers reported and had opposed protests against Spain. But, as he explained in his speech, he was convinced otherwise. "My inquiries were entirely outside of sensational sources . . . every time the answer was that the case had not been overstated." Thus, Proctor's report damaged Spain's claims against the rebels' propaganda and became a vital factor in convincing the American public, at least Washington officials, that war was necessary.

March 28, 1898

The naval inquiry reports the *Maine* was sunk by an outside explosion of unknown origin.

On February 17, the U.S. navy's court of inquiry began to investigate the sinking of the *Maine* in Havana harbor. President McKinley presented its report to Congress on March 28. The court reported that there was no evidence to fix responsibility but said the ship was probably destroyed by a submarine mine. Although McKinley asked Congress to consider the report carefully, the report that a submarine mine may have caused the explosion caused most Americans to blame Spain either because of intention or negligence. U.S. government officials did not believe Spain directly exploded the *Maine* but that Spain's failure to keep law and order in Cuba resulted in the destruction of the U.S. ship.

Nevertheless, the naval court had reached a wrong conclusion and so did the public. Seventy-five years later, a committee chaired by Admiral Hyman Rickover examined all the records of the *Maine*'s sinking. The Rickover report, which was published in 1976, said the explosion on the *Maine* resulted from internal combustion, not an outside bomb or mine.

March 28, 1898

A German naval bill begins expansion of the navy.

Nurtured through the efforts of Admiral Alfred von Tirpitz, the German navy planned eventually to surpass the British. The legislation of 1898 was extended by a second naval law on June 12, 1900, which authorized an additional rapid naval construction program for Germany.

March 31, 1898

Spain gives an unsatisfactory response to an American request for peace in Cuba.

Although the American request on March 27 did not forcefully urge the steps Spain should take, the Madrid government's response did not indicate that the Cuban insurrection would be concluded quickly.

Unfortunately, Secretary of State Sherman's illness in the spring of 1898 placed the State Department in the inexperienced hands of Assistant Secretary of State William R. Day. The assistant secretary had no diplomatic background and no experience in foreign relations. Consequently, his instructions to the U.S. minister at Madrid were imprecise. In asking Minister Woodford to obtain Spanish concessions the secretary wrote: "See if the following can be done": (1) an armistice by October 1, with peace negotiations through McKinley's good offices; and (2) the immediate end of the reconcentration program. Then Day continued, "Add if possible: (3) If terms of peace are not satisfactorily settled by October 1, President of the United States to be arbiter between Spain and insurgents." Day's message was ambiguous about both acts desired and consequences. McKinley particularly wanted Spain to recognize Cuban independence, but Day omitted this demand.

Regardless of Day's lack of clarity, Spain's response offered little hope for the end of hostilities. On March 31, Spain agreed to end the reconcentration program, a policy Captain General Blanco had been told to implement in November 1897. Regarding an armistice, Spain would accept one if the insurgents requested it. The rebels would not do this, as both

Madrid and Washington knew, because it would seem to be a surrender. Finally, Madrid had ignored McKinley's offer of good offices to settle the problems of Cuba.

U.S. Minister to Spain Woodford provided a good summary of Spain's March 31 response. He informed Day that Spain's offer did not mean peace but a continued "destructive, cruel, and now needless war." Although, as Woodford cabled McKinley on April 3, Spain would grant an armistice, it refused to grant the independence to Cuba necessary to end the conflict.

April 9, 1898

While preparing his speech for war against Spain, President McKinley learns that Captain General Blanco has suspended hostilities in Cuba.

Following his receipt of Spain's March 31 reply to the American request for peace in Cuba, McKinley consulted with his cabinet and decided to prepare a speech to deliver to Congress on April 11, requesting the use of armed forces in Cuba.

The president originally planned to speak to Congress on April 6 but delayed the speech to have more time to find out about Spain's future proposals for Cuba. In addition, England and other European powers had talked with Spain's Premier Sagasta and received a note regarding the armistice that Blanco instituted on April 7. The armistice proposal did not promise Cuban independence, however, and the insurgents rejected it. Thus, whether or not Blanco's armistice decree would have effectively solved the Cuban problem is not certain. Some observers in 1898 believed the armistice assured independence because Spain could not afford to begin fighting again. Others believed, however, that the "loyalists" in Cuba would not accept Blanco's armistice decree or Cuban freedom. Spanish honor was one of the obsolete attitudes still prevailing among Spain's upper classes, and the political surrender of independence could be won or lost only on the battlefield.

April 11, 1898

McKinley asks Congress for authority to use American armed forces in Cuba.

McKinley's decision to request extreme U.S. action resulted from Spain's unsatisfactory response to an American request to end the Cuban insurrection. His speech had been delayed to evacuate Americans in Cuba and to await possible effective action by Spain as had been sought by British and other European diplomats. Spain's announcement of a cease-fire without independence on April 7 did not seem sufficient to end hostilities, so the president went ahead with the speech of April 11.

McKinley's speech reviewed past attempts to end the Cuban insurrection and emphasized the damage to U.S. property and commerce in Cuba, as well as the tensions in America caused by pro-Cuban groups and gunrunners. The president said he needed congressional authority to use the nation's armed forces if necessary to bring order and stability to the island "on our doorstep." Near the end of his speech, he referred to Blanco's armistice of April 7, which the insurgents had rejected unless independence for Cuba was agreed to by Spain. Finally, McKinley did not directly ask for a declaration of war but told Congress it should decide on future American action.

McKinley's address received a mixed reaction both at home and abroad. While some saw it as a war message, others emphasized the last section, on the armistice in Cuba. Because the president avoided a direct recommendation for war, Congress had to choose war, negotiation, or continued inactivity by America.

April 19–20, 1898

Congress approves and President McKinley signs a joint resolution directing the President to use force to assure Cuban independence from Spain.

Following McKinley's message of April 11, Congress deliberated nine days before approving the joint resolution on Cuba. The resolution did not declare war but made it certain because Spanish honor would not permit its government to accept the American ultimatum to grant Cuban independence.

During the congressional discussions, the principal issue was how much authority to give to the president. On April 13, the House adopted a conciliatory resolution that McKinley had approved. This resolution permitted the president to intervene in Cuba to stop the fighting, empowering him to use force at his discretion. The strong influence of Speaker of the House Thomas B. Reed obtained a 325 to 19 vote for this resolution.

A stronger Senate proposal prevented quick action on McKinley's speech. On April 13, the Senate Foreign Relations Committee recommended three resolutions, each of which disappointed the president. The Senate resolutions stated that Cuba had a right to independence, demanded that Spain evacuate Cuba, and "directed and empowered" the president to use force if necessary to implement the resolutions.

On the Senate floor, two amendments were added to the Foreign Relations Committee's recommendations. The first was a minority resolution from the committee, which was known as the Turpie resolution. This amendment demanded that the president grant "immediate recognition to the Republic of Cuba." McKinley opposed recognition because he believed the rebels lacked a viable government. Democrats and Populists wanted to recognize Cuba's government and charged that the McKinley administration refused to do so because it wished to protect American bondholders who wanted to require the Cuban government to accept liability for $400 million of bonds. The Turpie amendment passed the Senate because Western Republicans joined the Democrats and Populists in passing the resolution by 51 to 37.

The second amendment added to the Senate's resolution on Cuba was proposed by Senator Henry M. Teller. The Teller amendment stated that the United States had no intention of exercising "sovereignty, jurisdiction, or control over Cuba" and the island would be left to the government of the "island and its people." The Teller amendment passed also, and on April 16 the Senate approved its joint resolution with the three Foreign Relations Committee recommendations and the Turpie and Teller amendments. The Senate vote was 67 to 21.

A joint House-Senate committee had to reconcile their differences. By this time, a war fever prevailed in the country so that Speaker Reed could no longer hold his followers to the conciliatory House resolution. Finally, at 1:15 A.M. on April 20, the congressmen reached a compromise. The House accepted the declaration that Cuba ought to be free; the Senate withdrew the Turpie amendment on recognition of Cuba's government.

During the final vote, the compromise resolution barely passed the Senate. The Populists and Democrats demanded the Turpie amendment and voted against the compromise. The Senate vote, therefore, was 42 to 35, although the support for war was greater than the vote indicated. The House approved the compromise by 311 to 6.

Thus, as finally signed by McKinley, the congressional joint resolution declared Cuba should be independent, demanded that Spain evacuate Cuba, directed the president to use force, and stated that the United States would not seek sovereignty over Cuba.

April 25, 1898

Congress declares that a state of war has existed with Spain since April 21, 1898.

Following passage of the congressional joint resolution on April 20, 1898, the State Department sent the Madrid government an ultimatum asserting that unless Spain relinquished its authority over Cuba by noon on April 23, the United States would use force to implement the terms of the congressional resolution. Spain could not honorably accept Washington's dictation of its policy in Cuba and broke off diplomatic relations on April 21. Subsequently, the U.S. congress formally recognized Spain's refusal to comply and, on April 25, declared that war had begun with Spain on April 21.

April 28, 1898

William Rufus Day replaces John Sherman as secretary of state.

Day had no diplomatic experience prior to his appointment as assistant secretary of state in 1897. While he was an assistant, he confided to a friend: "I see the newspapers talk about the diplomacy of this administration as 'amateurish' and I must confess that it is." Because Sherman's lack of experience in diplomacy matched Day's, McKinley had selected an incompetent team to handle the Spanish crisis.

During the spring of 1898, Day had become acting secretary of state because of Sherman's illness. As a result, the president decided on April 28 to name him as secretary after Sherman agreed to resign. Aware of his shortcomings, Day served only until the Spanish armistice was concluded in August. He resigned as secretary on September 16, 1898.

May 1, 1898

U.S. Navy is victorious over the Spanish fleet in Manila Bay, the Philippine Islands.

Commodore George DEWEY's naval squadron had prepared since February 25, 1898, to fight Spain at Manila in case of war. Dewey's ships were at their station off the China coast when, on April 25, the Navy Department notified Dewey: "Proceed at once to the Philippine Islands. Commence operations at once, particularly against the Spanish fleet. You must capture vessels or destroy. Use utmost endeavors."

Dewey left as quickly as possible for Manila, the light cruisers and gunboats of his Asiatic squadron steaming into the harbor near Corregidor Island just before dawn on May 1. The Spanish fleet outnumbered the six U.S. vessels, but Spain's ships had fewer guns and were old and rotting. Dewey ordered the first attack at 5:40 A.M., and by 7:35 Spain's ships were silent, three of them aflame. Later, at 11 A.M., Dewey's gunboats knocked out the shore batteries of Manila and the fight was over. The American squadron suffered no deaths and only eight sailors were wounded.

Although New York newspapers reported news of Dewey's victory on May 2, some observers feared the reports were false because no official word arrived until May 7. At Dewey's orders the cable lines from Manila to Hong Kong had been cut. As a result, Dewey had to send the revenue cutter *McCulloch* to Hong Kong to file his report to Washington. On May 8, the New York *Tribune* confirmed the victory and the nation celebrated.

The week's delay had caused tension; the report of the victory resulted in a vast array of cheers for a new American hero: George Dewey. Babies, streets, and hotels were named in his honor. Dewey was promoted. Congress honored him a vote of thanks and an elaborate sword. Elation over the victory became one factor influencing the American decision to retain the Philippine Islands, even though few Americans knew where they were before May 1, 1898.

May 19, 1898

Aguinaldo, leader of the Filipino independence movement, is brought to the Philippine Islands from Hong Kong.

Emilio Aguinaldo's arrival in the Philippines had been planned with Commodore Dewey in Hong Kong, prior to Dewey's leaving for Manila on April 25–26. The Filipino leader had gone into exile in Hong Kong by the terms of the armistice of December 27, 1897. E. Spencer Pratt, the American consul at Singapore, had consulted previously with Aguinaldo and suggested to Dewey that the Filipino rebel forces could

Dewey's naval squadron is victorious over Spanish fleet in Manila Bay. Copy of lithograph, 1899. National Archives

aid the American defeat of the Spanish army in the Philippines.

Later, much controversy centered around Aguinaldo's discussions with Pratt and Dewey. The Filipino leader claimed the Americans promised the independence of his country; Pratt and Dewey denied this claim. Technically and precisely, the Americans probably did not promise independence, because they lacked such authority. Evidence indicates, however, that between April and August 1898, the Americans spoke favorably toward Philippine independence and led Aguinaldo and his lieutenants to believe independence would result.

See January 9, 1899.

May 25, 1898

A U.S. Army expedition leaves San Francisco for the Philippine Islands.

On May 4, President McKinley approved a recommendation of Major General Nelson A. Miles to divert a U.S. army force to the Philippines to conquer and hold a land base so that Commodore Dewey could hold Manila in case a second Spanish fleet arrived. Previously, the army planned no operations in the Philippines, and Dewey's discussions with the Filipino leader, Aguinaldo, presumed that the rebel forces would be used against the Spanish army.

Following Dewey's victory on May 1, news reached Washington that Spain was preparing a naval squadron under Rear Admiral Eduardo de la Camaro y Livermore, to leave Cádiz for Manila. As a result, McKinley decided to send an army to support Dewey. Twelve thousand soldiers arrived in San Francisco on May 24, embarking the next day on the *City of Peking* transport, the first U.S. expeditionary army to the Philippine Islands.

On July 11, Washington learned that the Camaro fleet had been recalled to Spain. By that date, three additional U.S. transport ships had left San Francisco for the Far East.

May 29, 1898

U.S. Naval forces begin a blockade of the Spanish fleet at Santiago, Cuba.

Although the U.S. navy first planned to intercept the Spanish fleet coming from the Cape Verde Islands, Commodore Winfield S. SCHLEY had delayed his ships at Key West until May 19, by which date Spain's Admiral Pascual CERVERA y Topete had brought the fleet to Santiago. Consequently, Schley and Admiral William T. SAMPSON decided to blockade Cervera's fleet of four cruisers and three destroyers. The blockade required reinforcements by the army, however, and General William Shafter was ordered to undertake this task.

See July 3, 1898.

June 9, 1898

A commercial commission to China is requested by Secretary of State Day.

The State Department had become concerned by the rush of European powers to gain concessions and loans from China. American business interests envisioned a great future in the China market and became apprehensive of the activity of other nations in China following the Sino-Japanese war of 1894–1895. Early in 1898, the Committee on American Interests in China organized in New York and, at its urging, Chambers of Commerce in New York, Boston, San Francisco, Cleveland, and Philadelphia petitioned Congress and the State Department to protect American interests in East Asia.

Secretary Day's request to Congress on June 9 resulted from these business petitions. Through Secretary of the Treasury Lyman J. Gage, Secretary Day sought a congressional appropriation to pay the expenses of a commercial commission to China. Day's note to Congress stated that American manufacturing output "has reached the point of large excess above the demands of home consumption," and the "United States has important interests at stake in the commercial facilities in regions which are likely to offer developing markets for goods. Nowhere is this consideration of more interest than in its relation to the Chinese Empire."

Because Dewey's victory at Manila afforded an excellent opportunity for an American base near China, Secretary Day and other U.S. leaders saw a connection between the Philippines and China. On July 29, 1898, a San Francisco Chamber of Commerce petition asked President McKinley to keep the Philippines for America "with a view to strengthening our trade relations with the Orient." Or, as the president's chief campaign manager Senator Mark Hanna observed: with the Philippines as a base for American ships, "we can and will take a huge slice of the commerce of Asia. That is what we want."

See May 23, 1896; November 14, 1897; July 1, 1898.

June 11, 1898

The Hundred Days of Reform begin in China.

Western interests in China were elated by a series of reforms advocated by the Chinese scholar K'ang Yu-wei and a Cantonese group with foreign education. The Emperor Ch'ing Te-tsung accepted these reforms and permitted K'ang to enforce them.

The reformers planned to Westernize China. Their program included the rapid completion of the Peking-Hangkow Railroad, importing Western armaments, establishing a naval school, and creating other schools including a university. They ran into trouble, however, when K'ang tried to replace the six ministers and the Grand Council with an assembly and a constitution. These attempts endangered the entrenched interests of the dowager Tz'u-hsi and the Manchu military order.

When K'ang further proposed in September to institute a budget and end private sinecures, the conservative factions in the imperial court decided to take action to end the reforms.

See September 22, 1898.

June 17, 1898

German ships arrive at Manila and the Germans express interest in having a base in the Islands.

Dewey's defeat of the Spanish fleet at Manila brought warships of other nations to the Philippine Islands, where they waited anxiously to obtain special privileges such as they had gained in China. Although the Germans arrived the earliest and expressed their desire for a naval base and land leases in the islands, Great Britain informed Washington that it would annex the islands if the United States did not want them, and Japan indicated it would join a multinational protectorate over the islands. France also was willing to obtain concessions in the Philippines. Nevertheless, Germany's presence irritated Commodore Dewey the most because the German commander, Vice Admiral Otto Von Diedrichs, failed to observe Dewey's blockade regulations.

June 20, 1898

Guam is captured from the Spanish by the U.S. Navy.

Secretary of the Navy John D. Long ordered Captain Henry Glass to seize the island of Guam from Spain. Commanding the cruiser *Charleston*, Glass proceeded to Guam and easily overthrew the weak Spanish garrison based on the island.

June 30, 1898

The first U.S. Army troops land in the Philippine Islands.

In order that his ships could remain at Manila, Dewey needed a land base; U.S. army units had been sent on May 14, 1898. The first of these expeditionary forces landed on June 13 but did not occupy Manila until August 13. By June 30, Dewey had also brought the Philippine rebel leader, Emilio Aguinaldo, from Hong Kong to organize the native troops against the Spanish garrisons. Problems with Aguinaldo seem to have arisen early because Dewey wrote on June 30: "He is sorry our troops are here, I think."

July 1, 1898

Great Britain obtains special land concessions in China, completing a rush for spheres of influence inaugurated by Japan in 1896 and by the Germans on November 14, 1897.

On July 1, the British obtained a lease of Weihaiwei, following up an agreement of June 9, by which England acquired a 99-year lease of Kowloon Territory opposite Hong Kong.

Within a period of one year, China had to accept the following concessions:

1. Germans occupied Kiaochow peninsula on November 14, 1897.
2. Russia received a 25-year lease of Talienwan, the southern part of the Liaodong peninsula and Port Arthur.
3. Russia received rights to build a Harbin-to-Port Arthur railway.
4. France extorted a 99-year lease of Kwangchowan Bay and the territory nearby.
5. France received rights for a railroad to Yunan-Fu.
6. France secured a Chinese promise not to lease land bordering on Tonkin, Indochina.

7. Japan required China not to lease any part of Fukien Province.

The Chinese spheres of influence granted to Japan and the European powers endangered the 19th-century policies of the open door heretofore advocated by Great Britain and America. As soon as the United States ended the war with Spain, the State Department sought some means to restrict these concessions.

See September 6, 1899.

July 3, 1898

The Spanish fleet in Cuba is destroyed after the U.S. Army gains strategic positions to bombard Santiago and the fleet.

Following Admiral Schley's blockade of Cervera's fleet on May 29, U.S. army forces under General SHAFTER came aboard a transport ship in the vicinity of Santiago and disembarked ashore on June 25. The army of 17,000 regulars and volunteers including the "Rough Riders" (the First U.S. Volunteer Cavalry Regiment, under Colonel Leonard WOOD and Lieutenant Colonel Theodore ROOSEVELT) marched on Santiago. At the battles of El Caney and San Juan Hill on July 1, the army won the commanding heights east and north of Santiago, where its artillery could bombard both the city and Cervera's fleet.

Lt. Col. "Teddy" Roosevelt (with sword) leads the Rough Riders to the top of San Juan Hill, July 1, 1898

On July 3, Admiral Cervera attempted to run for the open sea. His seven ships were no match for the four U.S. battleships and two cruisers commanded by Admiral Sampson. During a four-hour battle along the coast of Cuba, the Spanish fleet was destroyed. The Spanish losses were 474 killed or wounded and 1,760 taken prisoner. The U.S. navy had only one seaman killed and one wounded. Santiago and its 24,000-man troops surrendered on July 17.

July 4, 1898

U.S. forces occupy Wake Island.

This island, 2,325 miles west of Honolulu, was first taken by the U.S. army's expeditionary forces on their way to reinforce Dewey's men at Manila. Later, the U.S. navy occupied the islands on January 17, 1899, under Commander Edward D. Taussig of the USS *Bennington*.

July 6, 1898

Congress annexes Hawaii by joint resolution.

Almost immediately after the first word of Dewey's victory at Manila, Congressman Francis G. NEWLANDS on May 4 presented a joint resolution of annexation to the House of Representatives. The strategic significance of Hawaii became clearer to more Americans after they learned about the Philippines. Consequently, the House Committee on Foreign Affairs quickly recommended approval of the Newlands resolution on May 17. With McKinley's support, it passed the House by a vote of 209 to 91 on June 15, 1898.

The Senate vote required more time. Anti-imperialist senators such as Justin S. Morrill, who was 88 years old, pleaded with the younger senators not to violate the republic's traditional principles against acquiring colonies—the curse, Morrill said, that destroyed the Roman republic.

The opponents of imperialism were a minority, however, and on July 6 the resolution passed by 46 to 21 with 26 senators abstaining.

President McKinley signed the annexation bill on July 7, and on August 12, 1898, the islands were formally annexed. In Hawaii, the white ruling classes enthusiastically favored U.S. annexation. A league of natives opposed annexation, claiming it was done without the consent of the people. Unlike what had occurred in Texas in 1846, Hawaii's leaders did not call for a state convention and a plebiscite to ratify the treaty of annexation.

July 13, 1898

Rear Admiral Dewey's men occupy Grande Island to keep it out of German hands.

Whether or not Germany's Vice Admiral von Diedrichs intended to take the Philippines' Grande Island, the German leader had irritated Dewey sufficiently to make the Americans suspicious. Grande Island lay at the entrance to Subic Bay, and Aguinaldo's forces had been prevented from taking the island by the position of the German ships. Dewey heard of the problem and sent the warships *Raleigh* and *Concord* to discover what von Diedrichs proposed. As the American ships approached, the *Irene,* Diedrichs's flagship, quickly withdrew and Dewey's seamen took over the island.

In contrast to the German violation of Dewey's blockade orders and other requests, French and British naval officers at Manila had been courteous and cooperative. When Dewey's report of the Grande Island incident reached America, U.S. resentment of Germany flared. The imperialists claimed that if the United States did not annex the Philippines, Germany would. Actually, the British, Japanese, and French were as eager as Germany to take the Philippines if they could. If America had given independence to the Philippines, it might have had to protect the islands from being taken by one of the other powers.

July 25, 1898

Puerto Rico is occupied by U.S. forces under General Nelson A. Miles.

The Spanish had few troops on the island of Puerto Rico and they offered only minor opposition to General Miles's men before they surrendered.

August 12, 1898

Spain is granted its request for an armistice, ending the war with America.

The Spanish position in Cuba became untenable following the fall of Santiago and the destruction of Cervera's fleet. Therefore, the Madrid government asked France to mediate a settlement. Jules Cambon, the French ambassador to America, requested U.S. peace terms on July 26. Less than two weeks later, Spain accepted the following terms:

1. Spain relinquished its sovereignty over Cuba and agreed to evacuate the island.
2. Spain ceded Puerto Rico and one of the Ladrone Islands (Guam) to the United States.
3. The United States would occupy Manila pending the determination of the future of the Philippines at the peace conference.
4. All hostilities were suspended and a peace conference would convene at Paris no later than October 1, 1898.

For results of the Paris Conference, see December 10, 1898.

U.S. soldiers learn that the Spanish have asked for an armistice. National Archives

August 13, 1898

Manila is occupied by American and Filipino troops.

The occupation of Manila had two significant factors. First, the occupation came one day after the armistice was agreed to between Washington and Madrid. Second, Filipino troops became involved in the move to replace the Spanish forces, even though the Spanish and American army officers made plans to keep Aguinaldo's forces out of the city. The plans to restrain the Filipinos failed because some Spanish troops tried to prevent the U.S. occupation and fighting resulted in parts of the city. The attempt to make Manila a strictly U.S. military base had become the American objective by August 13. Nevertheless, Aguinaldo's army did help to end the final Spanish hostilities in Manila. His army also occupied and repaired Spanish forts outside of Manila. The Spanish commander in Manila surrendered on August 13, 1898.

September 8, 1898

Japan offers to join America in jointly protecting the Philippine Islands.

In a diplomatic message to Washington, the Japanese recognized American control over the future of the Philippines. Therefore, if the United States did not desire to operate unilaterally in those islands, Japan offered to join America singly or "in conjunction with another power" in forming a "suitable government" under a "joint or tripartite" protectorate. America did not, of course, accept this offer.

September 9, 1898

The Filipino leaders proclaim an independent republican government.

This announcement followed Emilio Aguinaldo's proclamation of independence on June 12, 1898, soon after his return from Hong Kong to renew the Philippine insurrection. Aguinaldo became president of the Republic of the Philippines and Apolinario Mabini, a former associate of Rizal, became his chief adviser and the "mouthpiece of the revolution."

On September 15, a revolutionary assembly met at Malolos. It ratified the decree of Philippine independence on September 29, 1898.

For earlier developments of the Philippine insurrection against Spain, see December 30, 1896, and December 27, 1897.

September 18, 1898

An Anglo-French crisis begins at Fashoda in the Sudan.

Since 1896, British forces had advanced up the Nile, claiming the region for Egypt, while the French had pushed down the Sobat River from west-central Africa. On September 18, British forces under Sir Horatio Herbert Kitchener faced French forces under Jean Baptiste Marchand and both refused to evacuate Fashoda.

A conflict was barely avoided because each leader agreed to consult his government. On November 3, the French yielded by evacuating their forces and on March 21, 1899, renounced all territory along the Nile. The episode resulted in a continuing cool relationship between Paris and London as each nation sought to expand its imperial power. This antagonism did not change until 1907.

September 20, 1898

John Hay is Commissioned to replace William Day as Secretary of State.

Because he had never considered himself well qualified for the office, Day prepared to resign as soon as the armistice was made with Spain.

President McKinley requested John Hay to return from London, where he served as ambassador to England, and to take over as secretary. In contrast to both Sherman and Day, his two immediate predecessors, Hay was well qualified to be secretary of state. Hay had served as an assistant private secretary to President Lincoln (1860–1865) and in diplomatic posts at Paris (1865–1867), Vienna (1867–1868), Madrid (1869–1870), and London (1891–1898). He had been assistant secretary of state from 1879 to 1881, and served as secretary throughout the remainder of McKinley's presidency and under Theodore Roosevelt until his death on July 1, 1905.

September 22, 1898

The end of Chinese reform: the Empress Dowager Tz'u-hsi imprisons the Emperor.

The Hundred Days of Reform begun on June 11 ended because the nobles in power feared their special benefits would end. To eliminate the reformers' position Tz'u-hsi reasserted the political control she had held with Prince Kung in 1889. For China's internal political developments this move inaugurated a dispute between the conservatives and those who preferred to Westernize, a conflict that climaxed in the Revolution of 1911. In the meantime, China experienced serious difficulties with the "foreign devils" who were exerting greater control over China territory.

October 26, 1898

President McKinley makes a decision on the Philippines: "the cession must be of the whole archipelago or none."

Secretary of State John Hay wired to the American peace commissioners in Paris the president's decision that the whole of the Philippines must be ceded to the United States by Spain. Since July 1898, the McKinley administration had been divided about the future of the Philippines. When the issue was considered by the cabinet in July, three department secretaries favored and three opposed annexation. In favor of acquiring the islands were Secretary of Agriculture J. Wilson, Secretary of the Interior C. N. Bliss, and Attorney General J. W. Griggs; opposed were Secretary of the Navy John D. Long, Secretary of State William Day, and Secretary of the Treasury Lyman Gage.

Because McKinley could not decide, the armistice terms of August 12 left the "control, disposition and government of the Philippines" to be determined by the peace conference. President McKinley seems initially to have desired to take Manila and the nearby area for a naval base, but when he issued instructions to the peace commissioners on September 16, he wrote that we "cannot accept less than the cession in full right and sovereignty of the island of Luzon." But October 26, McKinley had decided that the United States should annex all or none of the Philippines, preferably all. The president came to envision U.S. annexation as a duty "which we cannot disregard" because the "march of events rules and overrules human action." As he wrote to the peace commission, the United States did not by "any desire or design" seek to gain the Philippines, but the "success of our arms at Manila" imposed an obligation on the American people. The duties, he said, are as becomes a great nation "on whose growth and career from the beginning the Ruler of Nations has plainly written the high command and pledge of civilization." Then he added: "Incidental to our tenure in the Philippines is the commercial opportunity to which American statesmanship cannot be indifferent." Thus, both God and mammon had ordained that America should annex the Philippines.

Clearly McKinley's rhetoric was not accurate. Alfred Mahan and the advocates of sea power and imperialism had favored the annexation of the Philippines for some time. The navy's war plans division had planned operations against Manila for several years. On February 25, the Navy Department ordered Dewey to prepare to attack the Philippines if war began. These were all decisions of men, not gods. McKinley was either ignorant of or deceptive about the foreign policy goals of prominent Republicans in his administration and in Congress.

Because most of the peace commissioners favored annexation of the Philippines, McKinley's decision was effectively carried out.

See December 10, 1898.

November 19, 1898

An anti-imperialist league is founded at Boston.

The anti-imperialists opposed the acquisition of overseas territory by the United States, excepting perhaps Puerto Rico. They especially opposed annexing the Philippine Islands, which were 7,000 miles from San Francisco and had a native revolutionary leader, Emilio Aguinaldo, who desired independence for his people.

The anti-imperialists had a strong following. The Boston League enlisted 30,000 members. Among the leading U.S. citizens who supported the league were former Presidents Cleveland and Harrison, Senator George Hoar, and the businessman Andrew Carnegie. As the Philippine insurrection developed between 1899 and 1902, the anti-imperialists became a major group dissenting against the U.S. war in Southeast Asia.

Uncle Sam's White Elephant. Cartoon reflects opposition to U.S. annexation of Philippines. *New York Herald*

December 6, 1898

The Vest Resolution is presented to Congress. It declares that the Constitution does not grant power to the federal government to govern a colony permanently.

This resolution offered by George C. Vest, a Democrat from Missouri, was designed to prevent the annexation of the Philippine Islands. Generally, Americans assumed that these islands were too remote to be considered for statehood.

The Vest resolution received considerable debate in Congress during December and January 1898–1899 but was never voted upon because it became tangled with the question of ratifying the Treaty of Paris. Probably Vest and his supporters realized that they did not have the majority support necessary to pass the resolution. The ratification of the Treaty of Paris rendered the Vest resolution obsolete.

See February 6, 1899.

December 10, 1898

The Treaty of Paris is signed by Spain and the United States.

The U.S. peace commissioners who began deliberations with Spain in Paris on October 1, 1898, were Senators Cushman K. Davis, William P. Frye, and George Gray; former Secretary of State William R. Day; and the owner of the New York *Tribune*, Whitelaw Reid. John Bassett Moore, an eminent international lawyer, was secretary to the commission. This group met with Spanish delegates for two months to settle two questions not provided for in the August 12 armistice terms: (1) the Cuban debt of $400 million in Spanish bonds and (2) the future of the Philippine Islands.

On the Cuban debt, the Americans insisted that Spain must assume the debt, while the Spanish tried to forestall this demand. First, they argued that America should assume the debt. Later, they asked for arbitration of the issue. Eventually, however, Spain had to accept U.S. terms and assumed responsibility for Cuba's past debts.

The Philippine question caused more difficulty. On October 26, the president finally instructed the commissioners to demand all of the archipelago or nothing, and most of the Paris delegates preferred all of the islands. Senator Frye objected, however, because he did not believe Spain would agree. Furthermore, because Manila was occupied after the armistice of August 12, the United States had no clear right of conquest. Frye recommended offering Spain $10 million to $20 million for the islands. Nevertheless, the Spanish prolonged the talks because they believed a Democratic congressional victory in November would soften American demands.

Following the elections, Spain agreed to cede the Philippines for $20 million. As a result the United States gained three territories in the Treaty of Paris: Guam, Puerto Rico, and the Philippine Islands.

1899

January 5, 1899

The United States opposes France's attempt to extend its concessions from China in Shanghai.

Between 1896 and 1898, England, Russia, Germany, and Japan forced China to grant them additional land and commercial concessions. When France sought further concessions during the fall of 1898, the American minister to China, E. H. Conger, became concerned because the United States had interests in preserving an open door at Shanghai. Conger learned about the French proposals on December 22, when the British minister asked him to join in protesting the French requests. After cabling Washington for direction, Conger received authorization from Secretary of State Hay to file a formal protest if France's request seemed to damage American interests.

On January 5, Conger formally notified the French minister that America objected to the extension of French privileges at Shanghai. Conger acted unilaterally, however, not jointly with England. Conger explained to Hay that American landowners, merchants, and missionaries in China opposed the French demands. Incidents such as these led to Secretary Hay's reaffirmation of the open door policy on September 6, 1899.

January 9, 1899

In Manila, Aguinaldo and U.S. Major General Otis fail to agree on terms to end antagonism between American and Filipino forces.

The officials of the Republic of the Philippines led by President Aguinaldo protested a decree of President McKinley's that extended Major General Ewell S. Otis's military control over the entire archipelago of the Philippine Islands. Aguinaldo claimed that American spokesmen had promised in May and June 1898 to give independence to the Philippines not only from Spanish but from any other foreign control. Yet General Otis followed McKinley's orders, which were based on the Spanish cession of the islands to America in the Treaty of Paris.

Whether Commodore Dewey or the U.S. consul at Singapore, Spencer, promised Aguinaldo independence is not certain. Probably he was encouraged to believe this in May 1898 because the Americans sought the insurgents' assistance against the Spanish army. Neither Dewey nor Spencer had authority to grant independence, however, and never put such terms in writing for Aguinaldo. At the same time, before August 1898, Americans who talked with the Filipino leaders probably disclaimed any American desire to annex the islands. In a December 1897 speech to Congress on Cuba and Spain, President

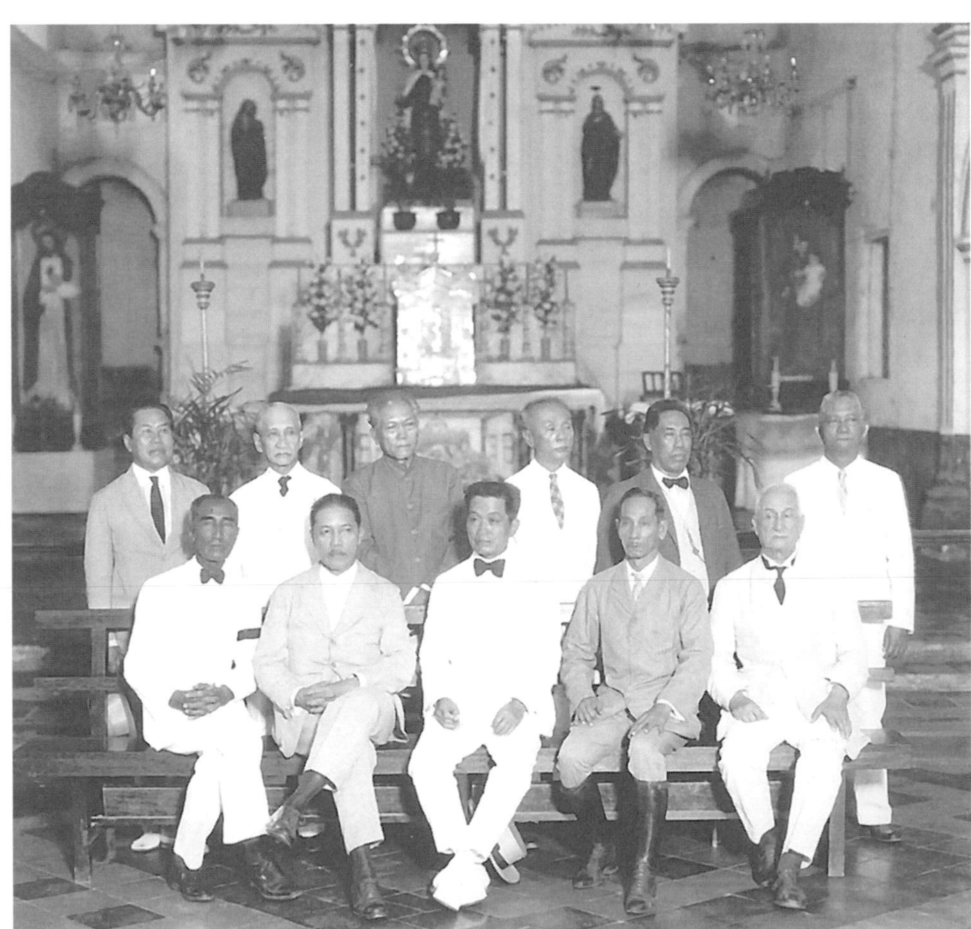

General Aguinaldo (seated center) and ten of the delegates to the first Assembly of Representatives. National Archives

McKinley had stated: "I speak not of forcible annexation, for that cannot be thought of, that by our code of morality would be criminal aggression." The president had later hesitated until October 1898 to instruct the peace commissioners to obtain the Philippines as part of the Treaty of Paris. Once he decided, however, McKinley used every effort to maintain American control of the islands.

Aguinaldo and his officers had, during the interim, proclaimed the Republic of the Philippines and organized a constituent assembly on November 29 that named Aguinaldo as president on December 23 and issued a republican constitution on January 23, 1899. None of these Filipino acts was recognized in Washington, and most Americans hardly knew they had occurred. Americans generally saw the Filipinos as illiterate, uneducated, and backward "little brown brothers" who had to be taught civilized manners by the United States.

To try to resolve increased disturbances between his forces and the Americans, Aguinaldo conferred with General Otis on January 9, 1899. He pleaded with Otis to grant some concessions toward the recognition of independence now or in the near future. Any type of reassurance, the Filipino leader said, would enable his followers to end their fear of American control over their nation. Nevertheless, Otis felt he had to obey his orders to the letter. The president gave him military authority but did not cite any concessions for the Filipino people.

The failure of Otis to yield to any degree led to further protests and demonstrations by Filipino nationalists against the Americans. Tensions increased that permitted any incident to break into full-scale war.

See May 19, 1898, and February 4, 1899.

February 4, 1899

Fighting breaks out in Manila between American and Filipino troops.

The failure of the conference between Aguinaldo and General Otis on January 9, 1899, led to greater tension, uncertainty, and insecurity between Americans and Filipinos in Manila. For several weeks General Otis restrained his men because President McKinley warned him to avoid a conflict until the Senate ratified the Treaty of Paris. The president feared that an immediate outbreak of war would enable the anti-imperialists to defeat the treaty because the administration argued in Washington that Aguinaldo did not represent the majority of Filipinos and a war was not expected.

The war was not delayed but began on February 4 after an incident where American guards on duty shot a Filipino soldier. Blame for the incident is controversial because the Filipino may have provoked the shooting that led to widespread fighting between the Americans and the Filipino Army of Liberation. The Filipino army consisted of from 15,000 to 40,000 men who fought against the Americans for a year before Filipino forces adopted guerrilla warfare in one-third of the 77 Philippine provinces. American forces were reinforced, reaching a total of 70,000 before the guerrilla war ended.

Fortunately for McKinley, the delay in fighting proved to be sufficient. News of the Manila events of February 4 to 6 did not reach Washington until after the Senate had voted to ratify the treaty on February 6.

February 6, 1899

The U.S. Senate ratifies the Treaty of Paris, annexing Guam, Puerto Rico, and the Philippine Islands.

President McKinley sent the Treaty of Paris to the Senate on January 4, 1899. During the next month, most of the Senate debate focused on the annexation of the Philippines. Senators such as George Hoar and Eugene Hale opposed annexation, but like other anti-imperialists they lacked an alternative proposal about what to do if other powers moved to take over the Philippines. Reports had appeared that both Germany and Japan wanted to annex the islands.

With no adequate answer to such a contingency, the anti-imperialists could not obtain sufficient votes to reject the treaty. On February 6, the Senate ratified the treaty by a vote of 57 to 27.

February 14, 1899

A resolution to grant independence to the Philippines is narrowly defeated by the Senate.

During debate on the Treaty of Paris, some senators had argued that the treaty must be approved to end the war with Spain. The Philippine question, they argued, should be held for future consideration. Accepting this viewpoint, Senator Augustuos O.

The Philippines, 1899

Bacon of Georgia had voted for the treaty but immediately after February 6 offered a congressional resolution to give the Philippines independence.

On February 4, fighting had begun in those islands between the U.S. army and Philippine forces. Bacon and other opponents of imperialism believed the fighting should end immediately and independence be given to Aguinaldo's government. Senator Albert Beveridge of Indiana and other pro-imperial senators spoke as strongly in favor of retaining the Philippine Islands.

The dispute over the annexation of the Philippines proved difficult during the next four years. Anti-imperialists argued in terms of U.S. tradition as opposing colonial control and being unconstitutional. The imperialists contended that it was the duty of the United States to civilize the world, and that the United States needed bases in the Western Pacific to promote American commerce and sea power. Neither side's arguments indicated any knowledge of Philippine history or culture. Such Filipino leaders as José Rizal, who had been educated in Spain, were not known to Americans. Thus, even anti-imperialists often envisioned the Filipinos as half-naked savages who lacked the benefits of Western technology and civilized life.

Whatever the status of the Filipino natives, Senator Bacon's resolution resulted in a tie vote in the Senate on February 14. The resolution failed to pass because Vice President Garret A. Hobart voted against it. Nevertheless, the evenly divided Senate vote indicates the deep divisions within the nation regarding annexation of the Philippines. The American imperial thrust after 1898 had strong supporters but equally strong opponents from the beginning, a factor heralding the persistent divisions within America regarding its 20th-century role in international relations.

For the outcome of the Philippine Insurrectionary War, see March 23, 1901, July 4, 1901, and July 4, 1902.

February 20, 1899

An Anglo-American Joint High Commission fails to settle the two basic disputes between England-Canada and America.

This commission resulted from a discussion between President McKinley and British Ambassador Julian Pauncefote in March 1898. The basic issues in contention were the Alaskan boundary and the revision of the Clayton-Bulwer Treaty of 1850 regarding an isthmian canal.

The commissioners met in Quebec and Washington between August 23, 1898, and February 20, 1899, but reached no agreement. The Alaskan boundary conflict was of immediate concern because of quarrels between gold prospectors in the Yukon. To head the British-Canadian delegation, London selected Baron Farrer Herschell (Lord Herschell), the lord high chancellor of Great Britain.

Herschell had been instructed to hold the excess demands of Sir Wilfrid Laurier and other Canadians in check by making concessions to America without "betraying" Canada, a difficult role to fulfill. The Canadians insisted on arbitration, but the U.S. delegation refused because it believed arbitration would divide the territory in dispute, giving up land that was rightfully America's.

An impasse resulted. After 18 weeks of fruitless discussion in Quebec and Washington, the meetings adjourned on February 20, 1899. Lord Herschell reported that perhaps after tempers cooled and informal negotiations were held, the commissioners might try again.

See October 20, 1899.

March 3, 1899

Congress establishes a committee to investigate Isthmian canal routes.

Although some concern about a Central American canal had been present previously, an incident during the Spanish-American War dramatized the value of such a waterway, making Congress more receptive to such proposals in 1899.

In three sessions of Congress (1895, 1896, and 1898), Senator John T. Morgan had sought congressional support for a canal in Nicaragua to be constructed by the Maritime Canal Company of Vermont with the cost guaranteed by U.S. government bonds. These proposals never passed the House of Representatives prior to the war with Spain.

During the Spanish-American War, the U.S. navy's need for ships in the Caribbean Sea demonstrated the canal's purpose. The navy had ordered the warship *Oregon* from San Francisco to assist naval action in the Caribbean. As the *Oregon* raced 12,000 miles past Cape Horn and around South America, newspaper accounts followed the ship's progress for 67 days. At times, ominous periods of silence occurred whenever communications were lost. Then rousing dispatches of praise followed when the *Oregon* reached ports at Peru or Chile. Finally, the battleship arrived at Florida and later helped the navy to blockade Santiago, Cuba. The *Oregon*'s voyage enabled businessmen, the National Board of Trade, and others to point out how a canal would have cut 8,000 miles from the San Francisco-to-Florida trip.

Subsequently, President McKinley's annual message of 1898 suggested urgent action to obtain a canal. After Canadian objections prevented signing of the Hay-Pauncefote Treaty of January 12, 1899, Senator Morgan's renewed attempt to approve a Nicaraguan canal obtained great support. The Senate passed Morgan's resolution on January 21, 1899, but opposition in the House prevented its enactment. Some congressmen complained that the bill granting bonds for the Maritime Canal Company threatened to be another Credit Moblier scandal such as the railroads caused during President Grant's administration. Consequently, William P. Hepburn introduced a bill to substitute for Morgan's; Hepburn's bill provided $115 million for the U.S. government to build and own the Nicaraguan canal.

Eventually, neither the Morgan nor the Hepburn bill passed Congress because a new factor arose: a proposal to reincorporate the New Panama Canal Company in the United States, permitting America to control a Panama canal. The New Panama Canal Corporation had purchased the rights and assets of the de Lesseps Company including the equipment and work completed. The company's U.S. attorney, William Nelson Cromwell, informed Congress that the French had finished two-fifths of the canal and that his investors held the concessions given by Colombia.

With President McKinley's backing, Cromwell persuaded Congress to establish a committee to study both isthmian routes. The bill of March 3, 1899, approved this commission, which replaced the 1897 commission set up by the president. This decision opened the way once more for the Panama route to supersede the Nicaraguan proposal.

On June 10, 1899, McKinley appointed the Isthmian Canal Commission with Rear Admiral John G. Walker as chairman.

See December 7, 1899, December 16, 1901, and January 18, 1902.

March 11, 1899

The Samoan Islands are divided by an Anglo-German-American conflict

On June 14, 1889, the three-power protectorate over Samoa established King Malietoa and a multinational council to rule the islands. Following Malietoa's death in 1898, the Germans attempted to install Mataafa as king. The British and American consuls protested because the 1889 pact specifically excluded Mataafa as ruler.

Malietoa's death also resulted in a tribal civil war in 1898 as followers of Mataafa and Malietoa Tanu, son of the deceased, each sought power.

On March 11, the U.S. consul, William L. Chambers, and the British consul decided to enforce the rule of Tanu even though the German consul, Dr. Raffel, supported Mataafa. British and American marines landed and the USS *Philadelphia* bombarded areas of the island held by Mataafa's forces. Sporadic fighting including the damaging of the German consulate continued until March 23, when English and

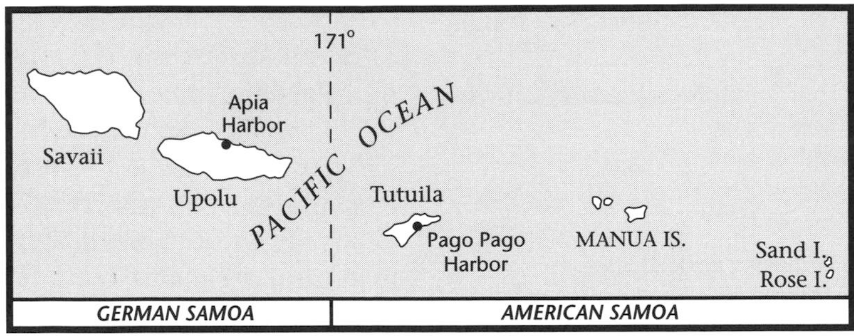

Samoa, 1899

American officials crowned Tanu as king. The Germans asked that a three-man commission investigate the Samoan problem. The commissioners began work on May 13, and the fighting stopped in Samoa.

See December 2, 1899.

July 29, 1899

The first Hague conference on disarmament adjourns. The United States signs a convention to join the permanent Court of International Arbitration.

The Hague Conference had convened on May 18, 1899, at the invitation of Czar Nicholas II of Russia. Its agenda was to consider disarmament, to limit methods of warfare, and to create a tribunal of international arbitration of disputes. The United States joined 25 other nations in the Hague Conference.

The one significant result of the conference was the establishment of the Permanent Court. The delegates sought to restrict or prohibit the use of poison gas, balloon-launched missiles, and other new instruments of war. The United States had long been an advocate of arbitration and encouraged the creation of the Permanent Court of International Arbitration. Consequently, at the final conference session on July 29, America signed that agreement.

In accepting the Permanent Court, the U.S. delegates insisted on a reservation regarding disputes in which the Monroe Doctrine would be involved. In other respects, they accepted the convention decision to resolve disputes by means of third-party mediation, international commissions, or an international court of justice at the Hague. Arbitration could not be compulsory, nor could it be extended to include questions of national honor or integrity.

Generally, the U.S.-British delegates Andrew Dickson White and Sir Julian Pauncefote cooperated during the Hague Conference. They prepared and lobbied for the International Court against German opposition. They also agreed in opposing a proposal to outlaw dumdum bullets, which were developed by the British at a foundry in Dum Dum, India. Their peculiarity was to expand on impact and create an ugly wound in the victim, a tactic that proved effective against the fanatical attacks of tribesmen in India and, later, the Philippines. Thus, the U.S. and British military opposed their prohibition although spokesmen of other nations believed the ghastly wounds were inhumane. The humanitarian interests of the other delegations won out at the Hague Conference, which prohibited dumdum bullets. The United States refused to accept this limitation, however.

The Hague Conference also defined several other laws of war including prohibiting the use of gas warfare or dropping bombs from balloons for five years and provisions for the better treatment of prisoners and the wounded.

August 14, 1899

Jacob G. Schurman, Chairman of the President's Philippine Commission, returns to America and reports in favor of keeping the Philippine Islands.

On January 20, Schurman had been appointed by President McKinley to head a committee to examine and recommend the future status of the Philippine Islands.

On August 14, 1899, Schurman returned from the Pacific and informed the public that while the Philippines might be given independence in the future, the United States should retain control of the islands and establish a territorial government to prepare the local populace for self-government at some indefinite future date. Schurman's commission was, therefore, preparing recommendations for a suitable means to govern the islands. This announcement greatly encouraged the imperialist groups in America who favored annexation of the Philippines.

On informing news reporters about his commission's decisions, Schurman emphasized America's need to join England and Japan in preventing the other powers from dismembering Chinese territory. "China," he said, "should maintain its independent position but its doors should be kept open."

See September 6, 1899.

August 15, 1899

A Russian ukase declares China's port of Talienwan would be open to all powers.

The czar's government had secured a 25-year lease of the Liaodong peninsula and Talienwan on May 7, 1898. The decree of August 15 indicated the czar did not wish exclusive use of the port but would allow all nations to use it on an equal basis. Advocates of the continued use of open door terms in China were pleased with the czar's decision and hoped other nations would do the same so that all China could remain open for equal commercial activity. The ukase was not carefully read, however, because although Talienwan was made an open port, Russian tariffs were to be collected there. The czar's response to Hay's open door note made it clear that Russia did not intend to follow the principle of equal rights in China.

September 6, 1899

Secretary Hay asks six other powers with Chinese interests to join America in reaffirming the Open Door Policy.

John Hay had become increasingly aware of the special land and commercial "spheres of influence" imposed on China by Russia, Germany, Japan, France, and England. Great Britain had suggested American cooperation in China during 1898, and after Hay became secretary of state England had a kindred spirit at the highest level of U.S. policy-making. The British government had come to realize the limited nature of its ability to continue as the principal power in China and sought U.S. cooperation in this area.

In August 1899, Hay had held discussions with his friend W. W. Rockhill, who had served in the U.S. diplomatic service in China and Korea (1884–1887) before becoming director of the Bureau of American Republics in 1899. With Rockhill's advice, Hay prepared a circular diplomatic note that reaffirmed the open door policies Great Britain began in 1842 after the conclusion of the Opium War. Hay's notes enunciated three basic principles regarding foreign activities in China:

1. that each nation would not interfere with trade of another nation in its Chinese "sphere of influence";
2. that present tariff duties should be retained at all treaty ports with duties collected for the Chinese government;
3. that all nations would be treated equally in harbor dues and other charges in any "sphere-of-influence."

Hay sent his original notes to London, Berlin, and St. Petersburg for their comment. Later, similar notes were sent to Paris, Rome, and Tokyo for their governments' acceptance.

For preliminaries, see July 1, 1898, and January 5, 1899; for the responses to Hay's notes, see March 20, 1900.

September 12, 1899

China's Minister to the United States protests against America's disregard for friendly relations with China.

China's minister, Wu T'ing-fang, protested to Secretary of State Hay that the United States was extending its anti-Chinese immigration laws and other discriminatory legislation to its new territories of Hawaii and the Philippines. As in prior Chinese objections to America's discriminatory immigration practices, including the state laws of California and other Pacific Coast states, Wu argued that friendly relations could not exist between China and America until the United States treated the Chinese justly.

Coming at the time when Secretary Hay was sending his "open door" notes, this complaint indicates two facets of U.S. policy: (1) Hay and the United States perceived the open door notes not as intended to benefit China but as intended to suit American interests; and (2) U.S. relations with China were no more friendly than the relations of other powers to China. Together these events and other facts about American policy toward China in the 19th century indicate the fallacy of the myth that American policy was the great benefactor of the Chinese. This myth was created by American missionaries who sought assistance from the U.S. public by romanticizing their good works in converting a small portion of China's large population to the Christian religion. Nevertheless, this myth had great influence on U.S. political perceptions of China, especially after 1931.

October 1, 1899

The report of the Venezuelan boundary arbitration is issued.

Set up under the Anglo-American agreement of November 11, 1896, the commission of six met in formal sessions in Paris from June to September 1899. The October 1 report awarded almost all the disputed region to British Guiana. Venezuela received the mouth of the Orinoco River and 5,000 square miles of land in the interior.

Venezuela was not satisfied with the award but did not immediately act to thwart it. On August 18, 1962, Venezuela took the case to the United Nations and requested an investigation.

October 12, 1899

The Boer War begins in South Africa.

British problems with President Kruger's South African republic were negotiated but not solved after the Jameson raid failed. Kruger feared that the British wished to annex the Transvaal; the British believed Kruger planned to drive them out of South Africa. After the war began, the Boers resorted to guerrilla warfare that prolonged the conflict until May 31, 1902, when the Treaty of VEREENIGING promised the Boers representative government in the future for their acceptance of British sovereignty at that time. The war was a difficult experience for Great Britain because it had to use 300,000 soldiers to deal with 60,000 to 75,000 Boers and to adopt ruthless methods to fight the Boer guerrillas. During the war, Britain also faced threats of French, Russian, or German intervention to help the Boers, but this intervention never occurred. It was also a challenging situation for some of Britain's new dominions, such as Australia and New Zealand, who had to determine the nature of their role in this new political arrangement.

Although the United States remained neutral during the war, U.S. policymakers favored Great Britain's cause.

See January 3, 1896.

October 20, 1899

Britain forces Canada to accept a modus vivendi on the Alaskan border controversy.

After the Joint High Commission had failed to resolve the outstanding issues between the English-speaking powers on February 20, 1899, London began to pressure the Canadians to accept a settlement on Alaska so that the isthmian canal issue could be settled. Finally, Joseph Chamberlain, the colonial secretary, threatened to formulate an understanding with America with or without Ottawa's approval, and Canada reluctantly accepted. The British were having trouble in South Africa, the Sudan, and China and could not accept what Chamberlain called Canada's "trumpery causes of irritation" with Washington.

As a result, the three parties agreed to a modus vivendi on the Alaskan boundary based upon lines proposed by Secretary Hay. By this agreement, the boundary covered three stretches of land routes to the goldfields, two of which favored the Americans; the third favored Canada. Because these routes were along the border where conflicts had taken place, the police of both nations would be in charge of local problems. Canada received a few square miles it had not previously owned, but Hay believed he had won a diplomatic victory in ending the conflict. The final settlement of the Alaskan border issue was completed on October 20, 1903.

November 20–28, 1899

Anglo-German discussions about possible cooperation fail.

These discussions took place informally when a visit of the Emperor William II to England enabled Lord Balfour, Joseph Chamberlain, and Count Bernhard von Bülow to discuss matters of mutual interest. Although these talks continued on a formal basis until March 1901, the two nations could not agree.

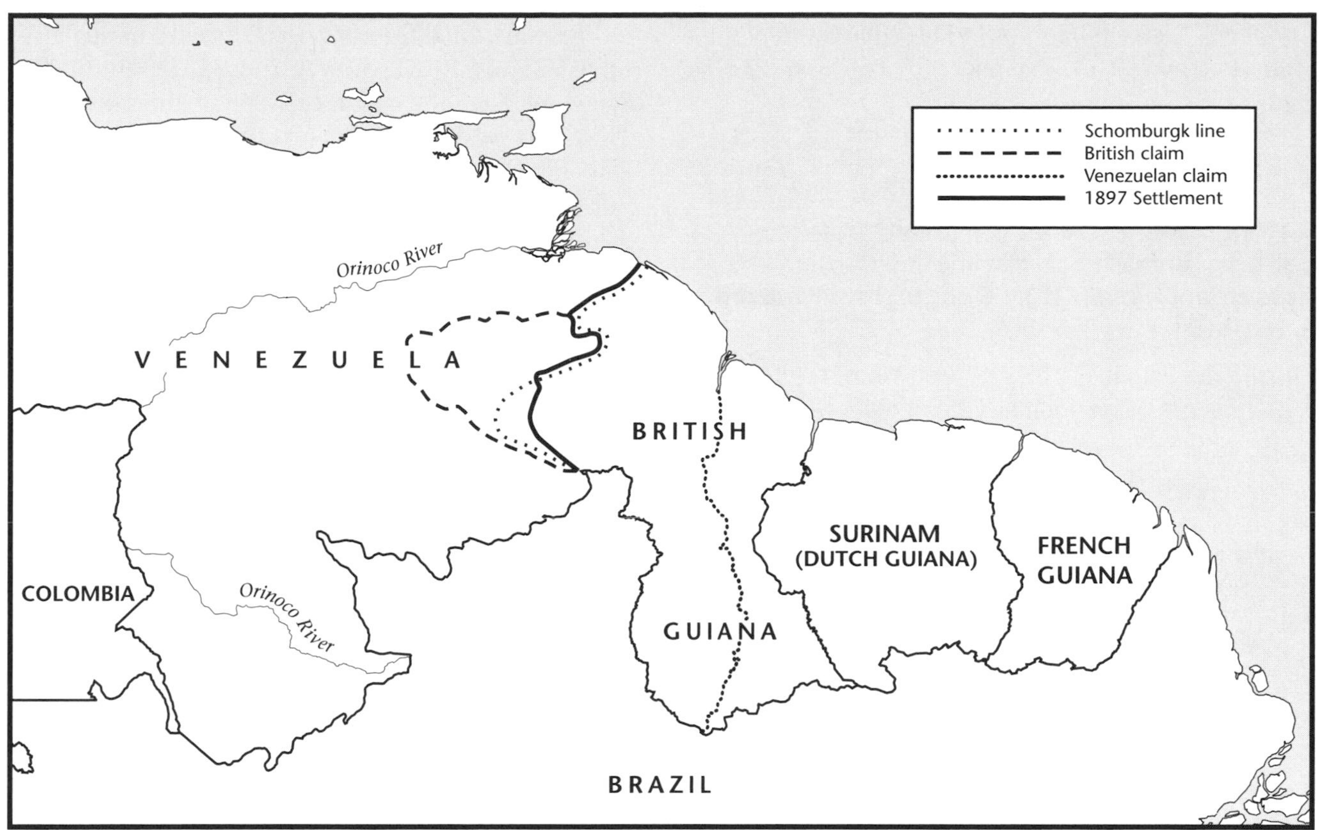

Venezuela Boundary Dispute

Of particular interest to Americans is the fact that, at least partly, the British gave consideration to American attitudes toward a British agreement with Germany. Britain's foreign secretary, Lord Lansdowne, cited German hostility to America as one "formidable obstacle" to an Anglo-German agreement.

December 2, 1899

An Anglo-German-American treaty partitions the Samoan Islands.

The Treaty of 1899 resulted from the crisis of March 11, 1899, which had brought a new three-power commission to study the Samoan problem on May 13. The American commissioner was Bartlett Tripp, who, on August 7, recommended to Secretary Hay that the 1889 pact should be terminated.

Hay agreed to change the status of Samoa, and negotiations leading to the Treaty of 1899 began. Great Britain agreed to allow the other two powers to partition the islands, and an Anglo-German treaty of November 14 settled that matter. Great Britain renounced its rights to Samoa in return for German compensation in Africa and the Tonga and Savage Islands of the Pacific. This cleared the way for a joint treaty to divide Samoa between the United States and Germany.

The Treaty of December 2 included the following terms:

1. The United States received all of Samoa east of 171st longitude, which included Tutuila and the excellent naval base of Pago Pago.
2. Germany received all islands west of the 171st longitude.
3. The issue of a German indemnity for the Anglo-American naval bombardment was given to arbitration. A November 7, 1899, convention referred this to arbitration by the king of Norway and Sweden.

The U.S. Senate ratified the partition treaty on January 16, 1900, and the claims convention on February 21, 1900. On October 14, 1902, the king found the United States and England at fault, and the United States paid $20,000 for German damage claims.

December 7, 1899

A Congressional bill for the United States to build an Isthmian canal without British agreement is offered by Congressman William P. Hepburn.

During the debate leading to creation of the Isthmian Canal Commission on March 3, 1899, Hepburn proposed a bill to appropriate $115 million for the United States to construct a Nicaraguan canal without requiring British consent. The Republicans had advocated a canal in their 1896 platform, and Hepburn believed Congress should undertake to implement that policy before the 1900 election. Although Hepburn's bill never passed, it had wide support in Congress and was a vital factor in convincing Great Britain to forsake Canada's concerns for the Alaska boundary and cooperate with Washington in the more vital area of the isthmian canal. On February 5, 1900, the Hay-Pauncefote Treaty was signed, leading to 10 months of public dispute in America over the merits of the isthmian bill.

See December 20, 1900.

1900

March 20, 1900

Although nations present evasive responses to Secretary Hay's "Open Door" notes, Hay claims their responses are "satisfactory."

On September 6, 1899, Hay requested that various nations join America in reaffirming the open door principles of equal commercial opportunities in China. By March 20, 1900, most nations had offered responses that Hay chose to interpret to the public as "satisfactory" and "definitive."

In fact, no nation had clearly accepted Hay's proposal. Great Britain, whose support seemed assured in 1899, sent a disappointing response. Lord Salisbury praised the idea of the open door but did not want it to apply to Kowloon Territory or Weihaiwei, two areas under British control. Later, Salisbury agreed to permit equal opportunity at Weihaiwei "dependent on similar assent by the other Powers in like circumstance."

Britain's qualifications were usually matched by other nations. Russia, however, used ambiguous language to reject the entire concept of the open door. Thus, no nation genuinely concurred with Hay's September 6 proposition. Hay was neither candid nor accurate in the statements he issued for publication on March 20.

Nevertheless, Hay's notes had two results. First, his notes extended U.S. recognition to "spheres of influence" because he asked each nation to provide equal commercial rights in its sphere. Second, the powers did acknowledge that China was allowed to levy and collect customs duties in their spheres. This recognized China's ultimate sovereignty, even though it was partly given by concessions to other nations.

The dubious question of American commercial rights remained. Although the United States had engaged in the China trade throughout the 19th century, Hay had hoped to encourage America to expand its commercial and investment rights in China. In 1898, American commercial interests in China were too small to be vital to American business. Only 1% of U.S. exports ($10 million out of $1,231 million of exports in 1898) went to China. Great Britain had one-sixth of its foreign commerce with China and controlled 70% of China's trade. Nevertheless, many American business interests and politicians believed that the United States could secure a larger market in China for its surplus products—sustaining the "myth of a huge Chinese market," a myth that has lasted well over a century.

Moreover, American missionaries fostered sympathy for their nation's duty to bring Christianity to China. To achieve these future goals, Hay desired to protect some of America's previous treaty privileges in China. His 1899 notes served to retain this possibility for Americans.

See April, 19, 1839.

April 12, 1900

The Foraker Act establishes civil government in Puerto Rico.

According to this congressional act, Puerto Rico became an unorganized territory and its residents became citizens of Puerto Rico. The president of the United States would appoint a governor general and a council. The council would be the upper house of the legislature, while a lower house would be elected by the people. Both the governor general and the legislature had veto powers. This act, which became effective on May 1, 1900, also extended the Dingley Tariff to Puerto Rico and levied duties that were 15% of amounts authorized in that tariff law.

May 31, 1900

U.S. and other foreign troops arrive in Peking to protect the diplomatic legations from the Boxer Rebellion in China.

The Boxers were an organization of Chinese nationalists who wished to eliminate foreign influence and strengthen the Chinese Empire. By 1900, they invaded Peking and their forces surrounded the foreign diplomatic legations, causing a threat that the China treaty powers chose to combat.

During 1900, foreign concern about the Boxers was slow to materialize. Beginning as a traditional Chinese secret society, the Boxer movement evolved in the 1890s in the northern Chinese provinces of Shantung and Chihili. Its name, *I-ho-Ch'iian,* could be translated as "Righteous and Harmonious Fists" ("Boxers"), for its objective was to harmonize the member's mind and body to prepare for combat. Using mystical Taoist concepts, the society's members followed rituals enabling them to be possessed of spirits that immunized them from death. Society members and Chinese who observed their public demonstrations claimed that after the rituals reached the point where they clenched their teeth and foamed at the mouth, their bodies became invulnerable to swords or bullets.

The Boxers imperiled the foreigners because their leaders also adopted the slogan "Overthrow the Ch'ing; destroy the foreigners." This movement's slogan reflected the dismay of the Chinese with Japan's victory in the war of 1894–1895 and the aggressive efforts of Western missionaries and military forces to expand their control in China. Combined with two years of poor agricultural harvests and floods in the Yellow River valley between 1896 and 1899, the problems of the Chinese in northern China became enormous, and the Boxers blamed the Ch'ing dynasty and the "foreign devils" for their ills.

Boxer attacks on Western civilians increased in Shantung during 1899 because Governor Yii Hsien supported the movement. After several diplomatic protests the governor was replaced, but when he visited Peking, the Empress Dowager Tz'u-hsi praised him and began herself to grant favors to the Boxers. By January 11, 1900, the empress issued a decree that referred to the Boxers as public-spirited persons who helped China. She gradually persuaded the Boxers to change their slogan to "Support the Ch'ing; destroy the foreigners."

With encouragement from the empress, the Boxers increased their attacks on foreign missionaries, merchants, and any Chinese who had been converted to Christianity or aided the foreigners. Since January, missionaries from Taujuan and various parts of Shantung had informed the diplomats in Peking that the attacks on their converts had multiplied. On May 17, 61 converts were massacred at villages 90 miles from Peking, and the next day a British chapel was burned to the ground 40 miles away. Yet until the Boxers attacked the Fengtai Railway Station on May 28, the diplomatic corps discounted these reports as exaggerated. By that date, the Boxers planned to move into Peking and unite with the Imperial Army against the foreigners.

Under these circumstances, 458 soldiers from the various nations represented in China began to arrive in Peking. The first contingent of 337 officers and men came on May 31, and included a contingent of U.S. Marines. On June 3, 89 German and Austrian sailors arrived to further augment the foreign guards.

The arrival of foreign forces in Peking only stimulated complaints and action by the Boxers. By June 20, the Peking diplomatic legation was under siege by the Boxers and the Imperial Army.

For results of the siege, see August 14, 1900.

June 12, 1900

A German naval law is passed by the Reichstag authorizing construction of 38 battleships in a 20-year period.

This naval program challenged British sea power. It passed the Reichstag during a period of antagonism toward the British, who had recently stopped the German ship *Bundesroth* because they claimed the

German ship carried contraband to help the Boers in their war against England.

July 3, 1900

Secretary of State Hay describes U.S. policy regarding China and the Boxer crisis.

Hay decided to inform the other nations with Chinese treaties that U.S. policy wanted to uphold a Chinese government. In a circular note to other foreign officers, Hay recognized that China's politics were in a state of anarchy in 1900. He believed that reparations with the foreign powers and creation of a new Chinese leader would solve the problems. The best interests of all nations, Hay argued, would be served by preserving Chinese territorial integrity. This would preserve the foreign nations' treaty rights and maintain equal and impartial trade with all parts of the Chinese Empire.

August 14, 1900

An international force lifts the Boxers' siege of the Peking diplomatic legation.

The 55-day siege of the diplomatic quarters in Peking was ended by a multinational expeditionary army that marched on Peking after the outside world heard the false report that the entire legation had been massacred.

Following the arrival of additional legation guards in Peking on May 31, the Boxer attacks on foreigners increased. On June 2, 40 Belgian railroad workers fled from Paotingfu; 7 were killed by Boxer troops. On June 3, two British missionaries were murdered in a village near Peking, and on June 4, the railroad lines between Peking and Tientsin were torn up, stopping all trains to Peking. According to a British historian, the head of the Peking diplomatic corps, Sir Robert Hart, and other diplomats had not thought the crisis was serious until June 9, when the Boxers burned the grandstand at the race track three miles from Peking. Because the race track was one of the privileged sanctuaries of the diplomats, its loss apparently caused them greater concern than the attacks on missionaries and their converts.

The diplomatic corps decided on June 9 to ask Admiral Sir Edward Seymour to send more troops from Tientsin. In response, on June 10 the admiral led a force of 2,129 international soldiers including 111 Americans, which left on five trains for China's capital.

Seymour's forces never reached Peking. The Boxers forced Seymour's expedition to turn back within 32 miles of Peking. Moving slowly to repair railway track, Seymour's trains had traveled halfway to the capital when Boxer soldiers attacked and stalled the international army on June 14. Three days later, Imperial Army troops reinforced the Boxers and Seymour ordered a retreat to Tientsin. Marching back slowly but in an orderly fashion, Seymour's men fought their way village by village while cavalry of the Imperial Army constantly harassed them. When it reached Tientsin on June 26, the expedition had lost 62 killed (4 Americans) and 232 wounded (28 Americans).

While Seymour's forces were fighting their way back to Tientsin, other foreign contingents captured China's Taku forts at the mouth of the Pei Ho River south of Tientsin. The campaign against the forts began on June 17 after the Chinese refused to surrender. The Chinese manned two forts on each side of the river where it narrowed to 200 yards. German engineers had rebuilt these forts, arming them with quick-firing guns manufactured by the Krupps. Thus, the forts had become strong, seemingly impregnable bases.

For the assault, the international forces included nine ships with 900 officers and men. The U.S. navy's ship, *Monocacy,* did not participate because its commander, Admiral Kempff, said his orders did not permit fighting the Chinese.

The British, French, and Japanese forces at Taku began their attack on the forts at night on June 17 because the guns of the fort aimed less effectively in the dark. By dawn, the allied forces made a dual attack: ships bombarded the forts while marines stormed the gun posts on land. Although the allied casualties were 172 men, the forts fell, opening the Pei Ho River to allied ships as far as Tientsin.

While the capture of the Taku forts took place, the diplomats in Peking tried unsuccessfully to negotiate with the Empress Dowager Tz'u-hsi. The plight of the legations heightened by mid-June because Christian refugees fleeing from the Boxers flocked to the diplomatic quarters. The Boxers put added pressure on the diplomats by firing sporadically at the legation walls. In addition, on June 29 the legation lost contact with Tientsin and the outside world when the Boxers cut the last telegraph lines out of Peking.

The worst lay ahead for the diplomats. On June 18, Baron Klemens von Ketteler, the fiery German minister, was attacked and killed by Boxers while on his way to negotiate with the Chinese. On June 20, Boxer and Imperial Army guns began regular bombarding of the legation residences and walls of the diplomatic quarters. The bombing continued every day except from July 17 to August 1, a period during which the empress tried to decide on her next step. Some of Tz'u-hsi's advisers wanted a full-scale offensive to drive out the foreigners; others believed such action would force the foreigners to launch a full-scale war on the Ch'ing dynasty.

The two-week delay by the empress allowed the legation to survive because it enabled foreign forces to regroup at Tientsin and launch a new expedition to Peking. Following the capture of the Taku forts on June 18, the allied leaders could not decide on a strategy. The allies had moved up the Pei Ho to Tientsin but hesitated because they received false news that the Peking legation had been massacred. After the telegraph lines were cut on June 29, rumors of the legation's destruction surfaced and seemed to be confirmed by a July 16 story in the London *Daily Mail.* Under the headline "The Peking Massacre," the *Daily Mail* reported that its Shanghai correspondent had word from "authoritative Chinese sources" that on July 6–7 the Boxers methodically destroyed the legation defenses and sent wave after wave of Boxers against its heroic defenders. Running out of ammunition, the report alleged, the legation guards made a valiant last stand at the British residences but were overwhelmed. Any foreigner left alive was "put to the sword in a most atrocious fashion."

For a week, the story of the usually reliable *Daily Mail* was accepted. The British prepared a memorial service at St. Paul's Cathedral for July 23. At the last moment, the service was canceled. The American State Department had received a secret coded telegram from its minister, Edwin Conger, dated July 22, which stated, "Quick relief only can prevent a general massacre." The legation was not destroyed on July 7. Not until October 20, 1900, did the London *Times* publish the source of the tragic lies published in the *Daily Mail.* The latter newspaper had unwisely hired a former forger and gun smuggler as its Shanghai correspondent, a man known as F. W. Sutterlee. The correspondent had fabricated his story for a handsome fee.

The story of the legation's fall delayed the international expeditionary force because its march on Peking appeared less urgent. Actually, the international army won its greatest victory on July 14, when it captured the walled city of Tientsin. The allied force of 14,000 men defeated a Chinese nationalist army of 22,000 that defended the city. Heroic action by Japanese soldiers who stormed the south city gates at 3 A.M. won the day, and the Chinese resistance was ended easily soon after. The Boxers' loss to an inferior army severely damaged their reputation.

Admiral Seymour did not follow up the victory at Tientsin because his sense of urgency ended when the false report of the Peking legation's demise was received. Only after couriers from the Peking legation reached Tientsin on July 28 did Seymour and the allied generals realize that their mission to free the legation remained plausible.

Nevertheless, the allied armies remained inactive until August 5, because they had no commander in chief. The German emperor had insisted that Field Marshal Count Alfred von Waldersee must head the international army, but the German troops and Marshal von Waldersee had not arrived at Tientsin, and they did not reach China until October.

Finally, on August 3, British General Gaselee told the other allied leaders that the British were not going to wait. His men, he said, were going to relieve the legation at Peking. If the other leaders wanted to come along, they could. All the remaining generals concurred with Gaselee, and the international army marched off on August 4. The force totaled about 18,000 officers and men: 8,000 Japanese; 3,000 British; 4,000 Russians; 2,500 Americans; and a few French, Germans, Austrians, and Italians.

Lacking a commander or long-term plans, the international generals continued on to Peking because their first two battles proved successful. They defeated the Chinese at Peitrang on August 5 and at Yangtsun on August 6. Moving forward, the armies captured Tungchow on August 12 when they also met couriers from the Peking diplomatic legation who gave them maps of the capital city and the legation quarters.

On August 14, the troops had reached the Peking city gates, where they decided to attack in four groups under the generals of their nations: Britain's General Gaselee, Russia's General Lineivitch, Japan's General Fukushima, and America's General Chaffee. Three of the main city gates were breached by 10 P.M. and the troops pressed into the city. Reaching the legation quarters, the British entered through a seven-foot sewer duct to the legation residences, while the Americans and Russians charged the Chinese defenders on the Chien Mien Wall above the Imperial Canal.

As the legation was being liberated, the empress and her court fled to Sian.

For the settlement of the dispute with China, see October 16, 1900, and September 7, 1901.

September 4, 1900

Russian troops move into Manchuria during the Boxer incident in Peking.

At Blagovestchensk on the Amur River, Russian army officials claimed that Chinese nationalist Boxers had bombarded Russian territory on July 14–15, 1900. In retaliation, Russian forces attacked the Chinese and chased thousands of civilians into the river, where they drowned or were shot. The Russians moved 100,000 soldiers into Manchuria. Consequently, the question of Russian withdrawal from Manchuria and its future rights in the province became a major international problem. The Japanese, in particular, protested Russia's activity in Manchuria.

See April 28, 1903.

October 16, 1900

England and Germany make an agreement on the "Open Door" in China.

Largely owing to British fears of Russian plans in northern China and Manchuria, Britain joined Germany in issuing a statement by which the powers would disclaim all territorial acquisitions in China and maintain equal trade rights (an "open door") in China. Other powers agreed to this statement, and the negotiations regarding the evacuation of the international force in Peking ruled out any attempt by one of the foreign nations to obtain territory from China. This Anglo-German agreement gave practical effect to the concepts Secretary of State Hay proposed as America's policy. Moreover, the British agreement with Germany represented the interests of various nations in avoiding an international scramble to divide up Chinese territory.

See September 4, 1900; for Hay's statement, see July 3, 1900.

November 6, 1900

William McKinley is reelected President.

The Republican Party had nominated McKinley at its convention on June 19. His Democratic opponent in 1900 was William Jennings Bryan. During the campaign the Democrats stressed imperialism as a major issue in opposition to Republican support for American expansion by gaining colonies in the Pacific Ocean and by building and controlling a canal in the isthmus of Central America. For most voters, however, domestic policies probably played the largest role in the campaign. The Republicans' slogan of "A Full Dinner Pail" emphasized the nation's general prosperity at the turn of the century. McKinley won 292 electoral votes to Bryan's 155.

December 10, 1900

Japan rejects an American request to negotiate with China for a U.S. Naval base in Fukien province, an area over which Tokyo had concession interests.

The U.S. navy had told Secretary of State Hay that it desired a coaling station at Samsah Inlet north of Fuchow in China's Fukien Province. Therefore, Hay instructed A. E. Buck, the American minister to Japan, to seek Japan's permission to negotiate with China for such a concession. Because the Sino-Japanese Treaty of April 26, 1898, prevented China from yielding any concessions in Fukien, Hay desired Tokyo's consent before talking with China about a naval base.

Japan's refusal to accept the American proposal ended Hay's pursuit of a U.S. base. Nevertheless, this attempt indicated that under the right circumstances, the United States might have joined the other powers that sought territorial privileges in China.

December 20, 1900

The U.S. Senate ratifies the Hay-Pauncefote Treaty on an Isthmian canal with amendments that are not acceptable to Great Britain.

Since the 1880s, the United States had attempted to alter or abrogate the Clayton-Bulwer Treaty of 1850 to free America to build and control a Central American canal. The British had been unwilling to negotiate until 1898, when Secretary of State Hay and Britain's ambassador, Sir Julian Pauncefote, agreed to discuss a canal treaty. The result was the first Hay-Pauncefote Treaty of February 5, 1900.

Throughout 1899, the treaty had been delayed because Canada opposed a canal treaty until America settled the Alaskan dispute. Because Prime Minister Salisbury accepted Canada's viewpoint, the treaty was not agreed to by Great Britain for more than a year.

During England's delay, a bill was introduced in Congress in December 1899 that provided for a canal without British permission. This prompted Pauncefote to urge Salisbury to reconsider his decision, and on February 5, 1900, the prime minister authorized Pauncefote to sign the treaty.

Nevertheless, the 12-month delay placed the Hay-Pauncefote Treaty before the Senate during a less favorable time—an election year. Anti-British groups in America claimed Hay had yielded too much to the British. They and other U.S. politicians argued that Hay did not insist on abrogation of the Clayton-Bulwer Treaty and limited America's freedom to defend the canal. Even Hay's good friend Theodore Roosevelt opposed the treaty without amendments. Roosevelt wanted treaty amendments to put the canal "wholly under the control of the United States alike in peace and war."

Treaty opposition was strong enough to persuade Secretary Hay not to seek a Senate vote on it during the spring of 1900. It was sent to the Senate following President McKinley's election victory on November 6. Yet there was an obvious need to amend the treaty to assure its passage. Therefore, Senator Cushman Davis, chairman of the Senate Foreign Relations Committee, accepted three amendments, although they significantly changed the treaty. These amendments specifically rescinded the Clayton-Bulwer Treaty, eliminated a clause that invited other nations to internationalize the canal, and permitted the United States to send armed forces to defend the canal if necessary. With these additions, the Senate ratified the treaty on December 20, 1900.

Great Britain could not accept the Senate amendments because they altered the substance of the treaty. Although Secretary Hay was disillusioned with the outcome and offered President McKinley his resignation, the president asked him to remain as secretary and to begin another series of talks with Pauncefote in London.

See December 16, 1901.

December 24, 1900

Turkey's government settles the American indemnity demand for property damage in 1895.

The American minister in Istanbul had protested regarding the damage by Turkish mobs to two American missions on November 15, 1895. The sultan did not respond immediately because of continuous disorders in Turkey in 1896 and 1897.

In 1900, the United States exchanged a series of diplomatic notes with the Turks and dispatched a naval ship to Istanbul to reinforce America's intentions. As a result, on December 24, Turkish officials met with U.S. Minister Lloyd Grissom, and the indemnity claim was resolved. To repay America for damages, the sultan's government deposited $83,600 in the Ottoman Bank to the account of the American Missionary Board.

1901

March 2, 1901

The Platt Amendment to regulate future relations between Cuba and the United States is added by Congress to an army appropriation bill.

In Cuba, a constitutional convention had adopted a document on November 5, 1900, that did not satisfy the War Department because it included no provision for special relations with the United States. Secretary of War Elihu Root and General Leonard Wood, who headed the American military government for the occupation of Cuba, insisted that the United States must be able to guarantee Cuba against internal disorder and foreign invasion. Consequently, General Wood rejected the Cuban constitution, and Secretary Root on February 9, 1901, sent Wood instructions that described the additional clauses for Cuba to include in the constitution.

McKinley and Root decided to ask Congress to accept these provisions because they allowed the United States to intervene in Cuba to maintain orderly government. Senator Orville H. Platt introduced these terms in Congress as part of the Army Appropriation Bill of March 2, 1901.

The Platt Amendment, which Cuba was required to accept before the U.S. army would evacuate the islands, made Cuba a quasi protectorate of America. Its main provisions were as follows:

1. Cuba could make no treaty with a third power that would impair its independence.
2. Cuba's public debt could not exceed the capacity of its ordinary revenues to repay.
3. The United States had the right to intervene in Cuba to preserve its independence, to maintain law and order, and to have Cuba discharge its foreign obligations.
4. Cuba would sell or lease land to America for a U.S. naval base. (This became the Guantánamo base on the southeast coast of Cuba.)
5. Cuba would execute the sanitation policies begun by the U.S. army to control disease.

On June 12, the Cuban constitutional convention appended the Platt Amendment to its document and the United States agreed to withdraw its troops and end the occupation. The American occupation ended on May 20, 1902, and on May 22, 1903, Cuba and America signed a treaty that incorporated the terms of the Platt Amendment.

March 23, 1901

Following a vicious guerrilla war, Aguinaldo is captured but war continues.

Following intensive warfare in Manila on February 4, 1899, Jacob Schurman, head of an American Presidential Commission, arrived in the Philippines and made a deal with Manila's educated citizens in the Philippine legislature, allowing them to replace the Spanish government and keep their private property. Schurman's deal divided the Philippine urban groups and large landowners from the rural, uneducated peasants who followed Aguinaldo. By 1900, Schurman was able to establish a civilian government in Manila while the U.S. army continued a guerrilla war against Aguinaldo's nationalists.

In October 1900, U.S. army General Ewell S. Otis led 126,000 soldiers in offensive operations north of Manila. As the Americans moved ahead, the Philippine nationalists fled from village to village before reaching jungles and mountains. Because the local natives supported the guerrillas, U.S. troops experienced anger and frustration because they could not tell friend from foe in the rural areas. This made Otis's offensive a cruel struggle. Both sides committed atrocities and used terror tactics. In America, anti-imperialists denounced the war as dehumanizing American soldiers, who used water torture and massacred women and children in villages. Later, Senator Lodge's Committee on the Philippines investigated these stories.

Nevertheless, the U.S. army gradually seized control of more and more of Luzon Island from the rebels. With Aguinaldo's capture on March 23, the Americans initially thought this would end the war. However, fighting did not stop as Philippine nationalists continued the struggle for another year before the U.S. gained control of the key islands and cities.

During the four-year war, 4,234 American soldiers were killed and 2,818 were wounded. On the Philippine side, an estimated 20,000 soldiers died as well as 200,000 civilians from pestilence and disease. Many more thousands were wounded.

See June 28, 1902, and July 4, 1902.

July 4, 1901

William Howard Taft becomes the first civil governor of the United States in the Philippine Islands—the insurrection of the Filipinos is nearly ended.

The U.S. war against Philippine independence forces had been waged since February 4, 1899. During this period the U.S. military government had controlled the Philippines, pursuing its efforts to suppress the rebellion. The military government terminated on June 21, 1901. President McKinley had appointed Taft to head the Second Philippine Commission on April 7, 1900. Under the guidance of Secretary of War Root, the commission established city government and gradually let Filipinos have some role in self-government. Soon after Aguinaldo's capture on March 23, the U.S. army commander moved toward giving Taft control of the government. For subsequent action on the Philippine government, see July 4, 1902.

September 6, 1901

President McKinley is assassinated.

Leon Czolgosz, an anarchist, shot the president while he was attending a reception at the Pan-American

Theodore Roosevelt, 26th president, speaking at Brattleboro, Vermont, in 1902. Library of Congress

Exposition in Buffalo, New York. McKinley lingered until September 14, when he died and Theodore ROOSEVELT took the oath of office as president.

September 7, 1901

The Boxer Protocol between China and the foreign powers settles the problems resulting from the siege of the Peking foreign legations and foreign occupation of Peking on August 14, 1900.

Following the rescue of the Peking diplomats, the Empress Tz'u-hsi fled to Sian, leaving negotiations with the foreigners to be carried out by Li Hung-chang, the venerable 77-year-old Chinese official who had dealt with the foreign powers in the 1860s and 1870s. These negotiations took more than a year because the foreign delegates argued among themselves about their demands against China.

For the United States, Secretary of State Hay sent W. W. Rockhill as a special agent to Peking. The United States had agreed to try to preserve the existing Chinese government and to keep Western indemnity demands as low as possible, proposing a lump-sum payment by China of $100,000.

However, Rockhill had to follow the lead taken by England and Germany in the discussions with Li. On October 16, 1900, an Anglo-German agreement with China became the basis for the other nations to reach a settlement. This agreement assured the continued existence of the Ch'ing dynasty under Tz'u-hsi. China lost no territory, but Chinese financial independence was limited by the Western nations. England, Germany, and the other foreign powers, including the United States, wished to retain the imperial government because there was no satisfactory alternative government able to uphold the treaties that the Ch'ing signed.

By September 7, the 11 nations with interests in China signed an agreement with China's representative, Li Hung-chang. The important terms of the Boxer Protocol were as follows:

1. The Chinese would execute 10 high Boxer officials for treason and punish 100 others.
2. China would pay the foreigners an indemnity of 450 million taels (about $333 million). The payments would be in gold and would be financed by a foreign loan paying 4% interest.
3. China would apologize to Germany for the murder of Baron Ketteler and erect a memorial to him at the place he was shot.
4. China would apologize to Japan for the murder of the chancellor of Japan's legation, Sugiyama.
5. Foreign powers would have exclusive control of the Legation Quarters in Peking with the right to make them defensible.
6. Foreign nations would occupy 13 ports including Tientsin to guarantee open communication with Peking.
7. China would levy a 5% effective tariff on foreign imports.
8. Chinese forts at Taku and between Peking and the sea would be razed.
9. Edicts to prevent the renewal of Boxer propaganda would be published.
10. Foreign troops would be evacuated from Peking on September 17, with the exception of the legation guards.

The Boxer Protocol did not deal with the Russian occupation of Manchuria, which the foreign representatives chose not to consider as a joint issue.

Although American missionaries and merchants in China wanted the United States to take a stronger role in China after the Boxer agreement, McKinley and Hay preferred to minimize America's action there. The United States received approximately $25 million of the Chinese indemnity but did not join the other powers in Tientsin. An American guard was kept in Peking and, as before the Boxer incident, a naval squadron was available at Shanghai and on the Yangtze River. Generally, however, the U.S. presence in China was not considered a vital interest by the State Department.

See January 15, 1907.

October 22, 1901

The second Pan-American Conference opens in Mexico City.

The chief significance of this meeting was that the movement to stimulate inter-American cooperation began conducting sessions at the invitation of Latin American nations. Proponents of Pan-Americanism had worked since the Washington Conference of 1889 to achieve this goal. The Mexico City sessions were held from October 22 until January 31, 1902.

Subsequently, two other conferences were held prior to World War I: the third conference was in 1906 at Rio de Janeiro; the fourth in 1910 at Buenos Aires. World War I along with the Mexican revolutionary upheaval delayed the convening of the fifth Pan-American conference until March 25, 1923, when meetings took place in Santiago, Chile.

December 2, 1901

The U.S. Supreme Court rules that Puerto Ricans are not U.S. citizens.

Two of the so-called Insular Cases were decided in 1901 regarding the status of Puerto Rico as a territory of the United States. The case of *De Lima v. Bidwell* was reported by the court on December 2, the court ruling that Puerto Ricans are not ipso facto citizens of the United States.

Earlier in 1901, a Supreme Court ruling in the case of *Downes v. Bidwell* had indicated the direction cases would take relative to overseas territory acquired by the United States in 1898–1899. In the Downes case, the court ruled that overseas possessions could be governed in a special way. In that case, the court permitted Congress to levy import duties on goods from Puerto Rico.

December 16, 1901

The U.S. Senate approves the revised Hay-Pauncefote Treaty.

Dejected after the Senate amended the first treaty he negotiated on the isthmian canal and the British rejected the changes, Hay nevertheless instructed the U.S. minister to England, Joseph Choate, to seek a new treaty with British Foreign Minister Lord Lansdowne and Pauncefote, who had returned to London. By the end of September, new terms were agreed to. After consulting again with Pauncefote in Washington, Hay and the British minister signed the treaty on November 18.

The Senate ratified the new treaty overwhelmingly on December 16. The treaty explicitly abrogated the Clayton-Bulwer Treaty and permitted the United States to build and control the canal. The United States would maintain the canal's neutrality, making it free and open to ships of all nations on equal terms. Fortifications were not mentioned in the treaty, but in a separate note of August 3, Britain conceded the right of the United States to fortify it. While some Anglophobes in America wanted a more abject resignation by England, most Americans welcomed the treaty's acceptance. In Great Britain, the feeling had grown in official circles that U.S. controls in the Americas could best serve Anglo-American friendship in the future. Therefore, England had accepted U.S. terms on the canal treaty.

See August 24, 1912.

1902

January 18, 1902

The Walker Commission recommends the Panama Canal route to Congress.

The Walker (Isthmian Canal) Commission, which President McKinley appointed in 1899, recommended the Panama route only after the Panama Canal Company lowered its price from $109 million to $40 million.

The commission's original report in November 1901 had recommended the Nicaraguan route because of the "unreasonable" terms that the New

Panama Company asked for its holdings and franchises in Panama. The commission, headed by Rear Admiral John G. Walker, had thoroughly considered all aspects of the two routes, including climate, health, water, legal rights, and the cost of construction and operation. Yet the commission had recommended the Nicaraguan route simply because of the Panama Company's asking price.

When the commission's first report went to Secretary Hay's office in November, it was assumed that it would remain secret until the president sent it to Congress. On November 21, however, William Randolph Hearst's *New York Journal* published the report. A Hearst agent had bribed one of Admiral Walker's secretaries for a carbon copy of the report. The *Journal* also published a copy of the commission's minority report, which extolled the Panama route. Indeed, anyone reading the commission's report could discern that from a technical standpoint the Panama route was better and that the French company's price had been the deciding factor against Panama.

After the news of the commission report leaked, the pro-Nicaraguan group moved as fast as possible to have Congress approve it. Early in December, Congressman William Hepburn introduced legislation to construct the Nicaraguan canal, and on December 19 the House agreed unanimously to consider the bill immediately after the Christmas holidays. During the ensuing weeks, the Panama Company decided to revise its price.

Following a session in Paris, the Panama Company's stockholders decided on a new asking price. Actually, the Walker commission report had been based on what company officers said was the considered worth of the Panama property. On January 4, Admiral Walker received the first definite price offer from the company. The price was $40 million, a sum that exactly matched the estimated value of the French holdings as listed by the Walker commission's report. Walker rushed over to the State Department with this news because he believed the company's offer significantly affected his commission report.

Although the House of Representatives acted on January 9 to approve Hepburn's Nicaraguan bill by 308 to 2, President Roosevelt decided to interview the commission members individually to determine their exact views under the new circumstances of the Panama Company's price of $40 million. These talks convinced Roosevelt, who had formerly preferred the Nicaraguan route, that the Panama route was the better. He called the entire commission to a secret meeting, and on January 18 they voted unanimously to support the Panama route. The commission's new conclusion was publicized on January 20.

The new situation caused some political and public turmoil. Until January 18, newspapers, politicians, everyone had seemed to favor the Nicaraguan route. As the *New York Herald* reported: "the Nicaraguan canal project is a purely national affair, conceived by Americans, sustained by Americans, and (if, later on, constructed) operated by Americans according to American ideas and for American needs." The Panama route was considered to be under foreign (French) influence.

Nevertheless, Roosevelt had made up his mind and decided to risk public censure to get the Panama route.

For the outcome, see June 26, 1902.

January 24, 1902

A Danish-American treaty provides for the American purchase of the Danish West Indies. Denmark later rejects the treaty.

Because there were rumors of Germany's desire to purchase the Danish West Indies, President Roosevelt agreed to offer to buy these islands. Consequently, a treaty was prepared and signed on January 24, 1902, to obtain the island for $5 million. The U.S. Senate quickly ratified the treaty, but the Danish parliament rejected the treaty by one vote. Roosevelt and Secretary Hay were convinced that the Germans had intervened in Copenhagen to persuade the Danish parliament against the sale of the islands. There is no evidence of the German activity in Denmark. It is known, however, that Germany's Admiral von Tirpitz desired the islands for strategic reasons.

January 30, 1902

England and Japan form an alliance.

This alliance sought cooperation between the two powers in East Asia. The allies agreed to preserve the independence of China and Korea from threats of other powers and from "disturbances arising in China and Korea." Great Britain recognized Japan's special interests in Korea.

The two nations also agreed to remain neutral if either went to war with a third power. If, however, a fourth nation joined the war, the ally would join the conflict. Finally, neither nation would make a treaty with another power without prior consultation.

In response to the announcement of the Anglo-Japanese alliance, France and Russia jointly declared on March 20 that they favored the East Asian principles of the alliance but would consult together to safeguard their interests in China.

March 9, 1902

Prince Henry of Germany visits Washington on a goodwill tour.

In January 1902, Kaiser William II announced that President Roosevelt's daughter would christen the imperial yacht *Meteor,* which an American company built. To join the ceremony, the kaiser's brother, Prince Henry, would visit America on board the yacht *Hohenzollern.*

Prince Henry's trip included a visit to Washington to try to improve German goodwill. Because of incidents with Germany at Samoa, Manila, China, and elsewhere since 1889, German-American relations were not satisfactory and U.S. opinion of Germany was cool. Nevertheless, as the December 1902 Venezuelan crisis would indicate, the goodwill visit accomplished little in the face of the kaiser's heavy-handed diplomacy.

May 20, 1902

U.S. troops withdraw from Cuba following the election of Tomas Estrada Palma as President.

After U.S. General Leonard Wood became military governor of Cuba on December 13, 1899, the Cubans adopted a constitution that included the Platt Amendment and established schools, civilian administrative units, and municipal governments. The Cuban constitution provided for a president and bicameral legislature patterned after America's government. By May 20, the United States believed Cuba was ready for self-government, and General Wood turned his authority over to Palma. American troops left for home the same day. Cuba was independent but under the careful watch of America, which could justify future intervention under the Platt Amendment.

See March 2, 1901.

June 26, 1902

Congress approves construction of a Panama Canal.

On June 26, the House of Representatives passed the Spooner Bill, providing for the U.S. construction of a canal at Panama. The act was named for Senator John Coit Spooner, who introduced the bill in January 1902 as a substitute for Hepburn's Nicaraguan bill. The key vote on the bill took place in the Senate on June 19, when, after an intensive two-week debate, it passed by a vote of 42 to 34.

The approval of the Panama route marked a complete reversal of public opinion, which in January favored the Nicaraguan canal. Factors influencing the change were (1) the lobbying efforts of the Panama Company's lawyer, Thomas Cromwell, and its chief engineer, the Frenchman Philippe Bunau-Varilla; (2) the backing of President Roosevelt and a key Republican leader, Senator Mark Hanna; (3) the behind-the-scenes support of engineer George S. Morison, who made the commission's minority report in November 1901; and (4) the volcano Momotombo, which erupted in Nicaragua on May 14, 1902.

Three dramatic events highlighted the change of support from Nicaragua to Panama. The eruption of Mount Momotombo on May 14, soon after a more disastrous eruption of Mount Pelee on Martinique on May 8, greatly disturbed many Americans. The Pelee disaster wiped out the city of Pierre, "the little Paris." The Nicaraguan explosion caused less damage but was accompanied by an earthquake, which supposedly caused a government dock to plunge into Lake Managua on the proposed canal route. Senator Morgan and other pro-Nicaraguan spokesmen denied the reports of disaster in that state but were not convincing. Second, on June 5–6, Senator Mark Hanna, the Ohio political boss who brought McKinley to preeminence, made one of his few and therefore very effective Senate speeches. Old, ill, walking with a limp, yet determined and well prepared, Hanna used a display of charts and enthusiasm to show that the Panama route was the best deal for the future. He convinced many senators and others. Finally, Bunau-Varilla, in addition to using his charming French mannerisms and engineering expertise to lobby for the Panama route, used a final ploy that probably affected some Senate votes. Because Senator Morgan had recently sought to deny the dangers of the Nicaraguan volcano, Bunau-Varilla decided to demonstrate that Nicaraguans themselves acknowledged the volcano's influence on their nation. Noting that the one-centavo Nicaraguan postage stamp showed Momotombo volcano "in magnificent eruption," he visited stamp dealers in Washington to find 90 stamps, one for each senator. Calling the stamp an "official witness of Nicaragua's volcanic activity," he sent one stamp to each senator for receipt on the morning of June 16, just before the deciding Senate vote. The Senate vote was close enough to make each of these three influences important.

The law of June 26, which Roosevelt signed two days later, included the following provisions:

1. appropriated $40 million to purchase property and canal rights of the New Panama Canal Company;
2. authorized construction only if a Colombian treaty gave the United States perpetual control over the canal right of way;
3. authorized the purchase of the Nicaraguan route if the Panama negotiations failed.

June 28, 1902

Secret Senate hearings on the Philippine War take place while the war is winding down.

In January 1900, Senator Henry Cabot Lodge was appointed chair of a special committee on the Philippine war. Lodge did not convene the hearings about alleged American atrocities in the war until January 1902, when he had to thwart a Committee on the Conduct of the War proposed by the anti-imperialist Senator George Hoar. When the hearings began on January 28, 1902, the war was winding down following two years of brutal conflict between the Americans and the Filipino guerrilla forces. On April 27, 1902, the last guerrillas surrendered on Samar.

Because the hearings were secret and the Philippine war was winding down, the hearings had little impact at that time. They did influence later congressional action to grant Philippine independence, and they also gave historians insight into the irony of a republican government fighting a war to prevent self-government by another people. The hearings included interviews with General Otis, Arthur McArthur, and Admiral Dewey, who were active in the war, as well as with the civilian governor, William Howard Taft, and a group of enlisted American soldiers.

Soon after the hearings concluded on June 28, Congress approved the Philippine Government Act, which was proclaimed on July 4, 1902. Therefore, the Lodge committee issued no report on the hearings.

June 28, 1902

Germany, Austria, and Italy renew the triple alliance for another six years.

The only reluctant partner in this alliance was Italy. To retain Italy's membership, Germany and Austria assured Rome they would recognize Italy's ambitions to gain Tripoli as a colony. Italian and Austrian relations were antagonistic at this time because of border disputes over national territory that each state claimed.

Soon after renewing the Triple Alliance, Italy agreed to an entente with France on November 1, 1902, assuring mutual neutrality if either nation were attacked by an enemy.

July 4, 1902

Philippine Government Act (Organic Act) is proclaimed by the President.

Constituting the Philippines as an unorganized territory, this act confirmed the president's appointment of the Taft Commission on April 7, 1900, and retained the commission to govern the islands. The act made the island's inhabitants citizens of the Philippine Islands and extended to them all of the U.S. Bill of Rights except the rights to trial by jury and to bear arms. The Filipinos could eventually elect an assembly, while the U.S. commissioners would act as the upper house of the legislature.

When this act became effective on July 4, President Roosevelt issued a proclamation ending the Philippine insurrection and granting amnesty to the rebels.

August 11, 1902

U.S. State Department opposes Romania's Jewish persecution, asking the signators of the 1878 Berlin treaty to act on behalf of the Jewish minority.

One aspect of Theodore Roosevelt's approach to foreign affairs issues was to appear to be vigorous in public protests that had little or no effect. Such was the State Department protest over the Jewish problem in Romania at the turn of the century because of the limits upon America's power to influence foreign domestic behavior. Public expectations often exceed the government's ability to resolve such unfortunate situations.

On April 6, 1902, Jacob Schiff of New York's Kuhn, Loeb and Company appealed to Secretary of State Hay to attend to the persecution of Jews in Romania. Anti-Semitic incidents had recurred during the 1890s in eastern European countries such as Romania and Russia, and Schiff thought Roosevelt should act on humanitarian grounds to oppose these activities.

Although Roosevelt and Hay knew that the United States could do little to change these internal problems in eastern Europe, Roosevelt asked Hay to examine the problem. Hay and the assistant secretary, Alvey Adee, found two ways to act that would not damage any diplomatic protocol but would seem to be effective action.

First, on July 17 Adee sent instructions to the American chargé in Bucharest to seek a naturalization treaty with Romania. In his orders, Adee told the chargé that he must "scrutinize most jealously the character of the immigration from a foreign land," noting that the United States "offers asylum to the oppressed of all lands" and has the "rights of remonstrance against the acts of the Romanian government." Subsequently, Hay used the words of Adee's note to the chargé to inform Schiff that a protest had been made, even though it had no influence in Bucharest. When the chargé requested that Romania's foreign minister negotiate a naturalization treaty, the Romanians refused to do so.

Adee took a further step to strengthen Roosevelt's image. On August 11, he sent a circular diplomatic note to the nations that had signed the Berlin Treaty of 1878, informing them that Romania had violated the humanitarian clauses regarding the rights of minorities because they persecuted Jews. Although the European nations ignored Roosevelt's message, it was published in the United States and helped the Republican campaign of 1902. In New York City some rabbis read it to their congregations on the Saturday before the election.

Secretary Hay wrote to Adee that "the President is greatly pleased with your circular and the Hebrews—poor dears! all over the country think we are bully boys, with a glass eye—as the ribald used to say." Hay instructed Adee to "please burn promptly" his note, but those directions were not carried out.

See July 16, 1903, for another, similar episode.

December 29, 1902

The "Drago Doctrine" of Argentina's foreign minister proposes that European nations cannot intervene in a country to collect debt payments.

For some time, Venezuela had failed to meet its debt payments to English and German creditors. Early in December, German and British warships blockaded the coast of Venezuela to collect their debts. President Roosevelt moved to end this crisis, and Argentina's Foreign Minister, Luis M. Drago, suggested an alternative long-term solution to European intervention.

In a note to the U.S. State Department, Drago suggested that the proper interpretation of the Monroe Doctrine should exclude foreign intervention when the "financial misfortune" of a nation made it impossible to pay a foreign debt. Drago urged the United States to accept the principle that "the public debt cannot occasion armed intervention nor even the actual occupation of the territory of American nations by a European power."

Soon after, Secretary Hay told Drago that his proposition closely resembled statements by President Roosevelt in his congressional address of December 2, 1902. Hay did not, however, touch on the central issue of whether or not default on a public debt could justify foreign intervention.

Drago's concept was related to a practice followed by some Latin American countries of including a "Calvo clause" in contracts awarded to foreign concessions. Named for an Argentine foreign minister who suggested the idea in 1886, this clause required foreign investors to renounce their right to appeal for the protection of their own governments for the execution of a contract. Calvo claimed that if foreign capital migrates, the alien investor has no appeal but to the courts of the nation to which it "migrates" for investment. American and other investors disliked such a clause, and if they signed such a contract, their lawyers asserted, they could not sign away their right to be protected by their own governments. The Calvo precept had not been accepted as international practice by other nations.

In contrast, the Drago doctrine was adopted in a modified form as international law by the Hague Convention of 1907. The modification added the exception that the debtor state could not refuse to accept and abide by the decision of international arbitration regarding debts due.

See February 13, 1903.

1903

January 22, 1903

The United States and Colombia sign the Hay-Herran Treaty, which grants America the right to build a canal in Panama.

This treaty required a year of frustrating negotiation for Secretary of State Hay and three Colombian ministers to the United States: Martinez Silva from March 1901 to the fall of 1901; José Vincente Concha from September to November 1901; and Dr. Tomás Herran. Each of these ministers proceeded cautiously with Hay and President Roosevelt and often required two or three weeks to clarify points with Bogotá.

Initially, Martinez worked closely with Hay and the lawyer for the New Panama Canal Company, Thomas Cromwell. Eventually, Bogotá feared that Martinez conceded too much to America by working with Cromwell. Concha, his replacement, spoke no English and had a nervous breakdown because of pressure from both Bogotá and the Americans. Concha had argued that Colombia should receive the $40 million intended for the Panama Canal Company, which, he said, could not sell its rights to America or anyone else. Concha's tactics irritated Hay and each believed the other was neurotic. Hay claimed that Concha had been sent home in a straitjacket in November.

When Dr. Herran arrived to replace Concha, the negotiations seemed ready to be finalized. Educated at Georgetown University, Herran had friends in Washington and worked well with Hay. He was cautious, however, and was disturbed by President Roosevelt's impetuous disposition. As a result, Herran checked often with his home office in Bogotá.

Hay finally told him in January 1903 that if he did not immediately sign the agreement, America would end the discussions and negotiate with Nicaragua. Herran yielded and the next day, January 22, he signed the treaty, even though Bogotá had instructed him three days earlier not to sign but to await further instructions. No one in Washington knew Bogotá's official feelings.

America favored the Hay-Herran Treaty and the Senate ratified it by a vote of 73 to 5 on March 17. The treaty provided that for a payment of $10 million and an annual rental of $250,000, the United States would obtain a 99-year lease with renewal options on a canal zone six miles wide. But Colombia did not receive any of the $40 million appropriated for the New Panama Company.

And the treaty failed, because the Colombian Senate rejected it on August 12, an action that precipitated an uprising in Panama.

See August 12, 1903, and November 3, 1903.

February 4, 1903

The U.S. Army undertakes an important reorganization as recommended by Secretary of War Root and approved by Congress.

Because the army had been unable to efficiently mobilize for the Cuban war, Root, soon after becoming secretary of war, undertook a study that indicated the need to reorganize the army for war purposes. Using plans that the European nations had adopted, the act of Congress of February 4 followed Root's proposals to create a chief of staff who was under the secretary of war and responsible for military discipline and army maneuvers. A general staff was instructed to develop war plans to be used when necessary.

During his term, Root also established an Army General Staff College at Fort Leavenworth, Kansas, an Army War College in Washington, D.C., and other intermediate schools between West Point and the War College for expanding the training of staff officers.

February 13, 1903

European nations accept a U.S. proposal to end their intervention in Venezuela and arbitrate.

Because Venezuela had refused to pay debts due to several European nations or to arbitrate a claims settlement, England and Germany instituted a naval blockade of Venezuela on December 1, 1902. The Venezuelan debts had been incurred by its various governments during the 19th century. On October 23, 1899, Cipriano CASTRO gained power in Caracas in a coup d'état but refused to recognize the nation's foreign debts. In addition, the European nations held damage claims against Venezuela for property losses during the 1899 revolution.

Early in 1901, Germany warned Castro that his financial contracts had to be met and informed Washington that Germany did not desire territory in Venezuela but wanted that nation to meet its obligations. Concurring with Germany, President Roosevelt in his annual message of December 1901 had stated that the Monroe Doctrine did not protect any nation from its fiscal responsibilities.

During 1902, Great Britain agreed to join Germany in blockading Venezuela because the British claims for debts were five times larger than Germany's. Before sending naval vessels, however, London and Berlin urged Caracas to arbitrate. When Castro refused, the two European powers sent warships to the Caribbean Sea, where the naval commanders issued an ultimatum to Castro to pay or agree to arbitrate. In retaliation, however, Castro arrested all British and German citizens in Venezuela, forcing the Europeans to install a "pacific" blockade of the Venezuelan coastline, in which they sank three Venezuelan gunboats and seized four others.

On December 9, Caracas asked the U.S. State Department to request a method of arbitration. The Europeans accepted this proposal on December 17, but exact terms for the agreement took some time to prepare. During the interim, tension developed because the Germans opened fire on a Venezuelan fort near Maracaibo, an act that inflamed U.S. opinion against the Anglo-German intervention. The blockade continued until February 13, before the Germans accepted the terms offered by the United States through its minister in Caracas, Herbert Bowen.

America's principal concern during this affair was to avoid territorial concessions by Venezuela. Although the Germans pledged not to demand territory prior to sending their navy, the British did not do so until January 1903, after Ambassador Herbert reported to London that U.S. opinion strongly opposed the blockade. In addition to his concern that territorial changes must not be required, President Roosevelt determined during this episode that a better method had to be devised to enforce the financial obligations of Latin American nations.

April 28, 1903

Although Russia halts its plans to leave Manchuria, the United States is not prepared to act to force Russia's withdrawal.

Russian forces had entered Manchuria during the Boxer Rebellion of 1900 but had agreed with China in 1902 to withdraw its army in three stages. Some Russian forces left during the fall of 1902, but in April 1903, the czar's government refused to continue to leave unless China accepted proposals giving Russia predominant rights in Manchuria.

Japan was the nation most concerned about Russia's hesitancy to leave Manchuria. Therefore, Tokyo urged its ally Great Britain to join it in demanding the Russian withdrawal. Because London was not interested in challenging the czar in northern China, the British asked the United States to provide leadership against Russia as a means to uphold the open door.

Although President Roosevelt and Secretary Hay both had an exaggerated fear of Russian policy in 1903, neither of them wanted to act forcefully for China's territorial integrity in Manchuria. The United States was interested in maintaining its equal access to commercial rights in all of China, but as Hay wrote to Roosevelt on April 28, 1903, the United States had no vital interests in Manchuria that were sufficient to fight for, nor could America do so. "If our rights and interests in opposition to Russia in the Far East were as clear as noonday," Hay wrote, "we could never get a treaty through the Senate, the object of which was to check Russian aggression."

Although some proponents of sea power and U.S. commerce in China advocated strong American action against Russia, neither Roosevelt nor Hay agreed. Realistically, the president observed that America could not go to war over Manchuria, and "I hate being in the position of seeming to bluster without backing it up."

As a result, on June 28, Hay met with Russia's ambassador, Count Cassini, simply to object to Russia's bad faith in not evacuating Manchuria. He told Cassini that he hoped Russia would rectify its policy as a means of maintaining U.S. friendship.

Privately, both Hay and Roosevelt indicated that Russia could not be trusted. "Dealing with a government with whom mendacity is a science is an extremely difficult and delicate matter," Hay noted in a memo to the president. Roosevelt agreed, for in a letter to a friend the president stated that the Russians had "extraordinary mendacity."

Without U.S. support and only a minimum of British backing, Japan vigorously protested Russia's Manchurian policy.

See August 12, 1903.

July 16, 1903

Roosevelt and Hay manipulate a U.S. citizen petition against Russia's Jewish persecutions to incite public opinion against Russia.

As in the case of Romanian discrimination against Jews in 1902, Jacob Schiff of New York sought support from the State Department in protesting against reports of a Russian pogrom against Jews that nearly destroyed the village of Kishinev on Easter Sunday of 1903. Hay told Schiff that an official protest to St. Petersburg would not be accepted because the affair was an internal Russian matter. He agreed, however, to speak with the Russian ambassador and to forward to the czar a petition signed by American citizens.

In June, Hay spoke to Ambassador Cassini about the Jewish protest. The ambassador became so upset that he impulsively called in American newsmen to oppose U.S. interference in Russian affairs. The czar, Cassini said, would never receive such a petition. Americans, he asserted, were reaching false conclusions about events in Russia without substantial evidence to support their accusations.

Cassini's press interview gave the Jewish persecution additional publicity and also enabled President Roosevelt to issue an official response that rebuked both Cassini and the czar in the matter of its persecution and its Manchurian policy. Roosevelt asserted that the United States had a right to express its "deep sympathy" for the "unfortunate Jews" in Russia. Moreover, he added, Russia did not act as a friendly power when it employed devious methods to bar Americans from Manchurian trade. Without any official notes to St. Petersburg, Roosevelt effectively aroused American opinion against Russia's domestic and foreign policies.

Neither Roosevelt nor Hay bothered to report official word they received regarding the czar's attempts to punish the local officials who carried out the Jewish persecution in Kishinev. On April 29, the Russian government removed from office the provincial governor, Lieutenant General von Raabe, and the police chief, Colonel Khanzheneff. Two or three lesser officials were also punished. The failure of Americans and their news media to report such action explains Ambassador Cassini's unwise attempt to grant a public interview in America, an effort that backfired.

See April 28, 1903.

July 25, 1903

Plans for a revolution in Panama begin at a meeting of prominent persons near Panama City.

Many of the leaders of the Panamanian government met on July 25 at a country estate to discuss a revolution by the Department of Panama for independence from Colombia. Those attending included Senator José Augustin ARANGO; Carlos Constantino AROSEMENA; an American, Herbert PRESCOTT, the assistant superintendent of the Panama Railway; the U.S. consul at Panama City, Hezekiah A. GUDGER; and two U.S. army officers who were engineers on the Walker Commission, Major William BLACK and Lieutenant Mark BROOKE. About 20 other Panamanians were also present at the meeting. The Walker Commission was the U.S. committee that studied alternative canal routes at Panama and Nicaragua.

Two other leaders were not present at this time. One was Dr. Manuel AMADOR GUERRERO, a physician for the Panama Railway, and James BEERS, the foreign agent for the railway. Beers was expected to return soon from New York City, where he had gone to consult with Thomas Cromwell, the lawyer for both the New Panama Canal Company and the Panama Railway and a person much interested in a possible revolution in Panama. The other absent leader was

Dr. Amador, who did not join the independence movement until August.

See October 17 and November 3, 1903.

August 12, 1903

Colombia's Senate rejects the Hay-Herran Treaty on Panama.

Although the U.S. Senate had quickly ratified the treaty of January 22, 1902, Colombia was not pleased with it. In January, Bogotá instructed Herran not to sign, but the minister did so because Secretary Hay had given him an ultimatum that America would drop the Panama route in favor of the Nicaraguan proposals if he did not sign. Whether or not Hay's threat would have been carried out cannot be known.

The Colombian government did not like the treaty's financial arrangements or the agreement that the Panama Canal Company could transfer its rights and property to the United States. In 1902, Herran had argued Colombia's case that the Canal Company's land rights could not be transferred. In accordance with the Colombian view, the Bogotá government wanted at least $25 million, not the $10 million allocated in the treaty of 1903.

Colombia also claimed the canal rental fee was unsatisfactory. The lease of the Panama Railway was $250,000 per year, and Bogotá believed the canal lease should be greater, not the same. It also objected that there would be no annual rental paid for the first nine years of the treaty. In addition to the rental and payments, Colombia desired more explicit clauses to affirm its continued sovereignty in Panama.

The Colombian senate's rejection on August 12 should not have surprised Roosevelt, as he later asserted. On several occasions the U.S. minister to Bogotá, Arthur Beaupré, informed Washington that the Colombians were angry about the treaty. Both on March 30 and May 4, Beaupré wrote to Secretary Hay about Bogota's opposition to, as well as public disapproval of, the treaty.

Hay had instructed Beaupré to tell the Colombian officials that no modifications of the treaty could be accepted. Moreover, Beaupré was told to inform Colombia that if the treaty were rejected, friendly relations between the two nations would be "so seriously compromised that action might be taken by Congress next winter which every friend of Colombia would regret" (Hay to Beaupré, June 9, 1903).

Therefore, even though Colombia disliked the treaty from the outset, Secretary Hay used threats and refused treaty revisions. These American attitudes were also reported in U.S. newspapers, making the Colombian decision more difficult to accept. On June 14, the *New York World* printed an unsigned article based on a conference between Cromwell, the Panama Company's lawyer, and Roosevelt. The *World*'s story said Roosevelt greatly preferred the Panama route. Roosevelt, the writer said, blamed the "greed of the Colombian government" for delaying the treaty. The *World* also reported that if the treaty were rejected, the state of Panama would secede from Colombia and make a treaty with America. President Roosevelt, it said, favored this plan in case Colombia rejected the treaty.

In part, the Americans misunderstood that the delay in Bogotá was due to Colombia's recent history. A three-year civil war in Colombia ended in November 1902 and brought a conservative, José Manuel Marroquin, to power. Hay thought Marroquin was a dictator with unlimited power. In fact, his powers were limited and his rule was precarious. In particular, his Liberal Party opponents in congress accused him of selling out to the United States. Moreover, both Marroquin and the Liberals were sensitive to Colombian citizens' deep feelings about national honor, a quality not always appreciated in Washington.

In June, Minister Beaupré informed Hay that the Colombian government was seeking a compromise to save face in the treaty debates. For example, if $10 million of the $40 million designated for the Panama Company could go to Colombia, Bogotá's government would support the treaty with no added cost to America.

Under different circumstances such a compromise might have succeeded. In Washington, however, Hay followed the advice of Thomas Cromwell, the Panama Company's lawyer. Cromwell persuaded Hay not to mix the Panama Company's rights with Colombia's treaty demands. As early as February 17, the United States had officially told the Panama Company that it would pay $40 million, and Cromwell used his influence to insure that his clients received the entire amount. The Colombian senate rejected the Hay-Herran Treaty on August 12.

Roosevelt's reaction to Colombia's rejection was said to be both emotional and racially antagonistic to Colombia. Hay suggested that a treaty should be made with Nicaragua. But the president insisted on the Panama route. Regarding Colombians, Roosevelt wrote to Hay: "We may have to give a lesson to those jack rabbits."

See November 3, 1903.

August 12, 1903

Japan protests Russia's failure to withdraw from Manchuria.

During the Boxer uprising of 1900, Russian troops occupied Manchuria, an action that Great Britain and Japan opposed. Under pressure of the Anglo-Japanese alliance, the czar had agreed with China on April 8, 1902, that the Russian army would withdraw in three stages over an 18-month period. Some Russian troops left during the fall of 1902, but in April the Russians balked at fulfilling the second stage.

With a minimal amount of British backing, the Japanese on August 12 insisted that Russia fulfill its 1902 agreement with China. The Russians complied temporarily on October 8, 1903, but soon thereafter the czar reinforced his determination to retain Russian rights in northern China. Czar Nicholas II had personal financial interests in the Yalu concessions and wished to guarantee their profit.

Therefore, while yielding somewhat to Japan in October 1903, the czar also sought to strengthen Russia's interests in Manchuria. On August 19, the czar removed Count Serge WITTE as his finance minister because Witte opposed Russian expansion in East Asia. Soon after, Nicholas defied Japan by establishing the viceroyalty of the Far East as a new Russian agency to deal with Asian affairs. When Russia hesitated to make its third and final troop withdrawal from Manchuria in 1904, the dispute led to the Russo-Japanese war.

See April 28, 1903.

October 8, 1903

A Chinese-American commercial treaty opens trade at two Manchurian cities.

Because Russia's occupation of Manchuria raised the question of the open door, Secretary of State Hay wished to reassert the U.S. concept as far as possible. In the treaty of 1903, the Chinese accepted the American view by opening the cities of Mukden and Antung for U.S. commerce. China's foreign minister, Chang Chih-tung, desired the treaty as part of China's attempt to get Western aid in counteracting Russia's influence. Nevertheless, Secretary Hay rejected Chang's proposal to link the U.S. treaty rights to the Russian withdrawal, which, since April 1903, the Russians had halted.

Initially, Russia opposed the Sino-American Treaty of October 1903 but yielded when Washington agreed not to insist on settlement rights in the new treaty ports. The U.S. Senate ratified the treaty on December 18, 1903.

The treaty with China recognized that America would use the open door in its treaty ports. It had no effect on the other foreign nations that sought spheres of influence in China. To keep an open door effectively, America would have had to join England and Japan against the other powers. The United States would not act jointly, however.

See April 28, 1903.

October 17, 1903

Plans for the Panamanian revolution are given to Dr. Amador by the Panama Canal Company's agent, Philippe Bunau-Varilla.

Following the July 25, 1903, meeting of Panama's leaders, the plot for an independence revolution developed significant backing. The leaders recruited Dr. Amador to the movement in August and sent him to New York to obtain assistance from the Panama Company's two chief American agents: the company lawyer, Thomas Cromwell, and the French engineer who represented French canal investors, Philippe Bunau-Varilla. Both Cromwell and Bunau-Varilla had lobbied the U.S. Congress to fund the Panama project in 1902.

On October 17, Amador had the last of several meetings with Bunau-Varilla in Room 1162 of the Waldorf Astoria Hotel, the place referred to by the Frenchman as the "cradle of the Panamanian revolution." Since his first meeting with Dr. Amador on September 22, Bunau-Varilla had also visited President Roosevelt at the White House and Secretary of State Hay at his Washington home.

As a result of his recent visits, Bunau-Varilla had specific plans for Amador to take back to his colleagues for their action. Although his visits with the president and secretary of state had evidently avoided precise commitments, these U.S. officials convinced Bunau-Varilla by implication that they would act effectively to permit the U.S. Navy to protect the rebels from being attacked by Colombian troops coming by sea to suppress any uprising. Amador knew that for $100,000 he could buy off the small garrison of Colombian troops stationed in Panama City as well as its commander general, Esteban Huertas. Amador's concern was that the rebels had no gunboats to defend Colón against reinforcements sent from Bogotá by sea. Bunau-Varilla knew by October 17 that the U.S. navy would protect the rebels along the seacoast.

In addition to the assurance of U.S. support, Bunau-Varilla outfitted Amador with the other perquisites of a successful independence movement: a proclamation of independence, a basic military plan, a scheme to defend Colón and Panama City, the draft of a constitution, a secret code for communication, and a national flag. Amador did not like the flag's design, but he took it. Later, his colleagues in Panama changed it to their liking. Bunau-Varilla told Amador the rebellion must take place on November 3, election day in the United States. Amador believed this was too soon, but Bunau-Varilla insisted because the American public's attention would be diverted on election day; thus, the affair in Panama would not be noticed.

The Frenchman had one final demand. Panama must name him—Bunau-Varilla—as the new republic's minister plenipotentiary to negotiate recognition by the United States and to make a treaty to build a canal in Panama. Again, Amador was reluctant to fulfill this demand, but Bunau-Varilla convinced him that his connections in Washington made it essential for Panama to use his good offices in Washington immediately after the rebellion began.

Following Bunau-Varilla's instructions as closely as possible, Amador returned to Panama, where he arrived on October 27 and set about advising his coconspirators of their need to act as the Frenchman had directed.

See November 3, 1903.

October 20, 1903

The Alaskan boundary dispute is resolved in America's favor despite Canada's opposition.

The U.S.-Canadian boundary dispute had been pending since October 20, 1899, when the British had accepted Secretary Hay's proposed modus vivendi. Finally, on January 24, 1903, Hay and Britain's ambassador, Sir Michael HERBERT, signed a convention that created a commission of three Americans and three Britons to resolve the issue. Although the commissioners were to be "impartial jurists," President Roosevelt selected Senators Henry Cabot Lodge and George Turner and Secretary of War Elihu Root as delegates. The British chose two Canadians and Lord Alverstone, the lord chief justice of Great Britain. As Hay remarked after learning of the British choice, "Everything now depends on . . . Lord Alverstone." As the only impartial commissioner, his attitude in the dispute would be imperative to obtain a settlement.

The six commissioners held their sessions in London between September 3 and October 20, 1903. The commission reached an agreement because Alverstone voted with the Americans and the U.S. delegates accepted some minor concessions in Canada's favor. Britain's prime minister appointed Alverstone because he expected him to be objective enough to realize the validity of the American claims. Nevertheless, during the meetings, the U.S. delegates let Joseph Choate, the U.S. ambassador in London, know that Alverstone was being too rigid on behalf of Canada. Choate informed Lansdowne and, within two days, Alverstone moderated his views accordingly. Lansdowne wanted to obtain better relations with America and had become alarmed when President Roosevelt publicly threatened to seek funds from Congress to "run the line on our own theory."

Nevertheless, the United States made a minor concession to Canada in order to appease Canada's delegates. The Americans agreed to concede the Pease and Wales Islands to Canada. This agreement gave Canada two islands they desired but continued to exclude all the ocean inlets in the Alaskan panhandle from Canada's possession. Maintaining control of these inlets was the principal American concern in the dispute.

With the cession of the Pease and Wales Islands, the commission finalized its report by a vote of 4 to 2. The two Canadians continued to oppose the settlement, but without London's backing the Canadian government had to be reconciled to the boundary decision. In 1908, Canada calmed down and named a mountain near the Alaskan boundary for Lord Alverstone.

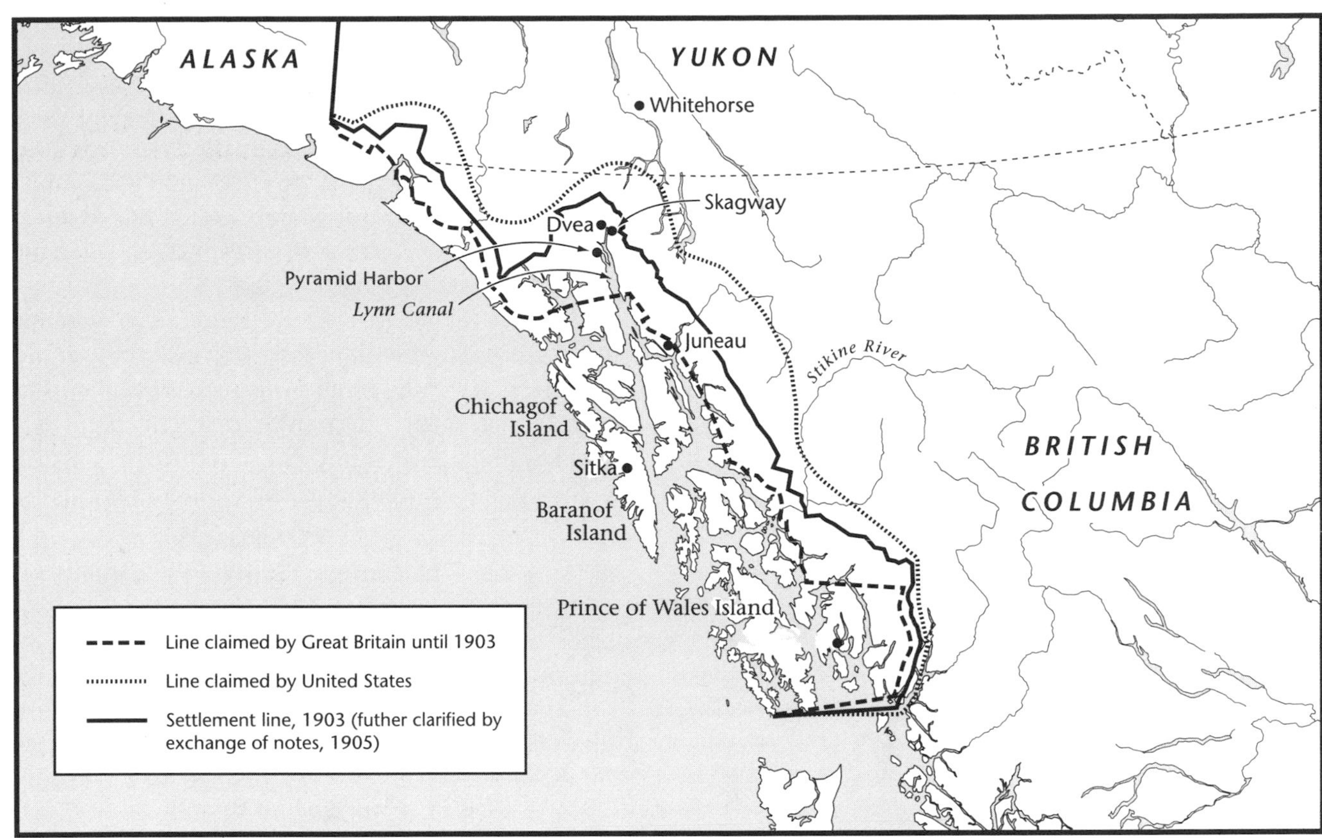

Alaska Boundary Dispute, 1898–1903

November 3, 1903

The United States is implicated in Panama's revolution against Colombia.

When a rebellion began on November 3, it was precipitated partly by Colombia's rejection of the Hay-Herran Treaty on August 12 and partly by the leaders of a group of Panamanians who devised independence plans on July 25. Furthermore, the Panamanian rebels believed they had secured a promise of aid from the White House and State Department when Dr. Amador returned with Bunau-Varilla's instructions on October 27.

The rebels could scarcely believe that they had White House support. Consequently, they devised a test of Bunau-Varilla's influence. They asked Amador to wire the Frenchman in secret code and report that because Colombian troops planned to arrive soon at Colón, a U.S. warship was needed immediately. Bunau-Varilla complied. He contacted his "personal friend," Francis B. Loomis, an assistant secretary of state, and learned that a U.S. warship would be sent in 24 hours. That same day, October 31, Commander Hubbard of the USS *Nashville* in Jamaican waters received orders to proceed immediately to Colón, Panama, where he should consult with the American consul and await orders. The *Nashville* reached Colón on the afternoon of November 2, and the revolutionary leaders knew that Amador's report from Bunau-Varilla was correct. Having already collected smuggled arms and ammunition and prepared the Panama City fire brigade as a military unit, they were ready to go the next day.

The November 3 uprising at Panama City and later Colón was almost bloodless. The only death was that of a Chinese shopkeeper who was killed when the Colombian gunboat *Bogotá* fired six shells on Panama City. The rebels' chief problem was the arrival of the Colombian ship *Cartagena* with 200 men on November 2, an unexpected Colombian move that, ironically, required the *Nashville*'s presence. On November 2, however, Hubbard had not yet received orders to act. Therefore, the rebel planners decided to send the two Colombian generals who arrived on the *Cartagena* to Panama City by train, promising to send the 200 troops soon after. The rebels controlled the

TR Intervenes in Panama. *New York Globe*

railway because both Superintendent James Shaler and his assistant had joined the rebel plot, together with almost all officials of the Panama Railway.

The Colombian generals fell for the rebel trap. Unaware who controlled the railway, the generals traveled to Panama City, but "engine failure" on the train prevented the 200 Colombian soldiers from leaving on the next train. Without their soldiers, the generals were arrested in Panama City on November 3 by Colonel Eliseo Torres, head of Panama's army garrison. Torres received $80,000 for his aid to the rebels.

By November 3 at about 10:30 A.M. the commander of the *Nashville* received his orders from the assistant secretary of the navy, Charles DARLING. He was told to retain "free and uninterrupted transit" of the Panama Railway and to occupy the railroad if it were threatened. Commander Hubbard was told to prevent any armed force, "government or insurgent," from landing at Colón, Porto Bello, or any other point. Acting in an unprecedented fashion, the United States ordered its naval officer to intervene in the domestic affairs of a foreign nation. While U.S. officials claimed they acted under earlier treaties to preserve transit rights, previous treaties did not indicate this meant interfering with forces of the government seeking to put down a rebellion.

By November 5, however, the rebels had succeeded with U.S. help. Hubbard prevented the Colombian troops from using the railroad to go to Panama City to fight the rebellion, and he stood by as arrangements were made to ship the Colombian troops home on a Royal Mail steamer, the *Orinoco.* That same day, November 5, a second U.S. warship, the *Dixie,* arrived at Colón.

Early on November 6, the Republic of Panama notified Washington that the new government was established and that Philippe Bunau-Varilla was its "confidential agent" in Washington. At 12:51 P.M. on that same day, the U.S. government formally recognized the new government of Panama.

November 18, 1903

American rights to construct and control a Panama Canal are granted by the Republic of Panama.

Just 12 days after the United States recognized the Panamanian government, Secretary of State Hay and Philippe Bunau-Varilla signed a treaty for U.S. rights to build a canal in the isthmus of Panama. The negotiators rushed the treaty because the Panamanian government had sent a commission to assist its minister in Washington, Bunau-Varilla. The minister correctly feared that if the commissioners arrived before the treaty was signed, they would offer opposition to the treaty terms he and Hay desired.

Learning that three Panamanian delegates had left Colón for New York on November 10, Bunau-Varilla hastened to draft a treaty. On November 13, President Roosevelt formally received Bunau-Varilla at the White House and immediately Hay and the minister discussed terms of a treaty. Hay sent Bunau-Varilla a modified copy of the Hay-Herran Treaty, but the Frenchman thought he should compose a new treaty that the U.S. Senate would be certain to approve. Therefore, Bunau-Varilla prepared a treaty and readily accepted all changes proposed by Hay. At 7 P.M. on November 18, Hay and Bunau-Varilla signed the treaty at Hay's home office on Lafayette Square.

Two hours later, Bunau-Varilla met the three Panamanian commissioners who arrived at the Washington railway station. As they stepped off the train, Bunau-Varilla informed them: "The Republic of Panama is henceforth under the protection of the United States. I have just signed the Canal Treaty." According to the Frenchman's account, the

Panamanians reacted in disbelief and consternation; then they were enraged. Dr. Amador looked as if he would faint. Federico Boyd insisted that Bunau-Varilla had acted illegally and without authorization.

Later, however, the three delegates met with Secretary Hay, who assured them that the United States would accept supplementary arrangements to correct any defects in the treaty. Nevertheless, the commissioners had been presented with a fait accompli.

For America, the treaty was exceptionally beneficial. As Senator Hernando de Soto Money of Mississippi remarked during the Senate debate on the treaty: "we have never had a concession so extraordinary in its character as this. In fact, it sounds very much as if we wrote it for ourselves."

Senator Money was nearly correct in his remark, for Bunau-Varilla did not care about Panamanian interests. In the U.S. Senate, the debate focused on how the treaty was obtained, not on the favorable treaty terms. The anti-imperialist Senator George Hoar denounced the U.S. role in Panama, even though he lacked the exact evidence available to later scholars. The arrival of a U.S. warship the day before the uprising, the hasty recognition of the Republic of Panama, and the rapid negotiations with the former lobbyist for the Panama Canal Company provided sufficient evidence of Roosevelt's interference in the Panamanian revolt to convince Hoar of the administration's duplicity.

Nevertheless, the opposition of Hoar and other senators was minimal. Most senators and most Americans cheered Roosevelt's aggressive tactics. Thus, on February 23, 1904, the Senate ratified the Hay–Bunau-Varilla Treaty by a vote of 66 to 14.

The important treaty terms were as follows:

1. The United States could build a canal through a zone 10 miles wide (the Colombian treaty had provided for 6 miles).
2. The canal zone would be held by the United States "in perpetuity" (the Herran Treaty was for 99 years).
3. Within the zone, the United States would exercise all rights, power, and authority as " if it were the sovereign of the territory . . . to the entire exclusion of the exercise by the Republic of Panama of any such rights, power, or authority."
4. Colón and Panama City were not part of the canal zone but the United States would control sanitation, sewerage, water, and public order in those cities.
5. America secured four islands in the Bay of Panama and had the right to expropriate any other land or water "necessary and convenient" for the building, operations, sanitation, or defense of the canal.
6. The United States guaranteed the independence of Panama.
7. The French canal company had the right to transfer its concessions and property to America.
8. Panama would receive $10 million on the exchange of ratifications and a $250,000 annual annuity beginning after nine years.

For Panama's agreement, see November 26, 1903.

November 26, 1903

The Panamanian government agrees to the Hay–Bunau-Varilla Treaty.

Bunau-Varilla's acceptance of the canal treaty without awaiting the arrival of the Panamanian commissioners led these delegates to refuse to support the agreement. The new government had wanted Dr. Amador, Federico Boyd, and Carlos Arosemena to check all clauses being negotiated by Bunau-Varilla.

What changes would have been made in the treaty if Bunau-Varilla had awaited the arrival of the three commissioners will never be known. As the Frenchman realized, however, without the freedom to act on his own, negotiation of a proper treaty would take many months. Thus, he preferred to avoid their interference.

Moreover, Bunau-Varilla treated the commissioners with constant disdain. He told them Colombia was sending a special mission to Washington to negotiate with the Americans, thus threatening them if they rejected his advice. He agreed with them to send the treaty to Panama by steamship. Then he cabled the text of the treaty to Panama's Minister of Foreign Affairs Dr. F. V. de la Espriella with a report of the "bad conduct" of the three commissioners with U.S. officials and President Roosevelt.

Most critically, however, Bunau-Varilla used a ploy that convinced the Panamanian leaders to accept the treaty. On November 25, he cabled de la Espriella that America would suspend protection of Panama and sign a new treaty with Colombia if Panama did not immediately ratify the treaty. The Panamanian leaders decided to ratify. They were not familiar

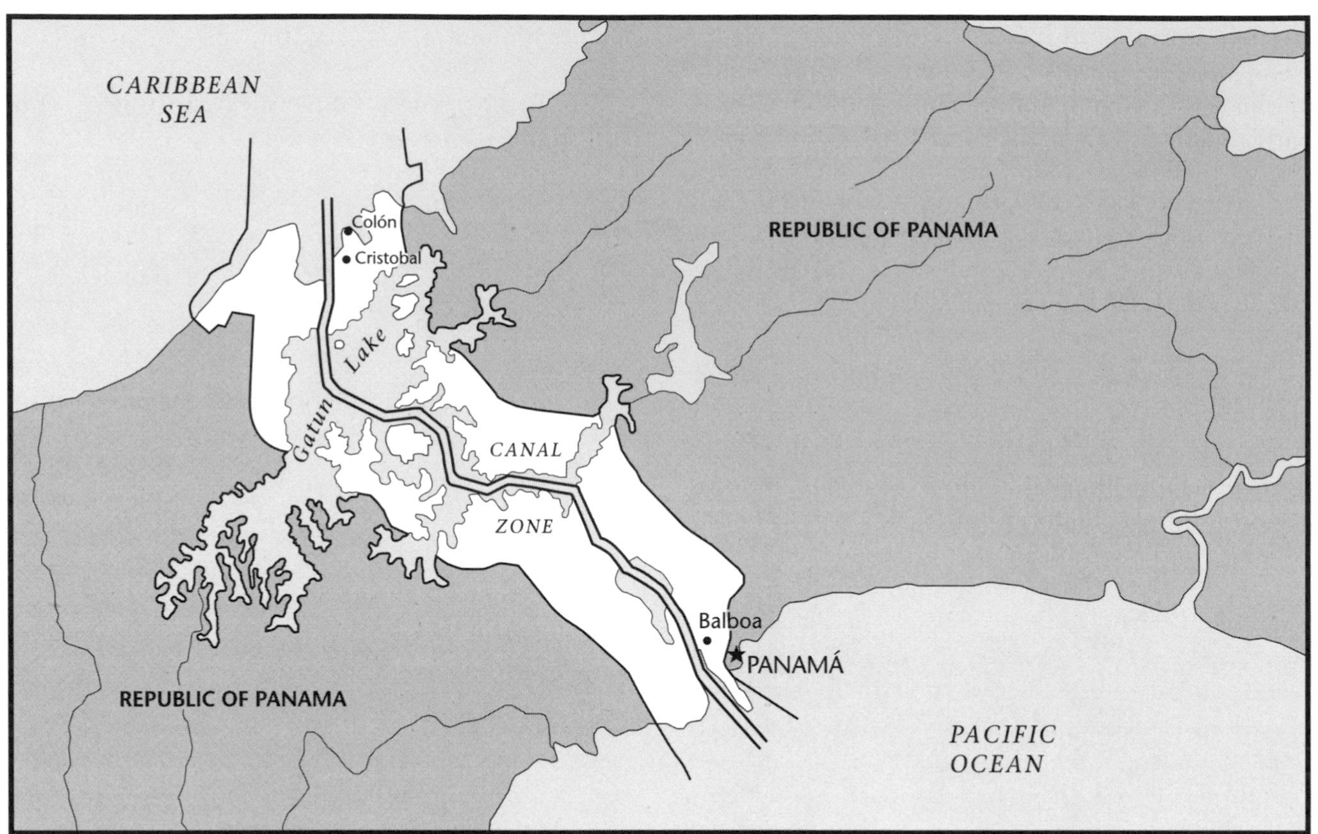

Panama Canal Zone, 1903

with Americans in Washington, but Bunau-Varilla had demonstrated his power by getting U.S. backing on November 2 and 3. The military weakness of Panama if it lost U.S. support seemed to require their compliance with Bunau-Varilla's demand. On November 26 they overrode Dr. Amador's reported opposition to the treaty and cabled Bunau-Varilla that the government approved the treaty.

Historically, the dubious circumstances of Bunau-Varilla's action cast a shadow over U.S.-Panamanian relations. The leaders of Panama claimed the treaty damaged their national interests by giving America too much authority in their land. Panamanian nationalists saw the treaty as illegal, unwarranted, and conceived by Roosevelt and Hay as well as Bunau-Varilla. In 1903, however, Roosevelt achieved his goal. America could build and control a canal in Panama.

December 17, 1903

The Wright brothers make the first heavier-than-air flight at Kitty Hawk, North Carolina.

The flight of the first airplane culminated a long series of studies and developments in aerodynamic theory and glider flights by such pioneers of flight as Octave Chanute, Samuel P. Langley, and Alberto Santos-Dumont. Orville and Wilber Wright had begun experiments in 1898 and tested gliders in 1901 at Kitty Hawk. Their 1903 plane weighed 750 pounds and carried a 170-pound, 12-horsepower gasoline engine. On December 17, they made four flights, the longest lasting 59 seconds and traveling 852 feet.

Soon after their success, the Wrights solicited military contracts for airplanes. They patented their aircraft on May 22, 1906. In 1908, they toured Europe and obtained a contract for a plane from the French government. On August 2, 1909, the U.S. army tested and approved a contract for an airplane.

1904

February 8, 1904

Russo-Japanese War begins.

Since August 1903, Japanese and Russian diplomats had discussed prior Russian agreements to evacuate Manchuria. During the talks, the czar's troops remained in Manchuria while additional forces moved across the Yalu River into Korea. The Russian maneuvers directly challenged Tokyo, and on February 6, 1904, Japan broke diplomatic relations with Moscow. The war began on February 8, when the Japanese fleet moved into the ocean area near Port Arthur and bottled up Russia's Asian fleet. War was declared officially on February 10.

For the outcome of the war, see August 9, 1905.

April 8, 1904

A British-French entente is formed.

This alliance between France and England ended a long series of imperial disputes between the two nations and provided Paris with an ally against Germany. The agreement recognized French rights in Morocco and British rights in Egypt. The allies provided mutual diplomatic support in extending their control in each area.

June 22, 1904

"Perdicaris alive or Raisuli dead!"—this Moroccan incident boosts President Roosevelt's public iamge.

Ion Perdicaris, a Greek native holding American naturalization papers, had been seized and held for ransom by a Moroccan chieftain named Raisuli. The United States sent a warship to the Mediterranean coast while the State Department negotiated for the release of Perdicaris.

Although the release of Perdicaris had been arranged, Roosevelt advised Secretary of State Hay to send a strongly worded protest for the U.S. consul in Tangier to deliver to the Moroccan chieftain. Included in Hay's note was the dramatic phrase "Perdicaris alive or Raisuli dead," which implied that the release of the American citizen was not certain.

In reality, Roosevelt was again demonstrating his ability to stir the U.S. public. The Republican National Convention was in session in Chicago, but with Roosevelt's renomination a foregone conclusion, the convention had become apathetic. The telegram to Tangier roused the delegates because, as intended, it was read to them as a display of the virile Republican president shaking a "big stick" at Morocco. The delegates cheered and celebrated the message of the president. As planned, the entire telegram from Hay to the American consul was not read. The remainder of the note warned the consul to act cautiously and not commit the American warship at Tangier to use force unless the consul received specific approval from Washington.

June 30, 1904

The United States is unsuccessful in preventing the British violation of the Chinese territory of Tibet.

In the fall of 1903, the British began military action to prevent "disorders" in Tibet, and by May 1904, they neared the capital city of Lhasa. On June 3, Secretary Hay asked Ambassador Choate in London to seek an explanation of the British purposes in Tibet, for they seemed to violate China's integrity and independence. Britain's only response to Choate on June 30 was the assertion that the Chinese had not acted effectively in Tibet and the British would impose such terms as they believed necessary to obtain order.

This exchange of information indicates that U.S. policy on the open door deviated from British interests in China. Nevertheless, President Roosevelt and other Americans incorrectly believed that British and American policy on China were the same, that is, to retain an open door and preserve China's territorial integrity.

See September 7, 1904.

September 7, 1904

Britain establishes a protectorate over Tibet.

Situated just to the north of India, Tibet had been an object of British and Russian designs since the 1880s. As China's government became increasingly weakened during the 1890s, Britain feared the czar's armies might move into Tibet as they had into Manchuria in 1900. Following several border incidents in 1901–1902, the British found an excuse to blame Tibet for treaty violations and sent in a military expedition under Sir Francis Younghusband. Winning a few minor battles, the British seized the capital city, Lhasa, on August 3, 1904. Thereafter, Tibet signed a treaty on September 7, accepting a British protectorship, although the legal fiction of Chinese sovereignty was maintained.

October 20, 1904

Chile and Bolivia officially end the War of the Pacific.

Since 1884, only a truce had prevented war between these two Latin American nations, and there were several periods of crisis that nearly led to hostilities. By the treaty of 1904, Chile gained possession of the Bolivian littoral on the Pacific coast but agreed to construct a railway between the port of Arica and La Paz for the use of Bolivia. Without the littoral Bolivia's territory had no outlet to the sea.

November 8, 1904

Theodore Roosevelt is reelected president.

Because the conservative Republicans dominated the party convention, the Republican platform scarcely indicated the political reform concepts associated with President Roosevelt's progressivism. The Democratic convention nominated Alton B. Parker on a platform that criticized business trusts and demanded greater regulatory powers for the Interstate Commerce Commission. Roosevelt won easily, gaining 336 electoral votes to Parker's 140. Subsequently, during his term of office, Roosevelt did begin a policy to break up the trusts and to enable the ICC to set fair railroad rates.

December 6, 1904

The Roosevelt Corollary to the Monroe Doctrine is asserted in the President's annual message to Congress.

Because of recent efforts of European powers to force Latin American nations to pay their financial debts, Roosevelt decided he should offer a U.S. policy designed to make certain that such obligations were met without risking European intervention in the Western Hemisphere.

In 1902–1903, the Anglo-German blockade of Venezuela caused difficulty in the Caribbean, and in 1904 a similar problem developed when Santo Domingo fell behind in its debt payments. Roosevelt agreed that European investors had the right to seek their governments' protection. Therefore, he told Congress, European intervention could be prevented only if America accepted the responsibility of "the exercise of an international police power" in the Western Hemisphere.

To achieve this end, the president stated that the United States should intervene in those states guilty of "chronic wrongdoing" to assure that they met their foreign obligations. The Monroe Doctrine, he said, could not be used by Latin Americans to ask the United States to allow them to avoid their financial obligations. Therefore, the United States had to act by overseeing the fulfillment of these duties to prevent European intervention.

Whereas the Monroe statement of 1823 had been designed to halt European intervention, Roosevelt's corollary proposed to justify American intervention in Latin America. Moreover, Roosevelt's proposal soon became not only theory but also American policy.

See February 7, 1905.

1905

January 22, 1905

Bloody Sunday—Russian troops kill 70 workers during a procession at St. Petersburg.

Father Gapon, a Russian Orthodox priest, led a group of workers who desired reforms of working conditions in a march toward the czar's palace to present a petition stating their requests. Russian soldiers fired on them, killing 70 and wounding 240. This bloodshed inaugurated further worker demonstrations and strikes in Russia that climaxed in a general strike.

See October 20–30, 1905.

February 7, 1905

President Roosevelt applies his corollary to the Monroe Doctrine to intervene in the internal financial problems of the Dominican Republic.

Throughout 1904 a crisis developed in the Dominican Republic because the government defaulted on bonds and loans due to European creditors. Approximately $10 million was due to American creditors and another $22 million was due to Belgian, French, German, Italian, and Spanish business interests. In October 1904, the Dominican Republic permitted an American agent to collect its customs duties at Puerto Plata in order to pay the debts due to a New York investment corporation. The Europeans objected to this preferential treatment and asked their respective governments to protest to Washington.

As a result, the Dominicans agreed to permit an American agent to collect their customs duties for all debts. This agreement followed President Roosevelt's message to Congress of December 6, 1904, during which he offered the Roosevelt Corollary to justify American action as a means of preventing European intervention.

To "legalize" U.S. activity, the United States and the Dominican Republic signed a treaty on February 7. This convention authorized an American collector to levy the Dominicans' customs fees and apply 45% to the national budget and 55% to pay the foreign creditors. Roosevelt immediately acted to send an agent to collect the duties, even though the U.S. Senate did not ratify the treaty for more than two years.

See February 8, 1907.

March 31, 1905

The first Moroccan crisis begins—Germany's Emperor William II speaks against French privileges in Morocco.

By forming agreements with Britain (April 8, 1904) and Spain (October 3, 1904), France moved to solidify its rights in Morocco. In February 1905, France issued a demand to the sultan of Morocco for a program of reforms in police affairs, banking, and communications that would have given the French a virtual protectorship over the country.

Because the French had studiously kept the Germans out of these activities, German chancellor Count Bernhard von Bülow wanted to exert his nation's rights in Morocco and to try to split the French-English entente. Therefore, von Bülow persuaded the kaiser to visit Tangier and deliver a public statement to the sultan advocating the economic open door policy and the sultan's right to independence and territorial integrity. A crisis resulted because the French protested this German interference in Morocco's affairs, raising the threat of possible war. Soon after, President Roosevelt would become involved in seeking to prevent war.

See July 8, 1905.

June 10, 1905

President Roosevelt persuades Russia and Japan to end their war by direct negotiations.

Roosevelt's major achievement in ending the Russo-Japanese War that began on February 8, 1904, was to contact Japanese and Russian officials and persuade them to accept direct negotiations. Roosevelt desired to keep Manchuria under Chinese sovereignty as a means of retaining a power balance in East Asia. Because Japanese forces proved to be victorious on land and sea, the president had to receive moderate demands from Japan so that Russia would not attempt to fight on until it was driven completely out of Manchuria and China.

Roosevelt had excellent and direct contact with Japan's leaders. Following Japan's decisive victory at Mukden in March 1905, Roosevelt conducted secret talks in Washington with Japan's ambassador, Baron Kotoro TAKAHIRA, and the president's old friend Baron Kentaro KANEKA, an influential Japanese businessman. The Japanese confided to Roosevelt that they wanted secret negotiations because a liberal group of Japanese would accept either a bilateral Russian agreement or a multinational Great Power agreement to give Japan commercial rights in Manchuria. They feared a more hawkish military faction in Tokyo, which wanted both territory in China and a Russian indemnity, demands that Roosevelt did not want Japan to make. The Japanese also confided to the president that Japan's resources and manpower were being exhausted by the war and they hoped to restrict their government's demands if Russia would agree to negotiations.

Although Russia was losing the war and having uprisings in St. Petersburg, Roosevelt had more difficulty in bringing the czar's government to the peace talks. Both the Germans and the French initially preferred to keep Russia in the war, hoping for an eventual Russian victory. In St. Petersburg, the Czarina Alexandra and the military officers also wanted to continue the fighting.

To obtain Russia's agreement, Roosevelt sent a new American ambassador, George von Lengerke Meyer, to Russia. The czar found Meyer to be "charming" and a "fascinating talker." Having visited with Kaiser William in Berlin while on his way to Russia, Meyer learned that the Germans now planned to urge the czar to seek peace. The Japanese fleet had destroyed 32 Russian ships on May 27–29 at the battle of Tsushima Straits, and the kaiser knew the Russians could not win. Consequently, with the kaiser supporting peace talks, Meyer on June 7 secured the czar's consent to negotiations. To achieve this, Meyer arranged a private conference with Nicholas II at which the czarina was not present.

Having both the czar's and Tokyo's agreement, Roosevelt on June 10 formally invited the two nations to a peace conference under U.S. auspices.

For the conference, see August 9, 1905.

July 7, 1905

Elihu Root replaces John Hay as secretary of state.

Secretary of State Hay's health had deteriorated steadily during the fall and winter of 1904. Consequently, President Roosevelt both from desire and necessity had assumed more direct responsibility for decision making as well as for personal diplomacy during early 1905. After several months of rest in Europe, Hay returned to America, but his health did not improve and he died on July 1.

Soon after Hay's death, Roosevelt asked Elihu Root to become secretary of state, and Root assumed those duties on July 7. A former U.S. attorney in New York, Root had served as secretary of war under both McKinley and Roosevelt (1899–1904) and had been a member of the Alaskan boundary tribunal in 1903. Root served as secretary of state until January 11, 1909, when he resigned in favor of his assistant, Robert Bacon, to have a few weeks' rest before being sworn in as senator from New York.

July 8, 1905

President Roosevelt intervenes in the Moroccan crisis, persuading France to attend an international conference.

Following Kaiser William II's inflammatory remarks during a visit to Morocco on March 31, 1905, a series of multinational discussions failed to settle the dispute between France and Germany regarding each nation's rights in Morocco. Germany insisted on protecting the sultan's independence and believed that Great Britain had encouraged France to take firm action against Berlin.

Although the United States had little direct interest in Morocco, Roosevelt accepted a request from his good friend the German ambassador to Washington, Herman Speck von Sternberg, to act as a conciliator. The German Foreign Office desired "open door" trading rights in Morocco and wanted France to recognize these principles. The Germans hoped Roosevelt would persuade Great Britain to drop its support of Paris and urge the French to accept a conference.

Roosevelt talked with the French ambassador, Jules Jusserand, but there were no results until early June, when the sultan of Morocco invited the powers to an international conference. The sultan's action alarmed the French because they believed it was a German scheme. On June 16, Roosevelt decided to approach the French and German ambassadors to avoid a war that no one wanted. He told Jusserand that France could gain nothing from a war and would likely lose to Germany. He asked the French ambassador to do something to help the kaiser save face so that the crisis would end.

Next, the president contacted the kaiser through Ambassador von Sternberg to praise William II for gaining the French consent to attend a conference that would avoid a potential war. Accepting von Sternberg's suggestion, the kaiser on June 28 agreed to a conference on the basis that whenever differences arose between France and Germany, the kaiser promised to back the decision that Roosevelt "should consider to be the most fair and most practical." The kaiser's promise convinced the French to accept a meeting because Roosevelt had gained the confidence of both sides in the dispute.

On July 8, both Germany and France accepted the invitation to a conference on Morocco.

For the results of the conference at Algeciras, see April 7, 1906.

July 20, 1905

The Chinese begin a boycott of American goods and services.

This Chinese boycott against the United States became the first large-scale expression of Chinese nationalism, a phenomenon that Americans, including President Roosevelt and many of his successors, failed to understand. In contrast to the Boxer

Rebellion, which favored the emperor's control over the Western powers, the Chinese nationalists combined pride in their country with a desire to modernize their nation in trade, technology, intellect, and politics. The nationalists adopted the patriotic notion prevalent in Western civilization, an idea expressed in the slogan "China for the Chinese." The slogan opposed all foreign control of China.

Although many Americans believed they had helped China through using the open door principles, the United States became one of the leading antagonists of Chinese nationalism. Unlike other foreign nations, the United States passed legislation that specifically discriminated against the Chinese by excluding them and other Asians from immigration to the United States and obtaining U.S. citizenship. In addition, on frequent occasions Americans had grossly mistreated Chinese students, merchants, officials, and travelers. In Boston in 1903, Boston police and immigration officials surrounded the entire Chinese colony of several thousand people and arrested all Chinese who could not produce registration certificates. Two hundred thirty-four Chinese were held overnight in one room too small for them to lie down in. Only 45 of them proved later to be potential deportees. In 1904, Chinese officials who had been invited to attend the St. Louis exposition were detained by immigration officers in San Francisco. They were kept on the wharf in a shed that was dirty and overrun with vermin. Some of the officials immediately chose to return home, one of them commenting that "the Americans are a race of pigs."

Since the 1880s, the Chinese had been irritated most by the law excluding further Chinese immigration. Their diplomats had tried but failed to change the law. Yet in 1904 Congress passed a law to renew the exclusionary act, extending its effect to Hawaii and the Philippine Islands. President Roosevelt wanted to amend the act to exclude only Chinese laborers and to permit students, merchants, and other capable Asians to enter the United States. But fearing political opposition in the Western states, he sent Congress a message on April 5, 1904, that favored extending the existing law.

Late in the fall of 1904, Chinese nationalist leaders began to organize plans for a boycott and anti-American demonstrations. They wanted to carry out their proposals because Chinese diplomats were discussing a new immigration treaty with the Roosevelt administration. The Chinese hoped that satisfactory treaty changes might be made, at least changes that would accord fair and courteous treatment of Chinese by U.S. consuls and immigration officials.

In the United States, news of the forthcoming boycott divided public opinion. Many Americans, especially those who joined the American Asiatic Association, favored changes in both the treaty and the immigration act. Cotton interests in the South and New England in particular feared the consequence of a boycott on their exports. Others, such as Secretary of War Taft, criticized our unjust laws toward China and our failure to act like a civilized nation toward those we were trying to civilize. Nevertheless, the United States did not agree to any changes in the Chinese immigration treaty. China's nationalists proceeded to promote the boycott, which began officially on July 20, 1905.

The anti-American demonstrations were large and effective, especially in the Chinese treaty ports. In Shanghai, all of the leading trade guilds favored the boycott, and at mass meetings they agreed to unite to sell the American goods they had, but to buy no more. In Amoy, a mass meeting formed a committee of 36 merchants who agreed not to buy from or sell to Americans, not to use U.S. ships, and not to attend U.S. churches or schools. Many Chinese servants quit working for American households. Placards condemning Americans were also posted. One sign said: "If you buy or sell American goods you are lower than a pig or dog." U.S. cigarettes were called "Pin Head" and the Chinese stopped smoking them.

The U.S. State Department immediately protested the Chinese boycott. The Peking government claimed it was doing all it could, but found it difficult to control the people. Prince Ch'ing, the government leader, told U.S. Minister W. W. Rockhill that the cause of the trouble was the immigration treaty. If America agreed to a less harsh measure, he said, "everybody will be pleased." During the fall and winter of 1905, the Chinese government generally condemned the boycott but did nothing to suppress it. Eventually,

President Roosevelt resorted to threats of war before the disturbances ended.

See March 6, 1906.

July 24, 1905

Russia and Germany sign a treaty for mutual aid in the event of an attack by a third power, but France prevents its enactment.

Kaiser William II and Czar Nicholas II agreed to an alliance, called the BJORKO TREATY, while they visited each other's yachts. The alliance would apply only to a European conflict and would not become effective until the Russo-Japanese War ended. Because France was involved in a dispute with Germany over Morocco, it refused to consider such a pact. Given the terms of the Franco-Russian alliance, the czar's officials concluded they had to abandon the German treaty. Nevertheless, its transaction during the summer of 1905 made the French more suspicious of German designs in both Europe and Morocco. Moreover, Germany made some concessions to France in Morocco because Berlin hoped Paris might accept the Bjorko Treaty.

July 29, 1905

A secret memorandum of understanding is signed in Tokyo by Secretary of War Taft and Japan's Premier Katsura—the Taft-Katsura Agreement.

In this agreement, the United States recognized Japan's special rights in Korea while Tokyo agreed to maintain an open door policy in Korea and Manchuria. President Roosevelt had proposed this arrangement in talks with Ambassador Takahira during the conferences that led to the peace discussions on the Russo-Japanese War.

At Roosevelt's direction, Taft signed the agreement with Katsura during a stopover in Tokyo when Taft was en route to Manila. The memorandum was simply an executive agreement not binding on either power. It was further supplemented by the Root-Takahira agreement of November 30, 1908.

In addition to accepting an open door policy in Korea and Manchuria, Japan disavowed any aggressive design on the Philippine Islands.

August 9, 1905

The Russo-Japanese Peace Conference convenes at Portsmouth, New Hampshire, with President Roosevelt serving as an intermediary.

As a result of Roosevelt's assistance, Russia and Japan had agreed on June 10, 1905, to engage in peace negotiations. However, petty quarrels between Tokyo and St. Petersburg nearly disrupted the start of the conference. First armistice terms and later selection of a conference site stalled the talks. An armistice was not obtained before the conference. The conference location was agreed to only after Roosevelt became disgusted by the tactics of the two belligerents. They could not agree to accept Paris, Chefoo, the Hague, or Washington. Roosevelt wrote to a friend: "I have been growing nearly mad in the effort to get Russia and Japan together. The more I see of the Czar, the Kaiser, and the Mikado, the better I am content with democracy, even if we have to include the American newspapers as one of its assets." The president persisted, however, and earned high praise from other diplomats for finally convening the conference after Portsmouth was agreed on as the meeting place.

Throughout the conference, Roosevelt guided but did not mediate the deliberations. The Russian delegates were Count Serge Witte and Baron Roman R. Rosen; the Japanese representatives were Foreign Secretary Jutaro Komura, Baron Kentaro Kaneko, and Kotoro Takahira. In addition to wining and dining the delegates to encourage their good humor, the president pressured Russia to accept Japan's demands and later made a personal appeal to Japan's Emperor Mutshito to break a deadlock by forcing the Japanese to make concessions.

The deadlock occurred because Japan desired all of Sakhalin Island as well as an indemnity payment. Between August 18 and 29, Roosevelt worked diligently to persuade the delegates to compromise before he appealed to the emperor to provide some means of reconciling the Japanese. The Russians were willing to give up southern Sakhalin but stubbornly rejected any indemnity. The emperor persuaded his officials to forsake the indemnity and to take part of Sakhalin Island. Once this obstacle was surmounted, the negotiations were successfully ended on August 30, and a peace treaty was signed on September 5.

Roosevelt achieved peace where everyone had predicted failure. Nevertheless, even though diplomats praised him and the Nobel Peace Committee awarded him a prize, the president reaped only resentment from the Russians and Japanese. The czar's officers contended they would have won if the war had continued and they regretted the loss of southern Sakhalin. In Japan, anti-American riots broke out because Roosevelt was accused of betraying Japanese interests. The Japanese government never told its people what the Japanese delegates told Roosevelt before the conference—that is, that Japan's resources were exhausted by June 1905. Although Japan received large gains from Russia in Port Arthur, Korea, Manchuria, and Sakhalin, Tokyo's leaders had made public their desire for a large indemnity, which they did not receive. Generally, Japan had established its right to be treated as a major world power.

The Treaty of Portsmouth was a critical landmark in East Asian diplomacy. Its important terms were as follows:

1. Russia recognized Japan's "predominant political military and economic interests in Korea."
2. Both nations evacuated Manchuria and restored Chinese administration *excepting* that Japan received the Liaodong peninsula and all Russian concessions in that area, including mining, railroads, and the right to have railway guards.
3. Russia ceded southern Sakhalin to Japan.

Before the conflict Roosevelt had hoped Japan would balance Russian power in East Asia; now he sought a Russia that would remain strong enough to slow Japan's drive for empire. Soon, however, only the United States could challenge Japan's effort to dominate the western Pacific and East Asia.

August 12, 1905

Great Britain and Japan renew their alliance, changing its original objectives.

In adjusting their alliance of 1902 to the new conditions in the Far East, this agreement went beyond simply maintaining the status quo in East Asia. Important new clauses added included the following:

1. Peace in India as well as East Asia would be maintained because Britain became concerned about Russian expansion in south Central Asia.
2. Territorial rights of each nation in Asia and India would be maintained.
3. In case of war in defense of territorial rights, the other ally would join in the conflict.
4. Britain recognized Japan's special rights in Korea; Japan recognized Britain's rights in Tibet.
5. China's general territorial integrity and equal trade (open door) were accepted by both parties.

This agreement recognized that British interests primarily were in India and Persia against Russia. Because Britain's East Asian interests were less vital, it yielded influence there to Japan, especially in northern China and Korea.

August 29, 1905

J. Pierpont Morgan sells the American China Development Company to China in spite of President Roosevelt's opposition.

The leading American financier of the early 20th century, J. P. Morgan headed a group of investors who obtained a Chinese concession in 1898 to build a railroad between Hankow and Canton. Although the group's attempt to add important branch lines failed because of foreign competition, Morgan's company contracted in 1900 to issue $40 million of bonds to build 710 miles of main line, 130 miles of branch lines, and 78 miles of siding. It also agreed with China not to transfer its rights to another group.

The incident leading to Morgan's resale of the American China Development Company began on December 23, 1904, when China's ambassador, Sir Chentung Liang-cheng, informed Secretary of State Hay that the Canton-Hankow railway concession was being canceled because a Belgian company had secured control of its stock. In addition, Chentung told Hay, the American company had completed only $10\frac{1}{2}$ miles of functioning track and a total of 28 miles of track.

In January 1905, Hay persuaded King Leopold II of Belgium to sell Morgan 1,200 shares of stock so that the American group could regain majority control and avoid China's revocation of the concession. The Chinese ambassador subsequently agreed to conduct talks with Morgan's representative. By June 1, the American corporate directors accepted a Chinese offer to buy the company's concession, bonds, and property for $6,750,000. The directors called a stockholders meeting for August 29 to finalize this pact.

When President Roosevelt learned of the arrangement, he disliked it. Desiring to retain U.S. rights on this important railway, Roosevelt tried to persuade Morgan to reject the sale. On August 7, and again on August 28, Morgan's yacht, the *Corsair,* steamed into Oyster Bay, near New York harbor, to visit Roosevelt at his summer home. Morgan told the president that the stockholders were pleased to get rid of the concession for the liberal sum to be paid for 28 miles of railway. Roosevelt's entreaties to retain America's diplomatic position could not restrain Morgan's business decision. While Roosevelt considered that the Chinese boycott of U.S. goods required U.S. business to stand firm, Morgan's judgment differed, and on August 29, the sale to the Chinese was approved by the stockholders whom Morgan represented.

On the boycott, see July 20, 1905.

October 20–30, 1905

A general strike in Russia paralyzes the government and forces Czar Nicholas II to promise to grant civil liberties and power to a legislative assembly, the Duma.

The general strike in St. Petersburg culminated nearly a year of crisis and protest that had been precipitated by the Russo-Japanese War. This so-called Revolution of 1905 did not bring substantial results because neither the czar nor his advisers desired political changes in Russia. The czar issued an October Manifesto that promised to convene the Duma and bring reform, but its provisions were not carried out during the next decade.

November 10, 1905

President Roosevelt issues an executive order to professionalize the Foreign Service.

This order provided for filling diplomatic vacancies by transfer or promotion from within the foreign service and by making appointments to the service through a process of selection and examination. Concomitant with the president's act, Secretary of State Root established a board to conduct written and oral examinations. This process involved all positions below the rank of ambassador or minister.

The following year, on June 27, 1906, Roosevelt and Root established regulations to bring all consular appointments and promotions under a similar method of selection.

Secretary of State Root also adopted a State Department file and document-location system that had evolved in the Department of War when he headed that department. This filing system enabled studies of department activity to be made more proficiently.

November 17, 1905

A Japanese-Korean treaty permits Japan to control Korea's foreign affairs.

By coercing Korea to accept this treaty, Tokyo consolidated the control over Korea that Russia had agreed to in the Treaty of Portsmouth of September 5, 1905.

See August 9, 1905.

1906

February 10, 1906

Great Britain's Royal Navy launches the *Dreadnought*, the first all-big-gun battleship.

With 10 12-inch guns, the *Dreadnought* was considered to be "unsinkable" and revolutionized naval warfare and launched a naval arms race. In May 1906, the Germans announced they would increase the size of their ships and also would widen the Kiel Canal to permit passage of the large new battleships.

March 6, 1906

American-Chinese tensions end when an imperial edict condemns the Chinese boycott's antiforeign sentiments.

Following the beginning of China's boycott of American goods and services on July 20, 1905, Chinese-American tensions escalated to the point where President Roosevelt ordered preparations for either war or a show of American military force.

As the crisis heightened between July and December 1905, neither Roosevelt nor Congress would offer changes to the Chinese sections of the immigration treaty. Statements of recrimination appeared from both Chinese and Americans. In September, Roosevelt sent William H. Taft to

Canton to discover some means to settle the dispute. When Taft's traveling party reached Hong Kong, local authorities warned them that the Chinese in Canton were in an uproar against America. Posters and placards in the city insulted Taft and other U.S. leaders. The viceroy of Canton planned to fete Taft at a banquet, but the viceroy became "too ill" to attend. Consequently, Taft had the opportunity to experience the Chinese feelings even though he did not understand the Chinese viewpoint. At a business luncheon in Canton, Taft urged the Chinese merchants to end the boycott because it was bad for business relations. Many Chinese businessmen had placed their respect, dignity, and justice above money, however. Chinese business groups joined the Singapore Chinese merchants who unanimously voted to support the boycott.

On December 18, the one violent incident of the boycott took place. Chinese nationalists in Shanghai wanted greater jurisdiction over the international settlements in their city. Their demands led to a riot and general strike. A mob burned the municipal police station and freed the prisoners. The foreign powers, including America, rushed troops to the scene and gunfire broke out. Twenty Chinese were killed; several Western soldiers were injured. Although the Shanghai incident was a general antiforeign demonstration, it resulted from the U.S. boycott and reflected anti-American feelings in China.

The tensions with Peking and the Shanghai incident inflamed public feeling in America and caused Roosevelt to decide to demonstrate his nation's power. He ordered an increased naval force to go to the Far East and sent troop reinforcements to the Philippine Islands, where they would be within 50 hours of the Chinese mainland. Twenty thousand soldiers were sent to the Philippines over a two-month period. From Peking, the American minister, W. W. Rockhill, informed Roosevelt that there was no serious problem in China. Nevertheless, Roosevelt knew the American public liked a demonstration of force. One religious leader, the Reverend S. H. Littell, informed Roosevelt that U.S. warships "running up the rivers every now and then would show the Chinese that we have our eyes on them."

On February 26, Roosevelt gave the Chinese diplomats a strong list of demands. He wanted Chinese guilty of crimes to be punished and all antiforeign movements to be sternly dealt with by China. He said the boycott was unlawful restraint of trade and must be suppressed by the Chinese emperor.

China's foreign minister, Prince Ch'ing, promised to meet Roosevelt's demands as much as he could. Therefore, on March 6, 1906, Ch'ing issued an imperial edict that condemned the antiforeign sentiments and called on Chinese students to "cultivate loyalty to the state." By this time, the principal effects of the boycott emotions had dissipated in China. Public demonstrations waned after December 18. Merchants went back to normal business; students returned to classes. But Chinese nationalist feelings did not end—they were just beginning to find expression.

One sidelight of the tensions is noteworthy. In a dissenting court opinion during a Chinese immigration case in 1905, Justice Brewer made a prophetic statement. The time had been, Brewer said, when Chinese students studied in America and its people built our railroads, and its commerce sought our trade. But, he added, "if all this be reversed and the most populous nation of earth becomes the great antagonist of this republic, the careful student of history will recall the words of Scripture, 'They have sown the wind and they have reaped the whirlwind,' and for cause of such antagonism need look no further than the treatment accorded during the last twenty years by this country to the people of that nation."

April 7, 1906

The Algeciras conference on Morocco ends.

Following President Roosevelt's successful effort in bringing France and Germany to a conference to settle their Moroccan dispute (see June 10, 1905), the conference convened at Algeciras on January 16, 1906. The American representative, Henry WHITE, maintained close contact with President Roosevelt.

Although the kaiser had claimed to want open door policies in Morocco, the controversy became an issue of power prestige between France and Germany. By February, the delegates reached an impasse, and, at White's suggestion, the president intervened by asking the kaiser to honor his promise to follow Roosevelt's proposal on the dispute. At first this request caused Speck von Sternberg some embarrassment because he had misconstrued Foreign Minister Bernhard von Bülow's promise as that of the emperor in June 1905. Nevertheless, the kaiser accepted Roosevelt's proposal to preserve confidence between Berlin and Washington.

Subsequently, an agreement was concluded on April 7, which included the following terms:

1. Morocco's independence and integrity were affirmed.
2. France would police the Algerian-Moroccan border.
3. A joint French-Spanish force would police the remainder of Morocco.
4. A state bank of international investors was established under French control but with other nations represented.

The U.S. Senate ratified the Algeciras Treaty on December 12, 1906, with the added proviso that the agreement could not be construed as U.S. involvement in European affairs.

July 18, 1906

America and Mexico cooperate to end a war between Salvador, Guatemala, and Honduras.

Following the outbreak of a revolution in Guatemala, hostilities spread into San Salvador and Honduras because Guatemala claimed those neighboring nations assisted the rebels.

Secretary of State Root decided to request Mexico's help in joining with Washington to offer the good offices of the two nations to end the dispute in Central America. The belligerents accepted this proposal on July 18. Two days later, delegates of the three nations agreed to have the Presidents of Mexico and the United States arbitrate both their present and future disputes. This arbitration plan was further extended on September 25, when delegates from Nicaragua and Costa Rica joined the other three Central American nations in a convention by which they would submit all future Central American disputes to be arbitrated by Mexico and the United States. Nevertheless, peace was short-lived in Central America. In 1907 war broke out between Nicaragua and Honduras.

See December 20, 1907.

July 31, 1906

Secretary of State Root promotes Pan-American cooperation at the Rio de Janeiro conference.

Speaking at the Third Inter-American Conference at Rio, Root urged the delegates to promote the "right impulse" and "right tendency" to develop the American continents as free, independent, and cooperative nations.

The secretary's speech correlated with several small steps he took to encourage Pan-American cooperation. In addition to visiting many Latin American countries, Root persuaded the U.S. Congress to deed land in downtown Washington, D.C., for use as a Pan-American Union Building. Andrew Carnegie donated money to construct that building. Root also assisted the Latin American republics in securing invitations to the Second Hague Peace Conference in 1907.

Although American actions during the early 20th century did not often fit the ideals Root described in his 1906 speech, his concepts are worth noting as a contrast to U.S. activity. In part, Root told the Rio Conference:

> We wish for no victories but those of peace; for no territory except our own; for no sovereignty except sovereignty over ourselves. We deem the independence and equal rights of the smallest and weakest member of the family of nations entitled to as much respect as those of the greatest empire; and we deem the observance of that respect the chief guarantee of the weak against the oppression of the strong. We neither claim nor desire any rights or privileges or powers that we do not freely concede to every American republic.

September 18, 1906

America intervenes in Cuba because an election dispute threatens to cause a civil war.

The election dispute began in 1906, when Cuba's Liberal Party claimed that fraud at the ballot boxes had enabled the Conservative Party candidate, Estrada Palma, to be reelected. Palma had been elected for a first term in 1902, shortly before American troops withdrew from Cuba. Following the 1906 election, the Liberal Party began a revolution in August because Palma's victory was objected to by General José Miguel Gómez, the Liberal Party nominee.

To settle the issue, Roosevelt sent Secretary of War William Howard Taft and Assistant Secretary of State Robert Bacon to negotiate with the Cubans. On September 28, Palma became angry and resigned as president. Further turmoil appeared certain, and President Roosevelt ordered U.S. troops to Cuba to maintain order. On October 13, Roosevelt appointed Charles E. Magoon, a former U.S. minister to Panama, as governor of Cuba.

Between 1906 and 1908, Magoon instituted a series of political and electoral reforms in Cuba. New elections were held on November 14, 1908, and Gómez, the Liberal Party candidate, won. Magoon resigned as governor and U.S. forces withdrew on January 28, 1909.

September 26, 1906

The United States Navy outlines its basic war plan strategy against Japan—Orange War Plan.

Shortly after its success in the Russo-Japanese War, Japan emerged as the "most likely enemy" of the U.S. navy's contingency war plans. These plans were prepared by the General Board of the Navy, its highest policy board, and made recommendations to the secretary of the navy. The General Board followed the sea power theories of Alfred Thayer Mahan, the American naval captain whose studies of sea power history and theory influenced German and British as well as American naval concepts.

In its general "Estimate of the Situation" in 1906, the General Board envisioned the Caribbean Sea and the Pacific Ocean as the regions where the U.S. fleet must gain control to fulfill American interests. In the Caribbean, the acquisition of Puerto Rico and the Panama Canal enabled America to become the dominant power. In East Asia, however, Russia's defeat in 1905, coupled with Great Britain's evident yielding to Japan in northern China and Manchuria, made the United States the one potential competitor of Japan for the Asian market and Pacific Ocean sea power.

Following these assumptions, the General Board decided the U.S. navy had to plan and equip the American fleet for a war against Japan in the western Pacific Ocean. While other color-coded war plans were prepared for other contingencies, the Japanese color code Orange became the navy's "most likely" plan against a future American opponent.

While Orange War Plan was not finalized until 1910, it originated during the summer of 1906. The plans disclosed the navy's concepts of war and view of U.S. national interests. The chief deficiency was the navy's failure to consult with the State Department in agreeing on the "national interest." While the State Department and President Roosevelt's views by 1906 did not visualize the possibility of the United States using force against Japan to keep an open door in Manchuria, the navy based its plans on the policy pronouncements of the president and secretary of state, pronouncements that did not always match the realistic assessments of U.S. diplomatic priorities. The State Department's most vital interest region was Western Europe, not East Asia.

The navy believed that the open door statements and Asiatic exclusion policies made the Pacific theater a region of great U.S. concern. At the same time, of course, U.S. navy leaders envisioned—what by 1910 became a fleet centered around 48 battleships—the largest proposed fleet for any nation.

Even for a large navy, the Pacific Ocean's demands were great. The United States would have to fight more than 7,000 miles west of San Francisco, a logistical and fleet problem of huge dimensions. President Roosevelt would possess a fleet of 16 battleships by 1907; the Orange War Plan sought a fleet three times as large. Although the large battleship fleet was never approved by Congress, Orange War Plan became the navy's basic contingency plan and dictated its concerns until the eve of World War II.

October 11, 1906

Asian racial discrimination reappears in California because San Francisco establishes separate Asian schools.

In the Pacific Coast states, anti-Asian laws had caused difficulties during the 1880s. These laws became generally tolerated by the Chinese and Japanese, and racial tensions subsided until 1905–1906, when a new influx of Asian immigrants caused certain American groups in California to urge discriminatory school laws. As a result, the California state legislature authorized school boards to set up separate schools for "Indian children and for children of Mongolian or

Chinese descent." Using this legislation, on October 11 the San Francisco School Board directed school principals to send "all Chinese, Japanese, or Korean children to the Oriental Public School . . . on or after October 15, 1906."

The Japanese government led the opposition to the school laws, protesting to Roosevelt's administration. The president could not control the school board but he intervened to work out a compromise.

See February 20, 1907; also see December 4, 1906.

December 4, 1906

Asking Congress to grant Japanese immigrants the rights of naturalization, President Roosevelt castigates California school laws as "wicked absurdities."

Since the passage of the discriminatory school law by the San Francisco Board of Education on October 11, 1906, Roosevelt had sent Secretary of Commerce and Labor Victor H. Metcalf to investigate conditions in California while informing the Japanese ambassador that he would deal with San Francisco.

On December 4, Roosevelt used the results of Metcalf's report to formulate his message on the situation to Congress. Metcalf had found the allegations of the California Exclusion League to be grossly exaggerated. To the league's charge of overcrowding of schools, Metcalf found there were only 93 Japanese pupils in all San Francisco schools; 25 of these were American citizens and 28 were girls. To the charge that the Japanese students were too old to associate with younger Americans, he found that 33 of the 93 were over 15 years old and only 2 were 20 years old. Most seriously, to the charge that the Japanese students were vicious and immoral, Metcalf had testimony from numerous teachers that the Japanese students were exemplary in conduct and generally desirable students.

Consequently, the president informed Congress that the California school segregation order was a "wicked absurdity." Japan, he said, had made remarkable progress toward modern civilization and had been generous in sending help to San Francisco during its recent fire and earthquake. In fact, the Japanese Red Cross sent more aid to the San Francisco disaster victims than all other countries combined. Therefore, Roosevelt requested Congress to pass legislation to confer the right of naturalization on Japanese in America. He also warned that if necessary, he would use the U.S. army to protect the Japanese in California from further violence.

Although the Japanese public appreciated President Roosevelt's message to Congress, the exclusionist groups in California accused the president of lack of patriotism and of destroying his own nation's civilization. Subsequently, Roosevelt had to adopt more conciliatory methods to calm the irrational situation in California.

See February 20, 1907.

1907

January 15, 1907

America's interest in supporting reforms in the Belgian Congo is conveyed to the Brussels government.

Secretary of State Root joined other nations in urging King Leopold II of Belgium to give control of the Congo to the Belgian parliament (see February 26 and May 2, 1885). This international action resulted from reports of the deplorable mistreatment of the native population in the Congo. First, in 1903, Sir Roger Casement of Great Britain conducted an investigation of the Congo and described the inhumane treatment of African tribesmen. In 1905, an international commission investigated these charges. This commission recommended that the Belgian government take control of the king's "possession" and abolish the virtual slavery being practiced in the Congo.

Early in 1907, the commission report began to be considered by the Belgian parliament. At this juncture, Secretary Root instructed the American minister to Belgium to inform the government that there was a "deep interest of all classes of American people in the amelioration of conditions" in the Congo. Root indicated that the United States favored Belgian annexation of the Congo. Later, on February 15, 1907, the U.S. Senate passed a resolution that favored reforms in the Congo.

The Belgian parliament debated and discussed the reform measures for over a year. Eventually, on October 18, 1908, the parliament made the Congo part of the Belgian territory, and King Leopold II relinquished his personal control of that region.

January 15, 1907

The United States remits part of the Boxer indemnity of 1901 to China.

On September 7, 1901, when the Boxer indemnity was fixed, Secretary of State Hay believed the indemnity was exorbitant but accepted it with the intention of later remitting that part of the sum not needed to pay American claims against China. During the next five years, a claims commission in the United States decided that losses to U.S. property and interests were $12,479,657.05 out of the $24,440,778.81 awarded to America in 1901. On January 15, 1907, Secretary Root communicated this information to the Chinese minister to America.

The Chinese gratefully accepted the American rebate and on July 14, 1908, informed America that the Chinese would use the money to provide scholarships for worthy Chinese students to come to the United States to study at institutions of higher education.

February 8, 1907

The U.S. Senate ratifies a convention with the Dominican Republic that gives America control of the Dominican customs duties.

President Roosevelt made and began to implement this convention with the Dominicans on February 7, 1905. The Senate delay in ratification resulted from debate on the precise treaty-making powers of the president. Some senators claimed Roosevelt should have consulted with and gained approval from them before intervening. Roosevelt argued that the foreign powers demanded payment of the debts, and European intervention could be prevented only by immediate American action.

During the two years preceding Senate action, Roosevelt's agents not only collected the Dominican customs, they also negotiated with the European creditors to scale down the Dominican Republic's debts from $22 million to $17 million, including the arrears in interest. By February 8, new treaty clauses were added to provide for an issue of 50-year Dominican bonds of $20 million at 5% interest and to guarantee the territorial integrity of an independent Santo Domingo.

February 20, 1907

Congress amends the Immigration Act to enable President Roosevelt to resolve the Japanese protests of discrimination.

Since October 11, 1906, Roosevelt had sought some means to retain Japanese friendship in spite of discriminatory practices in California. After requests to the San Francisco authorities were unsuccessful in ending Japan's objections to the separate school law, Roosevelt urged Congress to revise the immigration act and asked a California delegation to come to Washington to discuss the problem with him.

In February 1907, an eight-man group arrived in Washington, led by Mayor Eugene Schmitz, who incidentally was under indictment for political graft. Part of the problem was that adult Japanese were enrolling in public schools. In this matter, an agreement was worked out for enrolling Japanese children of proper ages and preparation in schools with white children. Roosevelt promised to approve amendments to the immigration act to restrict the influx of adult Japanese men.

On February 20, congressional legislation authorized the president to refuse entrance to immigrants with passports "to any other country than the United States." Roosevelt immediately applied this to Japanese coming from Hawaii, Canada, or Mexico but not directly from Japan. To complete his promise to further restrict Japanese immigration, he asked Secretary of State Root to negotiate an agreement with Japan.

Root's discussions resulted in an exchange of notes with Japan. Known as the "Gentleman's Agreement," the significant portion of the exchange was contained in a Japanese note of February 24, 1907. Japan promised to withhold passports from laborers intending to migrate to America and recognized America's right to reject immigrants with passports for travel elsewhere. The result of Japan's action was to cut back on Japanese immigration. During the next 15 years, only 8,681 Japanese arrived in the United States.

June 1, 1907

Great Britain's Committee on Imperial Defense recognizes that war with America is inconceivable. It approves concentrating British Naval units in European waters.

This committee recommendation was prepared by Admiral Sir John Fisher to meet the growing German threat by reallocating British naval strength. Fisher contended that England would never have a "parricidal war" with America. The views of Fisher and the Admiralty Committee on Imperial Defense were stated in a memorandum of June 1, 1907, entitled "Comparative Strength of Battleships and Armoured Cruisers of Britain, France, the United States, and Germany."

On the basis of these decisions, the Royal Navy abolished its Western Hemispheric base at Halifax and maintained one small cruiser squadron for annual visits at Britain's Caribbean islands. Consequently, the U.S. navy became supreme in American waters.

See September 26, 1906.

August 31, 1907

An Anglo-Russian entente is signed.

This agreement had been urged by the French because it completed the formation of the Triple Entente (Britain-Russia-France) in opposition to the Triple Alliance of Germany, Austria, and Italy, which was renewed in July 1907.

The conclusion of the Anglo-Russian pact hinged largely on an agreement about the Middle Eastern nation of Persia. The two powers divided Persia into three spheres: one in the north for Russia; one in the south for Britain; and a neutral middle sphere. Afghanistan remained neutral but under British guidance. In separate notes, the czar recognized British predominance in the Persian Gulf, while Great Britain agreed to revise previous agreements on the Straits of the Dardanelles between the Black Sea and the Aegean Sea to give Russia an outlet to the Mediterranean Sea.

October 18, 1907

The second Hague Peace Conference adjourns with few accomplishments.

Although President Roosevelt had suggested a second Hague Conference on October 21, 1904, the Russo-Japanese War postponed it. Finally, on June 15, 1907, sessions began at The Hague with the American delegation headed by Joseph H. Choate.

The process for arbitration was slightly improved and a draft of a convention for an international court was left for future consideration. The one notable act of the Hague conference was the adoption of a revised Drago Doctrine to limit the application of armed forces to collect national debts. Additionally, the Hague Conventions of 1907 expanded the rules of war that had been formally recognized at the 1899 conference.

The U.S. delegation supported Great Britain's proposals for disarmament and better machinery for arbitration and, in particular, worked for the establishment of a Permanent Court of International Justice. Few of these or other propositions made headway during 1907. The German delegates led the opposition to disarmament because they believed Britain wished to limit the German navy.

See December 29, 1902.

December 12, 1907

The U.S. Navy grows to become the world's second largest and begins an around-the-world cruise to demonstrate its power.

Originally, Roosevelt had announced that the fleet of 16 battleships would simply sail from Virginia to San Francisco, but after the fleet rounded South America and reached Lower California two days ahead of schedule, Roosevelt announced that it would continue on around the world.

The fleet visited Australia and Japan before going on to the Mediterranean, through the Straits of Gibraltar, and home to Hampton Roads, Virginia, where the ships arrived on February 22, 1909.

Roosevelt intended the cruise of the Great White Fleet to impress Japan with U.S. power and Congress with the need to continue to build up a larger naval force. Although the Japanese greeted the fleet in a most gracious and friendly fashion on its visit to Yokohama, Roosevelt wanted to let Japan know that his recent negotiations on Korea, Manchuria, and immigration did not mean America could not use force if necessary. William Randolph Hearst, whose "yellow journalism" had spread to San Francisco, denounced the "yellow peril" of Japan that was spreading across the Pacific and praised Roosevelt's action. Roosevelt, however, was not taken in by Hearst's propaganda. The president wrote to

"Isn't It A Daisy?" Uncle Sam admires his fleet of battleships. *Philadelphia Record*

Senator Lodge that he had to be polite to Japan to offset the "criminal stupidity of the San Francisco mob, the San Francisco press, and such papers as the *New York Herald*." Roosevelt did not believe there would be war with Japan, but it would be "no fault of the yellow press if we do not have it. The Japanese seem to have about the same proportion of prize jingo fools that we have."

His desire to obtain continued congressional support for the navy was the more subtle reason for the world cruise. Between 1901 and 1906, Roosevelt persuaded Congress to authorize a major naval increase of 10 battleships and 4 armored cruisers that, added to the naval buildup of the 1880s and 1890s, gave America a navy second only to Great Britain's. But by 1907, pacifist groups had sufficient support in Congress to jeopardize the continued funding of the navy construction program. In this debate, however, Roosevelt's cruise did not prove successful because Congress did not increase its support for a larger navy. Under President Taft, the General Board of the Navy requested a 48-battleship fleet, a size ardent Republicans could not support. As a result, naval appropriations experienced difficulty under Taft and President Wilson.

On the 48-battleship plan, see September 26, 1906.

December 20, 1907

Central American problems are again settled, this time by a Washington conference.

Following a war in Central America that ended on July 18, 1906, Secretary Root and the Mexican government had agreed to arbitrate future disputes in that area. Hardly was the ink dry on the treaty of September 26, 1906, before President José Santos Zelaya of Nicaragua prepared to invade Honduras.

Zelaya apparently hoped to force the other four Central American republics to federate with Nicaragua. To promote this scheme, he aided rebels in El Salvador and, after capturing the capital of Honduras, placed a loyal subordinate in charge of that government. By the summer of 1907, a general war threatened to break out in the region, and Mexico and America stepped in to bring the dispute to mediation.

To promote peace in the region, a Washington conference of the five republics met from November 13 to December 20, 1907. With the mediation of Mexican and American officials, the delegates refused to join a confederation but concluded several treaties to foster better relations. The most important of these was the establishment of a Court of Justice to be set up at Cartago, Costa Rica, to resolve local disputes. In other treaties, the five countries made Honduras a neutral state, agreed not to harbor revolutionary leaders of other states, and established several cultural institutions including a pedagogical institute for Central America.

Unfortunately, these efforts did not permanently solve the disputes in the region. The court expired after 10 years and was not renewed in 1917. In addition, the United States had to intervene in Nicaragua in 1909, because Zelaya continued to promote disturbances in Central America.

See December 16, 1909.

1908

February 10, 1908

The United States and France sign the first of a series of arbitration treaties made by America with 25 nations.

This treaty bound America and France to refer disputes that diplomacy could not settle to the Permanent Court of Arbitration set up by the First Hague Conference. The only questions to be excluded from arbitration were those relating to vital interests, independence, the honor of the two nations, or those that did not concern a third party. In 1908–1909, Secretary Root prepared 25 similar treaties of arbitration for the United States with all leading world nations. The treaty of February 10 was ratified by the U.S. Senate on February 19, 1908.

March 20, 1908

Secretary Root organizes the first geographic division in the Department of State.

The first modern geographic division was the Division of Far Eastern Affairs. Later, Secretary Knox followed this pattern by creating divisions for Latin America, Western Europe, and the Near East. These divisions were policy-making agencies staffed by permanent bodies of experts for their areas.

April 11, 1908

The Root-Bryce treaty provides for creating a definitive boundary between Canada and the United States.

Secretary Root and British Ambassador James Bryce agreed to procedures for reviewing all boundary questions since 1783 and using arbitration to settle any outstanding questions. A subsequent review by expert geographers and surveyors found only one issue to take to arbitration: the possession of the islands in Passamaquoddy Bay. This matter was resolved by an arbitration that gave Pope's Folly Island to the United States, an agreement made official by the treaty of May 21, 1910, which the U.S. Senate ratified on June 6, 1910.

April 11, 1908

Secretary of State Root and British Ambassador Bryce sign a treaty regulating fisheries in U.S. and Canadian waters.

This agreement provided for an International Fisheries Commission that would examine all fishery issues and prepare a system of regulations "for the protection and preservation of the food fishes in the waters of Canada and America." Together with the results of the later arbitration on fishing rights and liberties established through the convention of January 27, 1909, the lengthy arguments on fishing in the northeast waters were finally resolved. The Senate approved this treaty on April 17, 1908.

May 5, 1908

An American-Japanese treaty provides a five-year arbitration agreement.

This arbitration treaty was negotiated following the Taft-Katsura agreement of July 29, 1905, which achieved an understanding on East Asia between Washington and Tokyo.

The 1908 arbitration treaty provided that disputes "of a legal nature, or relating to the interpretation of treaties" would be referred to the Hague Permanent Court of Arbitration if normal diplomacy failed to settle the issue. The arbitration process would not include matters of vital interests, independence, or honor. Compared to the arbitration treaties negotiated with other powers, the treaty with Japan was more restrictive. The U.S. Senate ratified the Japanese treaty on September 1, 1908.

See February 10, 1908.

June 23, 1908

Persia's Shah Mohammed Ali overthrows the constitutional government.

On December 30, 1906, a liberal-nationalist movement in Persia had obtained recognition of a constitution to employ parliamentary means for limiting the shah's power. Backed by the Russian government, the shah moved in 1908 to end these restrictions. Although Great Britain preferred to promote the liberals in Persia, London acceded to the request of its Russian ally and deserted the liberal cause in Persia.

July 24, 1908

A "Young Turk" revolution in Turkey forces the Sultan Abdul Hamid II to restore the constitution.

Turkish reformers who sought to preserve the Ottoman Empire had begun an uprising in Macedonia on July 5, 1908. After government troops sent to destroy them deserted the sultan and joined the rebels, the sultan decided to reverse his policy by accepting the reformers. Niazi Bey, leader of the reformers, agreed to cooperate with Abdul provided he returned to the reform constitution of December 23, 1876.

Because the reformers claimed to promote the rights of national minorities within the empire, leaders of these national movements applauded the constitution and elected representatives for the new parliament, which met on December 17, 1908. While the "Young Turk" program provided hope for the future, the immediate results were not satisfactory. Radical nationalist leaders in Albania and other regions of the Balkans demanded complete autonomy, a position that led to the First Balkan War on October 8, 1912.

October 6, 1908

Austria annexes Bosnia-Herzegovina.

When Austria's Emperor Francis Joseph announced Bosnia's annexation, Serbia and Montenegro protested and mobilized their armed forces. Serbia sent 30,000 soldiers to the borders of Bosnia; Montenegro prepared its artillery to bombard Austria's naval installations in the Adriatic Sea. After Austria withdrew its navy to safe positions, the emperor sent 15 infantry battalions to Bosnia. Although Russia supported Serbia and Montenegro as "Slavic brothers," British, French, and German diplomats warned Russia to restrain its army. Russia complied and the crisis stalled during the winter of 1908–1909.

Although Austria began "military exercises" in Bosnia in March 1909, Moscow persuaded Serbia and Montenegro to end their mobilization and withdraw to pre-crisis positions. Austria's Foreign Minister Alois Aehrenthal met with Russia's Foreign Minister Alexander Isvolski to settle the crisis. Russia recognized Austria's annexation of Bosnia and Aehrenthal agreed to support the czar's effort to get trade concessions from the Turks in the Dardanelles. When Isvolski could not get concessions from Turkey, he condemned Aehrenthal for annexing Bosnia. Thus, tensions increased between Moscow and Vienna.

See October 8, 1912.

November 3, 1908

William H. Taft is elected president.

Taft was Theodore Roosevelt's personal choice for the Republican nomination at the time Roosevelt announced he would not seek another term of office. Thus, Taft easily obtained the nomination at the Chicago convention of the Republican Party on June 16. The Democrats again nominated William Jennings Bryan on July 7. There were few differences in the two party platforms. Both opposed monopoly business, and while the Democrats wanted to reduce tariffs, the Republicans promised to "revise" the tariff law. There were six other minor party candidates including the Socialist Eugene Debs, but the votes

President William Howard Taft, later Chief Justice of the Supreme Court. National Archives

they received did not influence the outcome. Taft won by more than 1.2 million popular votes, gaining 321 electoral votes to Bryan's 162.

November 30, 1908

The Root-Takahira Executive Agreement is exchanged between the United States and Japan.

As in the case of the Taft-Katsura agreement of July 29, 1905, this agreement was not a treaty but an executive arrangement that did not, technically, commit the incoming Taft administration, a fact that Japan may or may not have understood fully. It represented the culmination of Roosevelt's balance-of-power concept for East Asia, one that he undoubtedly expected Taft to uphold.

Here are the main parts of the agreement:

1. Both nations agreed to maintain the status quo in the "region of the Pacific Ocean."
2. Each nation respected the other's territorial possessions in the region.
3. The two nations would support "by all pacific means" the independence and integrity of China (note: this is not the "territorial integrity" of China).
4. If the status quo were threatened, the two powers would consult to consider what measures to take.

Roosevelt had by 1908 decided to recognize Japan's special privileges in Korea and Manchuria because he envisioned an Anglo-American-Japanese triad to dominate East Asia: Japan in the north; the United States and Britain in central and south China. Roosevelt dismayed some U.S. diplomats who opposed the conciliation of Japan. However, Roosevelt believed that it was in America's interest to realistically accept Japan's power in the East Asia region adjacent to the Japanese islands.

In 1907, Japan had secured treaties with France (June 10) and Russia (July 30), which accepted Japan's special rights in Manchuria. The Russian agreement permitted Japan to control the Chinese Eastern and Southern Manchurian Railroad.

December 4, 1908

A London naval conference prepares a convention to clarify rules of naval warfare.

Ten major naval powers, including the United States, sent delegates to London in 1908 to recommend rules of naval warfare and neutral rights. The resulting Declaration of London of December 4 specified rules of blockade, contraband, unneutral service, convoy, resistance to search and seizure, ship transfers to a neutral flag, destruction of neutral prizes, and compensation for released vessels and goods. Many commentators in England believed the code was too favorable to neutrals, although the House of Commons ratified it. The U.S. Senate ratified the convention and, on the beginning of World War I in August 1914, recommended that all belligerents adhere to the 1908 agreement.

1909

January 9, 1909

Root-Cortés negotiations lead to three treaties to resolve U.S.-Colombian disputes. Colombia later rejects the treaties.

On his way home from the Pan-American Conference at Rio de Janeiro in 1906, Secretary Root stopped at Bogotá because the Colombian government of General Rafael Reyes had indicated an interest in settling its current disputes with America.

Soon after, Colombia sent Enrique Cortés to Washington to negotiate with Root. After more than a year of discussions, Cortés, Root, and a representative of Panama's government agreed on three treaties. In a Colombian treaty with Panama, the independence of Panama was recognized and a boundary established. A treaty between the United States and Colombia transferred the first ten annuities on the Panama Canal from Panama to Colombia. And a third treaty between Panama and the United States approved these changes and began payments of Panama's annuity five years earlier than agreed on in the Hay–Bunau-Varilla Treaty of 1903.

Although the U.S. Senate approved the American treaties with Colombia and Panama, Colombia rejected them. On July 8 a revolution in Bogotá overthrew General Reyes largely because of opposition to the three treaties. The new regime of Carlos Restrepo denounced the treaties. Most Colombians were not willing to forgive or forget the collusion between Washington and Panama in the revolt of 1903.

January 27, 1909

America and Great Britain agree to take the northeast fisheries dispute to arbitration.

The fishery problem had persisted between Canadian and New England fishermen throughout the 19th century. A Joint High Commission had considered this matter in 1898, and subsequently Secretary of State Hay signed a treaty with Britain in 1902. The U.S. Senate eventually ratified the treaty in 1905 but altered it substantially, and the representatives from Newfoundland refused to accept it. A crisis arose because Senator Lodge of Massachusetts called for U.S. naval vessels to protect American rights, while, at the same time, Newfoundland denounced the modus vivendi of the issue under which the dispute had been functioning since February 15, 1888.

To avoid further friction with England and Canada, President Roosevelt proposed arbitration. As a result, Secretary of State Root and British Ambassador James Bryce prepared a treaty providing for arbitration. According to the 1909 agreement, the Permanent Court of Arbitration at The Hague would settle the question. Following Senate approval of the treaty on February 18, 1909, the Court of Arbitration studied the matter and issued its report on September 7, 1910. Although the decision was a compromise between the two opposing arguments, both New England and Newfoundland fishing interests accepted the decision. The Hague court decision was formally accepted by an Anglo-American convention signed on July 20, 1912.

January 27, 1909

Robert Bacon is commissioned as Secretary of State.

Bacon succeeded Elihu Root, who resigned to take a rest before entering the U.S. Senate. A former member of J. P. Morgan and Company (1894–1903), Bacon had served as assistant secretary of state from 1905 to 1909. He was secretary of state until Roosevelt's term expired on March 5, 1909.

February 8, 1909

A Franco-German agreement on Morocco averts a crisis in north Africa.

The agreement of April 7, 1906, at Algeciras between France and Germany had not fully resolved the dispute in North Africa. In 1908, the Germans supported Mulay Hafid, a rebel who deposed the Sultan Abdul Aziz, and a new crisis arose. The tension increased after September 25, 1908, when German consular officials at Casablanca held three German deserters from the French Foreign Legion. The French had to use force to retake the deserters.

Nevertheless, diplomats of the two nations resolved the problems. The Casablanca desertion issue was submitted to arbitration, and on February 8 an agreement was signed on Morocco. Germany recognized France's special "political" interests in Morocco, and Paris agreed to accept German economic investments in future concessions for Morocco. Two years later, on May 21, 1911, French actions prompted a new crisis in Morocco.

March 5, 1909

Philander Chase Knox is selected as secretary of state by President Taft.

A former lawyer for the Carnegie Steel Corporation, Knox served as attorney general of the United States from 1901 to 1904 and senator from Pennsylvania from 1904 to 1909. A prominent Republican leader, he was an unsuccessful candidate for the presidential nomination in 1908 because President Roosevelt backed William H. Taft. Knox served as secretary throughout Taft's four-year term of office, until March 5, 1913.

Together, Secretary of State Knox and President Taft personified the close relationship of diplomacy helping U.S. business interests in their advocacy of "dollar diplomacy." President Taft described this effort in his final annual message to Congress on December 3, 1912.

> This policy has been characterized as substituting dollars for bullets. It is one that appeals alike to humanitarian sentiments, to the dictates of sound policy and strategy, and to legitimate commercial aims. It is an effort frankly directed to the increase

of American trade upon the axiomatic principle that the Government of the United States shall extend all proper support to every legitimate and beneficial American enterprise abroad.

April 9, 1909

The Payne-Aldrich Tariff continues protectionism.

Although President Taft called this tariff a reform measure, former President Theodore Roosevelt and Senator Robert La Follette of Wisconsin had fought the law because it continued protective rates. The Republican Progressives in Congress had introduced the tariff act at lower rates. Before it passed, however, multimillionaire Senator Nelson Aldrich of Rhode Island attached 847 amendments to the bill, 600 of these providing increases. Consequently, the rates averaged 40.8% of value, lower than the Dingley Tariff of 1897 but still significantly protective of most U.S. products. Taft's acceptance of this bill was one factor causing progressive Republicans to look for a new presidential candidate in 1912.

May 24, 1909

America seeks admission to the banking consortium constructing a Chinese railway—dollar diplomacy in China.

Willard Straight, the acting chief of the Far Eastern Division of the State Department in 1909, readily accepted the dollar diplomacy interests of President Taft and Secretary of State Knox. Straight had disliked Roosevelt's post-1905 policies toward China because the Root-Takahira agreement recognized Japan's special rights in northern China and because in 1905 Roosevelt declined to join the other powers in providing a Chinese development loan.

In 1909, Taft and Knox accepted Straight's desires to persuade American bankers and businessmen to increase their Chinese investments. The first indication of Taft's dollar diplomacy at work occurred on May 24. With the approval of Secretary Knox, Straight wired the American minister to China, W. W. Rockhill, to insist on U.S. membership in a railway consortium. British, French, and German interests had signed a contract with China to build a railway south and west from Hankow into the provinces of Kwangtung and Szechwan: the Hukuang Railway. Straight told Rockhill to obtain U.S. rights under the open door policy so that American investors could join the project.

The U.S. demands in May 1909 dissatisfied the Europeans and delayed both the loan to China and the railroad construction. Great Britain was particularly upset because in 1905 Roosevelt had declined to participate in such loans. Now, at the final moment, Taft sought to gain U.S. membership in the consortium. Following much discussion, the United States finally received a 25% share in the investments on May 20, 1911. The delay actually destroyed the project, however. Because of the outbreak of the Chinese Revolution in 1911, as late as 1927 no work had been done on the U.S. section of the Hukuang Railway.

November 6, 1909

Secretary of State Knox proposes an international neutralization plan for Manchuria.

To promote American business interests in China and to counteract the spreading Japanese influence in northern China, Knox followed his May 24, 1909, effort to obtain American membership in the Hukuang Railway consortium with a proposal to extend U.S. commercial investments in Manchuria.

Willard Straight, who had aroused the interest of Knox and Taft in the Hukuang Railway, had recently joined a banking group that hoped to stimulate U.S. investment in China. Headed by the railroad magnate E. H. Harriman, this group included the J. P. Morgan Company, the National City Bank, the First National Bank, and Kuhn, Loeb and Company. Straight had traveled to London to talk with European bankers before going to China, where he contacted a Chinese official, His-liang, who hoped to promote American interests as a counterweight to the Japanese.

By October 2, Straight had China's permission to finance a railway across Manchuria from Chinchow to Aigun on the Amur River. Subsequently, Straight notified Secretary of State Knox, asking him to secure British, French, and German support for the proposed railroad.

On November 6, Knox invited the British to join America and other powers in promoting the Aigun-Chinchow railway and in internationalizing all railroads in Manchuria. If all the Western powers agreed, Knox believed Japan would be forced to give up its control of the South Manchurian Railroad as part of the international action. When fulfilled, this plan would prevent Japanese and Russian attempts to control Manchuria and allow American investors to construct railroads in Manchuria.

Unfortunately, Knox's plan did not fully account for the interests of Japan, Russia, and Great Britain. The British valued Japan's alliance and goodwill in East Asia and would not jeopardize it. Thus on November 25, Sir Edward Grey tried to let Knox down gently. He informed the American ambassador to England that the British accepted the general principle of Knox's proposal but that the time was not right for internationalizing the Manchurian railways. He suggested that Knox should begin by obtaining Japan's consent because it had the greatest interests in Manchuria. If Tokyo agreed, the other powers would be likely to accept the internationalization plan.

Not realizing the underlying rebuff of Grey's message, Knox continued on his foolhardy way. On December 14, the secretary sent his proposal to Japan, China, France, Germany, and Russia. On January 6, 1910, he gave American newsmen an optimistic report on the developments and the excellent cooperation the plan would provide to benefit the Chinese people.

The powers did not, however, respond in an optimistic tone. Japan and Russia sent Knox nearly identical notes rejecting the neutralization proposal. They also told Knox they had advised China not to sanction the Aigun-Chinchow project without Japan's prior consent. Finally on July 4, 1910, Japan and Russia signed a treaty to further define their respective interests in Manchuria. Not surprisingly, Great Britain agreed with its Japanese ally in rejecting the American plan. France stood by Russia and the Germans remained aloof from Knox's request.

Knox had not opened the Manchurian door to U.S. investors; he had seen it nailed shut with Americans on the outside. Yet as typical politicians, Knox and Taft did not report their error to the American public. They made as affirmative a case as they could, issuing a statement that the open door had been invigorated in China. The State Department, said the official report, was pleased that the new Russo-Japanese Treaty gave "an additional pledge of the stability of peace in the Far East."

Former President Roosevelt was disturbed by Taft's policy. On December 22, 1910, he wrote to Taft that Japan had vital interests in Manchuria and the American interests were "really unimportant." He told Taft that it was "near madness" to challenge Japan in Manchuria. To fight Japan in that region would require the combined strength of the British navy and the German army. Better, Roosevelt said, to abandon the worthless words "open door" in China.

December 16, 1909

The United States assists a rebellion against the Nicaraguan government of President Zelaya.

When an insurrection began in 1909 against Zelaya's government, Washington made no secret of its willingness to get rid of the Nicaraguan dictator, whose bellicose efforts since 1905 had caused intermittent disturbances in Central America. After two Americans were executed by the Managuan government, Secretary Knox on December 1 dismissed the Nicaraguan minister to the United States and issued a note explaining the American plan to give stability to the region by reorganizing Nicaragua's finances and getting control over the customs houses whose income enticed dictators to seek power.

With American aid, a group of Conservative leaders successfully led the insurrection against Zelaya. On December 16, the dictator fled to exile. During the next year, Knox negotiated his plan for "dollar diplomacy" with the new government.

See June 6, 1911.

1910

August 22, 1910

Japan annexes Korea, renaming it Chosen.

Japan's announcement that it would be the protector of Korea culminated a series of Japanese activities to gain control of this state. The annexation followed an attempt by Korean rebels to obtain full independence from Japan in an insurrection that began in July 1907. Japan suppressed the rebellion and forced the emperor to resign in favor of a Japanese figurehead.

September 20, 1910

A Chinese request for American loans is accepted by Secretary Knox, but U.S. bankers never finance them.

Again seeking to circumvent Japan's railway monopoly in Manchuria, the Chinese government asked the United States to make an *exclusively* American loan to permit Chinese currency reforms and to assist Manchuria's industrial development. Knox agreed but believed he should solicit the other powers for their participation in the loan. Japan and Russia refused because they claimed the rights to all industrial and other concessions in Manchuria. This effectively blocked loans by France and Britain, who were allies of Russia and Japan.

Knox tried to float the loan in America, but his attempt did not succeed. The industrial loan was issued but was recalled because of Japan's opposition. The currency loan was never issued.

October 5, 1910

A Portuguese republic is proclaimed following an insurrection in Lisbon.

The provisional government organized by Theophilo Braga led to the adoption of a liberal constitution on August 20, 1911.

1911

January 10, 1911

Honduras and America sign a treaty to permit the United States to control Honduran customs collections.

Following the overthrow of President Zelaya of Nicaragua in 1909, a rebellion began against the regime of General Miguel Dávila, whom Zelaya had placed in control of Honduras. With U.S. aid, former President Manuel Bonilla regained power after a war in 1910 ended in an armistice that became official on February 8, 1911. During 1910, Secretary of State Knox prepared treaties for both Honduras and Nicaragua. Knox believed that if the United States controlled their customs offices, the two nations would become more stable politically.

See December 16, 1909; for details of Knox's treaties, see June 6, 1911.

February 11, 1911

In renewing the Commercial Treaty of 1894, Japan agrees to regulate the emigration of laborers that it had accepted in the 1907 Gentleman's Agreement.

During the negotiations to renew the commercial treaty, Japan wanted America to eliminate the stipulation in the treaty of November 22, 1894, which stated that the United States could regulate the immigration of workers. Secretary of State Knox believed that the right to regulate immigration was an inherent part of national sovereignty, whether or not it was embodied in a treaty. Therefore, he readily agreed to drop the clause in exchange for Japan's declaration that as a condition of signing the 1911 treaty, the Japanese would maintain the controls that they "have for the past three years exercised in regulation of the emigration of laborers to the United States." This declaration made the 1907 agreement a more formal pact between the two nations.

May 12, 1911

W. Morgan Shuster, an American, arrives in Theran, Persia, to reform the Shah's finances.

The shah and parliament had invited Shuster to reorder Persia's economic practices, giving the American almost dictatorial power. Russia became suspicious of Shuster's position and soon intervened to take over most of Persia, excepting the southern coastline.

See November 29, 1911.

May 21, 1911

The second Moroccan crisis begins after the French Army occupies Fez.

Having narrowly averted a crisis on February 8, 1909, the French continued to seek greater control in Morocco. In order to end antiforeign disorders in April 1911, the French military advanced in Morocco and took the capital city on May 21 despite German objections. The crisis increased on July 1, when a German gunboat, the *Panther*, arrived at Agadir, and preparations for war began in France and England. Berlin and Paris agreed to negotiate, however, and by an agreement on November 4, 1911, Germany gave France complete control in Morocco. In return, France ceded part of the French Congo to Germany.

May 25, 1911

Mexico's dictator Díaz resigns in favor of the revolutionary government of Francisco Madero.

An uprising began against Porfirio Díaz on November 20, 1910, when Madero issued the Plan of San Luis

Potosi. This program called for the principle of no reelection as president under the 1857 constitution and implied there would be land reforms to break up the rule of the wealthy minority and foreign investors.

Díaz had not only encouraged the continuation of large estates by the Mexican upper class (1–3% of the population) but granted land concession to foreign investors, principally British and American, for agricultural export products or oil. The overthrow of Díaz endangered these investments, but Madero, a large landowner himself, did not move effectively to enact the reforms desired by more radical groups in Mexico. Within two years, Madero was criticized by both the radicals who desired greater reform and reactionaries who wished to maintain the economic system set up under Díaz.

See March 11, 1913.

June 6, 1911

The Knox-Castrillo convention with Nicaragua institutes the Knox plan to control that nation's finances and bring political order.

Shortly before intervening in favor of the rebellion to overthrow President Zelaya of Nicaragua on December 16, 1909, Knox outlined his plan to control the customs income of that state as a means of ending its internal disorders.

During 1910, Secretary Knox negotiated treaties with Nicaragua and Honduras to give effect to his "dollar diplomacy." The treaty with Honduras was signed on January 10, 1911, and with Nicaragua on June 6, 1911. The preambles to both conventions indicated that the American objective was to aid the republics in their request to rehabilitate their finances by providing loans guaranteed through control over the customs duties in order to stabilize the economies of each nation. The United States would serve as protector of the customs collection system and oversee repayment of the loans.

According to the treaties with Nicaragua and Honduras, these nations would loan funds from U.S. banks. These loans would be secured by customs duties established by consent of the U.S. government. The customs receiver would be chosen from a list provided by the U.S. banks and approved by the U.S. president. The receiver would annually report to both the United States and his own government. To keep the receiver honest, the local government and the U.S. government would protect him from corruption. Thus, by guaranteed loans, the two nations would achieve stable economic development and, thereby, stable government.

Secretary Knox experienced one problem, however. He did not have the backing of two-thirds of the U.S. Senate when he concluded his treaty.

Critics of the plan in the United States, Honduras, and Nicaragua proved to be obstacles to dollar diplomacy. When the U.S. Senate refused to ratify the treaties, trouble resulted in both Honduras and Nicaragua.

See January 9, 1912, and August 14, 1912.

July 7, 1911

The North Pacific Sealing Convention—the pelagic sealing issue is settled between Britain, Russia, Japan, and America.

The treaty of February 29, 1892, had provided only a temporary resolution of the sealing problem because there were no limits on seal killing. In 1906, President Roosevelt informed Congress that there was a need to end the "hideous cruelty" of pelagic sealing. By 1910, the seal herds had dwindled from 4 million to 100,000 creatures, and extinction seemed imminent.

In 1911, the four principal sealing nations agreed to meet in Washington to regulate sealing. Although the United States, British, and Russian delegates readily agreed to limits, the Japanese representative refused to do so. Finally, President Taft appealed directly to the Japanese emperor, and the Tokyo government moderated its demands so that a multinational convention could be finalized.

The treaty of July 7 contained the following provisions:

1. Pelagic sealing was prohibited north of latitude 30 degrees north, for a period of 15 years and thereafter until terminated by a one-year notice.
2. Great Britain and Japan received 15% of the skins taken off the shores of the United States and Russia.
3. The United States, Britain, and Russia each received 10% of the skins taken off the shores of Japan.
4. All sealing was strictly regulated.

In 1912, the U.S. Congress passed legislation to prohibit all killing of seals on land for several years to give the seal herds time to increase in size. By 1932, the herds on the Pribilof Islands had increased to over 1 million. The treaty remained in effect until October 23, 1940, when Japan abrogated the agreement.

Also see August 15, 1893.

July 26, 1911

President Taft signs legislation to offer reciprocal free trade to Canada; later, Canada rejects the measure.

Taft and Secretary Knox had reached an oral agreement with the Canadian ministry of Sir Wilfrid Laurier to obtain concurrent legislative approval for free trade between the two nations. This tactic would avoid the difficulty of most-favored-nation treaties with other nations and give Canada a method to annul the law if the act was not beneficial.

The principal reason for the agreement was that the Payne-Aldrich Tariff of 1909 subjected Canada to the maximum rates of the U.S. tariff and presaged a trade war between the two neighbors. Yet Taft had to persuade both houses of congress to pass reciprocal legislation for Canada, and Prime Minister Laurier had to do the same in his parliament.

In the United States, the House approved the reciprocal law with Canada on April 21, 1911, and the Senate did so early in July. During the congressional discussions of the legislation, however, some U.S. politicians made exaggerated statements. Former President Roosevelt, for example, said the measure "would make Canada only an adjunct of the United States."

These U.S. statements greatly disturbed Canadians, and the opponents of Laurier took full advantage to argue against the reciprocal bill. The question became a major issue during the Canadian general election of 1911. Because Canadian nationalists claimed that the question became one of "the Union Jack or Old Glory," Laurier lost to the Conservative Party. The newly elected parliament voted down the reciprocity program.

August 3, 1911

The United States signs general arbitration treaties with France and Great Britain: the Senate rejects them.

President Taft had expressed his desire to broaden the arbitration treaties obtained with 25 countries by Roosevelt and Root in 1908–1909. He believed this would best succeed with England, and Foreign Secretary Sir Edward Grey agreed to negotiate a new treaty.

During the summer of 1911, while an Anglo-American treaty draft was being finalized, France asked also to be allowed to form a new arbitration treaty. Taft reluctantly agreed, and on August 3, the United States signed treaties with both nations and also agreed to negotiate a treaty with Germany. The 1911 treaties provided arbitration of all disputes in which decisions were susceptible to "principles of law or equity." A joint commission of six would decide if the treaty were applicable to a particular dispute.

These arbitration treaties were blocked by the U.S. Senate. Senators and politicians in Roosevelt's Progressive wing of the Republican Party had begun to challenge President Taft for the nomination in 1912. In addition, Senator Henry Cabot Lodge argued that (1) the treaties with Britain and France would provide a precedent for similar treaties with less trustworthy nations; and (2) the senatorial right to approve a joint commission was not specified in the treaties.

The Senate added a long list of amendments to the 1911 treaties, but they were not voted on before Congress adjourned. When the new Congress convened in 1912, Taft decided not to contest the amendments with the Senate and withdrew the treaties from consideration.

September 28, 1911

Outbreak of the Tripolitan War between Turkey and Italy.

Before precipitating the war with Turkey, Italy had gained the approval of all the major European powers to acquire Tripoli, on the northern coast of Africa. Nevertheless, the Italian forces had a difficult time before they forced the Turkish surrender on October 18, 1912. By that date, Turkish problems had grown because of the outbreak of war in the Balkans on October 8, 1912.

November 29, 1911

Russia invades northern Persia.

Since the arrival on May 12 of Shuster, who endeavored to reform Persia's finances, the Russians had moved toward intervening to retain the hold on northern Persia granted them by the Anglo-Russian alliance of 1907. On November 5, the czar gave Theran an ultimatum that required the dismissal of Shuster. The parliament (majlis) refused. Consequently, on November 29, Russian forces moved into Persia in spite of British warnings. But the British did not wish to break their 1907 alliance with the czar and accepted the Russian occupation.

Subsequently, on December 24, a pro-Russian group took charge in Theran and closed the parliament. Russian influence became dominant in northern Persia until 1917.

December 11, 1911

The Ottoman-American development company withdraws its railroad application—the failure of the "Chester Concession."

An example of Taft-Knox "dollar diplomacy" in the Near East, the Chester project developed from a proposal by a group of New York financiers to construct a railroad from Aleppo to the port of Alexandretta, a 900-mile route. The project was named for Rear Admiral (retired) Colby M. Chester of the U.S. navy, who negotiated with Turkey in 1908 to obtain a railway line and to apply for a railway concession.

Chester obtained a favorable first hearing from the Ottoman Parliamentary Committee and returned to New York in 1909 to gain financial backing. In November 1909, the Ottoman-American Development Company was chartered in New Jersey, capitalized at $600,000. It also enlarged its plans to build other railways in Turkey.

Obtaining the active support of the State Department, Chester returned to Turkey where U.S. Ambassador Oscar Straus assisted his negotiations with the Ottoman authorities. Chester's principal obstacle in gaining the concession was the German government. Germany wanted no one to interfere with its Berlin-to-Baghdad railway concession in Turkey and successfully prevented the Turkish parliament from voting on the American project in 1910.

In September 1910, Knox sent the assistant secretary of state, Huntington Wilson, to the Ottoman Empire as an ambassador extraordinary to pay a courtesy visit to Sultan Mehmed V and to encourage the Chester project. In addition, American negotiations with Germany overcame Berlin's objections because the Americans modified their railroad plans to avoid competition with existing German rights. The American application went to parliament in May 1911, but a vote was delayed for six months.

By the summer of 1911, the New York financiers preferred to withdraw the application and regain the $88,000 of earnest money that they had presented with their application. When Knox learned of the planned withdrawal, he sent the chief of the State Department's Bureau of Near Eastern Affairs to New York to dissuade the company's officials. The company stockholders were interested in a Turkish project, but they wanted to modify the original concession to obtain mining as well as railroad rights. Therefore, they wanted to withdraw the current application. On December 11, the new U.S. ambassador to Turkey, W. W. Rockhill, informed the Ottoman government that the U.S. company had decided to withdraw its railway application. The Chester concession was not obtained in 1911.

The Ottoman-American Development Company now strengthened its finances and as the Ottoman-American Exploration Company asked President Wilson's administration for assistance in Turkey on July 1, 1913. Wilson's State Department officers did little to encourage the company, and Chester's contacts with the State Department did not resume until 1920.

See April 10, 1923.

1912

January 9, 1912

U.S. Marines land in Honduras to protect U.S. property.

In 1910–1911, Secretary Knox had negotiated with a revolutionary government in Honduras to work out its political problems and economic instability in a treaty signed on January 10, 1911. Knox had also promoted the end of a civil war that resulted in the election of President Manuel Bonilla on October 29, 1911. Opposition to the American loan-customs deal and the rejection of the 1911 treaty by the U.S. Senate caused further difficulties, and a new insurrection began late in 1911. To forestall this rebellion, President Taft sent U.S. Marines to Honduras to protect U.S. property by bringing order to the nation.

February 15, 1912

Yuan Shih-K'ai is elected provisional president of the Chinese Republic.

Yuan's election followed the abdication of China's boy emperor, P'u-i. The abdication followed the outbreak of a general revolution against the Ch'ing dynasty in October 1911.

In addition to Yuan, the principal revolutionary leader was SUN YAT-SEN, who had been elected president of the United Provinces of China at Nanking on December 30, 1911. In order to unite the country, Sun Yat-sen resigned in favor of Yuan so that China would be unified under a ruler in Peking.

June 20, 1912

The United States joins a six-power consortium to offer loans to the new Chinese Republican government.

Soon after the outbreak in October of the Revolution of 1911, Yuan Shih-k'ai requested a foreign loan. U.S., French, and British bankers prepared a loan plan in December, and on June 20, Russia and Japan joined the international group. Great Britain had hoped to exclude Japan and Russia from the financial programs in central and southern China by recognizing their control in both Manchuria and Mongolia. Secretary Knox disagreed, however, because he objected to spheres of influence.

When Yuan first asked for a loan, Secretary Knox hoped to cooperate with the new government, and the United States joined Britain, France, and Germany in talking with Yuan without recognizing his regime. Knox also urged the admission of Russia and Japan to the four-power group. This addition would further internationalize any agreement and, perhaps, restrain both Tokyo and St. Petersburg in the north.

On June 20, when Japan and Russia joined the four powers to negotiate the Chinese loans, they did so with the understanding that their rights in Manchuria and Mongolia would be recognized. At the same time, Great Britain reasserted its rights to a sphere of influence in Tibet. This was not what Knox intended, for it again affirmed Russian and Japanese claims in northern China. Moreover, during the discussion with Yuan, the six powers insisted on strict and direct supervisory powers over the Chinese customs and financial receipts.

Yuan hesitated to grant the powers their political demands. Both he and the other Chinese nationalists who led the Revolution of 1911 preferred to halt concessions of the Western imperial powers in China. Yuan believed Sun Yat-sen and other Chinese would denounce his regime if he yielded to foreign demands. The American minister in Peking, William J. Calhoun, reported to Knox on February 12, 1913, that "it is no longer a question of friendly international co-operation to help China, but a combination of big powers with common interests to accomplish their own selfish political aims."

Consequently, the negotiations between Yuan and the six foreign powers continued into 1913. After becoming president, Woodrow Wilson announced the American withdrawal from the consortium.

See March 18, 1913.

August 2, 1912

The "Lodge Corollary" extends the Monroe Doctrine to Japan and to foreign companies.

This addition to the Monroe policy of 1823 was contained in a Senate resolution offered by Henry Cabot Lodge. The resolution stated that the possession by a foreign corporation or association affiliated with a non-American government would be seen with "grave concern" by the United States, especially if it is a harbor or other place capable of use as a naval or military base.

Lodge's resolution resulted because a Japanese syndicate wished to purchase 4,000 acres of land in Lower California including Magdalena Bay. The Japanese Foreign Office asked Secretary of State Knox for an opinion on the transaction. Upon learning that the transfer of such land would cause a "great outcry" in America, Japan canceled the proposal.

Nevertheless, news of the inquiry leaked out and Senator Lodge decided to make political points from the incident. Although both President Taft and Secretary Knox believed Lodge's resolution was not necessary, he carried it to the floor of the Senate. Few senators could oppose the question, especially during a presidential election year. The measure passed the Senate by a vote of 51 to 4. Except for putting into words what any U.S. administration would have done anyway, the Lodge resolution had no substantial effect on future foreign policy.

August 14, 1912

U.S. Marines land in Nicaragua to protect American property and interests.

Because the U.S. Senate refused to ratify the Knox-Castrillo Treaty of June 6, 1911, a special arrangement was worked out to secure a U.S. loan to Nicaragua. Needing funds to avoid defaulting on a British loan on July 1, 1911, the government of Adolfo DÍAZ obtained a loan for $1.5 million from a group of New York bankers. As a replacement for the customs guarantee provided by the Knox treaty, the American banks were granted control of the National Bank of Nicaragua and the government-owned railway.

Dissidents in Nicaragua opposed the Díaz involvement with American banks and in 1912 began an insurrection to overthrow Díaz. To put down the revolutionary disorders, President Taft dispatched 2,500 marines to Nicaragua on August 14, 1912.

Although Knox negotiated a second treaty with Nicaragua to provide a permanent solution to that state's problems, the U.S. Senate again refused to approve the treaty. Consequently, while some of the marines were withdrawn from Nicaragua in December 1912, a sufficient number remained to guard the U.S. legation until 1925.

August 24, 1912

The Panama Canal Act exempts U.S. coastwise trade from paying tolls: Great Britain protests.

During the summer of 1912, a congressional bill authorizing Panama Canal toll charges after its opening in 1914 became a controversial measure. The British government opposed the act as a violation of the Hay-Pauncefote Treaty, which stated that the canal would be free and open to "all nations" on equal terms. The proponents of U.S. exemptions contended the treaty meant that all foreign nations would pay the same rates. Great Britain argued that all nations included America.

President Taft refused a British request for arbitration because the issue became involved in the presidential contest. At their respective national conventions during June, both Republicans and Democrats included in their platforms an endorsement of toll exemptions for U.S. coastal shipping. This made it impossible to negotiate with England and made certain the passage of the congressional act in August 1912. In 1914, however, Woodrow Wilson proposed a repeal of the 1912 legislation.

See June 15, 1914.

October 8, 1912

The first Balkan War begins when Montenegro attacks Turkey.

Montenegro's attack preceded a large-scale offensive against Turkey by armies from Bulgaria, Serbia, and Greece. Perceiving Turkish weakness after Italy conquered Tripoli (Libya) in 1911, Russia's Foreign Minister Isvolski helped Serbia and Bulgaria agree to a "friendship" treaty in January 1912 containing a clause for dividing any Ottoman territory they conquered. In August 1912, Greece and Montenegro joined the Serb-Bulgaria alliance and the four allies planned an invasion of Turkey. On September 30, the four Orthodox Christian allies gave an ultimatum to Turkey, demanding the sultan grant autonomy to all Christians living in the Ottoman Empire or be attacked. Turkey rejected the ultimatum and Montenegro attacked first on October 8, 1912. The other three Balkan allies launched their offensive on October 16, with armies twice the size of Turkish forces in the area.

When the Serbs attacked on October 16, their force of 76,000 engaged about 16,000 disorganized Turkish troops in the area and Kosovo was the first to suffer from Serb atrocities. Western reporters in the area described the Serb assault as the "systematic extermination of the Muslim population." The only Muslim survivors in Kosovo or Macedonia were those who quickly converted to Orthodox Christianity or fled for refuge into Albania's mountains.

By December the Orthodox Christian allies controlled all the Balkans outside of Istanbul before the Great Powers—England, France, Italy, Germany, and Russia—obtained an armistice to negotiate peace in London. The December armistice was violated in February, but in April the Great Powers obtained a second cease-fire and renewed peace talks in London. In the London Treaty of May 30, 1913, the Great Powers revived Albania as a Muslim province, a decision that led to the Second Balkan War.

See August 10, 1913.

November 5, 1912

Woodrow Wilson is elected President in a contest with two Republicans, the incumbent Taft and the Progressive Theodore Roosevelt.

Republican Progressives had become disenchanted with President Taft, who, Roosevelt claimed, did not act as a proper steward of public welfare. On January 21, 1911, insurgent Republicans formed the National Progressive Republican League, headed by Senator Robert M. La Follette. The Progressives wanted political reforms such as the direct primary and economic reforms such as a low tariff.

On December 23, 1911, Roosevelt decided to oppose Taft for the Republican nomination, and during preconvention primaries his progressive delegates won the votes of six states. During the Chicago convention, however, Taft's forces controlled the party machinery and excluded most of Roosevelt's delegates in contested convention votes. Consequently, following Taft's nomination on June 22, the reformers left the party organization and formed the Progressive, or "Bull Moose," Party. They selected Roosevelt as the Progressive candidate on August 5.

At its Baltimore convention on June 25, the Democratic Party was involved in a closely contested struggle before Woodrow Wilson defeated Beauchamp "Champ" Clark on the 46th ballot. All three candidates campaigned on domestic reform issues, particularly the best method to control or eliminate monopoly business.

President Woodrow Wilson and his granddaughter, Ellen Wilson McAdoo. Library of Congress

Wilson won a large electoral victory although his popular vote was a minority of the total. He earned 435 electoral votes to Roosevelt's 88 and Taft's 8. In the popular vote he received 6,286,214 to Roosevelt's 4,126,020 and Taft's 3,483,922. The Democrats also gained control of Congress.

X. WILSON AND WORLD WAR

The Mexican Revolution
Neutrality and Submarine War
Defeat of the Treaty of Versailles

1913

February 9, 1913

President Madero is overthrown by General Huerta. A new phase of Mexico's revolution begins.

Following Porfirio Díaz's resignation on May 25, 1911, Madero was elected president of Mexico but proved incapable of carrying out the land reforms desired by such revolutionary leaders as Emiliano Zapata in the south and Francisco Villa in the north. These leaders defied Madero while Felix Díaz, nephew of the former dictator, tried to take over in Vera Cruz. To protect his government, Madero turned to the federal army for help and asked General Victoriano Huerta to protect him. Díaz was captured and brought to prison in Mexico City from which he continued to conspire against Madero.

Using the U.S. Ambassador Henry Lane Wilson as their liaison, General Huerta and Díaz agreed to depose the president. Henry Wilson had an intense hatred for Madero and had opposed him throughout his term of office. Consequently, after aiding Díaz and Huerta in a coup against Madero on February 9, Wilson urged the other foreign representatives in Mexico City to seek Madero's formal resignation. When Madero refused to resign, Ambassador Wilson persuaded Huerta and Díaz to sign the Pacto de la Cuidadela, which made Huerta president. Cuidadela was the prison in Mexico City from which Díaz was freed by Huerta. Shortly afterward, on February 22, Madero was shot by Huerta's army officers.

Although Wilson immediately urged the State Department to accept Huerta's regime, President Taft demanded concessions from the new government before he would grant recognition. These concessions had not been agreed on by March 4, 1913, when Woodrow Wilson became president. Wilson set new standards for Mexico's government to attain before he would grant recognition.

See March 11, 1913.

March 5, 1913

William Jennings Bryan is commissioned as secretary of state.

Bryan was selected for this office because of his long service to numerous followers in the Democratic Party. He had been the Democratic presidential nominee in 1896, 1900, and 1908. At the Democratic Convention of 1912, he supported Wilson and thereby unified the old agrarian populists with the new reform section of the party. Although Bryan had once taken a world tour, he had few qualifications to serve as secretary of state. Yet as a traditional party spoilsman who filled whatever public offices he could with party followers, Bryan felt no need to be especially qualified to conduct foreign relations. Bryan served Wilson until June 9, 1915, when he resigned because he believed Wilson's policy was leading the country toward war and he wanted to work for a peace campaign.

March 11, 1913

President Wilson refuses to recognize Huerta's regime in Mexico: the nonrecognition policy.

In Mexico, the overthrow and execution of President Madero between February 9 and 22, 1913, brought

William Jennings Bryan, Secretary of State. Library of Congress

General Huerta and the former Mexican dictator's nephew, Felix Díaz, to power. Because President Taft refused immediate recognition of Huerta, the Mexican situation became one of Wilson's first problems as president.

Wilson undertook a thorough review of American policy with Mexico, which caused him to devise a new policy regarding recognition: the nonrecognition of a regime that lacked "constitutional legitimacy." Wilson's recognition standard permitted the United States to consider such circumstances as a regime's moral status, the political involvement of the populace, or the personal ambitions of the new ruler. Heretofore, as the State Department Counselor John Bassett Moore informed Wilson, the United States would regard "governments as existing or not existing. We do not require them to be chosen by popular vote . . . We look simply to the fact of the existence of the government and to its ability and inclination to discharge the national obligations." Moore's view was, in fact, the standard policy of all nations. As an example of his "new diplomacy," the president was determined to consider a new regime's legitimacy.

Traditionally there were two forms of recognition: (1) de jure, which constituted full acceptance of the new regime; and (2) de facto, which accepted the fact a change had taken place but did not confer full recognition.

Wilson's refusal to recognize the Huerta regime contrasted with Ambassador Henry Wilson's ardent support of recognition. The ambassador concurred with those Americans who held financial interests in Mexico in believing that Huerta would restore the policies of the Díaz regime, which had benefited foreign investors. President Wilson, however, did not like the bloody-handed regime of Huerta and sympathized with Mexicans who wished to end the policies of Díaz. President Wilson distrusted Ambassador Wilson's analysis of the Mexican situation because he had read the New York *World*'s March 7 story exposing the ambassador's complicity in aiding the Huerta-Díaz conspiracy of February 9, 1913.

On March 11, while he privately formulated his recognition criteria for Huerta's government, Wilson announced publicly that he would deal with Huerta's government on a de facto basis, deciding on recognition as future developments took place. He told newsmen: "We can have no sympathy with those who seek to seize the power of government to advance their own personal interests or ambitions." The president's formal decision on nonrecognition was made on August 27, 1913.

March 18, 1913

President Wilson withdraws U.S. participation from the Chinese Loan Consortium.

Wilson's decision to withdraw from the Chinese loan consortium was due partly to his support of the Chinese republic but more to the desire of American banking interests to withdraw from the profitless venture.

The day after Wilson's inauguration, three representatives of the American banks involved in the China loan met with the president. They explained that they had lost interest in the project and indicated they wished to withdraw unless the U.S. government specifically asked them not to do so. One of the three representatives was Willard Straight, who, in 1909, had strongly urged President Taft to use dollar diplomacy in China.

Neither Wilson nor Secretary of State Bryan believed he should ask the banking interests to remain in the consortium because, unlike Taft and Knox, Wilson and Bryan did not look with great favor on Wall Street banking interests or promoting commerce in China. In addition, J. V. A. McMurray, chief of the Far Eastern Division of the State Department, approved the president's decision to withdraw.

Wilson may be faulted, however, for leaving the consortium without first consulting with the five other powers involved in the negotiation. Wilson simply informed the news media that the government would no longer support American participation in the consortium. He had decided, he said, to find a better way to help the new Chinese government. He did so by recognizing the republican government of China.

In spite of America's withdrawal from the bankers' consortium, the five other powers proceeded to arrange a loan with Yüan.

See April 26, 1913; for recognition, see May 2, 1913.

March 20, 1913

In Shanghai, Sung Chiao-Jen, the Kuomintang leader is assassinated by men hired by Yüan Shi-K'ai.

Sung had become a leading critic of Yüan's military rule and in 1912 formed an opposition party known as the Kuomintang (National People's Party). Sung's power threatened Yüan because in the February elections, the Kuomintang won a majority of seats in the Chinese parliament. Sung therefore claimed his party should control Yüan's cabinet ministry. During these discussions, Sung's assassination on March 20 was carried out by assassins hired by Yüan. At the time, Yüan disclaimed any connection with the murder and fabricated charges against another republican leader, Huang Hsing. Not until Yüan's death did an investigation by a Shanghai Mixed Court prove his involvement in Sung's murder. The Kuomintang lived on, becoming the leading revolutionary organization during the 1920s.

April 24, 1913

Secretary of State Bryan launches an attempt to obtain "cooling off" arbitration treaties with all nations.

One of Bryan's first projects as secretary of state was to promote an idea he first proposed in 1905—to have all insoluble international disputes referred to an arbitration commission that would report back in one year, thereby permitting national emotions to cool off before further decisions were made. On April 24, Bryan sent a statement to all diplomatic representatives in Washington, D.C., offering bilateral negotiations to establish such treaties. Because each nation could accept or reject the commission's report, the treaties really provided a method of conciliation, not arbitration.

By the end of 1913, five Central American nations and the Netherlands had made treaties with America as proposed by Bryan. Eventually 30 nations signed these treaties with America during 1913 and 1914; 21 of them were fully ratified. The outbreak of World War I in 1914 spelled disaster for Bryan's peace campaign, although prior treaties continued to be in effect. Significantly, Germany made no arbitration treaty with the United States.

April 26, 1913

Western bankers agree to loan Yüan Shi-K'ai's government funds to prevent bankruptcy.

Although President Wilson withdrew U.S. participation from the loan consortium, England, France, Germany, Russia, and Japan agreed to provide China a "Reorganization Loan" of 25 million pounds sterling. Yüan accepted terms favorable to the bankers. The loans would be guaranteed by the powers' control of China's salt tax. Moreover, because the bonds floated at 90% with a 6% commission, China received only 21 million pounds but had to repay the entire principal at 5% interest until 1960, a total of nearly 68 million pounds.

Because opposition groups had begun to contest Yüan's dictatorial rule, his government was desperate to survive and needed money to keep the loyalty of the military. After obtaining the Western loans, Yüan took aggressive action to suppress the genuine republican leaders of the opposing Progressive and Kuomintang parties. By September 1, Sun Yat-sen and Huang Hsing fled to exile in Japan.

See also May 1, 1914.

May 2, 1913

President Wilson recognizes Yüan Shi-K'ai's government, the first recognition granted by a major power.

Wilson decided to recognize the Chinese republic soon after deciding on March 18 to withdraw from the banking consortium. He delayed the announcement, however, to consult with the other major powers to determine whether they would join the United States in recognizing Yüan's regime.

The other nations, especially Japan, tried to persuade Wilson not to grant recognition. The Japanese cited various indications that Yüan's regime was unstable: Yüan's opponents were ready to begin a civil war (a "second revolution" began against Yüan on July 8); Yüan had usurped power from the parliament in Nanking; Sun Yat-sen disputed Yüan's claim to be president; recognition would be interference in favor of Yüan; the leader Sung Chiao-jen had been assassinated by Yüan's supporters in March 1913.

Wilson's decision regarding Chinese recognition contrasted greatly with his decision regarding Huerta in Mexico. Wilson's decision was heavily influenced by American missionaries whose accounts of conditions in China were often more in their own interests than in the interests of the Chinese people as a whole.

See March 11, 1913.

August 10, 1913

The second Balkan War ends with the Treaty of Bucharest.

The London Treaty of May 30, 1913, did not end Balkan conflicts. After the Great Powers gave Serb occupied land to Albania, Serbia's King Peter asked Bulgaria to compensate Serbia with part of Macedonia that Bulgaria occupied. Bulgaria's King Ferdinand refused. To confirm Bulgaria's possession, Ferdinand launched attacks on Serbia and Greece. His surprise raids failed because Serb counterattacks took over most of Macedonia by July 17th. At the same time, Greece conquered land on its northern border with Bulgaria, and an invading Romanian army neared the gates of Sofia. Bulgaria accepted an armistice and delegates of the four countries met to negotiate peace in Bucharest. The Treaty of Bucharest gave Serbia all of Macedonia except for a narrow strip on Bulgaria's border. Greece extended its border north to the city of Doiran, and Romania secured South Dobruja. Bulgaria shrank to its size before the 1912 war.

Balkan tensions continued, with Austria and Russia watching to protect their interests in the peninsula. Because Russia backed the Serbs, whose territory doubled in size from the two Balkan wars, Austria believed the Slavic nations had gained the advantage in that region.

See June 28, 1914.

August 27, 1913

President Wilson informs Congress that his Mexican policy will be "watchful waiting" and nonrecognition of Huerta.

Since his public statement against the Huerta regime on March 11, 1913, Wilson had sent a personal representative to Mexico City, and his information convinced him that the Huerta regime was incapable of orderly government.

Although President Wilson and Secretary of State Bryan did not trust Ambassador Wilson's reports from Mexico, they hesitated to recall him and risk breaking relations with Mexico. Therefore, they obtained reports on Mexico from a personal acquaintance. President Wilson's friend William Bayard Hale went to Mexico and wrote to the president, between June 3 and August 24, confirming Wilson's distaste for Huerta. On July 9, for example, Hale informed Wilson that "General Huerta is an ape-like old man, of almost pure Indian blood. He may almost be said to subsist on alcohol. Drunk or only half-drunk (he is never sober), he never loses a certain shrewdness." Hale thought Huerta was a good soldier who "gloried in the exercise of power." In addition, Hale believed Mexico was politically corrupt and economically bankrupt.

Having received affirmation of their prior perceptions about Huerta, Wilson and Bryan dispatched a special representative to offer America's good offices to solve Mexico's problems. On August 4, Governor John Lind of Minnesota went to Mexico City as Wilson's agent. Lind had been instructed to offer friendship to Huerta and to urge him to stop the violence by conducting an election that would better serve the people of Mexico.

During these same months, the revolutionists who opposed Huerta tried to organize. Meeting at Guadalupe on March 26, they joinly asked Huerta to restore Madero's constitution and to appoint Venustiano Carranza as "first chief" of the government. Under Carranza in the north and Zapata in the south, civil war troubled Huerta's regime, but he refused the request of his opponents to appoint Carranza.

Thus, Lind's mission to Mexico came at a critical time for Huerta. The new regime took a strong position against U.S. advice. At first, Huerta said he would "absolutely ignore" Lind. Mexico's foreign minister, Federico Gamba, talked with Lind, however. Their discussions were not successful. Gamba insisted that if the United States were friendly to Mexico, it would send a new ambassador and receive Mexico's ambassador in Washington. He refused to compromise with Lind. The American offered a loan to Huerta if he would call a fair election, but Gamba refused. Consequently, as Wilson told Congress on August 27, Mexico rejected Lind's attempt to offer America's good offices in friendship.

In this context, Wilson declared that the United States would wait patiently and watch developments in Mexico. He urged Americans to leave Mexico. Although a bloody civil war seemed certain in Mexico, America would be neutral. But in less than a year, Wilson found it essential to stop watching and intervene in Mexico.

To evaluate President Wilson's nonrecognition policy toward the Huerta regime, one should note that English, German, and French foreign interests in Mexico City joined U.S. Ambassador Henry L. Wilson in supporting the reactionary regime of Huerta and Felix Díaz. President Wilson rejected their views and favored liberal changes in Mexico, that Huerta wished to prevent. Wilson's biographer Arthur Link refers to Wilson's policy as "realistic idealism" because the president's attitudes were tied to moralistic concepts that promoted changes designed to benefit the Mexican people. Wilson's objections to Huerta encouraged the liberal movement in Mexico. Thus, an understanding of Wilson's endeavor to place U.S. policy on the side of democratic progress in Mexico, and to reject reactionary policies, expands the significance of the moralist rhetoric the president employed to describe his attitudes toward Huerta's exploitation of the Mexicans with the aid of foreign powers.

See April 21, 1914, and November 13, 1913.

October 3, 1913

The Underwood Tariff is passed.

To end the Payne-Aldrich Tariff of 1909, President Wilson called a special session of congress to meet in April 1913 to revise the tariff bill downward. The bill passed the House easily but had to survive six months of debate from special interest groups in the Senate lobbying for tariff privileges. The Underwood-Simmons Tariff that passed provided for a cut in average rates from 40.8% to 27%, reducing duties on 900 items and creating new free items such as raw wool and steel rails. While partly protective, this was the first substantial reduction below 30% rates since the Civil War.

November 13, 1913

The British agree to accept President Wilson's policy toward Mexico, thereby easing tensions in Anglo-American relations.

Unlike Wilson in his decision not to recognize Huerta's regime, the British followed normal diplomatic practice by granting recognition. Wilson had become convinced, however, that Great Britain's minister to Mexico, Sir Lionel Carden, had actively supported Huerta. The president's special representative in Mexico, John Lind, reported that Carden helped Huerta assume the dictatorship on October 8, 1913. Furthermore, news reports linked Carden's views to Lord Cowdray's influence; Cowdray was an Englishman with large investments in Mexican oil and railroads. Historians now understand that these reports were exaggerated but, at the time, both Wilson and Secretary Bryan believed them.

The Anglo-American tension surfaced on October 23, when Washington newsmen obtained and published information that Wilson was "seething with indignation" at British policy in Mexico. Following his August 27 report to Congress, Wilson had been encouraged because Huerta scheduled a presidential election for October 26, and announced that he would not be a candidate. But Huerta's opponents had not ceased their rebellion. Having formed a group called the Constitutionalists, the revolutionary army captured the city of Torreón. This success permitted Huerta to close the Mexican Chamber of Deputies and to arrest 110 representatives who, he claimed, had favored the opposition army. On October 8, Huerta announced his assumption of absolute power in Mexico. Wilson believed Cowdray had organized the foreign financial interests to support Huerta's action. Although the president contemplated sending diplomatic notes to the European governments to denounce their Mexican policy, he decided instead to leak word to newsmen that he blamed British Ambassador Carden and his connection with Lord Cowdray for inspiring Huerta to seize complete control in Mexico.

Upon receiving this news report, Sir Edward Grey, Great Britain's foreign minister, moved quickly to repair any misunderstanding in Washington.

Desiring a rapprochement with America, Grey sent his personal secretary, Sir William Tyrrell, to speak with Wilson. In talks with the president on November 13, Tyrrell explained that his government's only desire was to protect British rights in Mexico. If Wilson wished, Britain would join America in an attempt to overthrow Huerta and would use pressure to persuade France and Germany to follow Wilson's direction.

Wilson was pleased. Although Grey disagreed with Wilson's policy, he subordinated his views to the president's to gain U.S. goodwill toward larger European problems. Thus, with British backing, Wilson isolated Huerta from major foreign support and the president could deal with the Mexican dictator as he wished, ending his policy of "watchful waiting."

See April 21, 1914.

1914

April 6, 1914

America and Colombia sign the Thomson-Urruita Treaty, but the Senate prevents its ratification.

After Colombia's rejection of the Root-Cortés Treaty of 1909, negotiations between the United States and Colombia did not recur until President Wilson took office. Negotiations for the new treaty were conducted largely in Bogotá between the U.S. minister to Colombia, Thaddeus A. Thomson, and the Colombian minister of foreign affairs, Francisco José Urruita.

The treaty of 1914 had four major parts. First, America expressed regret for its differences with Colombia in 1903. Second, Colombia received transportation privileges in the Isthmus of Panama. Third, the United States would pay Bogotá an indemnity of $25 million. Fourth, Colombia recognized the independence of Panama.

The U.S. Senate refused to accept the treaty of 1914. Former President Roosevelt denounced the agreement as "blackmail." Several Republican senators denied the need for America to apologize or to make an indemnity payment. Subsequently, on April 20, 1921, the Senate approved the 1914 treaty clauses to pay $25 million but refused to apologize to Colombia. The Senate of Colombia accepted these reservations and ratified the treaty on March 1, 1922.

April 21, 1914

American forces occupy and blockade Vera Cruz, Mexico.

America's intervention in Mexico resulted from President Wilson's decision in the fall of 1913 to replace Huerta as Mexico's ruler. Following Huerta's declaration of absolute power on October 8, 1913, Wilson arranged with Great Britain to pressure other foreign powers to adhere to the president's direction in Mexico. Wilson had become convinced that Huerta lacked public approval. He decided to assist the Constitutionalists in Mexico and to blockade the Mexican coast to stop Huerta from importing arms from abroad.

President Wilson contacted General Carranza in northern Mexico to offer support. Carranza and his followers wanted U.S. armaments but would not accept Wilson's direct support. The rebels also refused to make any concessions to Wilson, an omen that should have cautioned Wilson against direct intervention. It did not. On February 3, 1914, Wilson agreed to send arms to the Constitutionalists without any concessions except a statement by Carranza's agent in Washington, Luis Cabrera, that Carranza planned to use legal methods once he gained power.

The incident that led Wilson to intervene directly at Vera Cruz resulted from the American naval blockade of Mexico's eastern coast. On April 9, when a group of U.S. sailors went ashore at Tampico to buy gasoline, local soldiers captured and arrested them. Because the local commander, General Morelos Zaragoza, had not ordered the sailors' arrest, he apologized to the U.S. consul and ordered the sailors released. Zaragoza also sent a formal apology to Admiral Henry T. Mayo, who commanded the American squadron near Tampico. Mayo, however, considered the arrest an insult and asked Zaragoza to hoist an American flag and offer it a 21-gun salute.

Mayo's request for a flag salute became a cause of honor leading to American intervention. Under different circumstances, President Wilson might have ignored Mayo's request. But, as Wilson later explained, he supported Mayo because it was the "psychological moment" to act. Therefore, Wilson insisted on the salute; Zaragoza and Huerta were equally adamant in refusing the salute. For four days, from April 15 to 19, there was an exchange of notes between Washington and Mexico City on the question of honor as both governments refused to compromise.

Wilson stood firm because he manipulated the issue to justify an American intervention. The president had ordered the Atlantic fleet to Tampico on April 13 and the Pacific fleet to the west coast of Mexico on April 15. He also consulted with congressional leaders regarding the Mexican dispute. These latter discussions paved the way for Wilson's request to Congress on April 20 for punitive action against Huerta's government.

According to Wilson's biographer Arthur Link, the president's April 20 speech to Congress misrepresented the facts of U.S.-Mexican relations since February 1913. Wilson asserted that the Tampico incident was one of a series of Huerta's attempts to "show disregard for the dignity and rights of the Government." Huerta's rejection of Admiral Mayo's "simple" demands showed his contempt for the United States and indicated the corrupt character of his regime. The United States, Wilson said, did not want war but only to aid the Mexican people.

Because of Wilson's advance preparations, the House of Representatives acted the same day to pass a joint resolution that stated the president was "justified" in using the armed forces to enforce the demands made on Huerta. Although the Senate delayed action until April 22, it was not because senators objected to Wilson's proposal. Rather, Senator Henry Cabot Lodge believed the president needed greater authority to act against Mexico, and he attempted to amend the House resolution accordingly.

Wilson landed U.S. forces at Vera Cruz before the Senate passed the congressional resolution of support. A German merchant ship, the *Ypiranga*, approached Vera Cruz with a load of arms for Huerta, and at Admiral Mayo's request, Wilson ordered the naval forces to seize the city's customs house immediately. On April 21, Mayo's ships shelled Vera Cruz while nearly 1,000 marines quickly went ashore. The Mexican garrison of 800 men scattered throughout the center of town, where they opened fire on the Americans from rooftops and windows. By noon on April 22, the Americans had routed the Mexican forces, using Marine artillery and the guns of the battleship USS *Prairie*. When the fighting ended, the Mexicans had lost 126 dead and 195 were wounded; the Americans lost 19 dead and 71 were wounded.

Wilson's biggest surprise came soon after the intervention, because when Huerta severed all diplomatic relations, the Mexican people rallied against the U.S. forces. The U.S. invasion caused all Mexicans to forget Huerta and to fight for their country. While thousands of Mexicans volunteered for the army, mobs looted and destroyed U.S. consulates, burned American homes, and imprisoned American consuls and citizens. The U.S. army dispatched General Frederick N. Funston to Vera Cruz with an expeditionary force, and the War Department planned to mobilize the National Guard. A general war seemed to be imminent.

Fortunately, Wilson found an honorable way to avoid a war when diplomats from Argentina, Brazil, and Chile offered to mediate the American-Mexican dispute.

See November 13, 1913, and April 25, 1914.

April 25, 1914

President Wilson accepts mediation of the Mexican dispute.

Although Wilson was prepared on April 21 to send army forces to capture Mexico City, he changed his plans because of the widespread Mexican resistance to the occupation of Vera Cruz. In addition, both Latin American and world public opinion objected to or denounced Wilson's action on April 21. The president suddenly lost the image of a "moral" leader and instead appeared to be an aggressor ready to shed blood for a minor issue of etiquette.

Consequently, Wilson was privately relieved that envoys from Argentina, Brazil, and Chile offered to mediate on April 25. The president accepted quickly, and, under pressure from British, French, and German diplomats in Mexico City, Huerta concurred. Wilson had not, however, shelved his plans to eliminate Huerta. He hoped to use the A.B.C. mediation to end Huerta's control of Mexico.

See July 15, 1914.

May 1, 1914

Yüan Shih-K'ai assumes dictatorial powers in China.

Since receiving loans from the five-power consortium on April 26, 1913, Yüan had steadily moved to eliminate his political opposition and strengthen his one-man rule with military backing. After forcing his two major republican opponents, Sun Yat-sen and Huang Hsing, into exile, Yüan staged an election to become president of China. On November 4, he purged the elected parliament of its Kuomintang members and then dissolved parliament on January 10, 1914. Next, Yüan promulgated a "constitutional compact" that gave him full powers in China for 10 years. In 1915, he declared himself president for life.

Yüan's action in centralizing his power was not criticized at the time except by the small number of republicans who directly suffered. The banking consortium of foreign powers was pleased that he had restored order in China.

On November 7, 1913, Britain and Russia recognized Yüan's government. Both nations were rewarded: Britain gained the protectorship of Tibet, Russia, the protectorship of Outer Mongolia.

June 15, 1914

Congress repeals the Panama Canal Tolls Exemption Act of 1912.

Two factors persuaded President Wilson to change his views and lobby for repeal of the August 24, 1912, act exempting U.S. coastwise shipping from paying canal tolls. First, the British strongly opposed the law. Second, an article written by Wilson's friend, John H. Latané, for the *American Journal of International Law* argued against such exemptions. Subsequently, after a repeal bill was introduced early in 1914, Wilson sent Congress a special message. The president argued that even if the United States had not violated the Hay-Pauncefote Treaty, other nations believed that the exemption law was an act of bad faith by the United States.

The repeal bill caused extensive debate in Congress. Shipping interests, the Hearst newspaper chain, Irish-Americans, and a few politicians from both parties opposed the repeal. Wilson stood firm and was aided by Republicans such as Henry Cabot Lodge. Finally, the repeal bill passed in Congress. The vote in the House of Representatives was 247 to 162. In the Senate, after an amendment attached to the bill granted the abstract right to levy tolls favoring U.S. ships, the bill passed by 50 to 35. Wilson signed the repeal legislation on June 15; two months later the Panama Canal opened for the first time.

June 28, 1914

Austrian Archduke Francis Ferdinand is assassinated at Sarajevo.

The archduke was killed by Gavrilo Princip, a member of the Serbian Black Hand society. Austria protests the Serbian government's role in the plot. This episode ultimately led to the outbreak of World War I between July 28 and August 6, 1914.

July 15, 1914

General Huerta leaves Mexico; Carranza's Constitutionalists prepare to take over.

The U.S. intervention at Vera Cruz on April 21 spelled Huerta's doom because Carranza rejected an armistice offer and continued offensive action against Mexico City. Although Wilson's intervention and the A.B.C. mediation offer of April 25 played a role in the overthrow of Huerta, the strong popular support of Carranza and the Constitutionalists brought about Huerta's downfall. In this respect, Wilson's decision to provide arms for Carranza on February 2 may have been the decisive blow against Huerta.

After April 25, the Mexican situation resulted in a curious political theater: a peace conference under A.B.C. mediation at Niagara Falls and a continued assault by the Constitutionalists against Huerta's forces. Huerta hoped the mediation would preserve Mexico for the conservative forces of wealthy landowners and foreign investors; Wilson designed the peace meeting to effect Huerta's demise, although he anticipated that with Carranza's participation the fall of Huerta could be bloodless.

The civil war continued because except for the supply of arms and munitions, Carranza wanted Wilson and the Americans to get out and stay out of Mexico. While he sent some observers to Niagara to talk with the U.S. delegates, he refused any foreign intervention in settling Mexico's internal problems. For this reason, between April 25 and July 15, Carranza and his generals continued their successful military assaults on the cities of Saltillo, Mazatlán, and Zacatecas.

Indirectly, Wilson aided Carranza. During the A.B.C. conference, which opened on May 20, it became apparent that the South American delegates tended to favor Huerta's desire for conservative control of the provisional government in Mexico. Wilson learned of these attitudes and told the U.S.

commissioners that any attempt to continue a Huerta-style regime was unsatisfactory. The mediators, he said, should accept the Constitutionalists' victory and get rid of Huerta and his followers without further bloodshed. Furthermore, Wilson was willing to prolong the Niagara Falls sessions until everyone became certain that the Constitutionalists had won in Mexico. By the time the A.B.C. mediation conference ended on July 2, even Huerta realized he had to leave Mexico while he could. Thus, the conference agreement provided that (1) Huerta would resign and the United States would recognize whatever provisional government resulted; (2) the United States expected no indemnity for the Tampico incident; and (3) the provisional government would compensate foreigners for damage during the civil war.

Eight days later General Huerta appointed a Constitutionalist—the Chief Justice Francisco Carbajal—as minister of foreign affairs to form a new government. On July 15, Huerta resigned as president and named Carbajal to succeed him. Then he left for Puerta, Mexico, where the German steamer *Ypiranga* carried him to exile in Europe.

Within a month, on August 13, Carbajal agreed to turn Mexico City over to Carranza's representative, Alvaro OBREGON, whose army peacefully entered the city on August 15. Once Obregon had cleared the way, Carranza and his generals rode into Mexico City on August 20, 1914. The crowds cheered as Carranza, entered the National Palace and took charge of Mexico's government.

Only one cloud appeared during Carranza's victory. In June, General Francisco Villa broke with Carranza and headed north to undertake opposition to the new first chief of Mexico. Otherwise, once U.S. troops evacuated Vera Cruz, Carranza expected he had triumphed.

See November 23, 1914.

July 28, 1914

Austria declares war on Serbia.

Following the assassination of Austria's archduke on June 28, a month of diplomatic discussions failed to resolve the Austro-Serb dispute. On June 25, Serbia sent an evasive response to Austria's demands, and mobilization for war began in both nations. Finally, on July 28, Austria declared war on Serbia.

Further diplomatic attempts to avoid a general war ended on August 1, when Germany declared war on Russia and then on France two days later. World War I began.

August 4, 1914

President Wilson issues the first of 10 American proclamations of neutrality.

Signed and proclaimed between August 4 and November 6 as new declarations of war came from Europe, these decrees stated that the United States was neutral in the conflicts and sought to make clear what Americans and foreign citizens were permitted to do and what they could not do without risking prosecution for crime or expulsion from America.

In addition to the official declarations of neutrality, President Wilson appealed to Americans on August 19 to be "impartial in thought as well as in action." Both Wilson and Secretary of State Bryan attempted to be impartial, but this was often difficult. Two examples of their problem occurred soon after war began. The first case involved wireless radio stations that the Germans had erected at Tuckerton, New Jersey, and Sayville, New York. Initially on August 4, Wilson prohibited all radio stations from sending unneutral messages. The German embassy protested, arguing that the British and French controlled the Atlantic cable and sent military information via it. The Germans' only means of communication was their wireless stations. State Department counselor Robert Lansing found that the Hague Convention of 1907 had conflicting articles on the use of radios, and the British refused Bryan's suggestion to open cables and wireless to all belligerents on equal terms. Wilson decided to compromise. The U.S. navy took over the German wireless facilities and permitted Germany to send messages in code except for military orders. Coded messages had to be given to the U.S. government for censorship.

The second case concerned Bethlehem Steel Corporation's contract to build and deliver submarines, by sections, to the British. Counselor Lansing said international law forbade the sale of assembled submarines or hulls but not parts of these vessels. Wilson and Bryan believed this was legal quibbling and forbade these sales as contrary to strict neutrality. In addition, a third issue—the most difficult of all—involved loans to belligerents.

For the U.S. decision on loans, see August 15, 1914.

August 4, 1914

President Wilson offers to mediate the disputes that brought the Europeans to war.

Following Austria's declaration of war against Serbia on July 28, a general European conflict seemed imminent. Thus, soon after Germany and France went to war on August 3, Wilson prepared a memo offering American mediation now or at any time that "might be thought more suitable." The president's note was sent to the emperors of Germany, Austria, and Russia; the king of England; and the president of France. Although U.S. ambassadors in Europe thought the effort would fail, Wilson decided that an attempt needed to be made.

Every head of state replied to Wilson's note, but each claimed that he was not to blame for the war. As Secretary of State Bryan commented: "Each one declares he is opposed to war and anxious to avoid it and then lays the blame upon someone else." Before the day ended, England declared war on Germany.

August 5, 1914

The Bryan-Chamorro Treaty with Nicaragua grants canal rights to America.

By this agreement, the United States received an exclusive right to build any canal through Nicaragua. America also obtained a lease to the Great Corn and Little Corn Islands on the east coast and a 99-year (renewable) lease to build a naval base in the Gulf of Fonseca. The United States paid Nicaragua $3,000,000 to reduce its foreign debt and pay other expenses under U.S. supervision. Bryan's original treaty included clauses similar to those in the Platt Amendment providing for U.S. oversight of Nicaragua's foreign affairs, but the U.S. Senate eliminated these sections before it ratified the treaty on February 18, 1916. During the next decade, the United States would have a form of protectorship over Nicaragua.

August 6, 1914

Secretary of State Bryan asks all European belligerents to accept the naval rules of the Declaration of London.

Although the London Declaration of December 4, 1908, had not been ratified by the European powers, it spelled out rules of naval warfare and neutral rights on the seas more clearly and definitively than any other document. Moreover, from an American point of view, the London agreement favored the widest possible neutral rights of trade during wartime, a favor contrary to Britain's traditional desire to limit neutral trade with its enemies. For example, the London Declaration did not list cotton, rubber, wool, or copper as contraband—items the neutral United States could continue shipping. As during the European wars of 1793 to 1815, the U.S. objective was to retain and even enlarge its trading rights with all nations and to protect American shipping from the depredations of belligerent navies.

Germany's one problem—and a major one—would be its use of submarines, a new naval weapon whose regulations in naval warfare had never been clearly prescribed. Their unannounced sinking of merchant ships would ultimately lead to the U.S. declaration of war against Germany.

Not surprisingly, the Germans and Austrians readily accepted adherence to the Declaration of London, provided their enemies agreed also. The crucial response to the U.S. notes of August 6 was the British note of August 26. Great Britain agreed generally to follow the Declaration of London but had to make certain modifications in areas essential to "the efficient conduct of naval operations." The British cited their orders-in-council of August 20 that specifically permitted them to capture neutral ships destined for enemy ports and to take "conditional contraband" consigned to Austria or Germany. "Conditional contraband" meant certain items the British considered as necessary to add to the list given in the Declaration of London. The British response drew a U.S. protest.

See September 28, 1914.

August 11, 1914

An American request fails to persuade the warring nations to observe the neutrality of the Pacific Ocean and China.

On August 11, Secretary of State Bryan asked the European powers and Japan to keep the European war out of China and the Pacific. His request had been inspired by a Chinese suggestion on August 3. But Bryan enlarged China's proposal by including all Pacific islands as well as China proper.

Bryan's endeavor was unsuccessful. After declaring war on Germany on August 23, Japan objected to

Bryan's request and proceeded to seize Germany's leaseholds at Shantung and Kiaochow. Great Britain was willing to neutralize China in order to restrain Japan, but the British occupied the German islands in the Pacific. Thus, British and Japanese imperial designs prevailed.

August 15, 1914

President Wilson forbids American loans to any European belligerent.

The issue of loans to warring nations arose on August 6 when France appointed J. P. Morgan and Company as its agent to float a total of $100 million of loans in the United States. The Morgan Company asked the State Department's advice on the French loan as well as on one for the House of Rothschild in Paris.

Although Counselor Lansing explained that such loans were not unneutral under international law or U.S. statute, Secretary of State Bryan demurred. He had opposed such loans at least since April 17, 1907, when he addressed the First American Peace Conference: "money is the worst of all contrabands because it commands everything else." He advocated that the United States outlaw loans as a means to shorten warfare. In addition, he feared that when a loan was made, the investors inevitably favored the victory of that debtor nation, thus causing internal attitudes that were not neutral.

On August 15, Wilson accepted the secretary's view. Bryan issued a press statement that said: "in the judgement of this Government, loans by American bankers to any foreign nation which is at war is [sic] inconsistent with the true spirit of neutrality."

On August 15, there was little opposition to the ban on loans. Even the *London Economist* of August 22 called the action an "honour" to America and a "service to the world." Within several months, however, the connection between foreign loans and American foreign trade as a neutral right began to make the entire financial issue much more complicated, and Bryan would change his views on the subject.

See October 15, 1914.

August 15, 1914

The Panama Canal officially opens without ceremonies.

The various ceremonies planned for the opening of the canal had to be canceled because of the European war crisis that began in June. There had been plans for an international fleet of 100 warships, headed by the old U.S. battleship *Oregon,* to make the first trip through the canal on its way to the opening of the Panama-Pacific exposition in San Francisco.

The war between France and Germany broke out on August 3, the same day that a lowly cement boat, the *Cristobal,* became the first oceangoing ship to pass through the canal. Earlier, on January 7, an old French crane boat used in the canal construction since the 1880s had traversed the canal to the Pacific Coast. On the day of the "grand opening," the ship *Ancon* traveled the canal, but news of the occasion was buried in newspapers behind reports of the war in Europe.

August 20, 1914

The German Army captures Brussels and most of Belgium.

Violating the neutrality of Belgium, the Germans followed their Schlieffen Plan, which was designed to avoid French fortifications by attacking France through Belgium. On August 4, German General Alexander von Kluck had scattered the small but resolute Belgian forces and, after taking Brussels, the Germans continued to their farthest western advance at Nieuport on September 8, 1914. The resulting chaos in Belgium would bring on food shortages and charges of German brutality.

For the resulting Belgian food problem, see October 16, 1914.

August 27, 1914

U.S. intervention in the Dominican Republic appears to be working when a provisional president is elected: the "Wilson Plan."

Following the establishment of the American protectorate over Santo Domingo on February 25, 1907, disorder had been relieved for nearly five years. In September 1912, however, a revolutionary group created new problems by seizing two Dominican customs houses.

During 1913, Secretary Bryan's effort in Santo Domingo made matters worse, largely because he replaced knowledgeable State Department officials with political appointees ignorant of the region's problems. In addition, he appointed James M. Sullivan of New York as the minister to the Dominican Republic. A former prizefighter, Sullivan had underworld connections and became implicated in corrupt dealings in Santo Domingo in December 1914. Sullivan's only prior connections with the Caribbean at the time of his appointment were his New York financial friends who owned the Banco Nacional de Santo Domingo and hoped to control the U.S. customs collections in the island.

These unqualified personnel, together with Wilson's desire to expand democracy in Latin America, caused further difficulty in Santo Domingo. Attempting to treat Dominican problems as if they were problems in Kansas or North Dakota, Bryan instructed Sullivan to support the "constitutional authority" that in 1913 happened to be an ambitious, cunning leader, President José Bordas Valdes. Sullivan and Bryan tried to back Bordas even after a December 1913 congressional election defeated the president's party. Because Bordas sought to repress the opposition and ignore Congress, a new uprising began during the spring of 1914, making it clear to Wilson and Bryan that changes were necessary in Santo Domingo.

To try to end the disorders, the president on July 27, 1914, prepared what became known as the Wilson Plan to resolve the Dominican political dispute. The plan offered four basic stages of development: (1) all hostilities would cease; (2) all Dominican political factions would send delegates to decide on a provisional president; (3) new elections for a president and congress would be held under U.S. observation to determine that they were "fair and free"; and (4) the United States would recognize the new government, permit no more revolutions, and require subsequent changes to be made peacefully.

To supervise his plan, Wilson appointed a commission headed by a former governor of New Jersey, John Franklin Fort. The commissioners arranged an armistice in the Dominican civil war and, by using threats to disavow him, persuaded Bordas to resign. The disputing groups agreed to make Dr. Ramón Báez the provisional president on August 27. New elections followed on October 25–27, and General Juan Isidro Jiménez received a bare majority of the vote for president. Almost immediately, Jiménez's opponents protested that the election was rigged. The opposition claimed that General Desiderio Arias, who was widely known as the Dominican army's most corrupt officer, had employed deceptive methods on behalf of Jiménez.

The Fort Commission discounted the charges of corruption, approving the election as "absolutely free." On December 4, 1914, Jiménez and the newly elected congress took office. For a brief moment, Wilson believed Dominican affairs had been stabilized. But within two years, further U.S. intervention became necessary.

See November 29, 1916.

September 5, 1914

Declaration of London—England, France, and Russia agree not to make a separate peace treaty or to discuss peace terms except jointly.

This Allied agreement was designed to maintain Allied unity and sustain a two-front war against the Central Powers. Japan announced its adherence to the Declaration of London on October 19, 1915.

September 18, 1914

The Irish Home Rule Bill becomes law but by a simultaneous act will not come into force until the war ends.

The Irish bill had been ardently contested since its introduction by Prime Minister H. H. Asquith's government on April 11, 1912. The bill united Ireland and according to its opponents was unjust to the Protestants in Ulster. As a result, the bill was twice rejected by the House of Lords (January 30 and July 15, 1913). When the House of Commons passed it for the third time on May 26, the lords could not again veto it. Also, Asquith had agreed to a compromise excluding Ulster from Irish rule for six years. After war began in August 1914, parliament agreed to pass the Irish bill but to delay its operation until peace returned. Both the Irish and Irish-Americans were dismayed by the delay of Ireland's home rule.

See also April 24, 1916.

September 28, 1914

The United States protests British efforts to change the Declaration of London regarding neutral ships and naval warfare.

After the English rejected the U.S. request of August 6 to comply with the Declaration of London, State Department Counselor Lansing decided some note of disapproval should be sent to Great Britain. Therefore, with Wilson's approval, the U.S. ambassador to Great Britain, Walter Hines PAGE, was requested on September 28 to protest officially in London. The U.S. message said that Britain's failure to follow the declaration and to propose contrary rules would "greatly disturb" American opinion and cause a grave situation between the two nations. The United States urged England to reconsider because the terms of the 1908 declaration "represent the limit" to which the U.S. government could go in getting public support.

By September 28, therefore, the United States and Britain had laid the theoretical basis on which later complaints about violations of neutrality could be argued. Great Britain did not accept the Declaration of London but on October 29 proclaimed its own list of absolute contraband and its methods to capture neutral ships whose cargo was destined for enemy hands. Items placed on the contraband list included unwrought copper, iron ore, aluminum, rubber, gasoline, and oil. In private discussions with American officials, Britain's only concessions were to keep a "sense of proportion" in executing its claims and to respect U.S. trade in the framework of Anglo-American understanding. Subsequently, many questions of detail over neutral rights arose during the next three years, but no threat of war occurred with Britain over neutral rights.

Walter Hines Page, U.S. ambassador to Great Britain. Library of Congress

October 14, 1914

Bulgaria, Germany, and Austria successfully attack Serbia.

After World War I broke out in August 1914, the Serb army defended their country for 14 months because most of Austria's forces were moved to its north border to engage Russian troops in Galacia. The war situation changed by October 1915 because Russian troops were driven back by the Germans and Austrians, and Bulgaria joined the Central Alliance. Thus on October 14, Bulgarian forces invaded Serbia from the east to conquer Macedonia, while Germans and Austrians struck from the north to occupy Belgrade and Kosovo. To escape the Austrians, Serbia's King Peter and many Serb soldiers retreated to the Adriatic coast, where British naval ships evacuated them to the island of Corfu. Later, the British navy transported 120,000 Serb soldiers to the Greek city of Salonika.

See September 30, 1918.

October 15, 1914

President Wilson approves "credits" to foreign belligerent nations by private U.S. bankers.

A State Department announcement on October 15 clarified the notice of August 15 that prohibited loans to foreign belligerents. The October interpretation allowed banks to extend "credits" to warring nations for purchases of American goods.

The subtle but important difference between "loans" and "credits" originated with Secretary of State Bryan. In September, the French Ambassador Jules Jusserand indicated to Bryan that the ban on loans made it difficult for France to buy U.S. products. Without a credit line, French imports from the United States would soon cease. Shortly afterward, Roger L. Franham of National City Bank met with Bryan to ask his view about a banking credit of $10 million for France. Bryan accepted the distinction between a credit and a loan and informed Franham that a credit transaction was proper provided there was no advertisement of French bonds to be sold as collateral for the "credit."

Four days after the interpretation of "credit" on October 15, a newsman asked President Wilson if the recent notice did not alter the prohibition of a loan. "No," the president responded, "'loans' were contrary to 'true neutrality.'" A credit was an "easy exchange in meeting debts" due to American merchants. Since U.S. trade with belligerents was permitted as a neutral right, credits were approved because they were essential to any trade arrangement.

As a result of the October 15 interpretation, National City Bank provided France with a $10 million credit in October 29. Soon after, other belligerents obtained credits as well as unadvertised collateral bonds in America. These financial ties between the United States and Europe continued to grow during the next two years, with most of the credits given to England and France.

October 16, 1914

An appeal of the U.S. Ambassador to Belgium launches Herbert Hoover's food relief program.

The U.S. ambassador at Brussels, Brand Whitlock, informed the U.S. State Department and the U.S. ambassador to Great Britain, Walter Hines Page, that the Belgian populace was within two weeks of famine, and immediate aid was necessary. In peacetime, Belgium imported five-sixths of its food supply. Since the war began in August, German confiscation of Belgian food stores together with the British blockade of Belgium had caused approaching famine conditions for the people.

In London, Herbert Hoover heard of the impending Belgian tragedy and announced that he would organize a food relief effort. Subsequently, Hoover and Page together with Hugh Gibson, who acted as the liaison with Berlin, and Ambassador Whitlock in Brussels, instituted a food relief program that lessened Belgian food problems during the war.

This effort was not simple, however. Successful implementation required England's willingness to permit designated shipments to enter Belgium and Berlin's agreement not to siphon off the supplies to Germany but to permit them to reach the Belgian people. Finally, constant oversight in Belgium required Ambassador Whitlock's diligence in getting food from authorities to the people who needed it. Generally, the program was evaluated as a success after the war. While Hoover was most publicly associated with the effort, a considerable amount of its success was due to the negotiating efforts of Ambassadors Page and Whitlock and the liaison work of Hugh Gibson.

November 23, 1914

Following some delay, U.S. forces finally evacuate Vera Cruz.

Wilson did not order the rapid withdrawal of U.S. forces following Huerta's exile on July 15 because of Mexico's renewed political problems between Carranza and Villa. Although Carranza became provisional president on August 20, Villa appealed for support from Washington and made plans to control the Constitutional Convention scheduled to convene in October 1914.

President Wilson not only listened to Villa's pleas but was almost persuaded to support him. Unlike Carranza, Villa seemed willing to follow American advice. He also appeared to have developed strong military forces through an alliance with Emiliano Zapata in Morelos.

By November Wilson was not certain whom to support. Although Carranza retained much strength, Villa obtained control of the convention in October. After capturing Zacatecas and San Luis Potosí on September 25, Villa met with several generals including Obregon and agreed to an armistice and to conducting the convention sessions at Aguascalientes, not Mexico City. This suited Villa's plans to pack the convention after its session began on October 10. The convention adopted rules favorable to Villa, and by

October 14, he was able to name his followers the Conventionists and repudiate Carranza's claims to power. The convention's major action thereafter was to approve the land reform advocated by Villa and Zapata, called the Plan of Ayola. The convention then named General Gutierrez as provisional president to replace Carranza.

Carranza had not stood still, however. He rallied several generals to his banner and moved his capital to Puebla, where he rejected the convention's program and claimed full government authority.

Because of these political complexities, Wilson, who was greatly concerned at the time about the European war, decided to withdraw from Vera Cruz and become neutral in Mexico. It became difficult to detect whether Villa or Carranza's forces were the stronger, although Wilson initially favored Villa and the Conventionists. On November 11, Wilson wired both Carranza and Gutierrez that the U.S. forces would withdraw on November 23 because both Carranza and the convention had agreed to respect the foreign interests in Mexico. Wilson refused to surrender Vera Cruz to either faction, telling General Funston not to make arrangements with any Mexican representative. Funston should just leave the city without recognizing any authority to replace him. By one o'clock on the afternoon of November 23, Funston complied.

For the continuance of Mexican problems, see October 19, 1915.

November 24, 1914

Following a battle at Ypres, the war on Europe's western front becomes stalemated.

Between August and November, German forces continued their attack through Belgium in an effort to reach the English Channel and encircle the Anglo-French armies. A turning point came when Germany failed to capture Ypres, near the sea.

By the end of 1914, a stalemate had developed on the western front, and trench warfare became the predominant mode of continuing the combat. For three years, the line dividing the enemy armies did not vary by more than 10 miles. Offensive thrusts occurred often but produced little more than an appalling loss of life and very limited success.

1915

January 18, 1915

Japan submits 21 demands to gain predominance in China.

Soon after they declared war against Germany on August 23, 1914, the Japanese began discussions with the government of Yüan Shih-k'ai to obtain a preeminent position in Chinese affairs. Ever since the Sino-Japanese war of 1894–1895, the Western powers including the United States had restricted Japan's interests south of the Great Wall of China by acknowledging Japan's special rights only in Korea and Manchuria. With Europe at war, Tokyo decided to advance its geographic advantage to obtain special economic and political rights in China.

In December, China's foreign minister asked Japan for specific proposals; these were delivered to Yüan on January 18. The Japanese asked the Chinese to keep their proposal secret, but Yüan realized that he had to publicize them to get assistance from England or America to resist Japan's demands. As a result, the U.S. minister to Peking, Paul Reinsch, obtained a garbled version of the demands on January 21 and sent these to Washington.

Japan's demands against China were arranged in five categories as follows:

1. Group One—granting Japan full control of Shantung and Germany's former concessions in China;
2. Group Two—approving consolidation of Japan's special rights in Manchuria and eastern Inner Mongolia;
3. Group Three—giving Japan exclusive mining and industrial rights in the Yangtze valley, including the iron, steel, and mineral deposits around the industrial center of Hankow;
4. Group Four—forbidding China to cede or lease harbors, bays, or islands along the Chinese coast, thus protecting the province of Fukien as Japan's sphere of influence;
5. Group Five—granting Japan political rights throughout China, giving Japan control over schools, churches, and government officials.

For the U.S. response to these demands, see May 11, 1915; for China's acceptance, see May 25, 1915.

January 30, 1915

A German-American league is formed to end "foreign influence" in official life and to pass an arms embargo.

Founded in August 1914, the National German-American League joined Irish-American and other lobbying groups who wanted Congress to pass an arms embargo to prevent U.S. armaments from reaching England and France. The Allied blockade was preventing armaments from reaching Germany. The antimunitions concept also appealed to many Americans opposing U.S. involvement in European wars. Because of the vast population of hyphenated-Americans—foreign-born or first generation—it was difficult to know how many favored neutrality. (Public opinion polls were not available until the 1930s.) After surveying U.S. opinion in 1914, historian Arthur Link agrees with President Wilson's comment, "We definitely have to be neutral, since otherwise our mixed population would wage war on each other."

Consequently, during the congressional session of December 1914 to March 1915, the House and Senate committees refused to report on the arms embargo act. In the Senate, Senator Gilbert M. Hitchcock of Nebraska added an arms embargo amendment to the Shipping Bill, but it was tabled by a vote of 51 to 36. The German-American groups continued to press for an embargo in future sessions of Congress.

February 4, 1915

Germany declares a war zone around Great Britain.

During the fall of 1914, the German Admiralty concluded that the submarine was the only naval weapon they had to halt the merchant ships carrying supplies to Britain. Admiral Hugo von Pohl led the naval group that persuaded the emperor that Germany was justified in such attacks because England was violating international law on the high seas and because nations such as the United States had yielded to British interpretations of sea warfare. The United States had not, for example, insisted on Britain's following the Declaration of London.

As planned by German naval leaders, unrestricted submarine warfare would take place in a zone surrounding England. The submarines in the war zone would be authorized to sink merchant ships without warning and without taking undue pains to spare neutral ships. The February 4 decree said that after February 18 all enemy merchant ships in the war zone would be destroyed, "even if it may not be possible always to save their crews and passengers." In addition, neutral vessels in the war zone would be "exposed to danger" because, in view of the misuse of neutral flags by Great Britain and the hazards of naval war, "neutral vessels cannot always be prevented from suffering from the attacks intended for enemy ships."

On February 6, Germany sent its decree to all neutral nations, explaining that the action was taken because Britain violated international law on the high seas. The submarine warfare was simple retaliation for British "crimes." Neutral ships, the note said, could be assured of safety only by staying out of the war zone or using safe lanes indicated in the declaration.

See September 28, 1914; for the British blockade order, see March 1, 1915.

February 10, 1915

The United States protests Germany's war zone decree and Britain's misuse of neutral flags.

President Wilson issued an official protest against Germany's February 4 decree permitting submarine attacks in European war zones and Britain's January 31 admiralty order authorizing naval captains to hoist an American flag if their ships were in danger.

President Wilson informed Berlin that attacks on neutral vessels could not be justified unless Germany proclaimed and maintained an effective blockade of Great Britain, a situation not proposed in the February 4 decree. Sinking ships without warning, Wilson said, was an act "so unprecedented in naval warfare" that he could not believe Germany "contemplates it as possible." Denying the German claim that America accepted Britain's neutral violations, Wilson said he had protested these incidents and would protest Britain's misuse of the American flag. For Germany to attack and destroy American ships would be "an indefensible violation of neutral rights" and an act for which America would hold Germany to a "strict accountability." American ships should not be molested except under proper procedures of visit and search when they traversed Germany's proclaimed war zones.

On the same day, February 10, Wilson vigorously protested the British order of January 31 regarding neutral flags. The misuse of neutral flags was unjustified and would become a "serious and constant menace" if German submarines could not distinguish an American from a British ship. If the British continued their practice, they would share responsibility if U.S. vessels were lost.

Thus, Wilson protested both German and British actions in a balanced and neutral fashion. Maintaining such a posture became difficult in future months because the violations by each belligerent were different in substance.

February 15, 1915

The United States withdraws a proposal for a modus vivendi regarding submarine warfare and armed merchant ships.

On December 30, 1914, the *Persia,* an armed British merchant ship, was sunk by a German submarine. Subsequently, Robert Lansing, the State Department counselor, suggested a modus vivendi by European belligerents that could solve the submarine question. He proposed that Britain stop arming all merchant ships and Germany prohibit submarine attacks without warning on merchant and passenger ships.

In theory, Lansing's suggestion was excellent; in practice, neither belligerent would accept it. Colonel Edward M. House, Wilson's personal consultant, and Ambassador Walter H. Page explained that the modus vivendi would be impossible to monitor. For example, a defensively armed ship could not be distinguished from an offensively armed ship. Also, the 1915 submarine was a fragile craft and quite vulnerable to attack when on the surface. Lansing reported these difficulties to the press on February 15 and soon after withdrew the proposal, which the State Department had also relayed to Paris, Rome, Berlin, and Vienna.

Robert Lansing, State Department Counselor, later Secretary of State. Library of Congress

February 17, 1915

Wilson and the Democratic leadership withdraw their attempt to pass a federal shipping bill.

Although President Wilson strongly supported a Ship Purchase Bill to enable the federal government to buy vessels in order to increase the size of the U.S. merchant fleet and cut shipping costs, the opposition of the Republicans and seven insurgent Democrats prevented passage of the act. Opponents of the bill objected to the "socialistic" aspects of government ownership of a merchant fleet and to plans to buy German ships in order to quickly build up the American fleet. By February 17, Democratic leaders were unable to secure a majority in the Senate and agreed to end their effort for the present.

The purchase of German ships might have caused difficulty with Britain if the ship bill had passed. On January 14, 1915, the State Department asked Great Britain to permit the *Dacia,* a former German ship purchased by an American, Edward N. Breitung, to carry a load of cotton to Rotterdam. The British and the French both objected, contending that the transfer of any German vessels to American registry was aiding the German enemy.

Nevertheless, Wilson and Bryan contended that the transfer of ships was not unneutral. The State Department allowed the *Dacia* to leave Galveston, Texas, on January 31, but the French seized the vessel on February 27 and escorted it to a French prize court at Brest. The French purchased the ship's cotton cargo but condemned the *Dacia,* which became a French ship, the *Yser,* in August 1915.

March 1, 1915

Great Britain announces a blockade of all ships headed or destined for enemy ports.

Although the British blockade did not become official until the proclamation of an order-in-council on March 15, Foreign Minister Grey declared in the House of Commons on March 1 that the government was responding to Germany's "ruthless and illegal" underseas campaign by a blockade of German ports. British ships, Grey said, would take all commodities off captured ships. They would not confiscate goods unless they were subject to condemnation as contraband.

Together with the German announcement of February 4, the British order endangered neutral commerce by attacks from both sides in the European war. As in the case of the German decree, America protested Britain's "unprecedented" decision to stop all neutral ships bound for enemy ports. The British responded that they would act as generously as possible toward U.S. ships captured in the war zone.

April 20, 1915

The Armenians revolt because of massacres by Turkish forces in the Caucasus Mountain area.

The Turkish atrocities began because the Turks claimed the Armenians assisted Russian forces invading Turkey. The revolt failed, however, and by August 5 the Turks regained control of the city of Van, which the Russians and Armenians had occupied.

For prior Turkish attacks on Armenians, see August 26, 1896.

April 25, 1915

Great Britain begins the Gallipoli campaign against Turkey.

The British joined with Australian, New Zealand, and French forces to attack the Turkish forces because the Balkan area was considered a vulnerable place where the Western powers might gain support from Serbia and other nations against Austria. In addition, supplies could be sent to Russia by way of the Black Sea if Turkey were defeated.

The Gallipoli campaign was strongly urged by First Lord of the Admiralty Winston Churchill, but it became a disaster. The assault bogged down and the Western armies suffered from heat, lack of water, and disease. By January 9, 1916, the campaign was called off and the Allied forces withdrew.

May 1, 1915

The American ship *Gulflight* is torpedoed without warning by a German submarine.

Following the German submarine proclamation of February 4, 1915, Kaiser William II tried to maintain some restrictions on submarine attacks against neutral ships. This was difficult, however, because submarines could not effectively ascertain the nationality and cargo of a ship before attacking without surfacing, which greatly increased their vulnerability.

The *Gulflight* incident, which took three lives, began a series of U.S. protests against Berlin's submarine tactics, although the *Gulflight*'s case was soon overshadowed by the sinking of the *Lusitania* on May 7. In both cases the events demonstrated German plans to sink any ship in the war zone. Admiral von Turpitz had become convinced that the United States accepted Britain's neutrality viewpoints. He also believed America would do everything possible to avoid a war.

May 2, 1915

An Austro-German offensive against Russian forces inaugurates a gradual, persistent, and successful rout of the Russian armies during the next year.

In August 1914, the Russians had invaded East Prussia to fulfill their agreement with France to divert as many German troops as possible. By the late spring of 1915, however, the German and Austrian armies were prepared for a general offensive into Russia and Poland that would take them to Vilna by September 19. The Russians began to suffer from the lack of rifles, artillery, ammunition, and clothing, all problems that grew to disastrous proportions by the end of 1916.

May 7, 1915

The *Lusitania*, a British passenger ship, is sunk by a German submarine with the loss of 1,198 lives.

Although Secretary of State Bryan wanted the president to take steps to keep Americans off belligerent ships, Wilson upheld the U.S. right to travel on mer-

The *Lusitania* departs from New York harbor on her last voyage. National Archives

chant ships. Before the *Lusitania* left New York on May 1, the German embassy had published an advertisement in New York newspapers to warn Americans that they traveled at their own risk.

By May 7, the *Lusitania* reached the Irish coast, where it turned eastward bringing it directly across the line of fire of the German submarine U-20, commanded by Captain Walter Schweiger. The U-20 followed the *Lusitania* for an hour, discovering that the liner was an easy target because its captain did not use the zigzag pattern normal for merchant ships in the war zone. At 2:10 P.M., the U-20 fired one torpedo that hit the starboard bow and caused a large explosion. The explosion resulted because the torpedo hit either a boiler or the ammunition that the ship carried in its hold. A second torpedo was not necessary; the *Lusitania* sank in 18 minutes. Although a total of 761 passengers and crew survived, 1,198 died, 124 of whom were Americans.

Although the Germans correctly claimed the *Lusitania* carried ammunition in its cargo, the American public overlooked such details in their anger against the German attack on an "innocent" passenger ship. This incident became a turning point in American opinion about the war. Although Wilson and many others continued to seek peace, a substantial American group began to organize U.S. opinion to protect American rights and prepare for war.

In addition, diplomatic discussions between Wilson, Bryan, and the Germans developed tensions that brought the two nations to the verge of war.

See May 14, 1915.

May 11, 1915

Reacting to Japan's 21 demands of China, President Wilson refuses to accept any Sino-Japanese agreement that impairs the Open Door policy.

Between January and May 1915, the U.S. State Department closely followed developments in the Chinese-Japanese negotiations that began on January 18 with Japan's 21 demands on China. U.S. Minister Paul Reinsch sympathized with China and became China's unofficial adviser on diplomatic tactics between January and May 1915. Apparently Reinsch aided the Chinese diplomats as they skillfully lengthened and qualified Tokyo's demands while getting some support from both Washington and London.

In February and March, Secretary Bryan conducted his discussions with Japan's ambassador and foreign minister. While Bryan described American concerns about Japan's activity in China, he tended to recognize Japan's needs and to be solicitous toward Japan's view. Eventually, however, Bryan learned that the Japanese had kept secret their Group Five political demands on China. On February 18, Bryan confronted the Japanese with the conflict between their reports and news reports of the Group Five claims. The Japanese retreated by explaining that these political clauses were "requests" of China, not "demands."

In his note to Tokyo on March 13, Bryan strongly protested the Group Five demands, which sought political controls over China and its institutions. He also stated that the United States had grounds for protesting the demands but conceded that "territorial contiguity creates special relations between Japan and these districts" of China. Thus, he implied that in addition to Japan's rights in Manchuria as recognized by the Root-Takahira agreement, Japan also had rights in Shantung and East Mongolia. Generally, Bryan offered some conciliatory possibilities for Japan to consider in limiting its demands.

Between March and May, however, further specific aspects of Japan's demands on China caused both Great Britain and President Wilson to put more pressure on Japan to restrict its demands. The British reluctantly complained about Japan's demands in central China and the Yangtze area. They protested sufficiently, however, to cause Tokyo's elder statesmen, the Genro, to require Foreign Minister Takaaki Kato to accept British views and limit both Group Five and the Yangtze demands (Group Three).

Wilson gradually assumed a greater role in Chinese policy during April 1915, because he sensed that Bryan was allowing Japan to obtain more than was necessary in China. Reinsch sent alarming telegrams from Peking on April 13 and 14, stating that the Chinese believed America had deserted them by taking the side of Japan. In addition, he sent new texts of Japan's demands that differed in some respects from those the State Department had previously obtained.

Consequently in early May, Wilson sent a message to Tokyo and Peking that repudiated any U.S. approval of a Sino-Japanese agreement that impaired the open door. Robert Lansing, who soon replaced Bryan as secretary of state, had prepared this May 11, 1915, statement that declared that America "cannot recognize any agreement or undertaking" that may impair "the treaty rights of the United States and its citizens in China, the political or territorial integrity of the Republic of China, or the international policy relative to China commonly known as the Open Door policy." This memorandum squared with Wilson's statement to Bryan on April 14 that he wanted Americans to be the "champions of the sovereign rights of China."

Wilson's May 11 note had the effect of reserving American rights to object to any Sino-Japanese agreements at a future date. Eventually, the note led to the 1917 Lansing-Ishii agreement and the 1932 nonrecognition doctrine of Secretary of State Henry Stimson.

See May 25, 1915; on Group Five demands, see January 18, 1915; also see November 2, 1917, and January 7, 1932.

May 14, 1915

President Wilson strongly protests the sinking of the *Lusitania*, appealing to Germany on humanitarian grounds to abandon its submarine campaign.

Wilson's note reviewed various submarine incidents that had involved Americans. These included the case of the *Falaba* on March 28, in which one American died when a British liner sank; the *Cushing*, an American ship attacked by a German aircraft in the North Sea on April 29; and the *Gulflight*, the first U.S. ship torpedoed by a submarine, on May 1, 1915. Together with the *Lusitania*'s sinking, these events violated international law as well as the rights of humanity, and he could not believe the German government sanctioned such attacks.

Moreover, Wilson said, America had warned Germany it would be "strictly accountable" for the loss of American ships or lives on unarmed merchantmen. The United States would uphold the rights of its citizens to travel on belligerent merchant ships. The U.S. note to Germany ended by expressing confidence that the imperial government would make reparation for its illegal actions, disavow such acts of its submarine commanders, and prevent such attacks in the future.

During the discussions leading to Wilson's May 14 note, a serious break occurred between the president and Secretary of State Bryan. The secretary wanted Wilson to issue a simultaneous public message indicating that the United States anticipated that Germany would seek to accommodate American views and that the United States would be willing to submit the *Lusitania* case to arbitration. Counselor Lansing and other cabinet members persuaded Wilson not to issue this statement. Bryan then asked that the United States warn Americans not to travel on British ships in the war zone pending a settlement of the neutrality issue with Germany. Wilson rejected this idea. Finally, Bryan hoped that a message would be sent to England to reassert American trading rights that the British had violated. This, Bryan thought, would demonstrate America's evenhandedness in protesting neutrality violations by both belligerents. Once again Bryan was disappointed. Wilson did not want to "make it easier for Germany to accede to our demands." Therefore, any complaints to England would have to wait until the German issue was settled.

These disagreements between Bryan and Wilson were the first of a series of differences in which the president overruled the secretary of state. Eventually, the diverging attitudes led to Bryan's resignation on June 8, 1915.

For the outcome of the discussion with Germany on the *Lusitania* incident, see June 8 and July 21, 1915.

May 23, 1915

Italy declares war on Austria.

Italy had denounced the Triple Alliance on May 3, after gaining concessions from France and Britain. On August 28, 1916, Italy declared war on Germany as well.

In August 1914, Italy refused to join its allies, Germany and Austria, in the war because the Italians claimed Austria had taken the offensive against Serbia. The Italian government proceeded to negotiate with both the Central Powers and the Entente Powers to obtain the most favorable concessions before declaring war. Austria agreed to cede Trentino to Italy after the war, but Italy's foreign minister, Baron Sidney Sonnino, demanded the immediate cession of Trentino, South Tyrol, the districts of Gorizia and Gradisia, certain Dalmatian islands, and Trieste as a free state. Before Germany could persuade Austria to agree to these exorbitant demands, Italy signed the secret Treaty of London with Britain, France, and Russia. This treaty granted Italy all the demands listed above plus the southern part of Dalmatia and sovereignty of the Dodecanese Islands. During the peace conference of 1919, Italy became dismayed because it did not receive all the territories promised in 1915.

May 25, 1915

A Sino-Japanese treaty recognizes some of Japan's 21 demands on China.

The 1915 treaty had been agreed to by Peking on May 10 but was not signed until May 25. China skillfully gained many concessions from Japan through diplomacy, obtaining an effective boycott of Japanese goods by the Chinese people and receiving support for portions of the requests from British and American diplomats. Thus, the treaty did not give Japan the protectorate over China envisioned by the original 21 demands of January 18, 1915.

British and American opposition caused Japan to withdraw the Group Five political demands almost entirely. Nevertheless, Japan received Germany's Shantung concessions of the Group One demands. China secured loopholes and reservations that limited the effectiveness of both the Group Three demands and the Group Four demands regarding the Yangtze concessions and certain Chinese territory. Japan obtained all of the Group Two demands in Manchuria and eastern Mongolia, which it held to a large degree before 1915. In general, Japan achieved some new concessions but not many of the significant demands that would have given the effective control of China that Tokyo desired. These Japanese ambitions were not renounced, however, and later Tokyo's nationalists would employ different method to enlarge its position in China.

June 8, 1915

Secretary of State Bryan resigns because he believes Wilson's strong protests against Germany policy may lead to war.

The particular issue leading to Bryan's resignation was the second note on the *Lusitania* incident. A second protest was required because Germany's May 28 response to Wilson's May 14 note had not been satisfactory. While agreeing to pay indemnity for the *Cushing* and *Gulflight* incidents if an investigation proved their forces errored, Germany refused to do so in the case of the *Falaba* because its captain had tried to escape after having been asked to surrender by the German commander. Regarding the *Lusitania*, the Germans on May 9 expressed their regret for the loss of neutral lives. Concerning other matters, Germany claimed the British misuse of the *Lusitania* caused its destruction. They said the *Lusitania* had been armed as an auxiliary cruiser and ordered both to use neutral flags and to ram German submarines whenever possible. On prior voyages, Foreign Minister Gottlieb von Jagow argued, the *Lusitania* carried Canadian soldiers and a munitions cargo. Thus, the German government believed the sinking of the ship was fully justified. It asked the United States to investigate these aspects of the case fully before judging the

Germans. To obtain a final accounting, the Germans wanted all facts about the *Lusitania* to be known.

Secretly, the Germans had given new orders to U-boat commanders as a consequence of the *Lusitania* incident. Chancellor Theobald von BETHMANN-HOLLWEG had insisted that the emperor overrule the military leaders and take steps to keep America out of the war. Kaiser William II yielded, but on condition that the chancellor take responsibility for this unpopular act. The German public as well as the military believed U.S. action was unneutral toward Germany in favor of England and argued that to yield on its submarine policies would be disgraceful to Germany.

Nevertheless, the kaiser allowed Bethmann to change the policy by ordering the submarine commanders on June 1 and 5 not to attack neutral merchant ships or any passenger ships. As a matter of honor to the military, the orders of June 1 and 5 were kept secret. Not until September 1, 1915, were portions of the German order publicized.

Lacking knowledge of Bethmann-Hollweg's action, Wilson sent Germany a second strongly worded protest on June 9, saying that Germany must stop all submarine attacks. During a June 1 cabinet session, Bryan urged that a similar strong protest be made about British violations of neutral rights. Bryan became angry during the meeting and remarked that the "Cabinet seemed to be pro-Ally," a comment that caused Wilson to rebuke the secretary.

Counselor Lansing prepared the protest against Germany. The note rebutted the charge that the *Lusitania* was armed or had carried Canadian soldiers. More seriously, however, the U.S. note said the "principles of humanity" made any special detailed circumstances irrelevant. A passenger ship carrying more than "a thousand souls" who were not involved in the conduct of the war had been sunk without a warning to the men, women, and children who "were sent to their death in circumstances unparalleled in modern warfare." Wilson therefore appealed to "the humanity of that great [German] Government" to stop such violations of humane concepts.

Bryan not only objected to Wilson's strongly worded protest; he refused to sign the official note. He feared Wilson's note headed the nation toward war because it judged one nation's violations of neutrality more strongly than another's. Consequently, Bryan resigned for what he considered to be a matter of high principle. His resignation letter was sent to Wilson on June 8. That same day, Wilson's second *Lusitania* note was sent to Berlin, signed by Acting Secretary of State Robert Lansing.

June 23, 1915

Robert Lansing is commissioned as secretary of state to replace William J. Bryan.

Lansing had extensive preparation to serve as secretary of state. From 1914 to June 9, 1915, he was counselor of the Department of State and became acting secretary of state when Bryan resigned on June 8. Prior to 1914, Lansing's foreign relations experience included counsel for the Mexican and Chinese legations (1894–1895 and 1900–1901); counsel for the Alaska Boundary Tribunal (1903); counsel for the North Atlantic Fisheries Arbitration (1908–1910); and counsel for the American-British claims (1912). Lansing served as Wilson's secretary of state until February 13, 1920.

July 21, 1915

President Wilson's "last word" on the *Lusitania* ends the critical phase of the controversy with no satisfactory solution.

Wilson's final note regarding the *Lusitania* crisis in relationship to submarine warfare was a response to a German note of July 8 that granted some concessions on the issue of neutrality. Written by Chancellor Bethmann and Foreign Minister von Jagow, the Germans' note said they shared Wilson's principles of humanity but alleged that the submarine warfare was Germany's only means to answer British violations of international law. The note ended with several concessions: German submarines would respect American shipping and safeguard Americans on neutral vessels; if there were not sufficient American ships to carry U.S. passengers on the North Atlantic, the German government would guarantee safe passage on enemy liners sailing an American flag. In summary, the German officials hoped that the present discussions would result in an understanding with America.

Wilson's response to the July 8 German note was that concessions were "very unsatisfactory." Wilson said his protests were to benefit all neutrals, not just U.S. citizens aboard Atlantic ships. He suggested that submarines follow the rules of cruiser warfare as one method to adapt the new weapon to the rights of individuals. Germany, he contended, must find a means to permit freedom of the seas to neutrals. If neutral rights were again contravened by Germany, Wilson would regard the act as "deliberately unfriendly."

To the Germans, Wilson's note of July 21 seemed to be impertinent. The German news editors argued that Wilson fit his "ideas of humanity and neutrality to the business interests of his major electors." By selling munitions to England, the United States showed its desire to "profit as much as possible from the war." Because of these German attitudes, Chancellor Bethmann decided to submit the question of American damage claims to the Hague Court of Arbitration. The American diplomats agreed. Although U.S. public opinion objected strongly to German submarine tactics, the United States did not wish to go to war on that issue in 1915.

July 21, 1915

President Wilson plans military expansion, asking the war and navy departments to recommend an adequate national defense.

The *Lusitania* crisis with Germany persuaded the president to step up the nation's military preparations, a measure some Americans such as former President Theodore Roosevelt had advocated since August 1914. On July 21, Wilson asked Secretary of War Lindly M. GARRISON and Secretary of the Navy Josephus DANIELS to design an increased defense bill to present to Congress in December. To obtain a favorable public reception, Wilson publicly announced on September 3 that he desired the nation to consider measures of an adequate American defense in a rational, responsible manner.

July 22, 1915

The espionage activity of German agent Franz Rintelen von Kleist is disclosed to Wilson and Lansing. Von Kleist's actions are not publicized until April 1917.

On and after July 22, Wilson was kept informed of Rintelen's espionage activity. The German General Staff sent Rintelen to New York during April 1915 with a forged Swiss passport carrying the name of Emil V. Cache. Rintelen, who spoke fluent English, assigned several projects, among his authenticated ones being as follows:

1. attempting (unsuccessfully) to destroy the Welland Canal, which linked the Great Lakes and the St. Lawrence River;
2. creating facilities to build time bombs that could destroy ships in New York harbor;
3. forming a longshoreman's union that stopped munitions ships during a short strike;
4. spending $12 million to divert American arms to Mexico for assistance to a counterrevolution against Carranza.

Assistant Attorney General Charles Warren received reports on these and other matters in a Bureau of Investigation report on July 21. The Justice Department had been alerted in "James Bond" fashion. Late in June 1915, Rintelen vacationed in Kennebunkport, Maine, where he met a charming American, Anne L. Seward. Miss Seward gained Rintelen's confidence, and in a moment of intimacy, he bragged to her that as a German agent he had planned the destruction of the *Lusitania*.

Seward, who knew Secretary of State Lansing, sent him this information. Lansing dispatched his assistant, Chandler P. Anderson, to Maine, where he heard the story and asked the attorney general's office to check on it. After receiving the July 22 report, both Wilson and Lansing suspected that German Ambassador Johann von BERNSTORFF knew about Rintelen's activity. They chose, however, not to confront the ambassador with the matter.

Having also learned about Rintelen, British intelligence sent him a message in German code, asking him to return to Berlin as soon as possible. Not realizing the British had broken Germany's code, Rintelen sailed from New York on a Dutch vessel. According to plans, the British navy stopped the Dutch ship on August 13 near Dover and arrested Rintelen. The British held the agent until April 1917, when they turned him over to American authorities. American courts convicted Rintelen of violating U.S. neutrality laws and sentenced him to four years in prison.

July 29, 1915

President Wilson orders U.S. Marines to occupy Haiti to improve that nation's finances and political order.

For over a year, French and German officials had attempted to require Haiti to pay its debts of $24 million. Following a revolution in Haiti on March 5, 1915, the foreign representatives proposed a customs receivership as a method for collecting the money. The new Haitian president, Vilbrun G. Sam, objected and, with U.S. support, the receivership was rejected.

On July 28, a revolutionary group assassinated Sam and caused further disorder in Haiti. President Wilson ordered U.S. Marines to occupy Haiti on July 29, and a U.S. protectorate resulted. On September 16, a U.S.-Haitian treaty permitted America to control Haiti's tariffs, customs, and public debt for 10 years. Because of public concern about the German submarine issue, Wilson's action in Haiti was hardly noticed in America.

August 15, 1915

The *New York World* publishes German documents on its propaganda attempts in America.

A series of news reports in the *World* from August 15 to 23 exposed various attempts by Heinrich F. ALBERT, commercial attaché of the German embassy, to furnish "news" to American newspapers and to subsidize George S. VIERECK's newspaper *The Fatherland* and other German-American organizations. The German network had also bought a Connecticut munitions plant to stop its arms production from going to the Allies. None of these activities was criminal or violated U.S. neutrality laws, but anti-Germans in America now had further reasons to distrust Germany, pro-German organizations, or the German point of view in America.

The *World* received its material for publication from Secretary of the Treasury William G. McAdoo; Colonel Edward House, the president's confidential adviser; and Secretary of State Robert Lansing, with an agreement not to divulge the source of the material. Colonel House wrote to Wilson that publishing the material would help the president counteract pacifists such as former Secretary of State Bryan.

McAdoo had obtained the German documents from the U.S. Secret Service. A service agent, Frank Burke, had followed Albert in New York City on July 23, and the German left his briefcase on an elevated train. Burke snatched the satchel and ran off with it before Albert came back to the car to retrieve it. Burke took the case to the chief of the Secret Service, William Flynn, who turned it over to Treasury Secretary McAdoo. After conferring with House and Lansing, McAdoo agreed to give the documents to the *New York World*'s editor, Frank Cobb, for publication.

Lansing's willingness to publish these relatively innocuous documents may have been due to his knowledge of the German espionage activity of Franz Rintelen von Kleist on July 22. The Kleist affair was not disclosed, however, although both Lansing and Wilson knew about it.

See July 22, 1915.

August 19, 1915

Two U.S. lives are lost when the British passenger ship *Arabic* is sunk by a German submarine.

The *Arabic* carried 423 passengers and crew and was bound from Liverpool to New York when a German U-boat sank it as it steamed south of the coast of Ireland. There were no explosives on board, as in the case of the *Lusitania,* and most of the 44 casualties died from the torpedo's blast. Two of the 44 were Americans. This event led to increased tension between the United States and Germany, ending in new German concessions regarding future submarine warfare.

See September 1, 1915.

August 19, 1915

The British ship *Baralong* sinks a German submarine that awaits the evacuation of a British merchant ship.

The action of the *Baralong* was a startling example of the dangers that German submarines incurred when they used traditional methods of "cruiser warfare" to attack a merchant ship. Coming on the same day as the sinking of the *Arabic,* this British naval tactic was never effectively reported by U.S. newspapers. Wilson and Lansing learned about the incident on August 26, but they never accused the British of barbarities as they did the Germans.

On August 19, Commander Wegener of the U-27 stopped the British steamer *Nicosian.* Wegener waited

British ambassador to the U.S., Sir Cecil Spring Rice. Library of Congress

for its crew to evacuate their ship in lifeboats. Meanwhile, the British Q-ship *Baralong,* disguised as a tramp steamer and flying the American flag, happened on the scene. The *Baralong* moved to within 100 yards of the U-27, hoisted the British flag, and opened fire on the submarine, sinking it immediately. As crew members of the U-27 swam in the water, the *Baralong* shot as many of them as possible, making the British attack even more inhumane.

Wilson and Lansing were horrified by this incident but had no direct reason to protest. But they did use it to propose stricter measures against armed British merchant ships entering U.S. ports.

See September 11, 1915.

August 19, 1915

Britain's Ambassador to the United States announces that cotton will be placed on the contraband list, but England will purchase cotton to prevent lower prices.

Although the Wilson administration had delayed its vigorous protests about England's March 11 blockade decree because of the *Lusitania,* the British realized that when the *Lusitania* affair ended they would have to answer American protests unless the United States and Germany went to war. By July 1915, the threat of American-German war subsided and in the Southern states cotton interests were urging Wilson to protect their central European market. The British had captured 200,000 bales of cotton since March 11, and the Southern congressmen believed action against Britain was necessary.

To avert Southern displeasure while maintaining British maritime policies, Sir Richard Crawford, the British trade adviser in Washington, suggested a solution to the Foreign Office. The plan as described to Colonel House was (1) to declare cotton as contraband; (2) to purchase cotton at existing or better than market prices to prevent a fall in prices; and (3) to end eventually the blockade order of March 11 in order to comply with established principles of blockade.

Although neither President Wilson nor Secretary Lansing knew officially of the British plan, they were informed about it and gave their indirect approval. In addition, Crawford was allowed to work with William Harding of Alabama, a member of the Federal Reserve Board who specialized in cotton financing; with Benjamin Strong of the New York Federal Reserve Bank; and with Secretary of the Treasury William McAdoo.

The British ambassador, Cecil Spring Rice, now awaited the best opportunity to announce the new British policy. News of the *Arabic* sinking provided an excellent opportunity. While all Americans excepting Southern cotton experts focused on the *Arabic* protests against Germany, the British cotton policy was announced. News of cotton as contraband was published on Friday, August 20, and a few Southerners filed protests. On Monday, August 23, the British purchased cotton on the Liverpool, New York, and New Orleans exchanges, keeping the Friday price of 8 cents a pound. Furthermore, cotton prices rose steadily, increasing to 12 cents on October 15. The German purchasing commission bought 1 million bales on its account, partly helping the price increase.

Administration officials in Washington helped Britain avert a cotton panic. Secretary of the Treasury McAdoo declared the Treasury would loan $30 million to southern banks if necessary. William Harding of the Reserve Board told Southern banks not to raise interest rates because cheap credit would be available for Southern cotton growers.

Therefore, with Washington's concern and aid, the British solved a difficult problem affecting their maritime practices and the U.S. cotton trade. At the same time, they found a method to sever central Europe's cotton supply. Although it cost the British £20 million, their purchases were financed by American banks, thereby adding to the list of loans due to American investors (note: the 1915 exchange rate was one pound = between \$4.65 and \$4.86). These expenses added to Britain's trade deficit, which ran as high as \$75 million per month and caused the Allies a financial crisis.

See August 26, 1915.

August 26, 1915

President Wilson decides that "strict neutrality" on allied war loans requires the U.S. government not to prohibit or favor loans.

Wilson's decision of August 26 reversed the policies he had announced on August 15, 1914, and had qualified to permit "credits" but not loans on October 15, 1914. Although Wilson argued that his view related to "neutrality," both his critical attitude toward Germany during the summer of 1915 and the Allies' financial crisis undoubtedly influenced the president's new position, a position he never publicly announced or defended in person.

The Allies, especially as described by French and British delegates, had reached a monetary crisis within a year after the war began because their purchases of American goods and munitions had caused a trade deficit of \$1 billion by June 30, 1915, and was expected to reach \$2.5 billion by December 31, 1915. During the summer, the British approached American bankers and Secretary of the Treasury McAdoo with proposals for public loans to maintain the stability of their currency and to support additional purchases in America.

In August Britain and France raised £80 million worth of gold to ship to New York with a value of \$400 million in round figures, but different methods to finance future transactions were essential. To obtain better banking terms, the British and U.S. bankers required an indication that President Wilson would not oppose a loan or the revision of Regulation J of the Federal Reserve Board, which prohibited rediscounting of bankers' acceptance notes on the sale of munitions for export.

The Federal Reserve Board regulation of April 2, 1915, was largely in accord with good banking practice and the Wilson administration's views on foreign loans. Led by McAdoo and the pro-British Federal Reserve member from New York, Benjamin Strong, the board reconsidered Regulation J as well as the broader issue of whether or not the Federal Reserve Banks were public institutions whose decisions directly related to government neutrality. By September 7, McAdoo and Strong persuaded the board to rule in favor of Great Britain's wishes. Agreeing that they were not a public institution, the board repealed Regulation J and adopted Regulation R to permit bank rediscounts not to exceed the bank's capital stock and surplus.

Meanwhile on August 26, President Wilson changed his loan concept of October 15, 1914. On advice from both McAdoo and Secretary of State Lansing, Wilson agreed that in case of foreign loans, the government should take "no action either for or against such a transaction." While McAdoo and Lansing referred to their views on "strict neutrality" as meaning nonprohibition of loans, both men emphasized to Wilson that American economic prosperity would suffer if loans were not made. McAdoo wrote: "To maintain our prosperity we must finance it. Otherwise it may stop and that would be disastrous." Lansing agreed, saying it was in the national interest of the United States to permit such loans.

Always cautious about yielding to economic causes for his decisions, Wilson adopted the position that "strict neutrality" required neutrality in private business transactions. When, after August 26, Wilson was pressured to offer statements on behalf of the loans to assure their subscription, he yielded a bit more. On September 14, he permitted Lansing to inform reporters that "highly placed administration officials" did not object to the British loans and believed they were essential to the maintenance of America's foreign trade. Wilson would go no further.

Whether because of Wilson's refusal publicly to promote the loan or the American investors' awareness that such loans were dubious, the loan floated by a J. P. Morgan syndicate of bankers was not popularly accepted. Although the loan of \$500 million for five years had the exorbitant (for 1915) interest rate of 6%, it fell short of its goal by \$187 million. Only \$33 million was sold to ordinary investors. The bond issue was saved from disaster because six companies with large British contracts purchased \$100 million; of these six, DuPont, Bethlehem Steel, and Westinghouse bought $70 million.

The bond failure meant that in the future the Allies became more dependent on short-term loans from U.S. banks or long-term loans with first-class collateral. These measures provided no permanent solution to the Allies' financial problems.

September 1, 1915

Germany's ambassador pledges that submarines will not attack ocean liners without warning and safety to noncombatants unless the ship resists or tries to escape.

Ambassador Bernstorff's pledge resulted from discussions in Washington and Berlin following the sinking of the passenger liner *Arabic* on August 19. Knowing the American public opposed German submarine tactics but wanted to avoid war, President Wilson and Secretary Lansing used an indirect means to seek an accommodation with Germany. On August 22, Wilson's press officer issued a report to newsmen that the White House staff was speculating on what to do if the *Arabic* investigation indicated there was a deliberate German attack. If true, speculation was that the United States would sever relations with Germany. If not true, negotiations were possible.

At the same time, Lansing approved Assistant Secretary Chandler Anderson's suggestion for a meeting with Bernstorff to explain informally that if Germany abandoned submarine war, Great Britain would be the only violator of American neutral rights. Anderson met with Bernstorff at the Ritz Carlton Hotel in New York City and reported to Lansing that the ambassador "saw at once" the advantage of making London appear responsible for illegal acts unless Great Britain ended its war zone.

Following the *Arabic* incident, Bethmann and Foreign Secretary von Jagow decided to tell the Americans about their secret orders of June 1 and 5, which instructed submarine commanders not to torpedo passenger ships without notice and provisions for the safety of the passengers and crew. On August 25, the chancellor informed U.S. Ambassador James W. Gerard about the June orders.

Bethmann and von Jagow also sought Kaiser William II's approval to spare *all* passenger ships from submarine attacks. This proposal aroused the anger of the German admiralty, and von Tirpitz offered to resign as naval secretary. William rejected the Tirpitz resignation but supported Bethmann. Consequently, on August 28, the chancellor gave new orders to the submarine commanders and relayed these terms to Washington. The orders stated that until further notice "all passenger ships can be sunk only after warning and the saving of passengers and crews." In his note to Ambassador Bernstorff, Bethmann instructed him to negotiate as follows:

1. offer Hague arbitration for the *Lusitania* and *Arabic* incidents;
2. passenger liners will be sunk only after warning and saving of lives, provided they do not flee or resist;
3. United States to endeavor to reestablish free seas on the basis of Declaration of London.

Thus, by September 1, although the facts in the *Arabic* case remained too uncertain for a full German response, Bernstorff informed Secretary Lansing about the new submarine policy. Lansing persuaded Bernstorff to violate his orders from Berlin by preparing a statement for publication regarding all aspects of Germany's policy on submarine warfare. Known as the "*Arabic* pledge," Bernstorff's press notice of September 1 asserted that passenger liners would not be sunk without warning and safety for noncombatants. It stated that this policy was the German response to the *Lusitania* notes of the United States, which had been agreed to by the German government before the *Arabic* incident.

Bernstorff's notice pleased both Wilson and the American public. Wilson's diplomacy appeared to have won a major victory for humanity. The Charlotte, North Carolina, *Observer*'s editor wrote that "Wilson was a divinely appointed leader of the people." Indeed, German-American relations verged on their most complete understanding since the submarine campaign began in February 1915.

For new controversy, see October 5, 1915.

September 6, 1915

The Dumba Incident—American newspapers disclose Austrian sabotage plans on U.S. industries as based on documents captured by the British.

Doctor Konstantin Theodor Dumba, the Austro-Hungarian ambassador to America, had outlined proposed plans for Austro-German agents in America. The proposals were being carried to Vienna by

James F. J. Archibald, an American newsman paid by the German embassy, when the Dutch ship *Rotterdam* was stopped and searched by British authorities at Falmouth, England. The British found the documents in Archibald's cabin and arrested him. The documents were sent to Washington, where President Wilson learned about them on September 2. Exactly how the newspapers received copies of the reports is not known.

The most damaging published dispatch was a memorandum by Martin Dienner, a correspondent for the Cleveland *Szabadság (Freedom)*, a Hungarian American newspaper. Dienner suggested plots to cause strikes and walkouts in steel and munitions factories between Bethlehem, Pennsylvania, and Chicago. Paid foreign-language newspapers and union officials would stir worker discontent by asserting that laborers were slaves in industries whose products damaged their homelands. Other documents contained similar plots of pro-German activity in Middle Western states with large central European ethnic populations.

Appearing in newspapers just after Bernstorff's "*Arabic* pledge," the Dumba documents resulted in new anti-German sentiments among many Americans. Although Vienna recalled Ambassador Dumba, this act did not end American rumors about widespread German-Austrian subversive activity in the United States.

September 11, 1915

Secretary of State Lansing requires British armed merchant ships to make bond that their weapons are for defensive use, citing British merchant attacks on German submarines.

The *Baralong* affair of August 19, 1915, made Lansing acutely aware of various stories about British armed merchantmen that sought out and attacked German submarines. International law traditionally permitted armed merchant ships to defend themselves but not to act offensively in unprovoked attacks. On this basis, the United States had since September 1914 allowed British armed merchant ships to use U.S. ports.

On August 25, 1915, Lansing learned that a British steamer with a mounted 4-inch gun was prepared to enter Newport News, Virginia, for a cargo of coal. The secretary informed British Ambassador Cecil Spring Rice and the Virginia port authorities that the gun would have to be removed before the ship, the *Waimana*, left the U.S. port.

When the ambassador refused Lansing's request in a memo of September 10, the secretary on September 11 informed Spring Rice that because British ships had made offensive attacks on German submarines, the ship could not leave port unless Great Britain gave assurances that the *Waimana*'s guns were for defensive use only. To avoid a confrontation with the Americans, the British ordered the *Waimana* to deposit its gun at Newport News and sail unarmed on September 22.

Lansing pursued the matter further, however. He obtained President Wilson's consent to prepare rules that classified armed merchant ships as warships. The rules were to be announced as soon as the *Arabic* case was settled with Germany.

October 5, 1915

America and Germany reach the brink of war on the *Arabic* case; Ambassador Bernstorff's agreement maintains peace.

For the second time in two months, Ambassador Johann von Bernstorff had to exceed his instructions from Berlin to heal relations with the United States.

Following Bernstorff's "*Arabic* pledge" of September 1, German-American problems increased. In addition to the Dumba incident on September 6, the British liner *Hespernian* had been sunk. Although no American lives were lost, the incident caused tension until an investigation disclosed that a sea mine, not a submarine, may have caused the *Hespernian* to sink.

On September 7, more serious difficulties arose regarding the *Arabic* because the German Foreign Office reported its interpretation of the August 19 sinking. The German report disavowed responsibility for the *Arabic* disaster on the basis of testimony by Commander Schneider and the crew of the U-24, the submarine that had torpedoed the *Arabic.* Schneider testified to the German Court of Inquiry that he fired at the *Arabic* only after it turned toward the U-24 in preparation for ramming the submarine. This testimony conflicted with the version given by British officers, but Chancellor Bethmann and Foreign Secretary von Jagow believed they must accept Schneider's statement to uphold German naval

Germany's ambassador to the U.S., Count Johann von Bernstorff, and Hugo Munsterberg (left to right). Library of Congress

honor. (Later, historians would learn that Schneider's testimony differed from the U-24's log book.)

President Wilson and Secretary of State Lansing were concerned that the German report of September 7 also conflicted with previous German orders that submarines could not attack passenger ships as of June 1–5, 1915. Although Lansing wanted to threaten to break relations with Berlin, Wilson asked for confidential talks with Ambassador Bernstorff to attempt to settle the dispute. Lansing found the ambassador to be conciliatory and Bernstorff agreed to communicate America's two demands to Berlin:

1. Germany to disavow the submarine commander's attack. Wilson believed this was a test of good faith that Germany would stop attacks on passenger ships;
2. a clear restatement of the "*Arabic* pledge" of September 1.

Although Bernstorff recommended the German disavowal, the German cabinet of Chancellor Bethmann-Hollweg refused to disagree with the naval officers. Foreign Minister von Jagow informed Bernstorff that the "*Arabic* pledge" was no problem, but the disavowal of the naval commander could not be made. Von Jagow suggested that arbitration by the Hague might be sought. After further urging by Bernstorff, von Jagow's only concession was to inform Schneider that he had not followed explicit instructions. He could not disavow the commander.

Because Wilson and Lansing wished to avoid a break in relations but also understood Bernstorff's dilemma, they found a method to resolve the *Arabic* matter with the ambassador's approval. In order to let Bernstorff know the serious nature of the affair, the White House leaked a news story on October 3 that the German response on the *Arabic* was not acceptable and could bring a rupture in U.S.-German relations. Next, Lansing met with Bernstorff and suggested the proper wording for a German response that would satisfy the Wilson administration and prevent a diplomatic break.

As on September 1, Bernstorff cooperated. The ambassador wrote Lansing a note that clearly reaffirmed the September 1 "*Arabic* pledge." Then the ambassador stated that Germany both regretted and disavowed the attack on the *Arabic,* agreeing to pay an indemnity. Lansing presented Bernstorff's note to newsmen on October 5, informing them that the Germans had satisfied the American requests and that no future submarine attacks on passenger ships could be expected. By disavowing the attack rather than Schneider, von Bernstorff and Lansing avoided war in 1915. Foreign Minister von Jagow did not appreciate Bernstorff's effort and reprimanded him for exceeding his instructions.

William II made one additional secret change in Berlin that also resulted from the *Arabic* incident. The kaiser appointed Admiral Henning von Holtzendorff to replace the more bellicose admiral Gustav Bachmann as chief of the admiralty. On September 18, Holtzendorff agreed with the kaiser that all submarine activity should stop off the west coast of England and in the English Channel. This effectively halted submarine attacks on merchant ships except in the North Sea, an area seldom used by U.S. merchant ships. Germany adhered to this policy until January 31, 1917.

October 14, 1915

Bulgaria and Serbia go to war as the Bulgarians cooperate with an Austro-German campaign to gain control of the Balkans.

The conflict between Bulgaria and Serbia had been pending since August 1914. With the British and

French forces launching the Gallipoli campaign on April 25, 1915, Germany desired to keep Turkey active in the war. British and French forces obtained the consent of Greece to land forces at Salonika, but their efforts to bring Greece and Romania into the war against Austria, Germany, and Bulgaria were not successful. Britain and France declared war on Bulgaria (October 15, 16) as did Russia and Italy (October 19). During the next two months, Vienna and Berlin hoped to assist Bulgaria and Turkey in order to maintain their status in southeastern Europe. Until the British began to withdraw from Gallipoli on December 20, the Germans were also greatly concerned about keeping Greece and Romania out of the war. The British failure at Gallipoli had caused serious problems for the Allies in the Balkans with no positive benefits.

October 19, 1915

The United States recognizes Carranza's authority in Mexico.

American recognition of Carranza was based on the recommendation of a six-nation Latin American conference that had considered Mexican problems. The conference had convened on August 5, 1915, in an attempt to resolve nearly 10 months of the most bloody, destructive period of the Mexican revolutionary era.

By the time American forces left Vera Cruz on November 23, 1914, Carranza had gained control of all Mexican factions except those of Villa and Zapata. Having an overwhelming military advantage, Villa joined his northern forces with Zapata's southern armies, and at Xochimilco the two leaders planned a campaign to defeat Carranza's Constitutionalists. Unfortunately these two fiery generals were not able to solve their own differences, and in the Convention that convened in October 1914, the Villistas and Zapatistas complained bitterly of each general's perfidy and could not agree on reform measures.

Early in January 1915, the military tide turned to favor Carranza. On January 5, a Constitutionalist army under General Obregon struck against one of Villa's armies at Puebla, 70 miles southeast of Mexico City. Hundreds of Villa's men were killed by Obregon's machine guns in the narrow city streets and thousands were captured. Villa retreated north to Chihuahua while Zapata fled to Cuernavaca.

Having moved his headquarters to Vera Cruz, where he could easily be supplied, Carranza withdrew Obregon's forces from the area of Mexico City. While Zapata occupied the traditional capital, Carranza's armies besieged the Valley of Mexico, cutting off all supply routes to Mexico City. Obregon's men damaged the city water system and stopped all trains carrying food and water to relieve the needs of the populace. During the next three months, everyone in Mexico City suffered, including 2,500 Americans and 23,000 foreign residents.

Other foreign governments urged President Wilson to act, but he refused to intervene. When Secretary Bryan warned Carranza that he would be held personally responsible for conditions in Mexico City, Carranza promised to protect Americans as far as possible. Wilson hesitated to intervene until an incident on May 27 convinced him he had to act in some way.

On May 27, a trainload of 600 tons of corn had been sent to Mexico City by the International Relief Committee of Mexico City. Carranza's men stopped the train and seized the corn. On July 2, the president issued a personal appeal to all Mexicans asking them to unite behind some leader who would benefit the people and be accepted by the world powers. If unity could not be achieved, Wilson said, "this Government will be constrained to decide what means should be employed by the United States in order to help Mexico to save herself and serve her people."

Fortunately President Wilson allowed himself room to maneuver. On June 1, Carranza announced he would permit foodstuffs to enter Mexico City. On June 7, Carranza indicated he would welcome Wilson's mediation. The Constitutionalist armies, on June 14, began an offensive to retake Mexico City, thereby ending the siege.

In June and July 1915, Wilson and Lansing hoped to exclude Villa, Zapata, and Carranza as possible rulers of Mexico. In talks beginning August 5, with representatives of Brazil, Chile, Argentina, Bolivia, Uruguay, and Guatemala, Lansing received approval to call a meeting of all Mexican factions to convene a constitutional convention and establish a new government. The six Latin American representatives lauded this proposal because their conservative governments hoped to prevent revolutionary changes in Mexico. The proposal did not succeed, as Carranza rejected the concept of a meeting of all Mexican groups. He desired that Wilson should mediate on behalf of the Constitutionalists.

Although Wilson disliked Carranza's response, the president reconsidered his views regarding Mexico's difficulties. Wilson's new attitude became clarified by August 11, 1915. He now realized that Mexico needed to undergo revolutionary economic and social changes before it established a new constitution. A provisional government under Carranza could establish such reforms prior to the creation of a government in which the people would be ready to participate. Wilson's new policy involved the recognition of Carranza rather than using foreign intervention to set up a convention of a new political group to write a constitution.

Between August 8 and October 9, Wilson's problems were Carranza's insistence on avoiding a foreign conference and gaining the approval of the six Latin American nations to recognize Carranza. The first problem became settled because Carranza's armies decisively defeated Villa. On September 9, General Obregon captured Villa's headquarters at Torreón in northern Mexico, reducing Villa's control to the state of Chihuahua. With Zapata's armies limited to the state of Morelos, Carranza firmly controlled all of Mexico except these two states. Subsequently, he informed Wilson that he would meet with the Latin American representatives only to convince them he deserved recognition.

On October 9, Lansing convinced the six Latin American nations that Carranza's party controlled Mexico. After the other representatives agreed, the conference issued a statement recommending that Carranza's government be given de facto recognition. They agreed to meet again on October 18 to issue a joint decree by which the various American governments would recognize Carranza. This decree was issued on October 19. In addition to the United States and the six other Latin American nations, Colombia and Nicaragua joined in the statement that recognized Carranza's regime.

November 5, 1915

America protests Britain's gross violations of neutral rights.

On July 14, the State Department informed Great Britain that America considered the orders-in-council of March 11 to be illegal. A thorough protest of British practice had been delayed because President Wilson wished to resolve the more immediate issue of German submarine attacks on the *Lusitania* and *Arabic*. Following Bernstorff's "*Arabic* pledge" on September 1, Lansing and his staff prepared a 7,000-word complaint against British practices. President Wilson approved this paper on October 21 and Ambassador Page personally delivered it to Foreign Minister Grey on November 5. It was reported in English and American newspapers on November 8, and in German newspapers on November 5.

Lansing's lengthy report indicted Great Britain as a gross violator of international law. In particular, he claimed British methods of controlling contraband were in error because they detained ships unduly and seized ships with no substantial proof of contraband. Second, the British orders were wholly opposed to proper international conduct. The blockade zones were not effectively maintained, all ships were not treated impartially, and the operations against neutral ports such as Rotterdam were illegal. In addition, by accepting the March 11 order, British prize courts had made themselves unavailable to ships desiring to have neutral principles impartially applied. The United States, Lansing wrote, endeavored to act as a neutral and to uphold just neutral rights of all nonbelligerents. Therefore, it could not condone British practice. The United States urged Britain to change its policies to conform with the "sanction of the civilized world." No threats were made against Britain, but Lansing tried to appeal to the aspirations of humanity in persuading Britain to follow international law.

In sum, Lansing's protest restated Wilson's original ideal that neutrality was impartial toward both belligerents. The German submarine campaign cost human life and had been given priority in 1915. The British also had to realize that their illegal actions would not be condoned.

November 21, 1915

President Wilson approves further action against Germany and Austria regarding the *Lusitania* and the *Ancona* and continued reports of conspiracies in America.

The settlement of the *Arabic* case on October 5, 1915, did not conclude Wilson and Lansing's careful defense of neutral rights against the Central Powers. The *Lusitania* indemnity had not been settled, and the loss of nine American lives when the Italian steamer *Ancona* was sunk on November 7 by an alleged

Austrian submarine brought further problems in November and December 1915.

Lansing and German Ambassador Bernstorff had informally discussed the *Lusitania* indemnity on several occasions since July 1915, and some officials hoped the affair had ended. Germany had not, however, accepted responsibility except in offering to refer the matter to the Hague court. It might have ended there, until the sinking of the *Ancona* on November 7. This Italian passenger ship was sunk by shell fire and a torpedo without warning or without giving the passengers and crew time to escape. The submarine was actually a disguised German submarine, the U-38, and although this fact was not disclosed until after the war, many Americans in 1915 did not differentiate between Austrian and German attacks.

Thus on November 21, Wilson approved a note protesting to Austria as well as a note of inquiry to Germany about a final settlement of the *Lusitania* issue. The note to Austria (sent on December 6, 1915) was so severe it amounted almost to an ultimatum. Lansing asserted that the facts in the *Ancona* case clearly indicated the attack on the passenger ship was "inhumane" and "barbarous."

Regarding the *Lusitania,* Wilson wanted to settle the case on the basis of the *Arabic,* with Germany recognizing the need to pay an indemnity. Lansing had indicated this solution to Bernstorff on November 17 but obtained no response, although a speedy settlement was requested. On November 24, Lansing saw Bernstorff and demanded a quick reply. The German ambassador answered that his report on the November 17 request of Lansing went to Berlin by ordinary mail and was not yet answered by Foreign Minister von Jagow.

Finally on November 21, Wilson and Lansing agreed they should act to counteract the reports of German and Austrian conspiracies in America. For several months, Austro-German conspiracies had been uncovered. In addition to the affairs of Franz Rintelen von Kleist (July 22), Heinrich Albert (August 15), and Konstantin Dumba (September 6), news about an Austrian spy network had been published in October. Based on details provided by a defected Austrian agent, Joseph Goricar, the story disclosed Austrian plots to sabotage American munitions, chemical, and metals industries.

To end rumors of Austrian and German espionage, on December 1 Wilson asked for the recall of the German military and naval attachés, Franz von Papen and Karl Boy Ed, as well as the head of the German Trade Mission, Heinrich Albert. On the same day, the United States asked Austria to recall its ambassador, Konstantin Dumba, and its consul general in New York, Franz von Nuber.

December 7, 1915

Proposals to enlarge the U.S. Army and Navy highlight President Wilson's annual message to Congress.

Using recommendations of the War and Navy Departments, Wilson requested a five-year naval program of $500 million to construct 10 battleships, 6 battle cruisers, 10 cruisers, 50 destroyers, and 100 submarines. The regular army would be increased 40% to 140,000 men, and a reserve force of 400,000 would be recruited to serve two months a year for three years and, thereafter, as a reserve force. While Americans desired to remain neutral, Wilson wanted a force to support American principles and to back up his diplomatic activity.

Although the president had begun to promote preparedness on July 21, 1915, his proposals caused extensive debate in Congress. Democratic leaders divided on the question. Among the chief opponents

Wilson as Preparedness Doctor. Washington Star

were former Secretary of State Bryan and the House majority leader, Claude H. KITCHIN of North Carolina.

1916

February 22, 1916

The House-Grey peace plan is signed.

On December 28, 1915, President Wilson sent his personal adviser, Colonel Edward House, to Europe to explore the possibility of a peace settlement. After visiting Paris and Berlin, House talked in London with Britain's foreign secretary, Sir Edward Grey, and on February 22, Grey and House signed a proposal to obtain a negotiated peace.

House's peace plan was a tactic to allow the United States to support Britain and France more fully. As he outlined to Wilson on October 17, House conjectured that America should intervene in Europe in a way that would bring terms favorable to the Allied powers. To do so, Wilson would propose a peace conference. If the Central Powers refused to attend, the United States could give support to the Allies, perhaps even declaring war on Germany. If the Central Powers accepted, Wilson could arbitrate the conference decisions to favor the Allies. As part of House's proposal, America would make a secret understanding with the Allies so that whatever the German response, the Allies would benefit.

Colonel Edward House, president's special adviser. Library of Congress

Therefore, although House visited Berlin from January 25 to 30, and Paris from February 2 to 8, his intended purpose was to appear impartial prior to his meeting with British officials in London. Beginning on February 9, House met with Grey, Prime Minister H. H. Asquith, and Minister of Munitions David Lloyd George. The British did not fully comprehend House's intention. They suspected he wanted to assist Wilson's political fortunes for the 1916 election. Therefore, while agreeing that Grey could sign the understanding proposed by House, the British added several specific terms such as the transfer of Alsace and Lorraine from Germany back to France. Grey also added the critical exception that Great Britain would need its allies' agreement before joining a conference.

To British and French officials, the House-Grey memo meant little. The Allies believed they would soon defeat Germany and Wilson's interference was unnecessary. Certainly they did not wish to have Wilson arbitrate a peace settlement such as Colonel House suggested. House never comprehended the French-British attitudes. He enthusiastically returned to America to enlist Wilson's support as a peace arbitrator. Wilson approved the House-Grey memorandum on March 7, but no further action resulted from House's project.

March 7, 1916

Wilson's followers defeat the Gore-McLemore resolutions to limit Americans from traveling on armed belligerent ships.

During January and February 1916, a group of congressional Democrats challenged President Wilson's insistence on the right of Americans to travel on belligerent merchant ships without fear of attack. Wilson contended this was an international right of neutrality that Americans must guarantee.

In Congress, two resolutions were proposed to invalidate Wilson's stand. On February 15, Senator Thomas P. Gore of Oklahoma introduced an act to deny passports to Americans who planned to travel on armed belligerent vessels. In the Senate, opponents modified Gore's resolution to justify war against

Germany if an American died when a German submarine sank an armed vessel. In this form, the Senate voted to table the resolution on March 3 by a vote of 68 to 14. The House tabled it on March 7 by a vote of 276 to 142.

A House resolution by Jeff McLemore of Texas issued a more serious challenge. McLemore's resolution requested the president to *warn* Americans not to travel on armed belligerent ships, a proposition that seemed sensible to many Americans. Wilson, however, opposed any restrictions on America's "legal" neutral rights. Therefore, the president on February 24 published a letter he had sent to Senator William Stone in which he placed the burden on belligerents to be wary of neutral rights. To pass McLemore's resolution, Wilson said, would infringe on America's honor to uphold law and civilization.

> Once accept a single abatement of right, and many other humiliations would certainly follow, and the whole fine fabric of international law might crumble under our hands piece by piece. What we are contending for is of the very essence of the things that made America a sovereign nation. She cannot yield them without conceding her own impotency as a nation, and making virtual surrender of her independent position among the nations of the world.

With the aid of loyal Democrats, Wilson's position was upheld. The McLemore resolution lost in the Senate by a vote of 68 to 14, and in the House on March 7 by a vote of 275 to 135.

Headquarters of the U.S. forces in Colonia Dublan, Mexico. General John J. Pershing with his aide, Lt. Collins. National Archives

March 15, 1916

Mexican border incidents cause Wilson to send U.S. Army forces into northern Mexico to fight Villa.

In September 1915, Carranza's forces had gained control of northern Mexico except for the state of Chihuahua. General Villa began conducting bandit-style raids from his Sierra Madre hideouts, including raids into the United States.

Incidents in 1916 led President Wilson to order U.S. army forces to pursue and defeat Villa. On January 10, Villa's men captured a train carrying 15 American mining engineers whom Carranza and Mexican mine operators had brought in to reopen mines. Villa's men massacred the Americans. Although congressional resolutions were introduced asking Wilson to intervene, the president accepted Carranza's promise to punish the perpetrators of the crime. They were never punished, however.

On March 9, a second incident impelled Wilson to act. Crossing the American border, Villa's soldiers raided the town of Columbus, New Mexico. They shot up the town, killing 17 Americans. With congressional consent, Wilson ordered General John J. Pershing to lead a 15,000-man expeditionary force against Villa and mobilized 150,000 militia on the southern border. Pershing's men tracked Villa's forces across the Chihuahua desert but never caught them. Although Wilson asked Carranza to join in a cooperative campaign against Villa, the Mexican leader refused, claiming it was an internal matter for Mexican forces to handle.

On May 5, raids by Villa at Glen Springs and Boquilla, Texas, led to another invasion of Mexico by Pershing's men. Despite Carranza's objections, 8,000 American soldiers crossed into Mexico. This time there was a clash with Carranza's army at Carrizal. Fortunately, serious trouble was prevented because on June 25, Carranza released 17 American prisoners captured during the clash at Carrizal. Nevertheless, Pershing's army remained in Mexico to police the border until early 1917.

See February 5, 1917.

April 24, 1916

The Easter Rebellion in Ireland.

Disappointed that the Irish Home Rule Bill had been delayed, Irish radicals led by Sir Roger Casement started a new rebellion on September 18, 1914. Casement had been smuggled from exile into Ireland by a German submarine on April 20. Soon after, a week of fighting resulted before British troops suppressed the rebels. Casement and several other Irish leaders were tried and executed on August 3, 1916. Casement's execution had been protested by Irish-Americans who persuaded the U.S. Senate on July 29 to adopt a resolution appealing to England for clemency for Casement.

May 4, 1916

The *Sussex* pledge—Germany agrees not to permit submarines to attack any ships without warning.

The Germans finally abandoned their policy of submarine attacks by stealth as a consequence of further American protests following the sinking of the *Sussex* on March 24, 1915.

The *Sussex* was a French cross-channel steamer that was attacked and sunk by the German submarine U-29. Twenty-five Americans were on board the vessel and four were injured by the torpedo explosion. At least four other British merchant ships had been torpedoed during March 1915, although U.S. protests centered on the *Sussex*.

While Lansing advocated the threat of a diplomatic break with Germany, President Wilson softened the secretary's proposal and offered Germany the alternative of stopping all attacks without warning the intended victim ship. In a note sent to Germany on April 18, Wilson asked for the immediate declaration of Germany's intentions. To reinforce his views on the seriousness of this issue, Wilson delivered a special message to Congress on April 18. His speech asserted that America's rights as a nation and its sense of duty to all neutrals required that we "take this stand now with the utmost solemnity and firmness. I have taken it, and taken it in the confidence that it will meet with your approval and support."

In Berlin, Chancellor Bethmann was once again able to persuade the emperor to place further restrictions on German submarine warfare. Supported by the naval chief of staff, Admiral Holtzendorff, Bethmann convinced William II that keeping peace with America was more vital than the attacks on English shipping. In the "*Sussex* pledge," however, Bethmann included a significant caveat that President Wilson played down. The German note of May 4 agreed to abandon all attacks without warnings, but, the note added, the Germans expected that the United States would compel the British also to observe international law. If these efforts failed, the Germans reserved their liberty for future action.

Four days later, on May 8, a second note made specific explanations of Germany's action in the *Sussex* case. The Germans stated that the submarine commander made a mistake and was being punished. Furthermore, they offered to make a suitable indemnity for damages to Americans.

On May 8, Secretary Lansing sent a message to Berlin saying that Wilson accepted the German pledge to stop all attacks without prior warning. Wilson ignored the exception cited by the Germans but said he presumed that the German note did not really mean what it said. Rather, Wilson asserted, "Responsibility in such matters is single, not joint; absolute, not relative." Therefore, while Germany appeared to yield to Wilson, the German government could not ignore the relations between Washington and London.

May 9, 1916

The Sykes-Picot Agreement divides the Ottoman Empire into British and French "spheres of influence."

Since March 1915, British and French diplomats had considered the future of the Arab areas following their expected defeat of the Ottoman Empire. The secret agreement of May 9 gave Britain spheres in Mesopotamia, Syria, and the ports of Haifa and Acre. France received the coastal strip of Syria (later Lebanon), the Adana vilayet, Cilicia, and southern

Kurdistan with Kharput. Palestine would be under an international administration. Later, on April 21, 1917, Italy accepted the Sykes-Picot agreement in exchange for concessions in Adalia and Smyrna. Many of the agreements on the Near East were incompatible with one another and with British-French promises to Arab chiefs.

May 27, 1916

Wilson proposes a new diplomacy, a new world order, a major role for the United States in world affairs: his speech to a session of the league to enforce peace.

Following discussions that led to the House-Grey memorandum of February 22, 1916, the president thought much about conducting a conference to "end the quarrel" in Europe and establish a method to end militarism in the future. He and Colonel House had asked British Foreign Secretary Grey if the Allies were ready for a call to a peace conference, but Grey said the time was not right. Wilson believed the time should be soon, and while omitting a call to a peace conference in Europe, his speech of May 27 proposed an ideal process for finding a new diplomatic method for solving future "quarrels" and maintaining freedom of the seas.

Putting his sentiments into his May 27 speech, Wilson proposed not only a new diplomacy but also a future world order in which the United States would forsake its outmoded isolationism and become a leader in international affairs based on legality and a world organization. Americans, Wilson said, were no longer "disconnected lookers-on" but participants "in the life of the world. The interests of all nations are our own also. We are partners with the rest. What affects mankind is inevitably our affair as well as the affair of the nations of Europe and Asia."

Next, Wilson outlined fundamentals of world order and how to establish it. The three fundamental beliefs of Americans are (1) the right to self-government; (2) the same rights for small as for large nations; and (3) the right to have peace from aggression and disregard of the rights of peoples and nations. To effect these principles, Wilson believed the peace movement should proceed as follows: first, to allow current belligerents to settle their own immediate interests, for "we are in no sense or degree parties to the present quarrel"; second, to form a "universal association of nations" to secure free seas and to prevent wars begun without "full submission of the causes to the opinion of the world." He concluded: "God grant that the dawn of that day of frank dealing and of settled peace, concord, and cooperation may be near at hand!"

June 3, 1916

Congress authorizes the National Defense Act.

This was the first major result of Wilson's request for preparedness during his December 1915 message to Congress. It provided for a regular army of 175,000 men to be enlarged to 223,000 in five years. In addition, it approved a National Guard of 450,000 men; established Reserve Officer Training Corps at universities, colleges, and military camps; and provided for industrial preparedness.

Later, on August 29, Congress established a Council of National Defense under the chairmanship of Secretary of War Newton Baker. It prepared plans covering transportation, munitions, labor, raw materials, supplies, and other wartime requisites.

June 16, 1916

Wilson is nominated for a second term on a platform favoring internationalism abroad and a bold, progressive social program at home.

Wilson wrote the international sections of the Democratic platform. It stated that America had to use its power not only to be safe at home but to "secure its just interests throughout the world, both for this end and in the interests of humanity, to assist the world in securing settled peace and justice." The platform advocated membership in an association of nations to maintain peace and the freedom of the seas and a revenue tariff qualified to meet changing world conditions.

During the national convention, the Democrats emphasized that Wilson kept the nation out of war but defended neutral rights and maintained strict neutrality. The keynote address of Governor Martin H. Glynn roused the delegates by reciting the honorable tradition by which Washington, Adams, Jefferson, and Wilson defended neutral rights but refused to go to war. But, Glynn concluded, neutral rights and no war did not mean being unprepared to fight and die for the flag "when Reason primes the rifle, when Honor draws the sword, when Justice breathes a blessing on the standards they hold."

In addition to elating and exhausting the delegates, Glynn's rhetoric showed a willingness to fight when necessary. This accorded with Wilson's concepts: to defend neutrality and use diplomacy to protect American rights but to be prepared to fight if those rights were ignored or forgotten by another nation.

Even William Jennings Bryan supported Wilson in 1916. Although scorned by some Democrats in 1915, he returned to the party majority in 1916, praising Wilson's reform legislation and his labors for peace. Although often differing with Wilson, Bryan said, "I join with the American people in thanking God that we have a President who does not want this nation plunged into this war." Thus, Germany's "*Sussex* pledge" served Wilson well during the convention and the campaign of 1916.

June 16, 1916

China's Yüan Shih-K'ai dies: an era of "warlordism" begins in China.

During the two years of his military dictatorship after gaining full power on May 1, 1914, Yüan dissipated his position and brought on a series of local military uprisings. Most of Yüan's failure resulted from his attempt to create his family as the imperial inheritor of the Ch'ing dynasty. Throughout 1915, he staged a monarchical movement of "people's petitions" that solicited his enthronement. After several appropriate hesitations, he finally consented to become emperor and planned ceremonies to begin in 1916.

His attempt to claim the Chinese mandate of heaven failed. Japan rallied the Western powers, who advised Yüan not to become emperor. But the critical factor for his failure was the development of local military opposition led by Liang Ch'i-ch'ao. On December 25, 1915, Liang and his followers declared the independence of Yunnan Province. Yüan sent his army to suppress the rebellion. But as he did so, other military officers declared their opposition to Yüan and denounced his imperial claims. By June 16, eight southern and western provinces turned against Yüan as the local warlords took control.

Yüan first postponed and later renounced his enthronement, but his action was too late. He died a broken man and China's politics became decentralized into warlord factions during the next 10 years. The Chinese transition from an outmoded imperial regime to a modern political state entered a stage of pronounced nationalism without an accepted political philosophy to rally the backing of all Chinese people. While the fiction of a central power was maintained in Peking and supported by the Western treaty powers, Chinese politics reached their nadir of authority during the warlord period.

August 4, 1916

By treaty, Denmark cedes the Virgin Islands to the United States for $25 million.

There had been previous U.S.-Danish discussions for the sale of the Virgin Islands that were never carried to completion. In 1902 a treaty had failed because Denmark did not ratify the agreement. Therefore, in March 1915, the U.S. Minister in Copenhagen, Maurice Francis Egan, proposed new negotiations emphasizing that Germany might take over Denmark and use its Caribbean islands for a naval base. Lansing frankly told the Danish minister in Washington that the United States could not permit the transfer of the islands to another power, convincing him that their sale to the United States was proper.

In 1902, the Danish treaty had offered the islands for $5 million; in 1915, the Danes asked for $27 million. Wilson did not wish to bargain, however, because the U.S. navy envisioned the islands as an excellent naval base. Thus, when Denmark reduced the price by $2 million, an agreement was reached and a treaty signed on August 4. The United States ratified the treaty on September 7, the Danes in December 1916. America accepted transfer of the islands on March 31, 1917.

August 19, 1916

The Jones Bill grants independence to the Philippines when they establish a "stable government" but at no definite time.

Since 1912, the American consensus was that the Philippines should be given independence. The issue became not if but when and how to grant independence.

In 1912, Representative William A. Jones of Virginia introduced legislation to create a Philippine government and grant independence in eight years. Because President Taft believed the Filipinos were not prepared to "keep order," his Senate supporters blocked the Jones bill.

Knowing that President Wilson favored Philippine independence, Jones introduced a new bill in Congress in 1913. The second bill did not specify a certain date largely because of the intense opposition of American Roman Catholics who held concerns for the safety of the church and its property in the islands. In Manila alone the Catholic Church held $50 million worth of property. Philippine nationalists opposed church landholdings and wanted to nationalize these lands.

During the lengthy congressional debate on the Jones bill, Senator James P. Clarke of Arkansas introduced an amendment to free the Philippines in not less than two nor more than four years. Clarke represented American sugar interests that hoped to restrict Philippine sugar imports. The Catholic Church joined former President Taft, who opposed the Clarke amendment because he said the United States had a "duty" to introduce democracy in the island and four years was not sufficient time to accomplish that task. Eventually the Clarke amendment passed the Senate after Vice President Thomas R. Marshall broke a 41-41 tie vote. But the measure failed in the House because 30 Democrats voted against the amendment.

Without Clarke's time definition, the Jones bill passed Congress on August 19, 1916. It had little immediate effect in the Philippines but persuaded congressmen not to spend money for naval and military bases in the islands. The Jones act also provided an elective senate for the islands and established as the executive of the islands a governor-general, to be appointed by the president.

August 29, 1916

Congress approves the Naval Expansion Bill of 1916.

President Wilson had requested a naval building program in his annual message of 1915. This act authorized the expenditure of $91.2 million for 156 ships by July 1, 1919. The construction program included 10 battleships, 6 battle cruisers, 60 destroyers and torpedo boats, and 67 submarines. When completed, the United States would have what naval publicists called a navy "second to none."

The navy's planning had not yet considered the effects of German submarine warfare in 1914–1915. Its long-range program called for the additional building of battleships and battle cruisers after 1919, not for sufficient destroyers to challenge enemy submarines.

September 7–8, 1916

Congress passes measures to retaliate against British commerce.

Passed as amendments to the Shipping Bill (September 7) and Revenue Act (September 8), Congress took general measures to counteract new British limits on U.S. commerce.

On July 18, the British published a blacklist of 87 U.S. and 350 Latin American firms that allegedly traded with the Central Powers. British subjects were told not to do any business, direct or indirect, with these firms. Shortly before, on June 29, the British Ministry of Blockade announced that Britain would not allow transit of American tobacco for reexport to Germany or Austria except that paid for before August 4, 1916.

These two British measures, together with news that the British and French censored American mail that crossed the ocean and that the British had executed Irish leaders from the Easter Rebellion, caused extensive anti-British emotions in the United States by August 1916. As a result, a series of amendments were proposed in Congress to retaliate against the British. The two important amendments passed were (1) a bill authorizing the president to deny the use of U.S. ports to ships of nations denying ordinary privileges to Americans, an amendment also permitting the president to use armed force if necessary to enforce the law; and (2) a bill to prohibit the importation of any or all products from a country that discriminated against the products of American soil or industry or kept them from going to other countries in contravention of international law.

The one failure of the amendments was that they were not mandatory on the president. Consequently, Wilson hoped the threat of the retaliation would suffice. He told Lansing that he would wait until after the November election and then, if necessary, consider enforcing the retaliatory acts. The British also made some concessions by not strictly enforcing their measures and thereby prevented a serious conflict during the fall of 1916.

October 20, 1916

The German emperor requests President Wilson to take steps to mediate peace arrangements.

Kaiser William II sent Wilson a personal letter regarding a peace agreement. William wrote that in April Wilson had informed him the United States intended to offer its good offices to seek peace and he had expected it would be "far advanced towards the end of this year." He pointed out that the status of the war was such that Germany might be required to "regain the freedom of action that it has reserved to itself in the note of May 4th" unless some peace effort were soon undertaken. What the kaiser meant, of course, was that Germany might have to renew its restricted submarine warfare.

The kaiser and Chancellor Bethmann were uncertain how long they could continue to restrain the demands of the German General Staff for renewal of sub warfare. At Pless on August 31, they had stalled their military advisers against bringing America into the war. General Falkenhayn, who favored aggressive submarine war, had been replaced as chief of staff by General Paul von Hindenburg, who previously commanded the armies on the eastern front. With Hindenburg's consent the navy's desire for submarine war was overridden. However, Chancellor Bethmann had agreed that when the military situation in Romania improved or the status of the war changed, Hindenburg could call for a reconsideration of the submarine issue. In addition, William II agreed that the submarines could aggressively attack all shipping by using accepted warning *before* shooting tactics. An order to this effect published on October 15 resulted in a rapid increase in Germany's destruction of Allied shipping during the next month, as well as some incidents that required Wilson to protest.

In addition to the pressure from the General Staff, Bethmann and the emperor feared that if Wilson lost the November election, any hope for U.S. mediation would end. Wilson's Republican opponents were strongly pro-Allied and would be likely to side with the Allies. Consequently, the kaiser's letter to Wilson on October 20, although not directly saying so, hoped that Wilson would use the peace mediation to aid his presidential campaign and be offered before the election of November 7.

Wilson believed that the peace mediation should not be tied to the election campaign. Therefore, both before and after he received the kaiser's note, he had told Colonel House to inform Ambassador Bernstorff that no peace effort could be undertaken until, and unless, he were reelected. This disappointed Chancellor Bethmann, who began preparation for a separate German peace proposal.

The other part of the kaiser's note seemed generally to have been discounted by Wilson in October 1916, that is, William's reference to the excepting clause that Germany had included in its May 4 "*Sussex* pledge." This clause said that if Britain did not change its methods of sea war, the Germans reserved the right to reconsider their pledge. The October 20 letter sought to recall the attention of the Americans to this clause, a section that Wilson did not acknowledge in May or October.

See December 12, 1916, and December 18, 1916.

November 7, 1916

President Wilson is reelected in a close vote.

The 1916 campaign was hotly contested because the Republicans had healed their division of 1912. Theodore Roosevelt declined to run as the Progressive Party candidate but persuaded the Party's National Committee to unite around Charles Evans Hughes. Unfortunately, Hughes and the Republican Party had a lackluster platform and campaign. As a moderate progressive, Hughes hesitated to denounce Wilson's legislative acts, but he also feared advocating the anti-progressive views of the old guard Republicans. Although Theodore Roosevelt backed Hughes and urged him to come out in favor of war or a stronger anti-German policy, Hughes preferred the strict neutrality that Wilson followed. For many commentators on the campaign, Hughes lost more votes than he gained between July and November.

Therefore, Wilson's "He Kept Us Out of War" slogan, plus his willingness to prepare to fight if necessary, satisfied American voters. The final vote was close, the victory eventually depending on the California vote. Wilson won California by 3,773 votes and the election by 277 electoral votes to 254 for Hughes.

November 21, 1916

Austria's Emperor Francis Joseph I dies and is succeeded by the Emperor Charles.

The new emperor was known to advocate an end to the war, and his new foreign minister, Count Ottokar Czernin, undertook secret discussions regarding a separate peace in 1917 and 1918. These discussions irritated Berlin's officials but never succeeded.

November 27, 1916

With Wilson's consent, the Federal Reserve Board cautions member banks against investments in foreign short-term treasury bills. This resulted from evidence of British-French financial problems.

This federal reserve notice opposed suggestions that U.S. banks *accept and renew* without collateral short-term loans from Britain and France. It resulted in the Wall Street market sell-off of allied bonds and American war stocks and caused Great Britain to consider—but reject—going off the gold standard.

The impetus for this board notice was a meeting on November 18, 1916, during which Henry P. Davison of the House of Morgan explained the financial difficulties of France and England and suggested that American banks be urged to buy short-term Allied treasury notes that could be renewed again and again without repayment immediately. Davison also talked with President Wilson, who tried to be neutral regarding the Allies' financial problems. In addition, the Federal Reserve Board's governor, W. P. G. Harding, believed there was danger of a creditor's becoming too deeply involved with one debtor and expressed his concerns to Secretary of State Lansing and President Wilson. The president shared Harding's concern and suggested that Harding warn U.S. banks against unsecured loans during a war situation.

Whether or not Wilson and Lansing knew exactly how depleted British-French finances were by November 1916 is not certain. During October meetings in England, the dependence of these nations on American funds and strategic goods became clear to some U.S. financiers. At a Joint Anglo-French Financial Committee meeting between October 3 and 10, J. P. Morgan Jr. and his associate, Henry Davison, learned that French gold and dollar resources were totally exhausted and France needed £40–50 million during the next six months. Britain's situation was better because it held a secret gold reserve of £100 million, but by March 31, 1917, it wanted U.S. banks to loan $1.5 billion, a sum Morgan and Davison thought would be difficult to raise.

The British treasury gave the prime minister a gloomy report in October but believed that America's stake in the Allies' success required the United States to help the Allies. The British economist John Maynard Keynes stated in the treasury's report that, while Britain previously obtained two-fifths of its war funding in North America, it would have to raise four-fifths of its money in the United States in the future from unsecured public loans. While Keynes concluded that the British must avoid "any form of reprisal or active irritation" of the U.S. public, Foreign Minister Edward Grey contended that, while America should be treated with "greater civility," the British should make no concessions on any matter of principle. The United States, he said, would not proceed to extremes with Britain, but was "so dependent upon the British Empire, both as a market for American goods, on which, in present conditions, American prosperity depends, and also as a source of raw materials indispensable to American industry" that it would be "inexpedient" for Washington to change its commercial relations with Great Britain.

For British officials, the Federal Reserve notice resulted in only temporary alarm. On December 1, they withdrew their treasury bills from sale, but Ambassador Spring Rice reported to London that the State Department would not promote the Federal Reserve's warning, and that American irritations with England were only minor compared with what they could do to damage the Allies if they really chose to do so.

November 29, 1916

America institutes the full military occupation of Santo Domingo.

As authorized by President Wilson, Captain Harry S. Knapp of the U.S. navy proclaimed military control of the Republic of Santo Domingo, placing civilian officials and courts under control of the U.S. military governor. This action culminated the attempt of the "Wilson Plan" to bring constitutional democracy to the Dominican people. By the fall of 1916, Wilson's plan had not operated, causing American military and diplomatic officials to recommend military control as "the least of the evils in sight in this very perplexing situation." Wilson's plan of 1914 had overlooked the historical traditions in Santo Domingo that, like all heirs of the Spanish Empire, had no long-term experience of democracy. Consequently, U.S. intervention in 1913–1914 created as many problems as it solved. President Juan Jiménez had been elected in December 1914, but the Dominicans soon came to consider him a puppet of the United States, an evaluation that aided the opponents of Jiménez.

At least twice in 1915, Secretary of State Bryan acted to uphold Jiménez. Early that year, General Desiderio Arias, who had been an ally of Jiménez, resigned because U.S. officials had limited his authority as minister of war. When Arias threatened to rebel, Bryan instructed the president to accept his resignation because, if Arias caused trouble, America would exile him. On February 13, Bryan reinforced his promise by sending a gunboat to put down an uprising at Puerto Plata.

In April 1915, Bryan ordered Jiménez to permit Americans to clean up the Dominican finances. The U.S. State Department's Charles M. Johnson was given charge of the national revenues and the Department of Public Works. When the Dominican congress voted to remove Johnson and to impeach Jiménez, Bryan again intervened. He ordered Jiménez to ignore Congress because American troops would punish any "troublemakers." Jiménez became so unpopular that he asked to resign, but Bryan would not let him do so.

During the summer of 1915, Secretary of State Lansing undertook a different program for Santo Domingo. He sent a new minister to the island, William W. Russell, with instructions to give the American adviser, Johnson, complete control of the treasury and to place the native constabulary under an American commander. Realizing the Dominican congress would object, Lansing stated that the plan was an American right under terms of the U.S.-Dominican convention of 1907, an exaggerated extension of the treaty. Nevertheless, when Russell announced the plan on November 19, 1915, protests arose throughout Santo Domingo. Even Jiménez refused to accept it, leading President Wilson to order the delay of the plan to a more propitious moment.

By early 1916, a revolution seemed imminent. It began in April when General Arias proclaimed control of the Dominican army, and congress impeached Jiménez for violating the constitution. Jiménez rallied some loyal troops and, on May 5, 1916, U.S. Marines under Commander W. S. Crowley landed to help the president. Jiménez resigned on May 15 when Admiral William B. Caperton, who had pacified Haiti in August 1915, arrived to deal with General Arias. By July, nearly 2,000 marines and sailors occupied the strategic centers of Santo Domingo. General Arias surrendered, so there was little bloodshed.

Landing marines was easy; establishing economic and political order was difficult. During the next six months, Admiral Caperton and Minister Russell constantly argued with the Dominican congress and its presidential selection, Francisco Henriquez y Carvajal. On one occasion Russell arrested seven senators but released them because the State Department said that was going too far. More critically, neither the president nor congress would accept Lansing's plan of 1915.

On October 31, 1916, all U.S. officials responsible for Dominican policy met in Washington and recommended that the only solution was "the declaration of martial law and placing Santo Domingo under military occupation." Because Secretary of State Lansing agreed, President Wilson had little recourse except to concur with the unified decision of all his advisers. The order was sent to Captain Knapp, who issued the proclamation of military occupation in Santo Domingo on November 29. The occupation lasted until 1924.

See August 27, 1914, and July 12, 1924.

December 12, 1916

The German chancellor asks President Wilson to transmit Germany's peace offer to the belligerent powers.

Chancellor Bethmann had waited since October 20 for President Wilson to make a peace proposal. By the end of November, he doubted whether the president would ever act and therefore took independent action. During high-level discussions in Germany on December 6, Bethmann obtained the consent of Kaiser William and the General Staff to offer a peace proposal on one condition. The condition was that if he failed, the German navy would begin unlimited operations against armed merchant ships and consider a full-scale, unrestricted submarine campaign beginning at the end of January 1917.

Although Bethmann could not publicly report the condition imposed on him, he prepared a proposal to transmit through President Wilson. In his note to the president, Bethmann said he lamented the war but if the Allies rejected his peace offer, the Central Powers would finally win in a prolonged war. He asked that negotiations to end the war begin as soon as possible. He also sent similar requests to the Spanish and Swiss governments.

On December 14, President Wilson transmitted Bethmann's note to the Allied governments, informing them that he would be interested in learning their response. Wilson also indicated that entirely separate from the German proposal, he had a proposal that he would send to the Allies and to Germany on December 18, 1916.

December 18, 1916

President Wilson asks all belligerent nations to state their peace objectives for he believes they are generally similar and may result in peace negotiations.

Although Wilson and Colonel House had hoped to get peace negotiations started in May 1916, they delayed further plans once Wilson had been renominated for president in June 1916. The president did not want to make the matter a political issue during his reelection campaign.

Their May 1916 efforts disclosed to Wilson and House that the February 22 House-Grey memorandum was meaningless to the French and British. Britain's Foreign Minister Grey thought he had informed House of the difficulty they would have with the president's plan to interpose mediation. Perhaps because the plans made House overly enthusiastic, he did not understand this clearly until May 12, when he and Wilson conferred with Grey about a peace session. The French and British wanted to crush Germany and not return to a status quo ante bellum such as Wilson suggested.

After May 1916, Wilson realized that Britain and France were the major obstacles to his peace plans. They both wished to destroy all future German military threats and believed their planned 1916 offensive would counter German advantages. On September 28, Lloyd George, who would replace Asquith as prime minister on December 4, 1916, told a *New York Times* reporter that he had no use for neutrals and humanitarians who might "butt in" because "the fight must be to the finish—to a knockout." According to the British leader, "Peace now or at any time before the final and complete elimination of this German menace is unthinkable."

Despite Lloyd George's views, Wilson believed an attempt at mediation should be made. The Allied offensive on Verdun and the Somme in the fall of 1916 had not defeated the Germans. By November 18, the Somme attack ended after a seven-mile advance, and the Verdun struggle had gained only two miles. In addition, Wilson feared that if mediation failed, German submarine warfare might begin at any time. Germany's aggressive U-boat attacks during the fall of 1916 had already caused difficulties. On October 28, six Americans died when the British steamer *Marina* was torpedoed without warning, and on November 6 an unarmed liner, the *Arabia,* was sunk without warning although no Americans were on board.

To give his peace proposal a chance, the president protested but played down the attacks on the *Marina* and *Arabia.* Finally, Bethmann's December 12 note prompted Wilson to send the peace plea he had prepared to all belligerents on December 18, emphasizing that he did not offer mediation but urged each belligerent to state its war objectives. Wilson thought every warring power sought similar goals. Each wanted to protect weak nations, to secure its future peace, to end rival alliances, and to consider a "league of nations." Once the present issues of war ended, steps for future peace could begin. Neutrals as well as belligerents felt the terror of the war. Therefore, if each leader would state his war objectives in general terms, the way would be paved for a conference to resolve the details of the proposals. Wilson asked all leaders to be governed by their noble aims because their particular problems could then be settled according to those objectives.

December 26, 1916

Germany responds to Wilson's peace plea: (1) It will cooperate and suggest a meeting of belligerent delegates at a neutral area; (2) It cannot state peace terms at this time.

The German response to Wilson was short. It thanked the president for his "noble initiative" and offered to cooperate when the time for ending the war was reached. The Germans did not state their peace terms but agreed to meet immediately with delegates of other belligerent states at some neutral place in Europe. An interesting sidelight to Germany's message was a comment sent to Ambassador Bernstorff by German Foreign Secretary Arthur Zimmerman. He informed Bernstorff that he wished to meet in Europe to avoid the "experiences of Portsmouth," which "teach us that American indiscreetness and intermeddling makes it impossible adequately to conduct negotiations." The kaiser definitely did not want to have the president present at negotiating sessions. The Portsmouth reference was, of course, to Theodore Roosevelt's handling of the Russo-Japanese negotiations in 1905.

See August 9, 1905.

1917

January 10, 1917

The allied powers' response to Wilson's request offers peace terms so rigid they could only be won by further war.

The Allied response took some time to prepare because the Allies disliked Wilson's proposal but were not certain how to answer. Fortunately, Secretary of State Lansing offered them advice, which they closely followed in preparing their report. Without Wilson's knowledge (although the president became suspicious of the secretary at this time), Lansing wanted the Allies to understand that the U.S. note of December 18 was not a pro-German document.

Lansing had irritated the president on December 21 because he commented to newsmen about Wilson's proposal. The secretary told reporters that the United States wished to know each belligerent's war aims because America was "drawing nearer the verge of war." It was not a "peace note" but was designed "to get the belligerents to define the end for which they are fighting." Objecting strongly to Lansing's statement, Wilson forced him to call the reporters to clarify his words. Lansing added the assertion that America remained neutral but as a neutral nation wished to understand the peace objectives of the belligerents.

Soon after, Lansing conferred with British Ambassador Spring Rice and French Ambassador Jusserand and advised them regarding Wilson's December 18 note. America, he said, preferred the Allied war aims, understanding the Allies' desire to rectify certain European boundaries at Germany's expense. The Allies could reasonably demand changes for Alsace and Lorraine, a liberated Balkans and Poland, transferring Trentino to Italy, and expelling Turkey from southeastern Europe.

Relieved by Lansing's encouraging understanding, Allied representatives met in London to prepare a joint response to Wilson. Their January 10 note described the Central Powers' aggressive action in starting the war in 1914. Then they stated specific peace terms such as Lansing had proposed. Finally, they concluded that their hope was to reorganize Europe on a just basis to preserve future peace there.

The Allied terms required a military victory. Germany had specific terms as well, but they were not given in Germany's December 28 reply. On January 15, Ambassador Bernstorff stated certain German aims during a conversation with Colonel House. These included an independent Poland and Lithuania, unity of Serbia and Montenegro, annexing Liege and regions near Metz, Austrian rights in the Balkans, and negotiations to protect Belgium in future incidents. These German aims also required a prolonged war. By the time Bernstorff stated them to House, the German emperor had agreed to the renewal of unrestricted submarine war.

See January 31, 1917.

January 22, 1917

President Wilson's "peace without victory" speech outlines future U.S. concerns for collective security.

In order to launch an appeal to the people of Europe to protest their leaders' prolongation of the war and to stimulate their desire for peace now and in the future, Wilson addressed the U.S. Senate on the subject of a future league to maintain peace. His speech was, therefore, sent in advance to U.S. embassies in Europe so that it could be decoded, translated, and given to news reporters immediately after it was delivered to the Senate.

Wilson's speech was also another attempt to make Americans aware of their duty to become involved in maintaining a peaceful world. For peace to be achieved, Wilson argued, the present war had to be a "peace without victory." Neither belligerent alliance should first crush its enemies. "Only a peace between equals can last, only a peace that very principle of which is equality and a common participation in a common benefit."

Again outlining concepts of a "new diplomacy," Wilson argued that the present war cannot just be for a new balance of power. "There must be, not a balance of power, but a community of power; not organized rivalries, but an organized common peace." "Peace without victory" was the heart of Wilson's proposal. Victory would result in an imposed peace, a humiliation to the loser. Such a peace, Wilson said, was built on quicksand rather than on the sound foundation of equality and justice.

Finally, Wilson cited some specific essentials for a durable peace: self-determination, freedom of the seas, no alliances, government by the consent of the governed, and the moderation of armaments. These were principles accepted by forward-looking men and women everywhere, Wilson asserted. "They are the principles of mankind and must prevail."

One immediate consequence of Wilson's speech was opposition from senators who denounced collective security. On January 25, Senator William Borah of Idaho introduced a Senate resolution stating that the United States must follow Washington and Jefferson's principle of nonparticipation in European politics. Although Borah's resolution was tabled on January 30, it inspired Senator Henry Cabot Lodge to oppose an association of nations. Previously Lodge had concurred with Theodore Roosevelt and Elihu Root in supporting a league. Now, however, Lodge changed his opinion. On February 1, he told the Senate that second thoughts on a league convinced him that joining such an organization would sacrifice America's national sovereignty. Thus, he opposed Wilson's plan to combine a postwar league of nations and a peace without victory. The views of these two partisan senators would offer Wilson greater problems in 1919 and 1920.

January 31, 1917

Germany's Ambassador Bernstorff announces Germany will renew unrestricted submarine warfare on February 1, 1917.

The kaiser's decision to renew full-scale submarine attacks had been made on January 9. On January 31, Bernstorff informed Lansing about the change, stating that except for a period of grace for neutral ships in the war zones, all ships there would be sunk without warning after February 1. The United States could sail one ship a week to Falmouth, England, provided it was clearly marked and carried no contraband.

In a separate note to Lansing, Bernstorff stated that while the Germans agreed with the principles of Wilson's January 22 speech, the Allied response to Wilson's December 18 note demonstrated a desire to prolong the war. In addition, England continued to violate maritime law and neutral rights on the seas. Therefore, Germany had to renew its attacks to preserve its honor and combat Allied practices.

The German decision showed that Bethmann-Hollweg could no longer restrain the German General Staff. During the fall of 1916, Bethmann secured the kaiser's backing on condition that the British would also make concessions to America. The chancellor's attempt failed, and although his December 12 peace proposal stalled the military for another month, the Allies' rejection of peace negotiations on December 29 ended Bethmann's hopes for peace.

In January, Generals von Hindenburg and Ludendorff joined General Falkenhayn and the naval leaders in insisting that unrestricted submarine attacks should resume. They believed the submarines would knock England out of the war in five months and prevent supplies from reaching France for an Allied spring offensive. Moreover, they discounted any American challenge. The United States could not be mobilized quickly enough to influence the war. As naval minister Edward von Capelle asserted, "from a military point of view, America is nothing." Consequently, in a meeting at Pless on January 29, the kaiser agreed to the renewal of unrestricted submarine warfare, although this was not announced until January 31.

See October 20, 1916.

February 3, 1917

President Wilson breaks diplomatic relations with Germany, saying that any German attack on American ships or lives would require the protection of the American people.

Because Germany renewed its unrestricted submarine warfare, Wilson announced the breaking of relations with Germany. The one means open for Germany to avoid war was not to attack American ships or lives.

Although the German notice of January 31 allowed neutral ships to avoid attack by staying out of the war zones, Wilson had consistently maintained the U.S. neutral right to travel and trade in all sea regions without fear of unwarned attack. While

British violations of neutrality often destroyed or confiscated property, Germany's submarine methods threatened to sink all vessels and destroy lives.

Wilson reported to Congress that America's only alternative was to sever diplomatic relations and give Ambassador Bernstorff his passports. The president said he refused to believe Germany would again undertake such malicious attacks. "Only actual overt acts on their part can make me believe it now." If they did attack, the president would ask Congress to protect Americans in "their peaceful and legitimate errands on the high seas." He concluded: "God grant we may not be challenged to defend them by acts of willful injustice on the part of the Government of Germany."

On February 7, the U.S. Senate passed a resolution to support Wilson's diplomatic break with Germany. The vote was 75 to 5.

February 5, 1917

Mexico promulgates a new constitution on the same day that U.S. troops leave northern Mexico.

Between August and December 1916, General Pershing's forces in northern Mexico ended Villa's attacks across the border. Villa had, however, renewed his raids on Carranza's forces in central Mexico, keeping Washington constantly concerned about further violence against American towns.

On January 3, 1917, a group of American commissioners who had met with Mexican officials at Atlantic City, New Jersey, recommended that Wilson withdraw Pershing's men from Mexico. Carranza objected to the loss of dignity entailed in the U.S. intervention, and the Mexican convention at Queretaro was finalizing a new constitution. Wilson accepted the commission's recommendation and recalled Pershing's forces on January 12. This process was completed on February 5, when the last U.S. troops left Mexican soil. By this time, the threat of Villa's raids also ended because a campaign under General Francisco Murguia had decimated Villa's men and returned the U.S. Mexican border to normal.

The Mexican constitution, announced on February 5, resulted from a convention that had met since December 1, 1916, at Queretaro. The document represented both nationalistic and radical social viewpoints. It provided for universal suffrage, agrarian reform, restrictions on church power and property, minimum wages, an eight-hour day, and the curbing of foreign ownership of oil, land, and mines.

Although some Americans objected to the new Mexican constitution, Wilson sent Henry P. Fletcher as ambassador to Mexico to present his credentials and fully recognize de jure Carranza's government on March 3, 1917. On April 21, President Wilson received Mexico's Ambassador Ygnacio Bonilles in Washington.

February 24, 1917

The Zimmerman telegram: America learns that Germany proposes a Mexican alliance.

The United States learned of the Zimmerman message when British officials gave a copy of the telegram to Ambassador Page. The message of Foreign Secretary Arthur Zimmerman had been sent on January 19 to the German minister to Mexico, Heinrich von Eckhardt. Informing Eckhardt that Germany would renew submarine warfare, Zimmerman asked Eckhardt to propose that Carranza ally with Germany as soon as the United States declared war. Eckhardt could offer financial aid to Mexico as well as help in regaining territory lost to America in the Mexican War.

On February 25, Wilson received a copy of the telegram and was shocked but not surprised by Germany's action. U.S. newspapers published the telegram, and some Americans became more upset by the Zimmerman proposal than by the *Lusitania* sinking of 1915. The telegram seemed to confirm earlier American opinions about German duplicity.

March 1, 1917

A Franco-Japanese agreement recognizes Japan's rights to German concessions in China, rights that previously England and Russia had approved.

Japan's agreement with France completed its attempt to gain European recognition for supplanting German rights in China. The key agreement was the Anglo-Japanese agreement of February 16. In return for receiving German concessions in China and claims to German Pacific Ocean islands north of the equator, Great Britain obtained Japanese recognition of England's rights to all German islands south of the equator. Russia accepted Japan's rights in China proper by an agreement on February 20 just before

France completed the circle on March 1. Japan also agreed to urge China to declare war on Germany because this would legitimize its right to abrogate German possessions at the end of the war.

Thus, only the United States had refused to recognize Japan's demands in Shantung and China proper. The U.S. State Department urged China not to declare war.

See June 4, 1917.

March 4, 1917

Congress adjourns without approving the President's request to arm U.S. merchant ships.

On February 26, Wilson asked Congress to authorize an armed neutrality, leaving Congress only one week to consider the measure. He proposed the legislation because many U.S. shipping companies had cancelled their European voyages, while others asked if they could carry arms. Originally, on February 6, Wilson told shipping companies they could arm themselves without government aid. This proposal did not satisfy the shippers, however, and Wilson decided to request authority to arm ships and to receive $100 million for this expense.

Congressional resolutions to approve the president's request were submitted on February 26, but they were not passed quickly. Although the publication of the Zimmerman telegram hastened the House to approve the president's request on March 4 by a vote of 403-13, in the Senate four members filibustered the measure and prevented a vote. Senators Robert LaFollette of Wisconsin, George W. Norris of Nebraska, Albert B. Cummings of Iowa, and A. J. Gronna of North Dakota opposed the bill, claiming that arming merchant ships was tantamount to war.

To avert accusations that the Republicans caused the filibuster, Senators Lodge and Borah drafted a statement that said that, if a vote had been taken, the signators would have approved the armed ships bill. Seventy-five senators signed the statement. In addition, on March 18, at a special session of Congress, the Senate adopted a cloture vote permitting two-thirds of the Senate to stop debate on a measure.

On March 4, Wilson was incensed at the filibuster. He issued a statement saying that "a little group of willful" men in the Senate prevented action during a grave crisis and "rendered the great Government of the United States helpless and contemptible."

March 8, 1917

The U.S. Federal Reserve Board revises its November 27, 1916, statement on foreign loans to favor a "reasonable" amount of short-term bills.

The Federal Reserve Board action reflected a change between the fall of 1916, when Wilson desired to pressure Britain to alter its neutrality practices, and early 1917, when Germany renewed submarine warfare.

In the March 8 statement, the board said that the November note had been misunderstood. Because of the large volume of U.S. exports, short-term loans were essential to U.S. trade. The March statement pleased the Allies and the House of Morgan because Britain needed a $132 million loan. The board announcement also showed the drift of U.S. opinion in favor of aid to the Allies.

March 8, 1917

American forces intervene to prevent civil war in Cuba.

As on September 27, 1906, political turmoil arose in Cuba because of a disputed election. In 1912, the Liberal Party leader, José Gomez, lost the presidency to the Conservative leader, Mario Garcia Menocal. In 1916, Menocal ran for reelection against the Liberal Alfredo Zayas. The Liberals claimed election fraud, and forces led by ex-President Gomez rebelled on February 9, 1917. President Wilson sent marines to restore order and conduct another election. Gomez and the Liberals lost in the election of May 20, 1917, and President Menocal won another four-year term of office.

March 15, 1917

Czar Nicholas II abdicates in favor of his brother Michael, who abdicates on March 16 in favor of Prince Lvov.

The Russian czar abdicated because the nation's economy and government broke down during the winter of 1916–1917. Strikes, riots, and a troop mutiny in Petrograd (St. Petersburg was renamed in 1914) led to the formation of a provisional government under Prince George Lvov, to whom Michael gave authority on March 16. The new government included Paul Miliukov, a Constitutional Democrat; Alexander

Guchkov, an Octobrist; and Alexander Kerensky, a Socialist.

On March 18, the provisional government accepted Allied urging by pledging to continue the war against Germany. This was a fatal and unpopular decision. The Russian breakdown made the war a further strain on the economy as well as preventing social and political reform.

President Wilson learned about the revolution on March 15, and on March 22, American Ambassador David R. Francis formally recognized the new regime.

March 22, 1917

The Kaiser declares he cannot negotiate further with America.

Because of rumors that there would be neutral rights negotiations, the German Foreign Office told newsmen there would be no talks by Germany. The rumors came from Vienna, which still had relations with the United States.

The Berlin message of March 22 stated that the submarine war would be pushed aggressively. American ships in the war zone would have the same risks as any other ships. The message quoted the kaiser as saying, "Now, once and for all, an end to negotiations with America. If Wilson wants war, let him make it, and let him have it."

April 2, 1917

President Wilson calls for a declaration of War against Germany: Congress complies on April 6.

By the middle of March 1917, more and more Americans had reached the opinion that war against Germany appeared necessary. President Wilson moved to this decision only slowly and reluctantly. He knew the Allied war objectives were little better than those of Germany, but he also understood that the democracies would revert to a less militaristic stance after the war whereas the aggressive nature of the Prussian General Staff might continue if it were not defeated.

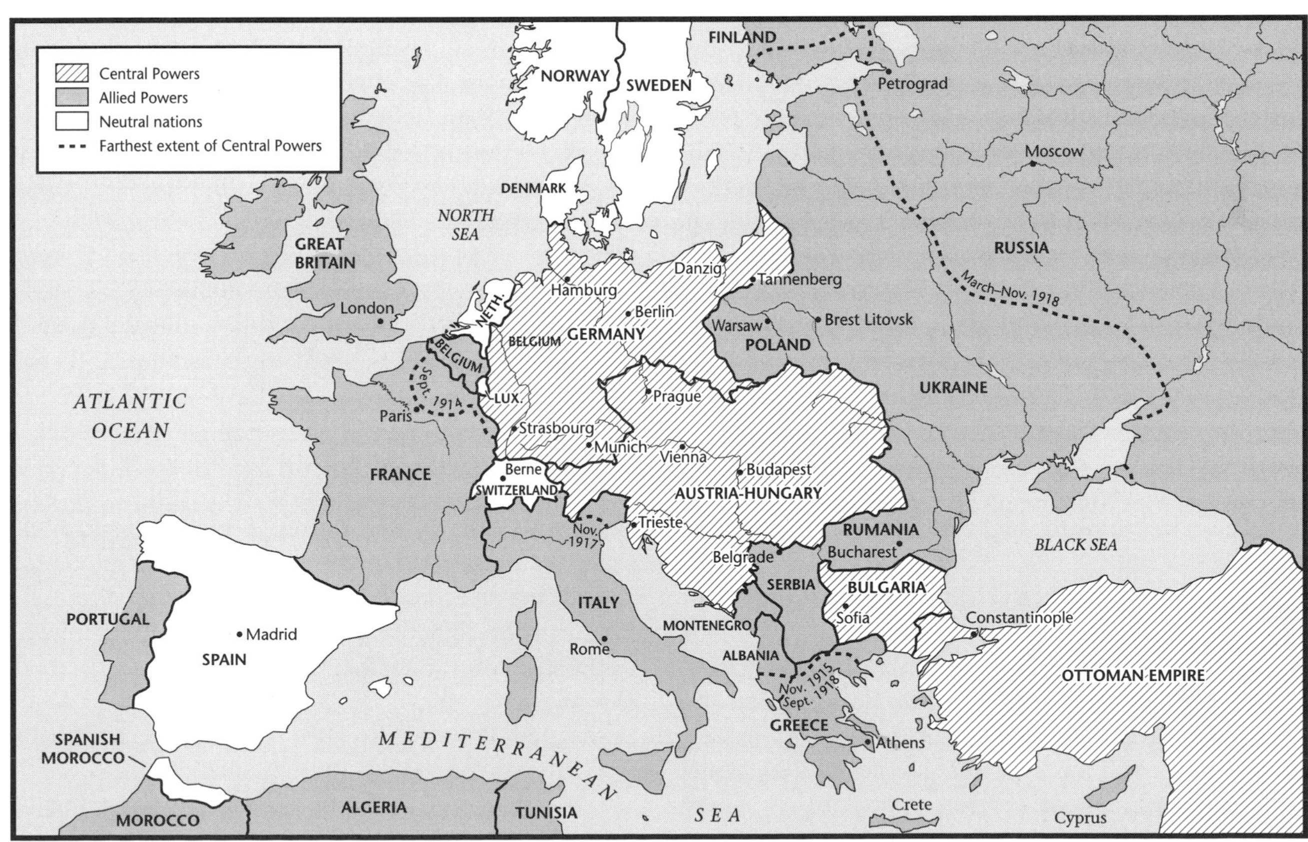

World War I

Public reaction to the news of German attacks on three U.S. ships between March 12 and 18 convinced Wilson and his cabinet members that war had to be declared. The *Algonquin* was the first American steamer sunk by a German submarine without warning on March 12. No lives were lost, however. Then in quick succession news of the sinking of the *City of Memphis* (March 17), the *Illinois* (March 18), and the *Vigilancia* (March 18) reached American newspapers and an outburst of public demonstrations ensued. On March 22, 12,000 people at Madison Square Garden in New York City cheered for war at a rally of the American Rights Committee. On March 31, thousands paraded at a Philadelphia meeting, while other mass meetings took place in Chicago, Boston, Denver, and Manchester, New Hampshire. The Socialist Eugene Debs and former Secretary of State Bryan were among the small minority denouncing the war fever.

While aware that it was best to act at the proper psychological moment, Wilson considered the situation carefully; first in solitude, later, on March 20, in a cabinet meeting. Exactly when he decided to ask for war is uncertain. That all cabinet members supported a declaration of war made the decision less difficult. Even two longtime peace advocates, Secretary of the Navy Josephus Daniels and Postmaster General Albert Burleson, spoke in favor of war. The most eloquent speech favoring war may have been Secretary of State Lansing's. The secretary had favored war against Germany for several months and believed that now the president had reached the best time to act. Wilson's valiant effort at armed neutrality had failed; Germany had carried out its submarine warfare as announced on January 31. In addition, Lansing believed the recent Russian overthrow of autocracy and the statements of German liberals against the vast power of the kaiser and General Staff indicated that forces of liberal democracy were appearing and the United States could lead this alignment for future peace.

Following the cabinet session of March 20, Wilson called for a special session of Congress on April 2. But he was still considering exactly what action he could ask for and how. By March 28, he decided that the United States had to join the Allies in war to end Germany's autocracy and enable the United States to become a leader of postwar peace efforts. These were the underlying themes of the president's April 2 speech to Congress, in which he asked for a declaration of war.

Wilson made his speech to a joint session of Congress at 8:30 P.M. on April 2. Reviewing events since February 1, he pointed out that Germany had made submarine war against neutral commerce, an act against all humankind. The United States, he said, could not submit to the German attacks, and armed neutrality did not function unless U.S. ships could shoot submarines on sight. Thus, the acts of the German government were in fact "war against the government and people of the United States," and America must accept the "status of belligerent which thus has been thrust upon it."

The president called for measures to help other governments at war with Germany, mobilize U.S. resources, and expand the armed forces "preferably through universal liability to service." The U.S. war aims were to vindicate peace and justice and establish a concert of power among the world's free peoples. The U.S. quarrel was with the few German leaders, not with the German people, who were pawns of their ambitious leaders. "We have no selfish ends to serve," Wilson declared, we desire no conquest, no indemnities, and no material compensation. "We are but one of the champions of the rights of mankind" and will be satisfied when these are made secure. We shall fight for things "nearest our hearts, for democracy, for the right of those who submit to authority to have a voice in their own Governments," for a concert of free people to make "the world itself at last free."

There was never doubt that Congress would support the president. On April 4, the Senate approved the war resolution by a vote of 82 to 6, as only five senators spoke against the war. The House discussions took longer because over 100 congressmen wanted to speak in favor of the war, while only 20 spoke in opposition. The House voted on April 6 to favor war by 373 to 50. Soon after, a messenger brought the resolution to the White House, where Wilson signed the act immediately at 1:18 P.M. President Wilson then signed a proclamation announcing the declaration of war against Germany as an Associate of the Western allies. He adopted the term "Allied Associated Powers" because he believed Americans were prejudiced against foreign alliances.

War was not declared against Austria-Hungary until December 7, 1917.

April 14, 1917

A Committee on Public Information is established by executive order of the President to unite the nation behind the war front.

The president appointed journalist George Creel to chair this committee, which included the secretaries of state, war, and navy. Secretary of State Lansing later had difficulties with Creel's aggressive propaganda tactics because he interfered with the State Department's news releases and tried to set up independent American propaganda agencies in foreign countries. As the war went on, the committee became controversial because many observers believed Creel went too far in "censoring" news and "playing" with the truth.

May 15, 1917

The Petrograd Soviet issues a peace proposal, appealing to socialists of all countries.

In contrast to the provisional government's decision to remain in the war, the Russian Communist Party leader NIKOLAI LENIN and the Petrograd Soviet advocated immediate peace. The Soviet peace formula may be summarized in one of its sentences: "Peace without annexation or indemnities on the basis of self-determination of peoples is the formula adopted unreservedly by the proletarian mind and heart." The Soviet called for a peace conference of socialists of all belligerent nations to form a future world peace.

In 1917, some commentators believed the Soviet's formula was inspired by Woodrow Wilson's appeal to the people of Europe in January 1917. Wilson, of course, believed democratic liberalism, not communism, was the best political means to achieve these ends.

May 18, 1917

The Selective Service Act provides for recruitment of American men into the armed forces.

This law provided for the registration and drafting into service of men between 21 and 35 years of age. Later, on September 23, 1918, the registration age was changed to be between 18 and 48 years. By June 5, 9,586,508 men had registered; a year later another 1 million 21 year olds were added. After the change in ages in 1918, another 13,228,762 men enrolled.

During the war, the U.S. army expanded from 200,000 to over 4 million. The U.S. navy's wartime strength was 500,000. A total of 2,084,000 U.S. soldiers served in France at some time, with 1,390,000 seeing active combat duty. The American Expeditionary Force was commanded by General John J. Pershing. U.S. naval forces in Europe were commanded by Admiral William S. Sims. The navy convoyed troop and merchant ships, chased submarines, and assisted the British fleet in the North Sea.

Because the United States remained an "associated," not an allied, force with Britain and France, Pershing demanded a distinct American sector on the Western front after U.S. troops began to arrive in France on June 26, 1917. Against Allied wishes, the United States received the Toul sector east of Verdun. The first American soldiers reached this sector on October 21, relieving French troops who had held the line.

Later in 1918, President Wilson agreed to the appointment of French General Ferdinand FOCH as supreme commander on the western front. Pershing disliked this arrangement and, on May 1, an Interallied Conference agreed to refer to a separate U.S. army for some sections in France. At other sectors, as during the German Somme offensive of 1918, U.S. troops joined with British and French forces.

May 26, 1917

Elihu Root is appointed head of a special U.S. delegation to visit Russia and give encouragement to the provisional government.

Secretary of State Lansing suggested a special mission to Russia on April 9, as part of an Allied attempt to maintain Russia's participation in the war. Britain and France had each sent delegations, and the American group could meet the new leaders of Russia and personally examine their situation.

Characteristically, while Paris and London sent pro-war socialists to represent their views, Wilson wanted to send persons from every walk of life in America. As a former secretary of state, Root held satisfactory credentials but was not sympathetic to recent developments in Russia. For the rest of the U.S. delegation, Wilson chose, among others, James Duncan, vice president of the American Federation of Labor, and Charles Russell, a right-wing socialist.

Following a four-week visit to Petrograd in July, the Root mission returned to the United States in August and made several recommendations that focused on the German danger in Russia. Alexander Kerensky, who became the leader of the provisional government in July 1917, emphasized this to the American and European delegates as a means for generating support and loans from the Western powers. Among the Root mission suggestions were (1) an educational campaign to persuade the Russian people to stay in the war and preserve democracy. (The Germans spent $3 million a month for intrigue in Russia. The United States should spend at least $5.5 million over one year through the Committee for Public Information for a news, film, leaflet, advertising, and speaking service); and (2) an effort to build the morale of the Russian army. The 13 million men in the army had never had an organization such as the Young Men's Christian Association to assist their physical, mental, social, and moral betterment. This was the largest area where the United States could help the Russian people, according to the Root mission.

In brief, the Root mission sought long-range means to an immediate Russian problem. It seemed not to have realized the complete breakdown of the social order that Russia had experienced over the previous one hundred years. Opposing the Root report, Secretary of State Lansing was concerned that, like prior revolutions, Russia's provisional government would be overthrown by a military group. To aid Kerensky's government, Lansing and the U.S. minister to Russia, David Francis, helped arrange $325 million of loans in America between April and November, 1917.

The provisional government failed to solve Russia's critical economic problems, however. The decision to continue to fight Germany and the government's failure to institute significant reforms caused its gradual loss of support in Petrograd.

For the resulting Bolshevik Revolution, see November 7, 1917.

June 4, 1917

America asks its allies to discourage a Chinese declaration of war on Germany.

Although the U.S. minister to China, Paul Reinsch, thought in February 1917 that he should persuade China to break off relations with Germany, Secretary of State Lansing disagreed when he heard of the minister's action. Reinsch assumed that President Wilson's February 3 request for neutrals to break relations with Berlin included China. Subsequently, he discussed the situation with Chinese officials who were willing to break off relations, provided that America promised to assist them and to grant a $10 million loan. When China broke relations on March 14, Lansing repudiated the minister's decision because he opposed giving special inducements to neutrals to act against Germany. Furthermore, Lansing believed China had enough difficulty protecting open door trade and its territorial integrity against other powers.

On June 4, Lansing informed the Chinese that their German relations should be secondary to their need to develop a modern economy in China and to persevere with open door trade abroad. He sent identical notes to England, France, and Japan, urging them to join him in keeping China out of the war. Lansing did not realize that Japan had agreed with Great Britain and France to take over German concessions in China and to encourage China to declare war in order to justify this (see March 1, 1917).

Because of the secret agreements, Japan and its European allies encouraged China to declare war on Germany, but the United States did not. In response to Lansing's note of June 4, Britain, France, and Japan indignantly disagreed that the European war was of secondary importance to China. The secret treaties of the other powers with Japan left the United States isolated. Moreover, the Japanese had negotiated secret financial aid to the Chinese military group ruling Peking. The combined influence of Britain, France, and Japan caused China to declare war on Germany in August.

See August 14, and November 2, 1917.

June 15, 1917

An Espionage Act is passed to punish and eliminate disloyal or treasonable activity.

This law stated that persons found guilty of aiding the enemy, obstructing army recruitment or causing troop insubordination, acting disloyally, or refusing service in the armed forces could be fined up to $10,000 and imprisoned for 10 years. Also, the postmaster general could prohibit use of the mail to newspapers, periodicals, and other publications that allegedly printed treasonable or seditious material.

While there was some opposition to the war by idealist socialists such as Eugene Debs and William Haywood, there was relatively little dissent compared with that of the War of 1812 or opposing the Philippine insurrection from 1899 to 1902.

July 19, 1917

The German Reichstag passes a peace resolution.

The peace resolution of July 19 showed the strength of Germany's liberal and socialist parties but did not affect the kaiser or his ministers. It also indicated the end of Chancellor Bethmann-Hollweg's coalition ministry of the center parties that had formed in August 1914. At that time the 110 members of the left-wing Social Democrat Party (SPD) joined the coalition as a method of fighting autocratic Russia and liberalizing the German government. The Russian Revolution of March 1917 ended part of this rationale and, during the spring of 1917, German parties in the Reichstag realigned. Philipp Scheidemann, the SPD spokesman, united with the Center Party of Matthias Erzberger and the Progressive People's Party of Friedrich von Payer to gain a majority in the Reichstag.

In addition to forming a committee to study constitutional reform, the new coalition overthrew Bethmann's ministry in early July and passed the July 19 peace resolution in an attempt to change German policy. The resolution asserted that the German people fought only for self-defense and should not attempt to annex territory or oppress other peoples. It advocated free seas and "economic peace." Finally, it said: "The Reichstag will actively promote the creation of an International Law Organization."

Unfortunately, the constitution of 1871 did not make the kaiser or his ministry responsible to the Reichstag. When Bethmann was overthrown, William II appointed a safe Nationalist Party member, Georg Michaelis, as chancellor. The executive branch controlled the government and opposed the Peace Resolution. In July 1917, German liberals realized that Germany had one of Europe's most autocratic governments.

August 14, 1917

China declares war on Germany to obtain western financial aid.

Following Yüan Shih-k'ai's death on June 16, 1916, many provincial warlords gained power. Two factions emerged in Peking to attempt to supplant Yüan. A group of liberal republicans led by Li Yüan-Lung failed in their attempt to revive the constitution of 1912 in Peking and set up an insurgent government in Canton under Sun Wen.

On July 12, 1917, an antidemocratic faction headed by Tuan Ch'i-jui and backed by Yüan's northern armies gained control in Peking. Tuan catered to Japanese and European interests to obtain money and to strengthen his army for an attack on Canton. Tuan became premier with Feng Kuo-chang as the figurehead president of China.

Soon after declaring war on Germany, Tung canceled all German concessions in China. This accorded with the secret treaties among Japan, France, and England because it established Tokyo's right to take over the former German regions. As Minister Paul Reinsch reported to Washington on March 1, 1917, when China declared war on Germany, it would "be entirely reactionary in character as far as Chinese political institutions and practices are concerned."

September 2, 1917

President Wilson asks Colonel House to create a group of experts to study problems for a satisfactory peace settlement—"The Inquiry."

Throughout the summer of 1917, many groups and individuals in Europe and America suggested a variety of proposals to establish a more peaceful world when World War I ended. Therefore, on September 2, the president told Colonel House that a group should systematically survey what different parties to the war expected in a peace agreement to enable America to formulate its position and "begin to gather the influences we may employ" from knowledge of other ideas.

In response to Wilson's request, House formed a group known as The Inquiry. Chaired by President Sidney E. Mezes of the College of the City of New York, the group included Dr. Isaiah Bowman, the director of the American Geographic Society; Walter Lippmann, from the staff of the *New Republic*; David Hunter Miller, an international legal expert; and two history professors, Charles Seymour and James T. Shotwell. For the group's most significant report see December 22, 1917.

October 6, 1917

The trading with the Enemy Act prohibits commerce with enemy nations and permits the takeover of alien property in the United States.

This law empowered the president to embargo imports and to establish censorship for material passing between America and any foreign nation. It also created the Office of Alien Property Custodian to oversee the possession and disposal of property held in the United States by residents of enemy nations.

November 1, 1917

The Balfour Declaration favors a home for the Jewish people in Palestine.

Regarding the desire of Zionists for a Jewish homeland, Britain's foreign minister, Arthur James Balfour, issued a statement that said the British government favored "the establishment in Palestine of a national home for the Jewish people and will use the best endeavors to facilitate the achievements of that object, it being clearly understood that nothing shall be done which may prejudice the civil and religious rights of non-Jewish communities in Palestine."

By the Sykes-Picot agreement of May 9, 1916, Britain and France had decided to place Palestine under an international administration. British armies took over Jerusalem on December 9, 1917. Its capture inaugurated a large-scale British offensive under General Sir Edmund Allenby assisted by Arab Legions led by Colonel Thomas E. Lawrence, who had captured Aquaba on July 6, 1917.

November 2, 1917

The Lansing-Ishii agreement is signed: America recognizes Japan's special interests in China; Japan declares respect for the Open Door.

After gaining the backing of the big three European nations for its acquisition of rights in Shantung and the Yangtze valley, Japan sent the Viscount Kikujiro Ishii to Washington on September 1, 1917, to obtain U.S. recognition of Japan's "paramount interest" in China.

An impasse resulted during the Lansing-Ishii talks because the Japanese desire for "paramount interest" conflicted with the American policy of preserving China's territorial integrity and equal trading rights. While it might have been preferable not to reach an agreement, the diplomats who were also allies in the war against Germany chose to exchange notes of ambiguous content that displayed no nation's policies but permitted each to claim that its proposals had been maintained.

The resulting agreement stated, therefore, that (1) the United States recognized that "territorial propinquity" allowed Japan to have "special interests" in China, "particularly in parts to which her possessions are contiguous"; and (2) Japan declared its respect for the open door and China's territorial integrity. Ishii emphasized item number one; Lansing emphasized item number two.

Neither Lansing nor Ishii publicly announced in 1917 a secret protocol agreed to by Japan on October 31. In this agreement, Ishii accepted Lansing's statement that neither country would "take advantage of present conditions" to seek special rights in China that would "abridge the rights of citizens of friendly states."

Because of the ambiguous character of the publicized agreement of November 2, the meaning of the Lansing-Ishii statements was greatly disputed. Lansing knew about Japan's treaty with China of May 25, 1915, and about Japan's agreements with England, France, and Russia between February 16 and March 1, 1917. He should have realized that special interests meant Japan's sphere of influence in Shantung, Fukien, and the Yangtze valley as well as Korea, Manchuria, and east Mongolia. As A. Whitney Griswold's study concluded, Lansing acted out of expediency. It is unclear whether or not Lansing and President Wilson realized in 1917 that their agreement negated their attempts to challenge Japan's rights during the Paris Peace Conference in 1919. Although Lansing and Wilson disclaimed knowledge of the secret allied treaties regarding China and Germany, the historical evidence indicates that they did know about these agreements.

See March 1, 1917.

November 7, 1917

The Bolshevik Revolution in Russia overthrows the provisional government of Kerensky.

Led by Nikolai Lenin, the Bolshevik revolution began on November 6 (October 24 by the old-style Russian calendar) when Soviet troops arrested members of the provisional government and took over their offices; Kerensky escaped but failed to organize a successful resistance. On November 7, the Second All-Russian Congress of Soviets gave all power to the Bolshevik Party. One slogan of the new government was "peace at any price," and the government sought to end the war with Germany as early as possible.

Lenin had returned to Russia from exile in Switzerland on April 16 and organized the Bolsheviks to oppose the provisional government. The Bolsheviks demanded "peace, land, and bread," reforms that the more moderate provisional leaders refused to institute until the war was over. Kerensky had replaced Prince Lvov as head of the government on July 20, but his willingness to remain in the war was contrary to the wishes of most Russians. The events of November 6–7 ended Kerensky's regime.

See March 31, 1918.

Nikolai Lenin. National Archives

November 8, 1917

Russia's Bolshevik government issues a peace decree to "all belligerent peoples and their governments."

The peace decree of Lenin's new regime represented two parts of the Bolshevik strategy for maintaining control in Russia and enlisting socialist revolution in other parts of the world. First, together with the Land Decree of the same day, it represented the practical, immediate Russian need to end the war at any cost so that social, political, and economic order could be restored within the country. Second, it represented the Bolshevik expectation that to succeed in Russia, communism had to be supported by the class-conscious proletariat of western Europe. As orthodox Marxists, both Lenin and Leon Trotsky believed that as Europe's most backward industrial nation, Russia advanced beyond its masses' political consciousness. Following the Petrograd Formula of May 15, 1917, the Bolsheviks urged workers of other nations to demonstrate for peace, overthrow their bourgeois governments, and form socialist regimes.

The Peace Decree of November 8 bore remarkable similarities to President Wilson's "peace without victory" concept. The Bolshevik decree called for a general peace conference, the conduct of "negotiations absolutely open before the entire people," and no territorial annexations in Europe or "in distant lands beyond the seas."

On November 27, Trotsky elaborated on specific aspects of the decree before a group of Allied military attachés in Petrograd. His main points included:

1. Russia desired general peace but would make a separate peace if the Allies refused.
2. Immediate armistice negotiations should begin.
3. If Allied governments did not respond to the decrees, Russia would appeal to the people of the nations at war.

Because the Allies refused to recognize the Bolshevik peace program, Lenin undertook separate talks with Germany. As Russia's commissar of foreign affairs, Trotsky led a campaign to aid foreign communist parties in subverting their governments and advocating peace. His methods were not secret because he wanted the world to know the Communists' ideological objectives. His decrees denounced secret diplomacy and released documents of the czarist foreign office that disclosed the secret territorial ambitions of the capitalist powers. Trotsky contended that the secret decrees demonstrated that the Allied and German statements about the war were "lies" that betrayed their citizens. The publication of the Allies' secret treaties began on November 23, 1917.

See December 3, 1917.

November 9, 1917

The State Department announces plans for a banking consortium to provide loans to China.

Lansing and Wilson had decided by November 9, 1917, to reverse one of their earlier policies toward China. That day, Lansing announced that the U.S. government was considering a new banking consortium of British, French, Japanese, and American banks to make loans to China. Since 1913, Japan had become China's principal source of loans, and America's European allies wanted the United States to enter into China's finances to prevent a Japanese monopoly. Consequently, Wilson was persuaded to change his 1913 policy by encouraging U.S. bankers to provide loans for China. This consortium was not finalized until October 15, 1920.

November 25, 1917

Rejecting the Bolshevik government of Russia, President Wilson continues to accept the provisional government's ambassador, Boris Bakhmetev.

The Wilson administration refused to accept the Bolshevik regime in Petrograd, recognizing Ambassador Bakhmetev as the representative of Russia. On November 11, Bakhmetev informed newsmen that he did not represent the Bolsheviks because they were but a temporary aberration. The liberal groups in Russia would soon regain control. Wilson concurred and on November 25 announced that the United States recognized Bakhmetev's official status. Wilson argued that the Soviet coup was illegal and did not represent the majority of Russia's people.

Even as Lenin solidified his power in Russia, Wilson and, later, President Warren Harding, recognized Bakhmetev as "ambassador of the Russian people." Bakhmetev became custodian of $56 million of the provisional government's funds at the First National City Bank of New York. Initially he used these funds to send nonmilitary goods to both Bolshevik and anti-Bolshevik groups in Russia. Later, however, he purchased military supplies that were sent to Admiral Kolchak and other "White" army leaders who sought to overthrow the Bolsheviks (Reds).

Bakhmetev continued to serve as Russia's "representative" until June 1922. After he resigned, the State Department recognized neither the Russian government nor the Union of Soviet Socialist Republics until 1933.

December 3, 1917

Russia begins peace sessions with the central powers at Brest-Litovsk.

Because the Allied powers ignored the Bolshevik peace decree of November 8, Lenin contacted German leaders and arranged an armistice and peace conference for the eastern front of the war. The peace conference with Russia, Austria, and Germany opened on December 3.

At the opening meeting at Brest-Litovsk, the Soviet delegation, headed by Adolf Joffe, submitted six points as the basis of negotiations, summarized as follows:

1. no forceable annexation of territory;
2. political independence to be restored to people backing independence;
3. referendums to be conducted for self-determination of a national government, the vote to be free to all residents of a territory;
4. minority rights to cultural independence and administrative autonomy to be guaranteed;
5. no war indemnities, and private losses to be paid by a fund raised in all belligerent countries;
6. colonial questions to be settled according to points 1 through 4 above.

Joffe also insisted that the conference sessions be open to the public.

For results of the conference, see March 3, 1918.

December 22, 1917

The inquiry—a group organized to advise Wilson on war aims—reports to President Wilson on territorial issues and the politics of war aims.

The Inquiry was formed on September 2, 1917, and its experts completed their most important report for the president by December 22. It was presented to Wilson on January 4, enabling him to consult it in preparing his Fourteen Points address on January 8, 1918.

The report indicated that there was a "universal longing for peace" among the common people of the world, who disliked the old diplomacy of secret treaties and armed forces. In addition, it said there was a great hope for a league of nations. Liberals and progressives in the United States and Europe should "show the way" not only in obtaining a better peace but as an "invaluable support for their internal domestic troubles." Thus, the group's report encouraged Wilson to advocate the liberal idea of a peace designed to aid the people of the world in resolving national and international social and economic goals.

1918

January 5, 1918

Prime Minister Lloyd George announces British war aims.

In a speech to labor union delegates, Lloyd George indicated that Great Britain recognized a need for a postwar organization to limit armaments and prevent war. Most of his address was concerned with specific territorial changes in Europe to rectify the wrong done to France in 1871 and to reorganize eastern and central Europe by national groups.

His territorial changes included an independent Poland; self-government for nations formerly controlled by the Turkish and Austrian Empires; restoration of all occupied parts of Belgium, France, Serbia, Montenegro, Italy, and Romania; and satisfaction for the national claims of Italy and Romania.

January 8, 1918

France requests American cooperation with an Allied intervention in Siberia: Wilson refuses.

Although on January 1, the British had telegraphed a request to Wilson to consider landing forces at Vladivostok, the French ambassador made the first formal request for American cooperation in Siberia on January 8.

French Ambassador Jules Jusserand requested U.S. aid because he said the Bolsheviks committed atrocities in Irkutsk against Russians who were loyal to the war effort. In reality, France and Britain feared the Russians would make a separate peace with Germany. In addition to endangering the large Allied loans made to the czar, a separate peace would permit Germany to shift soldiers from the eastern to the western front in Europe.

Wilson considered Jusserand's request but on January 16 informed the French that America could not support a Siberian intervention. The French request was the first of a series of Allied attempts to persuade Wilson to join an intervention in Russia. Wilson's policy on the Russian problem was stated as point six in his Fourteen Points of January 8, 1918.

See July 17 and September 1, 1918.

January 8, 1918

Wilson's fourteen points define his views of Allied war aims.

Wilson's speech to Congress on January 8 outlined America's 14 peace objectives in the context of recent developments in Europe and especially in Russia. Since March 1917, liberal and socialist groups had proposed their "new diplomacy" in contrast to the aggressive and militaristic objectives of European warfare. The German Reichstag resolution of July 19, 1917, the Petrograd Peace Formula of May 15, and in particular the Bolshevik statement of November 8, 1917, encouraged Wilson to state the position of liberal democracy in future world relations because the British and French had been reluctant to state their war aims although the Bolshevik's publication of their secret wartime agreements placed pressure on the Allies to assert their peace concepts as an answer to Trotsky's and Adolf Joffe's statements.

After Lloyd George's speech to the British labor unions on January 5 established some liberalization of Allied war aims, Wilson considered canceling his speech. Colonel House convinced him to proceed so that Wilson could become the "spokesman for the liberals of the world."

Wilson's speech to Congress began by reviewing recent diplomatic developments. Referring to the Brest-Litovsk negotiations and the Bolshevik statement of peace principles, Wilson criticized the Austro-German delegates at Brest-Litovsk because they followed a spirit of "conquest and subjugation." Before the Allies made peace with the Central Powers, they needed to know if the German-Austrian delegates spoke "for the Reichstag majority or the military party and the men whose creed is imperial domination." Wilson appealed to the democratic and nonsocialist Germans to rally the people for peace and not permit the socialists to gain control of the peace process.

Drawing on these introductory remarks, Wilson enunciated a program to make the world "fit and safe to live in" for every "peace-loving nation." "All the peoples of the world," he said, "are in effect partners in this interest... The program of the world's peace, therefore, is our program; and that program is the only possible program, as we see it."

Summarized to include the most significant or controversial phrases, Wilson's 14 Points were as follows:

1. "open covenants of peace, openly arrived at" with "no private international understandings," and diplomacy that shall be frank "and in the public view";
2. freedom of the seas except as they may be closed "by international action for the enforcement of international covenants";
3. removal of "all economic barriers," and equality of trade among "all nations consenting to the peace and associating themselves for its maintenance";
4. "national armaments... reduced to the lowest point consistent with domestic safety";
5. "a free, open-minded, and absolutely impartial adjustment of all colonial claims" based on the principle that "the interests of the populations concerned must have equal weight with the equitable claims of the government whose title is to be determined";
6. the "evacuation of all Russian territory" and settlement of Russian questions in free cooperation with other nations to give Russia "an unhampered and unembarrassed opportunity for the independent determination of her own political developments," and to "assure her of a sincere welcome into the society of free nations under institutions of her own choosing." The treatment of Russia by its "sister nations" will be "the acid test of their good will" as separate "from their own interests, and of their intelligent and unselfish sympathy";
7. Belgium to be "evacuated and restored";
8. French territory freed and restored and "the wrong done to France by Prussia in 1871... shall be righted...";
9. readjust Italian frontiers "along clearly recognizable lines of nationality";
10. the "peoples of Austria-Hungary" to be given the "freest opportunity of autonomous development";
11. "Rumania, Serbia and Montenegro should be evacuated," Serbia given access to the sea, and the relation of Balkan states to be "determined by friendly counsel along historically established lines of allegiance and nationality...";
12. sovereignty for the Turkish parts of the Ottoman Empire, but other nationalities under Turkish rule to receive the "opportunity of autonomous development"; the Dardanelles to be open to ships and commerce of all nations;
13. establishment of an independent Polish state to include "territories inhabited by indisputably Polish populations" and having free access to the sea;
14. formation of a "general association of nations" under covenants of mutual guarantees of "political independence and territorial integrity to great and small states alike."

Wilson stated that America did not wish to block Germany's legitimate power but asked Germans "only to accept a place of equality among the peoples of the world... instead of a place of mastery." American principles were based on peace and justice for all peoples and nationalities. The weak and the strong should, Wilson concluded, live on equal terms of "liberty and safety with one another." U.S. citizens fight for this and are "ready to put their own strength, their own highest purpose, their own integrity and devotion to the test."

See November 8 and December 3, 1917; for the "Reichstag majority," see July 19, 1917.

February 19, 1918

The Mexican government decrees that oil is an inalienable natural resource, levying taxes on all oil lands and contracts made before May 1, 1917.

The Mexican constitution of 1917 gave the nation the right to all subsoil resources that included oil (Article 27). Therefore, in addition to taxing oil lands, all prior oil land drilling had to be transformed into concessions for the Mexican state. British and American companies and their governments protested this decree but could not effectively act until World War I ended.

See January 20, 1920.

March 3, 1918

Russia and Germany sign the treaty of Brest-Litovsk to end their war.

The peace negotiations began on December 3, 1917, with Adolf Joffe representing Russia's Bolshevik regime. German demands were so severe that on February 10, Russia's Foreign Minister Trotsky declared the war over without any peace terms. The Germans renewed the war and after they had advanced to within 100 miles of Petrograd, Lenin insisted that negotiations for a treaty be renewed. The result was the Treaty of Brest-Litovsk, by which Russia lost Poland, Lithuania, the Ukraine, the Baltic provinces (Estonia and Latvia), Finland, and Transcaucasia. German troops occupied Finland and the major Ukrainian cities.

March 21, 1918

The Germans launch an offensive in the Somme area of France.

This German offensive was an all-out attempt to end the war as quickly as possible. Between March 21 and June 4, the Germans advanced far into France, reaching the Marne River, 40 miles from Paris, on May 31. At this point, U.S. troops of the 2nd, 3rd, and 28th Divisions joined French forces in blocking the Germans at Château-Thierry.

The Germans renewed their attacks in other theaters of war on June 9 in an attempt to integrate large forces north and northeast of Paris. They failed and the front became stabilized on August 6, when German efforts to cross the Marne River met little success

May 7, 1918

Germany forces Romania to sign the peace treaty of Bucharest.

A German-Austrian army launched attacks on Romania on August 6, 1917, and obtained a truce on December 6. Romania's delay of peace arrangements was ended by a German ultimatum on February 6 because Berlin wanted to end the eastern warfare.

In the Treaty of Bucharest, Romania ceded Dobruja to Bulgaria and the Carpathian passes to Austria-Hungary. Germany also obtained a 90-year lease on Romania's oil wells.

May 16, 1918

The Sedition Act amends the Espionage Act of 1917 to prohibit disloyal language and the promoting of disloyal action.

This law passed Congress because war dissenters were inciting Americans to disloyal actions that might injure the war effort. Under this law sedition included "false" statements interfering with the war; employing "disloyal, profane, scurrilous, or abusive language" about the U.S. government, the Constitution, the flag, or the armed forces; urging curtailment of war production; and advocating, teaching, defending, or suggesting disloyal acts.

The Sedition and Espionage Acts led to the arrest of many wartime dissenters. Socialist Party leader Eugene Debs, who ran for president five times, was sentenced to 10 years in prison for violating the sedition provisions of the Espionage Act. The laws, which have been viewed by many scholars as among the most serious infringements on civil liberties in U.S. history, had widespread popular support at the time.

Together with the Espionage Act of June 15, 1917, this legislation resulted in a series of "free speech" decisions by the U.S. Supreme Court after the war. In *Schenck v. U.S.*, Justice Oliver Wendell Holmes wrote a unanimous court opinion upholding the Espionage Act. Applying the "clear and present danger" ruling, he found that Schenck's pamphlets encouraged resistance to the draft. Holmes asserted that free speech is always under restraint, especially in time of war.

In the case of *Abrams v. U.S.*, a majority of the court found that pamphlets criticizing the U.S. Expeditionary Force to Siberia fell under the Sedition Act as invoking disloyalty in wartime. Although Justice Holmes dissented in this case, considering it not within the "clear and present danger," Justice John Clarke and the court majority applied the "bad tendency" test to justify Abrams's guilt.

For the significance of the Siberian intervention in applying the Sedition Act, see September 1, 1918.

July 17, 1918

Wilson agrees to send American forces to north Russia and Siberia to protect military stores and assist Czechoslovak soldiers trying to flee Russia through Siberia.

The issue of U.S. intervention in Russia required more and more of President Wilson's time in 1918. Almost every month since January 8, the British or French had requested U.S. aid, but the president refused consistently until late June. He opposed intervention because, as he had stated in point 6 of his 14 points, allowing Russia to settle its own problems was an "acid test" of Western attitudes of good faith toward self-determination. Some of his biographers believe Wilson learned during the Mexican intervention that such actions created more problems than they solved because of nationalistic opposition to foreign forces.

During these same months, Britain and France constantly plotted for a method to intervene against the Bolsheviks and, as they emphasized to Wilson, to maintain a second front against Germany. France especially desired to assist former czarist generals in their effort to defeat the Communist government, and France loaned money to the anti-Bolshevik groups. On December 23, 1917, an Anglo-French agreement divided southern Russia into spheres of action against the "Germans" to aid the former czarists against Lenin's peace plans. The British aided Aleksey KALEDIN, who planned a state for the Don Cossacks. This plan faltered on February 11, 1918, when the Cossacks repudiated Kaledin and he committed suicide. The French and British then shifted support first to General Lavr Kornilov, later to General Anatol Denikin. Britain also sent a few troops to Murmansk in northern Russia to protect military stores and to rally anti-Bolshevik and anti-German groups to assist the Allied cause.

The problem facing British-French plans was the lack of British and French soldiers to commit to the intervention in Russia. Thus, they sought troops from the United States and Japan, and even from a

Vladivostok, Russia. Soldiers and sailors from many nations are lined up in front of the Allies' headquarters building. Note different flags. National Archives

Czechoslovak legion that had helped Russia fight the Austrian armies until 1917. The Japanese were eager to move into eastern Asia but preferred not to move unless the United States agreed. Although President Wilson opposed Japanese action, the British persuaded Tokyo to send a cruiser to Vladivostok on January 12, 1918, to join them in blockading that port. On April 5, following the murder of a Japanese citizen in Vladivostok, a British-Japanese marine force landed to take control of the city. Vladivostok had been a storage area for Western supplies to Russia. By 1918, more than 800,000 tons of war matériel had stacked up in Vladivostok because the single-track Trans-Siberian Railway overburdened Russia's transportation system. This compared to the 160,000 tons held in north Russia in the spring of 1918.

For Wilson neither the large storage of supplies, the desire to intervene against Lenin, nor Japan's desire to intervene justified Allied action in Russia. By June, however, another development gained Wilson's sympathy for action: the plight of the Czechoslovak Legion in Siberia. The Czech Legion consisted of defectors or prisoners of war from the Austrian-Hungarian armies as well as those in the Russian army because they lived in Russian territory in Slovakia before the war. They had formed into one army in the Russian ranks against Germany, but after the Bolshevik Revolution began, the Czech Legion maintained its unity and discipline. It captured stores of arms and munitions that it previously had guarded, and sought some means to evacuate Russia to join the Western armies in France, where they could win independence for Czechoslovakia from both Austria and Russia at the peace conference.

The Czech Legion had been stationed in the Ukraine until 1918, and on March 16 the Soviet commander in Kiev authorized the Czechs to leave for France by way of the Trans-Siberian Railway and Vladivostok. During their journey, Soviet leaders often stopped the Czech train but usually allowed it to proceed.

On May 8, however, trouble began for the Czechs. First, the Soviet leaders told them the Allies desired to split their army so that one-half could go to Murmansk. This information was correct because the British hoped the Czechs would assist them in north Russia. The Czech leaders did not believe the Russians because the British had not bothered to send the Czechs direct information. Thus, the Czechs refused to divide and suspected that this was a Soviet attempt to divide and defeat them.

On May 14, the Czechs' suspicions seemed to be confirmed because the Soviets told them to leave the train and disarm. The Soviets stopped their train at the small town of Chelyabinsk, and negotiations began. While the Czech train awaited release, a trainload of Hungarians happened to arrive in the town. The Czechs and Hungarians normally despised each other, but the unexpected visit went well until a Hungarian soldier threw a heavy piece of iron at a Czech and apparently killed him. The Czechs immediately stopped the Hungarian train, captured the Hungarian who threw the iron, and lynched him.

The Czechs refused to be responsible to local rulers for the lynching, and just as trouble brewed, they intercepted a telegram from Moscow in which one of Leon Trotsky's aides ordered the Czechs to be drafted into a labor battalion for the Red Army. Trotsky had ordered that Russia shoot anyone trying to stop the disarming of the Czechs.

This series of events caused the Czechs to rebel and fight local Red Army troops. Consequently, although 15,000 Czechs reached Vladivostok on June 25, the remainder of the legion was stalled near Irkutsk. In addition, the Western powers failed to send ships to Siberia to evacuate the Czechs. Some Czechs took control of the city from the British, while others turned back to aid their brothers in central Siberia.

In mid-June 1918, the Czech leader Thomáš Masaryk visited President Wilson to describe his nation's desire for independence and the conditions in Siberia. As an articulate liberal democrat, Masaryk gained Wilson's sympathy, and by July 6, Wilson was ready to respond to the Czech pleas for aid. Wilson met with the secretary of war, the army's chief of staff, and the chief of naval operations, and they agreed to use a force of 7,000 Americans and 7,000 Japanese to intervene in Siberia.

Wilson's decision to commit American troops to northern Russia was based on a number of circumstances. During the war, Great Britain sent food and military equipment to Russia by way of Archangel and Murmansk, constructing an 800-mile railway that connected Archangel to the Trans-Siberian Railway near Petrograd. During the summer and fall of 1917, Britain sent 160,000 tons of war matériel to the Russian provisional government in northern Russia and it remained stored there in early 1918. The Russians had not paid for this equipment and Lenin rejected a British offer to exchange food for the military stores in the north.

In February 1918, the Soviet army gained control of Archangel, but at Murmansk the local Soviet was controlled by moderate socialists and cooperated with British Admiral Thomas W. Kemp, who commanded the British naval squadron. On May 24, the Allied Supreme Command at Versailles ordered British troops to take Archangel, and the U.S. navy's cruiser *Olympia* went to Murmansk to assist the movement. In early June, 600 British Royal Marines landed at Murmansk to prepare an attack on Archangel.

At this point, in June 1918, the British requested American troops to assist in northern Russia. Wilson agreed provided that the Supreme Allied Commander, Marshal Ferdinand Foch, stated that American troops at Murmansk were critical to the Allied war effort against Germany. Foch made the required statement, and on July 6 Wilson agreed to send U.S. forces to both northern Russia and Siberia.

Wilson's public statement announcing the dispatch of American forces to Russia was made on July 17. This press release gave Wilson's precise reasons for intervention in Russia. The north Russian troops were "to guard the military stores at Kola" in the peninsula where Murmansk was situated. The Americans would not "take part in organized intervention in adequate force from . . . Murmansk and Archangel." The United States would withdraw its forces if there were developments inconsistent with this policy. Regarding Siberia, Wilson's July 17 statement said that the United States did not intervene to disturb Russia or to win the war against Germany. "The United States could neither take part in such an intervention nor sanction it in principle." The American forces went to Siberia "to help the Czecho-Slovaks to guard military stores . . . , and to render such aid as might be acceptable to the Russians."

Wilson's memo of July 17 influenced Britain and France less than Wilson desired. In addition, the Japanese considered that Wilson's action approved their intervention in northern China and Siberia to control the Trans-Siberian Railway. However, Japan joined the intervention on its own terms, not Wilson's.

For results of the interventions, see September 1 and 4, 1918; June 27, 1919; and April 1, 1920.

August 8, 1918

An allied counteroffensive begins at the Somme and soon extends over all the western front.

After the German spring offensive was turned back at the Marne River between July 18 and August 6, the Allies prepared to strike at the Germans. British forces launched the initial attack on the Somme salient on August 8; their advances continued until the November 11 armistice.

On August 18, the French and a few American troops began an attack in the Oise-Aisne area, and on September 12, separate U.S. forces attacked first at St. Mihiel, later (September 26) at the Meuse-Argonne salient. During this final offensive of the war, more than 1,200,000 U.S. troops were employed.

See March 21, 1918.

September 1, 1918

General William S. Graves arrives at Vladivostok as Commander of American Forces in Siberia.

Following President Wilson's July 6 decision to commit U.S. troops to Siberia, 9,000 soldiers embarked from the Philippine Islands, arriving at Vladivostok on August 16. About the same time, Japan dispatched forces that by November 11 numbered 72,000, while the British sent 1,000 in August and another 1,000 in December. The Japanese forces took up positions along the Trans-Siberian Railway and the Chinese Eastern Railway between Irkutsk and Vladivostok.

Before leaving Washington, General Graves received instructions on his duties from Secretary of War Newton Baker. He obtained a copy of Wilson's July 17 press release and was told to protect the Czech Legion from German and Austrian prisoners of war but not to interfere in Russia's internal or territorial affairs. The American purpose was to aid the Czechoslovaks and not to intervene against the Soviets. Baker added a final warning: "Watch your step; you will be walking on eggs loaded with dynamite. God bless you and good-bye."

For results of the American expedition to Siberia, see April 1, 1920.

September 4, 1918

American troops arrive at Archangel, not Murmansk, because the British route them to the scene of military action without informing Washington.

In keeping with President Wilson's desire that the north Russian action have a military role under the authority of Supreme Allied Commander Foch, the French general and General Pershing sent 4,500 new American recruits from the 339th Infantry Regiment, the 337th Field Hospital Company, and the 310th Engineer Battalion. As specified by Wilson in his July 17 statement, these troops would protect the military stores at Murmansk but not participate in organized intervention.

The American forces embarked from Newcastle, England, on August 5 under the command of British officers. Before their ship reached Murmansk, the British commander, Major General F. C. Poole, wired the ship's captain, ordering him to go directly to Archangel. The Americans arrived at Archangel on the afternoon of September 4, and within 24 hours approximately one-third of them occupied combat outposts against Bolshevik troops and what the British claimed were their "German communist officers." Actually, the nearest Germans were in Finland, 500 miles from Archangel. The alleged presence of Germans was part of the British myth that justified military action in north Russia.

General Poole diverted the American troops to Archangel because of developments in that region since June 23, 1918, which had resulted in engagements between British and Bolshevik armies. Late in June, a British patrol riding the railroad south of Murmansk encountered Soviet soldiers en route to take control of Murmansk. The British captured the Bolshevik train, disarmed the men, and sent it south once again. Subsequently, the British took over the entire hundred miles of railroad between Murmansk and Kem.

The incident near Murmansk attracted the attention of Lenin, and the Soviets determined they should take control of that city. The Soviet commissar for foreign affairs, Georgy Chicherin, contacted the head of the Murmansk Soviet, Aleksey Yuryev, and demanded that he break with the English, who were to be considered as hostile as the Germans. Yuryev rejected Chicherin's advice, telling the foreign affairs

Americans frequently employed reindeer teams in getting about the Archangel region. National Archives

commissar that the English were less evil than the Germans. If Chicherin did not agree, it was only, said Yuryev, because the German ambassador was looking over Chicherin's shoulder. Chicherin became enraged. He denounced Yuryev as an "enemy of the people" and cut off further contact with him. Yuryev and the Murmansk Soviet proceeded to make a formal pact with General Poole, so that the British could claim to act in conjunction with an anti-Soviet in Murmansk.

At Archangel, however, the Bolsheviks had taken over in February 1918, and they began to move the British military stores south to Petrograd as quickly as the spring thaw and Russia's transportation system permitted. Because neither the czar nor the Soviets had paid for these stores, the British wanted to regain them. In May, the Allied War Council planned to direct one-half of the Czech Legion from Siberia to Archangel, but this plot failed. Therefore, late in June the British and French decided to capture Archangel. In July, the French sent a battalion to Murmansk, and General Poole proposed to attack Archangel as soon as possible. Poole had contacted a pro-czarist naval officer under the pseudonym Chaplain at Archangel, and Chaplain agreed to stage a rebellion at the same time that British naval units attacked from the sea.

On August 1, the Poole-Chaplain plot succeeded. While an international force of 1,500 British and French and 50 U.S. Marines from the *Olympia* attacked Archangel, Chaplain's supporters carried out a coup d'état against the local Soviets. The U.S. Marines and the *Olympia* had come to Murmansk on May 24. The Bolsheviks fled into the forests surrounding Archangel, where they erected barricades to defend themselves from the Allies.

At this moment, the fresh and green American soldiers were diverted from Murmansk by General Poole and arrived at Archangel. One-third were placed under the command of British General Finlayson and dispatched on a 100-mile trip by railroad boxcars to the front. Meanwhile, the group of 50 U.S. Marines that landed during the original attack on Archangel had seized an engine and railway cars at the suburb of Bakaritsa and chased the Soviet troops down the rail line for 75 miles. The Americans set up a defense line after the Russians burned a railroad bridge that stopped their train.

Although the action by American soldiers at Archangel violated Wilson's directions of July 17, the president did not find out about General Poole's orders until late in October. By that time, Wilson had become engrossed in the armistice discussions and could not immediately protest. The Americans remained in north Russia for another nine months.

See June 27, 1919, and July 17, 1918.

September 15, 1918

The Sisson Documents are published, purporting to demonstrate that the leaders of Russia's Bolshevik government—Lenin and Trotsky—are German agents. Although released by the U.S. Committee on Public Information, these documents are later found to be forgeries.

On September 15, newspapers throughout America began printing documents that the Committee on Public Information said demonstrated that Lenin's government was "a German government acting solely in the interests of Germany." Edgar Sisson, a U.S. newsman, visited Petrograd during the winter of 1917–1918, and obtained documents from three sources: (1) from Raymond Robins, an American Red Cross director who found pamphlets being distributed on the streets of Petrograd but did not believe they were authentic; (2) from a Russian newsman, Eugene Semenov (alias Kohn); and (3) from a former czarist army officer, Colonel Samsonov, who claimed to have original documents from the Bolshevik headquarters at the Smolny Institute in Petrograd. The documents given to Sisson by Samsonov were allegedly stolen during a clandestine raid on the Smolny headquarters on the night of March 2–3, 1918.

Believing he held explosive proof regarding German control of the Bolsheviks, Sisson left Petrograd on March 3. He left Russia by going through Finland with a group of refugees, having secreted the documents in the baggage of an unwitting Norwegian courier. The trip was arduous, and Sisson arrived in Washington with the documents on May 6. Sisson delivered the papers to George Creel and Secretary of State Lansing. Lansing decided not to release them to the public until the "proper" time. Subsequently, the papers were released in September when President Wilson ordered Creel to let American newspapers print them.

The Sisson papers were released without consulting with the State Department. Some U.S. Foreign Service officers doubted their authenticity. Secretary Lansing stated that he had preferred to wait to release them until a time that would damage the German war effort. Exactly how and why Wilson released the papers is not certain. Creel's committee arranged their distribution. Probably the president desired further support for his July decision to send U.S. troops to Russia.

The publication of the documents appeared to confirm the rumor that Lenin and Trotsky acted on behalf of Germany. There appears to be substance to the allegation that Lenin had been carried across Germany from Switzerland to Petrograd in a sealed German railway car. The papers claimed that the Bolsheviks had acted as German agents since 1914, and that Lenin withdrew Russia from the war in 1918 to assist Germany at the expense of Russian territory. These rumors, if true, would further justify the British, French, and American interventions against the Bolsheviks at Archangel, south Russia, and Siberia after July 1918.

Because of doubts about the documents' authenticity, Creel asked the National Board for Historical Service to appoint a committee to review them. In late September, the board appointed J. Franklin Jameson, editor of the *American Historical Review,* and Samuel Harper, Professor of Russian language and institutions at the University of Chicago. Jameson and Harper reported within a week that "we have no hesitation in declaring . . . the genuineness or authenticity" of 53 of the 68 documents examined. These 53 documents were the critically important ones.

The Jameson-Harper report and the Sisson documents were printed and distributed by Creel's committee in October 1918 in a pamphlet entitled "The German-Bolshevik Conspiracy." Other countries printed the documents in later editions.

Over the next two years, attempts to authenticate the documents were made by Sisson and Creel. In December 1920, however, Creel stopped the investigation because neither the White House nor Mrs. Wilson, who took charge during her husband's illness, would permit an examination of the original documents.

Between 1952 and 1956, the documents became public. Following thorough study, the historian George F. Kennan published an article demonstrating that the Sisson documents were forged. Writing in the June 1956 issue of the *Journal of Modern History,* Kennan showed that the documents contained technical errors of language, form, letterhead, seals, handwriting, and typewriting. Incidentally, historians Jameson and Harper later explained that in 1918 they had acted from a sense of duty to support the war effort against Germany.

September 29, 1918

Takashi Hara is the first commoner to become Japan's Premier.

Heretofore, Japan's government ministry had been headed by persons of noble birth. In 1912, Japan began the Taishō period following the death of the Meiji emperor and the ascension to the imperial throne of Yoshito. The Taishō era marked a period when Japanese politics became liberal and came under the control of leaders who represented civilian and business leadership, marked by Hara's becoming premier in 1918. The Taishō era ended on December 25, 1926.

September 30, 1918

The Allied armies defeat Bulgaria and liberate Romania.

After the British navy took Serb troops to Salonika, the Serbs joined French units to plan an offensive that began on September 15, 1918. The allied forces easily defeated the Bulgarians, who surrendered on September 30th. The French also liberated Romania from the Germans, while French and Serb troops captured Macedonia before linking up with Italian forces to capture Kosovo before entering Belgrade on October 11, 1918. Officials from the Austro-Hungarian Empire signed an armistice on November 3, 1918, before establishing the separate republics of Austria and Hungary. On November 29, 1918, Yugoslav (South Slav) leaders proclaimed the Kingdom of the Serbs, Croats, and Slovenes led by Prince Regent Alexander, who ruled for his father, King Peter. See September 12, 1919.

October 6, 1918

Germany seeks peace on the basis of Wilson's 14 points.

Facing the complete collapse of their armies after the Allied and Associated Powers offensive of August 8 proved successful, General Ludendorff and Field Marshal von Hindenburg advised the government on September 29 to seek peace and maintain some German advantage by an appeal to Wilsonian principles. On October 4, Prince Max of Baden gained control of the German ministry and asked the Swiss government to appeal to President Wilson for a peace treaty based on the 14 Points.

But Wilson did not yield as easily as the German officers had expected. The president delayed a direct answer to the Swiss and consulted with Marshal Foch to determine if the military situation justified an armistice. He also talked with British and French officials about peace and armistice terms.

Because of the later myth of the "stab in the back" by which German liberals, and not the army, "lost the war," the date of the Ludendorff-Hindenburg recommendation (September 29) and of Prince Max's gaining control of the ministry (October 4) is significant. In addition, the August 1918 offensive by the Western Allies had severely damaged the German army.

See November 11, 1918.

October 28, 1918

Theodore Roosevelt's articles opposing the League of Nations and advocating the unconditional surrender of Germany begin publication in the Kansas City *Star*.

Roosevelt's attitude is important in understanding American war aims because he was a spokesman for many Republicans and for other conservative groups that wanted the United States to be strong overseas but opposed Wilson's liberal international style of "new diplomacy."

Roosevelt's series of articles in the Kansas City *Star* advocated boisterous national egoism in foreign affairs through aggressive military power to further the "national interest," as opposed to Wilson's desire for international cooperation. Regarding the war situation, Roosevelt wrote: "This is our war, America's war. If we do not win it we shall some day have to reckon with Germany single-handed. Therefore, for our own sake let us strike down Germany."

Roosevelt had been critical of Wilson's foreign policies since 1914. For example, on January 22, 1917, he castigated Wilson's "peace without victory" speech. The former president said that "Wilson, by his support of a world league and a peace without victory, had become a rallying point for all the pacifists, cowards, and short-sighted fools which had plagued him since the war began."

October 28, 1918

Czechoslovakia declares independence from the Austro-Hungarian monarchy.

The Czechoslovak National Council had been organized in Paris on October 14, selecting Thomáš G. Masaryk as president and Edvard Beneš as foreign minister.

October 30, 1918

The British conclude an armistice with Turkey.

British forces, aided by Arab troops under Colonel T. E. Lawrence, began a major offensive action on September 18, 1918. The Allied army broke Turkish lines at Megiddo and advanced rapidly to capture Beirut (taken over by French naval forces) and Aleppo. In Istanbul, Turkey's Sultan Mohammed VI, who had taken office on July 3, dismissed his Young Turk ministers on October 13 and appealed to President Wilson for an armistice. Not hearing from Washington, he contacted the British naval commander in the Aegean Sea and arranged an armistice on October 30. The Turks were required to place all their territory at the disposal of Allied military operations.

November 5, 1918

Republicans win control of both houses of Congress in the midterm election.

The results of the congressional elections were especially significant because on October 25, President Wilson appealed to the electorate to vote for Democratic candidates who would support his policies at the anticipated peace conference. This appeal backfired because most observers disapproved of presidential interference in state elections, and the Republicans claimed Wilson violated the concept of a truce on politics during the war. Moreover, the election of November 5 seemed to repudiate the president's foreign policies, whether this assessment was correct or not.

In October, President Wilson believed it was essential to have backing for his concept of peace with justice. Many prominent Republicans, including former President Theodore Roosevelt, had denounced the 14 Points as too "soft" on Germany. A Republican Congress, they said, would force stronger surrender terms on the enemy.

To counter the Republicans, many of Wilson's advisers suggested he should not make the peace issue partisan but should back any nominee who desired peace with justice. Wilson disregarded their advice, making a costly mistake that united the Republican Party factions as they had not been united since their 1912 split.

November 11, 1918

Germany signs an armistice to end the war.

Following receipt of the German peace request on October 6, President Wilson undertook to ascertain that the German government represented the people, that the Allies would accept the peace terms, and that Marshal Foch determined an armistice was appropriate from the military viewpoint.

Regarding the German situation, Prince Max, the German chancellor, assured Wilson that his government held a controlling majority in the Reichstag. Further German developments between October 6 and November 9 confirmed this assessment. The German developments included (1) on October 28, a sailors mutiny at Kiel during which the seamen refused to go to sea to fight the British; (2) a revolt in Munich led by Kurt Eisner, an independent socialist who proclaimed the Republic of Bavaria on November 8; (3) the proclamation of the abdication of Emperor William II on November 9 followed by the proclamation of a German republic in Berlin under a ministry of the Majority Socialists led by Frederick Ebert and Philipp Scheidemann. The emperor fled to exile in Holland.

Day of jubilation as U.S. soldiers greet the Armistice at the front. National Archives

Second, Wilson sent Colonel House to Europe as his personal representative to conduct pre-armistice negotiations with the Allies. By November 5, the Allies agreed to accept Wilson's peace plans as the basis of peace with only two vital reservations: (1) the British insisted that Britain's interpretation of the freedom of the seas (Point Two) could not be given up but agreed to make it a subject of future discussion; (2) France demanded that Germany pay compensation for damages to civilian populations and their property and that "reparation for damages" must be obtained. Once the Allies agreed to these terms, only the military situation needed to be resolved.

Marshal Foch and the military commanders of the Allied and Associated Powers had final control over the armistice. Significantly, only General Pershing of the United States dissented seriously with the Allied commanders regarding the armistice issue. Following the normal U.S. military doctrine developed during the 19th-century Indian wars, Pershing wanted the Germans to be given no conditions for surrender. The European commanders, whose military doctrine was based on centuries of European conflict among often nearly equal opponents, believed, as Foch said, "One makes war only to get results"; that is, war is for political purposes only insofar as defeating the enemy's military and naval power serves political ends. These ends the European commanders had achieved, and therefore, in their view, an armistice with surrender terms was appropriate. General Foch met with a German Armistice Commission to settle the surrender terms.

Foch and the Germans agreed to surrender conditions, and at 11 A.M. on November 11, the armistice became effective and hostilities ceased. The important armistice conditions were (1) Germany would evacuate all occupied territory, the left bank of the Rhine River, and the bridgeheads at Mainz, Cologne, and Coblenz; (2) the Allies and the United States reserved the right to make damage claims; (3) the German submarines and fleet would be interned and German aircraft, tanks, and heavy artillery would be destroyed; (4) the treaties of Bucharest and Brest-Litovsk would be abrogated; (5) all prisoners of war and deported civilians would be returned; (6) the Allied blockade would continue until a peace treaty was signed; (7) Germany would turn over to the Allies 150,000 railroad cars, 5,000 locomotives, and 5,000 trucks.

At the time the armistice was made, the total of U.S. deaths was 112,432, more than half of these from an influenza pandemic at U.S. military camps. The battle casualties of the American Expeditionary Forces were 48,909 dead and 230,074 wounded. During the entire war in Europe, the estimated number of dead was 10 million, with 20 million more being wounded.

November 29, 1918

The American Peace Commission to the Paris Peace Conference is announced; President Wilson heads the delegation.

The president had announced on November 18 that he would go to Paris personally, but the names of the official delegates were not announced by the White House until November 29. In addition to Wilson, the group included Secretary of State Lansing, Colonel House, General Tasker H. Bliss, and Henry White, a Republican who was an able career diplomat.

The announcement that Wilson would attend resulted in protests from many Republicans and news editors; the delegation announcement received additional criticism from many of Wilson's opponents. The Republicans complained that although they controlled Congress, they had not been consulted or that there were better Republicans than Henry White to represent their views. Senator Henry Cabot Lodge, the chairman of the Senate Foreign Relations Committee, was the logical Republican choice, but Lodge and Wilson disliked each other intensely.

December 4, 1918

President Wilson leaves for Europe to make tour of the continent before the peace conference begins.

Wilson's tour of France, England, and Italy inspired a massive outpouring of public emotion that hailed the president as a messiah or prince of peace. Whether Wilson's peace ideals and the nationalistic aspirations of the crowds greeting him were compatible would become a question only after the Paris Conference began on January 12, 1919. Certainly, his efforts to limit the British, French, and Italian attempts to punish the Germans were not accepted by the same crowds that greeted him in December, 1918.

Wilson in Dover, England, 1919, receiving a warm reception. National Archives

December 14, 1918

The British "khaki" election—Lloyd George's coalition cabinet retains a huge majority by promising to punish German "war criminals" and making the central powers pay fully for the costs of the war.

The strongly nationalist-militarist atmosphere surrounding this post-armistice election sent Lloyd George to the Paris Peace Conference with a mandate to take revenge on Germany for the war. This contrasted strongly with the idealistic, nonpunitive approach that President Wilson desired. It closely resembled similar speeches by French Premier Georges Clemenceau, who vowed to punish Germany harshly.

In the December 14 election, Irish Nationalists of the Sinn Fein were elected to the British Parliament. The British had arrested Eamon De Valera and other Sinn Fein leaders, but their political organization triumphed nevertheless. The Sinn Fein members of Parliament declared Irish independence and refused to attend any sessions of Parliament in London.

December 17, 1918

French forces arrive at Odessa in the Ukraine on premier Clemenceau's orders to isolate and destroy Russian Bolshevism.

The French intervention at Odessa became the Allies' most disastrous operation in Russia from 1918 to 1920. Clemenceau, the most ardent anti-Communist of the Big Three, often chided Lloyd George and Wilson for their weakness in pursuing Russian intervention. The Ukraine offered Clemenceau the opportunity to demonstrate the proper anti-Bolshevism. Yet the French attempt ended in total failure and the desertion of many anti-Communist refugees in the Ukraine.

Clemenceau ordered the French intervention on October 27, 1918, contrary to the advice of General Franchet d'Esperey, the French commander in the Danube area who had led French and Greek forces to victory against the Bulgarians on September 30, 1918. The French premier replaced d'Esperey with the more optimistic General Henri Berthelot, who brought 1,700 French troops to Odessa on December 17.

In December 1918, Ukrainian politics were in near anarchy. Following the Bolshevik Revolution of November 1917, Ukrainian nationalists established an independent state and drove out the German and Austrian forces. Soon after, Soviet forces moved into Kiev to prevent the new government from operating. At Brest-Litovsk, Lenin agreed to evacuate the Ukraine, and German troops returned to pillage and loot the province. A Ukrainian nationalist, Simon Petliura, rallied the people and took control when the Germans withdrew on November 11, 1918.

During the winter of 1918–1919, Trotsky delayed sending the Red Army to the Ukraine because of the political problems. Petliura tried to create a dictatorship, numerous Don Cossack atamans fought each other to extend their personal power, and a former czarist officer, General Anatol Denikin, sent his officers to the Ukraine to set up an anti-Bolshevik Russian state. Among these many factions, the largest were Petliura's Ukrainian nationalists and the czarist group under Denikin's appointee, General Grishin-Almazov.

For the consequences of Clemenceau's intervention, see April 5, 1919.

1919

January 15, 1919

The Spartacists uprising in Berlin, during which the Communists fight to control the German capital city, ends.

On November 10, a coalition ministry of the Independent and Majority Socialists gained control in Berlin. Soon, however, the Independents joined the extreme left-wing communists (Spartacists) led by Karl Liebknecht and Rosa Luxemburg to seek dictatorial control and to use violence to effect a radical economic revolution. The majority Socialists (Social Democrats) preferred evolutionary not violent changes for Germany and proposed a national assembly to draw up a constitution.

To forestall control by an assembly, the Spartacists revolted in Berlin and attempted to duplicate Lenin's victory of November 1917. The Social Democratic leader, Friederich Ebert, decided to accept the aid of the German General Staff in putting down the uprising. This tactic met immediate success and the rebellion was silenced by January 15. Liebknecht and Luxemburg were arrested and executed on

January 15. Subsequently, a national constituent assembly was elected on January 19 and began sessions at Weimar on February 6, 1919. The Communists boycotted the election, in which the Social Democrats won 163 seats while other parties won 258.

In February, the Communists staged smaller uprisings in Berlin, Munich, and other cities, but they were suppressed. When a Soviet Republic was declared on April 4 in Bavaria, it was overthrown by the German army of the federal government.

January 18, 1919

The Paris Peace Conference formally opens.

The conference was attended by 70 delegates representing 27 victorious powers. The Germans did not gain recognition to join the discussions until the treaty terms were ready to be signed on May 7, 1919.

February 12, 1919

The Prinkipo proposal—a British-American suggestion—fails to end the Russian Civil War.

At discussions during the Paris Peace Conference in January 1919, Prime Minister Lloyd George and President Wilson agreed to invite all warring factions of the Red and White Russian armies together to settle their disputes. Georges Clemenceau absolutely refused to invite them to Paris, so Lloyd George proposed Prinkipo Island in the Sea of Marmara. Clemenceau agreed to this and the Big Three invited the various Russian factions to attend a Prinkipo conference on February 15.

On February 12, Lenin agreed to an armistice and meeting under prescribed conditions, but Admiral Kolchak and General Denikin, the two principal White leaders, refused. President Wilson learned later that Clemenceau had discreetly advised the pro-czarist leaders not to accept the proposal, undermining any slim hope that the conference might succeed.

February 14, 1919

At the Paris Peace Conference, President Wilson reads the covenant of the League of Nations drafted by a conference commission that he chaired.

Prominent among his 14 Points of 1918, Wilson believed that if a League of Nations were properly formed, it could work out in the long term any immediate shortcomings of the remainder of the peace treaty. Therefore, he wanted to secure the league agreement as quickly as possible using his political as well as diplomatic skills to have the delegates approve it. He obtained Italy's vote, for example, by promising the Brenner frontier in the Tyrol, an area where 200,000 Germans lived and a subject that later caused problems. Nevertheless, he won his point, and on January 25 the conference voted to make the League of Nations covenant part of the treaty. Wilson was appointed chairman of the commission to draft the league proposal. After laboring arduously for two

The "Big Four" at Versailles. (left to right) Premier Vittorio Orlando of Italy, Prime Minister David Lloyd George of Great Britain, Premier Georges Clemenceau of France, and President Woodrow Wilson of the United States

weeks, the commission offered its draft to the delegates on February 14. Although the draft underwent a few revisions, the commission report became the basis for the League of Nations as adopted in its final form on April 28, 1919.

March 2, 1919

The Third Communist International is founded in Moscow.

Lenin's government founded the Third Communist International because of the belief that it was important to the Bolsheviks' success in Russia to secure support from workers in other parts of Europe and the world.

The First International had been founded by Karl Marx in London during 1864 but was wrecked by a dispute between Marx and Michael BAKUNIN, who advocated direct action to create anarchy as the method to promote the working-class revolution. The Second International, organized in 1889, was dominated by moderate socialists who opposed violence and believed in the gradual evolution of socialism as part of economic democracy. The Second International split apart in August 1914, because most delegates joined their nations' war efforts.

Late in 1918, Lenin discovered plans begun in western and central Europe to revive the Second International. To counteract this possibility and bring the organization under Russian control, Lenin invited delegates from various European nations to send representatives to Moscow to establish the Third International. He especially hoped to get radical socialists from Germany to join the Russian organization.

During its sessions between March 2 and 6, 1919, 35 delegates attended. Most of them represented minority groups of the old Russian Empire. Five foreign representatives came from Germany, Austria, Norway, Sweden, and Holland. The radical German delegates came to oppose a new international group, hoping to keep Germans in control of the Second International. Nevertheless, the Russian delegates dominated the meeting and voted to organize the Third International under Bolshevik leadership.

March 4, 1919

Senator Lodge introduces a Senate petition signed by 39 Senators opposing the League of Nations in the form now proposed: the Republican "Round Robin Petition."

Lodge's petition had been prepared by several Republican senators following a meeting of February 26 with President Wilson. Recently returned from Paris, Wilson had hoped to answer all questions about the league from members of the House Committee on Foreign Affairs and Senate Committee on Foreign Relations. Although Wilson's friends thought the White House meeting went well, Republican Senator Frank Brandegee of Connecticut showed his group's discontent, telling newsmen, "I feel as if I had been wandering with Alice in Wonderland and had tea with the Mad Hatter."

Consequently, for Wilson the only surprise about Lodge's presentation on March 4 was that 39 signatories, over one-third of the senators, opposed Wilson's plan. Later in the evening of March 4, Wilson in a speech in New York City defiantly disclosed his tactics for the anticipated struggle in the Senate. He said there would be "so many threads of the treaty tied to the covenant that you cannot dissect the covenant from the treaty without destroying the whole vital structure. The structure of peace will not be vital without the League of Nations, and no man is going to bring back a cadaver with him." Apparently, Wilson did not believe the senators would reject the entire peace treaty.

March 21, 1919

A Socialist-Communist government is formed in Hungary; soon after, the Communist Béla Kun establishes a Communist dictatorship.

On October 17, 1919, Hungary declared complete independence from Austria and declared itself a republic on November 16. On March 21, Hungarian President Michael KAROLYI resigned to protest the Allied powers' decision to assign Transylvania to Romania. The same day the socialist Alexander GARBAI became president and Kun became minister of foreign affairs. Kun, who had come to Hungary from Russia in November 1918, soon crowded out the socialists and took full control.

See August 1, 1919.

April 5, 1919

French forces evacuate Odessa, leaving behind nearly 500,000 anti-Bolshevik refugees who crowded to Odessa to gain French protection.

Premier Clemenceau's October 1918 predictions that he could destroy bolshevism ended in disaster on April 5, when the French commander in Odessa received orders to evacuate southern Russia. The quick French exit resulted from the hopelessness of the French attempt to back anti-Bolshevik armies in the Ukraine and political circumstances in Paris that required Clemenceau to recall the troops or be voted out of office. If Clemenceau had followed General d'Esperey's advice in 1918, the French débâcle would have been avoided.

The French troops in the Ukraine faced internal disputes and anti-Bolshevik Russians who fought each other. Within the French army, Clemenceau's precise objective was not clear. Many French officers did not understand their mission, for as one French general told his men: "We are not here to fight. We cannot anyway since we are not at war with Russia." Other officers grumbled that no Frenchman who had survived Verdun or the Marne against Germany wanted to die in Russia.

Equally serious, the local Russian army leaders preferred fighting each other to fighting the Bolsheviks. Petliura, the Ukrainian national leader, dreamed of controlling an independent state; the White army General Grishin-Almazov wanted to save the province for the new czarist empire of General Denikin. The French could not decide which local leader to support, and attempts to compromise made their status more tenuous.

In the midst of the political confusion at Odessa, the Bolsheviks enlisted a competent military commander to conquer the Ukraine. He was Vladimir Antonov-Ovseenko, the officer whose Soviet troops had arrested the members of Kerensky's government in November 1917, and was a notable Bolshevik until executed by Stalin during the 1938 purges. In 1918, Antonov led Red Army forces in defeating the Petliurists and capturing Kiev on February 4. He then recruited a Cossack, Nikifor Grigorev, and sent him against the French position on the Black Sea.

The telling blow against the French became Grigorev's siege of Odessa, which began on March 12. The French had greater fire power because of their warships along the Black Sea coast. Within the city, troop morale was poor and the city suffered from typhus, food shortages, and overcrowding. Many local Ukrainians were anti-Bolshevik and flocked to Odessa for protection, but this only made living conditions there worse.

In Paris, newspapers and politicians first avoided printing reports on the difficulty in the Ukraine. In Britain, however, the Manchester *Guardian* reported the Bolshevik successes. Even Winston Churchill, whose anticommunism matched Clemenceau's, confessed that the Ukrainian experience had been a disaster and the French had aroused the ill will of most Russians.

French leaders soon had to admit their problems to the Chamber of Deputies. Marshal Foch confessed that Odessa was unimportant and that the only reason for keeping French troops there was to bolster army morale. Finally, on March 29, Clemenceau's delegate announced to the assembly that no more troops would be sent to Russia because an evacuation was being planned.

In Odessa, the April 5 evacuation notice caused panic in the city. Refugees rushed to the docks to secure passage out of the city. Exactly how many escaped is not known. The French took their troops aboard their warships and crowded 40,000 Russians on board before leaving. Many of the remaining refugees committed suicide; some died during the mad rush to board the ships. The fate of the rest was never reported.

According to the British historian John Silverlight, French news reports and memoirs on the Ukrainian incident are almost nonexistent. No official French reports were issued. The French attempt never achieved the heights of Clemenceau's anti-Communist rhetoric. The Odessa incident was the clearest instance of a direct Allied attempt to overthrow the Bolsheviks; it was a disaster.

April 10, 1919

A U.S. attempt to reach a settlement with the Bolsheviks fails: the Bullitt Mission.

Shortly after the White army generals rejected the Prinkipo conference on February 12, 1919, Colonel House and Secretary of State Lansing accepted William C. Bullitt's suggestion that Bullitt make a personal trip to Petrograd and Moscow to assess the situation. A State Department aide at the Paris Conference, Bullitt believed that every effort should be made to reconcile the Russians because Wilson's Point 4 of the 14 Points saw this as an "acid test" for creating goodwill among Europeans. Before sending Bullitt to Russia, the Americans obtained Britain's Prime Minister Lloyd George's sanction for the attempt.

On March 16, Bullitt held a personal interview with Lenin and reported to Paris that the Bolsheviks had agreed to terms of negotiation provided the Allies would accept them by April 10. Lenin's terms included an armistice by all Russian groups, amnesty to Russians who supported the Allies, the end of the Allied blockade of Russia, the withdrawal from Russia of Allied forces, and the opening of channels of discussion between Moscow and Paris.

Bullitt returned to Paris enthusiastic about his mission, but he found no ready audience for Lenin's proposal. The Big Four (Wilson, Lloyd George, Clemenceau, and Orlando) were in the midst of a crisis over French reparation demands. In addition, Clemenceau disliked the Americans' failure to consult with him before the mission began. Consequently, the Allied leaders never considered the merits of Lenin's offer and the April 10 deadline passed.

April 11, 1919

A Japanese proposition to include a statement on racial equality in the League of Nations covenant is defeated by the conference delegates: the U.S. delegates abstain in the voting.

One of Japan's principal objectives during the Paris Peace Conference was to obtain recognition for the equality of rights of Asians at world meetings, a proposition backed by the Chinese delegates. Although President Wilson supported Japan's proposal at conference meetings, he and Colonel House avoided debate on the issue in plenary sessions open to the public because of the anti-Asian antagonisms of some of the U.S. Western states.

Wilson endeavored to find some means to have the Japanese proposal approved without debate, but British and Australian delegates strongly opposed the racial equality amendment. Attempts to qualify Japan's statement sufficiently to satisfy the British were unsuccessful. Therefore, during the April 11 session of the peace commission, Wilson abstained from voting on Japan's proposal. In addition, as chairman of that day's session Wilson ruled that unanimity was necessary to approve Japan's proposal. Consequently, when the commission voted 11 to 6 for the statement, Wilson ruled it was not adopted.

Coincidentally, because Wilson's secret support for the Japanese proposal was not publicized, the Australian delegation told the Japanese reporters that the United States should be blamed for the defeat of the amendment. This news was published in Japanese newspapers, causing anti-American tirades similar to those regarding the California laws against the Japanese in 1905. Colonel House tried to stop the lies of the Australians but his efforts were constrained because Wilson had abstained in the vote of April 11.

April 16, 1919

Clemenceau and Wilson compromise on the Rhineland occupation after a British-American guarantee of French security is offered.

Late in March, 1919, the Big Four reached a deadlock on peace terms because of French-American disagreement regarding France's demands for security through its occupation of territory on the left (east) bank of the Rhine River and French desires for war reparations.

On April 2, President Wilson became ill from influenza, and by April 7 he made plans to leave the conference because of the French demands. Prime Minister Lloyd George saved the conference by proposing the British-American guarantee of French security. In addition, the principle of reparations would be accepted, but a special Reparations Commission would decide the exact terms after the peace treaty was concluded.

France considered the guarantee treaties to be vital to prevent a future German attack. To placate

Clemenceau, France could occupy the Rhineland and receive the coal of the SAAR Valley for 15 years. A plebiscite would determine the later fate of the region. More important, the United States and Britain agreed to conclude treaties with France by which they would "come immediately to the assistance of France as soon as any unprovoked movement of aggression against her is made by Germany." These treaties were signed on June 29, 1919, but were never ratified by the U.S. Senate or the British government.

April 17, 1919

The Hoover-Nansen proposal for Russian food relief is approved by the big three powers but on conditions the Bolsheviks cannot accept.

Herbert Hoover, who had effectively organized the Belgian Relief Prograrn, proposed on March 28, 1919, a similar relief effort to serve Russia's needs. He and the Norwegian explorer Fridtjof NANSEN thought this humanitarian effort was necessary for the Russian people.

Because Hoover's proposal came under consideration at the moment when Bullitt's proposal from Lenin was being denied, Colonel House argued that the food relief in exchange for a Russian armistice would be an alternative to simply rejecting Lenin's March offer. The Allied leaders accepted this idea but added other strings to entice Lenin to end the civil war. Food relief would be offered provided that hostilities had stopped, local governments in Russia could distribute the food, and the Food Relief Commission could control transportation in Russia to deliver the goods.

The conditions imposed by the Allies were unacceptable to the Russian government. A Red Army offensive against Admiral Kolchak had turned the war in favor of the Communists. In addition, Lenin would not agree to turn Russia's transportation over to a foreign group. Consequently, on May 20, Foreign Minister Chicherin refused the relief proposal. He informed Nansen that the Russian people appreciated his offer but feared the Allies' conditions were a trap to overthrow the Bolshevik regime. Later, in 1921, Hoover undertook a less politically conditioned relief program for Russia.

For the Belgian Relief Plan, see October 16, 1914; also see April 10, 1919.

April 23, 1919

Italian Premier Orlando protests Wilson's opposition to Italy's demand for the Tyrol and the eastern Adriatic coast.

In 1915, Italy joined France and England against Germany after a secret Treaty of London promised to give the Tyrol and Trentino and the eastern Adriatic coast to Italy. On February 14, 1919, Wilson acceded to Orlando's claims before the president realized that 200,000 Germans lived in the Tyrol and Yugoslavs occupied the Adriatic Coast. Wilson shifted his position on April 23 by denouncing the secret 1915 treaty as violating the principle of self-determination. At the height of Wilson's argument, Orlando protested and packed his briefcase, leaving Paris until May 6. Nevertheless, the Versailles delegates completed their work on the German treaty, leaving Italy and Yugoslavia to settle their disputes on the Dalmatian coast. See June 23, and September 12, 1919.

See February 14, 1919.

April 30, 1919

Japan's rights in Shantung are recognized by the big three despite China's opposition.

Although China had accepted Japan's rights in the Kiachow peninsula and Shantung by a treaty in 1918, Chinese delegates argued at Paris that China's participation in World War I canceled the German rights and therefore Japan's takeover of the German rights. Because France and Great Britain had previously recognized these Japanese rights, Woodrow Wilson was the only member of the Big Three (in Orlando's absence there was no Big Four) to advocate China's point of view.

As a compromise on this question, Wilson agreed that Japan could have the former German concessions provided that Tokyo return political control of the regions to China as soon as China's civil strife ended. As in the case of the Lansing-Ishii agreement of 1917, this section of the peace treaty was open to a variety of interpretations in the future. Furthermore, the Chinese rejected these peace terms. The United States sympathized with China even though there was no definite American national interest in China. Wilson challenged Japan in terms of abstract justice and without backing from other powers such as England or France.

Japan Allegedly Using League to Grab China. San Francisco Chronicle.

May 4, 1919

The May Fourth Movement begins in China.

This movement united students and Chinese workers against all foreign concessions in China, particularly those of Japan. Although China had only 2 million industrial workers in 1922, Chinese leaders had begun organizing labor groups. In May 1919, these groups joined Chinese students who had long agitated for a modern China that would overthrow the old Confucian authorities of the family and village elders. While traditional Chinese culture continued to thrive, the May Fourth attitudes challenged those ideas by using Sun Yat-sen's Three Peoples' Principles of nationalism, democracy, and livelihood to equalize land rights and modernize China's society.

June 23, 1919

Facing the alternative of an Allied invasion, Germany's republican government representatives sign the Treaty of Versailles.

The German delegates were presented with the Treaty of Versailles on May 7, but after reading its terms, Count Ulrich von BROCKDORFF-RANTZAU, who had been sent by Philippe Schiedeman's ministry, protested that the terms did not accord with conditions laid down by the Allies at the time of the November 11 armistice. Schiedeman's ministry resigned in protest, but a new coalition headed by Gustav BAUER accepted the agreement, and the treaty was signed on June 23. Because Germany's crews of naval fleet had scuttled their ships on June 21 rather than turn them over to the Allies, the victorious powers were determined to enforce the treaty.

The first section of the treaty provided for the League of Nations. All treaty signatory powers of the victor nations were members; additional members could join by a two-thirds vote. A permanent secretariate was set up at Geneva, and there was a two-chamber representative body: the General Assembly, in which all member states had one vote; and the Council, which consisted of the five great powers—Great Britain, France, Italy, Japan, and the United States. Member nations were to protect each other.

On July 7, the German government ratified the treaty. France ratified it on October 13; Great Britain and Italy on October 15; and Japan on October 30. The U.S. Senate refused to ratify the treaty.

See March 19, 1920.

June 27, 1919

American forces withdraw from northern Russia.

Immediately after the armistice on November 11, 1918, Secretary of War Baker urged Wilson to withdraw American troops from Archangel. Having learned of the unauthorized use of the troops by the British, Wilson agreed, but the withdrawal became impossible because of the freezing of the rivers and ports near Archangel. As a result, the American soldiers endured a miserably cruel winter in north Russia, huddled in blockhouses and alert against a possible Bolshevik attack. One American outpost was attacked, and the U.S. troops withdrew under dangerous conditions. This was the only actual engagement with the Bolsheviks following the August "conquest" of Archangel by the Allies. Nevertheless, the morale of the American troops deteriorated during the winter, and near mutinies took place in some units.

Even as the spring thaw began, the U.S. troop removal proceeded slowly. The Allied difficulties in north Russia had grown over the winter because the British and French commanders argued about which local political factions should be recognized. The British supported the pro-czarist Gregory Chaplain, who had assisted them in the takeover at Archangel, while the French backed a local Social Revolutionary, Nikolai Chaikovsky. The Social Revolutionaries gained control at Archangel, but when Chaikovsky left for Paris in January 1919, the Allies lost all local support. Meanwhile, the Bolsheviks rallied the peasants in the surrounding regions by opposing the "invaders" of the homeland. In this situation, President Wilson delayed the U.S. withdrawal out of deference to British requests to maintain some strength at Archangel.

U.S. Senate action finally stirred Wilson to speed up a program to bring the troops home from Archangel. The soldiers were largely from regiments out of Michigan and Wisconsin, and citizens from those states flooded congress with petitions. On February 14, Senator Hiram Johnson offered a resolution to withdraw troops from north Russia; this resolution failed to pass the Senate only because Vice President Marshall cast his tie-breaking vote against the resolution.

Three days later, Secretary Baker announced that American troops would leave north Russia as soon as weather permitted. Delay continued, however, because of British Minister of War Winston Churchill's attempt to persuade the Allied leaders at Paris to launch an attack south of Archangel, where they might link up with Admiral Kolchak's armies. Wilson opposed this action but did not speed up the U.S. withdrawal in order to placate Lloyd George, who was in political difficulty in Great Britain against Churchill's Conservative Party followers.

After Kolchak's army in Siberia retreated in May 1919, the British command overruled Churchill and began a withdrawal. The last American troops evacuated on June 27; the British and French stayed in Archangel until September 27, and at Murmansk until October 12, 1919. They turned Archangel over to a former czarist officer, General E. Miller, who held out against the Red Army until February 2, 1920.

At Archangel, the British and French lost 327 men; the American casualties were 139 from injuries or accidents.

July 10, 1919

The Senate Foreign Relations Committee receives the Treaty of Versailles but uses delaying tactics to allow its opposition to organize.

President Wilson had realized since the Senate "Round Robin Petition" of March 4 that he would have difficulty obtaining ratification of the Treaty of Versailles by the U.S. Senate. But he expected that the good sense of the senators and the necessity of having a formal peace treaty would persuade the Senate to accept the treaty as well as the League of Nations, which was a part of that treaty.

By July, Senator Henry Cabot Lodge, chairman of the Senate Foreign Relations Committee, and other senators were preparing a national campaign against the League of Nations. Although Lodge was willing to accept a league with reservations protecting American sovereignty, "irreconcilable" senators such as William Borah, Hiram Johnson, and Robert La Follette advocated rejection of any league. Six of the ten members of the Senate Foreign Relations Committee were irreconcilables, giving them an influence far in excess of their Senate following. The campaign to defeat the league received financial assistance from two millionaires, Andrew Mellon and Henry C. Frick.

Both the Lodge reservationists and the irreconcilables opposed the league because they believed that the collective security concept implicit in the league's ability to maintain peace sacrificed American national sovereignty. The reservationists would accept treaties for consultation and negotiation so long as all final decisions could be independently made by the United States. During the extensive Senate hearings arranged by Lodge to delay action on the treaty, other arguments were presented against the treaty and the league. Those heard frequently included these:

1. The treaty treated Germany too harshly and violated the 14 Points.
2. German-Americans believed the treaty betrayed their fatherland.
3. Italian-Americans wanted Fiume for Italy.
4. Irish-Americans claimed the British Empire could demand that Americans help subdue Ireland.
5. The treaty violated America's tradition of no foreign entanglements.

Europe Between Wars, 1919–1937

6. America was superior to other nations and should not treat them as equals.
7. European conflicts such as current wars between Hungary and Czechoslovakia or Greece and Turkey would involve America.
8. The Allied powers were not sufficiently grateful that America saved them by entering World War I.

The delaying tactics achieved their main goal. American enthusiasm for the league gradually subsided as more and more special interest groups attacked the Treaty of Versailles. To counteract his opposition, Wilson decided to launch his own publicity campaign.

See September 25, 1919.

July 31, 1919

Germany adopts the Weimar Constitution to establish a republican government.

The Weimar Republic was created at a time of severe crisis in Germany. The Allied blockade did not end until July 12, 1919, and had brought the populace to near starvation. Moreover, the Allies forced representatives of the Weimar Assembly to sign the Treaty of Versailles, which Germans believed violated the principles of the 14 Points, on which they had based their surrender in November 1918.

August 1, 1919

The Communist dictator of Hungary, Béla Kun, flees to Austria when Romanian forces attack Budapest.

Hungary had declared war on Czechoslovakia on March 28 to regain its Slovakian provinces. When Béla Kun's Hungarian army threatened to conquer Transylvania as well, Romania began a preemptive war and invaded Hungary on April 10. While Romania's army invaded successfully, Admiral Miklós HORTHY formed a counterrevolutionary movement that replaced Kun, who fled to Vienna on August 1.

After the Romanian armies withdrew from their occupation of Budapest on February 25, 1920, Horthy's followers took control and proclaimed a monarchy on March 23, 1920.

September 2, 1919

The American socialists split into three blocs: the Socialist Party, The Communist Labor Party, and the Communist Party of America.

Although there had been factions in the Socialist Party of the United States before 1914, the Bolshevik victory in Russia and Lenin's formation of the Third International in March 1919 caused the Socialist Party to split into three irreconcilable divisions in 1919. The old leadership of the Socialist Party (SP) retained majority control, espousing an evolutionary-style socialism related to American conditions and willing to work with trade unions. When the SP met in Chicago on August 30, 1919, one division developed because the moderates refused to seat John Reed and Benjamin Gitlow, who represented the left-wing faction.

This initial split caused another division when the radical socialists met in Chicago on September 2, 1919. One group, led by Louis Farina, extolled Russia's call to immediate revolution and to break relations with the moderates, the trade unions, and liberal reformers. They formed the Communist Party of America (CP), which, after much competition with other factions, gained the backing of Moscow's Comintern.

The second bloc in Chicago at the September 2 meeting was the Communist Labor Party (CLP), which was led by Reed. The CLP disagreed with the CP because it rejected the possibility of an immediate revolution in America and did not want to isolate itself from appeals to the majority of Americans.

The CLP endorsed the direct action of the International Workers of the World but condemned the American Federation of Labor as did most socialists. Unlike the CP, the CLP wanted to create an American movement that did not declare the unconditional loyalty to the Third International demanded by the Russian Bolsheviks.

According to historian Theodore Draper, the CP and CLP had approximately 40,000 members after September 2, 1919, with 23,744 paying dues to the CP. He believes that because 75% of these were native Russians or East Europeans, they joined out of national sympathy for Russia, not because they were ideologically committed to Bolshevism. The English-speaking members of the CP and CLP became leaders of the organizations, even though they made up only 10% of the membership.

September 10, 1919

Austria signs the Treaty of Saint-Germain, which ends World War I.

This treaty ratified the breakup of the Habsburg Empire, which had already been effected by revolution in various parts of the empire. Austria recognized the independence of Czechoslovakia, Yugoslavia, Poland, and Hungary. It also ceded Eastern Galicia to Poland, Trentino and South Tyrol to Italy, and Trieste and Istria to Yugoslavia. Austria had to pay reparations for the war and limit its army to 30,000 men.

September 11, 1919

U.S. Marines land in Honduras to quell an uprising.

Serious conflict began in Honduras in 1919 following an insurrection led by Rafael López Gutierrez, which overthrew President Francisco BERTRAND, the Conservative Party leader, who had been elected in March 1916. The U.S. forces prevented full-scale civil war but political disorders continued in Honduras, and the United States had to land more marines in 1924

See March 10, 1924.

September 12, 1919

A crisis begins when Gabriele D'Annunzio seizes Fiume.

Radical Italian nationalists such as D'Annunzio were ready to fight for Italy's right to Fiume and the entire Dalmatian coast, opposing any compromise with the Yugoslavs. Although D'Annunzio's capture of Fiume nearly precipitated war, conflict was averted in 1919. Rome and Belgrade settled the dispute over Dalmatia in the Treaty of Rapallo on November 12, 1920. Fiume became an independent city and the Yugoslavs abandoned all claims to the city. The treaty gave the Dalmatian coast to the Yugoslavs except for the city of Zara and part of Istria.

September 25, 1919

President Wilson has a physical breakdown during a nationwide tour seeking public support for the League of Nations.

The senatorial campaign against the League of Nations had become so pervasive that Wilson decided on September 4 to tour the nation to appeal to the good sense of the public for support. On August 19, the president had met with the Senate Foreign Relations Committee, to whom he proposed the method of adding "interpretive" reservations to the Treaty of Versailles that would not require action by the other signatory nations. The irreconcilables would not accept this or any other league covenant and the president realized that he had to find some means to change other senators' votes—namely, by appealing to their constituents.

Therefore, on September 2 he began a 9,500-mile tour during which he hoped to deliver 37 speeches in 29 cities, even though his personal physician advised against it. For over three weeks, Wilson's efforts appeared to be successful in arousing warm public support. By train, he traveled through Ohio, Indiana, and Illinois and into the Great Plains states. Sometimes his speeches were hastily prepared, and as he grew weary he resorted to uncustomary accusations against his opposition, calling them "contemptible quitters." In the Rocky Mountain and Pacific Coast states, demonstrations of acclaim exceeded those of the Midwest because the Western states had been his staunch supporters in 1916.

Heading back toward the east, Wilson's tour climaxed unexpectedly in Pueblo, Colorado, on September 25. The president had planned to continue to New England but he was exhausted and verged on a nervous breakdown. Therefore, he returned to Washington, where he suffered a stroke on October 2. The stroke paralyzed one side of Wilson's body and incapacitated him for seven and one-half months. During this period, the president held no cabinet meetings or visits with outsiders, including Colonel House and Secretary of State Lansing. The president's wife consulted with him and communicated his conclusions to administrative personnel.

Wilson's collapse ended his effort to obtain public backing against Lodge and the irreconcilables. In addition, the president and the moderates could not conduct direct discussions that might have led to compromise on the treaty.

For the outcome of the treaty fight in the Senate, see November 19, 1919, and March 19, 1920.

November 7, 1919

The "Palmer raids" begin: anti-Communist fears lead to Bureau of Investigation raids against American radicals.

With President Wilson's approval, Attorney General A. Mitchell Palmer ordered the Justice Department's Bureau of Investigation to examine socialist-communist agitation. On January 21, 1919, the Seattle, Washington, shipyard strike focused attention on alleged communist influence in America. Organized by the International Workers of the World (IWW), the Seattle strikers carried red flags and made anti-capitalist speeches. On February 6, the IWW called a general strike, a tactic that many Americans believed was communistic. Although there was no violence by the Seattle workers, Mayor Ole Hanson, who hated the IWW, claimed they plotted to overthrow the government. Local newspapers took Mayor Hanson's cue and when the strike ended on February 10, the Seattle *Star* headlines read, "Today the Bolshevik-sired Nightmare Is at an End"; the *Post-Intelligencer* asserted, "Our Flag Is Still There," beneath a cartoon showing the tattered red Bolshevik flag.

Other U.S. strikes and bomb plots plus several European events in 1919 appeared to be part of the Bolshevik world revolution. In February, an assassin unsuccessfully attacked French Premier Clemenceau; in March, Béla Kun's Communists held temporary control over Hungary, and Moscow announced the formation of the Third Communist International.

Bomb plots were disclosed in the United States. On April 28, Mayor Hanson's office workers discovered a bomb, and soon after, the Postal Department found bombs in 36 packages.

The most significant bomb attack was on Attorney General Palmer's home in Washington, D.C., on June 2. The fronts of Palmer's and his neighbor's houses were demolished. An anarchist pamphlet was discovered near Palmer's home. The booklet advocated terrorist methods to suppress the capitalist classes.

In July, Palmer prepared an assault on radical groups. He appointed William Flynn, chief of the Bureau of Investigation, to uncover the red network. Congress authorized $500,000 for a special General Intelligence Division (GID) of the Bureau, and Palmer named J. Edgar Hoover to head the GID. Hoover and Flynn prepared a file on 200,000 radically oriented individuals and 60,000 radical groups. The GID warned all Americans to beware of the communist danger to the American way of life. Hoover had found a career that ultimately gave him vast investigative powers, his division later being renamed the Federal Bureau of Investigation.

On November 7, the GID launched raids against radical groups, using deportation provisions of the Alien Law of 1918. Hoover estimated that 90% of all domestic radicals were aliens who infiltrated and corrupted the United States. The November 7 raid hit the Russian Peoples' House in New York City which allegedly attracted "atheists, communists and anarchists." The CID found several truckloads of radical propaganda and seized 200 men and women. According to the *New York Times* some of those arrested were "badly beaten by the police . . . their heads wrapped in bandages" when they were taken to the GID headquarters.

Simultaneous raids took place on the Union of Russian Workers offices in other cities, where 250 members of that group were arrested. Of the first 450 prisoners taken on November 7, 39 were held for questioning for up to five months; 411 were freed after court hearings with no charges being filed.

Additional raids followed throughout November. The process resulted in deportation orders against 246 aliens. On December 21, 1919, the Army transport ship *Buford,* which reporters christened "Soviet Ark," carried the radical aliens back to their European homelands. Most of these deportees had participated in terrorist acts or had a criminal record. Among those sent home were Emma Goldman, who "menaced the public order," and Alex Berkman, who had tried but failed to assassinate Henry C. Frick during the Homestead Steel strike of 1892.

For additional GID activity, see January 2, 1920.

November 19, 1919

The U.S. Senate rejects an amended Treaty of Versailles because Wilson asked his followers not to accept amendments.

While Wilson toured the nation to obtain support for the league, the Senate Foreign Relations Committee sent the treaty to the Senate on September 10, with recommendations for 45 amendments and 4 reservations. This was the beginning of a lengthy Senate debate on the treaty.

Beginning on October 2, Wilson sent notes to his followers in Congress but could not deal personally with the problems because of his illness. He wrote that he would accept some mild reservations but insisted on retaining Article X of the league covenant. This article required league members to aid other members against "external aggression," a clause that Wilson considered the essential part of collective security but that Senator Lodge believed would sacrifice the nation's independence of action during a dispute because the league members would decide who the aggressor was.

Article X became the focal point of Senate action in November because, with Democratic senators following Wilson's instructions, the 45 amendments of the Senate Foreign Relations Committee report had been voted down in the Senate. Senator Lodge followed this rejection by introducing 14 amendments that circumscribed American participation in league activity. Wilson opposed Lodge's proposals because he argued they would mean the "nullification of the treaty."

On November 19, the Treaty of Versailles with Lodge's 14 amendments lost by a vote of 39 to 55. Democratic votes defeated this version of the treaty because 42 Democrats joined 13 irreconcilable senators in rejecting it. Later that day, a Democratic proposal to ratify the treaty without any amendments failed to pass by a vote of 38 to 53.

Thus, Senate action on November 19, 1919, prevented passage of the Treaty of Versailles. The treaty could have passed with Lodge's 14 amendments if Wilson had agreed. This would have placed the few limits on U.S. participation in the league. The president, however, rejected Lodge's restrictions because he wanted a league in which America participated fully. Nevertheless, the vote of November 19 indicated that four-fifths of the senators would approve an amended treaty. Consequently, Senate leaders arranged for the reconsideration of the treaty.

See March 19, 1920.

November 21, 1919

The Wilson administration orders its peace commissioners to withdraw from Paris.

Four American peace commissioners had been designated in June 1919 to work with the Allied Powers in supervising the fulfillment of the peace treaties by Germany, Austria, and Turkey. The four U.S. delegates were Colonel House, General Tasker H. Bliss, Henry White, and Frank Polk.

Following the Senate rejection of the Treaty of Versailles, President Wilson and Secretary of State Lansing agreed that the U.S. commissioners should withdraw from work connected with the treaties. France and other Allies preferred to have the U.S. delegates remain, but Wilson insisted that they had no responsibility for fulfilling a treaty the Senate rejected.

Subsequently, while the commissioners served until December 7 to clear up technical details on which Clemenceau desired U.S. help, American participation stopped in early December 1919. After that date, only one U.S. member of the Reparations Commission remained in direct service on any peace agreement. The U.S. ambassador to France, Hugh Wilson, sat as an observer on the Council of Ambassadors in Paris but did not participate officially.

Wilson's decision to withdraw from the peace commission quickly heightened the American abdication of political responsibilities in adjusting Europe's postwar political problems. This policy of restricting American concerns in Europe was a policy followed by Wilson's successors after 1921.

November 26, 1919

A British-Irish war begins.

During the British election of December 14, 1918, Sinn Fein members won seats from the Irish districts and on January 21, 1919, declared they were members of an independent Irish parliament. The *Sinn Fein* leader Eamon de Valera escaped from British imprisonment and came to the United States, where he organized aid for the Irish rebellion. The British decided to suppress the Sinn Fein party, but proponents of independence began war against Great Britain.

See December 6, 1922.

November 27, 1919

Bulgaria signs the Treaty of Neuilly to end World War I.

By this treaty, Bulgaria lost its seaport on the Aegean Sea but was allowed an economic outlet. The Bulgarians had to recognize Yugoslavia's independence, pay reparations of $445 million, and reduce their army to 20,000 men.

December 24, 1919

Congress enacts the Edge Act, which allows U.S. banks to combine in financing foreign trade.

The House of Morgan and other American banking institutions desired to loan funds to European nations to assist their postwar reconstruction, but they preferred to spread their risks by forming banking consortiums. The Edge Act permitted the combination of finances by exempting banks from antitrust laws whenever they combined for foreign commercial benefits.

Soon after passage of the Edge Act, two banking corporations formed to finance foreign acceptance loans: the American and Foreign Banking Corporation and the Mercantile Bank of the Americas. These organized financial groups enabled the United States to dominate world trade and finance after 1920.

1920

January 2, 1920

The Red Scare in America continues when 2,700 persons are arrested during anti-Communist raids in 33 cities.

To learn better procedures because many of those arrested on November 7, 1919, went free, Attorney General Palmer consulted with officials of the Labor

An example of the "Red Scare" cartoons that found subversives everywhere. *Philadelphia Inquirer*

Department and the Immigration Office as he prepared the second raids. The secretary of labor signed 3,000 warrants for the arrest of aliens who belonged to the Communist Party or the Communist Labor Party. In addition, the Immigration Office changed its previous rules governing the arrest of aliens. Aliens no longer had the right to inspect the arrest warrants and be represented by counsel at the beginning of a deportation hearing. The new ruling stated, "Preferably at the beginning of the hearing . . . or at any rate as soon as such hearing has proceeded sufficiently in the development of the facts to protect the Government's interest," the alien could inspect the warrant and have counsel present.

The government had wide latitude in dealing with aliens because deportations did not involve a criminal proceeding but simply a hearing before an immigration officer. Moreover, the aliens' only appeal was for review by the secretary of labor or a federal writ of habeas corpus if the deportation process were manifestly unfair. This was a major reason Palmer used deportation rather than criminal action against the alleged Communists.

Thus, unlike the November raids, the January 2 raids included extensive plans. On one night over 4,000 suspected radicals were rounded up from 33 cities in 23 states. Virtually every Communist or left-wing group in the nation was hit and every leader was affected. Some arrests were with warrants, some were without warrants or any real cause. In Massachusetts 800 aliens were seized, and almost half of them were sent to the Boston Immigration Station for investigation. In New York, 400 were arrested; in Philadelphia, 100; in Pittsburgh, 115; in New Jersey towns, 500; in Detroit, 800; in Kansas City, 100. In Chicago, raids on January 1 and January 2 netted 425 prisoners. In the Far West, members of radical groups had been arrested during earlier IWW strikes, and only a few such groups remained there in 1920.

Despite his gross violations of the civil rights of some nonaliens as well as all rights of aliens, the American public considered Palmer to be the savior of the nation. The attorney general claimed he had "halted the advance of 'red radicalism' in the United States," and he predicted there would be 2,720 deportations. Palmer exaggerated both the red threat and the number of radical aliens. By the spring of 1920, the red hysteria of 1919–1920 ended; only 591 aliens were deported.

See September 2, 1919, and May 7, 1920.

January 20, 1920

A crisis with Mexico ends when Carranza compromises with the Petroleum Producers Association on oil permits.

A crisis arose in Mexican-American relations in 1919 because Carranza's government had neither ended all the social disorders in Mexico nor fulfilled its promise to protect oil holdings obtained before 1917 from the provisions of Article 27 of the constitution of 1917, which gave the Mexican government control over subsoil resources.

Two incidents during the fall of 1919 persuaded Secretary of State Lansing and U.S. Ambassador to Mexico Henry P. Fletcher to attempt a firm policy and possibly break diplomatic relations with Mexico to force Carranza to protect U.S. property and citizens from revolutionary nationalism in Mexico. The first incident was the kidnapping of William O. Jenkins, the U.S. consul at Puebla, Mexico, by Federico Córdoba, one of Carranza's opponents. Following Jenkins's release upon payment of a ransom, Mexican police arrested him on the charge of collusion with the rebels. On November 27, the Mexican government refused Secretary Lansing's demand for the release of Jenkins, causing Lansing to consider using this incident to apply pressure on Carranza.

Because Wilson's illness prevented his direct involvement, Lansing met with cabinet members, who advised him not to use the Jenkins episode to promote any drastic action against Mexico. Jenkins had a poor reputation as a land speculator in Mexico, and using his arrest to precipitate a crisis seemed unwise.

By November, a more serious issue provided a better reason for protesting against Carranza's failure to resolve the outstanding problems with the United States. The particular issue was a Mexican law that required government permits before new oil wells could be drilled in Mexico. American oil producers had hoped the Mexican senate would pass legislation to prevent Article 27 from applying retroactively to oil rights secured before 1917. Carranza opposed the bill, however, and it was defeated in October by a vote of 26 to 17 in the Mexican senate. In addition, the Mexican army began forcibly to close down oil drilling operations that lacked permits. The oilmen could have purchased the permits, but they mutually agreed not to do so because they feared the purchase of a permit would set a precedent validating Article 27.

The oil interests appealed to Secretary Lansing for help. Thus early in December, Lansing and Ambassador Fletcher used the oil permit issue to seek Wilson's approval for a strong policy to convince Carranza to accept concessions on Article 27. In addition to the oil issue, Lansing's appeal to Wilson cited Senator Albert B. Fall's report that Carranza's government was influenced by Bolsheviks who hoped to undermine the American way of life. Therefore, Lansing suggested to Wilson in his note of January 3 that Ambassador Fletcher should give Carranza one final opportunity to make concessions on the oil issue as a stronger American method for protecting the "lives, rights, and property of Americans." If Carranza did not comply with Fletcher's request within four weeks, the United States would break diplomatic relations. Lansing believed, however, that such strong inducements would force Carranza to yield to American rights.

President Wilson never approved Lansing's proposal. The president had received reports from friends such as Joseph P. Guffey, president of Atlantic Gulf Oil Corporation, which stated the Mexican situation was less acute than Lansing and Fletcher indicated. Guffey asserted that companies obeying the law had been well treated. Moreover, Wilson had become disenchanted with Lansing and since October 1919 had sought some means to obtain his resignation.

As soon as the Petroleum Producers Association members realized that Wilson would not exert pressure on Mexico, they appealed directly to President Carranza. In a note of January 15, the oilmen agreed to obtain provisional oil drilling permits provided that the Mexican government agreed that this acceptance would not "destroy or prejudice such rights as they may have." On January 20, Carranza accepted the oilmen's proposal. This temporary truce ended the crisis and satisfied the U.S. oil interests until a more definitive Mexican policy could be approved.

See February 13, 1920.

February 13, 1920

Robert Lansing resigns as secretary of state after President Wilson accuses him of conducting unauthorized cabinet meetings.

There was a growing rift between Wilson and Lansing after 1917. In particular, Wilson had irritated Lansing during the Paris Peace Conference when the president consulted with Colonel House rather than Lansing and gave the secretary a lesser role during the peace proceedings. After the president became ill in 1919, the secretary's role increased with regard to Russia and Mexico, but Mrs. Wilson kept him away from both the White House and the president. Because Lansing called and presided over several cabinet meetings in November and news leaked that he had considered asking the cabinet to advise the vice president to act temporarily as president, Wilson thought Lansing was disloyal.

Lansing's conduct had displeased Wilson even before the fall of 1917. He never liked Lansing's social habits and came to distrust his association with "reactionaries." Lansing's attempt to stimulate a strong Mexican crisis in 1919 convinced Wilson that his earlier dissatisfactions with Lansing were sound.

February 25, 1920

President Wilson appoints Bainbridge Colby as secretary of state.

Colby's appointment surprised many observers who anticipated the nomination of Frank Polk, the Secretary of State ad interim following Lansing's resignation.

Wilson selected Colby for his loyalty, not for his foreign policy experience, because the president expected to make the important policy decisions. Until 1916, Colby had been a progressive Republican. He refused to support Hughes and in backing Wilson for president brought many former Bull Moose Republicans into Wilson's campaign. During the war, Colby served on the Shipping Board, which represented his only foreign policy experience. Because of extensive Senate confirmation hearings, Colby did not begin official service as secretary of state until March 23, 1920.

March 19, 1920

A final Senate vote on the Treaty of Versailles again defeats the measure.

Following the Senate rejection of the peace treaty on November 19, Senator Lodge and several Democratic senators met to prepare a compromise on acceptable treaty reservations. Senator Borah ruined this attempt because he threatened to depose Lodge as the Senate majority leader and split the Republican Party during the 1920 election campaign.

Senator Henry Cabot Lodge is portrayed as the victor in the battle against the League. Library of Congress

Consequently, any possible compromise resolution could not be negotiated before a final vote on the treaty took place on March 19, 1920. Wilson advised the Democrats to oppose the resolution because it included Lodge's 14 amendments of November 19 plus an additional amendment in favor of Irish independence from Great Britain. Although 21 Democrats disregarded Wilson's advice, 7 more Democratic votes were needed to ratify the treaty with 15 amendments. The final Senate action on the Treaty of Versailles with amendments was 49 to 35. This defeat also meant the United States did not become a member of the League of Nations.

On Ireland, see November 26, 1919.

April 1, 1920

American forces evacuate Vladivostok, ending the Siberian expedition.

Although Britain and France used the Siberian intervention as an additional effort to assist the White anti-Bolshevik armies to overthrow the Communists, the Allied attempts were neither well-planned nor well-executed programs. Great Britain's plans focused on assistance to Admiral A. V. Kolchak, who established headquarters at Omsk; the Japanese objective was to secure power in Manchuria and eastern Siberia; while the American effort began as a venture to help the Czech Legions escape but ended by preventing Japanese ambitions in East Asia and China from getting out of control.

Thus for U.S. General Graves, his Siberian command became a diplomatic contest against Japan and Britain as well as a series of protests against the Don Cossack generals who spread terror in their attempts to become wealthy by looting Russian and Chinese peasants. By 1919, the British, Japanese, and Cossack generals believed Graves was pro-Communist because his opposition restricted their interference in local political and economic affairs.

The Japanese had initially gained much of their major objective in northern China and Siberia by the end of August 1918. Before Graves arrived, the British and Japanese had waged several minor battles against local Russian communist forces along the Trans-Siberian Railway. Defeating the Russians easily, the Japanese controlled the railway line as far west as Irkutsk, where the main forces of the Czech army

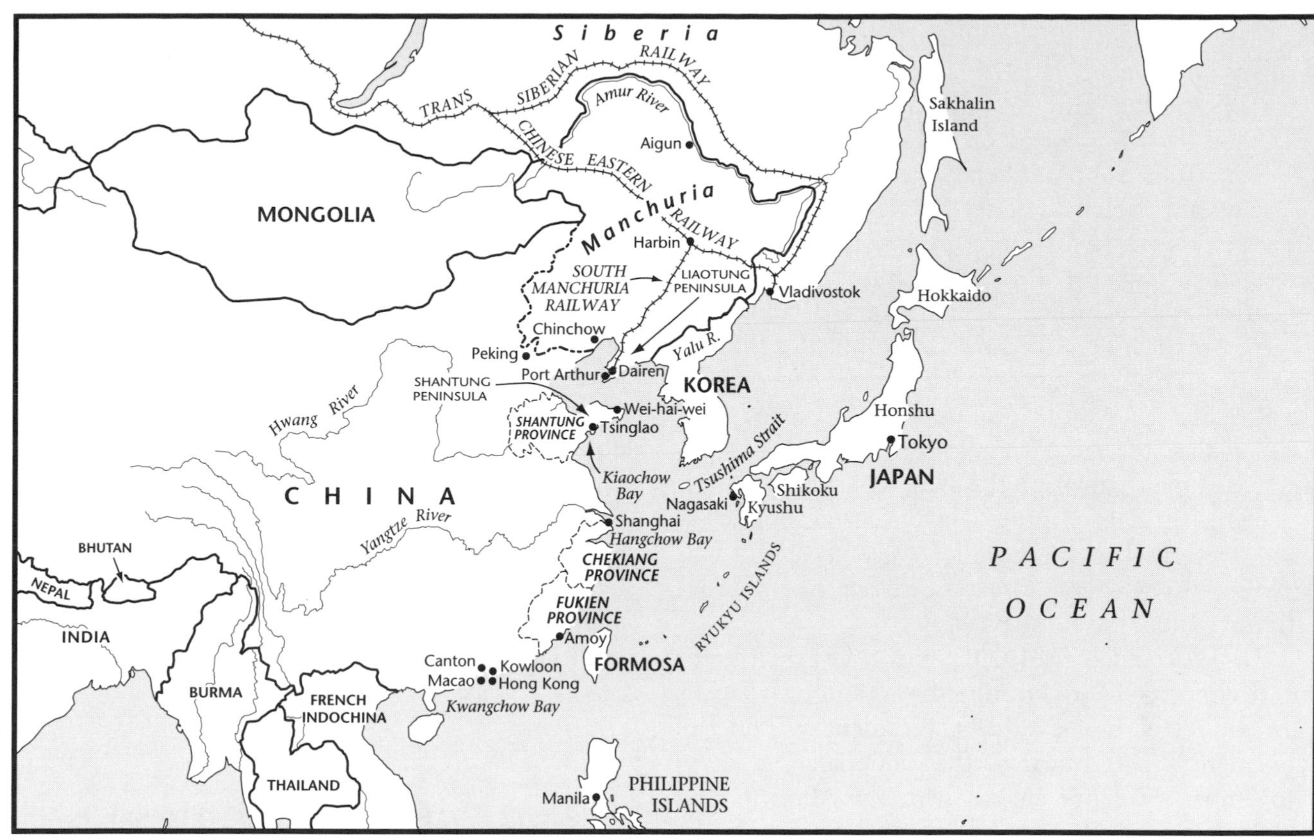

The Far East, 1919–1937

held control. Subsequently, a Japanese-British-American pact on January 9, 1919, established an Interallied Railway Agreement to keep the Trans-Siberian line operating. American forces assisted this railway effort until 1920. During the 18 months of Allied occupation the Japanese tried to consolidate their status in that area but reluctantly withdrew in October 1922, because America insisted. In 1922, the Soviet regional government in eastern Siberia thanked Washington for its friendly interest in forcing Japan to leave.

Great Britain's assistance to Admiral Kolchak's forces at Omsk was a more direct attack against the Russian communists. A former czarist naval officer, Kolchak moved into central Siberia during the fall of 1918 and became the supreme commander of the White army at Omsk. To protect and supply Kolchak with arms, the British sent 2,000 men under Colonel Ward. Yet the only British forces to fight Communists in the area of the Ural Mountains were an unusual naval gun crew. These sailors dismantled a gun from their cruiser, the *Suffolk,* at Vladivostok. They mounted it on an armored train and moved it 4,000 miles into Asia to aid Kolchak against the Red Army.

Unfortunately, Kolchak's policies were less imaginative than the *Suffolk*'s gun crew; thus, the admiral's anti-Communist campaign failed miserably. A typical counterrevolutionist, Kolchak did not understand the difference between the moderate agrarian socialistic Social Revolutionists (SR) and the radical Bolshevik Communists. The largest revolutionist group in Russia in 1917, the SR advocated peasant land ownership, but their moderate goals had succumbed to the Leninists. The SR preferred to fight the Communists, but the tactics of White leaders such as Kolchak, together with the Allied foreign intervention, caused the moderates to accept the Bolsheviks as the lesser evil. Kolchak tried to suppress the SR but ended by losing the support of the local peasants near Omsk, as well as the Czech Legion at Irkutsk. Eventually, Kolchak had many officers but few soldiers to fight in his army. By the end of April 1919, Kolchak's forces in Central Asia began retreating, and in August Great Britain withdrew all its support from the admiral.

Kolchak resigned as supreme ruler of the White armies on January 4, 1920. Local Soviet leaders in Irkutsk arrested him on January 15, and he was executed by firing squad on February 7, 1920.

American troops under General Graves did not directly aid Kolchak. They protected the Trans-Siberian Railway, a duty that resulted in one defensive engagement against the Bolsheviks. The incident occurred at a coal mine in Suchan near Vladivostok, where Americans guarded the coal supply for the railroad line. Because Don Cossack officers had engaged in atrocities against the local populace, trouble spilled over against the Americans as well. The U.S. troops increased their patrols in the area, which resulted in a shooting incident during which several Bolsheviks died. Nevertheless, this conflict was defensive in nature because General Graves ordered no offensive attacks against the Bolsheviks.

In 1919 and early 1920, General Graves became more concerned with limiting the actions of Japanese, British, and Cossack officers. President Wilson had considered withdrawing the Siberian force in November 1918 but agreed with the Allies to wait until the Paris Peace Conference determined the future of Russia. The peace conference had been unable to deal with Russia, and the Senate rejection of the Treaty of Versailles negated any possible U.S. influence on European-Soviet relations.

About the time that the Senate rejected the treaty in November 1919, the Czech Legion arranged its final withdrawal from Siberia. The Czechs had lingered at Omsk and Irkutsk through 1919 to assist Kolchak. They became disillusioned with the admiral's tactics, however, and in November 1919 completely withdrew assistance from the White armies and dealt with Communist leaders for safe transportation to Vladivostok. Although Japanese-American control of the railway in 1919 had given the Czech Legion the opportunity to leave, it did not begin its mass evacuation from Omsk and Irkutsk until December 1919. The Czechs experienced more difficulty now than they would have in 1918 because they had to convince the Soviets they no longer were aiding Kolchak. By helping the Soviets capture the admiral on January 15, they proved their point, and the day after Kolchak's execution, the Czech trains left Irkutsk. Finally in April 1920, at the same time that the American evacuation began, the Czech Legions boarded ships at Vladivostok. Two years after beginning their trek from Kiev, the Czechs left Siberia.

Actually, General Graves had given less attention to the Czechs than to the Japanese. The Japanese stayed on in Siberia, however, and did not leave in October 1922.

The historian George Kennan cites a later incident to illustrate the passive character of the U.S. intervention in Siberia. During the 1933 negotiations in Washington preceding U.S. recognition of the Soviet Union's Foreign Minister, Maxim Litvinov, raised questions about claims against U.S. destruction in Siberia from 1918 to 1920. The American officials showed Litvinov documents on the Siberian intervention, convincing him to withdraw his indemnity claims arising in Siberia. Litvinov gave President Franklin Roosevelt a public letter in which the Soviet Union waived any and all claims arising from U.S. military action in Siberia after World War I. The main result of American action in Siberia had been to limit Japan's presence.

May 7, 1920

America's Red Scare abates after Louis F. Post effectively explains the injustices of the Palmer raids.

The postwar red scare ended almost as abruptly in 1920 as it had begun in 1919. Not only had the Bolshevik threat declined in Europe by 1920 but Americans of both parties began to realize that the threat of communism had been exaggerated, and congressmen especially realized that U.S. civil liberties had been threatened by Attorney General Palmer's tactics between November 1919 and April 1920.

A significant role in ending this red scare was played on May 7 by Assistant Secretary of Labor Louis Post, who defended himself against impeachment charges made in the Rules Committee of the House of Representatives. Having been designated by Secretary of Labor Wilson to be the arbiter in the deportation hearings of the arrested aliens, Post soon realized that not only had the aliens' procedural rights been violated but also few of the aliens were Communists or radicals. Therefore, Post ordered the wholesale cancellation of deportation orders and released almost half of those arrested in January. These aliens, Post said, were "wage workers" who committed no offense and were not the aliens Congress "intended to comprehend in its anti-alien legislation." Post canceled 2,202 deportation orders.

Only 556 of the more than 4,000 aliens arrested in January were deported.

Post's action did not go uncontested. Palmer and American anti-Communist groups complained bitterly that Post was "coddling the Reds." In April, Representative Homer Hood of Kansas offered a resolution in Congress to impeach Post if the facts warranted. On May 1, the House Rules Committee, which had investigated Hood's charges, recommended that Post be censured for leniency.

At this point, Post demanded a personal hearing before the House Rules Committee. The committee complied, and on May 7, Post accomplished what few congressional witnesses have ever achieved. He presented testimony so eloquent and precise that the Rules Committee voted to suspend further consideration of his censure. Post offered detailed information to show how newspapers and superpatriots had manufactured a nonexistent Communist threat. During the January raids, he pointed out, only three pistols were found and two of these were .22-caliber guns, not the type suited for a revolution. He provided detailed information from the deportation hearings to demonstrate the Justice Department's high-handed and illegal arrest procedures. Finally, Post explained the exact differences between the disciples of Marx, Tolstoy, Proudhon, and Sorel, the principal philosophers of modern radicalism. He indicated how the ideas of these four men were arranged along the spectrum from democratic liberalism to violent, terrorist radicalism.

Post got his message across. Newsmen and their editors listened carefully enough to realize that the "Red Scare" tactics endangered Americans more than bolshevism. Post's vindication turned congressional attention to an investigation of Attorney General Palmer's illegal proceedings. Palmer denied the charges, of course, and blamed Post's "perverted sympathy for the criminal anarchists" for his failure to deport the aliens. By this time, however, the nation and Congress became apathetic about the issue as the 1920 presidential campaign began.

The renewed sanity of the public became clear in September 1920, when a terrorist attack took place on Wall Street. At noon hour on September 6, a large bomb exploded in front of the U.S. Assay Office across the street from the House of Morgan building. The bomb killed 29 persons outright, 4 more died in the hospital, and 200 others were wounded. Although Palmer revived charges of a radical plot, Americans reacted less drastically. While the New York police investigated, public opinion seemed to recognize that bomb attacks were insane plots that could not overthrow the government. The *Rocky Mountain News* ridiculed Palmer's charges. Palmer, the news editorial said, was "subservient to a bureaucracy. A great big secret-service army, composed largely of politicians is employed. The usual pinch of salt must be" added to Palmer's claims. The red scare had temporarily ended in America.

See January 2, 1920.

May 8, 1920

Japan agrees to American terms for a Chinese banking consortium.

In 1918, Secretary of State Lansing had proposed the creation of an international consortium to aid China. Lansing believed this banking group would implement provisions of the November 1917 Lansing-Ishii agreement by granting equal commercial opportunities in all China. Japan did not accept Lansing's interpretation of the 1917 agreement and refused to accept the proposed international group. The British and French accepted Japan's attitude because they desired to keep Tokyo from changing its alliance to join Germany after the war. Consequently, during the remainder of his term of office, Lansing was unsuccessful in forming a consortium.

When Bainbridge Colby became secretary of state, the United States began further discussions with Tokyo to arrange a banking group to aid China. Lansing's firmness toward Japan may have influenced Tokyo, but Colby's leadership finalized an agreement on May 8, 1920. Japan compromised because the bankers of the other three nations in the consortium exchanged notes with Tokyo indicating they would exclude loans from projects of special interest to Japan alone.

Bankers from the United States, Britain, France, and Japan signed a formal consortium arrangement on October 15, 1920. No important loans resulted from the 1920 agreement. Nevertheless, the treaty discussions disclosed the ineffectiveness of the Lansing-Ishii agreement, as well as President Wilson's desire to moderate Japan's position in China.

May 20, 1920

Wilson vetoes a joint resolution of Congress declaring the war is ended.

Because the Treaty of Versailles had been defeated on March 19, 1920, Congress proposed to end hostilities officially without a treaty of peace. President Wilson vetoed the bill because he was bitter toward those who had defeated the treaty and because he hoped to be nominated for a third presidential term and to make the treaty issue the principal issue of the campaign of 1920. But the Democratic Convention of June 1920 chose not to nominate Wilson as its candidate.

June 4, 1920

Hungary signs the Treaty of Trianon, ending World War I.

The uprising of Béla Kun and Hungary's war with Czechoslovakia and Romania delayed the conclusion of the Allied and Associated Powers' peace with Hungary. By the peace treaty, Hungary lost three-quarters of its territorial claims and two-thirds of its former inhabitants. Czechoslovakia received Slovakia; Yugoslavia gained Croatia-Slavonia and part of the Banat of Temesvar; Romania obtained Banat, Transylvania, and part of the Hungarian plain. Hungary had to pay reparations and could maintain an army of only 35,000 men.

July 7, 1920

The United States removes its trade restrictions on Russia but does not recognize Russia's Communist regime.

The Allied governments had restricted trade by their nationals with Russia after the Russian Revolution of November 1917, but when the British and French began negotiations to resume commerce with Lenin's government, American business and labor organizations also asked Washington to end its limitations.

On June 19, the State Department learned that the British proposed to reopen trade without recognizing the Soviet regime, and Secretary Colby recommended to President Wilson that the United States act similarly. Wilson agreed, and on July 7, the State Department announced that U.S. trade restrictions would be removed but that the United States could give no official support to its citizens engaging in commerce with Russia. The Wilson administration would not recognize the Soviet regime because, it claimed, it did not represent the will of the people. The United States also continued to restrict travel and mail sent to Russia.

August 10, 1920

The Wilson administration explains it cannot recognize Lenin's government because his regime is "based upon the negation of every principle of honor and good faith."

Composed largely by Secretary of State Colby, the August 10 note detailed why Wilson would not recognize the Soviet government and enunciated attitudes toward bolshevism that recurred in U.S. politics long after the United States finally recognized the Soviet Union in 1933.

The note of August 10 was technically a response to an Italian request for American aid to Poland during the Russo-Polish War. In this particular case, Colby said the United States was in favor of the territorial integrity of both states and could not accept Polish aggression in seeking land east of its ethnic region (the Curzon Line). The United States hoped the Russo-Polish War would end soon on the basis of national self-determination for both nations. (Polish armies had invaded Russia on April 25 in a vain attempt to conquer the Ukraine.)

Colby then shifted to a detailed explanation of why the United States could not deal with the Russian government until the Russian people were able to surmount their present crisis. Nonrecognition was not based on the political structure of Russia but on the fact that the present regime negated "every principle of honor and good faith," which made it impossible to have "harmonious and trustful relations" with the Communists. The ideology of the Bolsheviks prevented their agreement with a non-Bolshevik government with any moral standards. They instigated revolution in other nations and would abuse diplomatic privileges. "Inevitably, therefore, the diplomatic service of the Bolshevik Government would become a channel for intrigues and the propaganda of revolt." Colby and Wilson believed the Bolshevik regime could not last long because the Russian people would rise up and overthrow Lenin.

August 10, 1920

Turkey's Sultan signs the Treaty of Sèvres with the allied powers.

To obtain this treaty, an Allied force had to occupy Constantinople on March 16, 1920, where it defeated a group of nationalist Turks led by MUSTAPHA KEMAL (later Kemal Atatürk), who fought to maintain the unity of the Turkish Empire. The Allies exiled the nationalists, who moved their provisional government to Ankara on April 23. Nevertheless, the Allies supported the Sultan Mohammed VI, who agreed to the Treaty of Sèvres despite the opposition and protests of Kemal's government.

A Greco-Turkish war resulted on June 22 and continued through August 10, when the sultan accepted the peace treaty. Nevertheless, the Ankara government continued to fight Greece until July 24, 1923, when the Allied powers finally concluded the Treaty of Lausanne with the nationalist regime of Kemal.

September 5, 1920

Alvaro Obregón is elected President of Mexico, following a revolution against Carranza.

Between 1917 and 1920, Carranza became increasingly criticized in Mexico by more radical leaders who believed he did not use his presidential powers sufficiently to end Mexico's political disorder and economic problems. Consequently, when Carranza proposed a relative unknown, Ignacia Bonellas, as the candidate for president in 1920, Obregón led other revolutionaries in opposing Carranza's control of the election. Gaining support of generals such as Adolfo de la Huerta and Plutarco Elias Calles, Obregón organized a coup d'état and forced Carranza to flee Mexico City before being captured and shot on May 2, 1920. On September 5, Obregón was elected as president, but he was not officially installed until December 1, 1920. Obregón brought internal stability to Mexico and followed a moderate reform program including foreign policies to conciliate Britain and America.

See August 31, 1923.

November 2, 1920

Warren G. Harding is elected President as the Republicans also regain control of Congress.

President Wilson persuaded the Democratic Convention to endorse the League of Nations although it did not nominate him for a third term. The Democratic Party platform on the league actually qualified Wilson's previous ideas by agreeing to accept such reservations as were needed under the U.S. Constitution. The Democrats nominated James M. Cox, who promised to seek U.S. membership in the League of Nations.

The Republican delegates who met in Chicago had many divisions on an international organization, some supporting the league and others ardently opposed to it. The party platform straddled the issue, favoring an "organization to preserve peace." Because of the Republican divisions on both domestic and foreign issues, they chose an "available" man rather than the "best" man. The Republican candidate was Harding, a man who had no deep convictions about any issue, advocating a "return to normalcy." In the election, Harding won 404 electoral votes to 127 for Cox.

November 2, 1920

A California initiative resolution approves legislation to strictly prohibit Japanese from owning American land.

In the November 2 election, this initiative resolution passed overwhelmingly, further indicating anti-Asian racial prejudice in California. The proponents of the bill claimed that Theodore Roosevelt's 1907 Gentlemen's Agreement allowed too many loopholes for Japanese immigrants. As a means of forestalling the California action, President Wilson and Secretary of State Colby had begun negotiations to tighten the regulations with Japan but had reached no agreement in 1920.

See February 19, 1923, and May 15, 1924.

November 9, 1920

America opposes Japan's control of Yap, a Pacific island located on the projected site of cable lines.

During the Paris Peace Conference session of May 7, President Wilson neglected to insist that Yap Island be excluded from the former German islands mandated to Japan. Later, U.S. navy officers indicated that Yap was located on the cable route planned between Hawaii and the Philippines as part of the transpacific route from San Francisco to Asia. Subsequently, Lansing informed Japan that in oral reservations on the German islands before May 7, Wilson had mentioned Yap and the United States had to retreat to these reservations because there was an oversight when the Treaty of Versailles was being finalized.

Japan, of course, would not accept Lansing's objection, but until the spring of 1920, the State Department gave no further attention to Yap. The question reappeared when the State Department prepared documents for an international conference on electrical communications scheduled for October 8, 1920. Both the Netherlands, which was concerned about a cable line to the East Indies, and China called the State Department's attention to Yap as the center for the Pacific cable line. Therefore, at the conference session of November 9, Secretary of State Colby felt justified in objecting to Japanese rights at Yap because the United States had not ratified the Treaty of Versailles. During the fall of 1920, the question was not resolved. During the communications conference Great Britain supported Japanese rights to Yap while France urged the United States to settle the issue in direct discussions with Japan. At the Washington Conference of 1921–1922, the French suggestion led the United States and Japan to conduct bilateral talks which settled the matter.

See February 11, 1922.

November 23, 1920

The United States protests British control of oil rights and other economic concessions in the Middle East, asserting America's Open Door rights in that region.

With no American restraining policy on the peace terms that Britain and France secured from Turkey in the Peace Treaty of Sèvres, England and France established their mandated control over territory formerly part of the Ottoman Empire. Secretary of State Lansing had protested British policy in Persia in August 1919, and Secretary Colby also indicated dissatisfaction regarding British and French acquisitions in the region between the Persian Gulf and the Mediterranean Sea. Yet because the United States had only an ambassadorial observer at the peace sessions after December 1, 1919, American officials had little influence on Anglo-French decisions.

In answering one complaint by Colby, the British foreign minister on August 9 informed the secretary that provisions and terms of the mandated areas could "only properly be discussed at the Council of the League of Nations by the signatories of the Covenant."

Both Colby and President Wilson rejected the British attitude and prepared a memo for the British on November 2 to set forth American rights. Because the United States had played a significant role in the recent war, Colby said, it could not be denied a voice regarding the mandates or the equal commercial opportunities available to league members. The United States demanded equal commercial rights in the Middle East. On November 27, Colby forwarded notes to London, Rome, and Paris that insisted on U.S. rights to equal economic opportunity in the former Turkish Empire.

The U.S. protests related to the desire of Socony (Standard Oil Company of New York) to obtain oil exploration rights in the Middle East. The American protests in 1919 and 1920 began an American oil corporation challenge to British control of Middle East oil between 1919 and 1939.

See August 10, 1920.

December 11, 1920

Secretary of State Colby leaves on a goodwill tour of Latin America.

Colby's visit to South America was hailed as an attempt to encourage greater Pan-American cooperation. It was not very extensive, however, for Colby visited only three nations. In Brazil and Uruguay, he was generally well received. In Argentina, however, the crowds were small and the American entourage ran into criticism because of U.S. interventions in Haiti and Santo Domingo.

December 14, 1920

Senator Borah introduces a congressional resolution asking the president to invite Great Britain and Japan to attend a conference to establish naval limits and to reduce naval programs over the next five years.

Because the U.S. naval construction program of 1916 would give the United States the world's largest navy by 1923 unless reductions occurred, the threat of a naval race with Japan and Great Britain loomed as a possibility because those two nations proposed naval increases to at least maintain parity with the United States.

As national news media discussed the naval race and the U.S. navy proposed commensurate increases, Senator Borah decided to lead a movement to end what was looming as a costly naval contest by calling a conference of the naval powers to agree to restrict their navies.

For further data on the naval conference proposals, see January 25, 1921, and May 25, 1921.

XI. POLITICAL ISOLATION AND THE DEPRESSION ERA

Economic Global Concerns
Washington Naval Conference
Dawes and Young Plan

1921

January 7, 1921

The U.S. Navy's Orange War Plan against Japan is given tentative approval by the Secretaries of War and the Navy.

In accordance with their pre-1917 naval strategy for the Pacific Ocean, U.S. naval leaders reformulated their Orange War Plan with Japan as the most likely future American enemy. On March 29, 1919, Captain Harold E. Yarnell, head of the Navy War Plans Division, outlined a Pacific Ocean strategy that became the basis for the navy's and the Joint Board of the Army and Navy's strategic plans until May 11, 1939.

Yarnell did not envision a conflict in Europe, where Great Britain would be the only likely U.S. antagonist. Moreover, the United States held strategic advantages in a war against England that would not require a large U.S. naval force. In the Pacific, however, Japan's power had increased as a result of World War I, and the possibility of a U.S. conflict with Japan had increased proportionately. The tensions between the United States and Japan, Yarnell warned, were "permanent and cannot be arbitrated."

Based on Yarnell's analysis, Orange War Plan projected the need for a U.S. navy "second-to-none," capable of offensive action in the western Pacific, home waters of Japan. The navy also desired stronger fortifications in Hawaii and Guam, as well as the stationing of a large fleet in the Philippine Islands.

These navy plans conflicted with the State Department view of Europe as first priority for America. Although such differences were never seriously debated, they became apparent during the Washington Conference preparations of which Secretary of State Hughes took charge during the fall of 1921. The Orange Plan also laid the basis for the navy's opposition to the Washington Conference treaties of 1922, which limited the number of navy's battleships and placed a status quo on fortifications by the United States in the western Pacific islands.

January 25, 1921

Senator Borah offers a resolution to investigate what "constitutes a modern fighting navy—a navy with the type of ships and with air and submarine weapons" to be effective in future wars.

Borah followed up his proposal for a naval disarmament conference on December 14, 1920, with a January 25 resolution to determine whether U.S. defense policy should be changed.

The modern American navy that Borah suggested would include aircraft and submarines for coastal defense. As a nationalist, Borah did not want to weaken America's defense forces; thus, his resolution of January 25 asked the Senate Naval Affairs Committee to determine the influence of these new weapons on U.S. defense forces.

The submarine and the airplane had played important roles during World War I. As a result, some military observers believed these new weapons would transform warfare in the future. In America, two notable spokesmen for the new weapons were Brigadier General William MITCHELL of the Army Air Service and Rear Admiral William FULLAM of the U.S. navy. Both of these men provided information to Borah during January 1921, which contended that better and less expensive American coastal defense could be obtained with submarines and aircraft. Admiral Fullam argued that battleships would be useless in future wars unless they were protected by submarines and aircraft. In addition, a sufficient force of these new weapons would make America "perfectly safe from attack from any other country."

General Mitchell made even greater claims for the future abilities of airplanes in coastal defense. Airplanes, Mitchell stated, would sink any naval ships approaching within 100 to 200 miles of the North American continent. Mitchell also coined a slogan that appealed to Borah: "1,000 airplanes can be bought for the price of one battleship." As Borah informed Congress in February 1921, the nation was wasting $240 million by building battleships rather than aircraft and submarines.

To demonstrate the airplane's military potential, Mitchell urged the army and navy to test aircraft bombs against former German battleships. With the backing of Senator Borah and other congressmen, Mitchell overcame the navy's opposition and a test was held.

See July 21, 1921.

March 4, 1921

Charles Evans Hughes is commissioned as Secretary of State by President Harding.

Soon after his election in November 1920, Harding asked Hughes to serve as his secretary of state. Harding respected Hughes's advice on foreign relations and generally permitted him a free hand in foreign policy decisions. Hughes served as secretary until Harding's death and then for President Coolidge until March 4, 1925.

April 27, 1921

The Allied reparations commission reports that Germany must pay a total of 132 billion gold marks ($33 billion).

The Treaty of Versailles provided for a Reparations Commission to determine the exact amount Germany had to pay to the Allies for damages caused during World War I. The meetings of the commissioners, without delegates from America, began at Spa, Belgium on July 5, 1920, and formulated a tentative plan for German payments to France, Great Britain, Italy, Belgium, and the smaller nations that fought against the Central Powers.

President Warren G. Harding. National Archives

At the London Conference (February 21 to March 4, 1921), further discussions were held with German representatives to work out a payment schedule. The final figures for total costs were not set, however, until April 27. The Germans were also told in April that they had already fallen behind in their payments and must pay 1 billion gold marks by June 1, 1921. To do so, the Germans borrowed funds in London. But this was just the beginning of European difficulties in assessing and collecting German reparations.

See January 11, 1923, and September 1, 1924.

May 19, 1921

Congress approves the emergency quota act restricting immigration to the United States.

Disillusionment with World War I, fears that larger numbers of eastern Europeans with socialist-communistic beliefs would arrive, and a general xenophobic

Inspection at Ellis Island of new immigrants from Europe, early 1920s. National Archives

view held by 100% Americanists caused Congress to pass a law that broadly restricted immigration for the first time in the nation's history. The 1921 law limited the number of aliens admitted to the United States from a given country in one year to about 3% of the number of such nation's inhabitants in America in the 1910 census.

See May 15, 1924.

For prior immigration laws, see November 17, 1880, and July 5, 1884; May 12, 1888.

May 25, 1921

Congress approves the Borah resolution for a naval disarmament conference as an amendment to the Naval Appropriations Bill of 1921.

Borah's resolution of December 14, 1920, had been tacked on to the Naval Appropriations Bill on February 24. It passed Congress in that form with only four negative votes.

June 7, 1921

The Little Entente is completed by a treaty between Romania and Yugoslavia.

The Little Entente was designed to protect former nations of the Austro-Hungarian Empire and to forestall a possible restoration of Habsburg rule. On August 14, 1920, Czechoslovakia and Yugoslavia signed a treaty that became the basis of the entente. On April 23, 1921, the Czechoslovakian-Romanian agreement linked the triad of small powers created on former Habsburg territory.

July 2, 1921

The U.S. Congress passes a joint resolution declaring that hostilities with the Central Powers have ceased; President Harding approves the resolution.

This resolution resembled the one President Wilson vetoed in 1920 following the Senate's rejection of the Treaty of Versailles. The congressional resolution declared that the United States reserved all the rights and privileges provided by the Central Powers to the Allied nations under the treaties made during the peace conferences. The State Department used this resolution as the basis for separate treaties with Germany, Austria, and Hungary that were signed during August 1921 and promptly ratified by the U.S. Senate.

July 11, 1921

Harding's administration announces that preliminary requests have been made to invite the major powers to a disarmament conference.

The State Department's preliminary messages regarding the conference were sent on July 8 to Great Britain, France, Italy, and Japan. The public announcement of the invitations was made on July 11 to forestall the announcement that Great Britain would request a conference on the Far East to be held in London. The British Commonwealth ministers had been meeting in London since June 20 and agreed to seek a conference on the Far East in order to obtain an agreement that would terminate the Anglo-Japanese Alliance. Because Secretary of State Hughes wanted the conference to be held in Washington, where Americans would be closer to the conference process, he agreed with Great Britain to include the Far Eastern issues on the conference agenda.

Japan hesitated to accept conference participation because both the naval and Far Eastern issues vitally affected Japanese policies. Tokyo could not, however, afford to reject the British and American desire to hold a conference, and so Tokyo agreed to attend. In addition to the four large powers invited to the meeting on July 8, Hughes also sent invitations to the Netherlands, Belgium, Portugal, and China, each of whom agreed to be represented.

See November 12, 1921.

July 21, 1921

U.S. Air Service planes bomb and sink the "unsinkable" German battleship *Ostfriesland* during an army-navy test in Chesapeake Bay.

Since January 25, 1921, when Senator Borah requested an investigation of what constitutes a modern navy, plans had been devised to determine whether aircraft bombs could sink a battleship, as General William Mitchell contended. Consequently, on July 21, while

The *Ostfriesland* is hit by a bomb during tests. National Archives

the 27,000-ton displacement German battleship the *Ostfriesland* lay at anchor 60 miles off the Virginia coast, Army Air Service bombers dropped six 1,000-pound and seven 2,000-pound bombs, most of which scored direct hits on the ship. In $21\frac{1}{2}$ minutes the *Ostfriesland* listed to one side and plunged to its deep ocean grave.

Although Mitchell, Borah, and others were convinced that battleships had become obsolete, the Joint Board of the Army and Navy disagreed. Because the conditions were not "warlike" and no battleship defensive tactics were used, the board would admit only that there was a potential for future aircraft use in war. The battleships, however, remained as the board's choice to be "the backbone of American defense" as long as trade and transportation were used on the seas of the world. The air power versus sea power debate had simply grown to larger proportions. Significantly, however, Borah believed aircraft and submarines were the best weapons for protecting the coastline of an isolated America.

August 20, 1921

Russia agrees to admit an American relief administration (ARA) to provide food for its starving citizens.

The ravages of World War I and the civil war between the Bolsheviks and the various White armies left Russia in a disastrous economic situation, in which lack of food supplies and poor distribution systems combined to cause large-scale famine. In July 1921, the Soviet government called for aid from the workers of the world, and Herbert Hoover's relief organization responded immediately. The Hoover-Nansen offer of food relief in April 1919 had been affected by political problems between the Allied powers and Lenin's regime. But in 1921 there were direct contacts between Hoover's ARA and Maxim Litvinov, the Soviet's assistant minister of foreign affairs.

On August 20, Litvinov and the ARA agreed on terms for relief supplies to be distributed in Russia by ARA members. The ARA insisted on the right to distribute relief to make certain that the aid reached those in need. Although granting this authority to foreign representatives was humiliating to Soviet authorities, the need for food was so great that Litvinov had no alternative.

During the next year, ARA delegates brought food and medicine to distribute in Russia. Most aid went to the Volga River region, where the famine was the most serious. In December 1921, the All-Russian Congress of Soviets formally thanked the ARA for $66 million of assistance, a greater amount than all other sources combined gave to Russia after its July call for help. Unfortunately, the anti-Communist attitude of the ARA delegates, which caused them to treat all Russians with disdain, resulted in ill will among the Russian people despite their gratitude for the supplies.

November 12, 1921

At the opening session of the Washington Conference, the United States proposes that the naval powers scrap capital naval ships and accept a 10-year naval construction holiday.

Secretary of State Hughes surprised conference delegates and pleased the public by using his opening speech as conference chairman to urge the delegates to limit all naval forces not only by scrapping old naval ships or those under construction but also by accepting a 10-year naval construction holiday that would stabilize the great powers' naval ratios at 5 for Great Britain and America to 3 for Japan. Hughes's proposal to limit naval fleets had been carefully prepared and was approved by President Harding and the U.S. delegation. In addition to Hughes, the U.S. delegates were Republican Senator Henry Cabot Lodge and Democratic Senator Oscar Underwood, the leaders of their parties in the Senate Foreign Relations Committee, and Elihu Root, a former senator and former secretary of state.

During the conference preparations in September and October, Hughes had asserted State Department leadership, using the U.S. navy officers as experts to provide him with necessary information but rejecting the navy's strategic plans for an offensive American naval fleet capable of operating against Japan in the western Pacific Ocean (Orange War Plan). The navy plans had projected American needs for a battle fleet equal to the combined Anglo-Japanese fleets. After obtaining data on the existing naval fleets of the three major naval powers, Hughes proposed to freeze each nation's navy at existing ratios. This worked out to be the 5:5:3 ratio suggested on November 12.

The secretary of state believed his concept was a realistic assessment of the existing situation in the three-power naval race. According to data from U.S. naval intelligence, if each of the three powers completed its current naval construction plans, the ratio of capital ships in 1928 would give the United States 100; Great Britain, 108; Japan, 87. Assuming that the U.S. Congress appropriated all funds necessary for the navy program, the 1928 ratio would be 10:10:8.7, leaving Japan better off than the 5:5:3 ratio. But Congress did not appear willing to authorize the necessary navy funds. During the current 1921–1922 fiscal year, Congress had cut $332 million from the navy budget, and Senators Lodge and Underwood believed such cuts would continue. At the same time, Japan had increased its 1921 navy budget by $61 million, consistent with its recent increases of $177 million over the past four years. Furthermore, U.S. navy plans required congressional approval for increasing fortifications in the Philippine Islands and Guam, which the navy had unsuccessfully sought since 1907. In brief, these estimates meant that the 5:5:3 ratio would give American naval forces a better ratio than future U.S. prospects in Congress anticipated.

The Navy Department did not, however, accept Hughes's proposed ratio. On October 26, Secretary of the Navy Edwin Denby countersigned a protest to Hughes by the General Board of the Navy. The board report argued: "Our superiority today lies in these ships." Japan, it contended, respected only force, and if the United States cut out 15 capital ships as planned, "the temptation of Japan to take a chance becomes very great."

Yet according to Hughes and the State Department, U.S. interests in East Asia were not sufficient to prepare for war with Japan. Diplomacy that sought the support of Britain and other powers could contain Japan's aggressive intentions. Moreover, military operations should not be contemplated in the western Pacific because this region was not vital to U.S. security.

In November 1921, Hughes's policies had widespread support. And his naval limitation concept was generally accepted by the other nations' delegates at the conclusion of the Washington Conference on February 6, 1922. The four naval limitation principles he proposed on November 12 were as follows:

1. abandoning all capital shipbuilding programs, both actual or projected;
2. reducing the navy's size by scrapping older ships;
3. maintaining the existing 5:5:3 ratio of the three naval powers;
4. using capital ship displacement tonnage as the yardstick to measure the strength of navies, with a proportionate allowance for auxiliary combatant seacraft. Capital ships were those displacing more than 10,000 tons, i.e., battleships and heavy battle cruisers.

To attain these limits Hughes announced that the United States would agree to scrap 15 old battleships and 15 uncompleted ships on which $330 million had already been spent. In turn, Great Britain would have to scrap 19 old ships and 4 new Hood-class ships; Japan would lose 10 old ships, 7 capital ships under construction, and 8 being planned. Altogether, the three nations would eliminate 78 capital ships that were built or being prepared—a total of 1,878,043 displaced tons.

For the long term, Hughes proposed a 10-year holiday on building capital ships. After 10 years, ships could be replaced after a vessel was 20 years old, but no ship could exceed 35,000 tons.

Hughes believed his proposed agreement would stop all plans for offensive naval war. In addition, the naval competition would end and "enormous sums will be released to aid the progress of civilization." The national defense of each power would be adequate, and after 10 years the naval powers could consider a future course of further limitations.

For the conference results, see February 6, 1922.

December 16, 1921

The State Department and the Commerce Department agree to give foreign loan control to the State Department.

Secretary of Commerce Herbert Hoover had indicated that his department's Bureau of Foreign Commerce should have more jurisdiction over foreign commerce and loans. Secretary of State Hughes rejected this idea and wanted U.S. consular officers to retain their position in commercial affairs and the secretary of state to retain control over foreign loans. U.S. diplomacy had become a complex of economic and political problems, and Hoover believed the Commerce Department should have jurisdiction in economic affairs, including relations with foreign nations.

In spite of Hughes's authority over loans, Hoover's department expanded its overseas operations, and by the end of the decade many U.S. businessmen believed the Commerce Department could serve them better at home and abroad than the State Department. Hoover and Hughes worked cooperatively to encourage American bankers to set guidelines for judging foreign loans.

1922

February 6, 1922

The Washington Conference ends after agreements are signed on naval limitations and to freeze the status quo in the Pacific and east Asia.

Following the opening ceremonies on November 11, 1921, and Secretary Hughes's dramatic opening speech, which proposed drastic naval limits, the delegates met in both plenary and subcommittee sessions until early February. Many of the critical decisions were made in ad hoc meetings of the Big Three: Britain's Foreign Minister Lord Balfour; U.S. Secretary of State Hughes; and Japan's Minister of the Navy Admiral Baron Tomosaburo Kato. The conference resulted in the following treaties:

The aircraft carrier USS *Lexington*, shown here, and the *Saratoga* were built on the hulls of battle cruisers. National Archives

1. Five-Power Naval Limitation Treaty. This agreement prohibited the construction of new capital ships for 10 years and established national ratios for the possession of capital ships that displaced more than 10,000 tons: a ratio of 5 for Great Britain and the United States; 3 for Japan; 1.67 for France and Italy.

Because aircraft carriers displaced an average of about 25,000 tons, these ships received a special status based on similar ratios. The United States and Great Britain could construct 5 carriers (135,000 tons); Japan 3 (81,000 tons); Italy and France 2 (48,000 tons). A separate treaty clause permitted America and Japan to convert two battle cruisers under construction into 33,000-ton carriers. In 1928, the carriers USS *Lexington* and *Saratoga* were converted from the hulls of two battle cruisers. The carriers' value in naval warfare was uncertain in 1922. The U.S. navy's first carrier, the USS *Langley*, went into service in March 1922, but generally American naval officers denied that aviation would affect the status of the battleship fleet, an estimate that did not begin to change until the 1930s.

Agreement on the naval ratios presented fewer difficulties than might have been expected by outside observers. In fact, England had agreed to accept naval parity with the United States in private negotiations during the spring of 1921, when Britain's first lord of the admiralty, Lord Lee of Fareham, corresponded with Secretary of the Navy Edwin Denby. This critical change in British naval policy resulted from Britain's postwar belief that by establishing better relations with the United States, England could end the Anglo-Japanese alliance and have America assume the primary role of the Western power that restricted Japanese expansion in the Pacific and East Asia. This would give England primary responsibility for the defense of its empire on a line running from Singapore to New Zealand. The United States never accepted and may not have comprehended this shift in British foreign and defense policy after 1919. Nevertheless, Britain's change greatly influenced U.S. global strategy during the interwar years from 1918 to 1940.

The Anglo-American agreement on naval parity left Japan as the nation that had to be persuaded to accept a lower naval ratio. Japan reluctantly agreed to the ratio of 3 to 5 on the basis that the two English-speaking countries accepted the freeze on their fortifications in the western Pacific Ocean. America agreed not to fortify bases west of Hawaii, such as Guam, Samoa, the Philippines, and the Aleutians; England agreed not to alter its fortifications at Hong Kong or in the Pacific east of the meridian 110′ east longitude except those off the coasts of Canada, Australia, and New Zealand.

U.S. navy strategists disliked the limits on ships and fortifications because they anticipated having to fight Japan in a future war through offensive operations in the western Pacific. In fact, there was no expectation that the Navy's Orange War Plan against Japan would be funded by the U.S. government in 1922. As early as 1907, Theodore Roosevelt had decided the Philippines could not be defended from Japan, and while the U.S. navy continued to seek fortifications in the Far Pacific, these plans had never been approved. Furthermore, Senator Lodge and the Republican leaders in Congress reported that the navy could not expect to obtain appropriations for the 48-battleship fleet that its "second-to-none" program advocated or for the fortifications it desired in the Pacific. The special treaty clause that permitted two battle cruisers to be converted into carriers was recommended as the only means for the U.S. navy to obtain carriers in the near future.

With agreement made on freezing fortifications in the Pacific, the three naval powers accepted Hughes's original proposal almost intact. The one significant change resulted from Japan's desire to retain the *Mutsu,* a battleship it had just completed. Hughes and Lord Balfour eventually agreed to allow Japan to retain the *Mutsu,* while America and Britain could complete two new battleships to offset the *Mutsu*'s size.

The Washington Conference naval ratios applied only to capital ships. Hughes had hoped the ratios would be extended to all auxiliary naval vessels, but France prevented this. Claiming that submarines, light cruisers, and torpedo boats were essential to its defenses, France demanded an exorbitant tonnage for its auxiliary ships: 330,000 tons for light cruisers and 90,000 tons for submarines. Premier Aristide Briand asserted that France sacrificed in accepting a low capital-ship ratio and could not accept the same for its other "defensive" vessels. Because of French intransigence, the aircraft carrier was the only auxiliary ship limited by the Five-Power Treaty.

2. Five-Power Treaty on Submarines and Gas Warfare; no agreement, however, on air war. By this treaty the signatory powers accepted traditional principles of maritime warfare regarding the use of submarines in future war. They also agreed to outlaw the use of asphyxiating gases in war. An attempt by the British to abolish submarine warfare was not accepted by the conferees.

The conference subcommittee on aircraft in war could not reach agreement during the conference. Therefore, the treaty provided for a separate commission of jurists to meet at a later date in order to establish limitations on the use of aircraft and radios in warfare. For the results of this commission, see February 18, 1923.

3. Four-Power Treaty on Pacific Ocean Possessions. By this treaty, England, France, Japan, and the United States agreed to respect each other's rights in the Pacific and to consult together in the event of aggression by any nation in that region. Thus, the status quo on existing insular possessions and dominions in the Pacific was recognized, including Japan's agreement not to fortify its mandated islands. More significant, perhaps, was the agreement for consultation if any power were threatened by the aggression of another power. In such event, the four nations would "communicate with one another fully and frankly" to reach an understanding. The United States and Japan concluded a separate treaty on Yap Island on February 11, 1922.

The Four-Power Treaty's long-range importance was to substitute a multilateral pact for the Anglo-Japanese Alliance, which those two powers abrogated.

4. Nine-Power Treaty to Protect the "Open Door" in China and give China greater customs autonomy. The Chinese delegation to the Washington Conference did not obtain its four basic objectives. These were (1) release from the unequal treaties made during the 19th century; (2) restoration of its sovereignty over Shantung; (3) cancellation of its Japanese treaties of 1915 and 1918; (4) equal treatment by all nations.

Almost ignoring China's desires, Secretary of State Hughes worked to secure the multilateral approval of America's open door principles. Essentially, the United States achieved this within the context of the existing situation in East Asia. The Nine-Power Treaty agreed to the following:

a. to recognize China's sovereignty, independence, and territorial integrity;
b. to provide an opportunity for China to maintain a stable government;
c. to maintain the equal opportunity for commerce and industry of all nations in China;
d. not to seek special rights or privileges in China that abridged the rights of citizens of "friendly states."

Although clauses of the Nine-Power Treaty appeared to require the powers to end the spheres of influence and special privilege, it did not do so. French, British, and Japanese retained their existing spheres of influence in China in the minutes of sessions that reserved rights of the powers. Secretary Hughes reserved the rights of the United States to seek equal benefits in those areas, but this was rhetoric that did not influence the delegates. Like John Hay in 1899, Hughes substituted the outward appearance of an open door for the existing reality of the Japanese, French, and English spheres of influence, a tactic not suited to enlightenment of the American public, which found it difficult to understand.

The Nine-Power Treaty did not bind the United States or any other nation to defend the open door or Chinese territorial integrity. It was a statement of what each power would not do and depended on the good faith of each power for fulfillment.

The Nine-Power Treaty regarding Chinese customs raised Chinese tariff rates and gave China more administrative rights regarding customs duties and collections. A commission was also established to study the question of extraterritoriality in China. Any nation trading with China could sign this treaty.

5. Sino-Japanese Treaty on Shantung. Signed on February 4, this treaty gave China general economic control in the area for at least 15 years through Japanese loans to China for the Tsinan-Tsingtao Railway. Japan did agree to withdraw its troops from Shantung.

This treaty retained Japan's special rights and privileges in Manchuria. Although Hughes wanted Japan to abrogate these rights, neither France nor England would support the U.S. attempt to persuade Japan to relinquish them. Hughes could do nothing except assert the American right to pursue similar concessions in Manchuria if it desired.

6. Six-Power Treaty on Cable Rights in Former German Islands. Although the United States had been the only state to challenge Japanese power on Yap Island, where the cable rights were centered, the other powers with Pacific possessions signed a treaty to provide their rights to use former German islands for cables if the need arose.

The U.S. Senate ratified each of the Washington treaties that directly involved America. The only restrictive provision of the Senate was placed on the Four-Power Treaty. The Senate added a reservation for this treaty providing that "there is no commitment to armed forces, no alliances and no obligations to join in any defense." The provision required congressional approval before the president or State Department committed the nation to act in case of aggression in East Asia.

All nations except France had ratified the Washington treaties by July 28, 1923. The French Chamber of Deputies eventually ratified all the treaties except the Five-Power Treaty on submarines and gas warfare.

February 11, 1922

Japan and America sign a treaty that settles the Yap Island dispute.

In 1920, the United States disputed Japan's control of the former German island of Yap because it was located on proposed sea cable routes between Hawaii and the Philippines. The issue was not resolved until the American-Japanese agreement of February 11, 1922.

By this convention, American citizens received cable, radio, and residential rights and facilities on Yap on a basis of equality with the Japanese. In return, the United States recognized Japan's right to the mandated control over all former German islands north of the equator in the Pacific Ocean. This latter recognition had previously been accepted by the United States, but not in a formal treaty.

See November 9, 1920.

February 28, 1922

Great Britain ends its protectorship over Egypt.

An Egyptian Nationalist Party (WAFD) had grown in strength during World War I and undertook an insurrection on March 8, 1919. While fighting the WAFD rebels, the British also conducted an investigation of their problems in Egypt. The commissioners recommended independence for Egypt with guarantees that British interests would be protected.

Attempts to reach a compromise with the WAFD failed, and on February 28, the British unilaterally ended their protectorship in favor of King Fuad I, who assumed control on March 15, 1922. The British reserved the right to negotiate with Egypt to protect communications, defense policy, and protection of foreigners. These negotiations were carried on over a decade, and a treaty was not signed until 1936.

See August 27, 1936.

September 7, 1922

Secretary of State Hughes heads the U.S. delegation to Brazil, where that nation celebrates its centennial anniversary of independence. Hughes's speeches during the week's celebration urge greater Pan-American cooperation.

Hughes's most notable speech during his visit to Brazil was delivered at the dedication site for the American centennial monument. He urged the people of the Americas to understand that the United States held no imperial designs over its neighbors. The sincere desire of America was to see in "the hemisphere an abiding peace, the reign of justice and the diffusion of the blessings of a beneficent cooperation."

September 21, 1922

Congress passes the Fordney-McCumber Tariff, renewing U.S. protectionism but permitting the President to negotiate reciprocity.

The 1922 tariff reversed the downward trend of the Underwood Tariff of 1913, raising rates more than 25% higher than those of the Payne-Aldrich Tariff of 1909. While the minority of congressional progressives objected, their only success was the addition of Section 317, a clause allowing the president to raise or lower the tariff by 50% to obtain reciprocity tariff rates with other nations. The reciprocity provisions failed because both Britain and France wanted America to reduce its tariffs before negotiations began.

December 6, 1922

Proclamation of the Irish Free State.

The British-Irish War that began on November 26, 1919, led to several months of serious conflict in 1920. Finally, some order was restored after the British Parliament passed The Government of Ireland Act on December 23, 1920. This act divided the island into Northern Ireland and south Ireland with a council to represent the two parts. Members of the Sinn Fein party led by Eamon De Valera rejected the partition, but their insurrection was defeated by the moderate Dáil Éireann, led by Arthur Griffith.

The Dáil Convention adopted a constitution on October 25, 1922, that became effective on December 6 with William T. Cosgrave as President.

December 29, 1922

Secretary of State Hughes proposes that American experts prepare methods for German reparations payments.

Because European nations were experiencing problems repaying their American debts and collecting German war reparations, Secretary of State Hughes used a speech before the convention of the American Historical Association to offer U.S. assistance. Following the adoption of the London Schedule for Reparations on April 27, 1921, Germany found it necessary to delay or postpone its payments. On March 21, 1922, the Allied Reparations Commission reduced Germany's cash payments for 1922 from 2 billion to 720 million marks, but when this sum could not be paid, the commission suspended German payments for six months.

During the fall of 1922, the commission had to decide if the German defaults were "willful" or the result of monetary transfer problems. The British accepted Germany's argument that the rebuilding of its wartime economy and the inflation of German currency relative to gold marks caused transfer problems. The French delegation argued that Germany refused to raise taxes and to make the sacrifices necessary to meet its obligations. This "willful" default, the French said, justified the Allied use of military intervention to force Germany to pay.

Although America received no German reparations, Secretary Hughes became concerned as early as September 1922, and suggested to French Premier

Raymond Poincaré that a group of financiers ought to prepare Germany's payment schedule. Poincaré refused because he contended payment was a German, not a French, problem. Germany, he said, was obligated to pay the existing schedule.

On December 26, the Allied powers declared Germany had defaulted on its payments and opened the possibility of military action against the Germans. Hughes hoped to prevent a military conflict and, being scheduled to address the American historians on December 29, the secretary decided to publicly call on world opinion to help avoid a crisis between France and Germany. With President Harding's consent, Hughes proposed in his address that a group of "distinguished Americans" examine the problem and prepare a German payment plan. The European problem, he argued, was a world problem, and Americans "cannot escape the injurious consequences of a failure to settle [it]. . . . There will be no permanent peace," Hughes contended, "unless economic satisfactions are enjoyed. We should view with disfavor measures which instead of producing reparations would threaten disaster." Although Hughes rejected the contention that German reparations and European debts to the United States were linked, America wanted the reparations issue settled on its merits because its outcome would enable the United States to determine the Allies' capacity to pay their U.S. debts.

While many observers lauded Hughes's speech, the French did not. Poincaré became upset, claiming Hughes had condemned the military occupation planned for the Ruhr before it began. Thus France ignored Hughes and proceeded with its plans.

See January 11, 1923.

December 30, 1922

The Union of Soviet Socialistic Republics (USSR), is organized in Moscow.

During 1921, the Red Army under General Leon Trotsky defeated the White army forces trying to restore the czar's Russian Empire. The Red Army's victories permitted the Bolsheviks to consolidate their power in Moscow by organizing the Union of Soviet Socialist Republics. In 1922, the original USSR consisted of four republics: Russia, Ukraine, White Russia, and Transcaucasia. By 1937, eight more republics were added: Armenia, Azerbijan, Georgia, Kazakistan, Kirgistan, Tadjikistan, Turmenistan, and Uzebekistan.

1923

January 2, 1923

America and Japan formally cancel the Lansing-Ishii Agreement.

Following the acceptance of the Nine-Power Treaty at the Washington Conference on February 6, 1922, Secretary of State Hughes began discussions with Japan to formally cancel the Lansing-Ishii agreement of November 1917. That agreement included a clause that was crucial from the American viewpoint though it had been kept secret since 1917. In the secret clause Japan agreed not to seek special rights in China that abridged the rights of citizens of friendly nations.

On December 27, 1922, Japan's foreign minister sent Hughes a note accepting the cancellation of the Lansing-Ishii agreement. On January 2, 1923, Hughes wrote to Japanese Chargé Saburi in Washington formally responding and acknowledging America's agreement to abrogate the 1917 understanding. Because the Lansing-Ishii agreement was not a treaty, its cancellation required no Senate action.

January 11, 1923

French and Belgian troops occupy the Ruhr district after declaring Germany had defaulted on coal deliveries under reparations agreements.

The Allied Reparations Commission had debated the reparations issue and Germany's ability to pay throughout 1922. At the Second London Conference, on December 9–11, 1922, British Prime Minister Bonar Law offered to cancel Allied debts to Britain if changes were made regarding German payments, but French Premier Raymond Poincaré refused. On December 26, the Reparations Commission declared Germany at default on its debt but recommended no further action at that time.

In a meeting on January 9, the Reparations Commission again discussed the situation. The British delegation argued that the German default was not willful and military intervention should be avoided. To bolster its case, the British asked the U.S. observer at the commission, Roland W. Boyden, to offer his opinion. Boyden supported the British view and stated that the United States wished to prevent military action. This ploy failed to persuade the French, who, backed by the Belgians and Italians on the commission, voted that Germany had defaulted and, in particular, was behind in its coal deliveries. In spite of British objections, the other three European nations agreed to send troops to occupy the Ruhr district of Germany. They did so on January 11, 1923.

For the results of the Ruhr occupation, see September 1, 1924.

February 7, 1923

A Washington conference of Central American states results in a neutrality treaty that proves to be ineffective.

Secretary of State Hughes and the State Department's chief of the Latin American Division, Sumner Welles, had proposed a conference of Central American states to end the friction between Honduras, Nicaragua, and El Salvador. Each of these states accused its neighbors of assisting revolutionary plots against it.

In August 1922, Hughes arranged a temporary settlement of a crisis in Central America by sponsoring a meeting of the presidents of each nation on the USS *Tacoma* in Fonseca Bay, near El Salvador. To obtain a permanent agreement, Hughes invited the three states to meet at Washington on December 22, 1922. During the following sessions in December and January, the Central American delegates established a Central American Tribunal to act as an arbitration court. Five Latin American nations pledged not to assist or recognize a government set up by a coup d'état or to intervene "directly or indirectly, in the internal affairs of any other Central American republic."

Although they composed a model treaty that was signed on February 7, 1923, the signatory nations did little to make it effective. The past anxieties and problems persisted among these five states: Nicaragua, Honduras, El Salvador, Costa Rica, and Guatemala.

February 18, 1923

A Commission of Jurists at the Hague sign a treaty to regulate aerial warfare: an agreement never ratified.

Because the subcommittee on aircraft and radios could not reach agreement during the Washington Conference of 1921–1922, the delegates referred the issue to a special commission of experts. On December 11, 1922, the Special Commission of Jurists convened at the Hague to negotiate a pact, giving their particular attention to aerial bombing. John Bassett Moore, who headed the American delegation, also became commission chairman. Under his guidance a treaty was negotiated and signed (February 18) by delegates from France, Britain, Italy, Japan, the Netherlands, and the United States.

Essentially, the Hague pact proposed rules of air war based on traditional naval bombardment regulations. These rules restricted bombing "within bounds of military operations directed against combatant forces." Noncombatant areas were not to be bombed. In addition, the Hague rules anticipated a form of aerial war that some air power advocates were considering—terror bombing. The 1923 rules asserted: "Bombardment by aircraft for the purpose . . . of terrorizing the civilian population is forbidden."

Following the conference, the Hague Rules on Aircraft Bombing met a dismal fate. The U.S. State Department tried for four years to obtain an indication that the other powers would ratify the treaty, contending America would seek Senate ratification if the pact was accepted by other nations. Only Japan indicated it would ratify. The European nations decided aircraft were developing so rapidly that rules should not restrict this progress at such an early stage. Consequently, on April 9, 1928, the State Department placed the Hague agreement in the dead file. The attempt is notable as the first effort to restrict air raids by heavier-than-air planes.

February 19, 1923

The U.S. Supreme Court rules that America can deny naturalization rights to any immigrants except free white caucasians.

In the case of *U.S. v. Thind*, the Supreme Court gave general validation to state alien land laws that California had passed and 14 other states duplicated: Arizona, Arkansas, Delaware, Idaho, Kansas, Louisiana, Missouri, Montana, Nebraska, Nevada, New Mexico, Oregon, Texas, and Washington.

The court rulings reflected the xenophobia of the 1920s that was explicit in the Emergency Quota Act of May 19, 1921, and in the various state laws. Earlier, on November 13, 1922, the court had decided in the case of *Ozawa v. U.S.* that Japanese were not eligible to be naturalized. Later, in the cases of *Terrace v. Thompson* (November 12, 1923) and *O'Brien v. Webb* (November 19, 1923), the alien land laws of Washington and California were sustained as being constitutional and not violating the Japanese Treaty of 1911.

On the Japan-U.S. emigration agreement, see February 11, 1911; for California immigration restrictions, see December 4, 1906 and February 20, 1907.

April 10, 1923

The Second Chester Concession is granted by the Turkish government.

Admiral (ret.) Colby M. Chester had received but failed to fulfill an investment concession from Turkey on December 11, 1911. In May 1920, Chester asked the State Department to assist him in obtaining another Turkish concession for railway and mineral rights. Although Secretary of State Hughes discounted Chester's project, the U.S. Navy Department encouraged the plan and the U.S. high commissioner to Turkey, Admiral Mark Bristol, aided Chester.

On April 10, Chester seemed to have succeeded when the Ankara government granted Chester's Ottoman-American development company a concession to construct a railway and exploit mineral resources along its right-of-way. But Chester could not raise the financial backing in the six months allocated to him, and Turkey canceled the concession in December 1923. Chester's default left a consortium of seven U.S. oil companies as the only U.S. oil companies operating in the Middle East.

See July 21, 1928.

May 3, 1923

The Fifth International Conference of American States adjourns in Santiago, Chile.

Although Secretary of State Hughes had planned the meeting of the Fifth International Conference of American States, a lingering illness kept him home. He appointed Ambassador to Belgium Henry P. Fletcher to head the U.S. delegation. Future Secretary of State Frank Kellogg was also a delegate.

The convention met from March 25 to May 3, 1923, and agreed on two principal measures. First, it formed a commission of jurists to codify international law. Second, it adopted the Gondra Convention, an agreement to provide a "cooling-off" period for the nations in any dispute by first referring the issue to an inquiry committee for study and a report.

June 19, 1923

Great Britain accepts a plan to repay its U.S. war debts that becomes the basic model for American agreements with other world war allies.

The United States emerged from World War I as the Allies' major creditor nation, European nations owing nearly $11 billion to the U.S. government and private bondholders. During the period immediately following the Paris Peace Conference, British and French officials discussed with America the mutual cancellation of war debts, but the Wilson administration refused, a policy continued by Harding. In a message to Prime Minister Lloyd George on November 3, 1920, President Wilson made it clear that the United States would not cancel any debts or allow the Allies to correlate U.S. war debts with the reparations Britain, France, and other nations assessed against Germany for their war guilt.

Although Great Britain, France, and Russia agreed in February 1915 to unite their financial as well as military forces against the Central Powers, the United States persistently rejected this concept and listed the Allied war loans on a nation-by-nation basis.

Continuing to insist that the Allies must accept plans to fund their debt payments, Harding's Secretary of the Treasury Andrew Mellon asked Congress in 1921 for full authority to negotiate separate debt payments with each nation. Congress rejected this request but created a World War Foreign Debt Commission, with Mellon as the chairman, to negotiate agreements. This law was signed by Harding on February 9, 1922. It instructed the eight-member commission to settle all debts on a 25-year basis, at no less than 4.25% interest. Each national agreement would be submitted by the commission for ratification by Congress.

The commission's first major agreement was accepted by Great Britain on June 19, 1923, following several commission meetings with Britain's chancellor of the exchequer, Stanley Baldwin.

Although the British first refused to accept the terms of the congressional act of February 9, 1922, the commissioners worked out a method to circumvent the strict application of the 25 years at 4.25% interest, and Britain agreed to its terms. The commission made the funded principal less than the total debt and recalculated the accrued interest from 1918 to 1922 at 4.25%, rather than the original 5%. By also extending the payments of the funded amount over 62 years, the commission reduced the British debt in actuality while enabling congressmen and U.S. spokesmen to claim that there was no reduction or cancellation. The British debt with interest would be $11.1 billion, paying an average interest rate of 3.3%.

Similar treaties were made with 12 other nations between 1923 and May 3, 1926. Such nations as Italy and France received very low interest rates. France was charged no interest for the first five years and low rates thereafter, for a French interest rate of 1.6% on $4.025 billion; similarly, Italy's interest was 0.4% on $2.042 billion. The commission reported to Congress that its work had essentially ended on May 3, 1926, when a debt agreement was signed with Yugoslavia.

Because the debt commissioners and the congressmen who worked on the debt funding feared the consequence of being candid with the American people, they led the public to believe that the debt charges were not reduced. Herbert Hoover, for example, explained privately that the U.S. concessions were necessary during the negotiations. In public, therefore, the United States was referred to as "Uncle Shylock." In financial reality, the settlements reduced the Allied debts for 13 countries by 43.1% when calculated on the basis of the 4.25% interest supposedly required by the act of February 9, 1922, and the debt plus accrued interest of the original loans.

Nevertheless, these reductions left the European nations with large interest and principal payments to bear for a 62-year period. The cancellation of all war debts and German reparations may, ideally, have provided a sounder financial basis for Western Europe and the United States. This was not politically possible in the United States at the time. Thus, debts and reparations continued to plague the Western powers and Germany for another decade, leaving a reservoir of ill feelings among the nations concerned.

July 24, 1923

The Treaty of Lausanne concludes allied peace terms with Turkey's nationalist government of Mustapha Kemal.

The Turkish nationalists never accepted the Treaty of Sèvres of August 10, 1920, and Kemal continued at war with the Greeks, who were aided by a British force sent on September 16, 1922, to save them from complete defeat.

Following the landing of British troops, Kemal began to confer with the Allies. After several minor skirmishes, a peace conference began at Lausanne, Switzerland, on April 23, 1923. In the Treaty of Lausanne, Turkey ceded all non-Turkish territory lost during World War I except Eastern Thrace. Greece received all the Aegean Islands except Imbros and Tenedos. The British occupied Cyprus. Turkey again gained control of Istanbul, although Kemal retained the capital at Ankara.

During the 1920–1922 war, Kemal's armies also forced Sultan Mohammed VI into exile. On October 29, 1923, Turkey was proclaimed a republic with Kemal as its first president.

August 2, 1923

President Harding dies and is succeeded by Vice President Coolidge.

The president died in San Francisco while returning from a trip to Alaska. The cause of his death was listed as embolism. On August 3, Calvin Coolidge took the oath of office as president.

August 6, 1923

A U.S.-Turkish treaty of amity and commerce is signed.

During the Lausanne Conference between the Allied powers and Turkey (see July 24, 1923), the U.S. observers at the meeting negotiated a treaty with Turkey's new government. The American observers were Ambassadors Joseph C. Grew (to Switzerland) and Richard W. Child (to Italy) and the U.S. High Commissioner to Turkey Admiral Mark Bristol. The Turkish representative was Ismet Inonu.

The treaty of August 6 provided for the exchange of diplomatic officials; the most-favored-nation commercial treaty; the abrogation of all treaties between the United States and the Ottoman Empire; and the legal recognition of American educational, religious, and medical institutions in Turkey. The treaty engendered a lengthy dispute before the U.S. Senate rejected it.

See January 18, 1927.

August 31, 1923

America recognizes Obregón's regime in Mexico after he agrees to settle the oil issue of 1918.

Following his election on September 5, 1920, Obregón attempted to settle all foreign claims against Mexico in order to gain recognition. Since the revolution, which began in 1911, Mexico had been unable to pay its foreign debts and the bonded public debts that foreign investors held. Although the French and British held the largest share of these debts, they delegated the negotiations to representatives of American bondholders and bankers.

The United States held claims on Mexico in addition to the loan indebtedness. In 1919, a congressional subcommittee of the Committee on Foreign Relations, led by Senator Albert B. Fall, investigated all claims against Mexico and issued a 3,000-page report that both protested Mexico's outrages and compiled a list of claims. Among U.S. claims were those of citizens for damages since the claims commission of 1868; claims for violence, damage, and arbitrary decrees during the decade of revolution; land claims affected by Mexico's land reforms; damages to American interests under Article 27 of Mexico's 1917 constitution; and interest and principal on Mexican government bonds.

As a condition of recognizing Obregón's government, both Wilson and Harding had insisted that Mexico guarantee all claims. During the spring of 1923, Secretary of State Hughes persuaded Harding to send Charles Beecher Warren, the former ambassador to Japan, and John B. Payne, former secretary of the interior, to Mexico City to negotiate a settlement. After consulting with Thomas Lamont, the J.P. Morgan representative who had negotiated a bankers' agreement with Mexico on June 16, 1922, Payne and Warren began discussions with two Mexican commissioners on May 14, 1923, at No. 85 Bucareli Street in Mexico City. Two agreements resulted from the Bucareli Commission: a Special Claims Convention for losses between November 10, 1910, and May 31, 1920, and a General Claims Convention covering losses from 1868 to 1910. In addition, the commission produced an "extra official pact" of its conference minutes in which each side stated its policy on agrarian and subsoil issues. The result of the commission pact was to leave the issues of oil and land uncertain. The U.S. position reserved "all" the rights of U.S. citizens; the Mexican statement was that Article 27 of their constitution of 1917 was not retroactive if the persons with prior concessions had made "some positive act" that would manifest the intention of the owner "to use the oil under the surface." "Positive act" was defined broadly.

Initially in 1923, diplomatic relations appeared to have improved between Mexico and America. The claims conventions were ratified, and when an uprising by Adolfo de la Huerta threatened Obregón, the United States supported Obregón's government by selling him military equipment to suppress the rebellion.

In 1925, however, the Mexican congress passed new legislation regarding petroleum and land reform, causing the United States to protest. The new dispute again cooled U.S.-Mexican relations.

See February 19, 1918, and January 11, 1928.

September 27, 1923

Mussolini's attempt to conquer Corfu from Greece fails because of British intervention.

After several Italians were assassinated along the Greek-Albanian border on August 27, the Italians bombarded and occupied Corfu. Greece appealed to the League of Nations, and the League together with British pressure finally forced Italy to pull out of the island and restore Greek political rule. This was Mussolini's first attempt at military adventurism.

October 29, 1923

Turkey becomes a republic under President Mustapha Kemal.

Following the signing of the Treaty of Lausanne on July 24, Turkey's Grand National Assembly proclaimed the Republic of Turkey, naming Kemal—later given the title of Kemal Atatürk (Father of all Turks)—as president. Kemal ruled until his death in 1938, during which time he created a secular, nationalistic republic that differentiated Turkey from other Middle Eastern Muslim nations.

On April 20, 1924, the constitution of the republic was completed, stating that sovereignty of the nation resided in the Turkish people. The constitution specified that all Turks were equal under the law without distinction of race or creed. It also provided for freedom of the press, speech, and thought. Women were given the right to vote in 1934, a new law code was written to replace the Islamic Shariah courts, and a public law school was opened in Ankara, the capital of the republic. The Turkish army was trained in military schools where officers became strong supporters of Kemal's secular republic.

Although Atatürk ruled Turkey as a one-party state, Turkey retained friendly ties with Europe and became a partner after World War II.

See December 1, 1943.

December 20, 1923

Sinclair Oil obtains oil concessions in northern Iran; The project fails in 1925.

Following World War I, the Soviet Union ended the czar's treaties with Iran (officially Persia until March 21, 1935) and pulled out of northern Iran. Because the Iranian nationalists held strong anti-British attitudes, they asked W. Morgan Shuster, the American financier who had aided Iran in 1911, to help them. Shuster contacted Jersey Standard and Sinclair Oil regarding an oil concession in northern Iran. Jersey Standard withdrew, however, because of its connection with the British oil concession in Iraq.

Subsequently, on December 20, 1923, Iran granted the Sinclair Oil Company a concession. In exchange for 50-year oil rights in four of the five northern provinces, Sinclair arranged a $10 million loan for Iran and gave Iran 20% of the oil profits. Unlike Jersey Standard, Harry Sinclair planned to send oil through Soviet territory to avoid Britain's southern Iranian control. The Soviets agreed to accept Sinclair's plan provided the U.S. government recognized the Communist regime. But the United States would not grant recognition, and combined with its embroilment in the 1924 Teapot Dome oil scandal, Sinclair's fortune fell and it withdrew from the Iranian agreement in 1925.

Sinclair's attempt to exploit Iranian oil was one of two U.S. failures in Iran before 1940. In 1937, the U.S.-controlled Amiranian Oil Company received an oil concession from Iran's shah but had to surrender it within a year because of the company's financial problems.

In southern Iran, an Anglo-Russian oil company was formed after oil was discovered in 1908. During World War I, the Russians protected northern Iran from the Germans while the British navy remained in the Persian Gulf, where its new oil-burning ships refueled at Abadan's oil refinery. After the war, political disputes between Iran's shah and (Majlis) parliament resulted in conflicts in Tehran that led Iran's General Reza Khan Pahlavi to overthrow the Qajar dynasty of shahs. After Reza Khan became head of the Pahlavi dynasty in 1925, he tried to modernize Iran by introducing a secular law code, public education, and schools for women and promoting the ancient Iranian language to replace Arabic, the language of the Koran and Iran's mullahs. This action also changed Persia's name to Iran in 1935.

The Anglo-Russian oil company also ended during World War I being replaced by the Anglo-Persian (later Anglo-Iranian) oil company. Because Reza Khan wanted a greater share of the company's oil profits, the British increased Iran's share from 16 to 20 percent but this small increase caused controversy after World War II ended.

For Shuster see May 12 and November 29, 1911; for Iraq arrangement see July 21, 1928; for post-WWII see May 2, 1951.

1924

March 10, 1924

America sends additional marines to Honduras.

On September 11, 1919, the United States had sent marines to Honduras to prevent a civil war by supporting President Rafael Gutierrez. Since 1919, however, Gutierrez had moved to create dictatorial power, stimulating an insurgency led by Tiburcio Carias. On March 10, following the killing of Gutierrez by rebels under Carias, the United States ordered more marines to land in Honduras to suppress the disorders. Nevertheless, Carias's forces captured the capital city, Tegucigalpa, on March 31.

At this juncture, the State Department sent Sumner Welles to settle the dispute. On May 3, 1924, Welles met with representatives of Honduras's neighboring states, Nicaragua, Guatemala, and El

Salvador, and persuaded them to sign the Pact of Anapala. By this agreement, the neighboring states cut off aid to the insurgent forces. In 1925, Welles conducted elections in Honduras that prohibited revolutionary leaders from being candidates. The election was won by Miguel Paz BARAHONA. Unfortunately, the long-term Honduran political difficulties remained, and the United States had not established permanent order in the area. In 1933, General Carias became dictator of Honduras.

May 15, 1924

Congress passes a general immigration law including a clause to exclude "Orientals": Japan protests.

The Chinese and Japanese governments had been persistently irritated by the unequal treatment of their people by U.S. immigration laws. Beginning on May 19, 1921, when Congress passed the Emergency Quota Act, Japan protested the action as well as California's alien land laws. Tokyo did not object to control of immigration per se, but to the discriminatory treatment accorded Asians.

On the West Coast prejudices against Asians continued, although the 1907 Gentleman's Agreement and the 1911 Commercial Treaty with Japan virtually ended Japanese immigration. Between 1907 and 1922, the net increase of Japanese Americans was 16,096: those entering the United States and Hawaii numbered 171,584; those leaving, 155,488. Many of these immigrants were Japanese "picture-brides" sent by marriage brokers in Japan to wed Japanese American men, a custom most Americans did not understand. The influx of women had increased the number of Americans born of Japanese ancestry from 4,502 births in 1910 to 29,672 in 1920.

During these years, the West Coast Exclusionist League expanded its membership to Oregon, Washington, Nevada, and Arizona. Its activities secured state laws to prohibit "Orientals" from owning or leasing land.

By 1921, there was a crisis in American-Japanese relations because of the land and immigration discrimination. In Tokyo, U.S. Ambassador Roland S. Morris tried to negotiate a more restrictive gentleman's agreement with Foreign Minister Baron Shidehara. When drafts of the Morris-Shidehara proposals reached America in 1921, Senator Hiram Johnson of California and other Pacific Coast politicians strenuously objected and the project ended.

In Washington, Secretary of State Hughes and President Coolidge both urged in vain for congressional leaders to seek some compromise in 1924. Hughes wrote to Congressman Albert Johnson of the House Committee on Immigration to indicate that the exclusion of Japanese damaged U.S. relations with Japan. The Washington Treaties of 1922, Hughes stated, had improved U.S.-Japanese relations, and "fixing a stigma" on the Japanese would affront a friendly nation. Hughes pointed out that placing Japan under the European quota system would allow only 250 Japanese each year to enter America. After the House Committee ignored Hughes's pleas, the president suggested that Congress postpone the exclusion clause for two years while a treaty could be negotiated with Japan. But Congress rejected this proposal.

Consequently, despite objections of the State Department and president, Congress overwhelmingly passed the Immigration Bill of 1924 including the exclusion of "aliens ineligible to citizenship," a phrase especially designed to exclude Japanese. The House vote was 308 to 62; the Senate vote, 69 to 9. Coolidge signed the law on May 26, explaining that if the anti-Japanese measure had stood separately, he would have vetoed it. The president believed, however, that a general immigration law was necessary. For 30 years, the U.S. government had avoided a Japanese exclusion law; now it was a reality.

Although Secretary of State Hughes called Japan's Ambassador Hanihara to his office to attempt to minimize the effect of the congressional action, this was difficult to accomplish. Hanihara resigned as ambassador and returned to Japan in humiliation for failing to avert this insult. As representatives of the liberal political groups in Japan that opposed the aggressive methods of the military conservatives, Hanihara and Shidehara suffered a disastrous blow, which turned in favor of the more aggressive militarists during the next five years.

See November 2, 1920.

May 23, 1924

The Soviet Union abrogates most of the Czar's treaties with China.

Knowing that the Chinese revolutionaries had been urging the abolition of the "unequal treaties" forced on the Ch'ing dynasty between 1842 and 1914, Lenin's government announced as early as July 1919 that the Soviet Union would repudiate those treaties. By 1924, however, the Red Army had defeated the White armies in Central Asia. Now, Moscow was less willing to end all the czar's previous arrangements in East Asia. Therefore, while generally ending the czar's tariff and economic concessions with China, the Soviets worked out two exceptions with that country: (1) the Soviets retained control of the Chinese Eastern Railway to restrain Japanese interests in Manchuria; (2) Outer Mongolia continued to be a Soviet protectorate. This decision required that the Red Army intervene in Outer Mongolia to defeat refugees from Cossack and other White armies who were terrorizing the Mongolians. The Red Army suppressed these military bandits and placed a "friendly" ruler in control of Outer Mongolia under Soviet guidance.

May 24, 1924

The Rogers Act unites the U.S. Consular Service and Diplomatic Service into one branch of the State Department, creating the Foreign Service of the United States.

In 1919, Representative John Jacob Rogers of Massachusetts first offered legislation to unite the consular and foreign service branches. Secretary of State Lansing had advised Rogers that conflicts of jurisdiction had frequently taken place and necessitated the reorganization of the two branches. On May 24, 1924, the Rogers Act became law. It not only united these two parts of the State Department's overseas functions but also placed appointments to the Foreign Service on a merit basis.

On February 23, 1931, the Moses-Linthicun Act revised the Rogers Act to correct deficiencies of the 1924 legislation regarding classification of service officers and the appointment and promotion process. Together these enactments became the basis of the U.S. Foreign Service.

July 1, 1924

Secretary of State Hughes reaffirms America's refusal to recognize the Union of Soviet Socialist Republics.

Although Hughes, like President Wilson in 1917, said he was sympathetic toward the Russian people, he continued to refuse to grant diplomatic recognition to the USSR, although most European nations had done so. After Great Britain recognized the Bolshevik government on February 1, 1924, many Americans questioned U.S. policy toward the Soviet Union.

Subsequently, on July 1, Hughes issued a statement to clarify America's reasons for nonrecognition. The secretary's three basic reasons for not granting recognition were (1) the USSR's refusal to accept the debts of the Russian State and its repudiation of all prior Russian debts, including the $187 million loaned to the Kerensky government by the United States; (2) Moscow's attempt to seek the overthrow of the existing social and political order of the United States through the subversive activity of the U.S. Communist Party and the Workers' Party; and (3) the U.S. claim that the new regime had not yet been accepted by the Russian people.

See October 25, 1924.

July 12, 1924

In the Dominican Republic, Horacio Vasques becomes president following an agreement for the withdrawal of U.S. Marines.

Soon after taking office in 1921, Secretary Hughes endeavored to withdraw the U.S. Marines that President Wilson had sent to Santo Domingo in 1916. He appointed Rear Admiral Samuel S. Robison as the military governor, instructing him to prepare for free elections and ultimate withdrawal.

Initially, the Dominican people suspected some trick by Hughes. But in March 1922, the secretary sent word to the island that he would welcome emissaries to make an agreement in Washington. General Horacio Vasques and Federico Valasquez came to the United States and agreed on an evacuation plan. As a result, Hughes sent Sumner Welles to Santo Domingo as a special commissioner to arrange an election and the U.S. withdrawal.

The agreement for the transfer of independence to the Dominicans was signed on June 30, 1922. Thereafter, American rule was transferred to a provisional government on October 21, 1922, and preparations for a constitution and the election of a president were undertaken in 1923. The result was the election and inauguration of Vasques as president on July 12. The last U.S. Marines withdrew from the Dominican Republic on September 18, 1924.

September 1, 1924

The Dawes Plan seeks to solve the German reparations problem and end the Ruhr occupation.

On January 11, 1923, an international crisis began when French and Belgian troops occupied Germany's Ruhr District because Germany defaulted on its reparations payments under the Treaty of Versailles. Two consequences of this action were that Germany stopped all reparations payments and its economy collapsed, depreciating the value of the German mark to nearly nothing and causing staggering inflation. One result of the German economic plight was Adolf Hitler's beer-hall putsch in Munich on November 9, 1923. The fledgling Nazi Party protested that the German republican government could not effectively combat the Communist menace within and the French invaders from without. Hitler's putsch failed but gave the Nazis a prominence from which they profited after 1930.

The Ruhr occupation caused a stalement between France and Germany. Not only did reparations cease but also the German government encouraged passive resistance by the Ruhr workers, with the result that production of the coal and metallurgical industries declined precipitously in 1923–1924. France gradually realized that a new reparations scheme was necessary and, during the fall of 1923, David Lloyd George of Britain revived Secretary Hughes's proposal of December 29, 1922, for a commission of experts. On November 30, 1923, the Allied Reparations Commission agreed to form two committees: the first to find a method for restoring German financial stability; the second to repatriate German capital exports that had fled the country.

On the request of Louis Barthou, chairman of the Reparations Commission, Secretary Hughes arranged for Barthou to invite the Chicago banker Charles G. Dawes and the Chairman of the Board of General Electric Company, Owen D. Young, to serve on the currency stabilization commission and Henry M. Robinson on the committee on foreign German funds. Hughes cooperated unofficially in the appointment of the U.S. commissioners. Dawes became chairman of his group and its recommendations became known as the Dawes Plan. Other nations represented were France, Great Britain, Italy, and Belgium.

The currency commission met between January 14 and April 9, 1924. It submitted its report to the Reparations Committee, which accepted it and later agreed to make it effective on September 1, 1924. During the commission's study, Secretary Hughes studiously avoided the direct involvement of the State Department. Nevertheless, Hughes influenced the British and French acceptance of the Dawes Plan by visiting the Continent as president of the American Bar Association, leading a group of U.S. and Canadian lawyers on a pilgrimage to Europe between July 12 and August 2, 1924, at the time when the commission's report was under consideration. In particular, Hughes's visits with French Premier Édouard Herriot and President Poincaré seem to have persuaded the French to accept the Dawes Plan. When Herriot complained that accepting the plan would cause his cabinet to fall, Hughes told him it would fall if the German problems were not solved. If France rejected the plan, Hughes warned, no further American aid could be expected.

Consequently, France agreed and the European powers signed the Dawes Plan on August 30, 1924. The plan, which based its findings on what Germany could pay rather than on what it should be forced to pay, may be summarized as follows:

1. The Dawes reparation schedule would be temporary, to be made permanent following a review in four or five years. Thus, the total amount of reparations would be fixed later.
2. A five-year payment schedule required 1 million marks the first year and a gradual increase to 2.5 million annually in five years.
3. Bonds from a reorganized German railroad system and industrial bonds would underwrite German reconstruction and provide income for reparations during the five-year period.
4. A special Transfer Commission would collect German payments in marks and distribute the funds through the monetary exchange markets to preserve the stability of all national currencies, including Germany's.
5. Annual payments would be flexible to adjust to changes in economic circumstances in Germany and the nations collecting reparations.
6. Loans of $200 million would be extended to Germany, and the loan interest and amortization charges were to be included in the annual payments.
7. Germany's cash payments, payments in kind, payments for the occupation forces, and other charges

were unified into the one annual payment schedule.

Following approval of the Dawes Plan, Germany, Belgium, and France made agreements providing for the evacuation of Allied forces from the Ruhr District. At French insistence, clauses in these agreements recognized previous German defaults and the right of the Allies to use military sanctions if Germany defaulted again.

The Dawes Plan functioned as the reparations schedule until 1928, when a commission headed by Owen Young met to make permanent reparations arrangements.

For the Young Plan, see August 31, 1929.

October 25, 1924

The Zinoviev letter causes diplomatic tensions between Great Britain and the Soviet Union.

Within British domestic politics, the issue of recognizing the Soviet government continued to be controversial after Ramsay MacDonald's Labour cabinet extended de jure recognition to Moscow on February 1, 1924. The Labour cabinet signed a commercial treaty on August 8 that gave the Soviets most-favored-nation trading status. Together, these actions by MacDonald provided the election campaign of the fall of 1924 with a major issue that Stanley Baldwin's Conservatives capitalized on due to an unwise letter that Grigory Zinoviev sent on October 25.

Speaking on behalf of the Communist Third International, whose headquarters were in Moscow, Zinoviev wrote a letter to leaders of the British Communists that allegedly urged British subjects to provoke a revolution in Great Britain. The publicity about Zinoviev's message was largely responsible for Baldwin's victory in the elections of October 29, 1924. On November 21, 1924, Baldwin's ministry abrogated the August commercial treaties and adopted a hard-line policy toward the Soviet Union. The hostile British policy eventually caused a break in Anglo-Soviet relations on May 26, 1927.

See October 1, 1929.

October 28, 1924

France grants de jure recognition to the Soviet Union.

November 4, 1924

President Coolidge is reelected.

Although Robert La Follette bolted the Republican Party to run as the Progressive Party candidate, Coolidge easily defeated both La Follette and the Democratic Party nominee, John W. Davis.

1925

January 5, 1925

Secretary of State Hughes offers his resignation.

In November 1924, following the reelection of Coolidge, Hughes had notified the president of his intention to resign. The secretary had worked diligently for eight years as governor of New York and secretary of state. But as his expenses had exceeded his income during this period, he desired a better-paying job to provide for the future of his family. Hughes recommended Frank B. Kellogg to be his successor.

See March 5, 1925.

March 5, 1925

Frank B. Kellogg becomes Secretary of State.

Kellogg had been a senator from Minnesota (1917–1923) and ambassador to Great Britain (1923–1925). He had been trained as a lawyer and had once served as president of the American Bar Association. Thus, while his foreign experience was limited, he brought impressive credentials to the State Department. He served in this position until March 28, 1929.

March 13, 1925

The U.S. Senate ratifies the Isle of Pines Treaty with Cuba, ending one of America's problems with that island.

During World War I, American relations with Cuba were peaceful, owing largely to the profits obtained by the Cuban sugar industry during the war. In 1920–1921, however, sugar prices fell and Cuba's financial problems grew under the government of Alfredo Zayas. Following an election dispute in December 1920, General Enoch Crowder had been sent to Cuba by President Wilson to prevent a civil war. In new elections on March 15, 1921, Zayas won again but Crowder remained in Havana until 1923 to try to straighten out Cuba's finances.

Shortly before leaving office as secretary of state, Hughes revived a treaty negotiated originally in 1904 by which the United States renounced all claims to the Isle of Pines. The State Department had not requested Senate ratification because Senator Borah and others wanted to ensure the interests of some American citizens on the isle.

Hughes believed the issue should be ended and wrote to Senator Joseph T. Robinson to seek ratification in order to resolve an issue that harmed good relations with Cuba. With Robinson's aid, Borah's opposition was overcome and the Senate ratified the treaty on March 13, 1925.

June 27, 1925

The Geneva Protocol is signed. It prohibits the use of poisonous gas and bacteriological weapons of war. All the great powers ratify the pact except Japan and the United States.

At the 1925 Geneva Conference for the Supervision of the International Traffic in Arms, the United States proposed that nations prohibit the export of gases for war use. At suggestions from France and Poland, the conference drew up a protocol on non-use of poisonous gas and bacteriological methods in war.

Before World War II, many countries ratified the Geneva protocol. Japan and the United States were the two major powers that did not. In addition, some nations—including Great Britain, France, and the USSR—declared the protocol would not be binding if their enemies did not respect the prohibition. Although Italy signed the protocol, it used poison gas in the Ethiopian War of 1935.

In 1926, the Senate Foreign Relations Committee favored ratification. The Senate never voted on the pact because there was strong lobbying against it by the chemical industry. During World War II, however, President Franklin D. Roosevelt announced that the U.S. would not use "poison gas" unless the Axis power first employed it.

See November 25, 1969, and January 22, 1975.

August 4, 1925

U.S. Marines leave Nicaragua following the election of President Solorzano.

Secretary of State Hughes desired to remove U.S. Marines from their interventions in Latin American nations as quickly as possible. Nicaragua presented special difficulties because America had been its protector since 1914 without solving its political problems. In 1917, President Wilson had set up a Financial High Commission to reorganize the nation's finances. Under its guidance, British foreign debts had been satisfied and the debts due for American banking advances were paid by 1924.

Three recent developments had convinced Secretary Hughes that the marines should leave Nicaragua as soon as a new president was inaugurated in 1925. First, Nicaragua's finances appeared to be in order. Second, on February 7, 1923, the Central American Court of Justice was set up to keep peace in the region. And third, by the Pact of Anapala of May 3, 1924, the Central American states agreed to keep insurgent bands off their bases.

Unfortunately, the Nicaraguan election of 1924 demonstrated the difficulty for the United States of "teaching" democracy to Latin Americans. From the beginning, disputes raged between political factions. To prevent the Chamorro faction of the Conservative Party from winning, a coalition ticket led by the Conservative Carlos Solorzano and the Liberal Party's Juan Sacasa united their political groups. The coalition ticket won, but Emiliano Chamorro immediately protested election fraud and called for a new election.

President-elect Solorzano pleaded with Secretary Hughes not to withdraw the marines until a trained native constabulary could maintain order. Hughes agreed to provide six months' training, but between January 1925, when Solorzano was inaugurated, and August the training process lagged badly. Nevertheless, Secretary Kellogg like Hughes was anxious to withdraw U.S. troops to end the inter-American accusations about U.S. interference in other states. Therefore, on August 4, 1925, the U.S. Marines withdrew. Solorzano soon realized his fears about a new crisis if the United States withdrew. On October 25, a revolt led by Chamorro brought renewed political disorder to Nicaragua.

See May 12, 1927.

October 16, 1925

The Locarno Conference: Seven European nations conclude a conference with treaties to guarantee peace in western Europe.

The "spirit of Locarno," which prevailed among the European delegations between October 5 and 16, 1925, appeared to herald a new era of peace and cooperation. The delegates never talked of alliances but of cooperative pacts to avoid future war. On October 16, the delegates initialed the treaties of Locarno, which were formally drawn up and signed in London on December 1, 1925.

The principal parts of the treaties of Locarno were the following:

1. a mutual guarantee of the borders between Germany and France and Germany and Belgium;
2. arbitration treaties between Germany and Poland, Germany and Czechoslovakia, Germany and France, and Germany and Belgium; and
3. mutual assistance treaties between France and Poland and France and Czechoslovakia in case of attack by Germany.

1926

January 26, 1926

The U.S. Senate approves membership in the World Court but with amendments that make American acceptance unsatisfactory to the existing court members.

Secretary of State Hughes was an ardent advocate of a Permanent Court of International Justice for many years before 1919. Hughes's friend and fellow Republican Elihu Root had been on the jurist commission that prepared the court protocol approved by the Assembly of the League of Nations on December 13, 1920. As designed by the commission, nations not in the League of Nations could hold membership on the court.

In spite of his eagerness to have the United States join the court, Hughes delayed sending the matter to the Senate for approval until February 24, 1923. In his recommendation to the Senate, Hughes proposed that the United States join under conditions that did not involve America with the league but would give the United States equality in the proceedings of the court and the selection of judges. Although Hughes had anticipated that Senator Lodge's support for the World Court would expedite its acceptance, he had misjudged Lodge. The senator objected to features of the court that he interpreted as requiring compulsory arbitration and as involving the United States in enforcing court decisions. Hughes could not convince Lodge or other Republicans on the Senate Foreign Relations Committee that their views were incorrect. Therefore, although the House of Representatives approved court membership by a vote of 301 to 28, Lodge stalled the act in the Senate.

When the Senate adopted the bill on January 26, 1926, it approved amendments that prohibited the court's advisory opinions in a dispute and prevented a U.S. case from reaching the court without a two-thirds Senate vote. The International Court of Justice members would not accept the U.S. amendments and America dropped its application for membership.

May 18, 1926

The preparatory commission for a disarmament conferences opens its first sessions at Geneva.

Although several articles of the League of Nations Covenant touched on the issue of disarmament, Article 8 stipulated that league members recognized that the maintenance of peace required "the reduction of national armaments to the lowest point consistent with national safety and the enforcement by common action of international obligations." (Article 8 was a revised version of President Wilson's Point 4 of his famous 14 Points of January 8, 1918.) Additionally, in Part 5 of all the peace treaties—Versailles with Germany, Saint-Germain with Austria, Trianon with Hungary, Sèvres with Turkey, and Neuilly with Bulgaria—the victorious signatories stated their intention to prepare to limit armaments as well as observe the military, naval, and air limitations placed on the vanquished.

On May 19, 1920, the league created a Permanent Advisory Commission to advice on disarmament issues. Staffed by military officers from League Council members, these professionals viewed disarmament proposals in terms of whether they strengthened their forces or those of their allies and weakened potential enemies; consequently, they failed to make any significant progress on the reduction of armaments. In 1921, the League Assembly–sponsored Temporary Mixed Commission made up of mostly civilians undertook to exchange information regarding existing armaments and later to regulate private manufacture of armaments. While some information was published, no restrictions were placed on arms industries.

Following the provision for Germany's admission to the League of Nations at the Locarno Conference, disarmament advocates in the League's Assembly persuaded the League Council to invite 19 nations, including the United States, to attend a consultation meeting to prepare for a disarmament conference. The French government wanted the consultations to work out definitions and a prospectus prior to a formal conference.

The first preparatory commission met until November 26, 1926, but reached no conclusions. The principal dispute was between France's desire to obtain guarantees of security before disarming and the Anglo-American desire to disarm first and discuss security arrangements later. During the next five years, six more sessions of the Preparatory Commission argued this issue and a host of other general and detailed questions about arms and warfare. They achieved little. Finally on December 9, 1930, the Preparatory Commission recommended that a conference on general disarmament be held in 1932.

See February 2, 1932.

September 8, 1926

Germany is admitted to the League of Nations.

This action indicated that most nations believed that Germany was willing to fulfill its obligations under the Treaty of Versailles.

December 16, 1926

Great Britain announces a change in its China policy.

For some time, Great Britain had considered changing the 19th-century policy that made it the leader of foreign powers in pursuing political and economic concessions in China. As Chinese antagonism arose against the Western imperial powers, Britain decided that its interests required Chinese goodwill and an end to military ventures against the Chinese.

An incident at Shanghai on May 30, 1925, stimulated Chinese nationalist antagonism to a point where the British government decided a new policy was imperative. The Shanghai incident began when a crowd of 2,000 Chinese rushed a police station in the International Settlement to protest Western mistreatment of the Chinese. A British police inspector shouted for the mob to stop or be killed. When they did not halt, police fired on the crowd, killing 12 Chinese and wounding 17.

Because no foreign authorities took steps to investigate and punish the perpetrators of these killings, the Chinese populace began a series of demonstrations, strikes, and boycotts of Western products and businesses. Clashes took place between police and demonstrators in Canton, Hankow, and Kiukiang.

Following 18 months of such troubles, Great Britain issued a decree declaring a new policy toward China, designed to gain goodwill. On December 16, Foreign Secretary Sir Austen Chamberlain recognized that the growth of nationalism in China aimed at giving China an equal place among the nations of the world. England, he said, would meet this movement with understanding. He particularly called on the United States to join Britain in negotiating with China "as soon as the Chinese themselves have constituted a new government." This would permit China to increase its tariffs and to resolve all matters of foreign extraterritorial powers with Great Britain and other foreign nations.

December 25, 1926

Japan's Taishō Emperor dies; The Shōwa era begins under the Emperor Hirohito.

In contrast to the liberal political developments in the Taishō era, the Shōwa period gradually became militaristic and imperialistic, particularly after the Mukden incident of September 18, 1931.

See September 29, 1918, and also May 3, 1928.

1927

January 18, 1927

The U.S. Senate rejects a treaty of amity and commerce made with Turkey in 1923.

During the Lausanne Conference of 1922–1923, U.S. and Turkish delegates agreed to a treaty establishing diplomatic and commercial relations with the Turkish republic led by Mustapha Kemal (Atatürk). The treaty was signed on August 6, 1923, but action was delayed in the U.S. Senate because of strong opposition from religious opponents, an Armenian-American lobby, and political partisanship against Coolidge.

Following the Armenian massacres, which occurred during the 1890s under the Ottoman Empire, Armenian refugees in America formed a group that implored U.S. assistance against Turkish policy. By the 1920s, the Armenian ethnic organization had become one of many in the United States that opposed any conciliatory U.S. policies toward European nations. The Armenian-American group led by Vahan CARDASHIAN vehemently opposed the U.S. treaty with Turkey, using propaganda that presented a "Terrible Turk" view supposedly including all Turkish people, making no differentiation between those governed by the sultan's empire in the 1890s or the new, smaller Turkish nation of Atatürk following 1920. Atatürk's efforts to modernize and liberalize Turkish society were either ignored or discounted by Cardashian's followers.

Yet a few groups in the United States supported the treaty with Turkey by 1927. The moderate Armenian-American Society favored the treaty. In addition, while some U.S. missionaries opposed the treaty in 1923, they had become convinced by 1927 that the treaty would protect their educational, religious, and hospital organizations in Turkey.

In the U.S. Senate, however, a minority led by Senator William H. King of Utah strongly protested against the treaty. King claimed that the State Department had forsaken the Armenians in order to support U.S. investors in the Chester mission, which had temporarily gained concessions in Turkey. Although King's charges lacked substance, some politicians accepted them despite the State Department's denials.

The Turkish treaty was sent to the Senate by President Coolidge on May 3, 1924, but the vote on it was delayed to gain approval by a sufficient number of senators. The task failed, however, and in the vote on January 18, 1927, the Turkish treaty lost, 50 to 34, 6 votes short of the necessary two-thirds.

By 1927, U.S. newspapers and other groups had begun to publish more favorable reports about Atatürk's government. To establish relations with Ankara, the U.S. high commissioner to Turkey, Admiral Bristol, and Turkey's foreign minister, Tevfik Aras, signed a memorandum on February 15, 1927, agreeing to restore diplomatic relations on a friendly basis. Subsequently, on February 27, Joseph Grew was appointed U.S. ambassador to Turkey.

See October 1, 1895, and August 26, 1896.

January 27, 1927

Secretary Kellogg indicates America's willingness to end the Chinese treaties made during the 19th century.

In 1927, many factors inspired Kellogg to announce America's willingness to alter its tariff, customs, and extraterritoriality treaties with China. On May 31, 1924, the Soviet Union fulfilled earlier commitments to end the "unequal treaties" made by the czar with the Chinese. Incidents at Shanghai (May 30, 1925) and Canton (June 23, 1925) and Britain's announcement on December 16, 1926, of a new Chinese policy indicated the Western powers' desire to adjust to Chinese nationalism. Finally in January 1927, the House Committee on Foreign Affairs began congressional hearings on extraterritoriality in China, which revealed enthusiasm among religious mission societies in favor of such changes.

Therefore, on January 27, Kellogg asserted that the United States had been ready since 1922 to negotiate with China on customs duties, tariffs, and legal conditions in China. His statement concluded, "if China can agree upon the appointment of delegates representing the authority or the people of the country, we are prepared to negotiate such a treaty." The United States would conduct talks with China in conjunction with Britain and other powers or alone. The only obstacle preventing new treaties was the appointment of Chinese delegates to represent their people.

Gaining recognition for appropriate Chinese delegates was not easy. In 1925, a special tariff conference had tried to meet in Peking but experienced difficulty because of disputes among various political groups in China. In 1926, an extraterritorial commission had a similar problem. Until a stable political, judicial, and military authority was established in China, a treaty revision seemed impossible.

See April 11 and 12, 1927.

April 11, 1927

The United States joins four other nations in protesting Chinese attacks on foreigners at Nanking.

The Nanking incident of March 24, 1927, took place soon after Chiang Kai-shek's Nationalist forces captured that city from the Peking regime. For some time, China had experienced political difficulties and civil war. In addition to many local warlords who controlled certain provinces of China, there were three main political factions in China: a moribund successor of Yüan Shih-k'ai in Peking; and two Nationalist (Kuomintang) factions, one directed from Hankow, the other from Nanking in April 1927.

The antiforeign riots in Nanking were apparently encouraged by left-wing elements of the Kuomintang. The demonstrators burned the American, British, and Japanese consulates and 10 Christian mission buildings; looted foreign businesses and hospitals; and pillaged the homes of missionaries. Six foreigners were killed: one American, Frenchman, and Italian; and three Englishmen. British and American naval vessels on the Yangtze River helped a group of Standard Oil Company employees to safety by throwing a barrage of shells at Nationalist troops while the foreigners escaped over a city wall.

To protest the Chinese attack, the representatives of the United States, England, France, Italy, and Japan presented identical notes to the Nationalist foreign minister, Eugene Chen. The notes of April 11 demanded the punishment of commanders responsible for the attack and complete reparation for all damages. They also requested an apology from the commander of the Nationalist army and his written agreement to stop all agitation and attacks on foreign lives and property.

U.S. consulates were closed at Chunking, Changsha, Nanking, and Kalgan. The U.S. minister to China, John Van A. MacMurray, urged Secretary of State Kellogg to take strong action to deter further violence.

Neither Secretary Kellogg nor President Coolidge was willing to use force to carry out the April 11 demands. The War Department told Kellogg that 50,000 troops would be needed for the short route between Tientsin and Peking, but the secretary did not believe American interests were worth a war in China or the loss of any U.S. troops. As Coolidge told a press conference, the United States already had 13,200 American soldiers, sailors, and marines in China to protect 14,038 U.S. citizens. Kellogg believed the era of gunboat diplomacy in China had ended and that better relations had to be established with Peking.

April 12, 1927

In Shanghai, Chiang Kai-shek launches a white terror against China's communists that gives him full control of the Kuomintang (KMT).

Following the formation of the Chinese Communist Party (CCP) in 1921, Moscow directed CCP members to join a united front with the KMT under Sun Yat-sen for the purpose of abolishing foreign control and infiltrating the KMT.

After Sun Yat-sen died in 1925, the KMT-CCP alliance became precarious. CCP leaders such as Ch'en Tu-Hsiu suspected the KMT had bourgeois tendencies, while the KMT never fully trusted the Communist extremists. By 1927, the policy divergences in the united front increased as Chiang Kai-shek used Soviet help to create an impressive military force, while the CCP organized workers and peasants to control China. Nevertheless, even after Chiang sent his Soviet advisers home and purged the KMT of influential Communists, Soviet leader Stalin advised the CCP to cooperate with Chiang. Previously, Leon Trotsky, who led a bloc of Bolsheviks against Stalin, had opposed the CCP-KMT front, so Stalin had to prove its practicality to his adversary.

In 1926, therefore, Michael Borodin returned to Canton to represent the Comintern and urge the CCP to work with Chiang in forming a northern expeditionary army to capture Peking. In return for Chiang's promise to restrain the right-wing faction of the KMT, Borodin offered Soviet aid and agreed to restrict CCP opponents of the KMT. With his status secure in Canton, Chiang launched his campaign to control central and northern China. His men "liberated" Nanking on March 24, 1927. When the Nationalists conducted attacks on Westerners in Nanking, Chiang blamed the Communists. Thus, the same day—April 11—that the foreigners protested against the Nanking demonstrations, their representatives in Shanghai were working with Chiang to plot his bloody terrorist raids on the Communists.

On April 12, 1927, with the support of British police and anti-Communist Shanghai merchants, Chiang moved to eliminate the CCP and its worker allies in Shanghai. Beginning at 4 A.M., KMT forces attacked working-class headquarters throughout the city. All workers and union organizers in the buildings were either shot on the spot or marched into the streets to be executed. All CCP members were disarmed; over 700 CCP leaders were killed during the day.

The purge and disorders continued for several weeks. Eventually, the KMT forced businessmen to pay them money or be charged with treason. Chiang's dictatorship made the bourgeoisie pay a high price, but he "saved" them from communism. Similar purges were conducted by Chiang's men at Ningpo, Foochow, Amoy, Swatow, and Canton. Temporarily, at least, Chiang controlled the strongest political and military bloc in China.

May 12, 1927

The Peace of Tipitapa enables the United States to end political disputes in Nicaragua following the landing of U.S. Marines.

During the spring of 1927, President Coolidge sent a personal representative, Henry L. Stimson, to Nicaragua to settle a civil war that had developed and forced the president again to dispatch marines on May 2, 1926, to preserve order.

Nicaragua's problems began just three weeks after the U.S. Marines withdrew on August 4, 1925. The marines had been in Nicaragua since 1912, and the Coolidge administration believed they could leave following the election of President Carlos Solorzano, who took charge of the government on January 1, 1925. Two months after the marines left, Emiliano Chamorro, a long-powerful politician in Nicaragua, staged a coup d'état that forced Solorzano and Sacasa into exile. Chamorro claimed the election of Solorzano in 1924 had been corrupt and therefore invalid. Subsequently, the Nicaraguan senate selected Chamorro as president, and he took office on January 16, 1926.

The question of Chamorro's legitimacy arose because by the Central American Treaty of February 7, 1923, a revolutionary leader was not permitted to become leader of the government and new elections were required. The United States, while not a signatory to the 1923 treaty, had agreed to respect it and put pressure on Chamorro, who resigned on October 30, 1926. The Nicaraguan senate designated Adolfo Díaz as president on November 11.

U.S. forces in Nicaragua with captured "bandits." National Archives

Meanwhile, the Liberal Party began an insurrection against Chamorro and Díaz. Led by former Vice President Juan Sacasa, whom Chamorro had ousted in 1925, the Liberals had the support of General José M. MONCADA. Sacasa had also obtained the backing of President Calles of Mexico, who supplied the Nicaraguan Liberal insurgents with arms, ammunition, and soldiers.

Mexico's intervention became the principal reason why Secretary Kellogg recommended the dispatch of U.S. Marines, who reached Managua on January 6, 1927. Marine contingents also landed on February 20 on the west coast of Nicaragua to halt the influx of Mexican arms and to protect Americans who lived there. On January 12, Kellogg sent a memorandum to the Senate Foreign Relations Committee that used nearly hysterical terms to justify the intervention as resulting from Bolshevik plans to take over Central America under Mexican auspices.

To avert U.S. involvement in direct war on behalf of the Díaz government, Secretary Kellogg sent Henry L. Stimson to Nicaragua. Kellogg and President Coolidge instructed Stimson to keep Díaz in power but to offer new elections in 1928 in which Sacasa could be the Liberal Party nominee.

Meeting first with Díaz and later with Sacasa and General Moncada, Stimson worked out an agreement on May 12, known as the Peace of Tipitapa. The agreement provided for a general amnesty for the insurgents as well as the forces of Díaz. The soldiers would receive $10 for each serviceable rifle or machine gun. Any weapons not turned in would be forcibly taken by the U.S. Marines. Díaz's government would be recognized while new elections were prepared under the supervision of the United States.

During the next year, Americans worked out a peaceful election, held on November 4, 1928. Election regulations included closing all cantinas on election day, stationing at least one marine at each poll, and dipping the finger of each voter into mercurochrome to discourage repetitive voting. General Moncada won the election and became president.

One difficulty clouded Stimson's apparent success in 1927. A general in Sacasa's Liberal Party, Augusto C. SANDINO, rejected the Peace of Tipitapa. Condemning both Liberals and Conservatives in Nicaragua as well as the "imperialist Yankees," Sandino's small group of followers retired to the north and continued to fight. Following the election of 1928, Sandino withdrew to Mexico but in 1931 began further guerrilla warfare in northern Nicaragua. The Sandianistas were suppressed in 1933 and Sandino killed in 1934, but his followers continued sporadic fighting for many years.

See September 30, 1978, and July 17, 1979.

June 20, 1927

As the Geneva Naval Limitations Conference convenes, an immediate Anglo-American dispute begins.

President Coolidge invited the signatory powers of the 1922 naval treaty, which had already placed restrictions on battleships and aircraft carriers, to a conference designed to extend the naval limitations to their smaller warships. Although France and Italy refused to attend, the three major naval powers—Great Britain, Japan, and the United States—met on June 20.

At the first session of the conference, a dispute over cruisers arose between U.S. and British naval experts. U.S. Navy Admiral Hilary P. Jones presented the American view that cruiser tonnage should be limited to 300,000 tons for the U.S. and Britain, while the British admiralty asked for 600,000 tons. Furthermore, the British desired to have the tonnage split between heavy (10,000-ton) and light (7,500-ton) cruisers with 6″ guns, while the United States wanted to build heavy cruisers with 8″ guns. British naval strategy was to have many small cruisers to cover large areas of the ocean, while American naval planners desired fewer, heavier cruisers capable of long-range action in the western Pacific Ocean. Thus, even though U.S.-British war plans did not envision competition leading to war, their naval experts argued rather than cooperated in setting ship limits.

The principal reason for the failure at Geneva was that naval experts, not diplomats, dominated the proceedings. The head of the U.S. delegation was Hugh Gibson, ambassador to Belgium. Robert Cecil, the British chief of delegation, was not in the British cabinet and was recuperating from illness during the conference. Thus, Jones and Jellicoe, the naval experts, readily held control of the discussions and avoided limitations on the forces they cherished. Not surprisingly, therefore, the Geneva Conference adjourned on August 4 without any achievements.

November 11, 1927

France and Yugoslavia sign a "treaty of friendly understanding," linking Paris with the Little Entente network on Germany's eastern borders.

To gain greater security from future German aggression, French policy after 1919 included the attempt to form alliances with countries surrounding Germany. In order to bypass Article 18 of the League of Nations Covenant regarding alliances, the French negotiated "understandings" that technically were not military alliances. France created a network of such agreements with Belgium (1920), Poland (1921), Czechoslovakia (1924), Romania (1926), and, finally, Yugoslavia on November 11, 1927. (The Little Entente was formed by Yugoslavia, Czechoslovakia, and Romania in 1921.)

See June 7, 1921.

1928

January 11, 1928

A Mexican-American dispute over subsoil rights is resolved with the passage of a Mexican law that withdraws its claims.

Diplomatic relations between America and Mexico reached crisis proportions between 1925 and 1928. Following the election of President Plutarco Elias Calles in 1925, the Mexican legislature passed two laws based on Article 27 of its constitution of 1917. Because Article 27 gave all oil and mineral resources of Mexico to the state, U.S. and other foreign oil companies appealed to their governments to prevent the implementation of the Petroleum Law and the Alien Land Law passed in December 1925, claiming they violated the Bucareli Agreements of 1923.

The oil companies' appeals to Washington ran into two problems: theoretical and personal. The theoretical issue was Mexico's assertion of the Calvo Doctrine, a formula offered by Argentina's Carlos Calvo during the 1880s that declared corporations doing business in a foreign nation should appeal only to the native government's institutions, not to their home government. The United States had consistently opposed the Calvo Doctrine, and President Coolidge also upheld American investors' right to appeal to their home government. Coolidge stated his opposition to the Calvo theory in a public speech on April 25, 1927.

For Mexico, Minister of Foreign Relations Aaron Saenz challenged the U.S. arguments, calling them double standards when compared with America's internal sovereignty laws. In addition to citing U.S. state laws regulating property rights of foreigners, Saenz quoted Chief Justice John Marshall's court ruling: "The jurisdiction of the nation within its own territory is necessarily exclusive and absolute.... Any restriction on it, deriving validity from an external source, would imply a diminution of its sovereignty."

The more serious problem of U.S.-Mexican relations was personal, "being based on the conservative Secretary of State Kellogg's belief that all land reforms were communistic, and on the prejudiced U.S. Ambassador James R. Sheffield's intense and prejudiced disdain for all things Mexican." Kellogg and President Coolidge believed Mexican policy was directed by the USSR's Communist Third International. Kellogg informed the Senate Foreign Relations Committee in January 1926: "The Bolshevist leaders have had very definite ideas with respect to the role which Mexico and Latin Americans are to play in their program of world revolution. They have set up as one of their fundamental tasks the destruction of what they term American imperialism." While these accusations held no substantive basis to support them, they played into the continued fear of communism that began in the United States during 1919. The cause célèbre of the 1920s witch hunt had climaxed on August 23, 1927, when Nicola Sacco and Bartolomeo Vanzetti died in the electric chair in Charlestown, Massachusetts.

Nevertheless, such fears did not justify President Coolidge's appointment of an anti-Mexican ambassador to Mexico City. The least of Sheffield's faults was that he spoke no Spanish. Sheffield personified all the worst aspects of America's self-righteous, racist, and closed-minded elite. A former corporation lawyer and Yale University graduate, Sheffield complained in a letter to Nicholas Murray Butler: "There is very little white blood in the [Mexican] cabinet—that is it [the blood] is wholly thin." In addition, the Mexicans "recognize no argument but force" for, as Sheffield wrote to former President Taft, Mexico "is one of the only countries where the gun is mightier than the pen." In brief, Sheffield detested everything Mexican from Mexico City's high altitude to what he called its greedy, mixed-race, inefficient people.

Sheffield took on the "white man's burden," however. His duty was to uphold American principles of property rights abroad. The United States had 44% of its investments in Latin America, Sheffield contended, and those rights had to be protected from confiscation. "Any weakness in our attitude," Sheffield wrote to Kellogg, "is certain to be reflected almost immediately in other foreign countries."

In view of Kellogg's and Sheffield's attitudes, the U.S. adoption of a hard line of protests against Mexico's land laws was inevitable. By the end of 1926, it seemed that Mexico and America were on a collision course. Nevertheless, following his January 1927 report to the Senate Foreign Relations Committee, which explained his dispatching of marines to Nicaragua as an anti-Bolshevik measure (see May 12, 1927), Kellogg began a gradual retreat from the hard-line policy. Various groups in America attacked Coolidge's policies in Nicaragua and Mexico, including such disparate sources as the American Federation of Labor and the Ku Klux Klan, the *New York Times* and the Brooklyn *Eagle.* In Congress, strange bedfellows who criticized these policies were Senators Borah, La Follette, Burton K. Wheeler, and George Norris. Religious groups and academic interests also opposed U.S. intervention in Mexico and Nicaragua.

Senator Borah initiated action to thwart the Kellogg-Sheffield policies in Mexico. Although it was bad protocol, Borah sent a personal letter to Mexico's President Calles in January 1927, requesting him to explain Mexican policy. On January 25, 1927, the U.S. Senate unanimously passed a resolution recommended by the Senate Foreign Relations Committee, that asked President Coolidge to arbitrate all issues with Mexico. At least nine similar resolutions were introduced in the House of Representatives.

Although irritated that Borah had bypassed official channels, Coolidge decided on April 25 to placate Mexico, issuing a statement of concern to the Mexican people concluding that "we do not want any controversy with Mexico." About this time, Kellogg's assistant secretary, Robert E. Olds, took charge of Mexican affairs and assumed a more conciliatory attitude than Kellogg. The most significant result of these shifts in Mexican policy was the decision in September 1927 to remove Sheffield as ambassador in favor of Dwight W. MORROW.

Morrow's arrival in Mexico City inaugurated a complete change in U.S.-Mexican relations. A proponent of cooperation with Mexico, Morrow left his position at J. P. Morgan and Company and on his arrival in Mexico City demonstrated legal, social, and personal qualities that won over Mexico's president and the Mexican people. Morrow's biographer, Sir Harold Nicolson, wrote praisingly about his Mexican tactics:

> He applauded their food, their climate, their agriculture, their hats, their ancient monuments, the bamboo cages in which they kept their tame parrots, their peasant industries, their patriotism, their volcanoes, even their finances. Here at last was a North American who neither patronized nor sneered.

By November 1927, Morrow was ready for interviews with President Calles to discuss Article 27, the principal point of conflict with Mexico. On November 8, Morrow suggested that the questions of Article 27 and the land laws were not diplomatic but legalistic. Morrow noted that Article 14 of the 1917 constitution stated that no legislation should apply retroactively in Mexico. Perhaps, he said, the Mexican courts could inquire if Article 14 invalidated any law that affected oil rights contracted before 1925. Calles responded quickly, observing that perhaps a Supreme Court decree would settle the difficulty.

By November 17, the Mexican court ruled the law of 1925 was not constitutional. On December 28, the Mexican legislature passed a new law that applied Article 27 only to future subsoil concessions. The bill was signed by President Calles on January 3 and became effective on January 11, 1928. The oil issue was not permanently settled because new efforts to nationalize began again in Mexico in 1935. For the moment, however, Morrow and Calles had solved the most difficult problem between these neighboring nations. This solution opened the door for Morrow to assist in the settlement of church-state relations in Mexico.

See June 30, 1929.

February 6, 1928

The United States and France sign an arbitration treaty that revises the Root formula of 1908 that limited the use of arbitration.

Secretary of State Kellogg believed a new formula for arbitration was necessary that would no longer exclude such questions as national honor. Kellogg's formula excluded from arbitration only matters of domestic jurisdiction, third parties, the Monroe Doctrine, and the League of Nations. He signed the first of these new treaties with France on February 6. Before leaving office, 18 other nations signed new arbitration agreements with America. None of these were invoked during the next 50 years.

February 18, 1928

Charles E. Hughes defends the necessity of U.S. intervention in disorderly states during the final plenary session of the sixth Pan-American Conference in Havana.

Because of recent U.S. problems in Mexico and Nicaragua, the U.S. delegation went to the Havana Conference, which convened on January 16, fully expecting anti-American resolutions by Argentina, El Salvador, and other delegations. Charles E. Hughes had been selected to head the U.S. delegation to add stature to the American group and to provide the needed statesmanship during the expected difficult sessions.

Hughes fulfilled his duties in commendable fashion. Setting a theme during his opening conference speech, Hughes said America was not an aggressor. "Nothing could be happier for the United States than that all the countries of the Caribbean region should be strong, self-sufficient, fulfilling their destiny, settling their problems, with peace at home and the fulfillment of their obligations abroad."

The anti-American tone of many discussions remained, however, until the conference's final regular session. The question of the right of intervention in a nation had been discussed in the Committee on International Public Law, but no "balanced" view of the proper position had been agreed upon. The committee members agreed to delay the subject until the 1933 conference. Then, during the final session, Salvador's Foreign Minister, Gustavo GUERRERO, offered a resolution that stated, "No State has the right to intervene in the internal affairs of another."

A lengthy debate ensued because Hughes insisted that the opposition should be heard and the matter settled. For some time, Hughes listened to a variety of accusations against the "colossus of the north," as well as the efforts of some friends to defend the United States. By the time Hughes rose to speak, the potential vote on the Guerrero resolution was not certain.

Hughes convinced the delegates and the large crowd of visitors, mostly Cuban, to disapprove Guerrero's resolution. Asking the interpreter to translate each sentence, not to summarize, Hughes explained that he believed this critical decision should be delayed until 1933 so that a proper resolution could be studied. He restated his concept of U.S. policy in the Western Hemisphere. America, he asserted, yielded to none in its desire that all nations be independent and sovereign. "We do not wish to intervene in the affairs of any American republic. We simply wish peace and order and stability and recognition of honest rights properly acquired so that this hemisphere may not only be the hemisphere of peace but the hemisphere of international justice." He said U.S. citizens were in danger of their lives in Nicaragua. "Are we to stand and see them butchered in the jungle because a government . . . can no longer afford reasonable protection?" The United States had a right to protect its citizens and it would not forsake that. Nations must accept duties as well as rights. If all states recognized their duties and carried them out, interventions would not be necessary. Justice as well as rights was essential.

Hughes's speech proved to be so effective that Guerrero withdrew his resolution. Notably, however, Hughes's demeanor and attitude throughout the conference had contrasted sharply with the often arrogant, superior tones that Americans such as Theodore Roosevelt used toward Latin Americans or the moralistic tone Woodrow Wilson had employed. In this respect, Hughes's speech directed the evolution of U.S. policy away from U.S. intervention toward greater sensitivity and respect for Latin Americans.

See February 28, 1929.

May 3, 1928

Japanese and Chinese forces clash in Shantung because the Japanese intervene to block the northward conquests of Chiang Kai-shek's nationalist army.

Japan had briefly intervened in Shantung during May-June 1927 to stop the Nationalist army's march toward Peking. In April 1928, Japan again landed forces in Shantung and seized control of the railroads in that region. Japanese and Chinese forces skirmished for a week before Japan and Chiang's representatives met to resolve the issue. On March 28, 1929, the dispute was compromised and Japan withdrew its troops on May 20, 1929.

July 21, 1928

An American oil consortium receives a share of the international oil concessions in the former Ottoman Empire, especially in Iraq.

Because the Chester concessions had failed, the first successful U.S. oil concession in the Middle East was undertaken by a consortium of seven (later merged into two) U.S. oil companies.

Acting on his belief that the United States needed to secure future oil supplies, Secretary of Commerce Herbert Hoover met with oil company representatives in May 1921, encouraging them to seek oil rights under an open door policy in Mesopotamia. In November 1921, seven oil companies formed a consortium to negotiate with the British-owned Turkish Petroleum Company (TPC), which controlled oil concessions in Mesopotamia. The seven U.S. companies were Jersey Standard, SOCONY, Sinclair, Texas, Gulf, Mexican, and Atlantic.

Between 1922 and 1928, the oil consortium, led by W. C. Teagle of Jersey Standard, held talks with TPC while the British diplomats ironed out details of the postwar status of the former Ottoman Empire's territory. As a result, on July 21, 1928, the American group signed an agreement with TPC (later renamed Iraq Petroleum Company) that gave the Americans a 23.75% share of oil rights in former Ottoman territory. The other oil companies with shares of the TPC concessions were Anglo-Persia, Royal Dutch Shell, and French Petroleum. These members agreed not to pursue independent explorations for oil within a "Red Line Agreement" region that virtually encompassed all of the old Ottoman Empire except Turkey proper. The two U.S. corporations, which because of mergers by 1928 remained in the U.S. oil consortium, were Jersey Standard (Exxon) and Socony Vacuum (Mobil).

See December 11, 1911, and April 10, 1923.

July 25, 1928

The United States recognizes Chiang Kai-shek's nationalist government of China, signing a tariff treaty with the Chinese.

Between 1926 and 1928, the Kuomintang had severed its Communist influence and, on June 8, completed the pacification of most of central China by capturing Peking. In addition, Chiang's government had negotiated a settlement of the Nanking protests of April 11, 1927, by paying reparations for damages and accepting an American apology for the U.S. naval bombardment of Nanking.

The tariff treaties of July 25 ended previous unequal treaties and awarded China tariff autonomy *as soon as the other tariff-treaty nations did likewise.* Following the concurrence of the other powers, U.S.-Chinese trade would be on a most-favored-nation basis. Between July 25 and December 22, 1928, 12 other nations approved similar treaties with China. Nevertheless, because Japan delayed a new tariff agreement until May 1933, the U.S. treaty of 1928 did not go into effect for five years.

Sino-American attempts to end the unequal extraterritorial treaties did not succeed. The 1926 Commission on Extraterritoriality had met in Peking in 1926, but civil disorders prevented the commission's work between 1926 and 1928. In 1928, the Nationalist government unilaterally abrogated extraterritoriality treaties with Portugal, Italy, and Denmark but did not risk similar tactics against the larger foreign powers. U.S.-Chinese discussions on these legal matters lasted for another 15 years before the last unequal treaty ended in 1943.

See April 12, 1927.

August 27, 1928

14 nations sign the Kellogg-Briand Pact to outlaw war.

The signing of this treaty culminated the search for an easy solution to international problems that began after the U.S. Senate defeated the Treaty of Versailles in 1920. A Chicago lawyer, Salmon O. Levinson, formed the American Committee for the Outlawry of War, which urged nations to declare war illegal so that they would never again resort to it. Members of the committee included Senator William Borah, chairman of the Senate Foreign Relations Committee; philosopher John Dewey; and Charles C. Morrison, editor of the *Christian Science Monitor.* Two American officers of the Carnegie Endowment for International Peace also claimed that in 1927 they influenced Aristide Briand, the French foreign minister, to formulate a pact to renounce warfare. The two Carnegie officers were Nicholas Murray Butler, president of Columbia University, and James T. Shotwell, professor of history at Columbia University.

Shotwell drafted Briand's speech of April 6, 1927, and it became the basis for the peace pact. Briand believed that some sort of agreement with the United States would assist France in avoiding a future war with Germany. France was completing a Little Entente series of alliances with several small European nations, but Briand thought a negative pact condemning an aggressor nation as an outlaw would place the United States on the French side in a war. In this context, Briand's message of April 6 proposed to the American people and Washington officials that France was prepared to accept a Franco-American agreement to "outlaw war."

Even though Briand's speech was not offered through normal diplomatic channels, Secretary of State Kellogg responded on June 11 by informing newsmen that he was ready to consider Briand's proposal. On June 20, 1927, Briand sent Kellogg a draft proposal by which the French and the American people would mutually condemn the use of war and settle all disputes between their nations by "pacific means."

Belatedly, Kellogg and his State Department advisers now planned to ignore Briand's suggestion. Realizing that Briand hoped to gain some type of U.S.-French alliance, they hoped silence would quietly bury the French proposal. Peace groups in America would not be silent, however, and they pressured the State Department to accept Briand's offer. Levinson's committee promoted a letter-writing campaign, sending the State Department huge bags of mail in favor of outlawing war. Feminist advocates such as Carrie Chapman Catt and Jane Addams also organized a pro-treaty group.

Unable to ignore these public expressions, Kellogg consulted with Senator Borah, who agreed that a multinational pact on peace would prevent a treaty with France from being construed as a French alliance. On this basis, Kellogg answered Briand's note of June 20 in a December 28, 1927, note that said the United States accepted the French proposal and hoped all nations could be invited to join the movement to outlaw war as a method for settling disputes. In reality, of course, this ploy weakened a Franco-American treaty under the diplomatic principle that the more parties there are to an agreement, the less likely it is to be binding on any one power.

As drawn up by Kellogg on December 28, the peace pact proposed to abolish all war. There would be no reservations or qualifications to the treaty permitting a nation to justify war. The treaty would simply bind all nations to declare they were "renouncing war as an instrument of national policy." Ideally, there would be no war, no need for alliances, no need for armies and navies. It was a bold concept but far in advance of the capacity of nations to honor.

Kellogg's response placed Briand on the defensive. He did not want a multilateral treaty that sounded like the Sermon on the Mount. Yet Briand could not denounce Kellogg's suggestion. Briand had received the Nobel Peace Prize for negotiating the Locarno Treaty and his reputation would not permit him to back away from a peace proposal. Kellogg rejected Briand's proposal for the United States to sign a treaty with France before calling an international peace conference. Nor would Kellogg agree to add any statements about sanctions against an aggressor who violated the treaty. Kellogg's only qualification was made in a circular note to the Great Powers on June 23, 1928, wherein he said America accepted the "interpretation" that it would not be illegal for a nation to defend itself against violators of the league covenant, the Locarno treaties, or the French alliances.

Between April 23 and August 27, 14 nations accepted the Kellogg proposal as "interpreted" by the note of June 23. Great Britain accepted with a further qualification that excluded world regions vital to British security. Partly to persuade the United States to make a cooperative pact, partly because they did not desire the embarrassment of failing to accept the pact, the Great Powers accepted the Kellogg Pact.

Thus, on August 27, delegates of 14 nations assembled in Paris to sign the short, simple, two-article agreement. The U.S. Senate ratified the treaty on January 15, 1929. The other signatory nations ratified the pact by July 24, 1929, when President Herbert Hoover proclaimed the treaty to be in effect. Other nations later joined in signing the pact and, by 1929, 64 nations had accepted the peace pact that outlawed war.

Although Kellogg received the Nobel Peace Prize in 1930 for his work on the 1928 pact, the agreement never fulfilled its promise. Before 1929 ended, Soviet and Chinese troops went to war in Manchuria, and in 1931 Japan's attack on Manchuria inaugurated a decade during which the Kellogg-Briand Pact was repeatedly violated.

See November 11, 1927.

October 20, 1928

China's Kuomintang (KMT) promulgates organic laws creating the Chinese nationalist government.

By the laws of October 20, five administrative divisions of government were established under the jurisdiction of China's president and highest military authority, Chiang Kai-shek. Only the KMT party was legal, and as leader of the KMT's executive council Chiang was both the party and the government head. In brief, Chiang Kai-shek was the military dictator of China. Chiang's government resembled the Soviet Communist system that Sun Yat-sen established in 1924.

China had official political unity under Chiang. Nevertheless, followers of the Chinese Communist Party were actively organizing peasant support in Kiangsi Province under the leadership of Mao Tse-tung.

Herbert Hoover and his wife. National Archives

November 6, 1928

Herbert Hoover is elected president.

The Republican Party nominated Hoover at its convention in Kansas City on June 14. The Republican platform favored a federal farm board to assist farmers but rejected the McNary-Haugen act desired by the farm bloc but that Coolidge had twice vetoed. The party also favored the protective tariff and Coolidge's foreign policies.

The Democratic Convention selected Governor Alfred E. Smith of New York for its candidate. Regarding foreign policy, the Democrats wanted immediate independence for the Philippines and condemned the Coolidge policies in Central America.

Smith's loss was attributed partly to religious prejudice because he was a Roman Catholic. Together with his opposition to continued prohibition of alcohol, Smith's religion cost him the electoral votes of five Southern states. Hoover won by 444 electoral votes to Smith's 85, and the Republicans also retained control of Congress.

December 6, 1928

Border conflicts between Bolivia and Paraguay are a prelude to the Chaco war.

There had been unsuccessful attempts to settle the Chaco territorial dispute between these two nations before World War I, and their claims continued to stimulate friction. When armies of the two states clashed at the border on December 6, war seemed imminent. The Pan-American Conference offered to mediate and drew up an arbitration treaty on August 31, 1929.

Neither Bolivia nor Paraguay would arbitrate but they agreed to negotiate. On April 4, 1930, each side stated it would return to the status quo. The border skirmishes continued, however, and became full-scale war in 1932.

See June 14, 1935.

December 20, 1928

Great Britain recognizes Chiang Kai-shek's nationalist government of China.

In addition to recognition, Britain concluded a treaty with the Chinese that granted them tariff autonomy provided China abolished coastal and interior duties on English trade. This commercial treaty provided a partial release for China from the unequal treaties that the British instituted after the Opium War in 1842.

1929

January 5, 1929

A special Inter-American conference adopts treaties for conciliation and arbitration.

Meeting at Washington between December 10, 1928, and January 5, 1929, this special session of delegates from 20 Pan-American states adopted two treaties: one provided for arbitration of all juridical questions and set up a commission to handle such cases; the other provided methods to conciliate other categories of disputes. Of the 20 states, 16 ratified the arbitration treaty, which became effective on October 28, 1929; 18 ratified the conciliation treaty, which went into effect on November 15, 1929.

February 28, 1929

Secretary of State Kellogg "revokes" the Roosevelt Corollary to the Monroe Doctrine.

Kellogg's experience in Latin American affairs increasingly steered his thoughts to oppose U.S. intervention as a proper policy. He preferred the tone of respect if not the entire substance of Hughes's speech of February 18, 1928, which defended the right to intervene. Yet he had expressed anti-intervention views privately in a letter to Ambassador Robert Woods Bliss on April 10, 1928.

On February 28, 1929, as his term of office neared its end, he sent a circular letter of instructions to U.S. envoys throughout Latin America, expressing his favor for cooperation with Latin American nations. The United States, he said, had no right to enforce good behavior in Latin America as Theodore Roosevelt had implied in 1905. The Monroe Doctrine, Kellogg contended, was against Europe, not Latin America. "The Doctrine is not a lance; it is a shield."

Evidently, Kellogg's circular letter expressed views based on a study of the Monroe Doctrine by J. Reuben Clark, the undersecretary of state. Clark concluded that the Roosevelt Corollary could be justified on the basis of self-preservation but not in terms of the Monroe Doctrine. Clark's study was not publicized until 1930, when the Government Printing Office published it for the State Department. It is usually referred to as the Clark Memorandum.

March 5, 1929

Henry L. Stimson is commissioned as Secretary of State by President Hoover.

Stimson was well qualified to serve as secretary of state. Trained as a lawyer, he was a progressive Republican who admired Theodore Roosevelt. He served as secretary of war under President Taft (1911–1913); as a special presidential representative to Nicaragua during a crisis there in 1927; and as governor general of the Philippine Islands from 1927 to 1929. During the debate on the League of Nations in 1919, Stimson favored the Lodge reservationist position, although he believed Lodge permitted the irreconcilable Republicans to have too much influence in the Senate. Stimson was secretary throughout Hoover's term of office.

March 28, 1929

The State Department assists Standard Oil of California (SOCAL) to arrange oil concessions in Bahrain.

Located on several islands in the Persian Gulf, the Sheikhdom of Bahrain had been under British protection since the 1880s. On December 12, 1928, SOCAL purchased oil rights in Bahrain from the Gulf Oil Company but discovered that a British treaty with the sheikh required that the registration and direction of any oil company had to be British.

To obtain Britain's consent for the concession, SOCAL sought State Department assistance, and on March 28, the U.S. embassy in London undertook discussions with England to resolve the issue. During 1930, the British agreed that SOCAL could arrange a contract with Bahrain through its Canadian subsidiary, the Bahrain Petroleum Company, which was Canadian incorporated and British directed. This procedure complied with the British treaty requirements and permitted the American-owned company to invest in Bahrain. By 1935, SOCAL had 16 producing oil wells in Bahrain.

June 3, 1929

Chile and Peru settle a long-lived boundary dispute.

This dispute began during the 1870s, led to war in 1883, and eventually resulted in an uneasy truce and a break in diplomatic relations in 1910. In 1922,

Secretary of State Hughes learned that the two nations would accept his good offices to resolve their problem and invited their representatives to Washington.

Hughes worked with delegates of both nations, finally persuading them to agree to arbitration regarding a plebiscite to determine territorial ownership. After they agreed on July 20, 1922, they asked Hughes to act as the arbitrator. The secretary sought to dissuade them, but because both sides trusted Hughes's judgment, they insisted and Hughes accepted that duty.

With the assistance of William C. Dennis, Hughes examined all documents in the dispute from both Chile and Peru and decided a plebiscite should be held. He prescribed conditions for conducting the election, including the selection of a Plebiscitary Commission with delegates from each nation and a chairman named by the President of the United States.

President Coolidge named General John Pershing to head the commission, but its task proved hopeless. Both sides sought to move people in and out of the disputed land of Tacna and Arica, and the election was postponed several times. Although the election was not held, Hughes provided for continued negotiations by both sides.

Finally, the two nations resolved the question on June 3, 1929. Chile occupied Arica, Peru received Tacna. Chile agreed to allow Peru to use the port in Arica and gave Bolivia a railway outlet to the Pacific Ocean. Chile also aided Bolivia in its border dispute with Paraguay.

See October 20, 1883.

June 30, 1929

Ambassador Morrow assists in reconciling church-state relations in Mexico.

Following President Calles's election in 1925, controversy arose not only over subsoil properties but also about enforcement of the anticlerical articles of the constitution of 1917. The revolutionaries distrusted the power of the church in both political and economic affairs. Consequently in January 1926, Calles issued decrees to nationalize church property, close church schools, and stop the teaching activities of religious orders. In response, the Mexican bishops, with approval of the papacy, suspended all church services on July 31, 1926.

Three years of political-religious antagonism resulted in Mexico, leading U.S. Ambassador Morrow to seek a settlement not on a diplomatic but a personal basis. The U.S. ambassador believed Mexico's social order would be endangered until a settlement was reached with the church. To assist this process Morrow brought American Catholic Church representatives to Mexico for secret meetings in April and May 1928. These contacts inaugurated a series of proposals for a settlement of the outstanding Mexican disputes between Calles and the Mexican church authorities. The government reached a compromise with the Mexican Catholic Church leaders that, after the pope approved, became effective on June 30, 1929. On that day at Cuernavaca, Ambassador Morrow heard the cathedral bells peal for the first time in three years. He told his wife, "I have opened the churches of Mexico."

See January 11, 1928.

August 31, 1929

The Hague economic conference completes agreements that ratify the Young Plan on German reparations.

The agent general for reparations payments, who was the executive officer of the Transfer Committee set up in 1924, provided annual reports on German reparations under the Dawes Plan. In his fourth interim report on June 7, 1928, the agent indicated that an agreement for the final reparations schedules should be made soon. Through the foreign loans Germany had secured, they met the payments scheduled by the Dawes Plan in 1924, and the Transfer Committee believed Germany now had long-term paying capacity, a view that later historians have found to be unduly optimistic.

Nevertheless, the Allied powers began discussions for a second reparations meeting, with France especially eager to obtain a final settlement. Following negotiations, France convinced the Allies to link the reparations settlement to an agreement for the Allies to end their occupation of the Rhineland, and a new commission was agreed to on September 16, 1928. Germany objected because it wished to separate the evacuation issue, but, as usual in the 1920s, the German republic's views were overridden. The new commission added German and Japanese delegates to the 1924 Dawes Committee, which included Great Britain, France, Belgium, Italy, and the United

States. The principal U.S. delegate, Owen D. Young, chaired the commission.

The Young Committee met from February 9 to June 7, formulating a series of recommendations that became the basis of the final reparations settlement. The committee did not settle all details of procedure, however. These agreements necessitated the approval of political representatives of all the Allied nations of World War I. The political sessions were held at The Hague between August 6 and 31, 1929, when the preliminary agreements were signed by 15 governments, including Germany. The United States attended the Hague meetings only as an observer.

The Young Plan recommendations as changed slightly by the Hague delegates resulted in the following reparations agreements:

1. *Fixed total German liabilities.* The total reparations were divided into two categories: conditional and unconditional. The conditional payments gave Germany some possible relief in case of financial problems. The more critical unconditional payments could not be delayed and, as adjusted at The Hague, amounted to 673.8 million marks per year for 59 years. Payment in kind could only be made during the first 10 years.

2. *Linkage of reparations to U.S. debt requirements.* The agreement recognized that the conditional reparations could vary according to the charges the Allies had to make to pay their debts to the United States. Both Britain and France wanted the total annual payments to at least equal their debt payment to America.

3. *An end to safeguards on Germany.* Both the Transfer Committee of 1924 and other earlier organizations to oversee German payments were abolished. Germany was made solely responsible to determine that the Young Plan schedule was complied with when due.

4. *Creation of a Bank for International Settlements.* This bank acted as the intermediary between Germany and the Allies, changing all problems of payment into economic, not political, disputes. The bank would also stimulate international trade and exchange information on financial conditions with all parties to the agreement.

5. *Changes in earlier percentages for receipt of reparations.* In particular, Great Britain decided it needed more funds to meet its U.S. debts, and at the Hague conference asked for a higher percentage than it originally had been allocated. To provide more for the British, France agreed to reduce its total reparations in return for a larger percentage of unconditional reparations.

6. *Settlement of any dispute over the reparations payments by arbitration.*

7. *Evacuation by Great Britain, France, and Belgium of all their Rhineland Occupation forces by June 30, 1930.*

The Hague Conference agreements left certain matters open for further settlement by seven special committees that continued to work until November 1919. A jurists' commission drafted these reports into legal agreements and, between January 3 and January 20, 1930, a second Hague Conference settled those issues.

See January 20, 1930.

October 1, 1929

Great Britain resumes diplomatic recognition of the Soviet Union.

The Zinoviev letter's alleged interference in Britain's election of October 1924 resulted in generally bad relations with the USSR and a diplomatic break between the two nations on May 26, 1927. The Labour Party's victory in the elections on May 30, 1929, returned Ramsay MacDonald as prime minister, and new British discussions began with the Soviets. On October 1, the MacDonald government renewed relations with the Soviet Union on an official basis.

October 29, 1929

The Wall Street stock market plunge reaches disastrous proportions: date usually ascribed to the beginning of the worldwide Great Depression.

Although there had been signs of trouble in the stock market before October 29, the trading of 16 million shares in one day heralded a four-year period of price declines. By November 13, nearly $30 billion of market value of listed stocks had been lost. As John Kenneth Galbraith notes, the lost sum was greater than all the dollars in circulation in America in 1929. The international financial community of all nations suffered except for the Soviet Union, which was isolated generally from the capitalist financial structure. The low point of the Great Depression was reached in March 1933.

The stock market crash was only the beginning: The ensuing poverty is portrayed by these men, who built homes from scrap lumber at West Houston and Mercer Streets in New York City. Photo by Bernice Abbott, 1930s. National Archives

Of course, the decline in agricultural prices not long after the conclusion of World War I caused grave economic hardships, seriously disrupting the economies of many countries during the early 1920s. Consequently, historians have established different dates for the beginning of the Great Depression, although the U.S. stock market crash was the most dramatic episode.

International relations were affected as nations sought different solutions for their economic problems. The rise to power of industry-backed militarists in Japan by the early 1930s would cause problems for U.S. foreign policy.

December 2, 1929

Secretary Stimson invokes the Kellogg-Briand Pact to prevent a Sino-Soviet war. Although the pact is ignored, war is avoided because neither nation wants a conflict.

On July 10, 1929, Chinese Nationalist troops seized the Chinese Eastern Railway in Manchuria in an attempt to end the Soviet Union's control over the railroad. Chiang Kai-shek proposed to regain the Chinese rights in Manchuria that Russia, later the Soviet Union, and Japan had shared since 1896, with the Soviets controlling the Chinese Eastern Railway. The Soviets opposed the July 10 attack, and in November 1929 Soviet forces invaded Manchuria, where several armed skirmishes resulted with China's army.

Because the Kellogg-Briand Peace Pact had gone into effect on July 24, 1929, Secretary of State Stimson tested it by using the pact to avert a Sino-Soviet conflict. On July 25, Stimson called on Great Britain, France, Germany, Italy, and Japan to join America in a six-power commission acting under the Peace Pact to settle the Manchuria dispute. The other nations resented Stimson's interference, largely because he had not consulted them in advance, but also because they believed the request was not consonant with the pact.

On November 26, Stimson tried again. He sent identical notes to the five powers, asking them to publicly urge China and the USSR to observe the Kellogg peace agreement. Although all the powers except Italy ignored Stimson's note, the secretary assumed that silence was consent, and on December 2, he wired notes to the Soviet Union (by way of France since the United States did not recognize the Soviet regime) and China, admonishing them to follow the Peace Pact's obligations because both nations had signed the pact in 1928. Similar notes were sent to the antagonists by 37 other nations, but their efforts were pointless. China denied it had violated the pact; the USSR told the other nations to mind their own business.

By early December, aside from the Peace Pact, China and the Soviet Union undertook discussions to avert war. The latter was too concerned about its domestic Five-Year Plan to fight a war; China was too weak for a long struggle. On December 22, both nations accepted the status quo in Manchuria by signing the Protocol of Khabarovsk.

See May 23, 1924.

1930

January 20, 1930

The second Hague economic conference makes agreements that resolve pending reparations problems.

Convening on January 3, the Hague conference finalized details of the Young Plan recommendations of August 31, 1929. The important agreements of this conference were as follows:

1. A treaty between Germany and the World War I Allies ended all financial questions. German accounts under the reparations clauses of the Versailles Treaty would be fulfilled when Germany ratified the Young Plan as modified by the Hague Conferences ending August 31, 1929, and January 20, 1930. Germany agreed to implement the plan for the Bank for International Settlements which would receive its payments.

2. In a separate treaty, the United States and Germany on December 28, 1929, disassociated U.S. claims from other Allied claims. These included German payments for the occupation army and mixed claims of American citizens. The occupation payments would run to March 31, 1966, ranging between 16.4 and 35.3 million marks annually. The mixed claims would run until March 31, 1981, at 40.8 million marks per year.

3. Sanctions for German default were provided for. Although the Young Plan recommended that German good faith should replace the sanctions for nonpayment contained in the Dawes Plan, an incident during the fall of 1929 forced France to insist on the possibility of sanctions. In Germany, the Nationalist Party had obtained a plebiscite asking Germans to repudiate the war guilt clause and the financial obligations incurred by Germany in the Treaty of Versailles. The plebiscite vote of December 22, 1929, rejected the proposal by 20 million votes to 5.5 million, but France feared that a new German government might repudiate these treaty obligations. Consequently, the French insisted on adding a statement that expressed hope there would be no default but that in the event of a default, the creditor nations could appeal to the Permanent Court of International Justice. If Germany rejected the court's findings, the Allies reserved their "full liberty of action to force German compliance."

4. The Bank for International Settlements was set up in Basel as a Swiss corporation. The Swiss agreed to neutralize the bank's activity in both peace and war.

During the Second Hague Conference, the delegates also concluded reparations issues with the non-German members of the World War I Central Powers Alliance. These agreements included the following:

1. *Austria.* Excepting a few minor claims, all reparations claims against Austria were absolved and Austrian accounts with the Allied powers were closed.
2. *Hungary.* This nation was treated more harshly because of claims by Romania, Greece, Czechoslovakia, and Yugoslavia. A final reparations schedule was drawn up at the Hague Conference but was not finalized until April 28, 1930.

In 1924, Hungary had been assessed 200 million gold crowns to be paid over a 20-year period. The Hague Conference altered these payments to provide compensation to Magyar landowners whose estates had been confiscated by Czechoslovakia and Yugoslavia. The 20-year schedule of 1924 remained intact to 1943, but between 1944 and 1966, Hungary would pay 13.5 million gold crowns per year to its four creditor nations, part of these payments going from the Bank for International Settlements to the landowners whose property had been confiscated.

3. *Bulgaria.* This nation's reparations were reduced from the terms of the Treaty of Neuilly. Bulgaria would pay reparations until 1966 on a varied schedule: 10 million gold francs annually between 1931 and 1940; 11.5 million from 1941 to 1950; 12.5 million from 1957 to 1966.

February 6, 1930

An Austrian-Italian friendship treaty is signed; Mussolini begins a public campaign to revise the peace treaties of World War I.

Since 1927, Mussolini sought to coordinate Hungarian and other eastern European nations' proposals to revise the peace treaties in favor of the national demands of lesser powers of Europe. Austria agreed to this proposal as part of the treaty with Italy.

Mussolini's revision campaign resulted in the signing of the Rome protocol by Italy, Austria, and Hungary on March 17, 1934. These agreements provided closer trade relations and foreign policies to counteract France's organization of the Little Entente in eastern Europe.

April 22, 1930

The London Naval Conference delegates agree on a three-power treaty limiting cruisers, destroyers, and submarines.

To assure some success for the London Conference, Great Britain and the United States had carried on discussions during 1929. Designed to extend the Washington Naval Treaty of 1922 by limiting ships other than battleships and aircraft carriers, the conference preparations required a rapprochement between London and Washington to avoid the failure of the Geneva Conference of 1927 and create goodwill between England and America. On May 9, Secretary of State Stimson and British Ambassador Sir Esme Howard agreed that high-ranking diplomatic officers would attend the conference so that naval experts would not dominate as they had at Geneva. Later, from October 4 to 10, 1929, Prime Minister Ramsay MacDonald visited America for talks with President Hoover and to speak before a joint session of Congress. Although no naval agreements resulted, MacDonald's visit set the stage for closer Anglo-American cooperation during the 1930 conference.

In contrast to these positive preparations for the conference, other developments in 1929 presaged trouble. On August 12, the Japanese informed Washington and London that they would insist on a 10:7 ratio in all ship categories at the next conference. France also indicated its dissatisfaction with the 1922 ratios, contending that its long European coastline and far-flung empire required a larger French allocation of ships. Finally, U.S. and British naval experts continued to disagree about cruiser size, ratios, and whether or not tonnage was the proper method to determine naval allocations. In the United States, Allen W. Dulles, a lawyer who attended the 1925 and 1926 Geneva Conferences, proposed the use of a naval "yardstick" that would base combat strength on gun caliber, age, and tonnage of ships (see Dulles's article in *Foreign Affairs* for January 1929). U.S. and British naval leaders sought to develop such a technically based yardstick but could not agree on a satisfactory method of calculating combat strength.

President Hoover (center) signs the Naval Limitation Treaty. Herbert Hoover Library

Although the failure of these preparatory events left the success of the conference in doubt, Great Britain invited the five naval powers to sessions at London that opened on January 21 and continued until April 22. During the conference, Italy and France rejected agreements beyond those of the 1922 treaties, signing only the treaty to extend battleship limits. Japan, Great Britain, and the United States signed a three-power pact that included the following important agreements:

1. The 5:5:3:1.75:1.75 limits of 1922 battleships were renewed by the five powers and extended to December 31, 1936. Italy and France accepted this treaty but none of the remainder.
2. The tonnage ratio of heavy cruisers with 8-inch guns would be 10:10:7 until December 31, 1935, after which the United States could build additional cruisers that would make the ratio 5:5:3 once again. The United States agreed to this because in 1930 the U.S. naval construction program lagged greatly behind its 1922 limits and could not reach the 1930–1935 ratio before 1936. England did not rely on heavy but preferred light cruisers.
3. The ship ratio of light cruisers and destroyers would be 10:10:7. In both these categories of ships, Japan was near treaty limits by 1930; Great Britain had built to its small cruiser limits, but not to the destroyer limits; the U.S. navy lagged in its construction of both kinds of ship.
4. All three powers received parity in submarines.

Japan gained from the 1930 treaty, having received the 10:10:7 ratio for auxiliary vessels. Realistically, however, the British and Americans had limited Japan's naval program more than their own. The U.S. Congress in particular had cut the navy budget severely between 1922 and 1929. Although Congress approved a 15-cruiser program on February 13, 1929, none of these ships were far under construction in April 1930 and would not be completed until 1939, even if Congress continued to fund them. In 1922, the United States had negotiated from a position of naval strength; it held a weak position in 1930.

During hearings on Senate ratification during 1930, U.S. naval leaders largely opposed the London treaties, as they had opposed the 1922 agreements. The naval officer who defended the treaties was Admiral William V. Pratt. As a younger officer in 1922 Pratt saw the advantages in the limitation of battleships. Pratt strongly advocated the rapid development of an aircraft carrier task force, a concept forward-looking naval theorists preferred to battleships and heavy cruisers. President Hoover had appointed Pratt as a delegate to the London Conference, and subsequently he defended the treaties in the Senate hearings.

In each of the Big Three naval powers there were civilians who insisted that their nation's security had been impaired by the treaty.

> *Fredrick Hale* (before the U.S. Senate): "The British by the terms of this treaty have us hamstrung and hog-tied and there will keep us as long as limitation of armaments are the order of the day."
> *Winston Churchill* (before the House of Commons): "I am astonished that any Admiralty board of naval officers could have been found to accept responsibility for such a ham-stringing stipulation."
> *T. Inukai* (before the Japanese Diet): The government has "betrayed the country by entering into an agreement at the London Conference inadequate for Japan's defense needs."

It would appear, as H. A. L. Fisher wrote during the interwar years, that "in reality, security is a state of mind; so is insecurity."

During the conference the perennial French request arose for an Anglo-American security treaty. French Premier André Tardieu told MacDonald and Stimson that France could accept further naval limits provided it obtained some type of agreement to guarantee its security from future invasion. Although Secretary Stimson agreed to consider a consultative pact if one could be worked out, President Hoover refused negotiations regarding a guarantee treaty. He knew the U.S. Senate would reject such a treaty.

Despite objections from U.S. navy officials and other critics, the Senate ratified the London Treaty on July 24, 1930, by a vote of 58 to 9. The hearings on the Treaty had disclosed that the U.S. navy would require an additional $1 billion to begin to reach the 1922 Treaty limits. Such expenditures were unthinkable to senators during the first year of the "Great Depression."

September 6, 1930

In Argentina, the Democratic-Republican government is suspended when José Upiburu ousts President Irigoyen.

A democratic Argentine government, established in 1912, had instituted reforms such as factory acts, pensions, and regulation of workhouses. Hipólito Irigoyen had been elected president from 1916 to 1922, when Marcelo Alvear won a six-year term. In 1928, Irigoyen was again elected, but after the

Depression began he sought greater authority to deal with the nation's problems. Uriburu's coup d'état gave the conservatives control of the government. In 1932, the Conservative Augustin JUSTO was elected president. He undertook a successful recovery program. Nevertheless, unrest and opposition from Liberals and Radicals continued in parts of Argentina.

November 14, 1930

Japan's premier, Yūkō Hamaguchi is assassinated, marking a movement toward military control of Japan's government.

Against the wishes of Japanese naval leaders, Hamaguchi recommended that the emperor ratify the London Naval Treaty of April 22, 1930. A military fanatic shot the premier on November 14. Although another member of Hamaguchi's party, Reijiro Wakatsuki, became premier, Japan's party leaders were gradually subordinated to the influence of naval and military groups over the next 18 months.

See May 15, 1932.

1931

June 17, 1931

The U.S. Congress approves the Smoot-Hawley Tariff.

This law continued the American protective tariff policy, raising agricultural raw materials rates from 38% under the 1922 Fordney-McCumber Act to 49% and other commodity rates from 31% to 34%.

June 20, 1931

President Hoover offers to postpone all debt payments owed America if the Europeans postpone payments on debts due them.

The worldwide economic depression that began on October 29, 1929, combined with Germany's already shaky economy of the 1920s, caused severe economic problems for the German republic, including its inability to continue reparations payments after June 1, 1931. Since 1924, German reparations payments of about 5 billion marks had been managed largely with foreign loans, not with a surplus in the German budget or balance of trade. By the spring of 1931, as the German economy experienced greater difficulty and the Austrian Credit-Anstalt failed on May 11, gold and foreign-exchange funds began leaving Germany—many gold reserves going to the United States.

As the crisis became apparent, Hoover's fiscal advisers recommended that he call a moratorium on World War I debt payments to the United States provided the Europeans agreed to delay German reparations payments. Hoover agreed but first obtained the consent of 21 senators and 18 representatives of both major parties. With their concurrence, Hoover offered a one-year debt moratorium on June 20.

In making his announcement, Hoover emphasized the necessary interrelation of war debts, reparations, and the fiscal stability of both Europe and America. He hoped the moratorium would reestablish economic confidence and provide "political peace and economic stability in the world." The debtor nations had to recover their national prosperity. "I am suggesting," he said, "to the American people that they be wise creditors in their own interest and be good neighbors."

For the first time in America, Hoover's debt moratorium statement officially recognized the connection between American war credits and German reparations. Heretofore, U.S. presidential administrations, Congress, and the public refused to acknowledge the existence of the complexities of international finance. Many Americans objected to this analysis, believing national debts were the same as personal debts. To carry out Hoover's proposal, both the European governments and the U.S. Congress had to approve.

See July 24, August 11, and December 23, 1931.

July 24, 1931

A seven-power conference in London seeks to restore confidence in German finances.

In addition to the one-year debt-reparations moratorium proposed by Hoover on June 20, 1931, the Western powers needed to stop the withdrawal of foreign capital funds from German banks. The steady flow of gold and foreign-exchange notes from Germany continued until July, when the rate of flow began to double. As a result, the fiscal future of the other western European nations became shaky and gold funds began to leave England as well.

To end the fund outflow from Germany, England invited six other nations to send delegates to London. On July 21, the conference convened with representatives from France, Germany, Italy, Belgium, Japan, Great Britain, and the United States. Secretary of State Stimson and Secretary of the Treasury Mellon represented America, and their proposals formed the basis of the London agreements on July 24. The conference delegates asked their respective governments to use influence to maintain private and central bank credits in Germany at a stable level. They asked the Bank for International Settlements to establish a committee to study means to replace Germany's foreign capital. Finally, they recommended greater political cooperation with Germany to provide long-term German stability.

See August 18, 1931.

August 11, 1931

A committee of financial experts agrees on a plan to implement President Hoover's moratorium proposal.

Before this finance committee could be formed, a French-American agreement became necessary because the French government strongly objected to the moratorium suggested on June 20. Subsequently, the French delayed the agreement for two weeks as Secretary of the Treasury Andrew Mellon and U.S. Ambassador Walter Edge persuaded the French foreign minister to approve the moratorium.

According to the French-American agreement of July 6, the moratorium terms included the following:

1. Germany would be loaned funds for the unconditional payment schedule of the Young Plan as a form of continued payment during the moratorium.
2. The suspended payment loans would be paid in 10 years under a separate payment schedule to begin on July 1, 1933.

Although the two-week delay caused further problems for Germany, the committee of experts suggested by Hoover met in London on July 17. On August 11, the delegates accepted the one-year Hoover moratorium plan as qualified by the July 6 French-American understanding.

August 18, 1931

A committee of central banks recommends methods to help restore confidence in Germany's economy.

This committee of banking leaders evolved from the London Conference, which had adjourned on July 24. Headed by the U.S. delegate, Albert H. Wiggin, it became known as the Wiggin Committee. This group surveyed Germany's credit status and reported the following:

1. Germany's existing foreign credits should be maintained in line with the "standstill" agreement for all short-term credits.
2. All or part of the foreign capital that left Germany should be restored. Long-term loans should be made to Germany and its external obligations should be revised.

September 1, 1931

An international finance meeting in London arranges a "standstill" agreement on Germany's private short-term credits.

Following the announcement of the Hoover moratorium on war debts on June 20, 1931, a financial conference of bankers met in London to negotiate similar arrangements for private short-term credits. These credits had enlarged considerably since 1924, totaling approximately $5 billion, of which $1.7 billion was from U.S. banks.

On September 1, the British, French, and American financiers agreed to a six-month standstill on German payments. The standstill agreement became an annual affair, being extended to 1940 by U.S. banks under provisions that allowed liquidation of some funds with losses to the creditors. In 1940, the U.S. credit had been reduced, with losses, to $40 million.

September 18, 1931

The Mukden incident leads to Japan's occupation of a large part of eastern Manchuria.

According to Tokyo, the Kwantung Army guarding the South Manchurian Railway near Mukden had been startled by an explosion and had fired on Chinese soldiers fleeing from the site. This incident prompted the army to move on the night of

September 18–19 to defend itself from the Chinese troops at Mukden and elsewhere.

This version of the incident was fabricated by local Japanese officers, a fact that the Lytton Report by the League of Nations implied on October 2, 1934, and the Tokyo War Crimes Trials of 1946–1948 verified in detail. The later evidence shows that the Mukden plot was devised by Colonel Itagaki and Lieutenant Colonel Ishiwara of the Kwantung Army with the implied consent of its commander, General Honjo, and General Tatekawa of the Army General Staff. Although General Tatekawa was sent to Manchuria by the Tokyo authorities to prevent overt action by the Kwantung Army, Tatekawa arrived in Manchuria on September 18 but went directly to a geisha house without delivering his message. Consequently, following the explosion, Colonel Itagaki ordered his troops to attack the Chinese forces in Mukden and General Honjo launched a general attack in Manchuria. On September 19, the Kwantung Army seized Amtung, Yinghou, and Changchun. On the grounds of self-defense, the army advanced throughout the three eastern provinces of Manchuria, occupying them by February 5, 1932.

The Mukden incident resulted from a long series of Chinese-Japanese disputes going back to the war of 1894–1895. Japan gained dominance in eastern Manchuria between 1905 and 1929 while retaining the fiction of Chinese territorial integrity. The rise of Chinese nationalism challenged Japan following Chiang Kai-shek's unification of China in 1928. Subsequently, Chinese boycotts and demonstrations threatened the Japanese. Also in 1928, the Manchurian ruler Chang Tso-lin, who opposed Chiang Kai-shek, was killed when his train ran over a Japanese planted mine. He was replaced by his son Chang Hsueh-liang. The new Chang ruler was an avowed Chinese nationalist who received an appointment from Chiang Kai-shek as the commander in chief of the Northeastern Frontier Army and ruler of Manchuria, Jehol, and part of Inner Mongolia.

During the late summer of 1931, the Kwantung Army leaders advocated a more forceful policy against the Chinese, but the Japanese ministries of Hamaguchi and Wakatsuki desired to negotiate with China to maintain Japan's economic controls in Manchuria. Dissatisfied with the ministries' proposals, officers in the Kwantung Army fabricated an incident to justify their takeover in Manchuria.

In Tokyo, the Kwantung Army's offensive was popular with the public but divided Prime Minister Wakatsuki's government.

See December 10, 1931, and January 7 and 28, 1932.

September 21, 1931

The Bank of England is forced to abandon the gold standard.

Great Britain's economic difficulties had been exacerbated by the worldwide economic depression that disrupted the world trade on which British finances depended. When the British loss of gold reserves grew in 1931, the Federal Reserve Bank of New York and the Bank of France provided Britain with £25 million of credits, but these funds did not suffice to balance England's budget and balance-of-payments deficits. Therefore, in September the National Coalition Ministry was formed under Prime Minister Ramsay MacDonald and its members agreed to abandon the gold standard in face of the £100,000,000 budget deficit for 1931.

The devaluation of the British pound sterling caused England's currency to depreciate from $4.86 to $3.49 on the world exchange. The British action also affected other nations whose currency's value had been based on the pound sterling.

December 2, 1931

In El Salvador, Maximiliano H. Martinez creates a right-wing dictatorship, suppressing communism and liberal movements.

December 9, 1931

Spain adopts a republican constitution, abolishing the monarchy.

Spain did not participate in World War I, but its industrial development grew because of European demands for iron, munitions, and other goods. Liberal uprisings against King Alfonso XIII and favoring a constituent assembly began in 1917 but were staunchly repressed after General Miguel Primo de Rivera established a military dictatorship with the king's consent on September 13, 1923. Although dissolved in 1925, de Rivera's dictatorial government retained power because he became prime minister.

In 1929–1930, the economic problems resulting from the Great Depression caused new liberal agitation, leading to a series of military mutinies following de Rivera's death on March 16, 1930. The king finally agreed to hold elections during early 1931. The Republicans won an overwhelming victory in municipal elections on April 12 and in assembly elections on June 28, 1931. King Alfonso left Spain in April but refused to abdicate. Nevertheless, the constituent assembly accused the king of treason, forbade his return, and confiscated royal property on November 12, 1931.

The Spanish constitution adopted on December 9 gave universal suffrage, a single-house assembly, and a ministry responsible to the parliament (Cortes). On December 10, the Republican leader Alcala Zamora was elected president of Spain; Manuel Azana was elected prime minister.

December 10, 1931

The League of Nations council approves a commission (Lytton Commission) to investigate the Mukden incident of September 18–19, 1931; a U.S. delegate joins the commission.

Immediately after Japan's army occupied many Manchurian towns on September 19, Secretary of State Stimson and European diplomats hoped the conflict would be localized and settled quietly by Tokyo and Peking, just as the Sino-Russian dispute had been in 1929. But November talks had not begun between the antagonists, and the conflict spread when Japanese planes bombed Chinchow on November 9.

Stimson and President Hoover agreed to work independently of, but in concert with, the League of Nations Council. The council sessions, which convened on October 17, were momentous because a U.S. representative, Prentiss Gilbert, sat at the council table to consult with the league's members. The October meetings reached no solution to the dispute but urged China and Japan to negotiate and asked Japan to withdraw its occupation forces by November 16.

The council met again on November 16, but Japan had not complied with the request to withdraw. Therefore, at the suggestion of Tokyo's representative, Tsuneo Matsudaira, the council agreed to appoint an investigatory commission to visit Manchuria. China reluctantly agreed to the proposal because Japan's forces stayed in place, but Peking could secure no other assistance from the League of Nations.

Secretary of State Henry L. Stimson. Herbert Hoover Library

When the commission was being organized in December, Secretary of State Stimson approved, with Hoover's concurrence, the appointment of General Frank Ross McCoy to serve as a commission member. The earl of Lytton, a British delegate, became chairman of the league's investigation committee.

For its report see February 24, 1933.

December 23, 1931

A U.S. congressional resolution approves Hoover's debt moratorium after amending the law to declare that U.S. policy was not to reduce or cancel war debts.

When Hoover proposed a one-year moratorium on June 20, 1931, his consultation with 39 congressmen from both parties indicated that they sanctioned his proposal. By the time Congress convened for its next session in December 1931, the doubts and complaints had become evident. In particular, the popular feeling that the Europeans must fully pay their debts caused Americans who did not comprehend international finance to fear that the moratorium was a ploy eventually to abolish all debts.

Consequently, when the moratorium resolution was introduced to Congress on December 10, the opposition insisted on amendments saying (1) the one-year delay did not imply that the debts would be abolished, and (2) the postponed payments on the debts would be funded separately for future repayment at 3 to 4% interest, depending on the prevailing U.S. bond interest rate. Congress approved the amended resolution and President Hoover signed the legislation on December 23, 1931.

1932

January 7, 1932

Secretary of State Stimson announces the "Hoover-Stimson Non-recognition Doctrine" to protest Japan's aggression in Manchuria since September 19, 1931.

Heretofore, the only step taken against Japan by the League of Nations, England, and France was the league council's request that China and Japan negotiate and Japan withdraw. The investigation commission established by the league on December 10 only delayed possible action.

The possibility of economic sanctions against Japan had been discussed but avoided by the Europeans and the league. When the Europeans asked if the United States would join an embargo or other sanctions to punish Japan, Stimson informed them that America could not join cooperatively in an embargo because President Hoover opposed it. On November 19, however, Stimson notified the league council that the United States would not oppose an embargo or interfere with the league's attempt to employ such action. This was the closest the United States came to committing itself to cooperation.

Throughout December 1931, Japan stepped up its attacks in Manchuria, and on January 2, 1932, it captured Chincow, bringing its armies to the border of China's Great Wall in Jehol. The fall of Chincow persuaded Stimson to issue a policy statement that he and President Hoover had discussed as early as November 9, 1931. Stimson sent nonrecognition notes to Peking and Tokyo on January 7, 1932. The same day he informed the ambassadors of all the signatory nations of the Nine-Power Treaty of 1922 about the American action.

Stimson's nonrecognition policy was based on Japan's violation of the Nine-Power Treaty and the Kellogg-Briand Peace Pact. Although he did not solicit other nations to follow the U.S. policy, he hoped others might make similar protests against Japanese aggression. The basic clause of the nonrecognition statement was that the United States "cannot admit the legality of any situation de facto" or any agreement between China and Japan that impaired the treaty rights of Americans. In addition, Stimson asserted, the United States "does not intend to recognize any situation, treaty, or agreement which may be brought about by means contrary to the covenants and obligations of the Pact of Paris of August 27, 1928."

The Hoover-Stimson policy was moralistic in tone but had no constructive impact beyond putting the United States on record. Japan's reply to Stimson on January 16 employed diplomatic politesse to cloak its derisive repudiation of nonrecognition. Moreover by the end of January, Japan's new military offensive was preparing to thrust south of the Great Wall into China proper, a region where European and American interests exceeded those in Manchuria.

See January 28 and 31, and March 11, 1932.

January 28, 1932

Japanese troops land at Shanghai to compel China to stop its Japanese boycott.

The Japanese landed 70,000 soldiers at the international settlement in Shanghai, driving the 19th Route Chinese Army out of the region. Japan's forces controlled Shanghai until March 4, when China agreed to meet Japan's terms. In an agreement signed on May 5, a demilitarized zone was set up in Shanghai and the Chinese ended their Japanese boycott. Because of British and American protest, Japan withdrew its forces from Shanghai by the end of May.

The Shanghai attack rallied world opinion against the Japanese even though no one proposed taking any effective action to stop them. The Japanese air forces bombed civilian urban areas, terrorizing and killing men, women, and children. Most U.S. newspapers condemned the attacks as uncivilized or "insane imperialism." Few, however, supported proposals to boycott Japanese goods.

January 31, 1932

President Hoover and Secretary Stimson provide military preparations to protect Americans in the Pacific and China.

On January 31, three days after Japan landed forces at Shanghai, Hoover ordered the American Asiatic Squadron to move from Manila to Shanghai. This action paralleled a British decision to follow its protest of Japan's attack by sending two cruisers and additional marines to Shanghai.

About two weeks later (February 13), the American fleet arrived in Hawaii as part of the U.S. navy's winter fleet exercises conducted between California and Hawaii. Because these exercises occurred during the time Japan's military aggression expanded in China, Stimson and Hoover decided to keep the U.S. fleet based at Pearl Harbor rather than return to the Atlantic Ocean when their maneuvers ended.

Although the U.S. fleet movements were designed to demonstrate U.S. purpose in the Pacific, this was a hollow threat. During discussions about American army or navy capabilities in 1932, Secretary of the Navy Charles Francis Adams informed Hoover that U.S. naval experts advised against challenging Japan because the navy was not prepared to engage the Japanese navy if war began. This should not have surprised Hoover because he made the largest budget cuts in U.S. naval history when he approved the 1931–1932 budget. Disarmament on a unilateral basis could be rationally defended for isolated America provided the president and secretary of state did not risk war in the western Pacific. Of course, Hoover constantly restrained Secretary Stimson during the Manchurian crisis because the president never intended to risk war.

February 2, 1932

A disarmament conference convenes at Geneva.

In accordance with a proposal of the Preparatory Commission on Disarmament's recommendation of December 9, 1930, 60 nations met at Geneva to negotiate a general disarmament agreement. From the outset, the conference's success was doubtful. The draft treaty, which the Preparatory Commission had taken five years to draw up, did not resolve the basic disputes between French and German officials.

31st U.S. Infantry, one of several units, parade in China. National Archives

The Germans desired equality of armaments, and the French continued to insist on security guarantees prior to any disarmament.

In an attempt to get the conference to agree, the U.S. delegation, led by Secretary of State Stimson, offered a proposal on June 22, 1932, by which all nations would cut their armaments by one-third. This proposal was not successful. During debates on the concept, the delegates became aware that any military arms limit had to be correlated with political guarantees for the security of all nations from aggression. As France asserted, military cuts could not be accepted unless there were compensatory security pledges. The United States was not willing to make such a commitment. Therefore, the conference adjourned in July and the delegates decided to convene another session on February 2, 1933. During the interim, a special group tried to compromise the German and French demands.

See May 18, 1926, and December 11, 1932.

February 18, 1932

Under Japanese protection, the independence of Manchukuo (Manchuria) is proclaimed.

Initially, the state of Manchukuo included the three eastern provinces of Manchuria and the province of Jehol, areas the Japanese army occupied between September 19, 1931, and February 1, 1932. Local Manchu officers proclaimed their independence of China on February 18. Three weeks later, on March 9, the Japanese installed Henry P'u-i to replace the pro-Chinese Nationalist Manchurian ruler Chang Hsueh-liang. P'u-i, who had abdicated the Chinese throne in 1912, became the emperor of the K'ang Te reign for Manchukuo.

February 24, 1932

Secretary Stimson writes to Senator Borah stating that if any nation violates the 1922 treaties, it will no longer be covered by other 1922 treaty provisions.

Searching for a way to show clearly American discontent with Japan's aggression in Manchuria and Shanghai and to warn Tokyo that it risked the abrogation of all the 1922 treaty agreements, including limits on U.S. fortifications in the western Pacific islands, Secretary Stimson wrote a letter that Senator Borah agreed to publicize. The secretary's letter showed America's moral and psychological objections to Japan's action in East Asia but had no other immediate consequences. Stimson also hoped, apparently, to encourage Great Britain to undertake action to forestall Japan, but the British government took no effective action against Japan during 1931–1932.

Following Japan's attack on Shanghai on January 28, Stimson had frequent transatlantic telephone conversations with Sir John Simon, Britain's foreign secretary. Stimson urged Simon to obtain league sanctions against Japan in which the United States could cooperate under the Nine-Power Pact of 1922. The British did not wish to act directly, however, contending that they could function only with the League of Nations' agreements and recommendations. For this reason, Stimson's letter to Borah provided a forum for a public protest against Japan and an attempt to apply pressure on Europeans to do something. Of course, this tactic offered no official American commitment to assist in restraining Japan's aggression.

February 29, 1932

Great Britain enacts protective tariff legislation, ending the free-trade policy begun during the 1840s.

The protective tariff laws included a "corn law" guaranteeing British farmers about $1 per bushel for specified quantities of homegrown wheat.

In order to correlate the protective tariff acts with its imperial obligations, the British met with the Commonwealth countries from July 21 to August 20. During the Ottawa Imperial Economic Conference, agreements were reached for certain imperial preferential tariffs.

March 11, 1932

The League of Nations assembly adopts Stimson's nonrecognition statement to avoid the invocation of sanctions against Japan.

This league action was interpreted by some observers as support for the U.S. position in China. Actually, it was a British-French maneuver to forestall a league vote for sanctions against Japan that the smaller nations of the league advocated. Britain's foreign minister, Sir John Simon, proposed nonrecognition as a substitute for sanctions, and the league assembly adopted his resolution.

For further league action on the Manchurian crisis, see February 24, 1933.

May 15, 1932

The assassination of Japan's Premier Ki Inukai ends party government in Tokyo; reactionary military groups gain political control.

Japan's political leaders had been blamed by nationalist spokesmen for a weak foreign policy and for the economic difficulties created in Japan by the worldwide depression. Following the Mukden incident of September 19, 1931, military and so-called patriotic groups in Japan issued propaganda favoring a strong foreign policy abroad to solve the country's domestic economic problems.

Following Inukai's assassination, the new ministry consisted entirely of nonparty members, with the Viscount Makoto Saito as premier. Patterned on the German constitution of 1871, the ministry was responsible to the emperor, not the legislature (Diet). From 1919 to 1932, party leaders such as Hamaguchi, Wakatsuki, and Inukai governed with majorities in the Diet and favored the adoption of this system. Japan's military officers and nationalistic followers generally opposed the party system, asserting that the Japanese emperor should wield all power. In 1931–1932, the nationalistic and military factions gained the backing of Emperor Hirohito and disregarded the party structure in the Diet. This arrangement was opposed by Japan's liberal politicians, but they would not regain power until August 1945, when Japan's surrender ended World War II.

July 9, 1932

At the Lausanne Conference, the western European powers and Japan propose the reorganization of Germany's reparations debt.

The Lausanne Conference of 1932 became necessary because within a month after the seven-power agreement on Hoover's one-year moratorium, it became obvious that Germany's attempt to restore its economic stability would require more than one year.

During the fall of 1931, French Premier Pierre LAVAL met with President Hoover in Washington to discuss a longer period of moratorium. On October 25, Hoover and Laval issued a statement indicating that a longer moratorium would probably be necessary and asking the debtor nation, Germany, to request modifications in the Young Plan.

At Germany's request, a special Advisory Committee of the seven powers met in Basel to review the German debt status. On December 8 that group, which was chaired by Italian delegate Alberto Beneduce, reported:

1. Germany would not be financially able to resume payments in July 1932.
2. There was a need to adjust all world debts because the Young Plan did not provide for the extreme change in world finances that occurred after 1929.

Following the Advisory Committee's report, Great Britain invited the signatory nations of the Hague agreements of January 20, 1930, to meet at Lausanne on June 6, 1932, to discuss the debt-reparations problem. No American delegate attended the Lausanne Conference.

On July 9, the 13 governments represented at Lausanne signed an agreement that included the following:

1. The Young Plan of 1929 and the Hague agreements of 1929–1930 were terminated regarding reparations payments.
2. To replace the Young Plan, Germany would deliver bonds worth 3 billion gold marks (approximately $715 million) to the Bank for International Settlements. The bonds would bear 5% annual interest. Following a three-year delay, the bonds would be sold, provided that no issue was below 90% par. Bonds not sold in 15 years would be canceled and the minimum price would be charged to Germany, assuming its credit was restored; in effect, this plan eliminated nine-tenths of Germany's reparations liability because if all the bonds were sold, German costs would have been $2 billion, compared with the $25 billion due under the Young Plan.
3. The signatory creditor nations agreed to suspend all war debts payments among themselves.

Another clause provided that the agreements would become effective only after a satisfactory settlement was concluded between the signatory nations and their creditor nation (America). If the signatories could not settle with their creditor, the reparations would revert to their status before the Hoover moratorium of 1931. The ratification clause meant the

Lausanne pact was effective only if America renegotiated or canceled its war debts with the Europeans. The United States refused to do this. America was in the middle of the 1932 presidential election campaign, and both candidates stated they would not recommend America's compliance with the Lausanne agreements.

See December 15, 1932.

September 20, 1932

The Munro-Blanchet Treaty proposes America's gradual withdrawal from Haiti. Although Haiti's assembly rejects the treaty, President Hoover continues to relinquish U.S. control.

The United States had taken control over Haiti's political and economic affairs on July 29, 1915. Although Secretary of State Hughes reviewed U.S. policy toward Haiti in 1922, President Harding appointed General John H. Russell as high commissioner of Haiti, and American control continued for another eight years. Under Russell's guidance, Louis Borno became president of Haiti and followed U.S. directions until his resignation in 1930.

Between 1926 and 1929, several American investigations of conditions in Haiti publicized unfavorable circumstances regarding the U.S. occupation. Emily Greene Balch's *Occupied Haiti* (1927) contained a moderate but sound criticism of U.S. failings in Haiti. In 1929, both the Council on Foreign Relations and the Foreign Policy Association issued derogatory reports on American policy in Haiti. Finally, a series of strikes in Haiti during the fall of 1929 led President Hoover to ask Congress to appropriate funds for a commission to recommend procedures for American withdrawal from that country.

The resulting commission, chaired by W. Cameron Forbes, recommended a process that Hoover implemented over the next two years. Following the Forbes plan, Borno resigned as president on May 15, 1930, and Eugene Roy became interim president during a period when a new Chamber of Deputies was elected. In accordance with Haiti's constitution of 1918, which Borno had violated, the new chamber selected Stenio Vincent as president in November 1930. About the same time (November 1, 1930), General Russell resigned as the U.S. high commissioner and Hoover appointed Dana G. Munro as U.S. minister to Haiti.

Munro continued to grant more training and more responsibility to Haitians so that by October 1, 1931, Haitians controlled all domestic offices except fiscal and military positions. One year later, Munro negotiated a treaty with Haiti's foreign minister, Blanchet. The treaty provided that Haiti's Garde National would gradually replace the U.S. Marines, who would withdraw completely, except for a "training mission," by December 31, 1934. But fiscal operations would continue to be under U.S. supervision until Haiti's loans had been fully repayed.

On September 20, 1930, Haiti's National Assembly rejected the Munro-Blanchet Treaty. The Haitian representatives disliked the remaining U.S. strings on military and financial policies, desiring the complete withdrawal of all U.S. officials.

Despite the defeat of the treaty, President Hoover followed its basic provisions by relaxing U.S. controls. Franklin D. Roosevelt accepted Hoover's decision, and during his administration the U.S. Marines withdrew in 1934; U.S. fiscal officials left in 1941.

November 8, 1932

Franklin Delano Roosevelt is elected president.

On June 19 at Chicago, the Republican Party Convention renominated Herbert Hoover for president. Its platform advocated a balanced budget, the protective tariff, U.S. participation in an international monetary conference, preservation of the gold standard, and revision of the prohibition amendment.

The Democratic Convention selected Franklin D. Roosevelt, governor of New York, as its nominee. Flying to Chicago to personally address the convention, Roosevelt told the delegates: "I pledge you, I pledge myself to a new deal for the American people." The Democratic platform called for a balanced budget, a competitive tariff, a sound currency, repeal of prohibition, banking reform, and aid to farmers.

In the November balloting, Roosevelt secured 472 electoral votes to Hoover's 59. Roosevelt carried 42 of the 48 states.

December 11, 1932

The Five-Power Declaration retains German cooperation in the Geneva Disarmament Conference.

In July 1932, the Geneva Conference suspended its sessions and agreed to reconvene on February 3,

Franklin Delano Roosevelt. National Archives

1933. During the interim, a Bureau of the General Disarmament Conference was set up to explore issues raised during the sessions held from February 2 to July, 1932. This bureau met from September 21 to December 13, during which the disputes between France and Germany became so difficult that Germany's delegate, Baron von Neurath, asserted that his nation would not attend the 1933 sessions. The Germans wanted to be treated as an equal power rather than a "defeated" power.

The French-German dispute resulted in extensive negotiations leading to the five-power declaration of December 11 by Germany, France, Great Britain, Italy, and the United States. The declaration stated that the five nations resolved not to settle "future differences by a resort to force." It also asserted that at the disarmament conference the principle must be followed that Germany and the other nations that had been forced to disarm by the post–World War I treaties should be given "equality of rights in a system which would provide security for all nations." Under the terms of this declaration, Germany agreed to attend the February 3, 1933, meeting at Geneva.

December 15, 1932

France refuses to pay its U.S. war debts; Britain makes a conditional final payment: the virtual end of the Allied war debt payments to the United States.

Because America refused to cancel the war debts requested by the Lausanne Treaty, the December 15 installments came due on the war debts that European nations owed to America. The U.S. moratorium of June 20, 1932, had not been extended again by Hoover's administration. Hoover and Stimson realized few debtor nations could pay, but they hoped the majority would do so.

In December 1932, the British made a full payment of $95 million in gold but also sent the United States a note that effectively wrote off future payments. France defaulted on its payment of $20 million. Poland, Belgium, Estonia, Yugoslavia, and Hungary also defaulted. Greece made a partial payment on a blocked account. Full payments were made by Italy, Czechoslovakia, Finland, Latvia, and Lithuania. Nevertheless, the default of the major powers in future years led all nations but Finland to default. The incoming Roosevelt administration could do nothing to change the situation.

See July 9, 1932.